THE

PUBLICATIONS

OF THE

Lincoln Record Society

FOUNDED IN THE YEAR

1910

VOLUME 110

ISSN 0267–2634

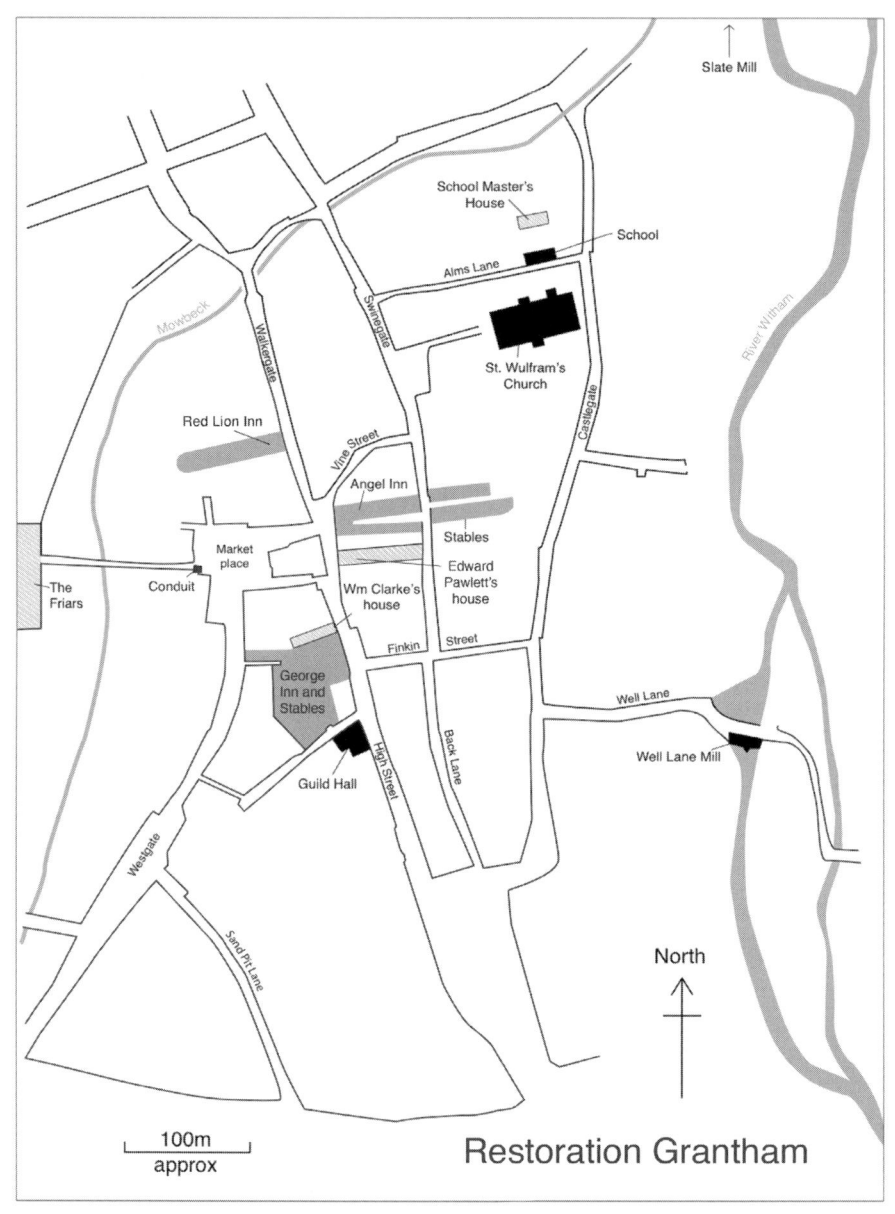

Map of Grantham in 1665.

BOROUGH GOVERNMENT IN RESTORATION GRANTHAM

THE HALL BOOK OF GRANTHAM, 1662–1704

EDITED BY
JOHN B. MANTERFIELD

The Lincoln Record Society

The Boydell Press

© Lincoln Record Society 2022

All Rights Reserved. Except as permitted under current legislation no part of this work may be photocopied, stored in a retrieval system, published, performed in public, adapted, broadcast, transmitted, recorded or reproduced in any form or by any means, without the prior permission of the copyright owner

First published 2022

A Lincoln Record Society publication
published by The Boydell Press
an imprint of Boydell & Brewer Ltd
PO Box 9, Woodbridge, Suffolk IP12 3DF, UK
and of Boydell & Brewer Inc.
668 Mt Hope Avenue, Rochester, NY 14620-2731, USA
website: www.boydellandbrewer.com

ISBN 978 1 910653 08 1

A CIP catalogue record for this book is available
from the British Library

Details of other Lincoln Record Society volumes are available
from Boydell & Brewer Ltd

The publisher has no responsibility for the continued existence or accuracy of URLs for external or third-party internet websites referred to in this book, and does not guarantee that any content on such websites is, or will remain, accurate or appropriate

This publication is printed on acid-free paper

Printed and bound in Great Britain by
TJ Books Limited, Padstow, Cornwall

CONTENTS

List of Illustrations	vi
Acknowledgements	vii
List of Abbreviations	viii
Editorial Note	ix
INTRODUCTION	xi
The Hall Book	xi
The Town of Grantham in the Late Seventeenth Century	xiii
The Corporation: Historical Background and Composition	xvii
The Charter of 1664	xxii
Strained Relations within the Soke	xxv
Responding to the Threat of Plague in 1665	xxvi
The Borough's Half Pence	xxviii
The Church and Religious Dissent in Grantham	xxxi
The Grammar School	xxxiii
The Borough and its Members of Parliament	xxxviii
The Charters of 1685 and 1688	xlv
Borough Governance 1689–1704	lv
The Red Lyon Saga 1662–1704	lv
Other Corporate Responsibilities	lix
Conclusions	lx
THE TEXT	1
APPENDICES	
1 Courts and Assemblies 1662–1704	486
2 List of Aldermen, Comburgesses and Second Twelvemen 1662–1704	488
Index of Personal Names	496
Index of Places	517
Index of Subjects	520

ILLUSTRATIONS

Figures from the Grantham Hall Book are by kind permission of Lincolnshire Archives, the Grantham Charter Trustees and South Kesteven District Council. Other photographs are copyright of John Manterfield, except Figure 5 which is copyright of Anne-Marie Kerr.

Frontispiece: Map of Grantham in 1665

1 The Grantham Hall Book	xii
2 Parish, Borough and Lordship Boundaries in Grantham, 1835	xiv
3 Map of Grantham Soke (from Turnor, 1806)	xv
4 First Court of Michael Taylor Alderman 31 October 1662 (HB, fo. 370r)	xxi
5 Town halfpence 1667 and halfpenny of Edward Pawlett, bookseller, 1666	xxix
6 Grantham St Wulfram's Parish Register detailing the proclamation of King James II (LAO, Grantham St Wulfram PAR/1/4)	xlviii
7 Thirteenth Court of John Coddington Alderman and Assembly 6 November 1688 (HB, fo. 714r)	liii

ACKNOWLEDGEMENTS

This present volume follows on from the earlier Lincoln Record Society volume *Borough Government in Newton's Grantham – The Hall Book of Grantham, 1649–1662*, published in 2016. That volume had had its origins in the 2012 'Gravity Fields' festival in Grantham, which was designed to celebrate the town's connections with Newton and had resulted in both the publication of the booklet, *Newton's Grantham – The Hall Book and life in a Puritan town*, published by Grantham Civic Society, and also publication on the 'Lincs to the Past' website (http://www.lincstothepast.com) of images with facing transcriptions of the Grantham Hall Book. This publication, covering the period 1662 to 1704, has followed on with the publication on the 'Lincs to the Past' website of transcriptions undertaken between 2015 and 2017.

The team of transcribers engaged in the work for LRS 106 has continued with some changes and I wish to record my thanks to Jan and Nigel Christmas, Josephine Hewitt, Anna Mauro-Pearce, Jackie Searl, Elaine Thurgood, Dr Amanda Topps and John Down, who had continued from the initial project in 2014. Marion Ellis, Barbara Manterfield and Christine Watkins joined the team of transcribers as the project progressed.

The relevant pages of the Hall Book were photographed by Trevor Goodale, whose contribution is acknowledged. Using these images, project team members completed their transcription independently. Accuracy was ensured by means of peer checking, prior to further checking by a second team member. All transcriptions then passed to the editor of this volume for extension and standardisation in order to facilitate publication on the 'Lincs to the Past' website, where each transcript occupies one page as per the original and is displayed opposite an image of the original. The transcripts of the nearly 500 pages for the years from 1662–63 to 1703–04 were published on-line by the end of 2017. The editor wishes to thank Dr Mike Rogers, then Collections Access Team Leader, Lincolnshire Archives, for his encouragement and support. Images of the Hall Book and its contents are reproduced by kind permission of Lincolnshire Archives and South Kesteven District Council. The editor wishes to thank Nicholas Bennett, our editor, for his assistance and encouragement. Any remaining errors and imperfections are my own.

Finally, and by no means least, I should again like to thank my wife, Barbara, not only for her considerable technical support in the preparation of the published material on-line and in this volume but also for her continued encouragement and support.

John Manterfield
December 2019

ABBREVIATIONS

CSPD	Calendar of State Papers Domestic
HB	Hall Book
HMC	Historical Manuscripts Commission
LAO	Lincolnshire Archives
LRS	Lincoln Record Society
LRS 83	Bill Couth (ed.), *Grantham during the Interregnum: The Hallbook of Grantham, 1641–1649*, Lincoln Record Society vol. 83 (1995)
LRS 106	John Manterfield (ed.), *Borough Government in Newton's Grantham – The Hall Book of Grantham, 1649–1662*, Lincoln Record Society vol. 106 (2016)
TNA	The National Archives

EDITORIAL NOTE

The Hall Book has continued to present all the usual challenges of transcription: unusual words, forms of English, abbreviations, word endings and the use of superscript, with much inconsistency of practice over the period examined partly owing to different clerks during the period of this volume.

Dates shown in the transcription of this volume have been standardised; dates between 1 January and 24 March are given with both Old Style and New Style years (for example, 4 January 1649/50). The language of the Hall Book is English, with the headings of some Courts given in Latin. This has been translated and summarised as, for example, The Sixth Court of A… B… with the dates standardised in English. The original text generally gives the headings for the lists of the names of the officials and the names of the Commoners at the start of each aldermanic year in Latin; this has been rendered into English along with *per hebdomadam* and *per mensem*, which have been shown as per week and per month accordingly. Less well-known Latin words have been translated and shown in square brackets. Phrases such as *Sub Pena* ['under penalty' or 'on pain of'] and *Contra Ordinem* ['contrary to the order', often specified with the book and folio reference] have been left but are shown in italics. A number of Courts conclude with 'By the Court' or in Latin *Per Curiam*; this has been omitted.

The transcription reproduces the original spelling except that missing words have been supplied and abbreviations silently expanded where their meaning is certain. The 'thorn' has been replaced by 'th'. The use of the letters 'i', 'j', 'u' and 'v' has been standardised. Punctuation has been modernised but capital letters have been retained as in the original. Abbreviated personal names have been extended but are otherwise transcribed as they appear with original spellings. Monetary sums appearing within the text have been given in either arabic or roman numerals as in the original and are standardised as 'li s d'. Where columns of tables appear in the text, for example in the last Court of the Aldermanic Year, all figures have been shown in arabic with dots and/or dashes omitted. Italics have been used for the marginal notes given in the Hall Book which generally summarise accurately the body of the text which in the transcription follows immediately below. The editor has attempted to follow the advice given in R. F. Hunnisett, *Editing Records for Publication* (British Records Association, 1977).

INTRODUCTION

The Hall Book

The earliest surviving book of minutes recording the discussions and decisions of the Alderman's Court of the Corporation of Grantham, Lincolnshire, covers the period from October 1633 to October 1704 and is known as the Hall Book. The volume, which now belongs to the Corporation's legal successor, South Kesteven District Council, is in the care of Lincolnshire Archives.[1] This edition relates to the years 1662–1704 and this spans some 60% of the period covered by the Hall Book. Specifically, the section covered in this transcription covers folios 370 to 780, which marks the end of the volume, albeit there is a discontinuity in the pagination between 519v and 600r with folios 520–599 being omitted. The 498 pages covered in this LRS volume therefore represent some 71% of the Hall Book's pages. The volume is made up of paper sheets, written in English with some headings in Latin, with a leather binding. It measures approximately 43.5 cm by 28.5 cm and is 11.5 cm from cover to cover (Figure 1). Owing to the span of years, this Hall Book volume reflects the handwriting of at least seven different Clerks, of which four served in the period 1662–1704.[2] On a few sheets, the ink has bled through leaving occasional small portions of the text illegible.

It is clear that during the time when the surviving Hall Book was being used, there existed at least five earlier minute books which are now lost.[3] These may have extended from the time of Grantham's Charter of Incorporation in 1463. The section of the Hall Book covering the period 1641 to 1649 was edited for the Lincoln Record Society by Bill Couth.[4] As noted in the acknowledgements, the Hall Book spanning the period 1649 to 1662 was edited by John Manterfield.[5]

---

[1] LAO, Grantham Borough 5/1 (hereafter cited as HB).
[2] William Hodgkinson 1660–80, Robert Parkins 1680–85, Samuel Proctor 1685–1700 and John Calcraft from 1700.
[3] HB, fo. 208v (11 January 1650) refers to the appointment of Mr Wilkinson as Headmaster of the Grammar School in Book 5. This appointment was made in 1605.
[4] Bill Couth (ed.), *Grantham during the Interregnum: The Hallbook of Grantham, 1641–1649*, LRS 83 (1995); hereafter cited as LRS 83.
[5] John B. Manterfield (ed.), *Borough Government in Newton's Grantham – The Hall Book of Grantham, 1649–1662*, LRS 106 (2016); hereafter cited as LRS 106.

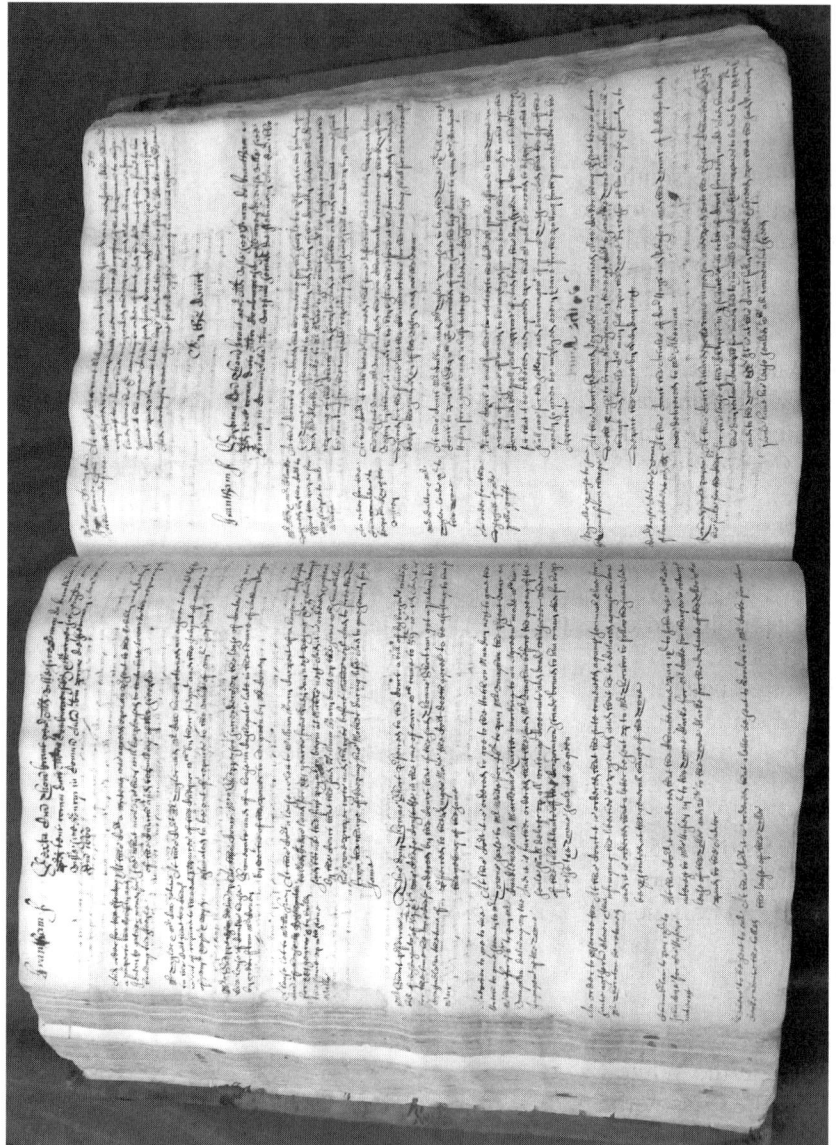

1. The Grantham Hall Book.

The Town of Grantham in the Late Seventeenth Century

As noted in LRS 106, the borough of Grantham itself covered an area of less than two-thirds of a square mile lying in the middle of the larger ecclesiastical parish of Grantham centred on the church of St Wulfram. The borough was bounded on its eastern side by the River Witham and the western and northern boundary was the stream known as the Mowbeck. The borough's southern boundary was the line of what is now known as Wharf Road and St Catherine's Road. Surrounding the borough were the separate lordships or liberties of Earlsfield to the southwest, the manor of Spittlegate, Houghton and Walton to the south and the manor of Harrowby across the River Witham to the east. To the north and northwest of the borough was the manor of Little Gonerby cum Manthorpe. These manors and liberties all formed part of the parish of Grantham. A small and extra-parochial area immediately on the west side of the borough was known as the Grange and was the former site of the Franciscan house known as the Friars or Greyfriars. The pattern of local boundaries is shown in the map drawn up in the 1830s as part of the evidence for the reform of municipal corporations (Figure 2).

The Corporation of Grantham had jurisdiction not only over the area of the old borough but also over the soke of Grantham, which included the villages of Barkston, Belton, Londonthorpe, Manthorpe, Great Gonerby, Denton, Harlaxton, Great Ponton, Braceby, Sapperton, Stoke Rochford, Easton and Colsterworth (Figure 3).[6] The Corporation was at pains to defend and assert its privileges in and over the soke at various times throughout the period of the Hall Book.

The street pattern in the later seventeenth century was broadly that which has survived today (Frontispiece). The principal streets of Castlegate, Swinegate, Walkergate (now Watergate), Market Place, Westgate and High Street lent their names to the six administrative wards overseen by the petty constables that formed the lowest level of the borough's government. From the Hearth Tax returns of 1665, the wards contained 346 properties and a further fifteen properties that were not rated on the grounds of exemption but it may be assumed had a single hearth. Additionally, there were further properties in the other liberties such as Spittlegate and Manthorpe that were also part of the parish. The relative size of houses (approximated from the number of hearths) in each ward is given in Table 1.

The Market Place ward, which included the major inns of the Angel, the George and the White (later Blue) Lion, had by far the largest numbers (11 and 15) of entries with six or more and 4–5 hearths respectively and also the smallest proportion of houses with just a single hearth. In contrast, Castlegate

---

[6] Edmund Turnor, *Collections for the History of the Town and Soke of Grantham* (London, William Miller, 1806).

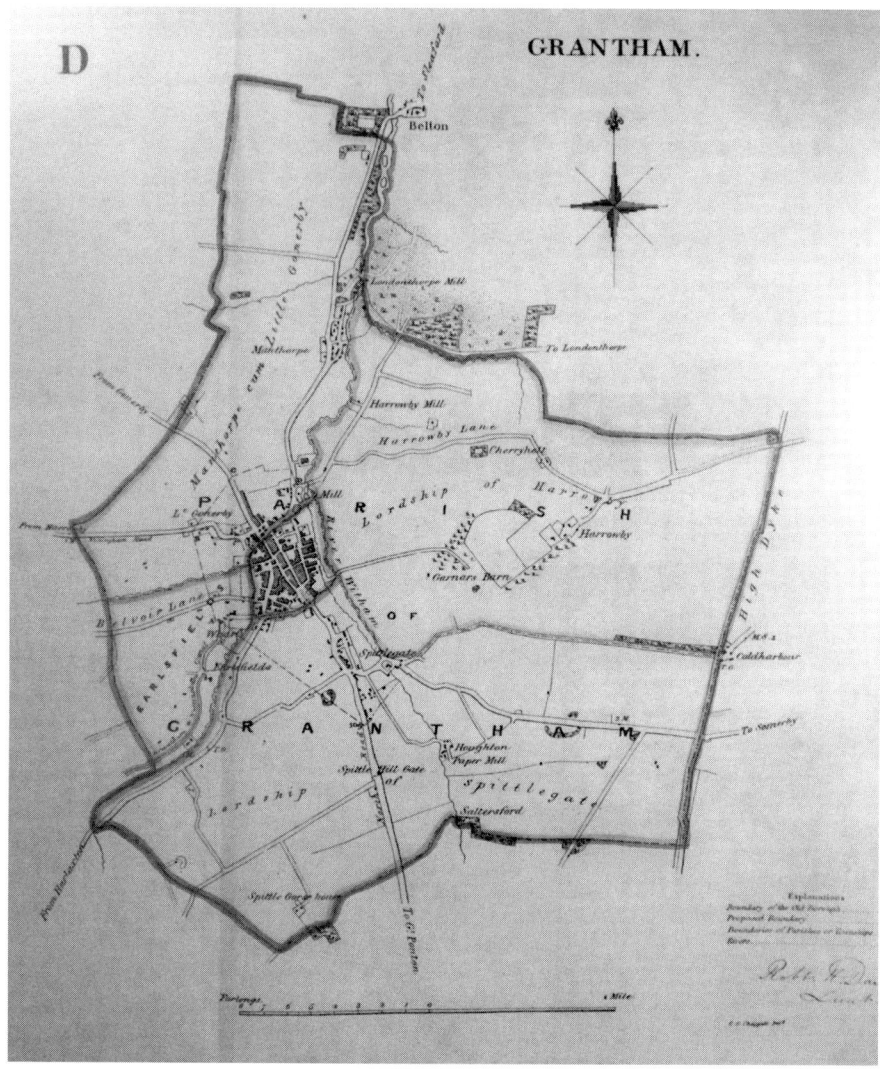
2. Parish, Borough and Lordship Boundaries in Grantham, 1835.

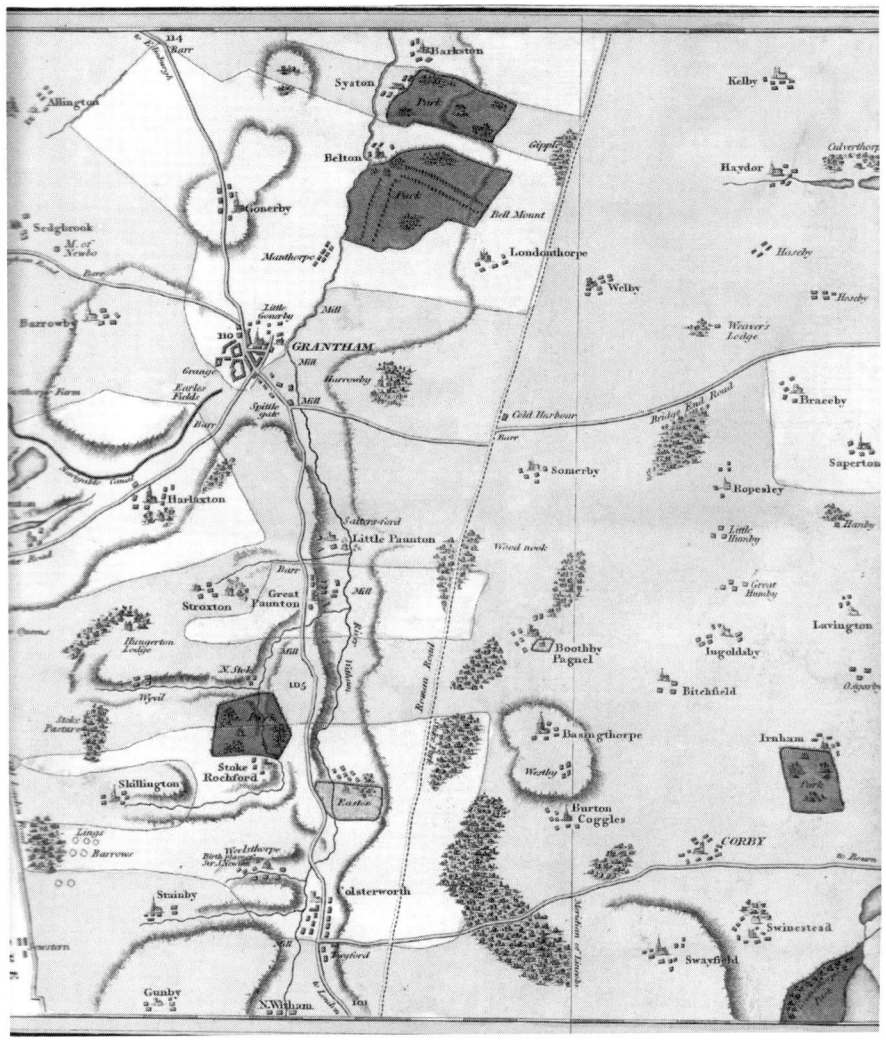

3. Map of Grantham Soke (from Turnor, 1806).

Table 1. House Sizes by Ward

Ward name	1 hearth		2–3 hearths		4–5 hearths		6+ hearths		Total	
	no.	%	no.	%	no.	%	no.	%	no.	%
Walkergate	10	50	7	35	2	10	1	5	20	100
Swinegate	25	46	19	35	8	15	2	4	54	100
Castlegate	43	60	21	29	4	6	4	6	72	99
Westgate	30	49	25	41	5	8	1	2	61	100
Market Place	20	26	30	39	15	20	11	14	76	99
High Street	33	52	22	35	5	8	3	5	63	100
Not rated	15	100							15	100
Total	176	49	124	34	39	11	22	6	361	100

ward, which included Well Lane, had over 60% of properties with just a single hearth and there were just four properties with six or more hearths.[7]

The physical appearance of the town in the late seventeenth century was described by diarist Celia Fiennes as 'all built with stone', although the evidence of extant buildings indicated that this may have been more accurately a stone ground floor and a half-timbered first floor. Some buildings were undoubtedly roofed with Collyweston stone tiles, others were thatched.[8]

The town's population may be estimated from the Compton Census of 1676, which records a total of 1,460 persons over the age of 16, indicating a total of 2,190 people, assuming one-third were children, or 2,430 if that proportion was 40%. This represents an increase from the figure of some 1,800–2,100 which had been estimated for the town in the 1640s.[9] Concerns about the harbouring of inmates and strangers and the fear of disease surface periodically in the 1680s and the Hall Book sets out the precautions enforced against the plague of 1665.[10]

---

[7] John B. Manterfield, 'The Topographical Development of the Pre-Industrial Town of Grantham, Lincolnshire (c1535–c1835)' (unpublished PhD thesis, University of Exeter, 1981), esp. Table 4.18, 199; LAO, Hearth Tax Return 17, fos 61–74.

[8] *The Journeys of Celia Fiennes*, ed. Christopher Morris, revised edn (London, The Cresset Press, 1949), 70; Manterfield, 'Topographical Development', 244–7.

[9] Anne Whiteman (ed.), *The Compton Census of 1676: A Critical Edition*, British Academy Records of Social and Economic History, New Series 10 (1986), 341; Arthur S. Langley, 'A religious census of 1676 AD', *Lincolnshire Notes and Queries* 16:2 (1920), 34; LRS 106, xiii.

[10] HB, fos 675r (7 April 1682) and 677r (22 September 1682) for inmates and 396r–402r *passim* (17 August, 15 and 21 September, 27 October and 15 December 1665) in respect of plague precautions.

The Corporation: Historical Background and Composition

Following its incorporation by Edward IV in 1463, the town's charters of incorporation, with subsequent confirmations and additions through letters patent issued by ensuing monarchs, defined the powers of the borough as well as its composition.[11] The charter of Charles I, dated 30 November 1631, established the Alderman's Court comprising the Alderman, twelve fellow Comburgesses (the First Twelve) who were to act with a Second Twelve and the other Burgesses. There was provision for a Deputy Alderman as well as reference to the Council's Common Clerk. The Charter of 1631 also gave the Corporation the power and authority to fashion, ordain and make 'laws, statutes and ordinances' as shall seem to them to be 'honest, useful and necessary for the general good and common utility of the said town or borough'. There was also explicit power to 'assess and tax reasonable sums within the said town or borough' to further all its public business including 'for the public and common good or utility of the said town or borough'.[12]

The Friday after St Luke's Day (18 October) marked the start of the civic year when an assembly was held in Corpus Christi chapel of St Wulfram's Church and the Alderman for the year to come was elected and sworn. On the following Friday the first court of the new Alderman was held in the Guildhall on the High Street. The First and Second Twelves were also sworn in together with the officials.[13] The list of officials (all unsalaried other than the Town or Alderman's Clerk) is headed by the Coroner, traditionally the Alderman in the preceding year, and the Escheator. The Coroner's duties included inquests into sudden and unexplained deaths and more particularly he determined what, if anything, accrued to the town in consequence of each of those deaths. Between 1662 and 1675, the Coroner's accounts were recorded in the Hall Book and they reveal a total of twelve accidental deaths, three murders and one suicide in the town and soke of Grantham. This level of detail is typical of that shown under the clerkship of William Hodgkinson.

The Escheator originally had a role in carrying out inquisitions *post mortem* to determine whether any lands reverted to the Crown if the tenant or landowner had died without heirs or the heir was a minor. The Escheator also accounted for the fines made in respect of defective weights and measures within the borough.

Two Churchwardens are also named annually. They served for overlapping periods of two years and at least one was a Second Twelve man. A more demanding role was that of Chamberlain, of whom two were appointed annually, one a Comburgess and the other drawn from the Second Twelve. The chronic shortage of funds on the part of the borough, with cash received being rapidly applied to repay existing loans and interest as well as meeting

---

[11] LRS 106, xiv–xvi.
[12] G. H. Martin, *The Royal Charters of Grantham 1463–1688* (Leicester University Press, 1963), 133–5.
[13] The structure of the Corporation and officials are more fully described in LRS 106, xvi–xix.

other debts, together with the annual preparation of accounts, meant that this was a challenging post and required the use of personal moneys to assist in cash flow. Accordingly, the Chamberlainship was usually held for a year at a time before the burden was passed on. The Hall Book contains regular reference to assessments being made for specific purposes such as meeting the Constables Bills, repairs to wells, streets or the church building.

The town's grammar school had been endowed by Edward VI with former chantry lands and these were managed by the Corporation. Rents were collected twice yearly by the two Collectors of the School House Rents who were responsible for paying the salaries of the Master and Usher. One Collector was drawn from a recently appointed member of the First Twelve and the other was usually a Commoner or member of the Second Twelve.

Two Chief Constables were usually drawn from the Second Twelve and they had a supervisory role over the two petty constables drawn from the Commoners in each of the borough's six wards. These ward constables were sent to gather in assessments and also to collect the goods of inhabitants that had been ordered to be distrained as fines or for non-payment of the assessments agreed by the Alderman's Court. Constables had oversight of the hooks, ladders and buckets that formed the borough's fire-fighting equipment and also were to report as required on those practising their trades who were not freemen of the borough or on those living as inmates in the town.

As well as the ceremonial side of carrying the maces in procession, for example, from the Guildhall to the church, the Serjeants-at-Mace acted as bailiffs of the liberties and one was also the gaoler of the borough's gaol in the Guildhall.

Other officials had specific roles in relation to the market, the pricing of corn or the leather trade. The two market sayers appear to have enforced market regulations and may have collected tolls and overseen the positioning of stalls. The corn prizers or pricers were involved in setting the maximum prices for grain. The four (occasionally three) leather sealers ensured the quality and grading of leather within the borough. The leather trade appears to have involved at least a fifth and possibly up to a quarter of the town's workforce in the later seventeenth century.[14]

Without doubt, the key official in the borough was the Town Clerk. With formal legal training and business experience, he not only kept the record of the proceedings in the Alderman's Court and was the writer of the Hall Book but also was responsible for the leases of Corporation property and the official communication with other bodies and specifically with the government in Westminster. In the period between 1662 and 1704, there were four town clerks in post. William Hodgkinson had been appointed on 11 May 1660 and served for upwards of twenty years when he was succeeded by Robert Parkins appointed

---

[14] LRS 106, xxvi–xxvii.

on 24 August 1680. Parkins was buried on 25 March 1685 and his successor Samuel Proctor was appointed on 24 July 1685. Proctor remained in post for over fifteen years and was succeeded by Mr John Calcraft on 17 October 1700. Whereas Hodgkinson and Parkins were generally detailed in their minuting of meetings, the entries made by Proctor and Calcraft are relatively less informative. Thus, under Hodgkinson, the average year amounted to a little more than 15 pages whereas under Proctor and Calcraft, the average year was some 11 pages. Under Robert Parkins the average year comprised just over eight pages of the Hall Book, with two years (1693–94 and 1696–97) comprising just five pages each. One obvious contrast between Hodgkinson and his successor is in respect of leases of Corporation property, particularly the school estate. Hodgkinson has some 70 references to leases of property (not counting the town mills, the Red Lyon (see below) or the leases of the tolls). His successor Robert Parkins has no such references in his period of office up to his death in 1685 and Samuel Proctor, Town Clerk from 1685 to 1700, has six such entries in all, although reference is made to a Book of Leases that was among the charters and documents handed over from the outgoing Mayor to the incoming Mayor in 1686 and 1687.[15] Perhaps the Clerk was simply recording decisions on the issue or termination of leases in a separate Lease Book.

Empirically, the standard of record keeping by Samuel Proctor in the 1690s appears much less detailed than that of William Hodgkinson in the 1660s. For the First Court of Alderman Simon Grant on 28 October 1698, the names of the attendees, First and Second Twelves, officials and Commoners are not even recorded. The names of Commoners attending the first courts of the aldermanic year are recorded by Hodgkinson for every year bar one. Where listed, between 1663 and 1692, the number of Commoners named ranges between 16 in 1675 and 37 in 1683, with a mean of 23.7, indicating that the governance of the borough was being conducted by 50 to 60 men out of some 300 households in the town in the late seventeenth century. This was similar to the situation in the 1650s.[16]

Newly-appointed freemen would be expected to take their place as Commoners in the Alderman's Court and would then hold successive posts, perhaps first as a constable in the ward in which they lived, then a junior office within the borough, progressing in due course to the Second Twelve and then to the First Twelve. The *cursus honorum* of Edward Pawlett, bookseller, between December 1660, when he was admitted a freeman, and his death in 1687 illustrates how a man could usefully contribute to his community. In October 1663 and 1664 he was sworn as a Constable and Commoner in the Market Place. In October 1665 and 1666 he was Churchwarden. On 12 October 1666 he was elected to the Second Twelve and rose in seniority, holding the offices of Chief Constable in 1668, 1673 and 1677, Key Keeper of the Common Hutch

---

[15] HB, fos 703v and 709r (29 October 1686 and 27 October 1687).
[16] LRS 106, xxi.

in 1666 and 1669 and Chamberlain also in 1669. On 9 January 1680, Edward Pawlett was promoted with two others to the First Twelve in place of three recently deceased members. In October 1680, Pawlett was made a Collector of the School House lands. His death in February 1687 prevented his attainment of the highest municipal office.[17]

Comburgesses held office for life or until their dismissal and vacancies were filled on the basis of seniority amongst members of the Second Twelve. Membership of that group in turn was filled by senior Commoners whose names appeared in a Kalendar of three names. Accordingly, the average age of the Comburgesses was older than the average age of the Second Twelve. Analysis of ages, based on known baptismal records and other declarations, or through estimating the age at which they were first sworn as freemen (at a minimum of 21 years), shows that the Corporation in the late 1670s comprised Comburgesses with an average age of some 48 years and a Second Twelve of an average of 34 years. The Comburgesses in October 1677 ranged in age from approximately 36 years to 68 years, whilst the Second Twelve were more closely spread in age from some 28 to 38 years.

The ejection of royalist sympathisers in 1647 had led to a town with clear Puritan sympathies and policies directed towards the 'Common Wealth' and 'Publique good' in the period to the Restoration in 1660.[18] The restoration of former royalists following the writ of Mandamus in March 1661 and the royal commission headed by Sir William Thorold had led to the resignation of two further members (William Clarke and Maurice Dalton) in October 1661, bringing a total of nine restored members. The Act for the Well Governing and Regulating of Corporations which received royal assent in December 1661 led to the appointment of county Commissions to require Corporation members to take an oath and subscribe their names and disavow the Solemn Oath and Covenant and to take the sacrament according to the rites of the Church of England. Two Comburgesses (John Simpson and George Briggs) and Matthew Wythey of the Second Twelve declined to subscribe and four non-responding Commoners were accordingly dismissed in August 1662 prior to the First Court of Alderman Michael Taylor with which this present volume commences (Figure 4).[19]

It is this relationship between the borough of Grantham on the one hand and the Stuart kings and central government on the other which forms one of the defining features of the Hall Book in the period through to 1688. The 1661 Act, as Halliday has observed, attempted to undo the changes wrought in the Civil War and Interregnum principally through the swearing by new men of new oaths to new regimes. The aim was to eliminate faction and to create unified corporate bodies throughout the country. However, it was the

---

[17] John B. Manterfield, 'Edward Pawlett of Grantham: A Provincial Bookseller 1660–1687', *Lincolnshire History and Archaeology* 29 (1994), 11–16.
[18] LRS 106, xxviii–xxix.
[19] LRS 106, xx.

4. First Court of Michael Taylor Alderman 31 October 1662 (HB, fo. 370r).

response by individuals within the local communities that shaped both those communities and the success of the Crown's policy. As noted, the Corporation Act led to the removal of just three of the 25 members (not counting any Commoners) of Grantham's Corporation. At 12%, this was a much lower proportion than some neighbouring boroughs. Boston lost 17 of 31 members including its Mayor (52%) and Leicester lost 53%.[20] At Lincoln in August 1662, the Commissioners displaced a significant proportion of the city corporation, namely seven aldermen, both the sheriffs, one coroner, one chief constable, eight common councilmen, one chamberlain, the sword bearer and the mace bearer and also the common clerk.[21] We cannot, of course, know how many of Grantham's governing elite may have sworn softly and remained disgruntled about disavowing the Solemn Oath and Covenant in the years following the Restoration but there is almost no evidence from the Hall Book of the depth of division seen in other towns such as Northampton which was wrought with faction. Certainly, William Clarke, Grantham's leading Puritan – and twice Alderman in the period 1647–60 – had removed to Loughborough and appears to have abstained from active involvement in Grantham matters.[22] After the swearing of oaths in Grantham in accordance with the Corporation Act in 1662, the Hall Book makes no specific reference to the oaths of allegiance and supremacy being signed. However, in the period from 1677 to 1688, there are over 30 references, of which over 20 fall within the period 1677–82. In December 1688, at the third Court of Edward Secker, the Alderman, Comburgesses, Second Twelve men and the Town Clerk all took their oaths of allegiance and supremacy except one John Gibson, a Second Twelve man who refused and was dismissed. It could, of course, be argued that from 1662 to 1677 the normal references to oaths having been sworn as and when new appointments were made included the oaths of allegiance and supremacy as a matter of course and that, accordingly, specific mention in the Hall Book was neither required nor necessary.[23]

The Charter of 1664

Corporate boroughs such as Grantham collectively returned more MPs than did the shire counties. In 1660 the House of Commons comprised 507 members, of which 388 were returned by 201 English boroughs and a further 19 members

---

[20] Paul Halliday, *Dismembering the Body Politic: Partisan Politics in England's Towns, 1650–1730* (Cambridge University Press, 1998).

[21] Sir Francis Hill, *Tudor and Stuart Lincoln* (Cambridge University Press, 1956; republished Stamford, Paul Watkins, 1991), 173.

[22] LRS 106, xlvi. Clarke wrote his will there in June 1671 before returning to Grantham at some point prior to his death in 1682.

[23] HB, fo. 716r (7 December 1688). The Charter of 1631, typical of those in other towns, makes several references to the routine taking of corporal oaths on the appointment of the Alderman and Comburgesses and other officers of the Corporation. The specific inclusion of the oaths of allegiance and supremacy may be viewed as an extension of oath-taking for civic officials.

were returned by 12 Welsh boroughs.[24] The boroughs were therefore of great interest to those seeking a career in Westminster. It was easier to influence the outcome of an election in a borough than in a county owing to the small number of electors; Grantham's 160 or so electors chose two Members whereas the county of Lincoln had an electorate of some 4,000 40-shilling freeholders.[25]

Charles II and his Court advisers were keen to explore ways of exercising control over the boroughs and over the election of MPs. As early as May 1661 a royal warrant proclaimed that charters of re-incorporation would name the initial aldermen, recorder and town clerk and that common council positions (in Grantham's case the Commoners) would only be filled by freemen, as was indeed already the case in Grantham. The warrant also specified that the election of MPs would be by the common council alone and also that the nomination of future recorders and town clerks would be retained by the King rather than merely requiring the king's approval of nominees. Over the next two years only a handful of new charters were granted to boroughs and in those the proposed provisions were diluted and the approbation clause was used more than a nomination clause. After a review in June 1663 the King cancelled the policy, opting instead for the approbation clause.

In Grantham, the restored Corporation was operating under the 1631 charter but was concerned over the actions in 1650 when the borough had bought from parliament the manorial fair and market tolls that had become available when the monarchy had been abolished. The Corporation had surrendered the tolls in August 1660 and the tolls were once more leased from the manor, held as part of the Queen's jointure, to the Corporation. Nevertheless, the Corporation was clearly concerned as to whether that charter fully protected its position. In April 1664, the Attorney General moved an action of *Quo Warranto* against the Corporation to initiate the process by which a new charter could be issued. The Alderman, Robert Calcraft, stated that 'this terme it was convenient to proceed to the renewing of it And for the raiseing of money it is thought necessarie if the Court approve thereof that some members of this Court might goe to the Gentry of the Towne and Country that are freemen of this Corporacion and to acquaint them that the Towne desires their aide advise and assistance in the obtaineing of the Chartor'. Two Comburgesses were to solicit gentlemen in the country and two others in the town. Within ten days the Alderman had raised £50 and Comburgesses Watson and Leeming had raised a further £50 10s secured on a bond. The Town Clerk with Mr William Parkins (the town's solicitor) and Comburgess Michael Taylor was to go to London on the town's behalf. Taylor reported back to the Court on 11 June 1664 that the

---

[24] B. D. Henning (ed.), *The History of Parliament: The House of Commons 1660–1690*, 3 vols (London, Secker and Warburg for The History of Parliament Trust, 1983), I. 104.

[25] Russell S. H. Newton, 'The Social Production of Gentility and Capital in Early Modern England: The Newtons of Lincolnshire' (unpublished PhD thesis, University of Durham, 2016), 312–13.

advice of Counsel and the Attorney General's clerks had been sought and the new charter was to have a confirmation of former grants and that there was to be 'a new proviso that the Kinge reserved the power to setle and confirme all Recordors and Towne Clarkes throughout England (except London) But the Towne may Elect and nominate and the Kinge confirme'. Expenses incurred to date of £6 5s 8d were to be reimbursed by the Chamberlain. Crown officers appeared helpful and the new Charter was finalised quickly and dated 10 June 1664. In April 1665, the Court was informed by the then Alderman, John Watson, that the 'Charter being lately renewed had caused the Towne to expend a hundred and twenty pounds out of the publike stocke' and it was agreed that an Assessment for this amount should be made.[26]

The collection of moneys to defray the cost of the new Charter turned out to be a prolonged process. The Alderman's Court issued an order for an Assessment of £80 in December 1665, with 21 assessors appointed to assist in gathering in the moneys in the town in two equal £40 sums due at Candlemas and Lammas-tide. The legal opinion of Mr Ellis was sought and he gave his opinion that the Assessment may be laid on all inhabitants of the Corporation. All was not plain sailing as Nathaniel Garthwaite refused to pay and his goods, in the form of a keg of soap, were distrained; just £30 had been paid in by the Constables by April 1666. The money was still being collected in July 1667 and in May 1670 it was agreed that the remaining £40 of the Charter Assessment be gathered. The first Court of Alderman Joseph Tomlinson in 1670 agreed that the Charter moneys be collected in by the Constables on pain of 20s per man. Mrs Secker was distrained two pewter dishes towards the Charter Assessment as late as September 1671.[27]

Grantham's Corporation was compliant in seeking the King's approval for the appointment of a new Recorder in November and December 1677 and a new Town Clerk in 1680. Alderman Michael Taylor informed the Court that he had been informed that 'the Right Honorable the Earle of Rutland our Recordor being very Auntient and sickley hath some thoughts to Surrender up his Pattent of Recordorshipp And if this Court pleased it was convenient to elect the Honorable the Lord Roos sonn and heire to the Earle of Rutland Recorder for life when there shall be occasion'. The Court did 'most Unanimously and freely consent And do hereby order that a Pattent of Recordorshipp for life be presented to the Honorable the Lord Roos upon Surrender of the former Pattent And that his Honour be received into this Corporacion with all the solempnities favour and respect that possible may be and as his Honours former Predecessors have beene received to the Grace of this Corparacion'. The King's approbation to the appointment was confirmed on 31 December 1677. Following William

---

[26] HB, fos 384v–385v (30 April, 9 May, 11 June 1664) and 394v (22 April 1665); Martin, *Royal Charters*, 20–2 and 157–69.

[27] HB, fos 402r (15 December 1665), 403v (6 March 1666), 404v (16 June 1666), 516Ar (20 May 1670), 601r (28 October 1670) and 607v (22 September 1671).

Hodgkinson's death in 1679, Sir Robert Carr, Member of Parliament for Lincolnshire, wrote to the Earl of Sunderland recommending Robert Perkins for his Majesty's approbation as Town Clerk of Grantham, but the Earl responded that the certificate had not yet come to him but he would take care to see it was despatched as soon as it did.[28]

Strained Relations within the Soke

As noted above, the Charters of Grantham had confirmed that the Alderman and Comburgesses were responsible for the administration of justice within the town and soke of Grantham and not the County justices. This caused some tension at various levels. At times the county sought a contribution from the town and soke to pay for repairs to the County Hall and gaol; the Corporation resisted any strict liability for this, sending a copy of the Charter to Lincoln in 1663. In 1688, when the question was again raised, the Corporation sought Counsel's opinion. In 1690 'a gratuity & no otherwise' of £15 12s 6d was made towards the building of the Lincolnshire house and gaol, presumably on the basis that from time to time Grantham borough and soke prisoners were housed there at the County assizes. Akin to liability for the upkeep of the gaol was the issue of whether members of the town and soke were liable to be summoned as jurors at Lincoln. This was raised in 1663 and again by the Under Sheriff in May 1689 but it appears that the Corporation was able to hold its position without much difficulty.[29]

More vexing and costly for the Corporation in 1665 was the issue of dissent within the soke. Alderman John Watson acquainted the Court in January 1665 that Comburgesses Robert Calcraft, senior and junior, Thomas Hanson, Michael Taylor and Richard Calcraft, together with Richard Black, bailiff of the liberties, were being sued by some persons in the soke for 'executeing the graunts and powers confirmed to the Corporacion by Charter And for committing & detaineing some of the Soakesmen in prison for severall contempts comitted in open Sessions'. It was unanimously agreed to defend this at the borough's expense. At the same meeting, a letter was produced from Captain Foster, solicitor to the Earl of Lindsey, Lord Great Chamberlain of England, supporting the Corporation in this matter and he was thanked accordingly. At the following Court in February, it was ordered that Mr William Parkins, the town's solicitor with the Town Clerk should appear to defend and maintain the rights of the Corporation. Two letters from the Earl of Rutland, one to Lindsey and the other to Mr Mountague, the Queen's Attorney, were produced in support of the

---

[28] HB, fo. 654v (6 November 1677); *CSPD, Charles II, 1677–1678* (London, HMSO, 1911), 534–5; *CSPD, Charles II, 1680–1681* (London, HMSO, 1921), 8.

[29] The issue of 'foreign' bailiffs seeking to exercise jurisdiction in the town and soke had also occurred during the Inter-regnum. See LRS 106, 172 and 232; HB, fos 373v (16 January 1663), 374v (2 March 1663), 716r and v (7 December 1688 and 18 January 1689), 717v (3 May 1689) and 726v (31 October 1690).

borough's position. In March, the Town Clerk reported further about the several vexatious suits commenced and the support received from the Earl of Rutland, Lindsey, Sir John Newton MP and Lindsey's solicitor. The Town Clerk had by now expended £18 5s 2d, £10 of which had been paid. It was ordered that the outstanding amount with a further bill should be repaid upon the first receipt of moneys. At the next Court in April, it was agreed that Serjeant Newdigate and Mr Ellis should be retained on behalf of the town for the next Assizes. In July the Town Clerk reported that a plea had been entered by the Town Clerk in the Court of King's Bench, as a result of which, the Town Clerk reported, the 'Soakesmen proceeds noe further'. His costs were now £15 13s 2d, which it was agreed should be paid by the Chamberlain on the first receipt of money. Mr Parkins had also incurred charges which he finally presented at a Court in June 1667 amounting to £6 13s 8d plus £4 due to him for two years' salary. The Corporation had succeeded in heading off the challenges from some in the soke but at a cost it could ill afford.[30]

Responding to the Threat of Plague in 1665

Part of the delay in gathering in the Charter money and dealing with the legal action from the sokemen was no doubt the result of the concerns and subsequent actions necessarily taken by the Corporation in dealing with a different external threat. The Great Plague in London had taken hold in the summer heat of June and July 1665. The University of Cambridge was closed as a precaution in late July and Isaac Newton had returned to Woolsthorpe by Colsterworth by early August 1665, returning to Cambridge in March 1666 and again taking refuge in Lincolnshire when there was a resurgence in the early summer.[31] Previous epidemics of pestilence and plague in Grantham had been dealt with since the 1580s by removing infected persons to isolation in the Pest House. This stood in Manthorpe Fields close to the River Witham and almost opposite the present-day Grantham General Hospital. The Pest House was part of the school estate and a clause in the earliest surviving lease of 1584 stated that 'if it shall happen or chance any time hereafter ... the Town and Borough ... to be visited with the plague called the pestilence or any other smiting disease or contagious sickness whereby it shall be thought good to divide the infected people from the whole', then for the 'better safeguard of the said Town', upon two days' warning all the tenants and dwellers within the said messuage or house were to depart to permit and suffer the infected or visited people to enter into the

---

[30] HB, fos 392r (5 January 1665), 393r (3 February 1665), 394r and v (17 March and 22 April 1665), 395r (8 July 1665), 397r (21 September 1665), 400r (27 October 1665) and 413r (10 June 1667).

[31] Rob Iliffe, *Newton: A Very Short Introduction* (Oxford University Press, 2007), 18; Newton himself stated that in the two plague years of 1665 and 1666 he was in the prime of his age for invention.

house.³² In March 1663, the Hall Book records that the Pest House should be repaired and this order was repeated a year later. Carpenter William Bury was to be paid 40s for work undertaken in 1665 but seemingly had to wait for nearly two years as he appeared at the Court in person to request a sum of 16s 7d that remained outstanding.³³

Evidence from administration accounts relating to those who had died during the plague outbreaks in Grantham in 1625 and 1637 show that infected persons were being shut up in their own homes, sometimes with a keeper to look after them. Richard Speedy, his wife Joan and two children had died in May 1637. Richard's brother, Henry, was the administrator of the estate and craved allowance in the accounts for boarding a surviving daughter, Elizabeth, in the time of the visitation. Hellen Selbie was paid five weeks' wages amounting to 20s for keeping 'the deceased's house and to order his three Children of which two then dyed'.³⁴

Clearly though, prevention was better than cure and the Hall Book details the arrangements put into place in 1665, just a generation later than the outbreak of 1637. On 17 August 1665, several weeks after the plague had begun to take hold in London, the Hall Book records, 'Whereas the Court this day takeing into consideracion the great mortalitie that is now in London and in severall places of this Kingdome by reason of the contagion of the Plague And that it is very requisite and necessarie that there should be good and sufficient Watch and Ward kept within this Burrough day and night to examine Passingers from whence they come so that by such meanes (& Gods almightie assistance) all suspected persons may be kept out of this Towne and the [sic] preserved from the said dangerous disease'. The watch was to be kept by every inhabitant householder upon pain of 10s to be levied by distress on anyone refusing or neglecting their duty. The Constables were appointed to see that the watch and ward were set and 'to give the charge to the said Watchmen as by the laws of this Kindome they are comanded and injoyned'.³⁵

At the next Court on 15 September, the Alderman felt that the order 'for keeping stronge Watch and Ward' was 'much neglected for want of some persons to Oversee the Watchmen that they doe their duty'. Accordingly, members of the First and Second Twelves were to oversee the Watchmen as Masters of the Ward and were freed from any watching during the day or night. Less than a week later, a further Court was held on 21 September at which the Alderman informed the Court 'that in this dangerous time of sicknes and mortalitie it

---

³² LAO, BNLW 1/1/35/398.
³³ HB, fos 375v (27 March 1663), 384r (11 March 1664), 403r (23 January 1666) and 411v (25 January 1667).
³⁴ LAO, LCC Ad. Acc. 25/186 (Richard Speedy).
³⁵ Paul Slack, *The Impact of Plague in Tudor and Stuart England* (London, Routledge & Kegan Paul, 1985); G. Melvyn Howe, *Man, Environment and Disease in Britain: A Medical Geography of Britain through the Ages* (Newton Abbot, David & Charles, 1972); HB, fo. 396r (17 August 1665).

is very requisite & needfull that the Corps of every person dying within this Burrough should be searched that it may be knowne what disease they dye on And by such meanes with the Aide and Assisstance of Almightie God the contagion of the Plague may be prevented in this Towne or otherwise the persons remaineing in such houses may be forthwith removed'. Four persons were appointed as searchers of corpses and any deaths were to be reported to the Alderman within half an hour so that the corpse could be searched. In the event, the measures appear to have had success and were scaled back on or after 27 October when it was noted that 'the Watch being now kept all night was being prejudiciall to the Watchmen by reason of the cold and the lenght [sic] of the nights' and so it was to be kept until 9 o'clock. On 15 December 1665, the Watch was reduced to six and members of the First and Second Twelves were discharged from watching in person.[36] Given Grantham's position on the Great North Road from London to York and Edinburgh, precautions were certainly prudent and necessary and the Corporation was no doubt thankful to the Almighty that plague had not decimated the town.

The Borough's Half Pence

During the 1650s, eight individual Grantham shopkeepers had issued farthings or halfpennies in response to the shortage of small change.[37] Change had again become scarce in the 1660s and at least six individual merchants in Grantham had begun to issue brass half pence or farthings. John Plummer, brazier, and Zachary Laxton, mercer, were responsible for farthings bearing dates of 1663 and 1664 respectively. Anthony Hotchkin, mercer, and Thomas Walton were responsible for farthings dated 1666, with Edward Pawlett, bookseller, and Henry Humes producing halfpennies in the same year. Town Corporations including Boston, Grantham, Stamford and Lincoln followed suit. Townsend notes that in Boston £20 worth of brass or copper half pence was ordered to be sent for on 4 October 1667. Spalding and Grantham half pence are also dated 1667 (Figure 5) and were to be exchanged by the Overseers of the Poor, as were Louth and Stamford which were undated. Lincoln City tokens are dated 1669 and were to be changed by the Mayor.[38]

The Hall Book sheds further light on the process of obtaining the half pence and the Corporation's motive and the difficulties that followed five years later when Charles II issued a proclamation to issue his own farthings. In December 1667, Alderman Thomas Short acquainted the Court that 'severall Corporacions have sett forth brasse halfe pence with the Townes Armes on them for the benefitt of the poore of the said Townes and that it might be very advantageous

---

[36] HB, fos 396v–397r (15 and 21 September 1665), 401r (27 October 1665) and 402r (15 December 1665).
[37] LRS 106, xxv.
[38] T. W. Townsend, *Seventeenth Century Tradesmen's Tokens of Lincolnshire: The Issuers*, Lincolnshire Museums Occasional Papers 2 (1983).

5. Town halfpence 1667 and halfpenny of Edward Pawlett, bookseller, 1666.

for this Corporacion to set forth halfe pence with the Armes of this Towne upon them and desired this Court to take the same into their consideracion Whereupon this Court haveing considered of the benefitt that may accrue thereby doth order that the present Chaimberlaine do send to London for brasse Halfepence with the Chequor of the one side and Grantham and the yeare of our Lord on the other side and to be written aboute the Rim, to be exchanged by the Overseer of the Poore And that the same be obtained as soone as may be'. On 20 January 1668, it was agreed that 20 pounds in weight be sent for. From the weight of the least-worn examples in the author's possession, it is estimated that this would amount to at least 4,600 halfpenny tokens. If we were to say

4,800 then that would represent a cash value of some £10. That this is indeed a reasonable estimate is supported in the two accounts detailed in the Hall Book in 1668. In the first on 26 June, the currency value of forty-six pounds weight of the Town's half pence is given as £21 2s 3d and on 22 October the currency value of forty pounds weight is given as £19 0s 0d. The disbursements in the first case amounted to £11 5s 9d, and in the second case £8 8s 2d was 'paid for them at London and Carriage down'. In other words, the Corporation was able to generate an income equating to about twice the cost of the halfpennies.[39]

Naturally with half pence also being produced by shopkeepers within the town, who realised that they too could benefit, the Corporation felt the income of its own tokens was under threat. In July 1669, the Alderman's Court recorded, 'Whereas the Court takeing this day into consideracion the great inconveniencie of severall sorts of brasse halfe pence in perticular mens name that are spread abroad and some of them not easely to be discerned who sett forth the same As also that the halfe pence the Corporacion hath sett out are laid up by severall Persons that their owne half pence may goe the better which is a great preiudice to this Corporacion For prevencion whereof for the future It is hereby ordered that Mr Alderman do cause proclamacion to be made in the Towne to prohibite all Persons in this Burrough from receiveing the brasse halfe pence of perticular men so that other halfe [*sic*] may not tend to the prejudice of this Corporacion'.[40]

Further half pence were sent for from the borough in batches of 40 pounds weight in October 1669, June 1670, October 1671 and May 1672.[41] Within months, Alderman John Lenton informed the Court that 'his Majestie was aboute setting forth farthings of his owne stampe and that all other halfepence would be prohibited for goeing And that till such time as the Proclamacion should come forth it was convenient that the Towne halfepence should passe in this Corporacion Whereupon it is ordered that all such Persons as take or exchange any of the Towne halfe shall have the same exchanged againe by the Chaimberlaine and shall for their so doeing be saved and kept harmles by this Corporacion'. Over the next three months a total of £113 of half pence were exchanged and £100 was borrowed from Mr Burnett on the security of the Schoolhouse lands. As late as April 1674, it was agreed that Mr Robert Cole 'have the Townes halfe pence that is in his hands changed by the present Chaimberlaine except to the value of xxs'.[42] It would appear therefore that there were upwards of 55,000 borough half pence in circulation in Grantham in the

---

[39] HB, fos 419r (20 December 1667), 500r (20 January 1668), 502r (26 June 1666) and 506r (22 October 1668). Fo. 512r (21 October 1669) details that 40 pounds weight represented £19 6s 6d in currency.

[40] HB, fo. 510v (16 July 1669).

[41] HB, fos 514r (29 October 1669), 516Br (23 June 1670), 610r (27 October 1671) and 612r (10 May 1672).

[42] HB, fos 613v and 614r (6 and 20 September 1672), 618r (1 November 1672) and 626v (10 April 1674).

early 1670s equating to some 200 per household on average, with additionally the halfpennies and farthings circulating from other Grantham merchants and tradesmen.

Examination of extant Grantham half pence indicates that five different dies were used during the course of the five years of their issue. Although the text on the Obverse 'A. HALF. PENY. TO. BE. EXCHAINGD' and on the Reverse 'BY. YE. OVERSEERS. OF. YE. POORE. GRANTHAM.1667' remains the same on the examples struck from the different dies, there are notable variations with the way in which the borough's arms are depicted. Some have a chequerboard or checky of five rows whereas others have five or six or even seven rows with the latter having two variants, one with seven rows as 3.3.3.3.3.3.3 and the other as 3.3.3.3.3.3.2 individual squares (Figure 5).[43] Although no individual manufacturer is named, the Hall Book confirms that the production of the borough half pence took place in London and was not undertaken locally.[44]

The Church and Religious Dissent in Grantham

The Municipal Corporations Act of 1662 had established a clear framework that those involved as municipal governors in Grantham and other towns were to be communicant members of the Church of England. In 1671 the Hall Book records that it was 'very necessarie' that all of the first and second Company 'should goe to the Church in their Gownes according to former order of this Court Whereupon it is ordered that the first and 2nd Company do every Sunday and upon every Christmas day upon the fifth day of November and the 29 May come to the Church constantly in the Gownes whether raine or any other foule weather happen upon paine to forfeite xijd. for every Offence'.[45] Not only were the Corporation members to wear their gowns but also the Chief Constables and Petty Constables should attend with their staves upon pain of 12d a piece. As we have seen above, the two Churchwardens were effectively Corporation appointees and the matter of raising moneys for repairs of the Church steeple, struck by lightning in July 1652, dragged on for several years and later other repairs too needed finance.[46] Such references in the Grantham Hall Book greatly outnumber references to any non-conformity or religious discontent. In 1669 the two Chief Constables, John Turner and Edward Pawlett, sought to be indemnified by the Corporation against legal action from one John Horner who was suing them for having been put in prison for having assembled with

---

[43] Townsend, *Tradesmen's Tokens*, 32.
[44] R. H. Thompson, 'Central or local production of seventeenth-century tokens', *British Numismatic Journal* 59 (1989), 198–211.
[45] HB, fo. 604r (9 March 1671). The 5 November and 29 May being the anniversaries of the discovery of the Gunpowder Plot in 1605 and of the entry of Charles II into London at the Restoration in 1660.
[46] LRS 106, xxxii–xxxiii.

others during the time of divine service. The Chief Constables argued that 'what they did was in execucion of their Office for finding him and many others assembled together under pretence of religious worships & contrarey to the lawes of this Kingdome during the time of divine service at the Church they did secure the said Horner and others in prison untill Mr Alderman for the yeare past and his Brethren had the examinacion of them And that their onely indeavor was to preserve the peace of his Majestie and the peace of his Kingdome and of this Corporacion'. The Alderman's Court agreed that local attorney Mr Secker might appear for them and that the Chief Constables should be saved harmless and indemnified from all charges, damages and expenses by reason of the said suit. John Horner was a shoemaker who had been made free as a foreign (not free-born) apprentice in 1661 and so would have been about 29 years old at the time that he was imprisoned in the town gaol.[47] In the event, Secker acted, incurring legal expenses of £4 4s 2d which were ordered to be paid as part of the Constables' bills for 1670–71 in that the Chief Constables incurred this in the execution of their Office and that they were 'acting for the preservacion of his Majesties peace and good of this Corporacion'. The Chamberlain appears not to have paid the final charges until February 1672.[48] Where exactly the 'pretence of religious worship' had been held is not known and the diocesan archives have no record of any licensed meeting place in Grantham until the mid-eighteenth century.[49] In any event, by the Declaration of Indulgence in 1672 Charles II sought to relax the penal laws against Protestant non-conformists and Catholics, much to the annoyance of Anglican clergy. Parliament responded in February 1673 with the Test Act, which deprived Catholics and non-conformists of public office. The Religious Census of 1676 gave the total number of adult communicants in Grantham as 1,460, comprising 1,440 conformists, five papists and 15 non-conformists. This represents 98.6% conformists, 1.4% in terms of dissenters and less than 0.4% as Roman Catholic. Grantham thus shows a higher degree of conformity than across the county as a whole, where 2.88% of the 88,107 population were non-conformists and 0.66% were papists. In Lincoln, which had a total from 13 parishes of 2,461 adults, nearly 5% were non-conformists and 0.66% papists. For Boston, the return was 150 non-conformists (5.6%) and 2,500 conformists (94.4%).[50]

Minor repairs to St Wulfram's Church in Grantham were financed by the Churchwardens who then claimed back their expenses, paid by the Chamberlains, after the end of the financial year. Where greater expenditure

---

[47] HB, fo. 514r (29 October 1669); LRS 106, 296.
[48] HB, fos 607r (4 August 1671) and 622v (16 February 1672).
[49] LAO, Dioc/Diss/1A/7 (1 November 1769) relating to a house in Sandpit Lane used by Particular Baptists.
[50] Arthur S. Langley, 'A religious census of 1676 A.D.', *Lincolnshire Notes and Queries* 16:2 (1920), 34, 50; Hill, *Tudor and Stuart Lincoln*, 181.

was anticipated, the Alderman's Court periodically agreed that there would be assessments made across the borough. Sums were collected from each household according to periodic 'rentals' or valuations of property and in the 1660s and 1670s on the personal wealth of the assessed goods of individuals. Between 1668 and 1695, 13 assessments were levied to raise amounts ranging between £20 and £80, with an average of some £20 8s 6d *per annum*. During the 1660s, the Alderman's Court stressed the urgency of repairs. In 1671 it was noted that the 'Church is very much out of repairs' and unless speedy action was taken 'part of it is likely to fall down', and in the following year 'the same is yet in great decay' and 'if speedy care be not taken the repaires of the said Church will be very chargeable'.[51] The amount of detail given as to the nature of the repairs is poor, although it was noted in March 1663 that the 'much ruinated and decayed' North Porch was to be repaired. In 1675 the repairs related to windows and the leads but later expenditure is recorded simply as for the repairs of the church.[52] One specific item that attracted support from the Earl of Rutland in 1663 was the setting up of the chimes, indicating a clock at the church in addition to one at the Guildhall. By 1694 the church chimes were 'now out of repaire' and the then present and succeeding Churchwardens were told that they should 'take Care that the said Chimes for the future be kept in good repair'. Mr Fisher, Churchwarden in October 1697, made a bargain with Edward Dickenson to keep the Hall Clock in good repair at 5s *per annum* and in March 1700 it was agreed that 'the Church Clock being broke Edward Dickenson undertakes to mend it for tenn shillings'. In 1701 a foreigner, John Fox, was admitted to his freedom having given security 'for the keeping the Church Clock and Chimes and the Town Clock in good repaires'.[53]

The Grammar School

Sam Branson observed that the second half of the seventeenth century was highly successful for the School, with many scholars who became national figures in later life, most notably, of course, Isaac Newton. Much of the success of the School was down to the ability of individual Masters and their assistant Ushers. Hugh Wilkinson was the Master from 1605 to 1645 and Henry Stokes, head whilst Newton attended, was in charge between 1650 and December 1663, when he resolved to go to Melton to be School Master there.[54]

Three masters held office in the 40 years between 1663 and 1703. Rev. Thomas Syston was appointed at the same Court as Henry Stokes's resignation was accepted. Town Clerk William Hodgkinson appears to have referred

---

[51] HB, fos 419v (10 January 1668) and 509r (8 April 1669).
[52] HB, fos 374v and 375v (2 and 27 March 1663).
[53] HB, fos 375v (27 March 1663), 741r (30 November 1694), 749r (29 October 1697), 756r (7 March 1700) and 761v (25 July 1701).
[54] S. J. Branson, *A History of the King's School, Grantham: 660 Years of a Grammar School* (Gloucester, Alan Sutton, 1988); LRS 106, xxxiii–xxxiv; HB, fo. 382v (8 December 1663).

back to the record of Stokes's appointment, as the words used to record Syston's acceptance are virtually identical. Syston 'with all thankefullnes accepted of the same and promised to bestow his paines and utmost indeavours for the Improvement of this Schoole whereby he might bring Glory to God and benefitt to this Corporacion'. Indeed, the conditions of service were spelled out, namely:

> that it shall be *ad bene placitum* of the Alderman Comburgesses and Burgesses of this Corporacion either for the further continuance of the said Mr Syston in his place of the Schoole Master of Grantham upon his good Behavior, orderly method of teaching and sufficiencey for learning and knowledge or otherwise to displace him for non abilitie of learning upon Evident proofe thereof whereof as yet noe ambiguitie or question is made. It is likewise deemed very requisite by the whole Court that it shall be in the power and Authoritie of the said Alderman Comburgesses and Burgesses of Grantham and their Successors either to place or displace any Schoole Master that now is or hereafter shall possess that place upon reasonable & sufficient cause as in their wisdomes and discretions shall be thought convenient or by the wisdomes and discretions of the most part of them.[55]

In January 1671, Alderman Joseph Tomlinson informed the Court that Syston had given him notice that a new School Master should be provided at Lady Day next, as he was hopeful that Sir John Brownlow would give him the Belton living and that he did not think that Sir John would let him continue with the School as well as hold the living. Sir John, however, was willing to allow Syston to have the living and to continue with the school but the Court decided to 'peruse the Article and Grant of the School and give Syston a further answer at the next Court day'. The response from the Court was that Mr Syston's proposal to continue with both was 'in noe way satisfactorie' but it was agreed that Syston should continue until Lady Day. In the event, Syston continued for a few more months, promising in May to resign 'at Midsomer next'. Eventually it was agreed in July that, in consideration of £10 paid to him by the Town, he would 'deliver unto the Alderman and Burgesses of this Burrough peaceable possession of the Colledge House and Schoole House of Grantham'.[56]

At the Alderman's Court on 10 July when Syston finally agreed his departure date, a letter from William Walker was read and the Court 'takeing into consideracion that he is a learned Person and a Schoole Master of great note and that it may be very advantageous to this Corporacion do with a free and unanimous consent elect the said Mr Walker Head Schoole Master within this Burrough'. Four days later, Alderman Richard Holley, appointed on 6 July

---

[55] LRS 106, xxxiv; HB fo. 382v (8 December 1663).
[56] HB, fos 602v (6 January 1671), 603r (n.d. January 1671), 605r (12 May 1671) and 10 July 1671. Thomas Syston was also rector of Bloxholm from 23 December 1667 to 23 March 1671 and rector of Belton from 17 December 1670 until his death on 14 December 1710: see LAO, Reg. 33, fos 95v, 137, 139v; Reg. 36, fo. 144.

following the death of his predecessor Joseph Tomlinson, had to inform the Court 'that Mr Walker was not willing to accept of the Head Schoole Masters place belonging to the Corporacion he haveing the proposicions performed with Mr Tomlinson the late Alderman promised him that was to have iij li vj s viij d added to this Sallary and some Roomes made convenient'. After discussion, 'takeing into consideracion as also that the said Mr Walker is a Worthy Person a learned Schollar and an able Schoole Master and is likely to improve the Schoole to the advantage of this Corporacion It is therefore at this Court ordered by an unanimous consent of this Court that the said Mr Walker be admitted' as Head Schoolmaster on terms that previous Masters had enjoyed plus the additional salary of £3 6s 8d and have some rooms made convenient for him.[57]

Walker was certainly experienced, having been Usher and then Master at Louth Grammar School from 1646 and then 1651–57. He was Rector and Schoolmaster at Welton-le-Wold from 1662 before being instituted as Rector in Colsterworth on 21 February 1663. He was the author of *A Treatise of English Particles* (1655). This became a standard school text, reissued until at least the fifteenth edition in 1720. Indeed, four editions published between 1673 and 1683, whilst Walker was Master of the Grammar School in Grantham, were published in London by Robert Pawlett, the older brother of Edward Pawlett, then a member of the Second Twelve and later Comburgess in Grantham. Walker's *Some Improvements in the Art of Teaching* (1669) saw four further editions between 1676 and 1687. Of particular note are three works by William Walker that bear the imprint 'Printed for Robert Pawlet at the Sign of the Bible in Chancery Lane near Fleet-street, and Edward Pawlet Bookseller in Grantham 1670'. These books are *An Explanation of the Rules of the Royal Grammar, Touching Heteroclisies or Irregular Declining of Nouns*; *An Explanation of the Royal Grammar, Touching the Preterperfect Tense* and *The Royal Grammar, Commonly Called Lylly's Grammar Explained*. Walker also wrote *A Modest Plea for Infant Baptism* (1677) and *Baptismon Didache, the Doctrine of Baptisms* (1678).[58]

Walker was certainly deeply learned but the Hall Book indicates that his physical health may not have been strong. Walker petitioned the Alderman's Court in November 1672 that 'the Season of the yeare being very cold and he weake it would be requisite that there were a Portell to the Schoole doore and a little house build on the side of the Schoole in the Garden with a Chimley in it which Roome would be very convenient upon many occasions And if this Court would be pleased to take care that the same be done he should thinke himselfe obliged to the Towne'. The Court ordered this to be built, with the money to be raised by a general contribution to which seven members of the

---

[57] HB, fo. 606v (14 July 1671).
[58] Nicholas Bennett, *Lincolnshire Parish Clergy c.1214–1968: A Biographical Register. Part II: The Deaneries of Beltisloe and Bolingbroke*, LRS 105 (2016), 70–1; Manterfield, 'Edward Pawlett of Grantham', 12.

First Twelve, seven of the Second Twelve and 15 Commoners contributed, there and then raising a total of £3 10s 6d.[59]

Walker died on 1 August 1684 and is buried at Colsterworth with the Latin inscription on his memorial gravestone, 'Here lie the particles of Walker'. The Master was supported by a second master, the Usher. Rev. Richard Poole had been Usher from January 1671 until Lady Day 1677 as he had obtained the living at Hough and he was succeeded as Usher by a man described in the Hall Book as being 'a very fitt person for the said place', namely Richard Calcraft son of Comburgess Mr Richard Calcraft. Richard Calcraft resigned as Usher from Lady Day 1687 when he was succeeded by Mr Thomas Mills.[60]

Walker's successor as Master in 1684 was the Vicar of North Grantham, Rev. Samuel Burnett, who had been appointed Vicar in 1670 and was licensed to preach within the diocese of Lincoln. Clearly, he was well known to, and trusted by, Corporation members and perhaps, as suggested by Sam Branson, it was envisaged that more responsibility was to be placed on the Usher. This may explain the appointment of Richard Calcraft and the overplus of the Head Schoolmaster's salary being paid in April 1686 to Mr Mills described as 'Assistant to the Master for his great care and paines he takes in looking to the Schoole'. Calcraft continued as Usher until Lady Day 1687, at which point Thomas Mills was formally appointed Usher. The arrangement whereby Mills received the overplus money from the Schoolhouse rents was confirmed by the Alderman's Court in September 1688 and August 1690. Concerns about the School under Burnett's headship may, however, be deduced from a Hall Book entry from August 1689 when it was ordered that 'Mr Cole, Mr Matkin, Mr Ireland, Mr Leivesly, Mr Robinson, Mr Beck, Mr Grant & as many of the first & second company as can meet doe speake to Mr Burnet about the afaires of the Schoole'. There is no entry giving the outcome of that conversation, although in March 1691 it was agreed that 'Mr Burnett is ordered to be continued Schoolemaster of this towne & to enjoy the profitts thereunto belongeing'.[61]

Thomas Mills, being obliged to reside at his living in Newton, was succeeded in March 1691 as Usher by Edmund Machin. Machin became curate to Mr Smith in Westborough and left to reside there in September 1697. The Hall Book states that 'upon the Request of Mr Samuel Coddington by his Friends in Court to Supply the said place he is unanimously chosen Usher of the Schoole of the said Towne and to enter upon the said place and perquisites at Michaelmas next'. In turn, Coddington himself gained a living in the country and 'could not

---

[59] HB, fo. 618v (8 November 1672).
[60] Bennett, *Lincolnshire Parish Clergy II*, 70–1; HB, fos 603r (n.d. January 1671), 650r (7 December 1676) and 704r (21 January 1687).
[61] Branson, *King's School Grantham*, 29–30 and 140; LAO, Reg. 33, fo. 128; HB, fos 60r (7 December 1676), 700r (30 April 1686), 704r (21 January 1687), 712v (28 September 1688), 719r (9 August 1688), 724r (29 August 1690) and 728r (6 March 1691).

attend the School att such times as necessary and desired to be dismissed from the said place' and Mr Charles Burnett (possibly a younger son of Rev. Samuel Burnett) was granted the post of Usher in 1699.[62]

Rev. Samuel Burnett proposed to step down at Lady Day 1702 and was given a gratuity of £20 for his voluntary resignation. It was agreed that Mr Charles Burnett should continue as Usher. In April 1702, Rev. John Troughton of Lowestoft was unanimously elected Schoolmaster subject to the same conditions as Mr Wilkinson, Mr Stokes and Mr Syston had accepted. Samuel Burnett was granted £4 per annum out of the Schoolhouse rents paid quarterly for three years if Mr Burnett lived so long.[63]

The Hall Book reflects the time spent by the Corporation in the management of the school estate. Three or four times a year on average, discussion took place about renewals of leases, new tenants and occasionally dealing with those in arrears. Where properties were in poor condition, an incoming tenant would sometimes promise to repair or rebuild the house, for example when William Beriffe took on the lease of a house in Swinegate formerly in the tenure of Henry Haire in January 1666. Again, when Mrs Wilkinson took on the lease of the 'House in Westgate burnt down by the late fire and since rebuilt by her' in October 1667, she was allowed to have a new lease from the expiration of the old lease at the old entry fine of 40s. At other times, where the entry fines were large, then a phased payment was agreed.[64]

In 1675 Town Clerk William Hodgkinson calculated that the total potential income from entry fines was £604 13s 4d and offered to raise a significant part of the town's debts if he had full power to let with fines certain all the houses and land belonging to the Corporation by Christmas next. This was agreed but in January 1676 a group of Comburgesses and Second Twelve men were ordered to examine the leases now to be made fine certain. It was said that there was a covenant for the fine certain not to be paid until the last year of the lease and the former orders of the Court were for that to be paid in the last five years whereas 'many pay their Fines haveing sixteene yeares to come in their Leases'. It was agreed that fines were to be paid before the expiration of the lease and all former orders about renewing leases were to be made void, repealed and revoked.[65]

---

[62] Nicholas Bennett, *Lincolnshire Parish Clergy c.1214–1968: A Biographical Register. Part I: The Deaneries of Aslacoe and Aveland*, LRS 103 (2013), 292; HB, fos 728v (27 March 1691), 748v (17 September 1697) and 753r (22 June 1699). Samuel Coddington was appointed Curate of Londonthorpe Chapel on 26 September 1698 and subsequently (7 November 1702) Master of Boston Grammar School (LAO, Reg. 35, fos 52, 89v).

[63] HB, fos 765v (27 February 1702), 766r (8 April 1702) and 766r (22 May 1702).

[64] HB, fos 402v (23 January 1666) and 414r (4 October 1667). James Long's fine of £3 6s 8d for a house in Castlegate was split with 33s to be paid on 24 June 1671 and 33s 4d on 1 May 1672, although he finally made full payment in January 1675: HB, fos 604r (9 March 1671), 634r (15 January 1675).

[65] HB, fos 635v (16 April 1675) and 642v (6 January 1676).

The Grammar School was not the only school in the borough. The former King's Chaplain Dr Thomas Hurst had, with three others, lent the town £2,000 on the security of a lease of the mills in 1649/50 and was a lessee of part of the Schoolhouse lands. In September 1666, Hurst was generous towards the town yet again. He informed the Alderman's Court that he was 'building of foure Schooles for the educateing and bringing up of poore Children in learning and other labor which may tend to the great benefitt and advantage of this Corporacion by setting the poore on Worke and keepeing them from an idle and loose kind of liveing'. A group of nine men chosen from the First and Second Twelves with five Commoners were to meet with Hurst about the settling of the schools and paying the School Dames. On 12 October the group reported that they had met with Dr Hurst, who had paid £40 to the town to generate 12d a week for 48 weeks. Hurst would also pay £40 more (previously pledged for the repair of the Alms-houses he had given to the town which he now undertook to repair himself) and give to the town £4 a year from the rent of six houses. In January 1667, Dr Hurst informed the Court that three schools would be sufficient and desired to know how the Court was proposing to meet the weekly costs of running the schools. Alderman Richard Leeming 'was pleased to let this court understand that a very worthy person at the Grange, Arthur Gorge Esquire, was pleased out of his good will for the releife of the poore to give x s in money every moneth, And that he had moved him in case the said money should be paid to Doctor Hursts Schoole dames towards their sallory that he would please to approve thereof.' A further 6d a week was to be paid by the Chamberlain as this, with the contribution from Arthur Gorge, would cover the computed running costs. In August 1670, Doctor Hurst was offering the Corporation £50, the interest of which was to go towards the salary of the School Dames.[66]

The names of the early teachers at Hurst's school or schools are not systematically noted in the Hall Book. In July 1690, Mrs Judith Smith, widow of Robert Smith, former church clerk, was appointed School Dame in succession to George Hutchin.[67] Clearly the Corporation was actively taking responsibility for the education of children within the borough to a greater or lesser extent, although the deliberations recorded in the Hall Book are not always consistent.

The Borough and its Members of Parliament

The right of election of the two Burgesses returned to represent the Borough of Grantham rested with the Freemen of the borough who had obtained that

---

[66] HB, fos 405v–406r (28 September and 12 October 1666), 411r (18 January 1667) and 517r (15 August 1670). Setting the poor on work had been a deliberate policy of Grantham's Puritan rulers during the Inter-regnum – see LRS 106, xxxviii–xxxix. For Thomas Hurst, see J. Peile, *Biographical Register of Christ's College, Cambridge, 1505–1905* (2 vols, Cambridge University Press, 1910–13), I. 295.

[67] HB, fo. 724r (4 July 1690).

freedom through patrimony (as the eldest son of a freeman), through apprenticeship to an existing freeman and less commonly through purchase. Women were not enfranchised. In the late seventeenth century, the normal cost of admission for a foreigner (someone not born in Grantham) was £10 and often this was remitted in part or in full if the prospective freeman offered, for example, to repair and maintain the Conduit or the town and church clocks. The Corporation also bestowed the freedom on local gentry who may have favoured it with loans and gifts. In essence therefore the Corporation controlled the freeman roll and hence the franchise.[68]

The election held for the Convention Parliament in 1660 had resulted in a landslide for the Royalist candidates, Thomas Skipwith, a lawyer and resident in Grantham House in Castlegate, and John Newton, who obtained twice as many votes as William Ellis, solicitor general in the Inter-regnum, and William Bury, also a lawyer and Cromwellian knight who had been MP for Grantham in 1654.[69]

The Corporation had been lobbied during 1661 on behalf of the queen mother (lady of the manor of Grantham) to consider her attorney general, Sir Peter Ball, and her treasurer, Sir Henry Wood, as candidates. The Corporation politely declined Sir Peter, noting that it was 'not in their power to make choice of a Burgesse without the consent of the whole Burrough'.[70] Sir Henry Wood was proving a more useful potential candidate in the negotiations over the town's lease of the tolls and the Town Clerk reported that he 'was very respectfull to this Corporacion and did Act very much for the good thereof'.[71] The Corporation was keen to raise money for the repairs of the Steeple and sought support from local gentry; a board naming benefactors was agreed by the Corporation in March 1661. Ellis subscribed £20 but in the event he did not stand for election, as John Newton and a prominent Cavalier, Sir William Thorold of Marston, were returned unopposed for the borough of Grantham from 17 April 1661. Thorold was born c.1591 and had been fined heavily by Parliament. At the Restoration he was appointed as a JP for Kesteven and as a commissioner for assessment in Kesteven. Thorold made a gift of £40 to the Corporation in October 1669. He remained one of Grantham's MPs until his death on 4 March 1678, John Newton remaining the other Member throughout the Cavalier Parliament which ran to 1679.[72]

Within Parliament as well as across the nation, there had developed, by the 1670s, a polarisation of court against country. In Lincolnshire, Sir Robert Carr had initially been elected as the court candidate and was connected by

---

[68] LRS 106, xxxvi; HB, fos 684v (29 September 1683) and 761v (25 July 1701).
[69] Henning (ed.), *The House of Commons 1660–1690*, I. 300–2 (Grantham Constituency). Skipwith and Newton received c.140 and c.120 votes respectively, with Ellis receiving c.40 votes and William Bury 20.
[70] LRS 106, 298.
[71] LRS 106, 300–11 (*passim*).
[72] Henning (ed.), *The House of Commons 1660–1690*, III. 558 (Sir William Thorold).

marriage to Henry Bennett, later Earl of Arlington, a leading member of the Cabal ministry. Carr was rewarded with the office of Chancellor of the Duchy of Lancaster but he incurred heavy personal debts as a courtier. After the fall of the Cabal, Carr moved into opposition. Opposing him was Robert Bertie, third Earl of Lindsey, Lord Great Chamberlain and Lord Lieutenant of Lincolnshire.[73]

The History of Parliament states that canvassing for Thorold's seat began in spring 1677, when Lord Roos, with the assent of Lindsey, proposed Sir Edmond Turnor of Panton as the court candidate. At Alderman Michael Taylor's fourth Court in December 1677 both the Earl and Lord Roos, together with Baptist, Lord Campden, were admitted to the freedom of the town and tendered their £40 apiece, 'which was by a free harty and generall consent of the whole Court returned againe to their Lordshipps'. At the same Court, Sir Robert Markham of Sedgebrook desired to be made free and tendered his £40, which he was 'very chearefully willing shall goe for the use of this Corporacion'.[74] Lindsey's political rival for the country, as opposed to the court, grouping was Sir Robert Carr of Aswardby who, with the support of John Newton (now brought over to opposition), was backing Sir William Ellys, Bt, for the Grantham seat. Sir William was the nephew and heir of the Parliamentarian judge, William Ellys, who had represented the borough in the 1650s. Sir Robert Carr had lent the Corporation £1,000, which was to be repaid at the rate of £100 a year over ten years out of the profits of the town's mills. Ellys apparently offered a similar sum, interest-free, also for ten years, even hinting that he might 'burn the bonds' if elected. Turnor may not have been in a position to match Ellys financially, although both could provide ale for potential supporters in local inns. Thorold actually died in the middle of a heated session in Parliament on 4 March 1677/8. A document originally from the Temple family of Stowe (published in the *Huntington Library Quarterly* in 1944) gives more detail of the by-election. The document states that they (Ellys and Turnor) 'began to drink & make entertainment in the town near 12 months before Sir William Thorold died whereby they spent great sums of money extravagantly'. Days before the election, Turnor dropped out and Sir Robert Markham was a last-minute choice as court candidate. It was stated that 'Sir Robert Markham never thought of standing before the election when [he] was invited thereto he went down on Saturday 9th of March, came to Grantham 10th /declared he would stand 11th /was elected on the 12th'.[75] Lindsey mustered the militia in Grantham in support of Markham on polling day, gaining 76 votes to 66 votes among ratepayers (those paying Lot and Scot).

---

[73] Clive Holmes, *Seventeenth-Century Lincolnshire*, History of Lincolnshire VII (Lincoln, 1980), 238–42.

[74] Henning (ed.), *The House of Commons 1660–1690*, I. 300–2 (Grantham Constituency); HB, fo. 656r (21 December 1677).

[75] Godfrey Davies, 'The By-Election at Grantham, 1678', *Huntington Library Quarterly* 7 (1944) 179–82.

The source then continues,

> And besides this Sir Robert Markham offers against 15 of Sir William Ellises voices that they were procured by notorious briberies which takes them off:

Sir Robert Markham had		Sir William Ellis had	
Good voices Residents paying Lot & Scot	76	Good voices Residents paying Lot & Scot	66
Residents that pay neither Lot nor Scot	14	Residents that pay neither Lot nor Scot	23
Foreigners Nonresidents	14	Paupers that receive collections	04
		Foreigners Nonresidents	18
	104		111

Controversy ensued when Alderman John Wing returned Markham as elected Member 'with the unanimous assent and consent of the freemen and commanalty', presumably by disallowing the four paupers and the 15 that Ellys had allegedly bribed. Holmes has commented that 'Lindsey's success in securing tame borough officers then proved its worth'.[76] Needless to say, the return of Markham was challenged by petition in the House of Commons submitted by Ellys on 16 March and again on 23 May, when a new Committee of Privileges and Elections was named. On 10 June the Committee reported that Markham was not duly elected and that Ellys was. Davies states that the question was then put to the House, to agree with the Committee, and a division took place. The Noes voted 179, the Ayes 167 and so the House, having rejected the Committee's report, agreed that Markham was duly elected. The consensus was that the real loser was Carr who, it was said, was in a state of great mortification and was struck off the Privy Council.[77]

Clearly the by-election and the mustering of the militia on polling day as well as the outcome had caused some tensions within the Corporation and its officers. Sir Robert Markham wrote on 9 July 1678 to Grantham's Recorder, Lord Roos at Belvoir Castle, advising that the Town Clerk, Mr Hodgkinson, was 'very penitent and very desirous, if possible, to regain your Lordship's favour'.[78] The response of Lord Roos is not known, but on 26 July Alderman Michael Taylor advised that Markham 'out of respect and kindnes which he hath to this Burrough and for to serve his Majestie and for the good & Welfare of this Corporacion is willing to become a Member of this Court' and his

---

[76] Henning (ed.), *The House of Commons 1660–1690*, I. 300–2 (Grantham Constituency); Holmes, *Seventeenth-Century Lincolnshire*, 242.

[77] Davies, 'By-Election at Grantham', 179; Holmes, *Seventeenth-Century Lincolnshire*, 242.

[78] HMC *12th Report, Appendix 5*, 'Manuscripts of the Duke of Rutland', Vol. II (London, HMSO, 1889), 52. Fletcher has noted that the Restoration militia served to enhance the social hegemony of the gentry but there is little further evidence in the Hall Book of the deployment of the militia within the borough of Grantham: Anthony Fletcher, *Reform in the Provinces – the Government of Stuart England* (New Haven, MA and London: Yale University Press, 1986), 323.

name was added to the Kalendar of Commoners, from which he was elected to the Second Twelve and then immediately chosen one of the First Twelve, duly taking his respective oaths. At the same meeting he was then nominated Alderman in the place of Mr John Wing, 'lately dismissed by a former order of Court for the reasons therein mencioned'. Comburgess Mr William Milles had also been dismissed.[79]

Within weeks, the so-called 'Popish Plot', concocted by Israel Tonge and Titus Oates, was whipped up by the Lord High Treasurer Danby. Tonge had revealed that in April Catholic conspirators had plotted to kill the King. The plot and subsequent trials of alleged conspirators led to the deaths of some 35 Catholics. Details of the plots and trials of those accused were described in contemporary broadsheets. Robert Pawlett of Chancery Lane, London, printed at least ten such broadsheets between 1678 and 1680 covering eight trials, most notably those of Edward Coleman, William Staley, Andrew Bromwich and William Atkins, and Robert Green, Henry Berry and Lawrence Hill. There can be little doubt that copies of these pamphlets and broadsheets found their way into his brother Edward Pawlett's shop in Grantham and we must assume that Grantham's ruling elite and local gentry were well informed of the latest news from the capital.[80]

The revelations of Danby's criminal correspondence with Catholic France led to his impeachment and fall from office. The King, anxious to prevent further revelations as to his secret diplomacy with France, prorogued Parliament on 30 December 1678 and dissolved it on 24 January 1679. Within a few days, on 29 January Alderman John Wing held his second Court at which John Newton of Hather Thorpe (now Culverthorpe Hall), son of MP Sir John Newton, desired his freedom and tendered down his £40, which was returned to him by the Court 'out of respect they beare both to his Father and himselfe'.[81] The same Court also made free John Thorold, esquire, son and heir of Sir William Thorold, knight and baronet, and also William Bury, esquire, son and heir of William Bury; it is not clear whether their tenders of £40 were remitted. The same Court also admitted four other men, including Rev. Richard Calcraft and Thomas Matkin, sons respectively of Comburgesses Mr Richard Calcraft and Mr Thomas Matkin. The Hall Book notes that the men took their oaths as free burgesses and also their oaths of Allegiance and Supremacy in accordance with the Corporation Act. Within a week, the Corporation had returned Sir William Ellys and Sir John Newton as its Burgesses in Parliament and Sir Robert Markham meanwhile had been returned as a Member for Newark.

The third Court of John Wing records 'takeing into Consideracon the order for 40li for every freeman and that the same is very prejudiciall to this Corporacon it was this day put to the Vote whether the said order should be

---

[79] HB, fo. 657r (26 July 1678).
[80] Manterfield, 'Edward Pawlett of Grantham', 13.
[81] HB, fo. 660v (29 January 1679).

abrogated and made void or stand confirmed And it was carried by the Major part of this Court that the said order stand confirmed to all intents and purposes whatsoever'.[82] The Corporation was, in effect, welcoming not only the income that gentry and nobility could bring into the town's coffers but also the influence of such friends in Westminster. At John Wing's next Court on 12 September 1679 a large body of men were enrolled as freemen. These 21 were either apprentices to Grantham freemen or were claiming freedom through patrimony. It is however clear that at least one of those made free was not the eldest son; Thomas Calcraft was described as 'one of the sones of Mr Richard Calcraft one of the Comburgesses of this Court'. Just a few months earlier, Richard Calcraft, clerk, 'eldest son of Mr Richard Calcraft one of the Comburgesses of this Court' had been made free, so Thomas was a second or third son. Other freemen appointed under Alderman John Wing included Sir Robert Carr on 3 October, whose 'great Kindnesses' in lending the borough £1,000 to be repaid over ten years without interest were duly noted. His steward Mr Bursleime tendered his £40 at the same Court, which was duly given back before he was made free. Myles Long of Sleaford, attorney, who had served Mr William Parkins senior, and Edward Secker, also an attorney, were also made free along with Comburgess Mr Thomas Matkin's brother, William, freed at the same Court.[83] Under the Aldermanship of John Wing's successor, Thomas Shorte, the Corporation twice discussed the circumstances under which a son other than the eldest could become free. On a vote in May 1680, it was agreed that the previous order that 'none but the eldest son of a Freeman should be admitted to his freedome and the Rest excluded' be ratified, 'provided neverthelesse that if the eldest sonn should happen to dye the second should be capable of his freedome and soe the Rest of the Children of Freemen as they should be in seniority of Age, after the death of their eldest Brother and not otherwise'.[84]

In May 1679, Parliament began consideration of the bill introduced by supporters of the Earl of Shaftesbury to exclude James, the King's brother, from succession on the King's death. James, Duke of York, had married the Catholic Maria of Modena in 1673 and by 1679 had publicly professed his Catholicism. When it appeared likely that the Exclusion Bill might pass, the King used his prerogative to dissolve Parliament, which had been prorogued on 27 May and did not meet before it came to an end on 12 July 1679. With a new Parliament summoned on 24 July 1679, Grantham returned on 21 August the same members, Sir William Ellys and Sir John Newton, apparently without a ballot. Although expected to meet in October 1679, King Charles prorogued Parliament until 26 January 1680. According to Holmes, popular feeling in Lincolnshire was 'predominantly "Whig" – suspicious of the executive, fearful of popery, favouring some scheme for the exclusion of, or limitations upon,

---

[82] HB, fo. 661r (20 June 1679).
[83] HB, fos 660v (29 January 1679), 661v (12 September 1679) and 662r (3 October 1679).
[84] HB, fos 666v (8 April 1680) and 667Ar (21 May 1680).

the duke of York, the Catholic heir to the throne'. Aware that the King might not meet this Parliament, Lord Shaftesbury launched a petitioning campaign to pressure the King, although the county of Lincolnshire does not appear to have participated in this. However, in late October 1679, when the Duke and Duchess of York passed through Kesteven on their way to Scotland, Lord Lindsey persuaded the members of the corporations of Stamford and then Grantham to welcome the retinue, although this visit of James is not referred to in the Grantham Hall Book. Lindsey pointedly commented that at Grantham, 'he did imagine that Newton & Ellis & the rest of his [Sir Robert Carr's] faction would have been brought in by him to have complimented his Royal Highnesse but not one of them appeared'. Lindsey did note, however, that 'the schoolmaster, one of our Friends, entertain'd him with speeches and verses well enough perform'd, but the Alderman and his Brethren also gave him a small Collation, not fitt indeed to be presented to him, but such as the place could afford'. The Earl also adds that 'My Lord Rutland was prevaild with so farr to sett aside his pique to that Town, which indeed has us'd him barbarously, as to wait upon the Duke there'.[85] Clearly the very modest collation was a measure of popular antipathy in Grantham towards the King's brother and the Court party in general.

The Privy Council issued a Circular Letter on 12 March 1680 to all corporations, requiring each to report back on its performance under the Corporation Act. Were the members of corporations taking the oaths, making their declarations, and had they annually taken the sacrament as prescribed and were records being kept accordingly? The Grantham Hall Book is silent as to both the Privy Council's letter and its reply to the Privy Council. In other boroughs and cities record keeping was sometimes found to be defective even where the Act's requirements were carried out regarding the oath taking and declarations. In some towns, there may have been deliberate oversight. Certainly, the first Court of Alderman Thomas Short in Grantham on 9 January 1679, recording the appointment of Thomas Ireland, Edward Pawlett and Christopher Thompson as Comburgesses, records that they 'at the same time tooke the Oathes of Allegiance and supremacey and the Oath and subscribed the declaracon and Received the Sacrament according to a late Act of Parlyament made for the well governing and Regulateing of Corporacions'. Grantham accordingly appears to have been compliant and was not exhibiting obvious signs of corporate dissent.[86]

Meanwhile in Westminster, under continued attack in the Lords and the Commons, Charles II prorogued Parliament and then dissolved it on 18 January 1681, calling for fresh elections for the next Parliament which was to meet in Oxford. Grantham again returned the same Members, Sir William Ellys and

---

[85] Holmes, *Seventeenth-Century Lincolnshire*, 244; LAO, CRAGG 2/30. The schoolmaster at that time was Samuel Burnett.
[86] Halliday, *Dismembering the Body Politic*, 124–31; HB, fo. 665v (9 January 1679).

Sir John Newton, for the Parliament which met for just one week in Oxford from 21 to 28 March 1681. An Exclusion Bill was again presented with popular support. Charles, having received the funding he needed from King Louis XIV of France, dissolved Parliament and the King began to rule without Parliament.

The Charters of 1685 and 1688

The 'Popish Plot' and the Exclusion Parliaments of 1679–81 led to the Crown taking a more stern view of the corporations. By mid-1683, the royal policy was to promote charter renewals nationwide. The use of the *Quo Warranto* writ encouraged corporations to humbly surrender their existing charters and be granted a new charter which contained clauses acceptable to the Crown and more specifically named the mayors, aldermen and common councillors, thereby ensuring that those in office were of suitable political persuasion. The leaders in turn would be expected to act as Justices of the Peace and uphold the King's laws. Moreover, Charles, by packing the governing bodies of the parliamentary boroughs, could in theory secure the election of a more subservient Parliament. Existing provisions regarding the appointment and approval of town clerks and recorders would be re-stated. In essence, the charter renewals reminded corporations where their authority originated. Halliday has stated that between 1660 and 1681, 85 borough charters were granted but in the five years from early 1682 there were a further 134 new charters granted.[87]

The Grantham Hall Book records John Coddington's Aldermanic year for 1683–84 as starting in the normal way as far as the seventh Court held on 13 June. At the eighth Court on 30 June 1684, 'Mr Alderman acquainted the Court this day he received A *Venire Facias* from the Sherriffe of Lincoln to shew cause wherefore the Alderman and Burgesses do use severall Franchizes and previledges within the said Towne.' At the same Court, 'Mr Alderman and his Brethren desired a free Voat for the present Surrender of the Charter of the same Burrough unto his most gracious Majesty. Which Voat was … with an Unanimous Consent passed that the Charter should be with all convenient speed sent up and Surrendred freely to his most gracious Majesty.'[88] In July the Corporation, realising that there would be costs associated with the renewal, agreed that £150 should be borrowed for the proceedings, with Alderman John Coddington, Comburgess Michael Taylor and Commoners Mark Nall, John Gasshe, Thomas Hutchin and John Weaver offering themselves to become bound for this sum which was to be secured on the borough's tolls and mills. It is interesting that Coddington and Taylor were the only members of the First or Second Twelves and the others were Commoners. Nall had been made free in January 1681 and Gasshe in November 1682. Thomas Hutchin and

---

[87] Halliday, *Dismembering the Body Politic*, 192–3; Holmes, *Seventeenth-Century Lincolnshire*, 247–8.
[88] HB, fos 690v (13 June 1684) and 691r (30 June 1684).

John Weaver were both cordwainers apprenticed to John Rawlinson and both were freed on 12 September 1679. Shoemaking was at the poorer end of the socio-economic spectrum and one must therefore wonder who, if anyone, was backing them financially to enable them to be bound for such a relatively large sum. At the same Court it was ordered 'that Mr John Coddington the present Alderman, Mr Robert Cole, Mr Thomas Ireland and Mr Robert Parkins the present Town Clark do go up to attend the King at London or Windsor' about the new charter with their expenses to be met from the £150.[89]

The outcome of this mission to the King is not recorded at the next Court in August, but at the following Court in September the sole business was the unanimous agreement that 'Captain Harrington be requested to take a Sudden journey to London on the Behalfe of this Corporacion In order to obtain a new Charter'. Town Clerk Robert Parkins was appointed to attend upon him (if he so please). Again, the cause of the urgency and any immediate outcome is not noted in the Hall Book.[90] Thomas Harrington of Boothby Pagnell was one of several local gentry who had assisted Grantham Corporation after the Restoration. In 1662 and 1663 he was one of several feoffees in connection with the sale of the Red Lyon and Dimsdale House properties. In 1674 he was made a freeman and in November 1676 he presented the Corporation with a large silver tankard which 'out of his respect and kindnesse to this Corporacion [he] was pleased to give unto the Towne for ever, and further out of his kindnesse promised that he would at all times serve this Corporacon to the Utmost of his power. Whereupon this Court doth accept of the said Tankerd and that Thancke be returned for soe great a favor given to the Corporacon and that they will be ready and willing to serve him in any thing that may be in their powers'.[91]

Harrington was under the political influence of the Earl of Lindsey, who as Lord Lieutenant had overseen the implementation of the Crown's policy in relation to the county's corporations. With the single exception of Grimsby, all had surrendered their charters, Lincoln in July 1684, Boston in November and Stamford in January 1685. Following the surrender, the last Hall Book entries under the Aldermanship of John Coddington were made on 24 October 1684. There are then no further entries until 13 March 1685, after the new Charter had been received in Grantham. A new Charter had been drawn up in December 1684 but King Charles II died on 6 February, to be succeeded by his brother as James II of England and VII of Scotland. He was proclaimed at Grantham on Tuesday 10 February and again, 'that the country might heare', on Saturday 14 February (Figure 6). Grantham's Letters Patent of Incorporation were finally granted on 25 February 1685, the third such grant of the new monarch. Grants

---

[89] HB, fos 691v (11 July 1684), 670r (Mark Nall, gentleman, freed 14 January 1681), 680r (John Gasshe freed 17 November 1682) and 661v (Weaver and Hutchin freed 12 September 1679).
[90] HB, fos 692r and v (8 August and 23 September 1684).
[91] HB, fos 371v (7 November 1662), 376v (26 June 1663), 632v (n.d. 1674) and 649Bv (3 November 1676).

for Newark, Stamford and Boston followed on 28 February, 3 and 9 March respectively. The City of Lincoln had received its grant from Charles II on 17 December 1684.[92]

The new Charter prescribed a Mayor, an aldermanic bench of 12 and a common council of 12, thereby replacing the Alderman and the First and Second Twelves of the old Corporation. The new Corporation was to have the rights and privileges of the old Corporation, although the appointment of the Recorder and his deputy were implicitly reserved to the Crown. Under this Charter, any member of the Corporation could be removed by the King by an order under the privy seal.

More significantly, the new Charter nominated those who were to serve for life as aldermen and as members of the Common Council. Those sworn in at the first Court of Robert Calcraft held on 13 March 1685 were as follows:

Aldermen	Common Council
Robert Calcroft Esquire mayor[1]	Mr Thomas Simpson[2]
Thomas Harrington Esquire	Mr Mark Nall
John Thorold Esquire	Mr John Smith[2]
Robert Fisher Esquire	Mr Edward Watson[2]
John Coddington gentleman[1]	Mr John Rollinson
Robert Cole gentleman[1]	Mr Samuel Prockter
Thomas Matkine gentleman[1]	Mr John Gasse
Thomas Ireland gentleman[1]	Mr Thomas Hutchine
Edward Pawlett gentleman[1]	Mr Richard Sentance
Thomas Fisher gentleman[1]	Mr Thomas Baly
John Robinson gentleman[1]	Mr John Newcome
Edward Bristow gentleman[2]	[Mr Thomas Chrichloe][3]
Simon Grant gentleman[2]	[Mr Arthur Taylor][3]

[1] Previously a Comburgess.
[2] Previously a member of the Second Twelve.
[3] Named in the Charter but not sworn and did not initially take their places on the Common Council.

Accordingly, 13 of the 25 men named (54%) had recent experience in the former Corporation prior to the surrender of the Charter. Twelve (46%) were new appointees. The newly enlisted Common Councillors had largely served as Commoners and, as noted above, Thomas Hutchin had been apprenticed to John Rollinson (Rawlinson), a cordwainer. Samuel Prockter or Proctor was new to the Corporation, becoming a freeman at the very first Court of Mayor Robert Calcraft in March 1685. Within four months, Proctor had been appointed in July as Town Clerk following the death of Robert Parkins.[93]

[92] Holmes, *Seventeenth-Century Lincolnshire*, 247; Martin, *Royal Charters*, 170–1; LAO: Grantham St Wulfram/PAR/1/4; Halliday, *Dismembering the Body Politic*, 350–3.
[93] HB, fos 649v (13 March 1685) and 696v (24 July 1685).

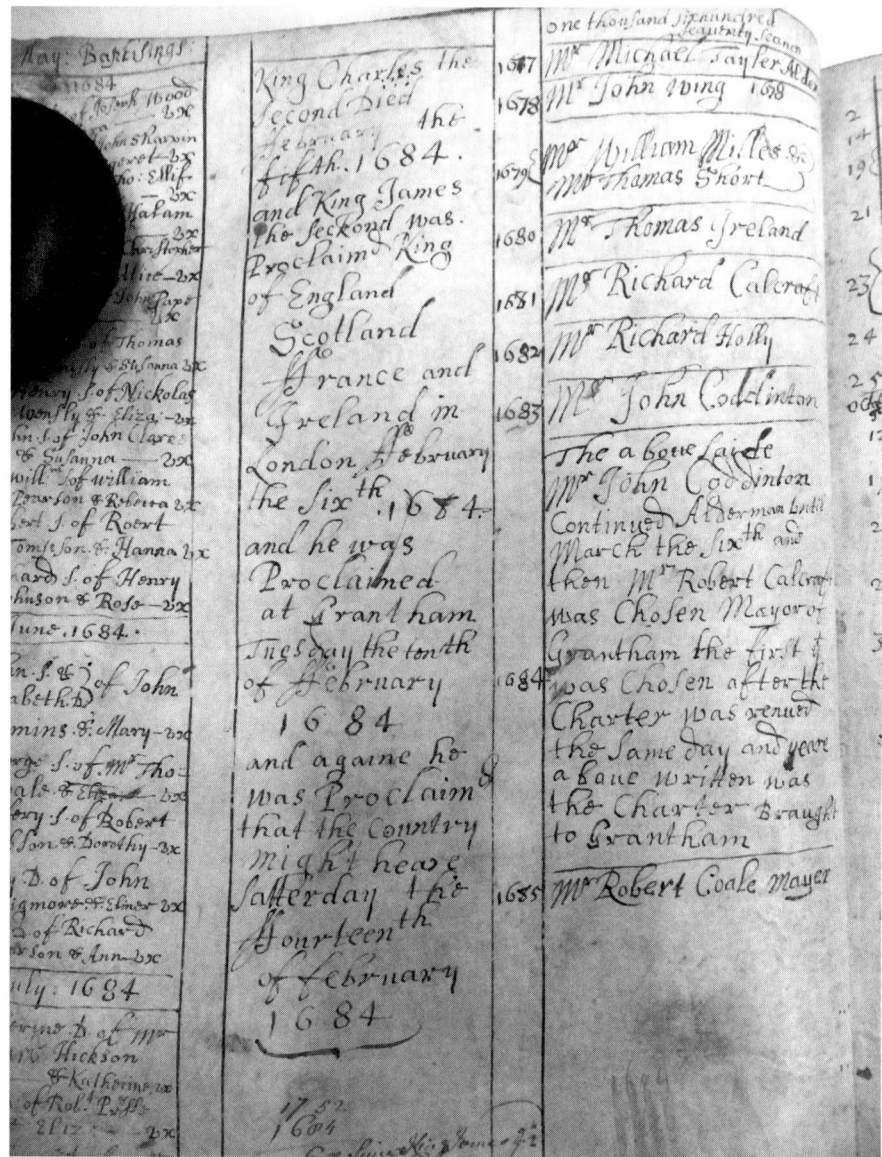

6. Grantham St Wulfram's Parish Register detailing the proclamation of King James II (LAO, Grantham St Wulfram PAR/1/4).

Of the three new members of the aldermanic bench, the earlier involvement of Thomas Harrington of Boothby Pagnell has been noted. John Thorold, the son of the late Sir William Thorold MP of Marston, was admitted a freeman in 1679. In June 1686, John Thorold was nominated as Mayor for the year beginning the following October but, in September, he urged, 'Severall reasons why he could not serve in the said place & Office, & allso Submitting himselfe to the auncient order of this Court in such case of Refusall'; Mr Thomas Matkin was elected Mayor in his place.[94]

Robert Fisher, although appointed and sworn in March, lasted only four months as a member of the new Corporation before his desire to be dismissed was agreed 'with an unanimous Consent'. One of the newly appointed members of the Common Council, Mark Nall, was Chamberlain for the year 1685–86 and, with Thomas Simpson, he presented their accounts in the Mayor's Court on 12 November 1686. He appears to have died shortly afterwards.[95]

Two Common Councillors were named in the Charter but did not take their places at the first Court. Thomas Chrichley or Chrichloe, a physician, had been active as a Commoner throughout the 1670s as a Colebuyer, Collector for the School Rents, Chamberlain and Churchwarden. He was promoted to the Second Twelve in November 1677 but was dismissed at his request in January 1680 on the grounds that he had obtained a licence to practise physic. In July 1685, the Mayor's Court agreed notice be given to Chrichloe and Arthur Taylor to appear at the next Court and, on their non-appearance in September, it was ordered that a warrant be made to distrain them. In October it was agreed that Mr Thomas Chrichloe and Mr Arthur Taylor were both unanimously chosen two of the Common Councillors, but still they did not appear. In September 1686, it was again agreed that a warrant be made out to distrain them. When the pair appeared at the next Court in October, they gave several reasons why they could not serve and take up their places and the Court thought fit to discharge them 'layeing down their Fynes'. Thomas Chrichloe paid his fine of £10 the following week whereas Arthur Taylor finally took up his place on 4 February 1687.[96]

So, in the face of these resignations and changes of membership, how successful, so far as Grantham was concerned, was the policy of Charles and James in seeking the surrender of its Charter in June 1684 and the issue of a new Charter establishing a new Corporation led by a Mayor in 1685? If the primary aim was to ensure a House of Commons more sympathetic to James II, then Grantham's two members returned to the Parliament on 4 April 1685 were the Tories Thomas Harrington and John Thorold who had defeated the Whig candidates Ellys and Sir John Newton's son John. In the run-up to the election, the Earl of Lindsey had written on 16 March 1685 to Lord Roos, now Earl of Rutland,

---

[94] HB, fos 701r (18 June 1686) and 701v (27 September 1686).
[95] HB, fos 696v (24 July 1685) and 704r (12 November 1686); LAO, LCC Wills 1686/ii/58.
[96] HB, fos 666r (23 January 1680); 697r–704v (*passim*) (1685–7).

As to Grantham, I hope your Lordship being Recorder, and Captain Harrington having it in his power to make an addition of freemen, there will bee no difficulty, but only in the choice of such freemen as will be firme to your Lordship's interest, and who really have a dependence upon you. A more acceptable service the Crowne cannott receive than the exclusion of the excluder, nor your Lordship and myself a more honourable revenge.[97]

Sir John Newton, father of the losing candidate, was briefed by John Fleck in Lincolnshire as follows: 'if you have not account from better hand, the Election at Grantham is over ... Sir William Ellys and my master Newton stood in Competition but were outvoted by the great numbers of Freemen made by the new major [Mayor] Mr Robert Calcraft. Since the procuring of the new Charter which hath raised great Animosities in the Towne all your old Friends of Grantham are dead as Mr Richard Calcraft, Mr [John] Wing and severall others ... and many others turned upside downe and all turned out of the borough court and common Councel now kept in the new Burrow [of] Grantham.'[98]

The evidence is that the new freemen, created within a month of the Charter taking effect at the first, second, third and fourth courts of Mayor Robert Calcraft, held on 13, 20 and 27 March and 3 April respectively, had swung the borough to the Tories. These four courts saw a total of 80 men enfranchised as freemen, including a baronet, nine esquires including the Earl of Lindsey's brother Peregrine and his son, Robert Lord Willoughby, 19 clergy, 19 gentlemen and 32 others. None were described as apprentices or eldest sons of other freemen.[99]

Thomas Harrington and John Thorold took their seats in King James's Parliament, which opened on 19 May. Shortly afterwards Danby was released from the Tower. Charles II's natural son, the Duke of Monmouth, who had been banished in the aftermath of the Rye House Plot, landed in Lyme Regis to lead a Protestant rebellion. He was proclaimed King in Taunton but was defeated at the battle of Sedgemoor on 6 July and quickly brought to trial. He was executed on 15 July. Some 320 of Monmouth's supporters were sentenced to death and 840 sentenced to be exiled into slavery. Holmes states that the revolt had no adherents in Lincolnshire, although the Earl of Lindsey took action against several dissenting ministers and gentlemen. Grantham's Corporation did not meet between 24 April and 24 July 1685.[100]

In November 1685, James II prorogued Parliament, which did not meet again. He pushed ahead with measures to permit Catholics to have the same

---

[97] Henning (ed.), *The House of Commons 1660–1690*, I. 300–2 (Grantham Constituency); HMC, *12th Report, Appendix 5*, 'Manuscripts of the Duke of Rutland', II. 87–8 (letter dated 16 March 1685).
[98] LAO, Mon 7/12/43(a) (8 April 1685); Russell S. H. Newton, 'The Social Production of Gentility and Capital in Early Modern England: The Newtons of Lincolnshire' (PhD thesis, University of Durham, 2017), 314.
[99] HB, fos 694r–695v (13, 20 and 27 March and 3 April 1685).
[100] Holmes, *Seventeenth-Century Lincolnshire*, 249; HB, fo. 696r (24 April and 24 July 1685).

civil and political opportunities as members of the Church of England in the face of increasing opposition from the Church of England. In a bold move, the Declaration of Indulgence in April 1687 offered similar rights to dissenters as to the Catholic minority. James was thus seeking support from those whom his brother Charles had purged from local positions following the Exclusion crisis. Local Tories were split, with a majority at a meeting in Sleaford in November 1687 refusing to support repeal of the penal laws and the Test Act. James added more Catholics to the county Commissions of the Peace.

In late April 1688, Mayor Thomas Ireland acquainted the court that the under-sheriff had served him in person a writ of *Quo Warranto* against the Charter to be returned by the fifteenth day after Easter Sunday. It was ordered that the Town Clerk go up to London to get an appearance in the Crown Office. The Town Clerk reported back to the court on 4 June that the Clerk of the Crown Office, appearing for the town, would take counsel for which £30 would be needed, to be borrowed by the Chamberlains as necessary. On 8 June, it was agreed that former Mayor Robert Cole would go up to London with the Town Clerk and the charters. The Corporation was thus actively resisting this *Quo Warranto*, unlike the previous one in 1685 where it had voluntarily surrendered them. His Majesty, by an order in Privy Council dated 7 June and read out at the Mayor's Court in Grantham on 25 June, responded by declaring that Robert Cole, together with former mayor Robert Calcraft and three other Aldermen, John Robinson, Simon Grant and Thomas Simpson, be discharged from their offices as Aldermen. 'Near the seventh hour after noon on the same day', the Mayor's Court met again to learn that according to His Majesty's letter under his signet manual dated 8 June, five men had been elected in the place of those dismissed. The new nominees were then unanimously elected by the court and took their accustomed oaths, including those of Allegiance and Supremacy. The appointees were Edward Secker, Edward Coddington, Nathaniel Garthwaite, John Poole, apothecary, and John Poole, haberdasher.[101] The men appointed were borough residents with some previous involvement in the Corporation though not as magistrates. Edward Secker, an attorney, had been freed in 1679. Edward Coddington was a mercer with a son of the same name, although it is not clear which of the two was the appointee. Nathaniel Garthwaite was a grocer who had been distrained for refusing to pay the assessment for the 1665 charter renewal. John Poole, haberdasher, had been freed in 1654 and had been an active member of the Corporation during the inter-regnum, but lost his place in 1662 on account of his refusal to subscribe his name to renounce the Covenant. His namesake, John Poole, apothecary, was a relative newcomer made free as a foreigner in 1672.[102] For the second time in less than four years, Grantham's Corporation was being filled by men nominated by the Crown.

---

[101] HB, fos 711r–712r (25 April, 4 and 25 June 1688).
[102] HB, fos 662r (Secker freed 3 October 1679), 611v (John Poole, apothecary, freed 16 February 1672), 403v (Garthwaite distrained 7 April 1666); LRS 106, 157 (John Poole, haberdasher, freed).

James was thus effectively trying to reverse what had been achieved by means of the new Charters issued between 1682 and 1687. Many royalist corporate members across England were being displaced by Catholics and dissenters. As Halliday has observed, 'corporate government around the country ground to a halt in the summer and autumn of 1688. This was the one period of true crisis in local government in the three generations after the restoration of the monarchy. It was not until 17 October 1688 that James admitted his dreadful political mistake and ordered that the corporations be restored to their previous condition.'[103] In August, Grantham, Boston, Grimsby and 28 other towns were to have charters renewed at His Majesty's charge and this was followed up with a Warrant signifying the King's pleasure that this same group were to have their charters pass the great seal without paying any fee.[104]

The new Charter of 1688 is dated 15 September and, as Martin has noted, seems not to have been acknowledged in Grantham. The text is known only from the Patent Roll in the National Archives. The writing shows many signs of haste in terms of literal errors and inconsistencies. The terms of the new grant included the clause that the King could remove any occupant of the offices named as well as anyone appointed to any other office by the Corporation. The King also had powers under the Charter to free members and future members from the provisions of the Acts of Supremacy and the Corporations and Test Acts, which would thus allow dissenters and Catholics to hold office in Grantham. The restitution of municipal liberties on 17 October annulled all grants and dismissals since 1679. Grantham therefore lost its Mayor and regained its Alderman, First Twelve of Comburgesses and Second Twelve, along with their former powers as set out in the Charter of 1664.[105]

So how did all this play out in Grantham? Mayor Thomas Ireland had held courts in July and August, and at the latter Thomas Cole had been appointed one of the 12 Aldermen and three Common Councillors had also been added (John Coddington, William Burbidge and Anthony Kirke). Edward Secker was nominated Mayor for the next ensuing year on 28 September, and then on 19 October he was formally elected and chosen and Thomas Ireland was discharged, indicating perhaps that the new Charter dated 15 September had not even arrived in Grantham or had it just been ignored?[106]

It is not clear from the Hall Book whether any further meetings or discussions took place in Grantham as it appears a sheet, now missing from the Hall Book, had been inserted. On 6 November, the thirteenth Court of John Coddington, Alderman, was held (Figure 7). The royal proclamation was made and the 'aunciant Courte which was in being at the time of the Surrender of

---

[103] Halliday, *Dismembering the Body Politic*, 238–9.
[104] *CSPD, James II, 1687–1689* (London, HMSO, 1972), 265–9 (warrant dated 6 September 1688).
[105] Martin, *Royal Charters*, 22–3, 214–33. Boston's charter was dated the same day and Grimsby's was dated 18 September: Halliday, *Dismembering the Body Politic*, 352.
[106] HB, fos 712r–713r (20 July, 10 August, 28 September and 19 October 1688).

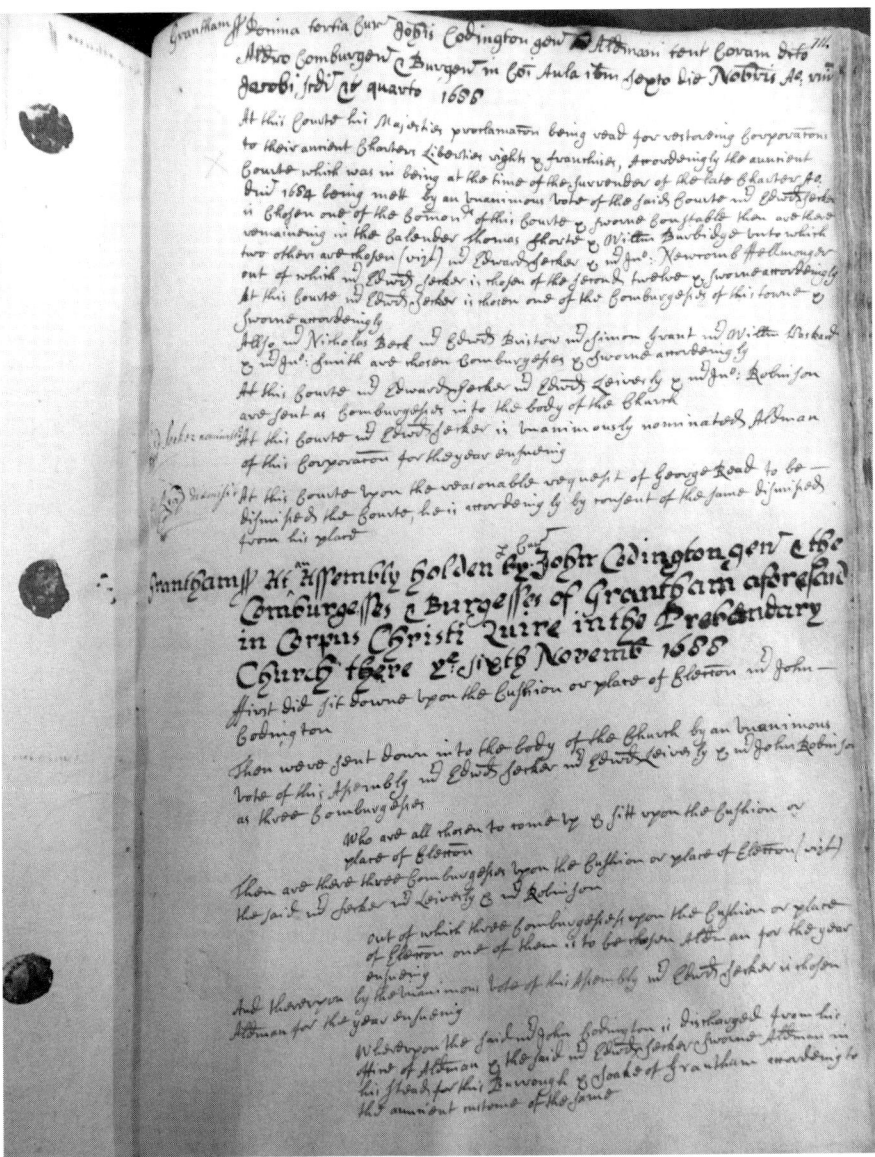

7. Thirteenth Court of John Coddington Alderman and Assembly 6 November 1688 (HB, fo. 714r).

the late Charter Anno domini 1684 being mett' chose Edward Secker from the Commoners to be a member of the second Twelve. He was then immediately elected and sworn a Comburgess. Four others, Nicholas Beck, Edward Bristow, William Haskard and John Smith, were also chosen and elected as Comburgesses. These four had previously been members of the Second Twelve prior to the 1685 charter surrender. The Court was followed the same day by an Assembly in Corpus Christi Quire and Edward Secker was duly elected Alderman. His first Court was held on 9 November and the vacancies on the Second Twelve were filled and Samuel Proctor the former Town Clerk was elected the 'continued Town clerke' and sworn accordingly. At the second Court, gaoler Thomas Quiningborow was restored to his post and in December the whole Corporation and Town Clerk took their oaths of Allegiance and Supremacy, excepting John Gibson of the Second Twelve who was dismissed. Normal service appears to have been resumed.[107]

William of Orange, the King's son-in-law, having accepted the invitation to save Britain from Catholicism, had landed in Torbay on 5 November; news of this would soon no doubt have begun to reach Grantham. By late November and early December there were fears of popular insurrection and civil strife in Lincolnshire. The Lincolnshire gentry met at Sleaford in mid-December and agreed upon an address to William, sending 'their unanimous thanks for his protection and assistance of the true Protestant interest'.[108] James's Queen and infant son had been sent to France on 10 December; William entered London on 19 December and James escaped to France three days later. As a post-script, at the Convention Parliament of January 1689, Sir William Ellys and Sir John Brownlow were unanimously elected. Ellys, who had been MP from 1679 to 1681, remained MP for Grantham from 1689 to 1713. He died at Nocton, near Lincoln, in October 1727, leaving £100 to the Corporation of Grantham. Sir John Brownlow, heir to his great uncle Sir John Brownlow and with an income of £9,000 per annum, rebuilt Belton House between 1685 and 1688. At various times, Brownlow was granted absences from the House of Commons owing to gout and pain from a stone. Brownlow entertained King William at Belton 'very nobly' in October 1695. His suffering and pain worsened and, on 16 July 1697, whilst at his uncle's house in Dorset, Brownlow shot himself. The coroner's jury found him *non compos mentis* and the estate passed according to his will, his widow holding Belton for life and then passing to his brother, with some £40,000 in ready money shared between his four surviving daughters, all of whom married into the nobility.[109]

---

[107] HB, fos 714r–716v (6, 9 and 16 November and 7 December 1688).
[108] Holmes, *Seventeenth-Century Lincolnshire*, 252–3.
[109] Henning (ed.), *The House of Commons 1660–1690*, I. 736 (Sir John Brownlow) and II. 262–3 (Sir William Ellys); *CSPD, William III, 1697* (London, HMSO, 1927) 264, 294.

Borough Governance 1689–1704

The last 15 years covered by Grantham's earliest surviving Hall Book amount to 129 pages, comprising some 648 items discussed at some 150 Courts. The period spans the proclamation of King William and Queen Mary in April 1689, the death of Queen Mary from smallpox in December 1694 and then the death of William III in 1702 following a fall from his horse, albeit that none of these events are referred to in the Hall Book. There is a passing reference to Queen Anne, in April 1702, when it was agreed that the town Waites be paid 10s for their attendance 'to play the Proclamacion and Coronacion day of Queen Anne'.[110]

During the 1690s, there were an average of just 9.3 courts per Aldermanic year, each covering on average some 32 items of business each year. This compares with an average of over 75 items per year in the period 1662–69 and over 50 items during the 1670s. As noted above, this may have been due to the attention to detail occasioned by the particular Town Clerk in office, Proctor and Calcraft leaving less detailed accounts than Hodgkinson and Parkins. Calcraft's appointment in place of Samuel Proctor, deceased, was approved by William III on 30 January 1701.[111]

The business of the Alderman's Court included the appointment of new freemen who were freeborn or who had completed their apprenticeships, although there was no repeat of external freemen being used to pack the electorate as seen in 1685. Accounts were presented by officeholders at the end of each year and, certainly in the 1690s, in less detail than had been the case in the 1660s. Typically they show a total of moneys received, a total of moneys disbursed and then the amount due to the accountant or to the town without any further breakdown. Corporation property was still let, normally on a 21-year lease with annual rents and entry fines which appear to have remained unchanged throughout the period covered in this volume. One property that formed part of the Corporation's estate was the Red Lyon in Walkergate, and the Corporation's management of this property throughout the period after the Restoration of Charles II deserves our attention.

The Red Lyon Saga 1662–1704

The Red Lyon stood roughly in the middle of the west side of Walkergate. It was a small inn which had been given in trust to the Corporation and Churchwardens in 1597 through the gift of Francis Trigge.[112] Unlike the school estate properties which were owned outright, the Red Lyon was held by

---

[110] HB, fo. 766r (30 April 1702).
[111] *CSPD, William III, 1700–02* (London, HMSO, 1937), 209.
[112] Trigge's major gift to the town is his library now housed in the south porch of St Wulfram's Church. See Brian Stagg, *The Trigge Library, St Wulfram's Church, Grantham – A guide* (Grantham, Independent Publishing Network, 2021).

feoffees. The building was occupied by a tenant. In June 1644, when the tenant was the then Alderman, Edward Christian, it was ordered that four members should take a view of Mr Alderman's house called the Red Lyon and seven other properties in and around the town, the leases of which had ended or were near expired, to ascertain their worth and how they could be let 'for the best benefitt & advantag' of the borough. Christian was a royalist and was purged from the Corporation in 1647 but restored in 1661. He resigned on 1 August 1662, being very ancient and weak. In November 1662, Alderman Michael Taylor reported that several feoffees in trust for the Red Lyon were dead and that it was necessary new trustees were nominated. Besides himself and five Comburgesses, others nominated included attorney William Parkins senior plus local gentry including Thomas Harrington of Boothby, William Welby of Denton and Robert Markham of Sedgebrook. The old deed was to be taken out of the Common Hutch on 2 February 1663 to make the new feoffees. In January 1665, a letter from Mr Christian was read, stating that the lease of the property was for 90 years; the Alderman's Court agreed to respite the granting of a new lease until the former lease had expired. In December 1665, the Corporation agreed to take legal advice from Mr Ellis and Mr Skipwith about the assessment for the Charter renewal and about 'the new feoffees for the Redd Lyon that a new lease thereof may be granted'. The order to seek Ellis's advice was repeated on 23 January 1666.[113]

Clearly, by April 1666 the Corporation wanted to see Christian out and he was unwilling to leave. It was agreed that a lease of ejectment against the tenant in possession be served and the Town Clerk would surrender the lease on request, thus allowing the title to come before the courts. The Clerk was to be saved harmless from any charges and damages. On the same day, the Alderman's Court agreed new feoffees comprising ten Comburgesses, together with the son of Alderman Thomas Hanson and Walter Leeming, son of Comburgess Richard Leeming. However, at the next Court in June, the Town Clerk reported that Mr William Bury, Counsel for the town, thought it 'very inconvenient' that the lease be made to the Town Clerk as it might 'take of his Evidence upon the tryall'. It was accordingly agreed that John Wing of the Second Company should have the lease for trying the Ejectment. The case was to be heard in Chancery and in November 1666, the Alderman's Court agreed that the feoffees were to be indemnified against any claims or damages and that three Counsel, William Ellis, Thomas Skipwith and William Bury, were to be retained for the town. The Town Clerk was to be paid £3 now due to him to defray his charges. The Town Clerk reported again at the next Court

---

[113] Details of Trigge's Charity, reproduced from the Reports of the Commissioners concerning Charities in 1836, are given in the *Grantham and Lincolnshire Red Book 1897* (Grantham, 1897), 54–6; LRS 83, 32 and 91; LRS 106, 300–1, 342; HB, fos 371v (7 November 1662), 373v (16 January 1663), 392v (5 January 1665), 402r (15 December 1665) and 403r (23 January 1666).

in January that the answer of the feoffees to the Bill of Complaint had been engrossed and that his bill now amounted to £10 12s 2d, of which £3 had been received. The balance was to be paid on the first receipt of moneys to the town. It was also agreed that the Clerk enter an Appearance in Chancery for two men, John Lenton and Edward Pawlett, who were presumably to act as witnesses.[114]

In June 1667, Alderman Richard Leeming reported that the trial against Mr Christian was 'brought downe' and that £10 was needed to defray expenses. The Court agreed that the Colebuyer, 'not haveing any occasion for the money at present', should lend the town the £10 for a quarter of a year until Henry Rudkin's rent due for the tolls would be paid. Cash flow clearly continued to be an issue for the Corporation at that point. In October the Town Clerk reported that he had obtained a deed and fine from the heirs of the surviving feoffees who were willing to come over to Grantham to give possession if the Court would indemnify them 'from any charge that Christian should putt to he being vexacious'. Six Comburgesses were bound accordingly, the Court bearing them harmless in turn. Legal proceedings were dragging on and costs continued to rise. In January 1668, the declaration of ejection was to be tried in the name of William Laine, he too being indemnified from all charges. By March 1668, the Town Clerk advised that Mr Christian was 'forced to relinquish all his right and title to the said Inn at Common law' but was now alleging that he and his father had laid out 600s for which they had not as yet been reimbursed. The Town Clerk reported that the costs now amounted to £58 0s 9d (the original gives £158, which is surely an error), of which £11 7s 6d had been paid, leaving due to him £46 13s 6d (also in error by 3d). A further £12, part of the fine paid by Widow Nidd for her lease, was to be paid to the Town Clerk in April.[115]

In June 1669, the Town Clerk reported that there had been a declaration by the Lord Keeper that there was little or no equity for the complainant Christian but 'in regard his father and he had beene Tennants to the said Inn for many yeares past did propound that he might be Tenant to the Inn aforesaid at the Rent of x li per Annum and to pay all the Arreares and to perform the said Covenants as formerly and to deliver up the lease which he had obtained from one Mary Fulwood one of the Heires of the late Surviveing Feoffees and then to have a lease for xxj yeares and at the Expiracion thereof to deliver up the possession and quite all his claime And that the Towne be reimbursed their money expended out of advancement of the Rent aforesaid'. The Town Clerk was still out of pocket in October 1669 when a further £10 was paid to him. £10 more was to be paid from the gift of £40 received from MP Sir John Thorold. An Assessment of £40 was then agreed in the following May for payment of

---

[114] HB, fos 404r and v (27 April and 16 June 1666), 410v (10 November 1666) and 411r (18 January 1667).
[115] HB, fos 413r (10 June 1667), 414r (4 October 1667), 419v (10 January 1668), 500v (27 March 1668) and 501r (19 April 1668).

the charges of the suit against Christian and, also, for the balance of the moneys owing for the Charter renewal.[116]

By June 1670, it was beginning to look as if the Red Lyon saga was at an end. Christian had clearly been ejected and Thomas Horsefield, who had married a daughter of Comburgess Thomas Hanson, desired to take a standard 21-year lease of the inn, along with two acres of land in the fields of Gonerby and Manthorpe, at a combined annual rent of £15. The town was to set the property in good and sufficient repair, as well as pave and plant the stables and pay the Chimley money (hearth tax). It was also stipulated that the tenant provide a sign for the inn. The Chamberlain was ordered to pay the Town Clerk £20 at the rising of the Court. The Town Clerk was still owed £38 and so, in March 1671, it was agreed that the Town Clerk be reimbursed at the rate of £10 per year. The new tenant was given encouragement in October 1673 as it was agreed that all public feasts and dinners be held at the Red Lyon. This would include the Alderman's Choice dinner and sessions dinners when the visiting judge was entertained, and by 30 September 1673 the account was cleared. Within a year Horsefield had left the Red Lyon, leaving his goods there. Mr Edward Pawlett, however, offered his services, but not paying any rent, so that the gates may be kept open to hold the custom the inn had. This was agreed and in January 1675 the Town Clerk, William Hodgkinson, took on a lease from the coming Lady Day for 99 years at a rent of £15 6s 8d on the proviso that all sessions dinners, venison feasts and visitation dinners were held there and that he, as tenant, keep the inn in good repair and that the inn be free from all manner of assessments. Three months later, Hodgkinson was released from his lease of the Red Lyon on the basis of his having power to raise moneys through letting town properties with fines certain.[117]

In March 1676, the Alderman had let the Red Lyon to one Mountague Stacey for seven years at £10 per annum and the town to set the inn into repair (as agreed by two indifferent men chosen by each party) and Mr Stacey to pay all assessments imposed on the property. Edward Pawlett agreed to sell the sign of the Red Lyon for £10 10s. By February 1686, Stacey was given six months to provide himself of another house. Two years later, Grantham's Recorder was to be consulted as to whether the deeds of the Red Lyon which had been settled in 1670 on trustees for the payment of £12 towards the schoolmaster and dames of the schools set up by Dr Hurst should be delivered to Hurst's grandson Lewis Hurst. In April 1688, it was ordered that the deeds should be put into Mr John Hurst's hands, he being one of the trustees.[118]

---

[116] HB, fos 509v (3 June 1669), 511v (7 October 1669), 514r (29 October 1669) and 516Ar (20 May 1670).

[117] HB, fos 516Ar (20 May 1670), 516Br (23 June 1670), 604r (9 March 1671), 624v (31 October 1673), 629r (29 July 1674), 634r (15 January 1675) and 635v (16 April 1675); see above in the context of managing the school estate.

[118] HB, fos 643v (10 March 1676), 646r (9 August 1676), 699v (26 February 1686), 710v (10 February 1688) and 711r (25 April 1688).

Whatever repairs had been carried out proved inadequate as, by June 1699, it was ordered that the Red Lyon be rebuilt. In March 1700, it was further ordered that the Red Lyon Inn should 'be this Spring pulled downe and rebuilt soe farr as is necessary and Convenient, William Niccolls to be bound to his good behaviour and care to be taken if possible to turn him out of Town if he will not come and take his freedome'. It appears that tenant Niccolls was not a freeman. Four years later, a new stable was ordered to be built at the Corporation's expense.[119] What the story of the Red Lyon exemplifies are the difficulties of property management in finding good tenants and the problems caused by bad tenants, including the delays and costs involved in litigation. It also demonstrates just how parlous was the town's financial position during the 1660s in living hand to mouth and even borrowing moneys from the Colebuyer.

Other Corporate Responsibilities

As described in *Borough Government in Newton's Grantham*, the Corporation oversaw the provision of many services, including an adequate supply of drinking water through the Conduit and the common wells. It also oversaw the repair of pavements and the town's roads. The town's mills were located on the River Witham; the North (or Slate) Mill was located near the confluence with the Mowbeck stream and the Well Lane (or Welham) Mill was situated further upstream. The mills were leased to a series of tenants and the Millmasters accounted for the income received and any larger items of expenditure. Periodically the mills were given as security for moneys borrowed on behalf of the town. Borough leases contained covenants obliging the town's tenants to grind their corn or grist at these two mills.[120]

In 1672 the Bishop of Lincoln and Sir Edmund Turnor were in Grantham and informed the Corporation that if a Manufacture was set up then they would add a stock to it to comb wool into yarn. Thanks were returned to the Bishop and Sir Edmund but nothing appears to have come of this suggestion. Sir William Ellys MP gave £20 to set the poor on work in 1690; the Corporation agreed to buy wheels and George Chantry was to be employed as overseer of this enterprise. By the next Court, the wheels had been procured and William Kirke reported that he had spoken to one Mr Bradfeild, a woolman, who had said that £20 was insufficient. The Court ordered that a letter be sent to Ellys with a copy of the will of George Dawson (who had given £60 *per annum* to the poor) asking for Ellys to give £20 *per annum*. Sir John Brownlow stepped in with £20 a year, which was increased to £30 by 1693. The location of this Manufacture is not stated in the Hall Book.[121]

---

[119] HB, fos 753r (22 June 1699), 756r (7 March 1700) and 777v (28 July 1704).
[120] LRS 106, xxxv–xxxix.
[121] HB, fos 614v (18 October 1672), 722v–723r (14 and 28 March 1690), 725r (23 October 1690) and 738r (17 November 1693).

Conclusions

The period from 1662 to 1704 witnessed much upheaval in terms of governance owing to the intervention from Charles II and James II and their policies towards corporations. By the end of the seventeenth century the governance of Grantham had reverted to the arrangements set out in the 1664 Charter. The framework thereby established continued through to 1836, when the provisions of the Municipal Reform Act of 1835 took effect. Nevertheless, the effectiveness of the corporate hierarchy reflected the abilities and interests not only of the ruling elite but also of the Town Clerk.

Clearly, the experiences of Restoration Grantham mirrored other corporate towns in Lincolnshire. The upheavals of the Civil War and the Parliamentarian and Puritan influences of the 1640s and 1650s had decisively ended with the Restoration. A period of relative stability followed but all Lincolnshire towns experienced crises of government in the latter third of the seventeenth century. Towns were unique and the determination of local communities to preserve their autonomy from the encroachment of outside forces is a recognised theme in the study of seventeenth-century history. Grantham, however, appears to have experienced less internal discord and strife and comparatively less religious dissent than other towns and cities in England, while still nodding to local gentry and being courted by them at times of parliamentary elections and accepting their gifts. In the end, the Crown under Charles II and James II was ultimately unsuccessful in gaining the influence it sought.[122]

In other aspects of the government of Stuart England, the Grantham Hall Book is silent. When in 1689 William III turned attention to private behaviour, justices in London, Middlesex and elsewhere responded by enforcing orders against swearing, drunkenness and profaning the Sabbath.[123] It is possible, of course, that the relative brevity of the records of Alderman's Courts by later clerks (in comparison with the detail surviving from William Hodgkinson) accounts for this and, perhaps more significantly, there are no surviving records from any Quarter Sessions for Grantham and the soke from this later period. Despite these lacunae, Grantham's Hall Book demonstrates clearly the internal and external factors affecting the town's population and governance.

---

[122] Norwich, with its large and active citizenry, was renowned by contemporaries for heated religious and political controversies: see John T. Evans, *Seventeenth-Century Norwich: Politics, Religion and Government, 1620–1690* (Oxford, Clarendon Press, 1979), 318–26. Dorchester had witnessed a steady dwindling of godly reformation but non-conformity was still a feature.

[123] Fletcher, *Reform in the Provinces*, 274–5.

THE TEXT

THE HALL BOOK OF GRANTHAM 1662–1663

[fo. 370r] **First Court of Michael Taylor, 31 October 1662**

Mr Michaell Taylor Alderman
First xij
Mr Robert Calcraft gentleman Comburgess
Mr Thomas Milles Comburgess
Mr Christofer Hanson Comburgess
Mr Gilbert Chantler Comburgess
Mr Thomas Short Comburgess
Mr Thomas Grant Comburgess
Mr John Watson Comburgess
Mr Thomas Hanson Comburgess
Mr Richard Leeming Comburgess
Mr Robert Calcraft Junior Comburgess
Mr Richard Calcraft Comburgess
Mr Joseph Tomlinson Comburgess

Second xij
Thomas Oldfeild
Richard Holley
John Lenton
Edward Coddington
Hugh Hutchin
Zachary Cox
George Short
Andrew Poole
Henry Humes
Edward Rawlinson
John Coddington
John Wing

Names of the Officers there

Coroner	Mr Gilbert Chantler	Keybearers	Mr Alderman
Escheator	Mr Richard Leeming		George Short
Church	George Short		Edward Rawlinson
wardens	Thomas Matkin	Prizers of	Francis Charity
Chaimberlains	Edward Rawlinson	Corne	John Taylor
	Robert Cole	Market Sayers	Christofer Walgrave
Collectors for	Mr John Watson		Edward Leivesly
Schoole Rents	John Turner	Leather	Robert Smith
Cheife Constables	Zachary Cox	Sealers	William Grococke
	Henry Humes		Edward Ulliott
Markett place	William Milles		John Inkerson
Constables	Thomas Calcraft	Towne Clarke	William Hodgkinson
High Streete	Richard Hauley	Serjeants at	Samuell Roades
Constables	William Bury	Mace	Richard Blacke
Westgate	Christofer Hanson	Gaoler	Richard Blacke
Constables	William Riseing	Bayliffe of the	Richard Blacke
Walkergate	George Read	Liberty	
Constables	William Laines	Church Clarke	William Newball
Swinegate	Richard Frisby	Belman	Ralph Osborne
Constables	Thomas Hatfeild	Scavengers	John Scot

| Castlegate | William Berriffe | Widdow Slater |
| Constables | Francis Charity | |

[fo. 370v]

Names of the Commoners of the Court there

Markett place   *Walkergate*
William Milles
Thomas Calcraft   George Read
Andrew Broome   William Laine
John Walker   John Dawson
John Turner   Richard Wintor
Robert Cole

High Streete   *Swinegate*
Richard Hauley
William Bury   Richard Frisby
Thomas Matkin   Thomas Hatfeild
John Goodson

Westgate   *Castlegate*
Christofer Hanson
William Riseing   William Berriffe
Edward Kenion   Francis Charity
William Palmer

Plate delivered to the New Alderman.
At this Court Mr Gilbert Chantler late Alderman delivers up to Mr Alderman that now is all the Towns plate being these peices following (vzt).

The horse Race Cupp	Mr Greenewoods Cann
Mr Archers Boll	Mr Batties Beaker
Mr Horsemans Boll	Two Tunns
Mr Kirkbys Boll	One salt with Cover
Mr Wheatelys Cann	13 Spoones Mr Greenewoords
One Wine Boll Mr Horsemans	The Waites 4 Cognizances

At the said Court Mr Chantler acquainted Mr Alderman that the Charters were at Mr Parkins & had beene there ever since they came from London.

Mr Chantler to perfect his Accompts for his time of Aldermanshipp.
At this Court Mr Chantlers bill of disbursments in the time of his Aldermanshipp was this [*sic*] read And the Court finding by his bill of particulars that he hath not accompted for his Receipts upon penall Statutes in the same yeare And also considering that it is requisite and fitt the same should be accompted for It is therefore ordered that Mr Chantler give an Accompt for the said Receipts and that the Chaimberlaine forbeare to pay his Bill of Disbursments till the said accompt be perfected.

Churchwardens day to Accompt.
At this Court George Short Churchwarden hath further day to give up his Accompts.

Chamberlaine day to Accompt.
At this Court Mr Robert Calcraft Chamberlaine in respect of the great buisnes of this day hath further time to give up his Accompts.

Markett place bill	05 17 00
Gathered	04 00 00
Remaines to gather which	01 17 00
Which they are ordered to cleare the next Court	
High streete bill	02 03 09
Gathered	02 01 02
Remaines to gather	00 02 07
Which is allowed to be abated & they are discharged	
Westgate bill	02 08 07
Gathered & paid	02 08 07
Which is the full Assessment & they are discharged	
Walkergate bill	00 19 04
Gathered	00 18 02
Remaines to gather	00 01 02
Swinegate bill	01 06 10
Gathered	01 06 06
Remaines	00 00 04
Castlegate bill	02 00 01
Gathered	01 18 06
Remaines	00 01 07

Which is allowed to be abated & they are severally discharged.

[fo. 371r]

A Confirmacion of the Order for refuseing to Accept of the places into any person is elected.
Whereas the Court this Day takeing into consideracion the benefitt and advantages of an order made the Nineteenth Court of Mr Gilbert Chantler Alderman for the imposeing of a penalty upon such persons as shall refuse to accept of such places and Offices into which they shall be respectively elected & chosen And for the more full expression and sure makeing and confireming of the said order It is this day fully ordered concluded and agreed upon by the whole Court that the said order shall from time to time and at all times for ever hereafter remaine continue and be in full force and vertue And it is hereby further ordered that if any person or persons shall at any time hereafter refuse to take upon him any place or Office whatsoever which he or they shall be chosen (except the Office of a Constable for which the law hath sufficiently provided for, that then

every such person or persons so refuseing shall according to the degree or place into which he shall be chosen forfeite all and every such summes of money as by the said order is injoyned according to the tenor purport true intent and meaning thereof any order heretofore made to the contrary thereof in any wise notwithstanding.

Constables Accompt.
At this Court the severall Constables gives a further Accompt of the Constables Assessment as followeth (vzt)

Mathew Wytheys Accompt to be examined.
At this Court Mr Thomas Grant, Mr Richard Leeming, Zachary Cox, Henry Humes, William Milles and John Turner are nominated appointed and ordered by this Court to examine the Accompts of Mathew Wythey late Gaoler of this liberty And to certifie their proceedinges therein the next Court day.

[fo. 371v] **Second Court of Michael Taylor, 7 November 1662**

New Feoffees in trust nominated for the Redd Lyon and Mrs Watsons house.
Whereas Mr Alderman this day acquainted the Court that there were formerly severall Feoffees in trust made for the disposeing and setling of the Redd Lyon & Mrs Watsons house to the uses by the donors will set downe and declared as also that most of them are dead and that it is very requisite and necessarie other Feoffees should be appointed Whereupon this Court takeing the same into consideracion they do nominate such persons to be Feoffees in trust for the uses aforesaid as is hereafter mentioned (that is to say) Mr Alderman, William Blith, Thomas Harrington, William Welby and Robert Markham, Esquires, William Parkins senior, Gentleman, and Thomas Milles, Thomas Grant, John Watson, Richard Leeming and Robert Calcraft Junior, Gentlemen, Comburgesses, And it is hereby ordered that a new deed be drawne and sealed by the severall Feoffees aforesaid according to the deed heretofore made.

Mathew Wytheys Accompt perfected.
At this Court Mr Thomas Grant, Mr Richard Leeming, Zachary Cox, Henry Humes, William Milles and John Turner returns an Accompt of Mathew Wytheys bill of disbursments whilst he was Gaoler according to an order of the last Court, wherein they acquaint this Court that there appeares to be due to him by his bill upon a true and just Accompt the sume of sixteene pounds & two shillinges whereof forty seaven shillinges is due to be paid by the Churchwarden Whereupon this Court also takeing into serious consideracion It is hereby ordered that the present Chaimberlaine do pay unto the said Mathew Wythey thirteene pounds and fifteene shillinges in manner following (vzt) five pounds part thereof to Mr Richard Leeming upon St Thomas next for the use of Mr Tyerman And nine pounds and fifteene shillinges the Remainder of his bill upon the five & twentieth day of December next And hereupon the said Mathew Wythey doeth

promise in open Court to leave the Gaole within two dayes now next ensueing and to deliver peacable possession to Richard Blacke the present Gaoler.

William Knewstubs & the Comon Waites accepted.
At this Court came William Knewstubbs and tendred his service to the Alderman and the rest of the Court and desired that they would be pleased to accept of him for one of their waites and to give him such allowance as he had formerly Whereupon this Court accepts of the said William Knewstubbs to be one of the waites for this Corporacion And it is ordered that the Chaimberlaine provide the Waites cloakes against the next faire.

The Comon Armes to be sold.
At this Court the Chaimberlaine is ordered to sell all the Common Armes belonging to this Towne to reimburse himselfe the money he laid downe for providing of the said Armes.

Marketplace Constables Accompts.

		li	s	d
Andrew Broome				
William Milles	Marketplace Constables their bill	05	15	00
	Abatements	01	02	00
	Remaines due to the Towne	04	13	00

Which they pay to the Chaimberlaine and they are discharged.

Churchwarden, Chaimberlyn, & Collector for Schoole Rent further day to accompt.
At this Court the Churchwardens Chaimberlaine and the Collectors for the Schoole Rent have further time to accompt.

[fo. 372r] **Third Court of Michael Taylor, 28 November 1662**

Accompts to be Examined.
At this Court Mr Thomas Grant, Mr John Watson, Zachary Cox, Hugh Hutchin, William Milles and John Walker are appointed and ordered by this Court to meete on Tuesday next at one of the Clocke to examine and take the Accompts of the Mill Masters, Chaimberlaine and the Collectors for Schoole Rent and to certifie their proceedinges therein the next Court day.

Mr Milles lease letten.
At this Court Mr Thomas Milles one of the Comburgesses of this Court takes a lease of the house he now liveth in scituate and being in Walkergate for one and twenty yeares from and after the expiracion of a former lease thereof yet in being in the name of one Robert Clarke Gent deceased And he gives to this Court Ten pounds for a fine to be paid upon the second day of February next ensuing And he gives in Earnest thereof xijd and is to give sufficient securitie for performance of the Covenants mencioned in

his lease and at the Expiracion of the terme aforesaid to leave the said house with all other buildinges and appurtences thereunto belonging as it is now build and repaired.

Assessment to be made for the Comon Armes.
At this Court there being a veiw taken of the Chaimberlaine Accompts, for money laid downe by him out of the Towns Stockes, for the Comon Armes which amounts unto nine pounds And part of them being sold by the Chaimberlaine It is therefore ordered that an Assessment of nine pounds be made and laid upon this Burrough to reimburse the Chamberlaine the money laid downe by him for the said Armes and to soldiers that carried them and for match and powder And it is further ordered that the Cheife Constables be Assessors and the petty Constables Collectors thereof.

Mill Masters appointed.
At this Court Mr Christofer Hanson and John Coddington are nominated and appointed Mill Masters for the Slate Mill.

Anthony Hodgkins made free.
At this Court came Anthony Hodgkins who served Mr Gilbert Chantler in the misterie of a Mercer and desired to be incorporated and made a free Burgesses of this Corporacion to whose request this Court doth condiscend whereupon he pay as being a forrainer five shillinges to the boxe and three shillinges to Clarke and Serjents and takes the oath of a free Burgesse according to the Antitient [*sic*] and laudable custome of this Burrough.

[fo. 372v] **Fourth Court of Michael Taylor, 2 January 1662/3**

Towns Milns lett to Henry Haire for one yeare.
At this Court it is ordered and agreed upon that Henry Haire shall have a lease of the Wellaine Mill and Slate Mill and all the appurtences thereunto belonging (excepting the Slate Mill close and the Wellaine Mill pingle for & during one whole yeare from and after the second day of February next ensueing upon the payment of 1612 li in manner and forme following vzt, the sume of thirty pounds upon every quarter day from the aforesaid second day of February and also the sume of twenty shillinges to be paid to the said Alderman and Burgesses their Successors and Assignes Weekely and every weeke for and during the terme aforesaid And it is further ordered that the said Henry Haire shall give bonds with two sufficient suerties vzt William Elston of Gunnerby and John Haire of Belton who being present in Court promiseth to give bonds with him for payment of the Rent and performance of Covenants for keeping the said Mills in good Repaires and at the end of the said terme to deliver the possession thereof to the Alderman and Burgesses or their Successors so well and sufficiently repaired as they shall be adjudged to be in repaires by foure Indifferent men at his entring upon the said Mills And also that he the said Henry Haire shall not at any time or times during the said terme detaine and keepe in either of the said Mills or in his custody any Corne or graine of any person or persons belonging to this Towne that is brought to be ground

above eight and forty houres nor take excessive tolle for the grinding thereof But upon Complaint made it shall be lawfull to take the said Corne away and to grind it elsewhere and to give such recompense for his takeing above his due tolle as shall be thought fitt by Mr Alderman and his Brethren And for the non performance of the Covenants aforesaid it shall be lawfull for the said Alderman & Burgesses or Successors or any of them within the said terme to put the said bond in suite to enter upon the said Mills and to have and enjoy them as in their former estate And lastly it is ordered by the said Court that they shall and will for and during the terme aforesaid do their utmost indeavours to injoyne the Inhabitants within this Towne to grind their Corne and graine at the said Mills And that it shall be lawfull for the said Henry Haire at anytime within the said terme to make use of the horse Mill putting the same into repaire And he is to have Articles of agreement and his bond sealed upon the second day of February aforesaid And he gives in earnest thereof xijd.

An Assessment to be made for Westgate Well.
At this Court it is ordered that an Assessment be made and laid upon the Inhabitants of Westgate the sume of xxs for the repaires of Westgate Well by the Assessors nominated & appointed by this Court for the Said Assessment vzt Henry Rudkin, William Palmer, William Bayly and Christofer Hanson.

Chaimberlaine to pay Mr Simpson bill.
At this Court Mr Alderman produces an [*sic*] note of Mr Simpsons Accompt whereby there appeares to be due to him 31s 3d And the Chaimberlaine is ordered to pay the same unto him with convenient speed.

[fo. 373r]

Churchwardens Accompt for the 50 li Assessment.

	li	s	d
George Short one of the Churchwarden gives an Accompt of the Church Assessment and he chargeth himselfe with the whole Assessment being	50	00	00
Whereof, he hath disbursed as by particulars appears	34	11	08
Remaines in arreare as also appeare by a bill	[blank]		
Abatements examined and approved of.	[blank]		

Churchwarden Accompt for the Quarteridge.

George Shorts Accompt for the Quarteridge to the Church his Receipts	26	00	00
He chargeth himselfe with Receipts for Burialls	07	05	00
And his Receipts for the Rent of lands	12	12	00
Whereof he hath disbursed	[blank]		
paid by him to the poore	[blank]		
Abatements approved of	[blank]		
Remaines in arreare which he is ordered forth to gather.	[blank]		

Churchwardens Accompt for Arreares.
John Scot give an Accompt of his arreares in his time
of being Churchwarden whereby he stands charged with   05 00 00
Abatements approved of   03 05 08
Remaines due to the Towne   01 14 04
Which he payes to the present Churchwarden & he is discharged.

Collectors for the Schoole Rents Accompt.
At this Court Mr Richard Calcraft and John Wing give an Accompt
for the Schoole Rent & they charge themselves with Receipt of   46 05 00
Whereof they have disbursed   41 19 04
Remaines due to the Towne   04 05 08
Which they pay to the Chaimberlaine and they are discharged.

Milne Masters Accompt.
At this Court Mr Michaell Taylor and Mr Joseph Tomlinson gives
an Accompt for the Milne proffitts whereof Mr Taylor chargeth
himselfe with the Receipts for nine weekes which amounts unto   15 14 01
And his disbursements are   16 10 04
And allowed for expences   00 01 08
Remaines due to him   00 17 11
Mr Tomlinson Accompts for one Moneth which comes to   05 08 11
His disbursments in the same time   02 10 07
Remaines due to the Towne   02 18 04
Which he pays & is discharged.

Chaimberlaine to pay Mathew Wytheys money.
At this [sic] it is ordered that the Chaimberlaine pay unto Mathew Wythey the money due to him upon the Receipt of the next quarters Rent for the tolles.

Marke Harnesse made free.
At this Court came Marke Harnesse a Forrainer and desired to be incorporated and made a free Burgesse of this Corporacion to which this Court doth assent whereupon the said Marke Harnesse layes downe his x li according to Auncient custome And this Court takeing the same into consideracion & also considering that he hath lived in the Towne severall yeares and hath beene a carefull & painfull man do give him backe againe v li And the said Marke Harness doeth pay his fees to Clarke and Serjents and takes the oath of a free Burgesse according to the Auntient custome of this Burrough.

[fo. 373v] **Fifth Court of Michael Taylor, 16 January 1662/3**

An order to pay Mrs Husseys money.
At this Court it is ordered that upon Mrs Bridgett Hussey letter the five pounds and seaven shillinges be paid unto her it being made appeare that the same is due to her for interest.

And an order aboute the County Hall.
At this Court Mr Alderman produceth a letter from Sir John Mounson and other Gentlemen aboute the Repaires of Lincolneshire Hall for the Towne and Soake to pay towards the same And Mr Watson this day acquainted the Court That Mr Terwhit one of the Gentlemen desired to see the Charter and if the Charter excused the said Towne and Soake they would be put the Towne to noe charge.

Mr Milles & Anne Still leases to be sealed & new feofees to be made for the Redd Lyon.
At this Court it is ordered that there be a meeteing at the Hutch upon the second day of February next to seale Mr Milles lease and Widdow Stills lease and to take out the deed of the Redd Lyon to make new Feoffees.

A peticion to the Queens Councill aboute Branstons Milne.
At this Court it is ordered that a peticion be sent up to the Queens Councill for the pulling downe Richard Branstons Mill and that the Councill will please to contribute towards the Repaires of the Gaole And it is also ordered that a letter of thankes be sent to Mercers Company for the continuance of the Lecturers place unto this Corporacion.

Mr William Gardner and Henry Coverly made free.
At this Court came Mr William Gardner and Henry Coverly and desired to be incorporated and made free Burgesses of this Corporacion and this Court grants their request whereupon the said William Gardner and Henry Coverly as Forrainers lay downe their ten pounds apeice according Auntient custome And this Court takeing the same into their serious consideracion and also considering that they have lived in the Towne severall yeares and are likely to be good Townsmen and to act for the good thereof do give the sume of iij li vjs viijd apeice backe againe And the pay their fees to Clarke and Serjents and takes the oath of freeman according to the Auntient and laudable custome of this Burrough.

Mathew Wytheys money to be paid him.
At this Court it is ordered that the Chaimberlaine upon the first receipt of money pay and satisfie Mathew Wythey the sume of money formerly ordered by this Court And that he likewise pay Mr Parkins his bill of disbursements.

An order to save Mr Humes harmles from Robinsons bond.
At this Court it is ordered that Henry Humes have his bond delivered in wherein he stood bound with Robinson for the viccars Tyths and that be acquited discharged saved harmles and indempnified from the aforesaid bond.

Accompts to be examined.
At this Court Mr Robert Calcraft Senior, Mr Richard Leeming, Mr Joseph Tomlinson and Hugh Hutchin are ordered to examine the Chaimberlaines Accompt & to certifie the same the next Court day.

[fo. 374r]

The Court promise to become bound for the Good of this Corporacion.
At this Court Mr Alderman produceth a particular of all the debts and disbursements of this Towne and also a particular of the Receipts and Revenues thereof whereby this Court may be fully satisfied with the Towns Condicion and Affaires and that such persons as are members of this Court may be incouraged to become bound for such sumes of money as occasions of the Towne shall require Whereupon Mr Alderman, Mr Robert Calcraft, senior, Mr Christofer Hanson, Mr Gilbert Chantler, Mr John Watson, Mr Thomas Hanson, Mr Richard Leeming, Mr Robert Calcraft, Junior, Mr Richard Calcraft, Mr Josph Tomlinson, Zachary Cox, Henry Humes, Richard Holley, Hugh Hutchin, George Short, John Coddington, John Winge, William Milles, John Turner, William Bury, and Thomas Matkin and the rest of this Court here present are very willing and contented to become bound as they shall be respectively chosen and requested thereunto for the good prosperitie well ordering and governing of this Corporacion

A particular of the debts owing by this Corporacion				A particular of the Disbursements of this Corporacion				A particular of the Revenues of this Corporacion			
	li	s	d								
Sir Robert Markham	250	00	00	For Interest money	66	00	00	Rent of tolles	50	00	00
Mr Ascough	100	00	00	To the Queens				Rent of the Mills	52	00	00
Mr John Welby	135	00	00	Auditor for Rent of	22	00	00	Schoole Rent	04	00	00
Mr William Welby	050	00	00	the Milns and tolles				Rent of the Mill close	03	13	04
Mr John White	100	00	00	Mr Welds Annuitie				Rent of the Mill pingle	01	00	00
Mr James Ashton	100	00	00	Aldermans sallary	10	00	00	Mr Lentons Rent	01	02	00
Mr Wright	100	00	00	Recordors sallary	02	00	00	John Wings Rent	01	02	00
Mr Babbington	100	00	00	Sollicitors sallary	02	00	00	Tanners Rent	00	06	08
Mr Hobson	050	00	00	Towne Clarke sallary	02	00	00	Shoemakers	00	05	00
William Milles	060	00	00	Serjents sallary	04	00	00	Constitucion			
Mr Greenwoods children	026	13	04	Gaoler sallary	01	00	00	The Rent of the Stalls	03	05	00
Darnils Children	010	00	00	Doctor Hursts Rent	02	00	00				
Richard Armestead	020	00	00	Lecturers Dinners	05	00	00				

[fo. 374v] **Sixth Court of Michael Taylor, 2 March 1662/3**

An order to sent [sic] *the Charter to Lincolne to free the Soake from Assizes.*
At this Court it is ordered that a copy of the Charter be sent to Lincolne at the Assizes to be produced to the Judge for freeing the Towne and Soake from the Assessment for the Repaires of the County Hall and from serving upon Juries at the Assizes.

North Church porch to be repaired.
At this Court it is ordered that if Mr Parkins will consent thereunto that the North Church porch shall be repaired with the money given by the Right honorable the Earle of Rutland after Mr Parkins money is paid to him out of the same.

Mr Alderman acquainted the Court with the Lord of Lincolns Will.
Whereas Mr Alderman this day acquainted the Court of the clause in the will of Doctor Sanderson late Lord Bishopp of Lincolne whereby he out of the great favor and respect he had to this Corporacion for the advancement of piety and Religion and the encouragement of the present viccars and of such as shall succeed them and to the end they may enjoy the company and society one of another and that they be conveniently setled in the certaine habitacions hath by his grace & favor by his said last will and testament given the sume of one hundred pounds towards the purchasing of a house within the parrish of Grantham for the use of the two vicars and so to be for the use of the vicars successively for ever as by the said Clause more fully appeares.

An Order for the selling Dimsdale house for the use of the viccars for ever.
Whereas Mr Alderman was further pleased to acquaint the Court that Mr Edward Dix one of the present viccars who being this day present in Court had made inquiry for a house in Grantham to purchase according to his Lordshipps will and that he could find noe so convenient as Dimsdale house being neare the Church And if the Towne would sell it the present vicars and the Executors of the Lord Bishopp would deposite for the purchase thereof out of the money given for that purpose the sume of Ninety pounds (they expecting the Corporacion will contribute something towards the purchase and repaires thereof as is desired by his Lordshipps will Whereupon this Court for the consideracion of ninety pounds aforesaid do hereby fully order and agree that Dimsdale house shall be convayed and setled upon the present vicars and their Successors for ever as shall be advised by Councill learned in the law And Whereas this Court takeing into serious consideracion the guift of the Lord Bishopp and the same to be imployed to so good and pious a worke As also for the happy Injoyment of the present learned vicars and their successors It is hereby ordered and agreed upon that x li part of the said 90 li shall be returned backe to the viccars towards the purchase of some other house to be added to Dimsdale and for the repaires of Dimsdale which to the viccars shall seeme most expedient.

Accompts to be examined.
At this Court it is ordered that Mr Hanson, Mr Richard Leeming, Zachary Cox, William Riseing and Francis Charitie shall meete upon Wednesday next and examine the Mill Masters Accompt and certifie the same the next Court day.

Cloth Markitt to be removed.
At this Court it is ordered that the Cloth markett be removed into Widdow Breilsfords corner it being formerly kept there.

[fo. 375r]

Money lent to the Towne by the Court.
At this Court the severall persons hereunder mencioned do lend the sumes of money hereafter written to the Towne towards the payment of the debts hereafter mencioned oweing by this Corporacion which said monies is to be paid againe unto the said persons by the Chaimberlaine upon the first receipt of money And all to be paid at one whole and entire payment

Mr Alderman	xxxxs	Mr Joseph Tomlinson	xxs	
Mr Robert Calcraft senior	xs	Zachary Cox	xs	
Mr Thomas Milles	xxs	Henry Humes	xxs	
Mr Gilbert Chantler	xxs	John Lenton	xs	
Mr Thomas Grant	xxs	Hugh Hutchin	xs	
['Mr John Watson xxs' *deleted*]		George Short	xs	
Mr Thomas Hanson	xxs	John Coddington	xxs	
Mr Richard Leeming	xxs	John Winge	xxs	
Mr Robert Calcraft Junior	xxs	William Milles	xxs	
Mr Richard Calcraft	xxs	William Riseing	xxs	Christofer Thompson xxs

An order for paying of money.
At this Court it is ordered that the sumes of money above mencioned be gathered up fortwith and to be paid by the Chaimberlaine as is hereafter set downe vzt, to the Gentlemen to whome the Mills are ingaged, xxx li to Mathew Wythey xiij li xiiijs To Mrs Hussey due for interest v li vijs To Mr Alderman which he was pleased to lay downe iij li vijs xjd and to Mr Parkins for money laid downe and for his sallary iij li xs.

A letter to be sent to the Deane of Winchester.
At this Court it is ordered that a letter of thankes be sent to the Deane of Winchester for his guift and respect to this Corporacion in setling an augmentacion of 50 li *per Annum* upon the South viccar.

Thomas Archer made free.
At this Court came Thomas Archer and desired to be made a free Burgesse of this Corporacion to which this Court doth assent whereupon he payes his ijs vjd to the Common box as free borne and his fees to Clarke and Serjent and takes the oath of a freeman according to the custome of this Burrough.

Thomas Taylor a Forrainer made free.
At this Court came Thomas Taylor a Forrainer and desired to be made a free Burgesse of this Corporacion to which this Court doth assent whereupon his [*sic*] layes downe his x li as being a Forrainer according to custome And this Court takeing the same into their consideracion and out of their respect to him being lately come to the Towne and marriing the widdow of Richard Hudson which payes his money to be a freeman as a Forrainer they give backe againe iij li vjs viijd And he payes his fees to Clarke and Serjents and takes his oath of a free Burgesse according to the custome of this Corporacion.

[fo. 375v] **Seventh Court of Michael Taylor, 27 March 1663**

Accompts to be examined.
At this Court it is ordered that Mr Thomas Hanson, Mr Richard Leeming, Zachary Cox, William Riseing and Francis Charitie do meete upon Tuesday next and examine the Mill Masters Accompt and that every person so faileing shall forfeite vjs viijd and make a returne of their proceedings the next Court day.

North Church porch to be repaired and Chimmes sett up.
Whereas Mr Alderman this day acquainted the Court that the Right honorable John Earle of Rutland hath beene pleased to give ten pounds towards the rebuilding of the steeple and repairing of the Church which now in the hands of Mr William Parkins the Sollicitor for this Corporacion, he being desirous to have the Chimmes set up with the same And whereas this Court takeing into consideracion that the North Church porch is much ruinated and decayed and that the Towne is lyable to a presentment for not repairing of the said porch It is therefore this day ordered with the consent of Mr William Parkins being present that the said monies shall be forthwith laid out for the Repaires of the porch aforesaid the Chaimberlaine paying out of the said x li, iij li xs to Mr Parkins for his sallary and money laid downe aboute Mr Pells guift and for Drinke xiiijs to Widdow Taylor when the workmen were building the steeple And it is further ordered that upon the first Assessment hereafter to be made for Repaires of the Church the Chimmes shall be erected and set up with part of the money raised by the said Assessment.

Mr Simpson to be set at liberty for the suite for tyth.
At this Court it is ordered that the Suite against Mr Simpson for tyth be referred to Mr Parkins for the setting of him at liberty upon Ingagement to pay the same hereafter.

Mr Welbys bonds to be renewed.
At this Court came Mr Richard Paxtons and acquainted the Alderman and this Court that Mr John Welby was willing to continue the money due to him in the Towns hand if they would renew their former bonds there being severall of the obligors lately dead which this Court taking into consideracion are willing to renew their bonds and returns thankes to Mr Welby for his respects to this Corporacion.

Pest house to be repaired.
At this Court it is ordered that the present Collectors for the Schoole Rents do take care that the pest house be repaired And that after Easter the Survayors for the High Wayes shall cause a day of Common worke to be at the Slate Mill for repairing of the Mill Banks.

[fo. 376r] Eighth Court of Michael Taylor, 24 April 1663

Ladders & hookes to be provided.
At this Court it is ordered that the Constables of every Ward doe provide hookes and ladders with all convenient speed to be placed in every streete to serve upon occasions and to give and [sic] accompt thereof the next Court day.

Mr Wright securitie to be renewed.
At this Court it is ordered that Mr Wright have his security renewed by the Towne as he shall thinke convenient if he will not approve of the Corporacion Seale.

Mr Welbys bond to be renewed.
Whereas Mr Alderman acquainted the Court this Day that Mr John Welby desired to have his bond of 130 li renewed there being some of the Obligors dead to which this Court doeth condiscend whereupon Mr Alderman, Mr Richard Leeming and John Lenton being present in Court are willing and contented for the good of this Corporacion to become bound unto the said Mr Welby for the 130 li aforesaid And in consideracion thereof of this Court doth firmely promise and ingage to save harmless and indempnified the said three persons and to graunt them such securitie for the same as they shall thinke convenient.

Mr Milles money to be paid.
At this Court William Milles acquainted Mr Alderman and the rest of the Court that he had very urgent occasions for his money which is in the Towns hand and desired that they would be pleased to helpe him to it, The which this Court takeing into consideracion do hereby order and agree that the Chaimberlaine shall pay the sume of money due to the said William Milles out of the monies to be raised by the sale of Dimsdale house.

Mr Brome charges to London to be paid by the Churchwarden.
At this Court it is ordered that the Churchwarden do pay unto the Chaimberlaine all such sumes of money as was paid to Andrew Broome to beare his charges to London aboute the Lecturers place.

Mill Masters Accompt.
At this Court Mr Thomas Hanson, Mr Richard Leeming, Zachary Cox, William Riseing and Francis Charitie do returne their proceedings for the examining of the Mill Master Accompt as followeth

	li	s	d
At this Court Mr Robert Calcraft & John Dye gives an [sic] of the proffitts of the Towne Mill & chargeth themselves with the Receipt of	56	00	02
And their disbursment to be	49	03	08
Remain Due to the Towne	06	16	06
Mr Christofer Hanson and John Coddingtons Receipts for the Towne Mill	10	14	04
Their disbursments	08	16	00
Remaines due to the Towne	01	18	04
James Fermans Receipts for the Slate Mill	09	11	09 ob
His Disbursments	09	05	08
Remaines due to the Towne	00	06	01

[fo. 376v] **Ninth Court of Michael Taylor, 26 June 1663**

Mr Alderman to receive iii li in part of his sallory of Mr Calcraft as Mill Master.
Whereas upon the reading of the Mill Masters accompt this day according to an order of the last Court there appeares to be in the hands of Mr Robert Calcraft Senior the sume of iij li xiijs iiijd And Mr Alderman acquainting the Court that he was in arreare of his sallory and if the Court pleased the [sic] would receive the same in part whereupon this Court doeth order that Mr Calcraft do pay the said iij li xiijs iiijd to Mr Alderman inpart of his sallory.

Dimsdale deed read & confirmed.
Whereas also upon the reading of the deed of sale for Dimsdale house this Court considering that it is requisite there should be more feoffees named It is therefore ordered that Sir William Thorrold, Sir John Newton, Erasmus Deligne, Thomas Harrington and William Blith Esquires shall be inserted in the deed as feoffees with the other Gentlemen and that the deed be ingrossed againe the next Court day.

Constables to bring in their bill of disbursments the next Court.
At this Court it is ordered that the Constable of every Ward do bring in a perticular of their disbursments this yeare the next Court day to the end an Assessment may be made for raiseing of the same according to former rules and orders of this Court.

Colebuyers Accompt.

	li	s	d
At this Court James Ferman gives up his Accompt as Colebuyer whereby he chargeth himselfe with the sume of	26	01	00
And his disbursments to be	01	08	04
Remaines to gather	00	02	06
Due to the Towne	25	19	00

And he payes the same downe in open Court to Mr Richard Calcraft and John Walker appointed Colebuyers by this Court for this next ensueing yeares and the said James Ferman is hereby discharged

An order for drawing kilns with lime or Morter upon paine of v li.
Whereas by a too late and sad experience it hath beene made manifest to this Court the great inconvenience and danger by Kilnes being neare to dwelling houses barns and outhouses which have of late caused severall families to be impovrished by a fire that happened upon the xxxjth day of March last past And whereas it is thought convenient and fully ordered by this Court for avoiding of such dangers for the future that all kilns within this Towne shall be well and sufficiently under drawne either with lime or Morter at or before Michaelmas next upon paine that every person offending contrary to this order shall forfeite five pounds of lawfull money of England to be levied by distress and sale of Goods And it is further ordered that the Constables of every Ward shall give notice to all such persons as have and use kilns within their Wards And also they are ordered to make a dilligent search at Michelmas next to see that this order be performed and to returne the Defaulters herein to the next Court after such search made as aforesaid.

[fo. 377r]

An order for Eleccion of the Alderman.
Whereas upon a mocion made by Mr Alderman and thereupon some speeches and propositions touching the proceeding therein concerning the putting downe into the Church and bringing upon the Cusheon such persons as the Court shall thinke most fitt for avoideing opposicion in the Church and for the peaceable and quiett proceedings in the Choice and Eleccion of the succeeding Alderman there should be this present Court as Nominacion of such persons as this Court should agree upon to be putt downe into the Church, that they might proceed to the setling three upon the Cusheon out of which the succeeding Alderman is to be chosen. Whereupon this Court agrees that Mr John Watson one of the Comburgesses of this Court shall upon the next eleccion day be sent downe into the body of the Church to make Mr Christofer Hanson and Mr Thomas Short three Comburgesses in the Church Out of which three Comburgesses in the Church it is in like manner agreed that Mr Christofer Hanson shall be brought upon the Cusheon to make Mr Robert [*sic*] and Mr Thomas Milles three Comburgesses upon the Cusheon or place of eleccion And that out of those three Gentlemen upon the Chusheon vzt, Mr Robert [*sic*], Mr Thomas Milles and Mr Christofer Hanson with

an unanimous consent and agreement of this Court Mr Robert Calcraft is nominated Alderman for this next ensueing yeare.

An order for keepeing of the Aldermans Feast.
Whereas this Court takeing into serious consideracion the great disorder unnecessarie charge and expense that have beene at every Aldermans choice Dinner by the admitting of the Generaltie of the freemen belonging to this Burrough And not only those that inhabite in the Towne but other freemen that dwell in the Country, And by and under the pretence of freemen severall persons out of the Country have resorted to the Aldermans choice Dinner so as that the present Alderman could not informe himselfe how to provide for any certaine number of persons, but have ever been put to an infinite trouble at such times And whereas this Court also considering that there is noe Corporacion neare unto them that have their feast kept in such manner but all in decencey and order, do this day move Mr Robert Calcraft the now nominated Alderman for this next ensueing yeare that he will please to take into his consideracion and onely provide a Dinner for such persons as are members of this Court and ~~the~~ such Gentry and other persons as he in his discrecion shall thinke most meete so as that the Aldermans Dinner may be kept after the same order successively, to which Mocion the said Mr Calcraft doth thereunto consent and well approves thereof, And for the good of this Corporacion he is willing to remitt his Aldermans sallory and to provide the feast at his owne proper costs and charges, onely desireing that the Court will please to pay Samuell Roades Serjent the three pounds for his wages which was formerly paid him by the Alderman Whereupon this Court returns thankes to Mr Calcraft for his respects and care to act for the good and welfare of this Corporacion And do hereby order and agree that the Chaimberlaine do pay to Samuell Roades his wages which the Alderman used to pay, in such manner as his other wages is paid him.

Mr Oldfeild dismissed from the 2 xij.
At this Court Mr Thomas Oldfeild one of the second twelve haveing formerly made it his request to this Court that they would please to dismiss him from the place of a second twelve man And also by a letter this Court to Mr Alderman showing that he hath very urgent occasions that he could not attend the Court as formerly whereupon by a vote of this Court he hath his request graunted him and is dismissed accordingly.

[fo. 377v] **Tenth Court of Michael Taylor, 31 July 1663**

The warrant approved against Andrew Poole for refuseing his place of second xij.
Whereas upon reading of the warrant against Andrew Poole for refuseing to accept of his place as a second twelveman, is this day allowed and approved of, and signed and sealed by the Alderman and Comburgesses, And hereby fully ordered that the Serjents and Constables do distraine of the Goodes and Chattells of the said Andrew Poole by vertue of the said warrant for the sume of tenn pounds And this Court doth likewise promise order and agree that the Serjents and all and every the Constables shall be saved

defended and kept harmeless of and from all suites troubles charges and incumbrances whatsoever touching or concerning the Execucion of the warrant aforesaid.

Constables Assessment.
At this Court it is ordered that an Assessment of xxij li be made for the payment of the Constables their bills of Disbursments an estimate being taken what those perticular sumes amount unto, And by reason of the late sad fier the Constables having beene at great charge for men watching at the fier and provideing new laddars and hookes which causeth the Constables bills to be increased, The Cheife Constables and under Constables are appointed Assessors and the under Constables Collectors thereof And it is ordered that the same Assessment shall be signed by the Alderman and some of his Brethren And if any person shall refuse to pay to the said Assessment, warrants to be made to the Constables to distraine for the same And after monies so collected to be paid into the hands of the Chaimberlaine and by him every Constable to hand his bill of disbursment paid And for the more legall makeing of the said Assessment It is ordered that notice shall be given thereof in the Church on the next Lords day of the time and place where the said Assessment shall be made to the end that such persons as are therein concerned may if they please be then and there present.

Robert Cole and Thomas Matkin chosen of the Second xij.
At this Court by full agreement of the same Robert Cole and Thomas Matkin are chosen of the second twelve to make that Company full And the said Thomas Matkin being present takes the oath incident to that place and Office according to auntient custome But the said Robert Cole being absent the takeing of his oath is respited till the next Court.

And now remaines in the Kallender of the second twelve
William Milles
John Turner
Christofer Thompson

[fo. 378r] **Eleventh Court of Michael Taylor, 1 October 1663**

A letter of thankes to be sent to Mercers Company.
At this Court it is ordered that a letter of thankes be sent to Mercers Company for the continueing the Lecturers place to this Corporacion As also for the presenting of Mr Elwood to the same he being a person of a peacable and quiett conversacion.

Mr Whites securitie to be renewed.
Whereas Mr Alderman this day acquainted the Court that Mr White desired to have his securitie renewed for the money he had in the Townes hand And he made choice of the present Alderman, Mr Leeming and John Coddington to become bound for the said debt, And Mr Alderman was also pleased to acquaint the Court that he was willing to

become bound with Mr Leeming and John Coddington for the same who being present in Court do likewise consent Whereupon this Court returnes thankes to Mr Alderman for readines to act for the good of this Corporacion And do hereby order and agree to save keepe harmles and indempnifie the said three persons for entring into the bond aforesaid And to give such other securitie for the same as they by their Councill shall be advised.

Andrew Poole distrained.
At this Court the two Serjents Samuell Roades and Richard Blacke and William Milles, Thomas Calcraft, Christofer Hanson, William Laine and William Berriffe, Constables, were sent out of this Court to distraine of the Goodes and Chattells of Andrew Poole for a fine of x li for refuseing to accept of the place of a second xijman according to the custome of this Bourrough And upon their returne they give an account of the Distresses taken, and many of them belonging to the trade of an Apothecary this Court could not value the prizes of them, upon which Mr Alderman sent for Mr Andrew Brome an Apothecarie who gave an account of the prizes thereof, as followeth vzt, one pestoll and morter, iiij li js, eight paire of brass scales and halfe a pound weight xxs a Runlet with some strong water in it xvjs, one searcy xxd five boxes vs, two pound of polypodia of the oake xvjd, a Bottle with some oyle in it iijs, a pound of Sarceyparilla vjs viijd, pound and a halfe of Orris Rootes ijs vjd, two pound and a quarter of Sena at xviijs, and a pound and foure ounces of Kasha fistola at ijs the value of the severall goodes above mencioned amounting in the whole unto vj li xvijs ijd Whereupon this Court takeing in the same into consideracion do order that the goods be safely laid up and secured, & that if the said Andrew Poole bring a Replevin they may be delivered to him again so as that there may be a triall upon the Replevin And this Court do hereby likewise fully order promise and agree to save beare harmles and indempnifie the Serjents and all and every the Constables aforesaid of and from all troubles costs charges damages and incumbrances whatsoever which shall or may happen or arise for or concerning the takeing and distraineing of all or any the Goodes above expressed.

[fo. 378v]

A tender of service by Boston Waites.
At this Court came one of the Waites that lately belonged to Boston and tendered his service for himselfe and others that were his partners and desired to be admitted Waites to this Corporacion whereupon Mr Alderman by the consent of the Court acquainted him that if he and his partners would come over at the faire and play the walking of the faire they should have the Benefitt as former waites had And in the meane time the Court would consider thereof and give them an answer the next Court day.

Mr Grant to receive vs viijd paid to John Wells for the Town.
At this Court Mr Grant acquainted the Alderman that John Wells late vintner at the Angell at his goeing away told him there was vs viijd oweing for Wine at the Venisson feast at the White Lyon and desired him that he would pay it which accordingly he did

on the Towns behalfe. Whereupon it is ordered that the Churchwarden pay the said vs viijd to Mr Grant upon the first receipt of monies.

The Serjent not to pay for his Dinner at the Lecturers Dinner.
Whereas Mr Alderman this day acquainted the Court that Mr Thomas Hanson expected to be paid for the Aldermans Serjent Dinner during the time the Lecture was kept there, which was not usuall neither hath the same beene paid these many yeares, and if it should be allowed now, it would be expected for the future and bring a further charge upon the Towne It is therefore thought convenient and hereby ordered that at all times when the Serjent waites upon the Alderman at the Lecture dinner he shall not pay for his Dinner being he is atendant upon Mr Alderman and the rest of the Lecturers.

Mr Wrights securitie to be renewed.
At this Court it is ordered upon a Mocion made by Mr Alderman on the Behalfe of Mr Wright that his securitie shall be renewed by the Towne seale upon the next meeteing at the Hutch.

Mr Cox to receive his money disbursed as Chaimberlaine.
At this Court Zachary Cox desired that the Chaimberlaine might pay him the money due to him upon his account as Chaimberlaine whereupon it is ordered that the same be paid unto him upon the first receipt of monies.

[fo. 379r] **Twelfth Court of Michael Taylor, 22 October 1663**

Mr Aldermans Accompt.
At this Court Mr Alderman doth account for all monies received by him upon the Common affaires of this Towne as upon penall Statutes &c as also of his payments and Disbursment on the publike

whereby he hath received and paid to the poore part	03 08 01
And his other payments to be	04 04 08
Soe due to him as paid and disbursed	00 16 07

Which he receives in open Court.

Coroners Accompt.
At this Court Mr Gilbert Chantler Coroner gives an Account for the yeare past and saith that one Elizabeth Wright of Belton within this Soake, being sicke for a longe time and by reason of age and weakenes fell downe by her Beddside as she was goeing to bedd, And through the extremitie of cold and Gods visitacion shee there suddenly died And he saith that noe profitt as accrewed to the Towne this yeare And further he hath not to accompt.

Escheators Accompt.
At this Court Mr Richard Leeming Escheator for the yeare past accounts and chargeth himselfe with the receipts of severall persons for light unlawfull and Defective

Weights and Measurers the sume of		01	07	04

And that he hath out of this paid himselfe his charges at every faire and
ijs to the Towne Clarke for his paines in attending every faire   00 04 06
amounting unto
So comeing to the Towne   01 03 02
Which he payes into the Chaimberlaines hands and he is discharged

Churchwardens & others day to Accompt.
Churchwardes hath time till next Court to perfect their Accompt Chaimberlaines hath the same time to give up their Accompts Collectors for Schoole Rents the same time to Accompt
The twelve Constables gives an Accompt of the Constables Assessment as followeth vzt

Constables Accompt.

William Milles				
Thomas Calcraft	Constables for Marketplace their bill	08	03	08
	Whereof they pay	07	08	00
	Rests to gather	00	15	08
William Bury	Constables for Highstreete their bill	03	15	08
Richard Hauley	Gathered and paid in	03	15	08
Christopher Hanson	Constables for Westgate their bill	03	13	00
William Riseing	Whereof they pay in	01	16	00
	Rests to gather	01	17	00

[fo. 379v]

George Read	Constable for Walkergate their bill	01	04	08
William Laine	Gathered & paid in			
Thomas Hatfeild	Constables for Swinegate their bill	01	18	00
Richard Frisby	Gathered and paid in			
William Berriffe	Constable for Castlegate their bill	03	02	07
Francis Charitie	Arreares allowed of	00	16	00
	Gathered and paid in	02	06	07

Constables Disbursments paid.
At this Court the Chaimberlaine payes the Cheife Constables and Under Constables their bills of Disbursments, excepting High Streete Constables upon reading of whose bills and finding them to amount to a considerable sume the Court doth take time to consider thereof and order that the
Chaimberlaine pay them at present   06 12 00
That is to Say to William Bury   02: 16: 00 in part of   03 14 11
And to Richard Hauly   03: 16: 00 in part of   04 16 11

Mr Chantler Accompt for his yeare as Alderman.
At this Court Mr Gilbert Chantler gives an Accompt of monies received by him upon the Affaires of this towne in the time of his Aldermanshipp as upon penall Statutes & As also for his payments and disbursments whereby

he hath received as appeares by perticulars the sume of	01	05	00
And his Disbursments to be the Sume of	03	15	01
So remaines due to him	02	10	01

[fo. 380r]

At an Assembly holden by Mr Michaell Taylor Alderman and the Comburgesses and Burgesses there in Corpus Christi Quire within the Prebendary Church there on Friday next after St Lukes day being 23 October 1663.

First did sitt downe the said Mr Michaell Taylor in Corpus Christi Quire within Prebendarie Church there
Next to him did sitt upon the Cusheon or place of Elleccion two Comburgesses vzt Mr Robert Calcraft and Mr Thomas Milles
Then was there in the Church two Comburgesses (to witt) Mr Christofer Hanson and Mr Thomas Short
Then was sent downe into the Church to these two Comburgesses one other Comburgesse (vzt) Mr John Watson
Out of which three Comburgesses in the Church one was chosen to come up and sit on the Cusheon or place of Eleccion one other Comburgesse (vzt) Mr Christofer Hanson
Then was there three Comburgesses upon the Cusheon or place of Eleccion vzt, Mr Robert Calcraft, Mr Thomas Milles and Mr Christofer Hanson
And then was remaineing in the Church two Comburgesses vzt Mr Thomas Short and Mr John Watson
Out of which three Comburgesses upon the Cusheon or place of Eleccion, vzt Mr Robert Calcraft, Mr Thomas Milles and Mr Christofer Hanson one is to be chosen Alderman for this next ensueing yeare
And so by an unanimous consent and vote of this Assembly Mr Robert Calcraft is chosen Alderman for the next ensueing yeare
Whereupon the said Mr Michaell Taylor dischargeth himselfe from the place and Office of Alderman according to Auntient custome And the said Mr Robert Calcraft now elected Alderman in his place and stead hath at this Assembly taken the oath of Alderman of this Burrough and Soake of Grantham according to the Auntient and laudable custome of the aforesaid Burrough.

And so this Assembly breakes up.

[fo. 380v] [Blank page]

THE HALL BOOK OF GRANTHAM 1663–1664

[fo. 381r] **First Court of Robert Calcraft, 31 October 1663**

Mr Robert Calcraft Alderman

First xij	2nd xij
Mr Thomas Milles Comburgesse	Richard Holley
Mr Christofer Hanson Comburgesse	John Lenton
Mr Gilbert Chantler Comburgesse	Hugh Hutchin
Mr Thomas Short Comburgesse	Zachary Cox
Mr Thomas Grant Comburgesse	George Short
Mr John Watson Comburgesse	Henry Humes
Mr Thomas Hanson Comburgesse	Edward Rawlinson
Mr Michaell Taylor Comburgesse	John Coddington
Mr Richard Leeming Comburgesse	John Winge
Mr Robert Calcraft Comburgesse	Robert Cole
Mr Richard Calcraft Comburgesse	Thomas Matkin
Mr Joseph Tomlinson Comburgesse	

Names of the Officers there

Coroner	Mr Michaell Taylor	Keybearers	Mr Alderman
Escheator	Mr Thomas Hanson		Henry Humes
Churchwardens	Thomas Matkin		Thomas Matkin
	Thomas Calcraft	Prizers of	Thomas Haskerd
Chamberlaines	Henry Humes	Corne	Richard Hauley
	William Milles	Markett	Christofer Hanson
Collectors for	Mr Joseph Tomlinson	Sayers	Robert Waineman
Schoole Rents	John Walker	Leather	William Grococke
Cheife Constables	Edward Rawlinson	Sealers	John Ingerson
	John Coddington		Robert Smith
Marketplace	William Bury		Edward Ulliot
Constables	Edward Pauley	Towne Clarke	William Hodgkinson
High Streete	Thomas Hatfeild	Serjents	Samuell Roades
Constables	Thomas Taylor		Richard Blacke
Westgate	Christofer Hanson	Gaoler	Richard Blacke
Constables	Anthony Hotchkin	Church Clarke	William Newball
Walkergate	William Riseing	Bellman	Ralph Osborne
Constables	William Laine		
Stonegate	Francis Charitie		
Constables	Edward Livesly		

Castlegate   William Berriffe
Constables   Thomas Archer

[fo. 381v]

Names of the Commoners of the Court there
Markett place
William Milles
Thomas Calcraft
John Walker
John Turner
Edward Pauley
Thomas Archer
High Streete
Richard Hauley
William Bury
Thomas Hatfeild
Thomas Taylor
Swinegate
Francis Charitie
Edward Leivesly

Westgate
Anthony Hotchkins
Christofer Hanson
William Berriffe
Edward Kenion
William Palmer

Walkergate
William Riseing
William Laine
Christofer Thompson
John Dawson
George Read
Castlegate
William Berriffe
Thomas Archer

The plate delivered.
At this Court Mr Michaell Taylor late Alderman delivers up to Mr Alderman that now is all the Towns plate being these peices following (vzt)
The horse Race Cupp
Mr Archers Boll
Mr Horsemans Boll
Mr Wheatelys Cann
Mr Horsemans Wine Boll

Mr Greenwoods Cann
Mr Batties Beaker
Two Tunns
One salt with Cover
Mr Greenewoods 13 spoones
The Waites 4 Cognizances

At this Court Mr Taylor acquainted the Alderman that the Charters were at Mr Parkins his house and beene there ever since they came from London.

Churchwardens & other day to accompt.
At this Court the Churchwardens Chaimberlaines and Collectors for the Schoole house Rent have further time to perfect their Accompts.

William Riseings Accompt as Constable.
At this Court William Riseing gives a further Accompt of his Constables

Assessment for Westgate which amounts to	03	13	00
Whereof he payes in	00	14	00
Arreares	01	03	00

And it is ordered that the said xxiii s be paid to the Constable upon the next Distribucion to the people in Westgate being due for them to pay.

[fo. 382r] Second Court of Robert Calcraft, 13 November 1663

Persons appointed to examine Accompts.
At this Court it is ordered that Mr Thomas Grant, Mr Joseph Tomlinson, Zachary Cox, George Short, William Milles, Thomas Calcraft, Edward Pauley and Francis Charitie do meete together to examine the Accompts of the Churchwardens, Chaimberlaines and Collectors for the Schoole Rents and to certifie their proceedinges therein the next Court day.

Constable to search Kilns if they be drawne with lime or Morter.
At this Court the Constables are ordered to search in every of their Wards, if the Kilns be well and sufficiently underdrawne with lime or Mortor according to a former order of this Court And to give an account thereof the next Court upon paine for every Constables faileing in the performance hereof to forfeite vs to be levied according to the custome of this Burrough.

An order for Mr Cox to receive his money.
At this Court Zachary Cox desired that the Court would please to order him the payment of the money which he disbursed when he was Chaimberlaine whereupon it is ordered by this Court that the present Chaimberlaine do pay the same unto him upon the first receipt of money.

Andrew Poole submitt & lays downe his fine for refuseing the place of 2nd xij.
At this Court came Andrew Poole the Apothecary formerly distrained of, for refuseing to accept of his place as one of the second xij being there setled and placed by the Comissioners in pursuance of the Act for the regulateing of Corporacions and afterwards confirmed by this Court, And in open Court this day submitted himselfe to the penaltie mencioned in the order for such as shall refuse to take their places being thereunto chosen, and to fullfill the said order laid downe his x li And desired that the Court would please to consider of his occasions, for they were so urgent that he could not possibly attend the service of this Court as it ought to be performed and therefore desired that they would please to dismiss him from the said place. Whereupon this Court takeing the same into their serious consideracion, and for the preventing of further proceedings in law and to continue peace have here in open Court ordered the said Andrew Poole the sume of v li part of his x li to be restored backe to him againe which the Chaimberlaine immeadiately pays downe to him And it is also ordered that the said Andrew Poole be dismissed the Court accordingly.

[fo. 382v] **Third Court of Robert Calcraft, 8 December 1663**

Persons to examine Accompts.
At this Court Mr Thomas Grant, Mr Joseph Tomlinson, Zachary Cox, George Short, William Milles, Thomas Calcraft, Edward Pauley and Francis Charitie do meete together on Friday next at foure of the clocke in the Afternoone to examine the Accompts of the Churchwardens, Chaimberlaines and Collectors for the Schoole Rents and to certifie their proceedings therein the next Court day.

Money to be paid to the Members of the Court which they formerly lent.
At this Court it is ordered that the Chaimberlaine upon his receipt of the next quarters Rent for the tolles, shall out of the same pay unto the Members of this Court the severall sumes of money which was lent by them in the time of Mr Michaell Taylor Alderman for the use of this Corporacion.

Mr Stoakes dismissed from being Schoole Master.
Whereas Mr Alderman this day acquainted the Court that Mr Stoakes the Head Schoole Master had sent him word that he intended to leave the said place and desired that the Towne would make choice of another person, for he resolved to goe to Melton and to be Schoole Master there, And Whereas severall Members of this Court have beene informed that Mr Stoakes hath for a certaine time indeavored to leave the Schoole void without giveing any notice to the present Alderman or this Court, The which, this Court taking into their consideracion, and to preserve the Schollars and to keepe the Schoole in request so as that the same may not be void, do hereby order that Mr Stoakes be dismissed and forthwith discharged from the place of Schoole Master within this Corporacion And that the Court may proceed to Elleccion of another person in his Roome.

Mr Syston chosen Schoole Master.
At this Court came Mr Systons chosen and elected this day by a generall consent to be Head Schoole Master within this Corporacion of the Free Schoole, And here in open Court as he was freely chosen, so he with all thankefullnes accepted of the same and promised to bestow his paines and utmost indeavours for the Improvement of this Schoole whereby he might bring Glory to God and benefitt to this Corporacion, Hereupon the said Mr Syston was made acquainted by this Court with the Condicions he comes in upon, being the same in all respects to that Mr Wilkinson and Mr Stoakes late Schoole Master came in upon which are in these words (that is to say) that it shall be *ad bene placitum* of the Alderman Comburgesses and Burgesses of this Corporacion either for the further continuance of the said Mr Syston in his place of the Schoole Master of Grantham upon his good Behavior, orderly method of teaching and sufficiencey for learning and knowledge or otherwise to displace him for non abilitie of learning upon Evident proofe thereof whereof as yet noe ambiguitie or question is made. It is likewise deemed very requisite by the whole Court that it shall be in the power and Authoritie of the said Alderman Comburgesses and Burgesses of Grantham and their Successors

either to place or displace any Schoole Master that now is or hereafter shall possess that place upon reasonable & sufficient cause as in their wisdomes and discretions shall be thought convenient or by the wisdomes and discretions of the most part of them, which being this day read was condiscended unto and approved of by all parties herein concerned And the said Mr Syston was this day setled and putt in possession of the free Schoole of this Burrough by the whole Court.

[fo. 383r] Fourth Court of Robert Calcraft 22 January 1663/4

Waites admitted.
At this Court came William Knewstubbs, George Kelham and James Moore and tendred their services to this Court and desired to be admitted Waites to this Corporacion, to which their desire this Court doth condiscend And order that they shall pay [*sic*] foure dayes in the weeke (vzt) Munday Wednesday Friday and Satterday, And that William Knewstubbs shall have a new cloake provided against the next Faire.

Mr Calcraft & Mr Humes abated x li of their Rent for the Soake.
This day Mr Robert Calcraft and Henry Humes acquainted the Court that all the Inhabitants of the Soake being free from Tolle, they could not make up the Rent they formerly agreed with this Court to pay, and desired to surrender up their lease, unless they might have some abatements, the tolles of the Soake amounting to above x li *per Annum* Whereupon this Court taking the same into their consideracions do order that they injoy the said lease for their full terme, And for the loss of such tolle as should be paid by the Soake the Court doth abate them x li of their Rent which agreement they accept of.

Chaimberlaines Accompt.
Robert Cole Chaimberlaine makes his Accompt	
And his Receipts (as by perticulars appeares) are	241 03 00
And his disbursements (as by perticulars also appeares) are	241 03 03
So this Accomptant hath paid more [than] recieved	000 00 03
Which he receives and is discharged.	

Churchwarden Accompts.
Thomas Matkin Churchwarden gives up his Accompt and chargeth himselfe	
to have received of the Quarteridge Assessment as appeares by the Booke	25 03 04
And for Bell and Burialls the sume of	04 02 04
And of the Earle of Rutland given towards rebuilding the Steeple the sume of	10 00 00
Total of his Receipts	051 18 04
And his disbursments (as by perticulars appeares) are	050 17 10

So remaines in this Accomptants hands which
he payes to the new Churchwarden the sume of   001 00 06

[fo. 383v] **Fifth Court of Robert Calcraft, 8 February 1663/4**

Money paid to the Members of this Court.
At this Court the Chaimberlaine payes the severall sumes of money formerly lent by the Members of this Court in the time of Mr Michaell Taylor Alderman.

A letter to [sic] sent to Mr Skipwith aboute the Chartor.
At this Court it is ordered that a letter be sent to Mr Skipwith the Deputy Recorder about the renewing of the Chartor and that 40s be sent for a fee for himselfe & Mr Mountague if Mr Skipwith thinke meete to joyne with him.

Henry Haire payes part of his Rent.
This Day Henry Haire payes in open Court the sume of xj li and promiseth to pay 9 li more within a weeke, and to give securitie for the Rent of the Millnes another yeare And to pay the Remainder of the Rent now in arreare And in the meanetime it is ordered that Mr Tomlinson and Richard Holley continue Milne Masters for a weeke and take an Account of the proffitts thereof this day and of the Corne there remaineing.

John Newton, Widdow Robson & Luce Dann placed in the Almshouses.
At this Court Doctor Hurst being present with the consent of Mr Alderman and this Court doth place John Newton, Widdow Robson and Luce Dann in the Almshouses that are now void.

Sixth Court of Robert Calcraft, 19 February 1663/4

Mr Richard Hurst admitted Tenant to Towers his lease.
At this Court it is ordered that Mr Richard Hurst be admitted Tenant to the lease formerly graunted by this Court to Thomas Towers of certaine lands belonging to this Towne at the request of Doctor Thomas Hurst being present at this Court.

Milne Masters appointed.
At this Court Hugh Hutchin and John Walker are chosen Mill Masters for the Slate Millne and Robert Cole and John Turner for the Towne Milne and to continue in the said places till next Court if they continue so long in the Towns hand.

Zachary Laxton, William Langley, Robert Little, Richard Durham and Edward Rudd made free.
At this Court came Zachary Laxton, William Langley, Robert Little, Richard Durham and Edward Rudd who had served their severall Apprentices within this Towne and

desired to be admitted Freemen of this Burrough (to which their desire this Court doth consent And hereupon they pay vs apeice (as forrainers) and usuall fees to Clarke and Serjents And take the oath for freemen according to the Auntient and Laudable custome of this Burrough.

xs paid for the repaire of Almshouses.
At this Court the Chaimberlaine pays xs to Mr Grant which he laid downe for the repaires of the Almshouses at Christmas Anno Domini 1662.

[fo. 384r] **Seventh Court of Robert Calcraft, 11 March 1663/4**

Leases to be forfeited for non payment of Rent.
At this Court the Chaimberlaine brought in a perticular of severall persons that are in arreare for Rent due to the Towne and acquainted the Court that they do refuse to pay the same It is therefore ordered by this Court that a reentry be made into the houses of such persons according to their leases upon their forfeiture thereof, And that their be new leases graunted to others.

Repaires of the Church to be veiwed.
At this Court it is ordered that the Churchwardens together with Workmen do veiw the decayes of the Church and how farr it is out of repaire and to take an Estimate thereof and returne the same the next Court day.

A lease lett to Jonathan Parnham of his house.
At this Court came Jonathan Parnham and takes a lease of the house he now dwells in together with a barne thereunto adjoyning for one and twenty yeares from the Expiracions of a former lease thereof in being, paying vij li for a fine in manner following (vzt) foure pounds part thereof upon the first day of May next and three pounds remainder of the seaven pounds upon the Nine and twentieth day of May next also ensueing And he gives in Earnest of the said contract vjd And is to give Covenants and bonds according to the former lease, and custome of this Burrough.

A lease lett to Hugh Holt of his house.
At this Court came Hugh Holt and takes a lease of this Corporacion of that part of the house he now dwells in which belongs to the Towne for one and twenty yeares from the Expiracion of a former lease thereof in being, paying a [sic] xj li for a fine upon the first day of May next ensueing And he gives in Earnest of this contract xijd And is to performe all such Covenants as are in the former lease heretofore made And to give securitie for the same according to the custome of this Burrough.

Bucketts to be provided.
At this Court it is ordered that the Chaimberlaine do provide Buckett with all convenience and to call of the Comoners for their proportion.

Haires house to be repaired.
At this Court the Chaimberlaine is ordered to take care that the house in Swinegate late in the tenure of Henry Haire be repaired and also the pest house.

Ladders to be set up.
At this Court the Constables are ordered to see that the Ladders and hookes be sett up in every Ward and to returne an Account thereof to the Alderman the next Court day.

[fo. 384v] **Eighth Court of Robert Calcraft, 30 April 1664**

Mr Tomlinsons promise for arreares of Rent.
Whereas at this Court there appeared by the Chamberlaines booke that there 44s due to the Towne for arreare of Rent out of the house now in the tenure of John Wing for two yeares in the time that Mr Bury or Mr Tomlinson had it in possession, And Mr Tomlinson acquainting the Court that Mr Bury told him the Rent was paid, and desired that the Court would please to respite the payment thereof till Mr Burys returne into the Country And if it did appeare that the Rent was unpaid and that Mr Bury refused or neglected to pay it, Mr Tomlinson promiseth to see the same satisfied and payd.

Chartor to be renewed.
At this Court Mr Alderman acquainted the Members thereof that the Kinges Attorny had sent downe a Quo warranto for the Towne to renew the Chartor and that this terme it was convenient to proceed to the renewing of it And for the raiseing of money it is thought necessarie if the Court approve thereof that some members of this Court might goe to the Gentry of the Towne and Country that are freemen of this Corporacion and to acquaint them that the Towne desires their aide advise and assistance in the obtaineing of the Chartor And that they will please to contribute towards the charge thereof, to which motion this Court doth consent And do hereby order Mr John Watson and Mr Richard Leeming to sollicite the Gentlemen in the Country and Mr Michaell Taylor and Mr Joseph Tomlinson for the Towne And in case the Freemen of this Towne refuse to contribute, And that then an Assessment shall be imposed upon them as shall be thought convenient, after the renewing of the Chartor.

An assessment of 60 li for repaires of the Church.
Whereas upon notice given to this Court this day that the Church is very much out of repaires and that Sir Edward Lake hath given order that if the Church be not speedily repaired that the Parish and Churchwarden shall be proceeded against in the Ecclesiasticall Courts The which this Court takeing into consideracion do hereby order that an Assessment of sixty pounds be laid upon this Parish and that notice be given thereof the next Lords day in the Church for the preventing of further inconvenience and danger at the next visitacion.

[fo. 385r] **Ninth Court of Robert Calcraft, 9 May 1664**

George Shorts Accompt to be perfected.
At this Court George Short Churchwarden hath further time to perfect his Accompts.

An order to take up 50 li towards renewing the Chartor.
This day Mr Alderman acquainted the Court that he hath obtained 50 li towards the renewing of the Chartor And that Mr John Watson and Mr Richard Leeming were bound for the same to Mr Tomlinson which bond was read in open Court and the money paid unto the Chaimberlaine and by him paid over unto the Towne Clarke to carry to London And it is hereby ordered that Mr William Parkins the Towne Sollicitor Mr Michaell Taylor one of the Comburgesses of this Court and the Towne Clarke do sollicite the Affaires of this Corporacion in sueing forth the Chartor this terme And it is likewise ordered that Mr Michaell Taylor shall have his charges allowed for all the time he shall continue at London on the Towns behalfe And that the Towne Clarke be allowed his charges being sent upon to London on purpose to sollicite the Towns Affaires.

Mr Watson & Mr Leeming bound for the 50 li.
Whereas Mr John Watson and Mr Richard Leeming of Grantham Gentlemen and Comburgesses of this Court do stand bound unto Mr Joseph Tomlinson of Grantham aforesaid in one obligacion bearing date the sixth day of May Anno Domini 1664 in the sume of 100 li condicioned for the payment of 51 li: 10s upon the sixth of November next ensueing the date hereof as by the same appeares which said sume was by the parties aforesaid taken upon the behalfe of this Corporacion for the renewing of their Chartor And paid to the Chaimberlaine in open Court as aforesaid And the parties before named became bound as aforesaid at the intreaty and request of this Burrough and for to advance the good and Benefitt thereof Now this Court do for themselves and their Successors firmely promise well and truly from time to time and at all times forever hereafter to save defend keepe harmles and indempnified the persons so bound as above said and either of them their and either of their heires Executors and Administrators of and from all and all manner of payments penalties forfeitures and suites of law whatsoever which shall or may happen arise or grow for or by reason of the said recited obligacion and Condicion thereupon written And to give such further Assurance with in such convenient time as shall be advised by Councill learned in the law.

An Assessment to be made for the Conduit.
At this Court it is ordered that an Assessment of twelve pounds shall be laid upon this Burrough for the repaires of the Conduit And Zachary Cox, Robert Cole, John Walker and Francis Charitie are nominated and appointed Assessors and the Under Constables Collectors thereof.

A contribucion to be made for the Chartor.
At this Court Mr Richard Calcraft is desired to joyne with Mr Tomlinson to collect the contribucion of the Towne towards the renewing of the Chartor in the place of Mr Michaell Taylor who is ordered to sollicite for the Towne at London.

Towns Clarke order to receive his 52s.
At this Court the Chaimberlaine is ordered to pay fifty two shillinges to the Town Clarke which is due to him as appeares by an order of Court in the time of Mr Gilbert Chantler Alderman.

[fo. 385v]

Henry Humes pays in Court the money due from him as Chaimberlaine.
At this Court Henry Humes payes to William Milles Chaimberlaine the sume of tenn pounds due from him upon his Account as Chaimberlaine and Henry Haires payes x li in part of his Rent for the Milles.

An order for the Elleccon of the succeeding Alderman.
For the more peaceable and quiett proceedings at the Church on the next Elleccion day for the succeeding Alderman It is ordered that upon the Elleccion day Mr Thomas Hanson be sent downe into the Church to Mr Thomas Short and Mr John Watson to make the three Comburgesses there Out of which three Comburgesses in the Church It is likewise agreed that Mr Thomas Short be brought upon the Cusheon and place of Elleccion to Mr Thomas Milles and Mr Christofer Hanson to make three Comburgesses there Out of which three Comburgesses on the Cusheon with a free and unanimous consent Mr Thomas Milles is nominated Alderman for the next ensueing yeare.

Tenth Court of Robert Calcraft, 11 June 1664

Mr Taylor Account of his proceeding at London aboute renewing the Chartor.
At this Court Mr Michaell Taylor gives an Account of the proceedinges the last terme in renewing the Chartor wherein he acquainted this Court that by advise of Councill and the Attorny Generalls Clarkes it was the best way to sue forth a confirmacion of former Graunts, for most Corporacion did the like, which Confirmacion was in the Recordors hands and he approved thereof, And that there was a new proviso in this Graunt that the Kinge reserved the power to setle and confirme all Recordors and Towne Clarkes throughout England (except London) But the Towne may Elect and nominate and the Kinge confirme, As also that one Mr Joseph Clarke is imployed to perfect the sueing forth of the Chartor He further acquainteth this Court that is [sic] charges in London on the Towne account came to xxxs and the Towne Clarke disbursments and charges came to iiij li: xvs: iijd which is in all vj li vs: iijd And that to make up the 50 li to be left with Mr Clarke, he lent iiij li and the Towne Clarke xxxxvs and iijd Whereupon

the Court doth returne Mr Taylor thankes for care and paines And hereby order that the Chaimberlaine pay Mr Taylor his iiij li and xxxxv s iiijd to the Towne Clarke upon the first receipt of money.

An Assessment of xij li to be made for repaires of the Conduit.
At this Court it is ordered that Mr Richard Calcraft, Richard Holly, Zachary Cox, William Milles, John Walker and Francis Charitie or any foure of them do Assess the sume of xij li upon the Inhabitants of this Towne for the repaires of the Conduit And to certifie their proceedinges the next Court day.

Mr Saule to be sued for xxx li.
At this Court it is ordered that the Towne Clarke do send for a writ against Mr Saule for xxx li which is due as securitie for Haire upon the Account of the Rent for the Milnes.

George Short to perfect his Accompt.
At this Court George Short Churchwarden hath further day to perfect his Accompt.

[fo. 386r] **Eleventh Court of Robert Calcraft, 1 July 1664**

George Shorts Accompt to be perfected.
At this Court it is ordered that Mr Thomas Grant and Mr Joseph Tomlinson do examine and perfect the Accompts of George Short Churchwarden and certifie the same the next Court day.

The tolles leased to Henry Rudkin for a yeare.
At this Court came Henry Rudkin and takes a lease of all the tolles belonging to this Corporacion (which was formerly lett to Mr Robert Calcraft and Henry Humes) to hold to him for one whole yeare from the first day of August comonly called Lammas day now next ensueing at the yearely Rent of fifty pounds to be paid at foure usuall dayes or Feasts in the yeare by even and equall portions And it is ordered that the said Henry Rudkin shall give sufficient securitie by bond with himselfe and others for the true payment of the said Rent as they shall grow due and payable at the severall dayes and feasts respectively.

The 250 li of Sir Robert Markham disowned to be the Corporacions debt.
At this Court came Mr Trevillian and Mr Berke and desired that this Court would please to give them and others that were bound with them some Counter securitie by the Towns seale or otherwise for the saveing them harmeles from the two hundred and fifty pounds they have paid to Sir Robert Markham Whereupon this Court takeing the same into their consideracions and finding by the Chaimberlaines Booke that the same 250 li never was paid into the hands of the Chaimberlaine for the use of this Corporacion according to the Auntient orders and customes of this Court And being this day put to the vote It is by the Major part of this Court fully ordered & agreed upon that the Towns seale shall not be given for their Counter securitie nor any other And it is hereby declared

that the said two hundred and fifty pounds is noe proper debt of this Corporacion And therefore disowned by this Court.

[fo. 386v] **Twelfth Court of Robert Calcraft, 22 July 1664**

Assessment for the Conduit delivered forth.
At this Court the Constables of every Ward received the Assessment for the repaires of the Conduit devided into their severall Wards And it is hereby ordered that the said Constables do collect the money thereupon assessed And pay the same to the Chaimberlaine the next Court day upon paine for every Constable neglecting herein to forfeit iijs iiijd to be levied to the use of this Burrough according to the Auntient custome thereof.

Mr Tomlinson takes a lease of John Winges house. Arreares of rent acquitted to him.
At this Court Mr Joseph Tomlinson takes a lease of the house wherein John Wing now dwelleth in the Markett place for xxj^{ty} yeares from and after the expiracion of a former lease graunted to Robert Smith paying the sume of 20 li for a fine and giveing securitie for the performance of Covenants according to the former lease And he gives in earnest xijd And whereas at present there is 44s in arreare for the Rent of the said house for two yeares past which the said Mr Tomlinson did formerly ingage to this Court that if the same appeared to be due he would see it satisfied And upon the renewing of this lease there is severall yeares to come before the comencement thereof Which this Court takeing into consideracion And also the readines of the said Mr Tomlinson to pay the Auntient fine by reason the Towne hath urgent occasions for money for renewing of the Chartor and that the same will be paid downe to the Chaimberlaine upon riseing of the Court It is therefore fully ordered and agreed that the said 44s be acquitted and released And that the said Mr Tomlinson and all other Tenants and persons whatsoever be freed and discharged from paying the same accordingly.

Zachary Cox takes a lease of his house.
At this Court Zachary Cox Takes a lease of the house he now dwelleth in for 21 yeares after the Expiracion of a former lease thereof in being to Henry Cole of Winthorpe in the County of Nottingham paying 25 li for a fine in manner following vzt 20 li to be paid downe to the present Chaimberlaine and 5 li upon sealing the said lease And to give securitie for the performance of the Covenants mentioned in the lease to be granted thereof And he gives in earnest xijd.

Mr Alderman to reenter of the Milles at Lamas next.
This day Mr Alderman acquainted the Court that Henry Haire was above 70^{ty} li in arreare for the Rent of the Milles and that if he be not prevented he would run further into the Towns debt whereupon it is ordered that the Alderman reenter upon the Milles at Lammas next for the Towns use And that the Towne Clarke send for a writt against Haire and his securitie for the Recovery of the Arreares.

Money to be sent to London aboute the Chartor.
At this Court it is ordered that the money rasied this day be sent up to London to pay towards renewing the Charter.

Thomas Cole & Daniell Quininborow made free.
At this Court came Thomas Cole and Daniell Quiningborow desired to be admitted freeman of the Corporacion, to which mocion this Court doe consent whereupon the said Thomas Cole as freeborne payes to the box ijs vjd And the said Daniell Quiningborow as a forrainer payes vs And they both take the oath of freemen and payes the fees to Clarke and Serjents according to Auntient custome.

[fo. 387Ar] **Thirteenth Court of Robert Calcraft, 2 September 1664**

Assessment for the Conduit to be collected.
At this Court it is ordered that the Constables of every Ward do collect the monies assessed for the Repaires of the Conduit and cleare the said Assessment within a fortnight now next ensueing upon paine for every Constable neglecting the same to forfeite iijs iiijd to the Common box.

George Short Churchwarden Cleares his Account.
At this Court George Short late Churchwarden cleares his Account of the 50 li Assessment & of the Quarteridge Assessment upon which Account there remaines due to the Towne 46s ijd which he payes downe in open Court to the present Chaimberlaine, and acquainting this Court that he hath beene at great expence and charge in collecting the said Assessments whereupon this Court considering of the charge and trouble he was at do hereby order the Chaimberlaine to pay him xxs towards his charges which is paid to him accordingly And the xxvjs vijd remainder of the 46s ijd the Chaimberlaine received in part of the iiij li which was lent by the Towne upon Mr Brownes goeing to London aboute the Lecturers place when Mr Starkey desisted from preaching and left the said place.

William Palmer to receive viij li xs & George Short to be discharged thereof.
At this Court George Short acquainted the Alderman that there is due to William Palmer for repairing of the Church in his time viij li xs which is ordered to be paid unto him by the present Churchwarden And the said George Short is discharged of the same And from the place of Churchwarden.

Mr Alderman relacion upon reentring of the Mills.
This Day Mr Alderman acquainted the Court that he had reentred upon the Milles for the use of the Towne within one weeke after Lammas Day And the reason that Henry Haire injoyed them that weeke was at the request of John Haire his securitie who ingaged for that weekes proffitt expecting to have received more money And Mr Alderman further acquainteth this Court that there is due and in arreare to the Towne upon Saules Account

and for part of this yeare the sume of 78 li : 8s And it is ordered that the securitie be arrested forthwith for recovery thereof.

A lease let to John Keale of a house in Spittlegate.
At this Court John Keale takes a lease of the house he now injoyes at Spittlegate for one and twenty yeares after the Expiracion of a former lease thereof in being to James Craddin paying viij li for a fine within a fortnight next ensueing And performing Covenants according to the former lease And he gives in Earnest thereof xijd.

Milnemasters chosen.
At this Court Mr Tomlinson and Edward Pauley chosen Milne Masters for the Slate Milne And Richard Holley and John Turner for the Towne Milne and to continue till next court day.

Mr Short time given to renew his lease till next Court.
At this Court Mr Thomas Short desires time till the next Court to renew his lease of the house he now dwelleth in Scituate in the Markett place.

William Milles chosen of the 2d xij.
At this Court William Milles is chosen of the second xij and takes his oath incident thereunto.
In the Kallender
John Turner
Christofer Thompson
William Bury

[fo. 387Av] **Fourteenth Court of Robert Calcraft, 14 September 1664**

Accounts to be Examined.
At this Court Mr Thomas Hanson, Mr Michaell Taylor, Mr Robert Calcraft, Richard Holley, Henry Humes, Edward Rawlinson, Robert Cole and William Milles are ordered to meete on Munday next at the Towne Hall by Nine of the Clocke in the morning to examine the Accounts of Mr Robert Calcraft and Edward Rawlinson as Chaimberlaines and to cleare the Constables Account for the Conduit Assessment.

Mr Cox pays the Remainder of his fine for his lease.
At this Court came Zachary Cox and payes downe in open Court the sume of v li remainder of the full sume due upon his lease as fine And John Keale likewise payes downe his fine of viij li.

Leases to be sealed at the Hutch.
At this Court it is ordered that the leases of Mr Tomlinson, Zachary Cox, Hugh Holt, John Keale and Jonathan Parnham and the lease formerly lett to Widdow Still and now

by consent of this Court made to Mr John Miller shall be sealed at the Hutch this this [*sic*] day upon riseing of the Court.

An order for makeing the Assessment for Constables bills.
At this Court it is ordered that an Assessment of xvij li be made & laid upon this Burrough for the payment of the Constables their bills of disbursments for the yeare past An estimate being taken what those perticular summes amount unto And the Cheife Constables & under Constables are appointed Assessors And the under Constables Collectors thereof And for the more legall makeing of the said Assessment it is ordered that notice thereof be given the next Lords day in the Church of the time & place where the said Assessment is to be made to the end that such as are therein concerned may if they please be there present.

Fifteenth Court of Robert Calcraft, 7 October 1664

Accounts to be Examined.
At this Court it is ordered that Mr Thomas Grant, Mr Thomas Hanson, Mr Michaell Taylor, Mr Robert Calcraft, Richard Holley, Henry Humes, Edward Rawlinson, Robert Cole and William Milles do meete on Tuesday next at twelve of the clocke in the Towne Hall to examing [*sic*] the Accounts of Mr Robert Calcraft Chaimberlaine and to certifie the proceedings the next Court.

Securitie given for Henry Haires debt for the Mills.
This day Mr Alderman acquainted the Court that Mr Saule hath given securitie for the xxx li oweing by Haire and that one Everitt of Welby is bound with him to him [*sic*] to pay xv li at Martlemas and xv li at May day next and xxs in part of the charges And he further acquainted the Court that John Haire of Wyvall hath given securitie to Mr John Welby for xxij li xs for three quarters Annuitie out of the Milles And is to give securitie for xvij li viijs to Doctor Hurst Remainder of the money due from Henry Haire to the Towne for the Rent of the Milles.

Mr Ireland made free.
At this Court came Thomas Ireland who hath lately taken the Inn called the George and being he is intended to settle in the Towne desired to be incorporated a freeman of this Burrough to whose request this Court doth condiscend whereupon the said Thomas Ireland being a forrainer laid downe his x li in open Court according to order of this Court desireing the Alderman & the rest of this Court that they would please to deale kindly with him & to give him some part backe againe The which this Court takeing into consideracion & that he is likely to make a good member of this Towne & not prejudiciall to any trade do order the Caimberlaine [*sic*] to pay him v li And thereupon he payes his fees & takes his oath of freeman according to Auntient custome.

[fo. 387Br] **Sixteenth Court of Robert Calcraft, 20 October 1664**

Mr Aldermans Account.
At this Court Mr Alderman doth Account for all monies received by him upon the Common Affaires of this Towne as upon penall Statutes &c As also for his payments and disbursments on the publike whereby he chargeth himselfe with the receipt of   00 12 00
And his disbursments in the same yeare amounts to   01 19 08
So remaines due to him as paid and disbursed   01 07 08
Which he receives in open Court.

Coroners Account.
At this Court Mr Michaell Taylor Coroner accounteth And saith that noe Casualties hath happened this yeare whereby any thing hath accrued to the Benefitt of this Corporacion And so he hath nothing to account for, and is discharged.

Escheators Account.
At this Court Mr Thomas Hanson Escheator for the yeare past accounts & chargeth himselfe with the Receipts of severall persons for light unlawfull and defective weights and
Measures forfeited by the Statute the sume of   00 15 08
And that he hath out of the same paid himselfe his charges at every Faire and ii s to the Towne Clarke for his paines in attending every Faire which amounts unto   00 04 06
So comeing to the Towne   00 11 02
Which he pays in open Court to the Chaimberlaine and he is discharged.

Churchwarden & Milne Masters further day to Account.
At this Court the Churchwarden, Chaimberlaine, Collectors for Schoole Rents and Milne Masters have time to perfect their Accounts till next Court.

The twelve Constables gives an Account of the Constables Assessment for the yeare past.

The Constables Account for their Assessment.
William Bury	Constables for the Markett place their bill	06 08 00
Edward Paulett	Whereof they pay in	04 17 07

Remaines xxx s v d which the said William Bury doth take in full of his disbursments for two yeares last past and cleares the bill aforesaid
Thomas Hatfeild Thomas Taylor Constables for the High Streete have further day to gather the said Assessment.

Christofer Hanson	Constables for Westgate their bill	02 13 06
Anthony Hotchkin	whereupon they pay in	01 15 11
	Remaines to gather up	00 17 07
William Riseing	Constables for Walkergate their bill	00 17 04

William Laine	Abatements allowed	00 00 10
	Gathered cleared and paid in	00 16 06
Francis Charitie	Constables for Swinegate their bill	01 05 08
Edward Leivesby [sic]	Abatements allowed	00 02 06
	Gathered cleared and paid in	01 03 02
Willaim Berriffe	Constables for Castlegate their bill	02 07 05
Thomas Archer	Abatements allowed	00 02 00
	Gathered Cleared and paid in	02 05 05

Sessions fines paid.
At this Court the Towne Clarke pays to the Chaimberlaine xxvs vjd which he received of severall persons for fines the last Sessions.

[fo. 387Bv]

Thomas Matkins Account as Churchwarden.
At this Court Thomas Matkin Churchwarden makes an Account for the Arreares
of the Quarteridge Assessment in his time which amounts to   07 00 06
Whereof there is still in arreare   03 08 06
So that he hath collected thereof   03 12 00
Which he hath paid into the hands of Thomas Calcraft the now
Churchwarden

Mr Parkins to pay xijd a Quarter to the Church.
Whereas upon the Examineing of the Arreares of Thomas Matkin it appeares to the Court that Mr William Parkins the Towns Sollicitor is set ijs a quarter to the Church for his seate which he doth thinke is too great a proporcion And desired the Churchwarden to acquaint the Court of it Whereupon this Court takeing into consideracion the readines of the said Mr Parkins to act for the good of this Corporacion And that he is overcharged do hereby order that the said Mr Parkins do pay onely twelve pence a Quarter for the future.

Mr Calcrafts Account perfected as Chaimberlaine.
At this Court Mr Thomas Grant, Mr Michaell Taylor, Mr Robert Calcraft, Richard Holley, Henry Humes, Edward Rawlinson, Robert Cole and William Milles do returne a relacion of their proceedinges aboute the Examineing of Mr Calcraft account as Chaimberlaine for vj li vs being one halfe quarters Rent for the tolles And they do declare that upon his Account there is due to him iij li xvijs vd from the Towne And upon the Adding of the vj li vs to this Receipts that then there remaines due to the Towne ii li: vijs: vijd which is sett at the foote of his Accout And that the same is to paid to the Chaimberlaine which being demanded the said Mr Calcraft cleares to this Court as followeth vzt lent to the Towne in Mr Taylors yeare xxs for two Assessments vs vjd

and remaineing in his hands xxijs which he payes to William Milles Chaimberlaine in open Court in full of his Account.

A bill of charges delivered against Saule.
At this Court the Towne Clarke delivered a bill of Charges for the suite against Mr Saule and the three Haires for the Rent of the Milles which charge comes to xxxiiijs and also iiijs viijd for freeing the Soake from the Assizes at Mid lent last And it is hereby ordered that the Chaimberlaine do pay the said sumes unto him which amount in the whole unto xxxviijs and viijd.

Constables Account for Highstreete for the Conduit Assessment.
Thomas Hatfeild	Constables for the High Streete	
Thomas Taylor	their bill for the Conduit	01 15 02
Abatements allowed		00 01 02
Collected and paid		01 09 05
Remaines to collect		00 04 09

Charles Wetherill a Forrainer made free.
At this Court came Charles Wetherill and desired to be made a freeman of this Corporacion to whose desire this Court doth condiscent whereupon he lays downe his x li according to Auntient custome desireing Mr Alderman and the rest of the Court that they would please to consider of his condicion for he was necessitated to borrow the money the which this Court takeing into consideracion & his willingnes to be a freeman & to submitt to the orders of this Burrough, do order that the Chaimberlaine pay him five pounds backe againe which he receives accordingly & returns thankes to this Court for the same, And payes his fees to Clarke and Serjents and takes the oath of a Freeman according to the Auntient custome of this Corporacion.

[fo. 388r]

At an Assembly holden by Mr Robert Calcraft Alderman and the Comburgesses and Burgesses there in Corpus Christi Quire within the Prebendarie Church there on Friday next after St Lukes day being 21 October 1664.

First did sitt downe upon the Cusheon the said Mr Robert Calcraft in Corpus Christi Quire within the prebenadere [sic] Church there
Next to him did sitt upon the Cusheon or place of Eleccion two Comburgesses vzt Mr Thomas Milles and Mr Christofer Hanson
Then was there in the Church two Comburgesses vzt Mr Thomas Short and Mr John Watson
Then was sent downe into the Church to those two Comburgesses to make them three one other Comburgesse vzt Mr Thomas Hanson

Out of which three Comburgesses in the Church one was chosen to come up and sitt on the Cusheon or place of Eleccion one other Comburgesse vzt Mr John Watson

Then was there three Comburgesses upon the Cusheon or place of Eleccion vzt Mr Thomas Milles Mr Christofer Hanson and Mr John Watson

And there was remaineing in the Church two Comburgesses vzt Mr Thomas Short and Mr Thomas Hanson

Out of which three Comburgesses upon the Cusheon or place of Eleccion vzt Mr Thomas Milles Mr Christofer Hanson and Mr John Watson one is to be chosen Alderman for the next ensueing yeare

And by an unanimous consent and vote of this Assembly Mr Thomas Milles is chosen Alderman for this next ensueing yeare

Whereupon the said Mr Robert Calcraft dischargeth himselfe from the place and office of Alderman according to Auntient custome And the said Mr Thomas Milles now elected Alderman in his place and stead hath at this Assembly taken the oath of Alderman for this Burrough and Soake of Grantham according to the Auntient and laudable custome of the aforesaid Burrough.

And so this Assembly breaks up.

[fo. 388v] [Blank page]

THE HALL BOOK OF GRANTHAM 1664–1665

[fo. 389r] **First Court of Thomas Milles, 25 October 1664**

Mr Thomas Milles Alderman
First xij
Mr Robert Calcraft Comburgesse
Mr Christofer Hanson Comburgesse
Mr Gilbert Chantler Comburgesse
Mr Thomas Short Comburgesse
Mr Thomas Grant Comburgesse
Mr John Watson Comburgesse
Mr Thomas Hanson Comburgesse
Mr Michael Taylor Comburgesse
Mr Richard Leeming Comburgesse
Mr Robert Calcraft Junior Comburgesse
Mr Richard Calcraft Comburgesse
Mr Joseph Tomlinson Comburgesse

2d xij
Richard Holley
John Lenton
Hugh Hutchin
Zachary Cox
George Short
Henry Humes
Edward Rawlinson
John Coddington
John Winge
Robert Cole
Thomas Matkin
William Milles

The names of the officers there

Coroner	Mr Robert Calcraft senior	Keybearers	Mr Alderman
Escheator	Mr John Watson		John Lenton
Churchwardens	John Lenton		John Coddington
	Thomas Calcraft	Prizers of Corne	John Plumer
Chamberlaines	John Coddington		Thomas Charles
	John Turner	Market Sayers	Robert Waineman
Collectors for	Mr Richard Leeming		William Scott
Schoole Rents	William Bury	Leather sealers	William Grococke
Cheife	John Winge		John Inkerson
Constables	William Milles		Robert Smith
Market Place	Thomas Ireland		Edward Ulliott
Constables	Edward Paulett	Towne Clarke	William Hodgkinson
High Streete	William Laine	Serjents	Samuell Roades
Constables	Thomas Archer		Richard Blacke
Westgate	Anthony Hotchkin	Gaoler	Richard Blacke
Constables	William Berriffe	Church Clarke	William Newball
Walkergate	William Riseing	Belman	Ralph Osborne
Constables	George Read		

Swinegate   Francis Charitie
Constables   Edward Leivesly
Castlegate   Thomas Gunnisson
Constables   William Scott

[fo. 389v]

Names of the Commoners of the Court there

Marketplace   Westgate
Thomas Ireland   William Berriffe
Edward Paulett   William Palmer
Thomas Calcraft   Edward Kenion
John Turner   Walkergate
John Walker   William Riseing
Anthony Hotchkin   George Read
William Laine   Christofer Thompson
Thomas Archer

                               Swinegate
High Street   Francis Charitie
William Bury   Edward Leivesly
Richard Hauley   Castlegate
Thomas Hatfeild   Thomas Gunnisson
Thomas Taylor   William Scott

The Towns plate delivered.
At this Court Mr Robert Calcraft late Alderman delivers up to Mr Alderman that now is all the Towns plate being these peices following vizt

The horse Race cupp   Mr Greenwoods 13 spoones
Mr Archers Boll   Mr Batties Beaker
Mr Horsemans Boll   Two tunns
Mr Wheatlys Cann   One salt with Cover
Mr Horsemans wine Boll   The Waites foure Cognizances
Mr Greenwoods Cann

Charters delivered.
At this Court Mr Calcraft delivers up to the present Alderman the severall Charters belonging to this Corporacion.

Mr Tomlinsons account as Milne Master.
At this Court the severall Millmasters gives an Account of the proffitts of both the Milles as
followeth   Mr Tomlinson one of the Millmasters for the
Slate Mill chargeth himselfe for foure weekes with   06 17 01

And that his disbursments in the same time are	03 04 07
Remaines due to the Towne which he pays in Court	03 12 06

Mr Holleys Account for the Millnes.
Richard Holley one of the Mill Masters for the Towne

Mill chargeth himselfe for five weekes with Receipt of	10 07 07 ob
And that his disbursments in the same time are	03 16 02
As also paid to the Chamberlaine	04 00 00
Remains due to the Towne which he pays in Court	02 11 05 ob

Edward Paulet day to Account
At this Court Edward Paulet Mill Masters hath further time to perfect his Accounts.

[fo. 390r]

John Turners Account.
At this Court John Turner another of the Mill [*sic*] for the Towne Mill

chargeth himselfe for five weekes with Receipt of	08 05 02
And that his disbursments in the same time are	02 15 04
And in money oweing vizt Mrs Katherine three stricke of mault	00 09 00
To Thomas Milles Felmonger one stricke	00 03 00
Remaines due to the Towne which he payes in Court	04 17 10

At this Court John Turner further accounteth and saith that in one of the five weekes there was twelve strickes of mault left in the mill which was disposed of and Remaines to be paid for as followeth To Widdow Breilsford eight strickes Humphrey Fishar three strickes and remaineing unsold one stricke which said severall sumes of money this Court doth order that the said John Turner do collect and gather the same and cleare his Account the next Court day.

Collectors for the Schoole Rent their Account.
At this Court Mr Joseph Tomlinson and John Walker do Account for the Schoole house Rents

& their receipts are	46 05 00
And that their Disbursments & Arreares are	46 02 04
Remaines due to the Towne	00 02 08

which they pay in Court & are discharged.

Jonathan Parnham to receive xxxs for worke done at the new house.
At this court it is ordered that the Chaimberlaines pay xxxs to Jonathan Parnham for stone worke done at the house in Swinegate where Henry Haire lately dwelt.

Accounts to be examined.
At this Court it is ordered that Mr Thomas Grant, Mr Michaell Taylor, Mr Richard Leeming, Richard Holley and Edward Paulett do meete at the Towne Hall on Tuesday next at one of the Clocke in the Afternoone to examine the Accounts of William Milles Chaimberlaine And the Accounts of Thomas Hatfeild, Thomas Taylor, Christofer Hanson and Anthony Hotchkin Constables for the yeare past And to certefie their proceedings the next Court day.

Mr Short in Arreares of his Rent.
At this Court the Collectors for the Schoole Rents demanded xxs of Mr Thomas Short for one yeares Rent due for the stipend of the Schoole Master which the said Mr Short then acknowledged to be owing And also xxs for the yeare before that Mr John Watson laid downe for him and past it in his Accounts whereupon Mr Short promised to pay the said xxxxs the next Court day.

Constables to pay the Towne Clarke for last yeares bills.
This day the Towne Clarke acquainted the Court that he delivered the Constables of every Ward their bills for the collecting of the Constables Assessment and made warrants upon the same And upon giveing up their Accounts they forgott to him for the makeing of them And he is likely to loose the same unless this Court will be pleased to order him the payment thereof Whereupon it is ordered by this Court that the Constables of every Ward do pay the same to the Towne and insert it in their Accounts for the yeare to come.

Churchwarden hath time to give his Accounts.
At this Court the Churchwarden hath further time to perfect his Accounts.

Comon Box opened.
At this Court the Common Box was opened and xxvs taken out and paid to John Coddington the present Chaimberlaine.

[fo. 390v]

At an Assembly holden by the Comburgesses & Burgenses of Grantham aforesaid in Corpus Christi Quire within the Prebendarie Church there on Satterday the fifth Day of November Anno Domini 1664 after the decease of Mr Thomas Milles late Alderman and for the election of a new Alderman in his place and stead according to the Auncient custome of this Burrough.

First did sitt downe upon the Cusheon or place of Election Mr Christofer Hanson and Mr John Watson in Corpus Christi Quire within the prebendarie Church there
Then were there in the Church two Comburgesses vzt Mr Thomas Short and Mr Thomas Hanson

Then was sent downe into the Church to those two Comburgesses to make them three one other Comburgesse vzt Mr Richard Leeming

Out of which three Comburgesses in the Church one was chosen to come up and sitton the Cusheon or place of Election one other Comburgesse vzt Mr Thomas Hanson

Then was there three Comburgesses upon the Cusheon or place of Election vzt Mr Christofer Hanson, Mr John Watson and Mr Thomas Hanson

And then was there remaineing in the Church two Comburgesses vzt Mr Thomas Short & Mr Richard Leeming

Out of which three Comburgesses upon the Cusheon or place of Election vzt Mr Christofer Hanson, Mr John Watson and Mr Thomas Hanson one is to be chosen Alderman for the residue of this ensueing yeare for this Burrough of Grantham in the place of Mr Thomas Milles late Alderman deceased

And so by the consent and Vote of this Assembly Mr John Watson is chosen Alderman for the residue of this yeare yet to come And The said Mr John Watson being so elected Alderman as aforesaid for the Remainder of this yeare did at this Assembly take the oath of Alderman according to the Auntient and laudable custome of this Burrough.

An [sic] so this Assembly breakes up.

[fo. 391r] **First Court of John Watson, 14 November 1664**

Mill Masters to perfect their Accounts.
At this Couurt it is ordered that John Turner and Edward Paulett do perfect their Accounts as Mill Masters the next Court day.

Accounts to be Examined.
At this Court it is ordered that Mr Thomas Grant, Mr Michaell Taylor, Mr Richard Leeming, Richard Holley and Edward Paulett do meete at the Towne Hall on Wednesday next at one of the Clocke in the Afternoon to examine the Accounts of the Chaimberlaine and Constables And to certifie their proceeding therein the next Court day.

A lease of the Milles let to Mr Robert Calcraft & Mr Richard Calcraft for foure yeares.
At this Court Mr Robert Calcraft and Mr Richard Calcraft takes a lease of the Towns Milles for foure yeares from the Eleaventh day of November last past at the yearely Rent of one hundred and forty pounds to be paid quarterly by even and equall porcions And for the setting of the said Milnes in repaire it is hereby ordered that the Towne beare one halfe and the said Mr Robert Calcraft & Mr Richard Calcraft the other halfe of all manner of charges that shall be expended in repaireing of the same And also it is agreed upon that the said Gentlemen shall injoy the said milnes during the said terme under the yearely Rent aforesaid And that they shall be freed from all payments taxes or imposicons whatsoever (excepting the tithe due for the said milnes) And if any contagion or plague shall happen (which God forbidd) that then if they the said Mr Robert Calcraft and Mr Richard Calcraft shall sustaine any loss the same to be

determined on both parties by two indifferent persons And it is further ordered that if Mr Robert Calcraft and Mr Richard Calcraft do quarterly and every quarter pay the proportion due to the Gentlemen to whome the Milnes are ingaged at the time the same shall acrue due And the Remainder to the Towne and giveing in their Acquittances that then the said payments shall be as good and effectuall as if the same had beene paid to the Towne And they shall be discharged and freed thereof accordingly And that this Court shall and will do their Utmost indeavors to compell the Inhabitants of this Burrough to grind all their Corne and Graine at the Milles aforesaid.

Haires house to be rebuild.
At this Court it is ordered that the Chaimberlaine and the Collectors for the Schoole Rent with the Assistance of Mr Tomlinson do take care for the rebuilding of the house in Swinegate late in the tenure of Henry Haire for to preserve and secure the Walls that are newly erected.

The oath of Attendance taken to Mr Alderman.
At this Court the severall members thereof do take the oath of Attendance to Mr Alderman (excepting Mr Michaell Taylor that desired absence from Court upon some especiall occasions And could not have the opportunitie to returne again during the sitting of the Court And also Mr Christofer Hanson, Mr Gilbert Chantler, Mr Thomas Short, Edward Kenion, William Palmer and Christofer Hanson junior who were absent And therefore it is ordered that upon their Appearances the next Court they do take the said oaths according to the Auntient custome of this Corporacion.

Constables to make a returne of Ladders & hookes.
At this Court it is ordered that the Constables of every Ward do returne an Account the nex[t] Court day of the laddars and hookes in every Streete And to get the same branded that they may be knowne to be the Towns and for the use and benefit thereof.

[fo. 391v]

Mr Tomlinson Escheator.
At this Court Mr Joseph Tomlinson takes the oath of an Escheator in the stead of Mr John Watson now elected Alderman.

William Clarke & others sues the Towne for the 250 li borowed of Sir Robert Markham which is disowned to be a Towne debt.
Whereas Mr Alderman this day acquainted the Court that the Corporacion was sued in the Exchequer by Mr Clarke, Mr Trevillian, Mr Dalton, Mr Becke and others for 250 li taken up by them upon pretence to be disposed for the use of this Burrough which hath lately beene examined and is found to be disposed to uses not appointed or allowed by order of any Aldermans Court kept for the ordering and setling the affaires of this Corporacion And therefore utterly disowned and disapproved of by this Court

And for the defending of the said suite it is ordered that Mr William Parkins the Towns Sollicitor do appeare and answer the said suite as shall be advised by Councill learned in the law And that the charge thereof be allowed and paid upon the publike account of this Burrough to injoine the paid persons to give a true and faithfull Account of the aforesaid two hundred and fifty pounds.

[fo. 392r] Second Court of John Watson, 5 January 1664/5

Mill Masters to perfect their Accounts.
At this Court John Turner and Edward Paulett have further time to perfect their Accounts against the next Court day.

Chaimberlaines Account
At this Court William Milles Chaimberlaine giveth up his Accounts &
he chargeth himselfe with Receipt of	311 04 00
And [h]is disbursments to be	311 09 07
So paid more than received	00 05 07

Which is ordered to be paid him by the present Chaimberlaine & he is discharged.

Richard Poole fined for grinding from the Milnes.
Whereas upon Complaint made this day to the Court that Richard Poole hath ground one Quarter of mault from her Majesties Milles contrary to Auntient orders It is therefore ordered and agreed that the said Richard Poole be distrained of for xxvjs viijd at the rate of iijs iiijd the stricke for the said offence Whereupon Thomas Ireland, William Lane, Thomas Archer and Edward Leivesly were sent with a tickett from this Court to make a Distresse And upon their returne they bring into Court severall pewter dishes And whereas upon the Appearance of Richard Pooles wife who layed down the said fine of xxvjs viijd and upon her submission and promise not to offend and more It is ordered by consent of this Court that the said fine shall be returned to her againe which is done in open Court accordingly.

William Marshall fined for the like offence.
Upon the like Complaint William Berriffe, Francis Charitie and William Scott Constables have distrained of William Marshall And it is ordered that his distresse shall be detained untill he lay downe his fine and submit to the Court.

Constables to be saved harmeles for distraineing of them.
At this Court it is ordered that the said Thomas Ireland, William Lane, Thomas Archer, Edward Leivesly, William Berriffe, Francis Charitie and William Scot Constables and every of them shall be saved harmeles and indempnified from all trouble & incumbrance whatsoever that shall or may happen for or concerning the takeing or leyveing the distresses above said or either of them.

A suite comenced by the Soake against the Towne.
Whereas Mr Alderman this [*sic*] acquainted the Court that Mr Robert Calcraft Senior, Mr Thomas Hanson Mr Michaell Taylor Mr Robert Calcraft Junior and Mr Richard Calcraft Comburgesses and Richard Blacke Bayliffe of the libertie were sued by some persons in the Soake for executeing the graunts and powers confirmed to the Corporacion by Charter And for committing & detaineing some of the Soakesmen in prison for severall contempts comitted in open Sessions Wherupon it is ordered by the unanimous consent of this Court that the said Comburgesses and Richard Blacke shall defend the said suite at the proper cost and charges of this Bourrough which shall be allowed and paid from time to time as occasion shall require And that they shall be saved harmeles and indempnified by this Court from all costs troubles and damages whatsoever which shall or may acrue to them or any of them by reason of the suite aforesaid.

[fo. 392v]

A letter from Captain Foster aboute the buisness of the Soake.
At this Court Mr Alderman produced a letter from Captain Foster Sollicitor to the Right honourable the Earle of Linsey Lord Great Chaimberlaine of England which was read in open Court wherein he shews his afection and readines to serve this Corporacion in bringing some persons of the Soake before his Majestie and his Councill to answer their Combinacion against the Goverment of this Towne whereupon it is ordered by consent of this Court that a letter of thankes be sent to the said Captain Foster for his respects And to desire him to sollicite the said buisnes on the behalfe of this Burrough.

A letter read from Mr Christian about the Redd Lyon lease.
At this Court Mr Alderman likewise produced a letter from Mr Christian aboute the lease of the Redd Lyon for ninety yeares the which this Court taking into consideracion do hereby order that the graunting of a new lease shall be respited till the expiracion of the former lease now in being.

Chaimberlaine to pay xxs to take of an Attachment concerning Sir Robert Markhams money.
This day Mr Alderman acquainted the Court that Mr Bury on the behalfe of Mr Clarke and others had gotten an Attachment against the Towne Clarke to injoyne him to appeare at the suite of Mr Clarke Mr Dalton and the rest that were bound for Sir Robert Markhams money And that before they accept of an Appearance they demand xxs of him It is therefore ordered by this Court that he being not concerned but as the Towns Officer that he be saved harmles and freed of all Charges by the Towne And that the present Chamberlaine do pay the said xxs.

Mr Holleys Account for the Towne Milne for a Moneth.
At this Court Mr Richard Holley Mill Master for the Towne Mill gives an Account for one moneth &

that he received	06	15	02
And that his Disbursments are	03	10	04
Remaines due to the Towne	03	04	10

Which he pays to the Chaimberlaine in open Court.

[fo. 393r] **Third Court of John Watson, 3 February 1664/5**

Mr Paulett account as Milne Master.
At this Court Edward Paulett one of the late Mill Masters for the Slate Mill

giveth up his Accounts and chargeth himselfe with	13	12	04
And that his disbursments are	12	01	07
Whereof he payes to the Chaimberlaine	01	03	01
Remaines to account for till next Court day	00	07	08

At this Court Mr Tomlinson and the rest of the Mill Masters have further time to perfect their Accounts.

William Marshalls fine returned backe.
At this Court came the wife of William Marshall and laid downe the fine of xxvjs viijd for grinding Mault from the Towne mills and upon her humble request to this Court and her promise not to offend any more in the like nature It is ordered that the said fine be returned to her againe with the distresses formerly taken by order of this Court which is accordingly restored.

Severall suites comenced by the Soake against the Towne.
Whereas Mr Alderman this day acquainted the Court that divers persons of the Soake have brought many vexacious suits against severall members of this Court for executeing the powers and trusts granted to this Corporacion by Charter in Comitting some of the said persons to prison for contempts done in open Sessions and moved this Court that the said Gentlemen might be saved harmeles from the said suits it being done upon the publike concernment of this Burrough whereupon it is ordered by the Court that all and every the said Gentlemen shall be saved harmeles & indempnified from the said suits at the publike charge of the Corporacion And for the defending thereof it is ordered that Mr William Parkins the Towns Sollicitor and the Towne Clarke do joyne together and give Appearances to the said suits and to defend and maintaine the rights of the said Corporacion And for the raiseing of money which will be laid out this terme It is also ordered that Mr Robert Calcraft and Mr Richard Calcraft do pay to the present Chaimberlaine the sume of fifteene pounds out of the Rent of the Mills which is to be repaid againe upon the first receipt of money And the said Chaimberlaine is likewise ordered to pay x li thereof to the Towne Clarke to carry to London to defray such Charges as shall happen upon the Account of this Towne by reason of the said suits.

A letter produced from the Earle of Rutland aboute the Soake.
At this Court Mr Alderman produced two letters from the Earle of Rutland one directed to the Earle of Linsey Lord great Chaimberlaine of England and the other to Mr Mountague the Queens Attorney wherein his Worshipp is pleased to intreat their favours to vindicate and maintaine the Auntient Rights & prividges of this Corporacion And to cause some of the said Soakesmen to be made exemplarie for their contempts and disobedience to the Authoritie confirmed to this Burrough by his Majesties Chartor.

[fo. 393v] Fourth Court of John Watson, 17 March 1664/5

Edward Paulett further day to account.
At this Court Edward Paulett one of the late Mill Masters hath further to perfect his Accounts.

John Turner to gather Arreares as Mill Master.
At this Court John Turner another of the Milne Masters payes to the Chaimberlaine xxxiiijs due at the foote of his Account And he hath further time to collect the money due for three stricke of Mault from Mrs Katherine And to give an Account for one stricke of Mault that was left in the Tubb in the Milne undisposed of at present.

Mr Tomlinsons Account as Mill Master.
At this Court Mr Tomlinson gives an Account as Milne Master and chargeth himselfe with the

receipt of the sume of	05 00 01
And his disbursments to be	01 16 00
Remaines and paid to the Chaimberlaine	03 04 01

Mr Trevillian to receive a Quarters Rent for the Milnes.
At this Court it is ordered that there be one quarters Annuitie paid to Mr Trevillian out of the Mills And that Mr Robert Calcraft and Mr Richard Calcraft shall have the charges allowed them which they lay forth for the repaires of the mills on the Towns behalfe according to the former order and agreement of this Court.

Mr Ireland to receive his bill for Wine & Sessions Dinners.
At this Court Thomas Ireland desired that he might have the bill paid him for Wine and other provision made for the Comissioners at severall times as appeares by his bill Whereupon it is ordered by this Court that the Chaimberlaine do pay of and discharge the said bill.

Mr Bury to receive Rent for Widdow Ashbys house of the Overseers of the Poore.
At this Court came Mr William Bury and desired that the Overseers for the Poore might pay him the Rent due for Widdow Ashbys house in Swinegate according to a former

agreement made on her behalfe It is therefore ordered that the Overseers for the Poore do pay Mr Bury the Rent that is now due to him.

Mr Richard Hurst to injoy the meadow of the lande in Gunnerby feild for one yeare after his lease ended.
At this Court came Mr Richard Hurst Sonn of Doctor Hurst who is present Tennant to the Towne for the Schoole house land in Gunnerby feild formerly demised to Thomas Towers for the use of Doctor Hurst or his Assignes and desired that he might inioy onely the meadow belonging to the said lease for one yeare next after the Expiracion of the said demise the late tennants in possession haveing inioyed the same for one yeare since the said lease did comence according to the custome of the feilds of Gunnerby as the said Tennants alleadgeth To which desire of Mr Hurst the Court doth condiscend and order that he injoy the said meadow ground for one yeare after the determinacion of the lease aforesaid as the late tennants held it after the comencement thereof.

[fo. 394r]

Persons appointed to veiw the repaires of the Colledge lease.
At this Court it is ordered that Mr Grant, Mr Tomlinson, Richard Holley and William Bury do veiw the houses in the Church Laine now injoyed by the said Mr Hurst that they be left in sufficient & tenantable repaires as is Covenanted by the former lease lett to Richard Butler And to certifie their proceedinges therein to this Court before the bond of the said Richard Butler be delivered up.

The Pumpes to be repaired by the guift of halfe Crowns.
At this Court it is ordered that the halfe Crowns given for the yearely repaires of the Wells belonging to this Towne be hereafter yearely laid forth for the repaireing of the same according to the Donors guifts And that they shall not be disposed of to any other use whatsoever.

The Towne Clarke gives an Account of his proceedinges the last terme of the suites betwixt the Towne and Soake.
At this Court the Towne Clarke gives an Account of his proceedings at London the last terme o[n] the behalfe of this Corporacion and of the delivery of severall letters to the Right Honourable the Earle of Linsey lord Great Chaimberlaine of England and to Mr Mountague the Queenes Attorny and to Sir John Newton one of the Burgesses in Parlyament for this Burrough to acquaint the said Worthy Persons of the injurey of severall Soakesmen that despise & contemne the goverment of the Corporacion in disobeying the Authoritie thereof in not executeing warrants for the raiseing of money to repaire the Kinges Gaole belonging to this libertie and for the maintenance of Prisoners committed to the said Gaole As also of severall vexacious suits comenced against divers of his Majesties Justices of the peace of this Burrough for comitting some of the Constables of the Soake in open Sessions for their contempt in not submitting or

traverseing the Indictments against them for disobeying the warrant for repaires of the said Gaole And that the said Soakesmen did not onely sue the said Justices at Common law for falce ymprisonment but for the same cause indicted them in the Crowne Office to inforce them to expend great sumes of money to vindicate and maintaine the rights and prividlidges of this Burrough confirmed by his Gracious Majestie which the said Soakers by their unjust practices indeavor to take away. All which unworthy Actinges the Earle of Linsey was pleased to take into his consideracion and did promise to do the Corporacion what service he could to uphold their Auncient Rights and to discourage all such disobedient persons And that Mr Mountague was pleased to declare that the Justices need not to doubt anything for they had the law equitie and the favour of the Judges in the cause And that he would be ready to serve the Towne at any time to his power And likewise that Sir John Newton and Mr Bartue the Earle of Linseys sonn and Captain Foster the Earle of Linseys Sollicitor and Mr Christian were all of them very Active willing & ready to serve this Corporacion and to maintaine the Goverment and incourage the Governors thereof in the executeing of their Auncient immunities and privilidges. The Towne Clarke also acquainted this Court of the charge he expended on the behalfe of this Towne the last terme as appeares by his bill of Perticulars which comes to xviij li vs ijd And upon this bill there is due to him viij li vs ijd And also xxxviijs & viijd for charges against Saule Haire & others as appeares by an order at the last Court of Mr Calcraft Alderman which comes in all to x li iijs xd and he desires that this Court will please to order him the payment thereof. Whereupon it is ordered that the Chaimberlaine do pay the same unto him upon the first receipt of monies.

William Palmer to receive xxs in part of his sallory.
At this Court it is ordered that the Chaimberlaine pay xxs to William Palmer in part of his Sallory.

[fo. 394v] Fifth Court of John Watson, 22 April 1665

John Turner further day to Account.
At this Court John Turner and Edward Paulett late Millmasters have further time to perfect their Accounts.

Widdow Still payes in Court xx li for the use of Edward Still Children.
At this Court came Anne Still Widdow Executrix of William Still late of this Burrough deceased and paid twenty pounds into the hands of the present Chaimberlaine by the consent and approbacion of the Court for the use of Edward Still and William Still sonnes of Edward Still of this Towne and Brother of the said William Still deceased to be imployed for the use of the said Children and being given to them by the last will and testament of the said William Still as by the same may more fully appeare Whereupon it is ordered that the said twenty pounds shall be imployed to and for the use of Edward Still and William Still aforesaid And that securitie be given for the same by the Towns seale at the next meeteing at the Hutch.

Serjent Newdigate & Mr Ellis to be retained against the Soake.
At this Court it is ordered that Mr Parkins the Towns Sollicitor do retaine Serjent Newdigate and Mr Ellis this terme for the next Assizes on the behalfe of the Towne against the Soake And that the Chaimberlaine do pay him ten pounds to follow the Affaires of the Corporacion this terme.

An Assessment to be made for renewing the Charter.
Whereas Mr Alderman this day acquainted the Court that the Charter being lately renewed had caused the Towne to expend a hundred and twenty pounds out of the publike stocke And that it being an equall libertie and privilidge to the [sic] all the Inhabitants and Freemen of this Corporacion it ought to be paid againe by an Assessment Whereupon it is ordered that an Assessment of 120 li be made and laid upon this Burrough for reimburseing the money formerly laid out by the Chaimberlaine for renewing the Charter And that Mr Thomas Hanson and Mr Michaell Taylor Comburgesses, Richard Holley and Hugh Hutchin of the second Companie and Thomas Ireland and Edward Paulett be Assessors for the same And the Constables Collectors thereof.

Richard Blacke to receive xxxijs for executeing severall warrants.
At this Court it is ordered that the Chaimberlaine do pay xxxijs to Richard Blacke Bayliffe of this libertie for his fees in executeing severall warrants wherein the buisnes of this Burrough were concerned.

Hamlett Brumpton made free.
At this Court came Hamlett Brumpton who lately married Widdow Goodson And being a Forrainer he layd down x li according to Auntient custome and desired be admitted a Freeman of this Corporacion & that the Court would be pleased to [sic] favourable to him & restore him part of his ten pounds againe To whose desire the Court doth condiscend unto in admitting him to be free And considering that his wife hath followed the trade of a Sadler And that he is noe prejudice to the Towne do returne him v li againe And he takes the oath of a Freeman & pays his fees according to custome.

[fo. 395r] **Sixth Court of John Watson, 28 July 1665**

Mr Pell Guift to be called in & lett to others.
At this Court it is taken into consideracion that severall of the persons to whome money were lent upon Walter Pell Esquire his guift have left of tradeing and do make noe use the[reof] And that it is convenient the same should be called in and lent to other Tradsmen in pu[rsuance] of the Donors conveyance It is therefore ordered that the said monies be demanded of the persons that received the same and notice thereof given to their securitie to pay in their severall sumes And if they make default of payment being often requested formerly thereunto that then the Towne Clarke is ordered to send for processe against them to hasten in the said monies.

Mr Saule to be sued for charges.
At this Court it is ordered that Mr Saule of Rippingale be prosecuted upon his bond for the charges of suite expended upon the first Accion commenced against him by this Corporacion.

Mr Welbys securitie to be renewed.
At this Court William Bury Carpenter is desired by Mr Alderman and the rest of the Burgesses here present to enter into bond with Richard Holley and John Lenton to Mr John Welby for 50 li which is due & oweing to him by the Corporacion And that they & he should have securitie to beare them harmeles from the same Whereupon the said William Bury being present in Court is willinge & contented to become bound with them It is therefore ordered that a new bond be made And the old one to be delivered up and brought here in Court to be cancelled.

An Assessment to be made for repaires of High Streete Well.
At this Court Christofer Hauley brings in a perticular he hath expended and laid for the repaires of the High Streete well and also acquainted this Court that the same is now ought [sic] of repaire and the charge already expended and now to be laid forth will amount to above 3 li 10s 0. It is therefore ordered that an Assessment of 3 li 10s be laid upon High Streete and Castlegate And that Edward Rawlinson, Thomas Matkin, Thomas Taylor and Richard Hauley be Assessors thereof.

Severall persons appointed to examine Accounts.
At this Court it is ordered that Mr Thomas Grant, Mr Thomas Hanson, Mr Joseph Tomlinson, Richard Holley, John Turner and Thomas Ireland do meete on Thursday next at the Towne Hall at one of the Clocke in the Afternoone to examine the Accounts of the Chaimberlaine, Churchwarden, and Miln Masters and Thomas Taylor and Thomas Hatfeild Constables for High Streete and to give an Account of their proceedings the next Court day.

The Towns Armes to be looked up.
At this Court it is ordered that the Towns Armes be looked up And that were any is sold the money may be collected by the Chaimberlaine This day Edward Paulet and John [sic] have further time to perfect their Accounts.

The Towne Clarke gives an Account of his proceedings at London the last terme of the Suite betwixt Towne & Soake.
This day the Towne Clarke gives an Account of his proceedinges at London the last terme in the affaires of this Corporacion And of the Accions commenced against severall members of this Court by some Inhabitants of the Soake wherein he by the advice of Mr Skipwith the Recorder to move the Court of Kinges Bench for the takeing of or respiteing the Indictments in the Crowne Office till Michaelmas terme And upon the mocion the Judges haveing before given a rule to plead or Judgment it could not be stayed unless the Attorny Generall would appeare and discharge them And by reason

thereof he was compelled to plead the generall issue And the plea given the Soakesmen proceeds noe further And he also acquaints this Court that the charge expended this terme as by perticulars appeares comes to 15 li xiijs 2d And not gone to London but on the Towns Account And therefore desires the Court to consider of it whereupon it is ordered that the Chaimberlaine pay him his bill of xv li xiij s ijd & xxs towards the charge upon the first receipt of money.

[fo. 395v] Seventh Court of John Watson 17 August 1665

Accounts to be taken for the Milns.
At this Court it is ordered that Mr Thomas Grant, Mr Thomas Hanson, Mr Joseph Tomlinson, Mr Richard Holley, Robert Cole, John Turner and Thomas Ireland do meete at the Towne Hall on Wednesday next at one of the Clocke in the Afternoone to examine the Accounts of Mr Robert Calcraft & Mr Richard Calcraft for the proffitts of the Towne Milns from the time, they entered upon them they being this Court admitted Accomptantes and not Tenants according to former order of this Court.

A lease lett to Mr John Miller of a house & land in Manthorpe.
At this Court Mr John Miller takes a lease of a certaine house & land in Manthorpe belonging to, the Schoolehouse for one & twenty yeares from and after the expiracion of a former lease, to him made and now in being, paying the sume of thirty pounds for a fine at or before Michaelmas, next and giveing securitie to performe and pay all Antient Rents and Covenants heretofore, made And he gives in earnest of the said bargaine ijs vjd.

A lease lett to Mrs Watson of her house.
At this Court came Mrs Martha Watson widdow and relect of Edward Watson late of this Burrough Sadler deceased and acquainted this Court that her husband in his life time had laid forth considerable sumes of money in repairing the house shee was dwells in, which belongs to this Corporacion And that her lease being now almost expired shee makes it her humble request to this Court that they would please to consider of her Condicion and to grant her a new lease of the said house The which this Court takeing into consideracion and being very sensible of the repaires of the said premisses do hereby order that Mrs Watson shall have a new lease made for one & twenty yeares of the house aforesaid under the Covenants and agreements formerly used, for which respect & favour she returns many thankes to this Court.

The tolles lett to Henry Rudkin for one yeare.
At this Court came Henry Rudkin and desired to take a new lease of the tolles for another yeare if the Court will please to consider of his loss the last yeare and of the present calamitie of the times and to abate him some part of the former Rent The which this Court takeing into consideracion do hereby grant him a new lease of the tolles belonging to this Corporacion as they were formerly letten to him for one whole yeare

from the fifteenth day of August last payd at the yearely Rent of xxxxv li to be paid at foure times in the yeare by even and equall porcions And it is also ordered that the said Henry Rudkin shall give sufficient securitie by bond with himselfe and others for the true payment of the said Rent at the dayes & times respectively that it shall grow due and payable or with in a weeke after And further that he shall injoy the Outners tolles till the Court day.

Mr Richard Holley chosen a Comburgesse.
At this Court Mr Richard Holley by a generall & Unanimous consent of the same is chosen of the first Companie and doth take his oaths incident thereunto.

An order for the next Eleccion of the succeeding Alderman.
For the more peaceable and orderly proceeding at the Eleccion of the next succeeding Alderman It is at this Court ordered that upon the next eleccon day Mr Robert Calcraft Junior shall be sent downe into the Church to Mr Thomas Short & Mr Richard Leeming to make three Comburgesses there Out of which three Comburgesses in the Church it is likewise agreed that Mr Richard Leeming be brought upon the Cusheon or place of election to Mr Christofer Hanson and Mr Thomas Hanson to make three Comburgesses there Out of which three Comburgesses on the Cusheon with a free and unanimous consent Mr Thomas Hanson is nominated Alderman for this next ensueing yeare.

At this Court it is ordered that the Constables do bring in the bills of Disbursments next Court Day that an Assessment may be made for the same.

[fo. 396r]

An order for setling the Watch & Ward.
Whereas the Court this day takeing into consideracion the great mortalitie that is now in London and in severall places of this Kingdome by reason of the contagion of the Plague And that it is very requisite and necessarie that there should be good and sufficient Watch and Ward kept within this Burrough day and night to examine Passingers from whence they come so that by such meanes (& Gods almightie assistance) all suspected persons may be kept out of this Towne and the [sic] preserved from the said dangerous disease In pursuance thereof it is at this Court fully ordered and agreed upon that every Inhabitant householder and such persons as are of Abilitie and strength shall from time to time as it happens and falls to them by house Roe keepe the said Watch and Ward in their owne proper persons Upon paine for every man refuseing or neglecting to performe his duty herein to forfeite xs to be levied by distresse and sale of Goods for the use of this Corporacion according to the Auntient custome thereof And for the more compleating & fullfilling of so good and needfull a Worke It is hereby also ordered that the Constables of every Ward as it shall come to them by order one after another give timely notice & warning to the Inhabitants within their wards of the time they are to appeare and performe the said duty And to see the said Watch & Ward sett and to give

the charge to the said Watchmen as by the laws of this Kingdome they are comanded & injoyned And if any failer shall be in any Person contrarey to the true intent & meaning of this order that then the Constables shall returne an Account thereof the next Court after such neglect that this order may be put in effectuall execucion as abovesaid.

Eighth Court of John Watson, 15 September 1665

A Reentry made upon the Millns & care to be taken for the Towne Goods.
At this Court it is ordered that the Chaimberlaine do take care for the disposall of the Wood and Mill Stone that belongs to the Towne, being that the Gentlemen to whome the Millnes are ingaged have made their reentry upon the same upon the fifth day of August last past And have from that time & still doe continue the takeing of the profitts thereof.

Money to be deducted out of Mr Robert Calcraft Account as Miln Master.
Whereas upon reading and examineing the Accounts of Mr Robert Calcraft & Mr Richard Calcraft concerning the proffitts of the Towne Milnes since the sixteenth of November last and observing that they account for horsehire and meale vjs a weeke for winter and iiijs a weeke for Sumner which is thought to be too much by this Court and that a lower rate might be made thereof Whereupon it is ordered by and with the consent of the said Mr Robert Calcraft & Mr Richard Calcraft being present in Court that there be a deduction made out of the said Account And that Mr Robert Calcraft haveing a horse both Winter and Sumner be allowed vs a weeke for Winter and iijs vjd for Sumner from the first day of May last past And Mr Richard Calcraft to have vs a weeke for winter his horse being noe longer in the Towne service.

Leases to [sic] sealed at the Hutch.
At this Court it is ordered that there be a meeting at the Hutch on Wednesday next at one of the Clocke in the Afternoon to seale leases.

John Turner chosen of the 2d xij.
John Turner chosen of the second Company, In the Kallender: Christofer Thompson, William Bury and John Walker.

[fo. 396v]

An order for the first and second Companie to be Masters of the Ward.
This day Mr Alderman acquainted the Court notwithstanding the order made the last Court for keeping stronge Watch and Ward the same is much neglected for want of some persons to Oversee the Watchmen that they doe their duty and great care being now to be had by reason the contagion is broke out in severall places And it is very convenient the first and second Company do oversee the Wards in the daytime and to be freed from any other charge of watching whereupon it is ordered that the first

and second Companie do order as the same shall come to their Turns be Masters of the Ward for that day and to take care that the Watchmen do dilligently observe their Offices And that the Gentlemen being so Masters of the Ward shall be freed from any charge of Watching day or night whatsoever during the time the same shall continue.

An Assessment for the Constables bills.
At this Court it is ordered that an Assessment of xiiij li be made and laid upon this Burrough for the payment of the Constables their bills of disbursments an estimate being taken what these perticular sumes amount unto And the Cheife Constables and under Constables are appointed Assessors and the under Constables Collectors thereof And for the more legall makeing of the said Assessment it is ordered that notice be given thereof the next Lords day in the Church of the time and place where the said Assessment shall be made to the end such persons as are therein concerned may if they please be there present at the makeing of the same.

Thomas Fishar, Thomas Frith, Richard Bristow, William Bristow, William Hayes, Jermin Richardson made free.
At this Court came Thomas Fishar, Tanner, late Apprentice to Mr Dalton, Thomas Frith, Butcher, late Apprentice to Mr Christofer Hanson, Richard Bristow, Apprentice to Mr John Fearon, Cordwainer, William Bristow, Apprentice to Thomas Charles, Baker, William Haynes [*sic*] Apprentice to Thomas Gunnesson, Cooper, and Jermin Richardson, Apprentice to George Short Apprentice [*sic*] And desired severalley to be admitted & made Freemen of this Corporacion to whose request this Court doth condiscend whereupon the said Thomas Fishar, Richard Bristow and William Bristow as freeborne do pay to the Box ijs vjd apeice And the said Thomas Frith, William Haynes and Jermin Richardson as Forrainer do pay to the Box vs a peice & all of them pays their fees to the Clarke and Serjeants & severally take oaths of Freemen and other oaths incident thereunto according to custome And thereupon they are admitted Free Burgesses of this Corporacion.

[fo. 397r] **Ninth Court of John Watson, 21 September 1665**

An order to renew Mr Shorts leases.
At this Court Mr Thomas Short acquainted Mr Alderman and the rest of the members of this Court that he had beene at great charges in rebuilding the house in the Marketplace and another in the High Streete which he hath in lease from the Towne As also that he suffered much damage and loss in the time of Warr when he was one of the Cheife Constables for this Burrough And his said lease being now almost expired he makes it his desire to this Court that they will please to consider of his Condicion and to grant him a new lease thereof The which this Court takeing into their consideracion do order that Mr Thomas Short have a new lease of the said houses under the Covenants and Rents auntiently used.

An order for the Searching of all Corps And that noe strangers be entertained without Mr Alderman Lycence.

Whereas Mr Alderman this day acquainted the Court that in this dangerous time of sicknes and mortalitie it is very requisite & needfull that the Corps of every person dying within this Burrough should be searched that it may be knowne what disease they dye on And by such meanes with the Aide and Assisstance of Almightie God the contagion of the Plague may be prevented in this Towne or otherwise the persons remaineing in such houses may be forthwith removed And also that noe Inhabitant within this Burrough shall entertaine or receive into their houses any Strangers without first acquainting Mr Alderman or his Bretheren, that thereby all dangerous and infectious person may be kept out, All which being taken into consideracion by this Court It is hereby ordered that there be foure Persons nominated and appointed to be searchers of such Corps as shall be within this Burrough And that the Inhabitants in whose house any person shall dye shall within halfe an houre at most give notice thereof to Mr Alderman to the end the Corps may be searched And also that noe householders or Inhabitants do receive into their houses any strangers or other Persons suspected to come out of an Infected place without giveing notice to Mr Alderman for the time being that the said persons may be examined, upon paine for every person offending contrarey to this order or any clause or sentence therein concerned to forfeite forty shillings of lawfull money of England to be levied according to the Auntient custome of this Burrough And it is also ordered that notice hereof be given in every Ward by the Belman this Afternoone.

Leases to be sealed.

At this Court it is ordered that Mr Millers & Mrs Watsons leases and Widdow Stills securitie for the Children be sealed at the Hutch upon the riseing of the Court.

William Palmer to receive his sallory.

At this Court William Palmer is ordered to receive his yeares sallory from the Chaimberlaine upon the first receipt of money.

And an order for the Towne Clarke to receive his money.

Whereas the Towne Clarke this day acquainted the Court that there is due to him from the Towne for the buisnes of the Soake and against Haire 10 li 16s 10d as appeares by his bill And also that it is all laid out by him and not a fee reckoned And therefore he desires that the Court will please to order him the payment of it as speedily as may be by reason he hath occasion for it this terme Whereupon it is ordered by this Court that the Chaimberlaine do pay the sume unto him upon the first receipt of money.

[fo. 397v] **Tenth Court of John Watson, 6 October 1665**

Arreares of Dimsdale to be paid.

At this Court it is ordered that the Chaimberlaine do pay halfe a yeares rent for Dimsdale House which was due upon resigneing the same for the use of the viccars.

The order for Mr Shorts lease abrogated.
Whereas upon reading of the order made the last Court for the granting of a lease to Mr Thomas Short of two houses belonging to the Burrough It is objected against & moved that it might be putt to the vote of this court whether or noe the said order should stand & be confirmed or revoked And being voted It is by the Major part of this Court hereby ordered that the said order is and shall be void and of none effect to all intents & purposes whatsoever.

An Agreement made for the Assessments of Mr Thorrold & Mr Ellis for Church and Poore.
This day Mr Alderman acquainted the Court that he had spoke with Robert Thorrold & William Ellis Esquire concerning their assessments to the Church and Poore of this Parish for their lands in Harrowby and Dunsthorpe And that Mr Thorrold was willing to pay foure pound a yeare & Mr Ellis forty shillinges to make up six pounds which formerly used to be paid And they desired that the same might be agreed upon for the future rather than to be in trouble or have any further charge Whereupon this Court taking into consideracion that the said Gentlemen may be very advantageous in doeing good for this Corporacion do accept of the said proposicion And hereby order that the said agreement of vj li per Annum shall continue and be yearely demanded by the Churchwardens and Overseers for the Poore and to be by them equally received for the use of the Parish.

Severall Persons appointed to determine the suite against the Haires.
At this Court it is ordered that Mr Alderman, Mr Thomas Hanson, Mr Michaell Taylor, John Lenton, George Short, Robert Cole, John Walker, Thomas Ireland and Thomas Archer or as many of them as shall meete upon notice to them given heare & determine the suite comenced against John Haire and Simon Haire for xvij li viijs debt due to this Corporacion And to make such end & accept such sumes of money as they shall thinke convenient rendering an Account of their proceedinges the next Court Day.

Eleventh Court of John Watson 19 October 1665

This Court adjourned for want of the Appearance of six Comburgesses.
Whereas a Court was day summoned to be held and the same called And distresses sent out for severall that were absent And divers of the Comburgesses being out of Towne or upon urgent occasions that they could not possibly appeare and attend the buisnes of this Court there where not six Comburgesses present And by reason thereof noe Court could be held according to Auntient custome and orders It is therefore agreed by the Assembly now meete that the Accounts and buisnes [sic] of this Day be respited till next Court. And so this Assembly breakes up.

[fo. 398r]

At an Assembly holden by Mr John Watson Alderman and the Comburgesses of Grantham aforesaid in ~~for~~ Corpus Christi Quire within the Prebendarie Church there upon Friday next after St Lukes day being the xxth day of October *Annoque domini* 1665.

First did sitt downe upon the Cusheon or place of Election the said Mr John Watson in Corpus Christi Quire within the Prebendarie Church there
Next to him did sitt upon the Cusheon or place of Eleccion two Comburgesses vizt Mr Christofer Hanson and Mr Thomas Hanson
Then was there two Comburgesses in the Church vzt Mr Thomas Short and Mr Richard Leeming
Then was sent downe into the Church to those two Comburgesses to make them three one other Comburgesse vzt Mr Robert Calcraft Junior
Out of which three Comburgesses in the Church one was chosen to come up and sitt on the Cusheon or place of Eleccion one other Comburgesse vzt Mr Richard Leeming
Then was there three Comburgesses upon the Cusheon or place of Election vzt Mr Christofer Hanson, Mr Thomas Hanson and Mr Richard Leeming
And then was there in the Church two Comburgesses vzt Mr Thomas Short and Mr Robert Calcraft Junior
Out of which three Comburgesses upon the Cusheon or place of Election vzt Mr Christofer Hanson, Mr Thomas Hanson and Mr Richard Leeming one is to be chosen Alderman for this next ensueing yeare
And so by an unanimous consent and vote of this Assembly Mr Thomas Hanson is chosen Alderman for this ensueing yeare
Whereupon the said Mr John Watson dischargeth himselfe from the place and Office of Alderman according to Auntient custome And the said Mr Thomas Hanson now elected Alderman in his place and stead hath at this Assembly taken the oath of Alderman for this Burrough and Soake of Grantham according to the Auntient and laudable custome of the Burrough aforesaid.

And so this Assembly breakes up.

[fo. 398v] [Blank page]

THE HALL BOOK OF GRANTHAM 1665–1666

[fo. 399r] **First Court of Thomas Hanson 27 October 1665**

Mr Thomas Hanson Alderman
    First xij
Mr Robert Calcraft senior Comburgess
Mr Thomas Short Comburgess
Mr Thomas Grant Comburgess
Mr John Dalton Comburgess
Mr Michaell Taylor Comburgess
Mr Richard Leeming Comburgess
Mr Robert Calcraft junior Comburgess
Mr Richard Calcraft Comburgess
Mr Joseph Tomlinson Comburgess
Mr Richard Holley Comburgess
Mr Christofer Hanson Comburgess
Mr Gilbert Chantler Comburgess

2d xij
John Lenton
Hugh Hutchin
Zachary Cox
George Short
Henry Humes
Edward Rollinson
John Coddington
John Winge
Robert Cole
Thomas Matkin
William Milles

The names of the officers there

Coroner	Mr John Watson	Keybearers	Mr Alderman
Escheator	Mr Robert Calcraft Junior		John Lenton
			William Milles
Churchwardens	John Lenton	Prizers of Corne	John Pape
	Edward Paulett		Thomas Charles
Chamberlaines	William Milles	Market Sayers	Thomas Cole
	John Walker		Christofer Hanson Junior
Collectors for Schoole Rents	Mr Richard Holley Anthony Hotchkin	Leather Sealers	William Grococke John Ingerson
Chiefe Constables	George Short Robert Cole		Robert Smith Edward Ulliott
Market place Constables	James Kirchival William Laine	Towne Clarke	William Hodgkinson
High Streete Constables	Robert Gibson Edward Leivesly	Serjents	Samuell Roades Richard Blacke
Westgate Constables	John Plumer Thomas Fisher	Gaoler	Richard Blacke
Walkergate Constables	George Read Francis Charitie	Church Clarke	William Newball

| Swinegate Constables | Thomas Gunnison Hamlett Brumpton | Belman | Ralph Osborne |
| Castlegate Constables | William Scott Richard Bristow | Beagle | John Scott |

[fo. 399v]

The Names of the Commoners of the Court there

Markettplace
William Laine
William Berriffe
John Walker
Thomas Ireland
Thomas Calcraft
Anthony Hotchkin
Thomas Archer

High Streete
Robert Gibson
Edward Leivesley
William Bury
Richard Hauley
Thomas Hatfeild
Thomas Taylor

Westgate
John Plumer
Thomas Fishar
Edward Kenion
William Palmer
Christofer Hanson

Walkergate
George Read
Francis Charitie
Christopher Thompson

Swinegate
Thomas Gunnison
Hamlett Brumpton

Castlegate
William Scott & Richard Bristow

The Plate delivered up.
At this Court Mr John Watson late Alderman delivers up to Mr Alderman that now is all the Towne plate being these pieces following vizt

The horse Race Cupp
Mr Archers Boll
Mr Horsemans Boll
Mr Wheatelys Cann
Mr Horsemans Wine Boll
Mr Greenewoods Cann

Mr Greenewoods thirteene spoones
Mr Batties Beaker
Two Tunns
One Salt with Cover
The Waites foure Cognizances

At this Court Mr Watson delivers up to Mr Alderman the severall Charters belonging to this Corporacion.

Mr Watsons Accompt as Alderman.
At this Court Mr John Watson late Alderman doth account for all monies received by him upon the Common Affaires of this Towne upon penall Statutes etc. And also of his payments and disbursments on the publike whereby he chargeth himselfe as by

perticulars appeares with the receipt of	03	06	00
and that is disbursments amounts to	02	04	01
So remaineing due to the Towne	01	01	11

Which he payes to the Chaimberlaine & is discharged.

Coroners Accompt.
At this Court Mr Robert Calcraft senior, Coroner accompteth And saith that no Casualtie hath happened this yeare whereby any thing hath accrued to this Corporacion And so he hath nothing to account for & he is discharged.

Collectors for the Schoole Rents further time to Account.
At this Court Collectors for the Schoole Rent have further time to perfect their Accounts.

[fo. 400r]

Escheators Accompt.

At this Court Mr Joseph Tomlinson Escheator for the yeare past accounteth & chargeth himselfe with the Receipt of	00	18	10
And that out of this he hath paid himselfe his charges at every faire and ii s to the Towne Clarke for his paines in attending every faire which amounts to the sume of	00	04	06
So remaineing due to the Towne	00	14	04

Which he payes to the present Chaimberlaine & he is discharged.

Henry Haires Suite agreed.
At this Court Mr Alderman and the rest of the Gentlemen to whome Henry Haires debt was referred to by order of the last Court to make an end of the same and to give an Account thereof do hereby declare their agreement to be as followeth vizt That there being xvij li viijs due to the Towne John Haire & Simon Haire shall pay xij li thereof, And whereas Simon Haire haveing beene long in prison at Lincolne upon the said debt and both of them alleadgeing their povertie and being not likely any part thereof from Henry Haire do make it their humble request to this Court that they would please to accept of the said xij li in full satisfaccion of the said debt and to Assigne over Henry Haires bond to them to see if they obtaine any part of it from him The which this Court takeing into consideracion do hereby accept of the said xij li and order the said bond to be assigned over to John Haire & Simon Haire.

Mr Parkins to deliver a bill of charges.
At this Court Mr Watson produced a letter from Mr Parkins the Towne Sollicitor that he hath expended aboute vj li charges in the suite betwixt the Towne and Soake more then he received whereupon it is ordered that Mr Parkins draw up his bill of charges and then this Court will consider of the same and order him the payment thereof.

Mr Lenton charges to be paid which he expended on the Towns behalf.
At this Court it is ordered that the Chaimberlaine pay xxijs vd to Mr Lenton for charges laid downe by him when he was arrested at Mr John Welbys suite for a debt due to him from this Towne and iiijs to Mr Holley for the charge of the New bond given to Mr Welby.

An order for the disposall of Mr Thorold & Mr Ellis his money to the Church and Poore.
This day the Towne Clarke acquainted the Court that he had received iiij li of Esquire Thorold Bayliffe for the Church and Poore and desired to have the Courts order for the paying of it Whereupon it is ordered that he pay xxs to the Churchwarden to make up three pounds with the xxxxs he received of Mr Ellis And the remaineing three pounds to the Overseers for the Poore And it is hereby also ordered that the said vj li shall be equalley devided betwixt the Churchwardens and Overseers for the poore yearely & every yeare during the payment thereof.

Charles Darniles money to be paid.
At this Court came Charles Darnile and desired Mr Alderman and the rest of the Court that they would please to order him the payment of the Tenn pounds due to him from the Towne for he had very urgent occasions for it at present. Whereupon it is ordered that the Chaimberlaine pay the same unto him upon the first receipt of money.

Persons appointed to Examine Accounts.
At this Court it is ordered that Mr Robert Calcraft senior, Mr Thomas Grant, Mr John Watson & Mr Michaell Taylor Comburgesse, Hugh Hutch [*sic*], George Short, Robert Cole and William Milles of the Second Company & William Bury, Thomas Ireland, John Walker and Anthony Hotchkin Comoners do meete on Wednesday next to examine the Accounts of the Churchwarden & Chaimberlaine and to returne an Account thereof the next Court day.

[fo. 400v]

A letter Mr Ascough sent for to call in his 100 li & Mr Grant & Mr Taylors promise to procure it for the Towns use of another Person.
At this Court Mr Thomas Grant and Mr Michaell Taylor produced a letter from Mr Ascough which is openley read wherein he demands the speedy payment of the 100 li that is in the Towns hands and the interest for the same for halfe a yeare And if the same be not paid presently he will put his bond in Suite And the said Mr Grant &

Mr Taylor were pleased to acquaint this Court that out of an Affection which they beare to this Corporacion & to maintaine the Creditt & reputacion thereof and to free the Towne from charge they will do their indeavour to take up a 100 li & pay Mr Ascough and become bound with Mr Dalton & Mr Bearne for the same as formerly upon securitie from the Towne to beare them harmless. For which respect this Court returns them thankes And do hereby order the use money to be paid And that they shall have an order of Court or any other Sufficient securitie as Councill shall advise for saveing them harmles for any such bond that they shall enter into for the use of this Corporacion.

An Account of the Constables Assessment for the yeare past.
The twelve Constables gives an Account of the Constables Assessment for the yeare past.

Thomas Ireland			
Edward Paulet	Marketplace Constables their bill	04 13 06	
	Abatments allowed of	00 06 00	
	Gathered cleared and paid in	04 07 06	
William Laine			
Thomas Archer	Highstreete Constables their bill	02 12 00	
	Cleared and paid in		
Anthony Hotchkin	Westgate Constables their bill	02 00 07	
William Berriffe	Abatements allowed of	00 00 09	
	Cleared & paid in	01 19 10	
William Riseing	Walkergate Constables their bill	00 16 04	
George Read	Cleared & paid in		
Francis Charitie	Swinegate Constables their bill	01 01 10	
Edward Leivesly	Abatements allowed of	00 01 00	
	Cleared & paid in	01 00 10	
Thomas Gunnisson	Castlegate Constables their bill	01 12 06	
William Scott	Abatments allowed of	00 00 06	
	Cleared & paid in	01 12 00	

At this Court it is ordered that the present Overseers for the poore do pay xs to Stephen Simpson for severall weekes table for Henry Ferman.

[fo. 401r] **Second Court of Thomas Hanson, 27 October 1666** [*rectius* 1665]

The procurement of the 100 li to pay Mr Ascough.
This day Mr Thomas Grant and Mr Michaell Taylor acquainted the Court that they had procured a 100 li to pay of Mr Ascough And that they indeavored to have paid it into the hands of the Chaimberlaine that he might have repaid it to Mr Ascough And he being not to be found they pay it themselves for the Towns use which was done before the present Alderman as he is pleased to relate to the Court and as appears by the old bond was read in Court & cancelled And therefore they desire that the present Chaimberlaine by order of this Court may enter the said mone[y] into his Booke of

the Receipt and payment of the said 100 li to Mr Ascough that the Accounts of this Corporacion may stand perfect As also that they & Mr Dalton & Mr Bearns may be saved harmles & indempnified from the new bond they have entred into for the said 100 li Whereupon it is ordered that the Chaimberlaine do enter the said 100 li received and paid into his booke of Accounts And that this order hereunder written shall save the said parties harmeles from the new bond they have given for the Towns use being by a free and unanimous consent of this Court moved & declared to be the sole & proper debt of this Corporacion.

Mr Grant, Mr Dalton, Mr Taylor & Mr Bearns to be saved harmles from the bond they have entred into for the payment of Mr Ascough debt.
Whereas the above named Thomas Grant, Maurice Dalton, Michaell Taylor and Thomas Bearns of this Burrough of Grantham Gentlemen do stand bound unto Robert Chamberlaine of Morton in this County Yeoman in one obligacion bearing date the third day of October last in the sume of two hundred pounds Condicioned for the true payment of a hundred & three pounds upon the fourth day of Aprill now next ensueing which said principall sume of money was by the parties aforesaid borrowed and received of the said Robert Chamberlaine and paid for the onely proper use and behoofe of this Burrough to Mr Ascough for a debt formerly owing by this Corporacion And the parties before named became bound as aforesaid at the intreaty and request of his [*sic*] Burrough Now this Court do for themselves and their Successors firmely promise well & truly from time to time and at all times for ever hereafter to save keepe harmeles & indempnifie the said Persons so bound as aforesaid and every of them their & every of their Heires Executors and Administrators of and from all and all manner of payments penalties forfeitures & suits of law whatsoever which shall or may happen arise or grow for or by reason of the said recited obligacion and Condicion thereupon written And to give such further assurance in such convenient time as shall be advised by Councill learned in the law.

The Watch taken of till nine a clocke at night The Constables to walke the Towne And noe Strangers to be received without Mr Alderman Approbacion.
At this Court Mr Alderman was pleased to relate that the Watch being now kept all night was being prejudiciall to the Watchmen by reason of the cold and the lenght [*sic*] of the nights And that of late it hath beene much neglected As also it would be very convenient that the Watch migh[t] be kept every night till nine of the Clocke and then the Watchmen to be discharged And the Constables of every Ward to warne every Person from entertaineing any Strangers or Passingers after five of the Clocke without speciall order Whereupon it is ordered that the said Watch be taken of, till nine of the Clocke at night And the Constables do walke the Towne & give notice that noe Stranger or Travellor be received into any house without the order and permission of the present Alderman Under the penaltie of a former order heretofore made for the same purpose in the time of Mr John Watson Alderman for the yeare last past.

[fo. 401v]

Mr Butlers bond assigned over to Mr Hurst for the repairing of the Colledge Houses.
At this Court came Mr Richard Hurst that hath by Assignement and admittance of this Court taken the lease of the Schoole house land formerly let to one Thomas Towers for the use of Doctor Hurst and this day made it his request to the Court that the former Tennants to whome the said premisses were demised might repaire the houses belonging to the said lease, they being very much out of repaire, And that the new Tennants are not able to live in them unless they be speedily repaired And if this Court will please to assigne over the bond of the late Tennants for performance of Covenants, he the said Mr Richard Hurst will do his indeavours at his owne proper cost and charges to cause the said houses to be repaired And that he will free the Towne from any trouble or charge by reason of the said Assignment And after he hath reccived satisfaccion for repaires of the said premisses that then he will give sufficient securitie for keeping the said premisses in repaire And to leave the same in good repairacion at the end or other determinacion of his present lease Whereupon the Court takeing the same into their consideracion do hereby order that the said bond and lease be assigned over to him the said Mr Richard Hurst And that it shall be lawfull for him to sue the same he performeing and fullfilling all & every the promises & Agreements aforesaid.

The Constables to returne an Account of the Ladders & Hookes.
At this Court it is ordered that the Constables returne an Account of the Ladders & hookes in their severall Wards the next Court day upon paine of iii s iiii d apiece.

The Chamberlaine to collect the money for the Towns Armes.
And that the Chamberlaine make inquirie for the Armes formerly belonging to the Towne and for the money for them that are sold And that he take care the Tanners seale their Leather in the Towne Hall that the Rent may be paid As also that John Coddington pay unto the Chaimberlaine iij li ijs viijd for the Hay of the Milne Pingle And that he be allowed thereout for getting the said Hay & fencing the Close the last yeare ij li xijs viijd.

Time given to the Chaimberlaine and others to perfect their Accounts.
Mandamus to be paid for by the Gentlemen.
At this Court it is ordered that the Churchwardens, Chamberlaine & Collectors for the Schoole Rents have time to perfect their Accounts till next Court. And that the charge of the Mandamus formerly obtained by some Gentlemen of this Burrough be paid by them & not by the Chaimberlaine.

[fo. 402r] **Third Court of Thomas Hanson, 15 December 1665**

Persons appointed to Examine the Church Wardens Account.
At this Court it is ordered that Mr Robert Calcraft, Mr Joseph Tomlinson, Robert Cole, William Milles, Thomas Ireland and Robert Gibson do meete on Tuesday next by nine of the Clocke in the Morning to examine the Accounts of John Lenton Churchwarden and to returne their proceeding therein the next Court day.

And order that xs shall be spent as the Judges passeth through this Corporacion & noe more without Mr Aldermans consent.
Nor noe Wine to be Expended at Sessions Dinners without the like consent.
Whereas upon reading of the Chaimberlaines Accompt to the Court this day it appeares that there hath beene divers sumes of money paid for Wine Bisketts & Beere at the comeing by of the Judges through this Corporacion As also great sumes laid downe for Wine at Sessions Dinners more then hath beene Expended heretofore, the charge thereof being always at an uncertainetie, And to the end & intent that a certaine sume may be laid forth and be a rule for all Chaimberlaines for the future It is at this Court fully ordered and agreed upon that noe Chaimberlaine for the time to come shall not lay forth or expend at any one time that the Judges shall pass through this Corporacion above the sume of ten shillinges unless Mr Alderman for the time being shall see cause for the Expending of a greater sume, nor lay forth any more money for Wine at any Sessions Dinner except it be by Speciall Direction from Mr Alderman for the time being that then the present Chaimberlaine of this Burrough shall lay forth the same & not otherwise upon any such Accounts before mencioned whatsoever.

An Assessment of 80 li to be made for the Chartor.
Whereas Mr Alderman this day acquainted the Court that the Towne stood great need of money for paying of the Interest money and other publike charges And that it is very convenient an Assessment should be made for the charges expended for the Chartor Whereupon it is ordered that an Assessment of Eighty pounds shall be laid upon the Inhabitants of this Burrough to be paid at two equall payments vizt forty pounds at Candlemas & forty pounds at Lammas for and towards the defraying of part of the charge for reviewing the last Chartor And it is further ordered that Mr Ellis & Mr Skipwiths advise be had aboute makeing the said Assessment, & for new Feoffees for the Redd Lyon that a new lease thereof may be granted.

Thomas Milles admitted Tennant to his Fathers House.
At this Court came Thomas Milles Felmonger & desired to be admitted Tennant to the Messuage or Tenement in Walkergate formerly demised to Thomas Milles Comburgesse & Father to the said Thomas Milles whereupon it is ordered that the said Thomas Milles be admitted Tennant during the Remainder of the terme yet to come & that he give bonds for performance of Covenants which he in Court promiseth to perform & doth nominate his Bond given vizt George Read & Richard Hauley.

THE HALL BOOK OF GRANTHAM 1665–1666 73

The Watch reduced to Six And the first & 2 Companie discharged.
At this Court is taken into consideracion that hath beene kept during the time of the Visitacion at London & being observed that severall other places hath of late left of the said Watch or taken part of It is this day ordered that the Watch of this Towne be reduced to six till further order And that the first & 2d Company be freed & discharged from watching in person as they were appointed by former orders of this Court.

Chamberlaine to pay vij li vs to Wm Laine for Stills Boy to be deducted againe.
At this Court it is ordered that the Churchwarden do pay xxs unto the Chaimberlaine laid downe by by [*sic*] his Predecessor for part of the charge for the Chimes As also that the Chaimberlaine pay vij li vs to William Laine Cordwainer for takeing Edward Stills Boy an Apprentice which said sume & all other charges of placeing him is to be deducted out of the xx li formerly putt into the Towns hand.

[fo. 402v] **Fourth Court of Thomas Hanson, 23 January 1665/6**

John Lenton Accompt as churchwarden.
At this Court John Lenton Churchwarden for the yeare last past gives an Account of the Quarterly Assessment to the Church of the Bell money and other

Receipts whereby he chargeth himselfe with the sume of	37 14 10
And his disbursements to be	38 05 10
Arreares not allowed of, which he is ordered to gather up	00 04 08
Remaines due to him which the next Churchwarden is ordered to pay the sume of	00 11 00

[*The receipts figure above is only partly legible; 'xiiijs' allows the sum to balance*]

William Berriffe takes a lease of the house late in the tenure of Henry Haire.
At this Court William Berriffe takes a lease of the house in Swinegate late in the tenure of Henry Haire which belonges to the Schoole house for one and twenty yeares from the five and twentieth day of March next ensueing Yeilding and paying yearely & every yeare during the said terme the sume of ten shillinges at foure usuall feasts or termes in the yeare at ijs vjd a feast And he the said William Berriffe doth here promise to rebuild the said house sufficiently with good timber & other materialls And to leave the same so rebuild at the end of the said terme And to performe such other Covenants as formerly hath beene given And he gives in earnest thereof xijd.

Mr Leemings bill of 6 li 15s 3d to be paid by the Chaimberlaine.
At this Court Mr Richard Leeming produced a bill of vj li xvs iijd due to him for Sessions Dinners & for Wine then, & at severall other meeteinges which bill was openly read in Court & there allowed and approved of. And by this Court it is ordered that the said vj li xvs iijd be paid to Mr Leeming by the present Chamberlaine upon the first receipt of money.

The Beacon money to be paid by the Constables.
This day the Cheife Constables acquainted Mr Alderman & the Court that there was an Assessment of xviij li xviijs vjd laid upon the Towne & Soake for rebuilding the Beacon and house formerly used within this libertie in pursuance of the Deputy Leiftenants warrant And that the Towns proportion came to ij li xiiijs xd ob & at this Court they desired to know whether they should make an Assessment for it at present or the Constables to lay it downe and insert it in their Accounts Whereupon the Court takeing into Consideracion that the Sume is too smale to make an Assessment for, at present & also the charge & trouble that will be in the collecting of the same do hereby order that the Cheife Constables and Petty Constables do lay downe the said ij li xiiij s xd ob & that they shall be reimbursed againe out of the next Constables Assessment.

Overseers for the Poore to pay all such sumes of money as the Collectors for the Schoole house have laid downe for the Poores harbor.
At this Court it is ordered that the present Overseers for the Poore do pay unto the Collectors for the Schoole house Rents all such sumes of money as have beene laid downe by them or their Predecessors for the Rent of Peekes house allowed for keeping widdow Selby & the Rent of Widdow Parkins house And the said Collectors are to returne an Account thereof.

The Tanners Rent to be Collected.
At this Court it is ordered that the Chaimberlaines Booke be looked over to find out how many yeares the Tanners are in Arreare of the Rent for the Towne Hall And upon setling of the same the Tanners are to be called upon for the payment of the said Rent & all Arreares.

[fo. 403r]

At this Court the Collectors for the Schoole Rents have further time to Account.

Camberlaine [sic] *to pay 40s to Widdow Simpson.*
At this Court it is ordered that the Chaimberlaine pay forty shillinges to Widdow Simpson for works done at the Church by her husband in his lifetime.

An order that there be noe Dinners at Visitacons [sic].
Whereas upon reading of the Account of John Lenton Churchwarden to the Court this day it appeares That there hath beene more money expended at Visitacions than heretofore for dinners which have not beene usuall, the charge thereof if not prevented will yearly increase, for prevention whereof for the future It is this day ordered by the Court that noe Churchwarden or Churchwardens for the time to come, shall expend or lay forth any money for dinners at the visitacons [*sic*] for themselves or others when the same is held in this Towne but such ordinarie expenses as hath formerly beene allowed for drinks and other necessaries auntiently accustomed to be expended at such times And hath beene used by their Predecessors when noe dinners were expected.

Persons appointed to make the Assesment of 80 li for the Chartor.
At this Court it is ordered by a general consent that an Assessment of Eighty pounds be made and laid upon the Inhabitants of this Towne for and towards the defraying of part of the charge laid out for reviewing Of the last Chartor And that Mr Robert Calcraft senior, Mr Thomas Short, Mr Thomas Grant, Mr John Watson, Mr Michaell Taylor, Mr Richard Leeming, Mr Robert Calcraft junior, Mr Richard Calcraft, & Mr Joseph Tomlinson, Comburgesses, Robert Cole, Hugh Hutchin, John Coddington, John Winge, Thomas Matkin & John Turner of the second Company, Thomas Ireland, Edward Paulett, William Laine, Christofer Thompson, John Walker and John Plumer, Comoners, shall be Assessors and Makers of the said Assessment And the Cheife Constables of this Burrough shall be the Collectors of so much of the said Eighty pounds as is to be paid by the first and second Company and Gentry And that the Under Constables of every Ward within this Burrough shall collect the residue of the said Assessment which shall be imposed upon all or any of the Inhabitants aforesaid And if any Person or Persons being an Inhabitants [sic] within this Towne shall be obstinate and refuse to pay the money which they or any of them shall be assessed That then the money due to be paid by any such persons refuseing or obstinate partie by force of the said Assessment shall be levied by the Constables or some of them by distresse & sale of the Offendors goods rendring the Overplus thereof (if any be) to the party distrained And it is further ordered that the Eighty pounds be divided into two payments vizt forty pounds thereof as from Candlemas last and the other forty pounds at Lammas next And that the Gentlemen & Assessors before named or the major part of them do meete at the Towne Hall on Thursday next by one of the Clocke to make the said Assessment & before the making thereof It is ordered that Mr Ellis his advise be had for the legall assessing of the same, as also aboute the Feoffees for the Redd Lyon.

Collectors for the Schoole Rents to pay 40s to William Bury.
At this Court it is ordered that the Collectors for the Schoole Rents do pay 40s to William Bury Carpenter for timber & worke done at the Pesthouse as appeares by his bill.

[fo. 403v] **Fifth Court of Thomas Hanson, 6 March 1665/6**

The Collectors to pay noe more money to the Poore.
At this Court it is ordered that the Collectors for the Schoole Rents do forbeare paying or allowing any more money to Mr Richard Hurst for any of the houses in the Church Laine And that the money already paid shall be returned backe againe by the Overseers for the Poore.

Mr Ellis his oppinion for making the Assessment for the Chartor.
This day Mr Alderman acquainted the Court that he with severall of his Brethren had beene with Mr Ellis for his advice aboute making the Assessment for the Chartor And that is [sic] oppinion & advice is that an Assessment may be made & laid upon all the Freemen being Inhabitants within this Corporacion And in case of neglect or

refusal of payment of the money assessed upon any such Person that then it may be lawfull to levey the same by distresse & sale of goods. And in pursuance of his advice The Assessors appointed by order of the last Court have made an Assessment which they produce in Court and being this day oppenly read it is fully confirmed allowed & approved of, And the Constables of every Ward hereby ordered to collect & gather the same with all convenient speed.

William Bury to repaire the Marketplace Pumpe.
At this Court it is ordered that William Bury Carpenter do repaire the Pumpe in the Marketplace according to his Agreement formerly made in that behalfe.

Sixth Court of Thomas Hanson, 7 April 1666

Thomas Slater admitted Tennant to John Keales lease at Spittlegate.
At this Court came Thomas Slater & desired to be admitted Tennant to a lease formerly leased to John Keale of Spittlegate belonging to the Schoole house of this Burrough which he hath assigned to him by the said John Keale, which this Court takeing into consideracion the said Assignment, and that the said Thomas Slater is likely to be a good Tennant do hereby admit & allow of the said Thomas Slater to be Tennant to the premises for and during the Remainder of the terme yet to come & unexpired And he gives here in Court by way of Attornement five shillinges.

Nathaniell Garthwaite distrained for his Assessment to the Chartor.
This day the Constables being called to give an Account of the Assessment for the Chartor William Laine Constable for the Marketplace acquainted the Court that Nathaniell Garthwaite did absoelutely refuse to pay his Assessment for the Chartor Whereupon it is ordered that the said William Laine together with Robert Gibson, John Plummer, Thomas Fishar & Edward Leivesly do goe forthwith from this Court to distraine the goods & Chattells of the said Nathaniell Garthwaite for the said Assessment And that they & every of them shall be saved harmless & indempnified from all charges damages or incumbrances whatsoever which shall happen or arise aboute the takeing of the said distresse In pursuance of this present order the said Constables do immeadiately goe from this Court & distraine the goodes of the said Nathaniell Garthwaite vizt one Kigg of sope to the value of xs which they bring here in Court to be kept for a reasonable time before sale be made thereof.

[fo. 404r] Seventh Court of Thomas Hanson, 27 April 1666

The Constables to give an Account of the Assessment to the Chartor.
At this Court it is ordered that the Constables of every Ward do appeare before the Alderman Comburgesses and Second Companie on Thursday next at one of the Clocke in the Afternoone to give an Account of their severall Assessments for the Chartor And

then to cleare the same upon paine for every Constable faileing herein to forfeite forty shillinges to be levied according to the custome of this Burrough.

Mr Chantler dismissed the first Company.
Whereas the Court this day takeing into consideracion that Mr Gilbert Chantler one of the Comburgesses hath above a yeare and three quarters last past beene in the Gaole of this libertie for severall debts laid upon him And in the said time hath not indeavored to satisfie the same whereby he may take his said place and be helpefull to carrey on the Affaires of this Corporacion, but doth altogether continue useles for the good thereof As also for divers other good and notable causes this Court thereunto moveing have thought fitt & convenient to remove the said Gilbert Chantler from the place of a Comburgesse And according to Auntient custome of this Burrough do dimiss [sic] & knock him of from the place of a Comburgesse aforesaid.

A lease of Ejectment to be sealed for the Redd Lyon.
At this Court it is ordered that the deed of Feoffment For the Redd Lyon be sealed with all convenient speed And that a lease thereof be made for the bringing of an Ejectment against the Tennant in possession And for the compleateing of the same It is ordered that a lease be made to the Towne Clarke (he surrendring the same upon request) whereby the title may be tryed And it is hereby likewise ordered that the Towne Clarke shall be saved harmles and indempnified of & from all charges damages and incumbrances whatsoever that shall or may happen for or by reason of the comencement of the said Accion of Ejectment or carrieing on of the said Suite.

New Cole Buyers chosen.
At this Court it is ordered that John Walker late Cole Buyer do give up his Account the next Thursday at the meeteing abovementioned
John Dye & Edward Paulett Chosen new Cole Buyers.

New Feoffees appointed for the Redd Lyon.
At this Court it is ordered that Mr Robert Calcraft senior, Mr Thomas Short, Mr Thomas Grant, Mr John Watson, Mr Michaell Taylor, Mr Richard Leeming, Mr Robert Calcraft junior, Mr Richard Calcraft, Mr Joseph Tomlinson & Mr Richard Holley Comburgesses, George Hanson son of Mr Thomas Hanson Alderman and Walter Leeming son of Mr Richard Leeming Comburgess be nominated and appointed Feoffees in trust for the Redd Lyon.

Jonathan Parnham to be punished for a new erected Cottage.
At this Court it is ordered that Jonathan Parnham be bound over to the Sessions for setting up a new erected Cottage contrarey to the Statute in that case made and provided.

[fo. 404v] **Eighth Court of Thomas Hanson, 16 June 1666**

William Bury to repaire Markett place Pumpe.
At this Court it is ordered that William Bury Carpenter do repaire the pumpe in the Markettplace according to an order & Agreement made the fifth day of September 1651.

John Wing to have the lease of the Redd Lyon for trying the Ejectment.
This day the Towne Clarke acquainted the Court that Mr William Bury Councill for the Towne concerning the Redd Lyon thought it very inconvenient that the lease of the said Redd Lyon should be made to him as Towne Clarke by reason it might take of his Evidence upon the tryall or other the concerns of the Towne Whereupon it is ordered by and with the consent of John Wing one of the Second Companie that the lease of the Redd Lyon be let to him (he surrendring againe upon request) And the said Court do hereby promise to beare him harmles from all charges damages & incumbrances whatsoever that shall or may happen by reason of the same or of the Accion of Ejectment that shall be brought in his name for Recovery thereof.

Mr Snow to have xxxxs for his care & paines in obtaineing the last Chartor.
This day Mr Michaell Taylor one of the Comburgesses of this Court produced a letter from one Mr Leonard Snow one of the Clarkes to the Attorny Generall which showeth that he had taken a great deale of care and paines upon the reviewing of the last Chartor And that he did not reckon or account for one penny for himselfe but referred it wholey to the Towne Upon examineing of his bill & the Court finding it to be true As also upon the relacion of Mr Taylor that he was instruementall & did take paines in obtaineing the said Charter This Court do hereby order him xxxxs And that a letter of thankes be sent to him with money.

An order for the Eleccion of the Succeeding Alderman
For the more peaceable and orderly proceedinges at the Eleccion of the next succeeding Alderman It is at this Court ordered that upon the next eleccion day Mr Richard Calcraft shall be sent downe into the Church to Mr Thomas Short and Mr Robert Calcraft Junior to make three Comburgesses there Out of which three Comburgesses in the Church It is likewise agreed that Mr Robert Calcraft Junior be brought upon the Cusheon or place of Eleccion to Mr Christofer Hanson and Mr Richard Leeming to make three Comburgesses there Out of which three Comburgesses upon the Cusheon with a free and unanimous consent of this Court Mr Richard Leeming is nominated Alderman for the next ensueing yeare.

Thomas Hodgson lease to be sealed & he to have Abatement if the sicknes shall happen as God forbidd.
At this Court came Thomas Hodgson & paid downe his x li for his new lease of the tolles & desired that he might have his lease sealed with all conveniencie And that the Court would be pleased to insert a Covenant in his lease (that if the sicknes or contagion of Plague shall happen in this Towne) which God forbidd that then they will please to

abate him some part of his yearely Rent as shall be then thought convenient whereupon it is ordered that his lease shall be sealed at the Hutch the next sealing And if the said Contagion shall happen as God forbidd that then he shall make his Applicacion to the Aldermans Court And there receive abatement according as his cause shall required [*sic*].

The Constables payes in part of the Assessment for the Charter.
At this Court came severall of the Constables & pays part of the money of the Assessment for the Chartor in manner following vizt the Cheife Constables ix li xs Marketplace vj li HighStreete iij li ijs Castlegate xiijs And they & the rest of the Constables are ordered to cleare their bills by the next Court And then to give a full Account thereof, Walkergate & Swinegate bills cleared.

[fo. 405r] **Ninth Court of Thomas Hanson, 31 August 1666**

Markett place Pumpe to be repaired.
At this Court it is ordered that William Bury Carpenter do repaire the Market place Pumpe within one weeke next ensueing under the penaltie of his Agreement formerly made with this Corporacion.

Keybearers takes a lease of Sandford house.
At this Court the Keybearers takes a lease of a house in the High Streete belonging to the Schoole house for xxj yeares from and after the expiracion of a former lease thereof in being and now in the tenure of John Sandford paying the sume of ix li for a fine at or before Michaelmas next And giving securitie to pay and performe all Auntient Covenants heretofore made And they give in earnest thereof xijd.

Edward Paulett takes a lease of George Hansons House.
At this Court Edward Paulett likewise takes a lease of a house in the Market place belonging to the Schoolehouse for and on the behalfe of George Hanson who is now present Tennant, for xxj yeares from and after the Expiracion of a former lease thereof in being paying the sume of vj [li] xiijs iiijd for a fine and giveing sufficient securitie to pay and performe all former Rents and Covenants And he gives in earnest thereof xijd.

John Walkers Account questioned as ColeBuyer.
At this Court John Walker produced his Accounts as ColeBuyer for two yeares last past which was this day read and being taken notice of, and observed that the said Account was in Generall termes and not in perticulars and finding the Stocke to fall much short of what was made and accounted for, do hereby order that the said John Walker do produce and give a better Account the next Court day and that to be in perticulars upon forfeiture of five pounds.

Henry Rudkin takes a lease of the tolles for a yeare.
At this Court came Henry Rudkin and desired to take a new lease of the Tolles for another yeare if this Court would please to consider of the smale trading buying and selling of Goodes that is likely to happen this yeare by reason of the late Contagion and of the present Warrs with the Dutch And to abate him some part of his former Rent The which this Court takeing into their Consideracion do hereby grant a new lease of the Tolles belonging to this Corporacion unto the said Henry Rudkin for one whole yeare from the fifteenth day of August last past at the yearely Rent of forty pounds to be paid at foure times in the yeare by even and equall portions, and under such other Covenants as they were formerly letten to him, And that he shall injoy the Outners tolles till the Countday And it is further agreed that the said Henry Rudkin nor any imployed by him shall molest or trouble any of the Inhabitants of Denton for tolle for the Cart and Carriages goeing or comeing over a High Way in Denton Feild which is by them repaired at any time during the present demise And he gives in earnest thereof ijs vjd.

[fo. 405v] **Tenth Court of Thomas Hanson, 28 September 1666**

Persons appointed to settle the sallory due to Schooledames in Doctor Hurst houses.
At this Court came Doctor Thomas Hurst and acquainted Mr Alderman and the rest of the members thereof that he was building of foure Schooles for the educateing and bringing up of poore Children in learning and other labor which may tend to the great benefitt and advantage of this Corporacion by setting the poore on Works and keepeing them from an idle and loose kind of liveing And also desired that some Persons might be appointed to treat aboute the setling of the said Schooles and paying of the Schooledames their Sallory Whereupon this Court returns thankes to Doctor Hurst for his respect to his Towne and for his Care for the poore thereof And it is hereby ordered that Mr Alderman, Mr Thomas Grant, Mr Michaell Taylor, Mr Robert Calcraft, Mr Joseph Tomlinson and Mr Richard Holley of the Comburgesses, John Lenton, Hugh Hutchin, and Robert Cole of the second Company, Anthony Hotchkin, Edward Paulett, Richard Hauley, Thomas Fishar and William Laine Comonners, do meete on Wednesday next at one of the Clocke in the Afternoone to treat with Doctor Hurst aboute the setling of the aforesaid Schooles and paying of the Schoole Dames And that they draw up there proceedinges therein and give an Account thereof the next Court day.

John Walkers Account further questioned and proved false.
At this Court came Richard Poole and gave in Informacion concerning the Accounts of John Walker as ColeBuyer for two yeares last past that whereas he accounteth for Eighteene load of Coles the first yeare at xx li he did not buy or lay in above a xj or xij load that yeare and that he the said Richard Poole and his wife can testifie the same upon oath by which it sufficiently appeares to this Court that the Accounts of the said John Walker are false and Unjust It is therefore ordered that he be proceeded against for the imbezilling and wastling of the Stocke of money intrusted with him for the buying of Coles for the Poore being contrarey to the donor's Guift.

An Assessment of xv li to be made for the Constables disbursments this yeare.
At this Court it is ordered that an Assessment of fifteene pounds be made & laid upon this Burrough for the payment of the Constables their bills of disbursments for this present yeare an estimate being taken what those perticular sumes amount unto, And the Cheife Constables and under Constables are appointed Assessors and the Under Constables Collectors thereof.

Mr Becke to have viij li for takeing Stills Boy Apprentice.
At this Court it is ordered that Mr Becke have viij li out of the money raised by the lease of John Sandfords house for the takeing Edward Stills Boy an Apprentice.

James Ferman fined xijd for Winnowing in the Streetes.
At this Court it is ordered that the Constables levey xij [*sic*] of James Ferman for Winnowing Corne in the Streete contrarey to an order of this Court in that behalfe made.

[fo. 406r] **Eleventh Court of Thomas Hanson, 12 October 1666**

Account of Doctor Hurst guift to the Schoole Dames & money to be given at Christmas & Easter.
At this Court Mr Alderman and the rest of the Gentlemen appointed the last Court to treat with Doctor Hurst aboute the foure Schooles for educateing of poor Children and for the payment of the Schoole Dames do here give an Account thereof as followeth First that Doctor Hurst formerly paid forty pounds into the Towns hand to purchase xijd a weeke for ever for 48 weekes in a yeare to be paid to the said Schoole Dames, And hath since paid 40 li more which he obtained from the Commoners out of the Breife money for damage which he sustained by the said fire) and laid out by the Chaimberlaine, which 40 li was deposited to purchase xijd a weeke for ever for 48 weekes in a yeare as aforesaid being an Addition to the said Schooles, six weekes being deducted in every yeare for Holydayes at Christmas Easter and Whiteson tide And whereas Doctor Hurst formerly purchased 40s per Annum to be paid for the repaires of the Almshouses that he gave to the Towne, he doth now give the said 40s per Annum to the said Schooles as a further Addition & doth take the repaires of the said Houses upon himselfe with funds being computed with the rent of six houses which he also gives to the said Schooles at the yearely Rent of 4 li For the Schooles dames to let and receive the Rents to their owne use is in all about x li per Annum to be paid to and received by the foure Schoole dames for ever, And that the payments on the Towns part is ijs viijd per weeke (that is to say) viijd a weeke to every of the said foure Schoole dames And the said Gentlemen further acquaints this Court that Doctor Hurst desires for the incouragement of the poore Children and to find them necessaries, to imploy them in labour, this Court would please to allow them some part of the Dole at Christmas and Easter to buy flax wooll and other materialls that may be needfull for them Whereupon this Court taking the same into their consideracions as also that the said money is given to the Poore and the said Children being the poore of this Towne and that if any part be taken from the

Parents it will be given to the Children do hereby order and agree that the sixth part of the Dole at Christmas and Easter be given to the Schooles aforesaid to and for the use of the said Children.

Leases to be sealed at the Hutch.
At this Court it is ordered that upon the riseing thereof there be a meeteing at the Hutch to seale the Keybearers and George Hansons leases.

Mr Lenton & Mr Hutchin chosen of first Company.
At this Court Mr John Lenton was Chosen one of the first xij in the roomth of Mr Robert Calcraft deceased who accordingly takes the oath of a Comburgesse and of a Justice of peace according to Auntient custome, Hugh Hutch [*sic*] likewise chosen of the first xij in the roomth of Gilbert Chantler lately deceased and takes the oaths aforesaid.

Thomas Ireland, Edward Paulett chosen of the 2d Company.
At this Court Thomas Ireland and Edward Paulett was chosen of the Second Company in the roomths of the said Mr John Lenton and Mr Hugh Hutchin who accordingly tooke their oaths incident to their said place and office.
In the Kallender
Christofer Thompson
William Bury
John Walker

[fo. 406v] **The last Court of Thomas Hanson, 19 October 1666**

Mr Aldermans Account.
At this Court the said Mr Thomas Hanson Alderman doth account for all monies received by him upon the Comon affaires of this Towne upon penall Statutes As also for his payments and disbursments this yeare on the publike buisnes of this Towne And he chargeth himselfe with

receipt of	03 19 00	
And that his disbursments are	01 07 06	
Remaines due to the Towne	02 11 06	

Which is paid to the present Chaimberlaine.

Mr Watsons Account as Coroner.
At this Court Mr John Watson Comburgesse and Coroner of this Burrough and Soake of Grantham for the yeare now past accounteth & saith That as Casualties happened this yeare there was one Henry Sooley of Sapperton who being under Age and for severall yeares troubled with the falling sicknes and goeing forth in the day time into the feild to looke after his fathers Catle one of his fitts takeing him fell downe into a little water on his face and for want of helpe to turne him over or to looke after him he then and there perished and suddenly died And that the Jury summoned & sworne to inquire the

cause of his death found it death by Casualtie and thereby nothing did accrue to the benefit of this Burrough The said Coroner further accounteth and saith that there was one Richard Waite killed at Denton by one Nathaniell Meres And the Jury impannelled and sworne found that the said Nathaniell Meres did wound the said Richard Waite with a Scye in both thighs neare the Belly and the Wounds to be six Inches wide and two Inches Deepe or thereabouts and also wounded on this necke with a Musquett that all the blood was felled downe his Backe, and that it was Wilfull Murder And that the he fledd for it And they also found him possessed at the time of the murder comitted of two Cowes and a Calfe which goodes are in the custodie of the Constables of Denton aforesaid who tooke an Inventorie of his Householde goodes, And the said Nathaniell Meres hath made his escape and hath not since be heard of.

Mr Calcraft Account as Escheator.
At this Court Mr Robert Calcraft Escheator for the yeare past accounteth and chargeth himselfe with receipt of severall Persons for light unlawfull and defective weights and Measures the sume of   00 07 03
And that out of this he hath paide himselfe his charges at every faire ijs vjd
and ijs to the Towne Clarke for attending every faire which comes in   00 04 06
all to
So remaines due to the Towne   00 02 09
Which he payes to the present Chaimberlaine and he is discharged.

Church Warden Collectors for Schoole Rent & Constables have further time to perfect their Account.
At this Court the Churchwardens, Collectors for Schoole Rents and the Petty Constables for their assessment have time till next Court day to perfect their Accounts.

[fo. 407r]

Constables Account of the Charter Assessment.
At this Court the Cheife Constables and Petty Constables gives their for the first Assessment for
the Chartor.   li   s   d
George Short   Cheife Constables their bill   15 13 08
Robert Cole
                    Arreares   03 04 00
                    Remaines & paid   12 09 08

William Laine   Market Place Constables their bill   13 08 08
William Berriffe   Lost upon sale of the distresses
                    Remaines & paid

Robert Gibson	High Streete their bill	03 13 00
Edward Leivesly	Arreares	00 11 00
	Remaines & paid	03 02 00
John Plumer	Westgate their bill	03 02 02
Thomas Fishar	Arreares	00 04 06
	Remaines & paid	02 17 06
George Read	Walkergate their bill	02 18 06
Francis Charitie	Arreares	00 01 00
	Remaines & paid	02 17 06
Thomas Gunnison	Swinegate their bill	01 05 00
Hamlet Brumpton	Arreares	00 02 00
	Remaines and paid	01 03 00
William Scot	Castlegate their bill	01 16 00
Richard Bristow	Arreares	00 17 00
	Remaines & paid	00 19 00

And it is ordered that the said Assessment be entred into the Booke of Assessment and a perticular of those that are in Arreare.

[fo. 407v] [Blank page]

[fo. 408r]

At an Assembly holden by Mr Thomas Hanson Alderman and the Comburgesses and Burgesses of Grantham aforesaid in Corpus Christi Quire within the Prebendarie Church there &c on Friday next after St Lukes day being 20 [*recte* 19] October 1666

First did sitt downe upon the Cusheon or place of Election the said Mr Thomas Hanson in Corpus Christi Quire within the Prebendarie Church there
Next to him did sitt upon the Cusheon or place of Election two Comburgessess vizt Mr Christofer Hanson and Mr Richard Leeming
Then was there in the Church two Comburgesses vizt Mr Thomas Short and Mr Robert Calcraft
Then was sent downe in the Church to those two Comburgesses to make them two, three one other Comburgesse vizt Mr Richard Calcraft
Out of which three Comburgesses in the Church one was chosen to come up and sitt on the Cusheon or place of Election one other Comburgesse vizt Mr Robert Calcraft

Then was there three Comburgesses upon the Cusheon or place of Election vizt Mr Christofer Hanson, Mr Richard Leeming and Mr Robert Calcraft

And then was there in the Church two Comburgesses vizt Mr Thomas Short and Mr Richard Calcraft

Out of which three Comburgesses upon the Cusheon or place of Election vizt Mr Christofer Hanson, Mr Richard Leeming and Mr Robert Calcraft one is to be chosen Alderman for this next ensueing yeare

And so by an unanimous vote and consent of the Assembly Mr Richard Leeming is chosen Alderman for the next ensueing yeare

Whereupon the said Mr Thomas Hanson dischargeth himselfe from the place and office of Alderman according to Auntient custome And the said Mr Richard Leeming Alderman now elected in his place and stead hath at this Assembly taken the oath of Alderman of this Burrough and Soak of Grantham according to the Auntient and laudable custome of the Burrough aforesaid.

And so this Assembly breakes up.

[fo. 408v] [Blank page]

THE HALL BOOK OF GRANTHAM 1666–1667

[fo. 409r] **First Court of Richard Leeming 26 October 1666**

Mr Richard Leeming Alderman

First xij	2d xij
Mr Christopher Hanson Comburgess	Zachary Cox
Mr Thomas Short Comburgess	George Short
Mr Thomas Grant Comburgess	Henry Humes
Mr John Watson Comburgess	Edward Rawlinson
Mr Thomas Hanson Comburgess	John Coddington
Mr Michaell Taylor Comburgess	John Winge
Mr Robert Calcraft Comburgess	Robert Cole
Mr Richard Calcraft Comburgess	William Miles
Mr Joseph Tomlinson Comburgess	John Turner
Mr Richard Holley Comburgess	Thomas Matkin
Mr John Lenton Comburgess	Thomas Ireland
Mr Hugh Hutchkin Comburgess	Edward Paulett

Names of the Officers

Coroner	Mr Thomas Hanson	Keybearers	Mr Alderman
Escheator	Mr Richard Calcraft		Robert Cole
Churchwardens	Edward Paulett		Edward Paulett
	William Laine	Prizers of	Richard Branston
Chamberlaines	Robert Cole	Corn	Richard Bristow
	Anthony Hotchkin	Market Sayers	George Hanson
Collectors for	John Lenton		Thomas Cole
Schoole Rents	Edward Leivesly	Leather Sealers	Robert Smith
Chief Constables	John Coddington		William Jordan
	Thomas Matkin		Edward Ulliott
Market Place	John Plumer		John Inkerson
Constables	Thomas Fishar		
High Street	Hamlett Brumpton	Town Clarke	William Hodgkinson
Constables	Thomas Charles	Serjents	Samuell Roades
Westgate	Robert Gibson		Richard Blacke
Constables	Francis Charitie		
Walkergate	George Read	Gaoler	Richard Blacke
Constables	Thomas Gunnisson		
Swinegate	William Scott	Church Clarke	William Newball
Constables	Edward Bristow		

Castlegate	Thomas Frith	Belman	Ralph Osborne
Constables	William Bristow		

[fo. 409v]

The Names of the Commoners of the Court there.

Market place	W[est]gate
John Plumer	[Rob]ert Gibson
Thomas Fishar	Francis Charitie
Thomas Calcraft	Edward Kenion
John Walker	William Palmer
William Laine	
Thomas Archer	Walkergate
Anthony Hotchkin	George Read
William Berriffe	Thomas Gunnisson
Edward Leivesly	Christopher Thompson
High streete	Swinegate
Hamlet Brumpton	William Scot
Thomas Charles	Edward Bristow
William Bury	
Richard Hauley	Castlegate
Thomas Tayler	Thomas Frith
	William Bristow

Plate Delivered.
At this Court Mr Thomas Hanson late Alderman delivers up to Mr Alderman

The Horse Race Cupp	Mr Greenwoods xiij Spoones
Mr Archers Boll	Mr Batties Beaker
Mr Wheatelys Cann	Two Tunns
Mr Horsemans Wine Boll	One Salt with a Cover
Mr Greenwoods Cann	The Waites foure
Mr Horsemans Bolle	Cognizances

Charters delivered.
At this Court was also delivered up to Mr Alderman the three Charters Boxes with all the Charters
vzt.

	Escheators Pattent
The Exemplificacion of Edward 4 Charter	James Charter
Henry the 8 his Charter	Charles 1 Chartre of Confermacion & for Wooll Market & Court of pleas
Edward the vj his Chartre *pro* Schoole	Charles 2 Chartre of Confermacion
Elizabeth her Charter of Conformacion [*sic*]	Librarey writeinges

Judge Dyers Award
Stamford writeing

Town Armes
A Writeing with many seales

Thomas Charles and Edward Bristow made free.
At this Court came Thomas Charles Baker Apprentice to Edward Bristow and Edward Bristow his sonn and desired to be admitted Freemen of this Corporacion to which this Court doth condiscend Whereupon the said Thomas Charles as a Forrainer payes to the Box vs and William Bristow as free born payes ijs vjd & the fees to Clarke & Serjents and takes their oathes of Freemen according to the custome of this Burrough.

[fo. 410r]

Chaimberlaines to lend v li to the Churchwardens for the payment of William Palmers debt.
This day George Short acquainted the Court that William Palmer had obtained against him a judgement for v li xijs due to him for work done at the Church when he the said George Short was Churchwarden which by a former order of this Court he was promised to be freed from, and that the same should be paid, and want thereof the said William Palmer doth threaten to take out Execucion against him he therefore desires that this Court would be pleased to order the payment of the said debt, which this Court taking into consideracion and to avoid further charge and trouble and haveing v li in their hands of Mr Pells money not yet disposed of do hereby order that William Milles late Chaimberlaine pay the said v li to Robert Cole the present Chaimberlaine And that he lend the said v li to the Churchwarden for two moneths to pay William Palmer which accordingly was lent and received by the said William Palmer in open Court And the present Churchwardens are hereby also ordered to repay the said v li at the two moneths end to be disposed to and for the uses limitted by the Court.

Constables Account.
At this Court the severall Constables gives an Account of the Constables Assessments for the

yeare past as followeth vzt	li	s	d
Market Place Constables their bill	04	18	00
Cleared and paid			
High Streete Constables their bill	03	05	01
Cleared and paid			
Westgate Constables their bill	01	17	05
Walkergate cleared and paid	00	12	01
Swinegate Constables their bill	01	00	03
Cleared and paid			

Castlegate Constables have till next Court to perfect their Accounts

Chamberlaine to pay 50s to discharge the Constables disbursements.
Whereas upon examineing of the Constables Assessment and their severall disbursements it appears that the Assessment will not discharge their payments by 50s Whereupon it is ordered that the present Chaimberlaine Robert Cole do lay down the said 50s and that the same be repaid againe by the next Constables Assessment.

Persons appointed to examine Accounts.
At this Court it is ordered that Mr Thomas Grant, Mr Thomas Hanson, Mr Michael Taylor and Robert Calcraft do meete on Wednesday next at one of the Clock in the Afternoone to examine the Chaimberlaines Account And to make a returne of their proceedinges therein the next Court day.

[fo. 410v] **Second Court of Richard Leeming, 10 November 1666**

Feoffees to be saved harmles aboute the Redd Lyon.
At the Court it is ordered that all the Feoffees to whom the state of the Redd Lyon is now convayed and for the tryall of which an Accion of Ejectment is now brought in the name of the said Feoffees, they and every of them be saved harmles and indempnified of and from all Incumbrances claimes of charge or charges damages and costs of suite whatsoever that shall or may happen either at the Common Law or in Chancery or in any other Court whatsoever against the said Feoffees or any of them by reason of the said trust And it is further ordered that for the prosecucion of the said suite William Ellis, Thomas Skipwith and William Bury Esquires be retained as Councill for the Towne and the Towne Clarke as Attorney and Sollicitor And that the present Chaimberlaine pay unto him iij li being now due for Thomas Hodgsons Rent to defray part of the charges of this terme in the Accion as aforesaid and in the cause in Chancery at the suite of Edward Christian in whose name the several Feoffees are supenaed to defend the his pretended Tenant right to the said Redd Lyon.

Thomas Tomlyn admitted Tenant to his House in Manthorpe.
At this Court came Thomas Tomlyn and desired to be admitted Tenant to a house in Manthorpe which he formerly held by lease from this Corporacion and is of late taken by the Keybearers and Comoners of the Towne and he haveing repaid the said fine intreats his admicion The which the Court taking into their consideracion and that he hath held it for severall yeares past do hereby admit of the said Thomas Tomlyn to be Tenant of the premises for the remainder of the terme yet to come and unexpired giveing Securite for the Rent and Repaires And he gives by way of Attorniment xijd.

William Palmer to be paid in full of the execucion against George Short.
At this Court it is ordered that the 40s remaineing in the hands of Mr Thomas Hanson late Alderman and paid unto him by Robert Thorrold Esquire for his halfe yeare payment towards the Church and Poore, be paid unto William Palmer in full discharge of a Judgment against George Short late churchwarden for a debt due from the Towne.

Samuell Roades to receive the Arreares of his Sallory of the Chaimberlaine.
At this Court it is ordered that the present Chaimberlaine pay xiijs unto Samuell Roades for his Arrears of the last yeares Sallory.

Mr Hutchin to be destrained of, for not takeing his place of Comburgesse.
At this Court it is ordered that Mr Hugh Hutchin appeare the next Court day and take upon him the place of Comburgesse or lay down his fine of xv li according to a former order of this Court or else that a warrant be sent forth to levey the said fine.

Chaimberlaines Account.
The Account of William Milles Chaimberlaine his Receipts	161 02 02
His disbursements	161 07 01
Remains due to him	00 05 01

Whereupon the said William Milles is discharged and the present Chaimberlaine ordered to pay unto him the said five shillinges and a penny.

[fo. 411r] **Third Court of Richard Leeming, 18 January 1666/7**

The Town Clerkes Account aboute the Redd Lyon.
At this Court was read the bill in Chancery against the Feoffees in Trust at the suite of Edward Christian concerning his pretended Tenant right to the Redd Lyon and also the answer of the said Feoffees to the said bill of Complaint which is ordered to be ingrossed The Town Clerke also produced his bill of Charges expended last terme both about the suite at Common law and Chancery which amounts to 10 li 12s 2d and acquainted the Court that he had received in part thereof 3 li and there remaines due to him 7 li 12s 2d whereupon it is ordered that the same be paid unto him upon the first receipt of moneys.

Doctor Hurst Schools dames to be paid out of Esquire Gorges x s a moneth.
At this Court came Doctor Hurst about settling the payments to the Schoole dames for teaching of poor Children and acquainted this Court that he formerly intended to set up foure schooles but haveing since considered that three will be sufficient, he desires to know from this Court how the weekly payments thereof may be settled whereupon Mr Alderman was pleased to let this court understand that a very worthy person at the Grange, Arthur Gorge Esquire was pleased out of his good will for the releife of the poore to give xs in money every moneth, And that he had moved him in case the said money should be paid to Doctor Hursts Schoole dames towards their sallory that he would please to approve thereof, at which time his answer was he left it solely to Mr Alderman and the Court and that it would be pleaseing to him to have it so disposed of, Whereupon this Court returns thankes to Esquire Gorge for his respects and favours to this Town and do hereby ordered [*sic*] that the same to be paid to the uses aforesaid the whole yeares charge amounting to vij li xvjs 0d and the xs a month being computed, and vjd a weeke to be paid by the Chaimberlaine will near make up the said charge, And it is further ordered (that if with conveniencie it may be) the Milles be Assessed

vjd a weeke and added to the said Schooles to take of the vjd a weeke paid by the Chaimberlaine.

Jonathan Parnhams Lycence to assigne over his lease & Mr Walles admittment.
At this Court came Jonathan Parnham and desired Lycence to assigne over his lease to Mr William Walles The which this Court takeing into consideracion as also that the said Mr Walles is likely to prove a good Tenant do hereby give Lycence to the said Jonahtan Parnham to assigne over his lease to the said Mr Walles And do also admit of Mr Walles to be Tenant And he gives to Mr Alderman by way of Attornement xijd.

Persons appointed to examine Accounts.
At this Court it is ordered that Mr Thomas Short, Mr Thomas Grant, Mr Robert Calcraft, Mr Richard Calcraft, Mr Joseph Tomlinson, Robert Cole, George Short, Thomas Fishar and Thomas Archer do meet on Wednesday next at two of the Clocke in the Afternoon to examine the Account of Edward Paulett Churchwarden and to returne their proceedings therein the next Court Day.

Gaoler to be paid the Sessions Dinners.
At this Court it is ordered that the Chaimberlaine pay xxxiiijs to Richard Blacke for two sessions Dinners and further charges in carreing home Mrs Darker when the Redd Lyon deed was sealed.

Appearance to be entered in Chancery for Mr Lenton and Mr Paulett.
At this Court it is ordered that the Towne Clerke enter an Appearance in the Chancery for John Lenton Gent and Edward Paulett at the suite of Edward Christian about the Redd Lyon.

[fo. 411v] **Fourth Court of Richard Leeming, 25 January 1666/7**

Churchwardens Dinners at Visitations to be taken into Consideracion.
Whereas upon the reading of the Churchwardens Accounts this day it appeares that severall sumes of money is expended for dinners at the Visitations which is a great charges to the Towne, And the Churchwardens being present acquainted this Court that it is observed in all places for the opportunitie of the Ministers and Churchwardens meeting together and the Sidsmen to treat concerning their presentments and other buisnes of the Church Whereupon it is ordered that the Charge already past be allowed And that the said charge for the time to come be taken into consideracion and that Mr Dix be advised with, for easeing the Towne of the said charge.

Mr Pauletts Account as Churchwarden.
At this Court Edward Paulett gives up his Account as Churchwarden for the last yeare
and that his receipts are   30 16 00
His disbursements   32 08 10

Remainder due to him   01 12 10

Which said sume is ordered to be paid unto him by the present Churchwarden.

Mr Lenton to be paid the arreares that he could not collect as Churchwarden.
At this Court Mr John Lenton Churchwarden for part of the yeare 1664 & 1665 brought in a note of Arreares due to the Church which upon his Account he charged himself with to gather up. And the said persons being either dead or removed out of Towne he cannot receive the said monies which note being this day read and the sume thereof amounting to xs and the Court being sensible that the same cannot be gotten do hereby order that the present Churchwarden pay unto the said Mr Lenton the aforesaid xs.

Mr Aldermans Account as Collector for the Schoole Rents.
At this Court Mr Alderman past his Account as collected for the Schoole Rent for part of the yeares 1664 & 1665 whereupon William Bury was inioyned to
assist him and they charge themselves with receipts of   46 09 00
And their disbursements and Arrears to be   40 04 11
Remainder due to the Towne [correct sum due should be 06 04 01] 00 04 01
Which they pay to the present Chaimberlaine and are discharged.

Mr Holley & Anthony Hotchkin account for the Schoole Rents.
At this Court Mr Richard Holley and Anthony Hotchkin gives up their Accounts as Collectors for the Schoole Rents for the yeare past
And they charge themselves with Receipts of the sume of   45 15 00
And their disbursments & Arreares to be   45 14 04
remaines due to the Towne   00 00 09
Which they pay to the present Chaimberlaine and are discharged.

William Bury paid for repaireing the Markett Place pumpe.
This day William Bury Carpenter desired that this Court will be pleased to order him the payment of xvjs vijd which hathe beene due to him this two yeares for repaireing the Pest house whereupon it is ordered that the present Chaimberlaine pay unto him the said xvjs vijd now in Court.

[fo. 412r]

Mr Hanson to Account for the collection for the sufferers at London.
At this Court Thomas Hanson late Alderman brings an Account of the Collection for the said fire that happened at London the funds thereof come to xx li xvs vjd which he is desired by the Court to pay unto Doctor Sanderson or Mr Procktor be returned to London with the rest of the Collections which they are empowered to receive by the Byshopp within this diocess they being Register thereof.

Mr Milles to have the money due to him upon his Account.
This day William Milles the late Chaimberlaine acquainted the Court that in his time he paid iiijs vjd for Trays which was broke when the Watch was kept to preserve the Towne from infeccion when the sickness was in London And that the same ought to be paid by the Constables and he being vs out upon his Account desired that the Constables might be ordered to pay him the said iiijs vjd Whereupon it is ordered that the present Chief Constable do pay the same to Mr Milles and insert it in their Account for the yeare.

Widdow Fishar admitted Tenant to Widdow Bliths House being a relacion to Mr Ducker the donor.
At this Court came Margaret Fishar and desired to be admitted Tenant to the house Widdow Blith lately lived in which was given to the Towne by one Mr Ducker her fathers owne Uncle whereupon this Court takeing into consideracion that she being a relacion to the said Mr Ducker and if any of his kindred should be in want of a habitacion that the Towne ought out of respect and not otherwise to place such relations And whereas one Luce Dann did take care and looke to Widdow Blith in her sickness and did dwell with her and paid the Rent for the said house and laid out some money in repairing the same it is therefore ordered that the said Margaret Fishar do pay unto the said Luce Dann the money laid out by her for repaires of the said house and that after payment thereof the said Luce Dann have time till Lady Day next to provide herselfe another house And that then the said Margaret Fysher be admitted Tenant to the house aforesaid giving securitie for the Rent and repaires and to leave the possession thereof peaceably to the Towne when shee shall be herewith required And that she shall not take any person or persons into her familie with [*sic*] the consent of the Alderman and Burgesses in open Court first had and obtained.

Chaimberlaine to lend 40s to the Churchwardens to pay Mr Palmer.
At this Court it is ordered that the Chaimberlaine lend 40s more to the Churchwardens for the paying of the Execucion against George Short late Churchwarden at the suit of Mr William Palmer for worke done at the Church which makes up vij li that the Churchwarden is indebted to the Chaimberlaine for debt and charges due upon the said Execucion.

John Trueman a forrainer made free.
At this Court came John Trueman a Joyner and a stranger in this Town and desired to be admitted a free Burgess of this Corporaion Therewith this Court takeing into their consideracion as also that there is none of that trade in the Towne do admitte of him to be a free Burgess whereupon he lays downe his x li according to custome and this Court considering that he will not be prejudiciall to any freeman of this Corporacion by reason of his trade do give him again iij li vjs viijd out of his x li And he pays his fees to the Clarke and Serjents and the oath of a freeman according to the Auntient and laudable custome of this Burrough.

[fo. 412v] **Fifth Court of Richard Leeming, 8 May 1667**

Widdow Simpson debt to be paid.
At this Court it is ordered that then [*sic*] the Churchwardens receive the next xxs of Robert Thorrold Esquire towards the Repaires of the Church that they then pay the same unto Widdow Simpson for a debt oweing to her for worke done at the Church by her husband in his lifetime.

Richard Bristow to be distrained for xxs
At this Court it is ordered that Richard Bristow be distrained for xxs for not passing of the Account as Constable for last yeare And that what money remaines in his hands shall be paid unto Robert Gibson for his disbursments as Constable in the said yeare.

Assessment to be made for repaireing the Conduit.
This day Mr Alderman acquainted the Court that the Conduit was very much out of repaires and that the Suthorne [?Syphon] was decayed and that unless it be speedy repaired the Water will not continue Whereupon this Court takeing the same into their consideracion and that it is for the Generall good of the whole Towne do hereby order that an Assessment of fifteene pounds be made and laid upon this Burrough of Grantham for the repaireing of the said Conduit And that Mr Michaell Taylor, Mr Richard Calcraft, Mr Joseph Tomlinson, Mr Richard Holley, Robert Cole, Thomas Ireland, John Turner, John Plumer and Thomas Fishar be Assessors and the Constables of every Ward Collectors thereof.

An Account to be taken for repaires of the Church.
At this Court it is ordered that an estimate be taken for the decayes of the Church and what sume may be raised for setting the same in Repaire and after the said estimate so taken that an assessment be laid upon this Parish for the raiseing of money to sett the said Church in sufficient repaires.

An order for the Elleccion of the succeeding Alderman.
For the more peaceable and orderly proceedinges at the Eleccion of the next succeeding Alderman It is at this Court ordered that upon the next Elleccion day Mr Joseph Tomlinson be sent downe into the Church to Mr Thomas Short and Mr Richard Calcraft to make three Comburgesses there Out of which three Comburgess in the Church It is likewise agreed that Mr Thomas Short be brought upon the Cusheon or place of elleccion to Mr Christofer Hanson and Robert Calcraft to make three Comburgesses there Out of which three Comburgesses upon the Cusheon with the consent of this Court Mr Thomas Short is nominated as Alderman for this next ensueing yeare.

[fo. 413r] **Sixth Court of Richard Leeming, 10 June 1667**

Mr Parkins the Towne Sollicitor desires payment of his bill and sallory.
At this Court came Mr William Parkins Senior the Towne Sollicitor and acquainted Mr Alderman and the rest of this Court that he hath laid out aboute the suite betwixt the Towne and Soake the sume of vj li xiijs viijd besides the money formerly received As also that there is iiij li due to him for two yeares sallory.

A Tryall to be had for the Redd Lyon.
This day Mr Alderman acquainted the Court that the Tryall against Mr Christian for the Red Lyon was brought downe and that there must be some money raised for the defraying of the charges at the Assizes which being considered by this Court for the more speedy raising of x li for the purpose aforesaid it was thought fitt that the Cole Buyer not haveing any occasion for the money at present nor will not till the time of yeare for buying of Coles might lend the Towne Whereupon it is ordered that the present Cole buyer do lend and pay x li to the Chaimberlaine for the Townes use for a Quarter of a yeare till Henry Rudkins rent be due for the tolles, And that upon the next quarters Rent paying by the said Henry Rudkin and received by the Chaimberlaine be againe fortwith paid to the Cole Buyer to be imployed for the buying of Coles according to the will of the Donor.

Churchwardens not to pay Osborne ijs vjd unless he keeps people out of the Alyers.
Whereas upon reading of the Churchwardens Account this day it appears that there is ijs vjd a yeare paid to the Saxton for keeping young people out of the Alyers on Shrove Tuesday which he hath neglected to do and doth rather give libertie to them It is therefore ordered that unles he doth keep them out of the Alyers as he formerly used that the Churchwarden forebeare paying him the ijs vjd any longer.

Mr William Parkins Junior made free.
At this Court came Mr William Parkins the eldest Sonn of Mr Parkins the Townes Sollicitor and desired to be admitted a free Burgesse of this Corporacion he being free borne which this Court doth condiscend Whereupon the said Mr Parkins payes to the Box ijs vjd and the fees to the Clarke and Serjents and takes the oath of a Freeman according to the Auntient custome of this Burrough.

Robert Moore, John Beamond, Lambert Portwood made free.
At this Court came Robert Moore Butcher Apprentice to John Scott, John Beamond Apprentice to Michaell Taylor Baker and Lambert Portwood Apprentice to Stephen Simpson Roper who have severally served their Apprenticeshipps and desired to be admitted free Burgesses of this Corporacion to which this Court doth condiscend whereupon the said Robert Moore, John Beamond and Lambert Portwood as Forrainers do pay vs a peice to the Box and fees to the Clarke and Serjents and do take the oath of Freemen according to Auntient Custome.

Mr Hutchin to be distrained for his fine.
At this Court it is ordered that Mr Hugh Hutchin be distrained for the fine of xv li for refusing to take upon him the place of a Comburgesse.

[fo. 413v] **Seventh Court of Richard Leeming, 12 July 1667**

William Bury to give bond for keeping Markett Place pumps in repaires.
At this court it is ordered that Mr William Bury Carpenter gives sufficient Bond to the Towne for the repaireing of the Markett Place Pumpe and for the keeing [sic] of his mother according to an Agreement formerly made with this Court.

Richard Bristow distrained for a fine of xxs for not clearing his Account as Constable.
At this Court the Bayliffe of the libertie and the Constables went and distrained of the Goodes of Richard Bristow for a fine of xxs for not paying his Account as Constable for the yeare past and they tooke by way of distresse foure pewter dishes and a Pye plate which remaines in the custodie of the Bayliffe for the fine aforesaid.

An order for payment of vj li to William Palmer for the Conduit.
At this Court it is ordered that the vj li which shall be due to William Palmer at Lammas next be paid unto him with all convenient speed and that in the meanetime he take care for the repaireing of the Conduit.

The Chartor Assessment to be setled.
At this Court it is ordered that the Assessors for the Chartor Assessment do meete on Tuesday next at foure of the Clocke in the afternoone to settle the said assessment.

Feoffees for the Townes land to be renewed.
At this Court it is ordered that upon rising of the Court there be a meeteing at the Hutch to examine the Townes writeings and for the makeing of new Feoffees for the land belonging to this Corporacion.

Edward Pawlett Account as Colebuyer.
At this Court Edward Paulett [sic] gives up his Account as Colebuyer as followeth vizt.

	li	s	d
Receipts	19	08	00
Disbursements|	09	05	00
Remaines	10	03	00

which x li he lent to the Chaimberlaine according to a former order of Court and the iijs he payes downe in open Court and he is discharged.

William Knewstubbs admitted Church Clarke.
At this Court came William Knewstubbs and desired to be admitted Church Clarke to which the Court doth condiscend, and he takes the oath incident to the said place.

An order for the raiseing of xviij li for the Constables Bills.
At this Court is ordered that an Assessment of Eighteene pounds be made and laid upon the Burrough for the payment of the Constables their bills of disbursments for this present yeare and estimate being taken what those perticular sumes amount unto And the Cheife Constables and Under Constables are appointed Assessors and the Under Constables Collectors thereof.

[fo. 414r] Eighth Court of Richard Leeming, 4 October 1667

A new lease lett to Mrs Wilkinson.
At this Court came Mrs Wilkinson and desired to take a lease of a House in Westgate which was burnt downe by the late fire and since rebuilt by her Whereupon this Court takeing the same into their consideracion As also the charge shee hath beene at in rebuilding the said House and of her present necessitie haveing sustained great losses herselfe by the said late fire do hereby lett her a new lease thereof for one and twenty yeares from the Expiracion of her former lease at the old fine of forty shillinges and under her former Rent and Covenants And she gives in earnest thereof xijd.

Hugh Hutchin Gentleman dismissed from that place of a Comburgesse.
At this Court came Hugh Hutchin formerly chosen one of the first Company and refused to take upon him the said place for which he hath beene distrained for a fine of fifteene pounds and goodes taken near to that value and he now alleadgeing many thinges to this Court that he cannot accept of the said place and therefore makes his earnest request to this Court that they would please to dismiss him of the said Office and to returne him his distresse againe Whereupon this Court considering thereof As also that he being formerly dismissed the Court upon his request and that upon the regulacion he was brought in againe Upon the perswasion of friends do at this Court dismiss him from the said Office and returnes his distress backe to him and thereupon he returnes thankes to the Court for their respect and favour to him.

A lease lett to Henry Rudkin of the tolles.
At this Court came Henry Rudkin and takes a new lease of the tolles belonging to this Corporacion from this fifteenth day of August last past for and whole yeare at the Rent of forty two pounds and eight shillinges whereof he payes downe xxxxviijs in court and is to pay the forty pounds at foure times in the yeare by even and equall porcions And under the same agreement they were lett to him the last yeare And that he shall injoy the Outner tolles till the Count day And he gives in earnest thereof ijs vjd.

The Towne Clarkes Account about the Redd Lyon.
The Towne Clarke this day acquainted the Court that he had obtained a deed and fine from the Heires of the surviveing Feoffees for the Redd Lyon and that they were willing to come over to Grantham to give possession if this Court would please to give them securitie to beare them harmles from any charge that Christian should putt to he being

vexacious The which this Court takeing into their consideracions As also that they cannot legalley be troubled for the performeing of their trusts which the law injoynes them to do this Court desires Mr Alderman, Mr Thomas Short, Mr Thomas Hanson, Mr Michaell Taylor, Mr Robert Calcraft and Mr Richard Calcraft that they would be pleased to be bound to the Heires of the surviveing Feoffees, for the saveing them harmles from any charge that Christian shall putt them unto by reason of the Settlement of the said Inn And that this Court will beare them harmles from any charge or trouble that shall happen by reason thereof Upon which intreaty the Gentlemen before named are contented to become bound as aforesaid.

[fo. 414v] **Ninth Court of Richard Leeming, 18 October 1667**

Zachary Cox dismissed the Second Company.
At this Court came Zachary Cox one of the Second Company and desired Mr Alderman and the rest of this Court that they would please to dismiss him from the said place and Office, to whose request this Court doth condiscend and he is dismissed accordingly.

Severall Persons have time to renew their leases.
At this Court came Widdow Nidd, Thomas Bristow and James Longe and desired time to renew their severall leases of the Houses and lands they hold of this Corporacion to which this [*sic*] doth condiscend and do give them time till Christmas next to consider thereof.

Mr George Short chosen of the First Company.
Whereas Mr George Short is this day chosen of the first Company and being present in Court the oaths incident to the said place was tendred to him which he refused to take but desired time to consider of them till next Court Whereupon this Court doth at present order that his fine forfeited upon his refusall be respited and doth give him time till next Court day to returne his absolute answer.

Christopher Thompson chosen of the Second Company.
Whereas Christopher Thompson is this day likewise chosen one of the Second Company and being present the oathes incident to the said Office was also tendred which he absolutely refused to take Whereupon it is ordered that a warrant be made to levey the sume of ten pounds by him forfeited for refuseing to take upon him the said Office according to a former order of this Court.

Mr Humes chosen of the first Company.
At this Court Mr Henry Humes is chosen one of the first Company within the roome of Mr Hugh Hutchin lately dismissed.

William Bury chosen of the second Company.
At this Court William Bury is chosen one of the Second Company in the roome of the said Mr Humes.

In the Kallendar
John Walker
Anthony Hotchkin
William Palmer

[fo. 415r] **Tenth Court of Richard Leeming, 25 October 1667**

Christofer Thompson hath time given till next Court to take his place.
This day Christofer Thompson was called upon to take his place in the Second Company according to the Elleccion the last Court Whereupon he desired the favor of the Court that they would please to give him time whilst the next Court to consider thereof and then he would either take his place or lay downe his fine of x li to whose request this Court doth condiscend and give him time accordingly.

Mr Alderman further time to Account.
At this Court Mr Alderman hath further time to perfect his Accounts as to his Receipts and Disbursements on the publike Account of this Corporacion.

Coroners Account.
At this Court Mr Thomas Hanson Coroner accounteth and saith that as touching Casualties happening this yeare that there was one Christofer James did kill one Samuell Crostwaite with a Rapure And that the Jury impannelled to inquire how the said Samuell Crostwaite came to his death found the said Christofer James guilty of Wilfull Murder. And the said Coroner further accounteth and saith that there was one Elianor Noble killed by the fall of a barne of Katherine Pearesons widdow And that the Jury upon their verdict found it chance Medley.
And the aforesaid Coroner also accounteth and saith that there were John Walpoole and John Greene drowned in the Milne River as they were washing themselves and of sudden fell into a deepe pitt of Water and for want of helpe to get them out they there perished And that the Jury found it death by misfortune And further he hath not to account for and therefore he is discharged.

Escheators Account.
At this Court Mr Richard Calcraft Escheator for the yeare past accounteth and chargeth himself with Receipts of severall persons for light unlawfull and
Defective weights and Measures the sume of   00 05 00
And that out of this he hath paid himselfe his charges at every faire which is ijs vjd and ijs to the Town Clarks for attending every faire which comes to   00 04 06
So remaines due to the Towne   00 00 06
which he payes to the present Chaimberlaine and is discharged.

Chaimberlaines & other Officers further time to Account.
At this Court Chaimberlaine, Churchwardens Collectors for School Rents Chiefe Constables and Under Constables have further time till next Court to perfect their Accounts.

[fo. 415v] [Blank page]

[fo. 416r]

An Assembly held by Richard Leeming Alderman and the Comburgesses and Burgesses of Grantham aforesaid in Corpus Christi Quire within the Prebendarie Church there as on Friday next after St Lukes day being the 25 October 1667.

First did sitt downe upon the cusheon or place of Election the said Mr Richard Leeming in Corpus Christi Quire within the Prebendarie Church there
Next to him did sitt upon the Cusheon or place of eleccion two Comburgesses vizt Mr Christofer Hanson and Mr Robert Calcraft
Then was there in the Church two Comburgesses vizt Mr Thomas Short and Mr Richard Calcraft
Then was sent downe into the Church to those two Comburgesses to make them three one other Comburgesse vizt Mr Joseph Tomlinson
Out of which three Comburgesses in the Church one was chosen to come and sitt upon the cusheon or place of eleccion one other Comburgesse vizt Mr Thomas Short
Then was there three Comburgesses upon the cusheon or place of Eleccion vizt Mr Christofer Hanson, Mr Robert Calcraft and Mr Thomas Short
Then was there in the Church two Comburgesses vzt Mr Richard Calcraft and Mr Joseph Tomlinson
Out of which three Comburgesses upon the cusheon or place of Eleccion vzt Mr Christofer Hanson, Mr Robert Calcraft and Mr Thomas Short one is to be chosen Alderman for the next ensuing yeare
And so by an unanimous consent and vote of this Assembly Mr Thomas Short is chosen [nominated] Alderman for the next ensuing yeare

Whereupon the said Mr Richard Leeming dischargeth himselfe from the place and Office of Alderman and according to auntient custome And the said Mr Thomas Short now elected Alderman in his place and stead hath at this Assembly taken the oath of Alderman for this Burrough and Soake of Grantham according to the Auntient and laudable custome of the Burrough aforesaid.

And so this Assembly breakes up.

[fo. 416v] [Blank page]

THE HALL BOOK OF GRANTHAM 1667–1668

[fo. 417r] **First Court of Thomas Short, 1 October 1667**

Mr Thomas Short Alderman

First xij	2d xij
Mr Christofer Hanson Comburgess	John Coddington
Mr Thomas Grant Comburgess	John Winge
Mr Thomas Hanson Comburgess	Robert Cole
Mr Michaell Taylor Comburgess	William Milles
Mr Richard Leeming Comburgess	John Turner
Mr Robert Calcraft Comburgess	Thomas Matkin
Mr Richard Calcraft Comburgess	Thomas Ireland
Mr Joseph Tomlinson Comburgess	Edward Paulett
Mr Richard Holley Comburgess	William Bury
Mr John Lenton Comburgess	Christofer Thompson
Mr George Short Comburgess	
Mr Edward Rawlinson Comburgess	

The Names of the Officers there

Coroner	Mr Richard Leeming	Keybearers	Mr Alderman
			Thomas Matkin
			William Bury
Escheator	Mr George Short	Chaimberlaines	Thomas Matkin
			John Plumer
Churchwardens	William Bury	Prizers of	Edward Archer
	William Laine	Corne	John Beamond
Collectors for	Mr Henry Humes	Markett	Robert Waineman
Schoole Rents	Anthony Hotchkin	Sayers	Thomas Hodgson
Cheife	William Milles	Leather	Robert Smith
Constables	Thomas Ireland	Sealers	George Wray
			Edward Ulliott
			Thomas Marshall
Markettplace	Thomas Charles	Towne Clarke	William Hodgkinson
Constables	Thomas Archer	Serjents	Samuell Roades
			Richard Blacke
Highstreete	Hamlett Brumpton	Gaoler	Richard Blacke
Constables	John Pape		

Westgate Constables	Henry Coverly Francis Charitie	Church Clarke	William Knewstubbs
Walkergate Constables	John Still Thomas Cole	Bellman	Ralph Osborne
Swinegate Constables	Edward Bristow Nicholas Becke		
Castlegate Constables	Thomas Frith William Bristow		

[fo. 417v]

Names of the Commoners of the Court

Marketplace
Thomas Charles
Thomas Archer
John Walker
William Laine
Anthony Hotchkin
William Berriffe
Edward Leivesly
Richard Bristow

High Streete
Hamlett Brumpton
John Pape
Richard Hauley
Thomas Taylor

Castlegate
Thomas Frith
William Bristow

Westgate
Henry Coverly
Francis Charitie
Edward Kenion
Thomas Fishar

Walkergate
John Still
Thomas Cole
George Read
Thomas Gunnisson

Swinegate
Edward Bristow
Nicholas Becke
Christofer Hanson
William Scott

The Towne plate remains in the hands of Mr Leeming late Alderman.
This day Mr Alderman acquainted the Court that Mr Alderman for the last yeare doth detaine the Towns Plate for the indempnifieing him from a debt that he bound for on behalfe of the Corporacion And that he will not at present deliver up the said Plate so as to charge the present Alderman.

Chartors delivered.
At the Court Mr Leeming the late Alderman delivers up the three Chartor Boxes with all the Charters vzt

The Exemplir of Edward 4 Charter   King Charles Charter of Confirmacion
Henry the 8 his Charter   Kinge Charles 2d Confirmacion
Edward the vj his Charter for the Schoole Librarey Writings
Elizabeth her Charter of Confirmacion   Townes Armes
Judge Dyers Award   A writing with many seales
Stamford writeing
Escheators Pattent
James Charter

Henry Rudkin to pay the Rent in Court.
At this Court Henry Rudkin was sent for to give an Account how he hath paid his Rent for the tolles for the last yeare And upon his appearance he saith he hath paid all but vj li which he promised to pay unto Anthony Hotchkin the late Chaimberlaine who being now discharged and a new one elected It is this day ordered that the said Henry Rudkin do forbeare paying the said vj li to any Person but to Thomas Matkin the now Chaimberlaine And that for the time to come he pay his Rent in open Court so as the same may be disposed of, by order of this Court and not otherwise.

[fo. 418r]

Mr Leemings Account as Alderman.
At the Court Mr Richard Leeming gives an Account of his Receipts
and disbursments as   li   s   d
Alderman the last yeare wherein he chargeth himselfe with Receipt of   03   12 00
And his disbursments to be   01   19 11
So there Remaines due to the Towne   01   12 01
Which is paid to him in part of his debt due from this Corporacion.

Robert Coles Account as Chaimberlaine.
At this Court Robert Cole gives up his Account as Chaimberlaine for the last yeare
wherein he Chargeth himselfe with Receipt of   48   16 06
And is [sic] disbursments to be   54   13 02
Remaines due to him upon his Account   06   03 04
Which is ordered to be paid unto him upon the Receipt of money by the next Chamberlaine.

Persons appointed to examine Accounts.
At this Court it is ordered that Mr Grant, Mr Taylor, Mr Robert Calcraft, Mr Richard Calcraft, Mr Tomlinson, Mr Holley, Robert Cole, Edward Paulett, Thomas Fishar and William Berriffe do meete on Wednesday next at one of the Clocke in the Afternoone to examine the Accounts of the Churchwardens and Chamberlaine and to returne their proceedinges therein the next Court day.

The tolles assigned over to the Gentlemen that are ingaged for the debts of the Corporacion.

Whereas there is severall members of this Court bound for the perticular debts of this Corporacion and as yet have noe Counter Securitie but the orders of former Courts and they being made long since the Gentlemen that are bound made it their request to the Court that they would please to give them securitie by the Towne Seale or Assignement of the lease of the tolles Whereupon the Court takeing the same into their consideracion do hereby order that the said tolles be assigned over to the severall Persons that are ingaged for the Townes debts for the saveing of them harmles from the same And that the Assignement be drawne against the next Court.

Constables Account.

At this Court the severall Constables gives an Account of the Constables Assessment for the last yeare as followeth vzt

Marketplace bill	06 02 04
Abatements not allowed of	00 05 08
Collected and paid in	05 16 08
High Streete bill	03 04 11
Abatements not allowed of	00 02 04
Collected and paid	03 02 07
Westgate bill	02 07 02
Abatements not allowed of	00 02 05
Collected and paid in	02 04 09
Walkergate bill	00 18 06
Abatments allowed of	00 00 06
Collected and paid	00 18 00
Swinegate bill	01 08 10
Abatements allowed of	00 00 08
Collected & paid	01 08 02
Castlegate bill	02 08 00
Abatements not allowed of	00 10 08
Collected & paid	01 17 04

[fo. 418v] **Second Court of Thomas Short, 15 November 1667**

The order for Assignement of the tolles confirmed.

At this Court it is ordered that the order made the last Court day for assigneing over the tolles to the Gentlemen that are ingaged for the Townes debts for their Counter securitie be this day confirmed and that there be a meeteing at the Hutch upon breakeing up of the Court to Seale the said Assignement.

Anthony Hotchkin Account as Chaimberlaine respited.
At this Court is ordered that the Account of Anthony Hotchkin as Chaimberlaine be respited as to the vj li paid to Mr Leeming for his sallory by reason he detaines the Townes plate And that the vj li which is in the hands of Henry Rudkin the Farmor of the tolles be paid to the present Alderman in part of his sallory.

Constables to cleare their Assessment.
At this Court it is ordered that the Constables of every place do forthwith cleare their severall bills of the Constables Assessment and pay the same in to the present Chaimberlaine and such as cleare their Accounts the Chaimberlaine is hereby ordered to pay of their bills of disbursments and not otherwise.

An Iron Grate to be bought for the Conduit.
At this Court it is ordered that the Chaimberlaine provide an Iron Grate for the safetie of the Conduit Cocke and that the same be done with all convenience.

Mr Chaimberlaine & Mr Hobson use money paid.
At this Court it is ordered that the x li due from Henry Rudkin for the last Quarters Rent of the tolles be paid as followeth (that is to say) vj li to Mr Grant and Mr Taylor which they laid downe for Mr Chaimberlaines use money And iiij li to Mr Richard Calcraft for Mr Hobsons use money.

Collectors for the Schoole Rents to cleare their Accounts.
At this Court it is ordered that the Collectors for the Schoole House land do cleare their Accounts for the next Court day And that William Laine pay in all such moneys as remaines in his hands upon his Account as Churchwarden.

[fo. 419r] **Third Court of Thomas Short, 20 December 1667**

Townes Halfe to be sett forth.
Whereas Mr Alderman this day acquainted the Court that severall Corporacions have sett forth brasse halfe pence with the Townes Armes on them for the benefitt of the poore of the said Townes and that it might be very advantageous for this Corporacion to set forth halfe pence with the Armes of this Towne upon them and desired this Court to take the same into their consideracion Whereupon this Court haveing considered of the benefitt that may accrue thereby doth order that the present Chaimberlaine do send to London for brasse Halfepence with the Chequor of the one side and Grantham and the yeare of our Lord on the other side and to be written aboute the Rim, to be exchanged by the Overseer of the Poore And that the same be obtained as soone as may be.

An order against Water Carts with shodd Wheeles.
Whereas the Court this day takeing into consideracion the great damage that is done by the water Carts of William Fearon and others haveing Irons aboute the Wheeles

which doth breake up the pavements in the streetes and in the Well laine hath done very much hurt for prevention whereof for the future It is hereby ordered that notice be given forthwith to the said William Fearon and such other person or Persons that use the like water Carts to forbeare goeing any longer with shodd Wheeles, but such as are made without Iron And that if the said William Fearon or any other Person or Persons whatsoever shall offend contrary to this order after Plowday next, he and they receiveing proffitt by carrieing of Water for other people, that then every such Person shall forfeite five shillinges aweeke for every weeke so offending to be levied of their goodes and Chattells for the use of this Burrough.

Henry Rudkin to pay his Rent to the Chaimberlaine.
Whereas Henry Rudkin the present Farmor of the tolles belonging to this Burrough is in Arreare vj li for the Rent of the said Tolles for the yeare past Which vj li Mr Leeming the late Alderman pretends was promised to be paid to him And since the said promise made if any were Mr Leeming detaineing the Townes Plate for a debt due to him form this Corporacion and this Court valueing the said plate to amount to the full of his debt and much more and the said Henry Rudkin haveing not paid the said vj li It is therefore at this Court fully ordered that the said Henry Rudkin forbeare paying the said vj li to Mr Leeming and he pay the same to the present Chaimberlaine for the Townes use and the Chamberlaines Acquittance shall be his sufficient discharge.

Castlegate Constable to cleare his Account.
At this Court it is ordered that Constable for Castlegate cleare his Acount the next Court day upon a paine of xs.

[fo. 419v] **Fourth Court of Thomas Short 10 January 1667/8**

An Assessment of xxx li to be made for repaires of the Church.
Whereas William Bury the present Churchwarden this day acquainted the Court that the Church is very much out of repaires and that unlesse some speedy care betaken for repaireing thereof part of it is likely to fall downe which may be prevented by raiseing of a finale Assessment to be laid out for the repaireing of it Whereupon this Court takeing the same into their consideracion doth hereby order that an Assessment of xxx li be made and laid upon this Parish for the laid out for repairacion of the said Church And that notice thereof be given in the Church the next Sunday to the Inhabitants of this Parish of the time and place when and where the said Assessment shall be made that noe excepcions may be taken at the makeing thereof.

Mr Alderman & other Gentlemen appointed to waite upon Sir William Thorrold aboute the Subscripcion.
At this Court Mr Alderman and Mr Richard Calcraft are desired to goe to Stamford to Sir William Thorrold and to take the Towne Clarke with them to intreat Sir Williams

favour to subscribe his sume to the subscripcion for the getting this Auntient Corporacion out of debt and to give an Account of it the next Court.

The title of the Redd Lyon to be tryed in the name of William Laine.
At this Court it is ordered that William Laine be putt in as Lessee in the declaracion of Ejectment for the Redd Lyon And that he be saved harmles and indempnified from all charges and damages that may happen by reason thereof.

Henry Rudkin to be sued for Arreares of Rent.
At this Court it is ordered that if Henry Rudkin refuse to pay the vj li remaineing in his hands for Arreares of Rent for the last yeare that an Accion be brought against him for recovery of the same.

Sessions dinners to be taken into consideracion.
At this Court it is ordered that the Charge of Session dinners be taken into consideracion the next Court day.

The Constables to assist the Overseers for High Streete Well.
At this Court it is likewise ordered that the Constables of High Streete and Castlegate do assist Christofer Hauley and of the Overseers for High Streete Well to collect the Assessment laid upon the said Streetes for the repaireing and scouring of the Well aforesaid.

The Cage to be made lesser.
At this Court it is ordered that the Cage be removed under part of the cover of Marketplace Pumpe and made lesser then it were.

[fo. 500r] Fifth Court of Thomas Short, 20 January 1667/8

[*The date is partly crossed through and if it was written as 20 January, it is unlikely to have been correct as the previous Court was held just ten days earlier and the next Court is 27 March, a much longer interval than normal.*]

The Conduit to be repaired.
This day Mr Alderman acquainted the Court that the Conduit was very much out of repair and that if some speedy care was not taken the same would fall to ruine Whereupon this Court takeing the same into their consideracion do hereby order that an estimate be taken what repaires are necessarie and the charge thereof and an Account given of the same the next Court day that an Assesment may be made for the raiseing of money to be laid out in the repaireing thereof.

Henry Rudkin to pay his Rent in Court.
Whereas also upon the Examineing of the payments of Rent by Henry Rudkin for the tolles it appeares that most of the said money is laid out for other uses then what is

ordered by the Court And to prevent the same for the future and that interest money may be duly paid It is ordered for the time to come that the said Henry Rudkin do pay his Rent in open Court to the then Chaimberlaine to be by him laid out and disposed of as the Court shall direct from time to time and not otherwise.

William Laine to collect the Arreares of the Church Assessment.
At this Court it is ordered that William Laine the late Churchwarden do collect and gather the Arreares of the Church Assessment and that he pay the same to the present Churchwarden to be by him laid out for and towards the repaireing of the Church.

Castlegate Constables to perfect their Accounts.
At this Court it is ordered that Mr Lenton late Collector for the Schoole Rents and the late Constables of Castlegate do cleare their Accounts the next Court day upon paine of xxs apeice.

Henry Coverly & Marke Harmes [sic] Overseers for Westgate Well.
At this Court Henry Coverly and Marke Harnes are appointed Overseers for Westgate Well and they are hereby ordered to take care from time to time that the said Well be sufficiently repaired and scoured so as that it may be usefull to the Inhabitants of the said Streete.

Anthony Hodgsons Account passed.
At this Court it is ordered that the Account of Anthony Hotchkin [sic] the late Chaimberlaine be this day past and that the same be entred into the Chaimberlaines Booke of Accoun[ts] and the sume of money due to him upon his Account be paid with all convenient Speed.

Townes halfe pence sent for.
At this Court it is ordered that xx li weight of the Townes halfe pence be sent for this weeke And that the same shall from time to time be exchanged by the Chaimberlaine the benefitt and proffitt thereof accrueing to this Corporacion.

[fo. 500v] **Sixth Court of Thomas Short, 27 March 1668**

John Pateman compounds for Meres Goodes that killed one Waite.
At this Court came John Pateman Brother to the wife of Nathaniell Meres who was found guilty the last Sessions of Manslaughter upon the body of one Richard Waite of Denton within this libertie and the said John Pateman desired to compound for the estate reall and personall of the said Nathaniell Meres for the good of his sister there being some debts oweing which cannot be recovered untill a Composicion be made and he also desired this Court to be favourable to his Sister in regard there is one bond of xx li due from one Thomas Parnham of Somerby which upon the payment of vj li gott a release from the said Nathaniell Meres for the said xx li, but it is disputable whether

the said release be good or not that makes her in some hopes of the Recovery thereof it being the greatest part of her estate Whereupon this Court in consideracion of the sume of foure pounds of lawfull money of England well and truly paid or secured to be paid doth hereby grant bargaine & sell unto the said Widdow Meres all the estate reall and personall of her late husbands To hold to her, her heires Executors or Administrators forever without rendring any Account thereof for the same And it is hereby likewise agreed that if shee recover the Remainder of the debt due from Thomas Parnham that then shee shall well and truly pay in to this Court the sume of xxs for the use of this Corporacion without any fraud or further delay.

The Towne Clarke gives an Account of the suite aboute the Redd Lyon.
This day the Towne Clarke acquainted the Court of his proceedinges at London the last terme upon the title of the Redd Lyon, that Mr Christian after severall mocions made was forced to relinquish all his right and title to the said Inn at Common law and stands to his equitie in the Chancery he alleadgeing that he and his Father have laid out 600s which they are not yet reinbursed and hath nothing else to alleadge for his title so as that if the Towne prove that he hath had satisfaccion either by his lease or letters Pattents, Councill is of oppinion he must necessariely be outed The Towne Clarke also acquaints this Court of the Charge that hath beene expended in the said suite from the first which as by the perticulars appeares comes to 158 li 0s 9d [*sic*] &c there hath beene paid thereof to him xj li vijs vjd and that here remaines due to him 46 li 13s 6d which he desired this Court will take order for the payment of the same Whereupon it is ordered that speedy care be taken for the provideing money to pay of the said bill and for paying of the charge that shall happen the next terme.

An Assessment of v li for repaires of the Conduit.
At this Court it is ordered that an Assessment of five pounds be made and laid upon this Burrough of Grantham for the present repaires of the Conduit being for the generall good of the towne, And Mr Richard Calcraft, Robert Cole, Henry Coverly & Thomas Cole are appointed Assessors thereof and the Constables in every Ward Collectors and that they give an Account of the makeing of at the next Court day.

[fo. 501r] **Seventh Court of Thomas Short, 19 April 1668**

John Poole admitted Tennant to Thompsons lease.
At this Court came John Poole and desired to be admitted Tenant to a house in Walkergate formerly leased to Christofer Thompson which he hath assigned over to him And this Court takeing the same into their consideracion as that the said John Poole is likely to be a good tenant doth hereby admitt and allow of the said John Poole to be Tenant to the said premisses for and during the Remainder of the terme in the said lease yet to come and unexpired he giveing Thomas Bearnes to be a Bondsman with him for the performance of Covenants And he gives her [*sic*] in Court by Way of Attornement ijs vjd.

Widdow Nidd renews her lease.
At this Court came Widdow Nidd and takes a lease of a certaine house in Swinegate & land in Allington feild belonging to the Schoole House for xxj yeares from and after the Expiracion of a former lease thereof in being paying the sume of xiij li vjs viijd for a fine in manner following (that is to say) xij li upon the xxvijth day of Aprill instant and xxvjs & viijd at Michaelmas now next ensueing and giveing securitie to pay and performe all Auntient Rents and Covenants heretofore made And shee gives in earnerst thereof xijd.

Widdow Winge compounds for her husbands Goods he being found a felo de se.
At this Court came Widdow Winge late wife of John Winge of Denton who was found *felo de se* and desired to compound for the personall estate of the said John Winge for the good of her Children And there being many debts oweing by him shee desired the favour of this Court to take a reasonable Composicion that shee may be enabled to pay the said debts And Whereas one Edward Gunby of the said Towne made it his humble request to Mr Alderman and his Brethren to acquaint the Court this day that there is x li due to him upon bond from the said John Winge and unless this Court would be pleased to releive him and order the said Widdow Winge either to pay him his money or give him securitie for it he is likely to loose his whole debt which is the greatest part of his livelihood Whereupon this Court considering that a moderate Composicion being for the good of the Widdow and her Children and enable her to pay her debts and especially the x li to Edward Gunby, for the consideracion of vj li xiijs iiijd and of her giveing securitie to the said Edward Gunby doth grant bargaine and sell unto the said Widdow Winge all the personall estate of her late husbands To hold to her and her Executors Administrators and Assigns without rendring any Account thereof for the same And it likewise agreed that shee give securitie by bond with her Brother Christofer Filding for paying of the said vj li xiijs iiijd upon the Nine and twentieth day of September now next ensueing.

William Bury to pay vij li to the Chaimberlaine that was formerly lent to the Churchwarden.
At this Court it is ordered that William Bury Churchwarden do pay the vij li formerly lent by the Chaimberlaine for payment of a debt due to William Palmer for worke done at the Church And that the vij li together with xij li part of the fine of Widdow Nidds lease be paid by the Chaimberlaine to the Towne Clarke in part of his Charges expended aboute the Redd Lyon.

[fo. 501v] **Eighth Court of Thomas Short, 28 April 1668**

Widdow Nidd payes x li in part of her fine.
At this Court came Widdow Nidd and paid xij li [*sic*] in part of the fine due from her for the lease she tooke of this Corporacion.

The fine of Bristows lease to pay use money.
This day Mr Alderman acquainted the Court that there were severall Persons in Arreare of their use money and that he was dayly called on for the same and desired that some speedy care might be taken for payment thereof Whereupon it is ordered that the lease of Thomas Bristowes of Spittlegate be lett the next Court day And that the money raised upon the said lease be disposed of towards the payment of the interest money in Arreare and for noe other use whatsoever.

William Bury to pay vij li to the Towne Clarke which was formerly lent by the Chaimberlaine.
Whereas the former Chaimberlaines of this Towne have heretofore lent vij li to the Churchwarden for the payment of money due to William Palmer for worke done at the Church and upon lending thereof it was agreed by a former order of this Court that when an Assessment was made for repaires of the Church the said vij li should be repaid to the Towne as soone as there was so much money raised out of the said Assessment And whereas by a late order of this Court It was agreed that an Assessment of xxx li should be made by William Bury Churchwarden and then likewise ordered that the first vij li that could be raised out of the said Assessment should be paid to the Towne for the said money lent by the Chaimberlaine And the said William Bury haveing since made the said Assessment and received the greatest part thereof doth delay the paying of the said vij li contrarey to the orders of this Court Whereupon it is ordered that the Towne Clarke shall have the said vij li in part of the charges due to him from the Corporacion And if the said William Bury shall refuse or neglect to pay the same that then the said Towne Clarke shall have libertie to sue for the said vij li he bearing the Charge himselfe.

Colebuyers appointed for thensueing [sic] *yeare.*
At this Court Thomas Cole and Nicholas Becke are appointed Colebuyers for the ensueing yeare.

[fo. 502r] **Ninth Court of Thomas Short, 26 June 1668**

Treasurers appointed for the Subscripcions.
At this Court it is ordered that John Coddington, Robert Cole, Thomas Matkin and John Turner be Treasurers for receiveing of all such money as shall be raised by way of Benevolence towards the getting this Auntient Corporacion out of debt.

Persons appointed to examine Accounts.
At the Court it is ordered that Mr Grant, Mr Richard Calcraft, Robert Cole and John Turner do meete and examine the Accounts of William Laine late Churchwarden and returne there proceedinges therein the next Court day.

Thomas Bristow renews his lease.
At this Court came Thomas Bristow and takes a lease of a house and land at Spittlegate belonging to the Schoole House for xxj yeares from and after the Expiracion of a former lease thereof in being, paying the sume of xxvj li for a fine and giveing securitie to pay and performe Auntient Rent and Covenants And he gives in earnest thereof ijs vjd.

An order for the Elleccion [sic] of the Succeeding Alderman.
For the more peaceable and orderly proceedinges at the Eleccion of the next succeeding Alderman It is at this Court ordered that upon the next Eleccion day Mr Richard Holley be sent downe into the Church to Mr Richard Calcraft and Mr Joseph Tomlinson to make three Comburgesses there Out of which three Comburgesses in the Church It is likewise agreed that Mr Richard Calcraft be brought upon the Cuisheon or place of Eleccion to Mr Chirstofer Hanson and Mr Robert Calcraft to make three Comburgesses there Out of which three Comburgesses upon the Cusheon Mr Robert Calcraft is nominated Alderman for this next ensueing yeare.

Mr Grants Account of the Townes halfe pence.
At this Court Mr Grant gives an Account what proffitt hath accrued to the Towne by

	li	s	d
by [sic] six and forty pound weight of the Townes halfe pence His charge	21	02	03
His disbursments –	11	05	09
Remaines due to the Towne –	09	16	06

Which he payes unto Thomas Matkin the present Chaimberlaine.

Anthony Hodgson [sic] chosen of the 2d Company.
At this Court Anthony Hotchkin is chosen one of the second Company in the roome of Zachary Cox lately dismissed the Court at his request
In the Kallender
John Walker
John Plumer
Thomas Charles

[fo. 502v] **Tenth Court of Thomas Short, 8 July 1668**

An order for what time the Churchwardens and Overseers for the poore shall be freed from the Colleccion.
Whereas upon the reading the Account of William Laine late Churchwarden for some Arreares that are to collect It is observed that the Overseers for the Poore are freed from their Colleccions for the payments to the Church and poore for a yeare and a halfe And the Churchwardens and Sidesmen for three yeares which is thought to be very unreasonable Whereupon for the setling the same for the future It is ordered that the Overseers for the Poore shall be freed to the payments to the Church and Poore as to the Quarteridge to the Church Assessment for one yeare from the Comencement of their

time to the end thereof. And that the Churchwardens be freed from the like charge for two yeares from the takeing upon them the said places by reason of their continuance of trouble for two yeares as Churchwardens and Sidsmen and not any longer.

John Turner to be freed from the Colleccion to the Poore for seaven yeares for takeing a Poore Boy Apprentice.
At this Court John Turner acquainted Mr Alderman and the rest of the Court that he had taken a Poore Boy of James Fancourts Apprentice and that he hath beene with him two yeares And upon takeing the said Boy an Apprentice It was agreed by the then Alderman that he should be freed from his Colleccion to the Poore for seaven yeares during the continuance of the Boys terme by reason he tooke him without any Charge to the Towne and found him Cloaths And the said John Turner now desired that an order in pursuance to the said Agreement may be entred into the Court Booke Whereupon it is ordered that the said John Turner for the takeing of the said Boy an Apprentice and the provideing of him Cloths and other necessaries for the said terme shall be acquitted of his Colleccion for two yeares past and shall likewise be freed for five yeares now next ensueing.

Mr Christofer Hanson dismissed from the place of a Comburgesse.
Whereas Mr Alderman this day acquainted the Court that Mr Christofer Hanson one of the Comburgesses of this Court had moved him to desire the Court to dismiss him from the said place of a Comburgesse upon which Mr Tomlinson and Mr Cole was desired by the Court to goe to Mr Hanson and to wish him to come to the Court and to desire the same himselfe And upon their returne they give this relacion that he was very weake and Auntient and therefore desired his dismission and that he had formerly acquainted Mr Alderman with it Whereupon it is ordered that the said Mr Hanson be dismissed from the said place and he is dismissed accordingly.

William Laines Account of the Arreares of the Church Assessment.
At this Court William Laine late Churchwarden gives an Account of his Arreares
the charge whereof amounts to	05 18 01
disbursments since	02 19 11
Arreares still remaineing	01 18 06
Remaines to the Towne	00 19 08

At [*sic*] it is ordered that the Arreares & the sume of xixs viijd be paid to Mr Edward Paulett late Churchwarden being due to him upon his Account.

[fo. 503r] Eleventh Court of Thomas Short, 31 July 1668

Hugh Smith admitted Tennant to Tomlyns lease.
At this Court came Hugh Smith and desired to be admitted Tenant to the house and premisses leased to Thomas Tomlyn he haveing made the said Hugh Smith Executor Whereupon this Court admitts of him And he gives by way of Attornement ijs.

Widdow Dyes Account for her late Husband as Colebuyer.
At this Court Widdow Dye wife of John Dye lately deceased who was Colebuyer for the last yeare and brought in the Account of her late husband of his Receipts and disbursments

as Colebuyer whereof his Receipts was	12	15	00
Out of which disbursed for Coles	10	08	08
Remaines	02	01	04
And he gives Account of the increase of the stocke in the said yeare which comes to	02	12	01
So there remaines for stocke for Coles	15	07	00

Which shee payes to Thomas Cole the new Colebuyer and is discharged.

The Towne Clarkes Account against Mr Fancourts for Mr Pells money.
At this Court the Towne Clarke gives an Account that Mr Fancourts Thomas Hatfeild and Richard Frisby to prolong time and to delay the paying in of Mr Pells money have pleaded *non est factum* Whereupon it is ordered that the Towne Clarke give notice to Mr Fancourts and the rest to give satisfaccion to Mr Alderman and his Brethren within a fortnight or otherwise proceedinges to be against them to tryall for recovery of the said money.

Thomas Bristow payes the fine of his lease.
At this Court came Thomas Bristow and payes in xxj li xvjs the Remainder of his fine of his lease, iiij li iiijs being paid before for the Rent of the tolles, And for the paying of some interest money It is ordered that the x li due from Henry Rudkin for the Rent of the tolles the xvth of August next be added to the said xxj li xvjs And for the raiseing of iij li xs more to make up xxxv li vjs this Court desires John Plumer the present Chaimberlaine to lay downe the same to which the said John Plumer doth condiscend And for the repaying of the said iij li: xs It is ordered that the same be paid out of the fine to be raised by Widdow Matkins lease And it is further ordered an Account being taken what interest money is in Arreare, that the severall sumes of money hereunder written be paid in part of Arreares and that Mr Chomley, Mr Chaimberlaine and Mrs Clarke be paid at present and the rest to stay till Henry Rudkin pay the said x li.

Interest money paid.

	Arreares due	Arreares paid in part
Mr Welby	12 00 00	07 10 00
Mr Chomeley	15 00 00	12 00 00
Mr Chaimberlaine	06 00 00	03 00 00
Mr Ashton	09 00 00	03 00 00
Mrs Clarke	15 00 00	06 00 00

[fo. 503v] **Twelfth Court of Thomas Short, 21 August 1668**

Henry Rudkin to pay his Rent.
At this Court Henry Rudkin was sent for to pay his Quarters Rent due for the tolles the fifteenth day of August instant and he appearing in Court It is ordered that the said Henry Rudkin pay his Rent to the Chaimberlaine at or before Michaelmas next to be disposed of, according to an order made the last Court for the paying of use money and to and for noe other use intent or purpose whatsoever.

The tolles assigned over to severall Persons that are ingaged for the debts of this Corporacion.
Whereas this Court and Henry Rudkin who formerly had a lease of the tolles belonging to this Burrough not agreeing for the lease of the tolles this yeare It was moved by severall Persons ingaged for the publike debts of this Corporacion that Mr Grant, Mr Taylor, Mr Holley and Mr Humes being Gentlemen ingaged with others might take care for receiveing the money that shall be raised by the said tolles Whereupon it is ordered that the said Mr Grant, Mr Taylor, Mr Holley and Mr Humes with others that are ingaged do take care and imploy Persons to receive the money due for the tolles belonging to this Burrough And that they pass their Accounts monthly in open Court and pay all such money as remaines in their or any of their hands to the Chaimberlaine for the time being And the said Chaimberlaine is hereby also ordered that he shall not dispose of any part of the said money to any publike use whatsoever till all the interest money for which the said Gentlemen and others are ingaged and the Rent to the Queenes Majestie be first satisfied and paid that is due to her for the said tolles any order heretofore made to the contrarey notwithstanding.
And if the Chaimberlaine shall at any time hereafter dispose of any of the money raised by the tolles till the interest money and Queenes Rent be first paid as aforesaid that then it shall be lawfull to and for the Gentlemen ingaged as aforesaid to receive the profitts of the said tolles and dispose thereof to the uses before mentioned giveing an Account of all such Overplus of money as shall remaine in their or any of their hands and paying the same to the Chaimberlaine for the time being for the use of this Corporacion.

Nicholas Becke, Isaacke Hall, Thomas Rowley, Edward Archer, George Kenion, Henry Godley, John Middlebrooke made free.
At this Court came Nicholas Becke, Izaacke Hall Forrainer Apprentice to Edward Watson Sadler, Thomas Rowley Apprentice to Thomas Charles Baker, Edward Archer Apprentice to John Walker Taylor, George Kenion Apprentice to his Father Edward Kenion Glasier, Henry Godley Apprentice to his Father Bryan Godley Butcher and John Middlebrooke Apprentice to Thomas Hatfeild Butcher and desired to be admitted free Burgesses in this Corporacion they haveing severally served seaven yeares Apprenticeshipp to the said severall trades within this Burrough to whose requests this Court doth condiscend Whereupon the said Izaacke Hall and Thomas Rowley as Forrainers do pay their vs a peice to the Common Box And the said Nicholas Becke Edward Archer George Kenion Henry Godley & John Middlebrooke do pay ijs vjd

apeice to the Box as Freeborne and payes their fees to Clarke & Serjents and takes the oath of Freemen according to the Auntient custome of this Burrough.

[fo. 504r] Thirteenth Court of Thomas Short, 15 September 1668

An order for payment of Richard Blacks bill.
At this Court Richard Blacke produced a bill of iij li xvjs vjd due to him for Sessions dinners for the Grand Jury and acquainted the Court that part of it had beene oweing aboute two yeares Whereupon it is ordered that the Chamberlaine pay the said iij li xvjs vjd unto the said Richard Blacke upon the riseing of Court.

An order for raiseing xviij li for payment of Constables bills.
At this Court it is ordered that an Assessment of xviij li be made and laid upon this Towne of Grantham for the payment of the Constables their bills of disbursments for this present yeare an estimate being taken what the same amounted unto, And the Cheife Constables and Under Constables are appointed Assessors and the Under Constables Collectors thereof And it is also ordered that notice be given in the Church the next Sunday of the time and place of makeing the said Assessment that such Persons as are therein concerned may if they please be there present.

An order for payment of the Recorders Sallory.
Whereas the Towne Clarke this day acquainted the Court that the Recorder desired they would please to take some care for the payment of the Arreares of his sallory which comes to iij li and his Clarkes to vs Whereupon this Court doth order that the present Chaimberlaine do pay the same to them before the keepeing of the next Sessions.

Michins Rent setled.
Whereas there hath beene a dispute about the Rent of Michins house and land in the Sands for many yeares past he inioying onely halfe the House and the other not being inhabited and for the setling the same for the future It is ordered that the part of the House that is empty and that the land is of too High a Rent he shall be abated yearely xiijs iiijd and that the Collectors Booke be rectified accordingly.

John Scot to have xs a weeke for collecting the tolles.
At this Court it is ordered that John Scot shall have for his care and paines in collecting the money due for the tolles belonging to the Corporacion the sume of xijd a weeke allowed him and that the same be paid him by the present Chaimberlaine weekely.

[fo. 504v] **Fourteenth Court of Thomas Short, 2 October 1668**

Constables charge at Sessions to be paid out of the Constables Assessment.
Whereas it being this day moved that it is the practice of all the Constables in the Country that appeare at Sessions to putt such charges as they then expend upon the Townes Account where they serve as Constables and deduct the same out of the money raised by way of an Assessment for the paying them their disbursments And being taken into consideracion by this Court It is held a very just and proper way by reason they serve on the behalfe of the publike Whereupon it is ordered for the time to come that what charge the Constables of the Towne shall expend for their dinners at the Session or Sessions shall be paid and allowed to them againe out of the money raised by the Constables Assessment.

A lease of part of the plow lett to Thomas Matkin.
At this Court Thomas Matkin takes a lease of part of the House called the plow which was formerly demised to his Father being parcell of the lands belonging to the Towne for one and twenty yeares from and after the Expiracion of a former lease thereof yet in being paying the sume of viij li for a fine the next Court day upon sealing of his lease And he gives in earnest thereof xijd.

John Plumer Chaimberlaine reimbursed viij li.
At this Court it is ordered that the Eight pounds raised by the lease of the said Thomas Matkin shall be paid into the hands of John Plumer Chaimberlaine for the reimburseing him the money laid out by him on the Townes Account out of the money raised by the profitt of the tolles belonging to this Corporacion.

The Subscripcions to purchase the Milles.
Whereas Mr Alderman this day moved the Court that it was his desire to have the subscripcion pursued and that if there were some way found out for the disposall of the money by purchaseing of the Milles the Subscribors would give more chearefully Whereupon it is ordered that all such moneys as shall be raised by the subscricions shall be paid for the redeeming of the Milles (if they can be obtained) and for want thereof to be disposed to and for such uses as the Major part of the Benefactors shall thinke convenient and to and for noe other use intent or purpose whatsoever.

Waites Compiscion [sic] *money to be collected.*
At this Court it is ordered that John Pateman be called upon for the foure pounds due for the Composicion made by him for his sisters husband Waite of Denton that was found guilty of Manslaughter.

[fo. 505r] **Fifteenth Court of Thomas Short, 16 October 1668**

John Shootewell to be made free.
At this Court came John Shootewell Forrainer and desired to be admitted a Freeman of this Corporacion And he doth at this Court promise and agree to and with the Alderman and Burgesses to repair the Pipes in the Conduit feild for bringing the Water to the Conduit at his owne proper cost and charges for three yeares now next ensueing with all manner of Plummers worke whatsoever.

Thomas Cole fined xs for uncivill words.
Whereas upon the makeing of the said John Shootewell free Thomas Cole a Comoner of this Court did crave leave to speake in Court for to prevent the Freedome of the said John Shootewell and upon debatement thereof this Court thought it reasonable he be may [sic] made free and the said Thomas Cole replied that there was not a man in Court that spoke on the behalfe of Shootewell that did care whether the Towne did sincke or swome which words did tend much to the opposicion of the Goverment of this Corporacion and for prevention of such offence by severall orders of this Court the same are made finable Whereupon this Court takeing the same into their consideracion do hereby impose a fine of xs upon the said Thomas Cole for the misdeameanour aforesaid and doth order that if he do not pay the said xs the next Court day that then the same be levied by distresse and sale of his goodes for the use of this Corporacion.

Mr Rawlinson chosen of the first Company.
At this Court Edward Rawlinson is chosen one of the first Company and doth take oaths incident to the said Office.

John Plumer chosen of the 2d Company.
At this Court John Plumer is likewise chosen of the second Company and doth take the oath incident to the said place and office.
In the Kallender
John Walker
Thomas Charles
John Pape.

[fo. 505v] **The last Court of Thomas Short, 22 October 1668**

The Subscripcions to be pursued and the disposall of the money.
Whereas Mr Alderman this day moved the Court that it was his desire the Subscripcions should be pursued, and that if there were some way found out for the disposall of the money by purchaseing the Milles the Subscribors would give more chearefully Whereupon it is ordered that all such monies as shall be raised by the Subscripcions shall be paid for the redeeming of the Milles if they can be obtained and for want thereof

to be disposed to and for such uses as the Major part of the Benefactors shall thinke convenient and to and for noe other use intent or purpose whatsoever.

The Ingagers for the Townes debt to have the proffitts of the tolles.
At this Court it is ordered that Mr Grant, Mr Taylor, Mr Holley, Mr Humes and the rest of the Gentlemen that stands ingaged for the debts of this Corporacion shall inioy the proffitts of the tolles for one whole yeare from the day of the date hereof and to dispose of the profitts to the uses mentioned in a former order made at the twelveth Court of this present Alderman as by the same relacion being had may more fully appeare.

Henry Rudkin to be sued for the Rent of the tolle.
At this Court it is ordered with the consent of Henry Rudkin now present that he pay his Quarters Rent to John Plumer the present Chaimberlaine on Satterday next and for non payment it is also ordered that the Towne Clarke shall proceed against him at law for recoverey thereof.

John Pateman to be [sic] *pay Waites Composicion.*
At this Court it is ordered that John Pateman be called upon for the foure pounds due and made by him as a Composicion for the estate of his Brother Waite of Denton that was here convicted of manslaughter.

John Still admitted Tennant to a house in Walkergate demised to Mr John Miller.
At this Court came John Still and desired to be admitted Tenant to a lease formerly made to Mr John Miller of a house in Walkergate and Mr Taylor being present in Court and Executor to Mr Miller desired that he might be admitted Whereupon the Court admitts of the said John Still to be Tenant giveing securitie for Rent and repaires And he gives by Way of Attornement to Mr Alderman xijd.

Mr Aldermans Account for Passingers.
At this Court Mr Alderman doth account for all monies received by him on the Common Affaires of the Towne as upon penall Statutes &c As also for his payments and disbursments on the Account of the publike And he chargeth himselfe with the Receipt upon penall Statutes

which he gave to the Poore as he received it the sume of	00 07 06
And his disbursments in the same yeare to amount unto	07 11 07

Which is paid to him in open Court.

[fo. 506r]

Mr Alderman Account for the Conduit.
At this Court Mr Alderman also accounteth for his Receipts and layinges forth aboute the Repaires of the Conduit and he chargeth with the Receipt of the Conduit Assessment the sume of   05 01 04

And his disbursments to be	07	00	00
Remaines due to him	01	18	08

Mr Aldermans Account for halfe pence.
Mr Alderman further accounteth for forty pound weight of Townes

halfe pence to be	19	00	00
Paid for them at London and Carriage downe	08	08	02
For building the Crosse	08	15	11
To the Chaimberlaine	03	00	00
Remaines due to him upon the Account	01	04	01

Mr Aldermans Account for the Cage.
Mr Alderman also accounteth for the Receipts and layings out for repaireing the Cage and he chargeth himselfe with Receipts for the

lead that was on the Cage	02	08	06
And his disbursments to be	02	18	06
Remaines due to him upon this Account	00	09	06

Mr Aldermans Account for Sessions fines.
And lastly Mr Alderman accounteth for his Receipts of Sessions fines and the charge of one Sessions dinner & he chargeth himselfe with

Receipt of	02	12	08
And his disbursments to be –	02	00	00
Remaines due to the Towne –	00	12	08
So as there is due to Mr Alderman upon the severall Accounts disbursments to Passingers excepted	02	19	07

At this Court the Coroner, Churchwarden and the Collector for the Schoole Rents have further time to passe their Accounts.

Escheators Account.

At this Court Mr George Short Escheator for the yeare past accounteth and chargeth himselfe with the Receipt of severall Persons for light unlawfull and defective weights & Measures forfeited by the Statute the sume of	00	09	00
And that out of the same he hath paid himselfe his charges at every faire and ii s to the Towne Clarke for his paines	00	04	06
Remaines to the Towne	00	05	06

Which he payes in open Court and he is discharged.

Chaimberlaines Account.
At this Court Thomas Matkin one of the Chaimberlaine for the yeare past accounteth for his

Receipts and disbursments on the Common Affaire of the Towne and
he chargeth himselfe   92 01 03
And his disbursments to be   91 07 03
Remaines due to the Towne   00 14 00
Which he payes in open Court and he is discharged.

[fo. 506v]

The twelve Constables gives an Account of the Constables Assessment as followeth

Thomas Charles Thomas Archer	Constables for the Markett place their bill	09 15 06
	Abatements –	00 04 00
	Collected and paid in	09 10 06
Hamlett Brumpton John Pape	Constables for High Streete their bill	03 12 05
	Collected and paid in	
Henry Coverly Francis Charitie	Constables for Westgate their bill	02 16 11
	Abatements –	00 02 04
	Collected & paid in	02 14 07
John Still Thomas Cole	Constables for Walkergate	00 17 00
	Collected & paid in	
Edward Bristow Nicholas Becke	Constables for Swinegate their bill	01 11 01
	Abatements	00 01 05
	Collected and paid in	01 10 01
Thomas Frith William Bristow	Constables for Castlegate their bill	02 09 00
	Collected & paid	

At this Court the Common Box was opened and xviijs taken out for the Towns use.

[fo. 507r]

At an Assembly holden by Mr Thomas Short Alderman and the Comburgesses and Burgesses of Grantham aforesaid in Corpus Christi Quire within the Prebendarie Church there &c on Friday next after St lukes day being 23 October 1668.

First did sitt downe upon the Cusheon or place of Eleccion the said Mr Thomas Short in Corpus Christi Quire within the Prebendarie Church there

Nest to him did sitt upon the Chusheon [sic] or place of Election one other Comburgesse vzt Mr Robert Calcraft

Then was there in the Church two Combursses [sic] vzt Mr Richard Calcraft and Mr Joseph Tomlinson

Then was sent downe into the Church to those two Comburgesses to make them three one other Comburgesse vzt Mr Richard Holley

Out of which three Comburgesses in the Church one was chosen to come up and sitt upon the Chusheon or place of Election one other Comburgesse vzt Mr Richard Calcraft

Then was there two Comburgesses up the Cusheon or place of Eleccion vzt Mr Robert Calcraft and Mr Richard Calcraft

Then was there in the Church two Comburgesses vzt Mr Joseph Tomlinson and Mr Richard Holley

Then was sent downe into the Church to those two Comburgesses to make them three one other Comburgesse vzt Mr John Lenton

Out of which three Comburgesses in the Church vzt Mr Joseph Tomlinson, Mr Richard Holley and Mr John Lenton was chosen to come up and sitt upon the Cusheon or place of Election in the Roome of Mr Christofer Hanson who was dismissed upon his request one other Comburgesse vzt Mr Joseph Tomlinson

Then was there upon the Cusheon or place of Election three Comburgesses vzt Mr Robert Calcraft Mr Richard Calcraft and Mr Joseph Tomlinson

Then was three [sic] two Comburgesses in the Church vzt Mr Richard Holley and Mr John Lenton

Out of which three Comburgesses up on the Chusheon or place of Election vzt Mr Robert Calcraft, Mr Richard Calcraft and Mr Joseph Tomlinson one is to [sic] chosen Alderman for this next ensueing yeare

And so by an unanimous consent and vote of this Assembly Mr Robert Calcraft is chosen Alderman for this next ensueing yeare

Whereupon the said Mr Thomas Short dischargeth himselfe from the place and office of Alderman according to auncient custome And the said Mr Robert Calcraft now elected Alderman in his place and stead hath at this Assembly taken the oath of Alderman for this Burrough and Soake of Grantham according to the Auntient and laudable custome of the Burrough aforesaid

And so this Assembly breakes up.

[fo. 507v] [Blank page]

THE HALL BOOK OF GRANTHAM 1668–1669

[fo. 508r] **First Court of Robert Calcraft, 22 October 1668**

Mr Robert Calcraft Alderman

Mr Thomas Short Comburgess
Mr Thomas Grant Comburgess
Mr Thomas Hanson Comburgess
Mr Michaell Taylor Comburgess
Mr Richard Leeming Comburgess
Mr Richard Calcraft Comburgess
Mr Joseph Tomlinson Comburgess
Mr Richard Holley Comburgess
Mr John Lenton Comburgess
Mr George Short Comburgess
Mr Henry Humes Comburgess
Mr Edward Rawlinson Comburgess

2nd xij
John Coddington
John Winge
Robert Cole
Thomas Matkin
William Milles
John Turner
Thomas Ireland
Edward Paulett
Christofer Thompson
William Bury
Anthony Hotchkin

The Names of the Officers

Office	Name	Office	Name
Coroner	Mr Thomas Short	Keybearers	Mr Alderman
			William Bury
			Thomas Ireland
Escheator	Mr Henry Humes	Prizers of Corne	Thomas Hodgson
			John Beamond
Churchwardens	William Bury	Markett	George Hanson
	Thomas Charles	Sayers	Thomas Hatfeild
Chamberlaines	Thomas Ireland	Leathers	George Wray
	William Berriffe	Sealers	Edward Ulliott
			Henry Wright
			Thomas Marshall
Collectors for Schoole Rents	Mr George Short [name left blank]	Towne Clarke	William Hodgkinson
Cheife Constables	John Turner	Serjents	Samuell Roades
	Edward Paulett		Richard Blacke
Marketplace	Henry Coverly	Gaoler	Richard Blacke
	Nicholas Becke		
High Streete	Thomas Cole	Church Clarke	William Knewstubbs
	Edward Bristow		

Westgate	Hamlett Brumpton	Belman	Ralph Osborne
	Thomas Frith		
Walkergate	Thomas Hodgson	Beagle [sic]	John Scott
	John Still		
Swinegate	William Bristow		
	Francis Bristow		
Castlegate	Henry Godley		
	Thomas Rowley		

[fo. 508v]

The Names of the Commoners of the Court there

Markettplace	Westgate
John Walker	Thomas Frith
Nicholas Becke	Edward Kenion
William Laine	Thomas Fishar
William Berriffe	Francis Bristow
Edward Leivesly	Walkergate
Francis Charitie	John Still
Thomas Charles	George Read
Hamlett Brumpton	Thomas Gunnisson
Thomas Cole	Swinegate
Edward Bristow	Christofer Hanson
Thomas Hodgson	Henry Godley
High Streete	Castlegate
Richard Hauley	Thomas Rowley
John Pape	
William Bristow	

Chartors delivered up.

At this Court Mr Thomas Short late Alderman delivers up the three Chartor Boxes with all the Chartors vizt

The Exemplir of Edward the 4 Chartor	Kinge Charles 1 Chartor
Henry the Eight his Chartor	Kinge Charles 2 Chartor
Edward the vj his Chartor per Schoole	Librarey writeinges
Elizabeth her Chartor of Confirmacion	Townes Armes
Judge Dyers Award	A writing with many seales
Stamford writeinges	
Excheators Pattent	
James Chartor	

Accomptants further time.
At this Court Mr Richard Leeming Coroner, William Bury Churchwarden, John Plumer Chaimberlaine and the Collectors for Schoole Rents have time till next to perfect their Accounts.

Subscripcions to be gathered.
At this Court it is ordered that John Turner and Edward Paulett Cheife Constables do collect what money they can Upon the subscriptions and to give an Account of their proceedinges the next Court day.

[fo. 509r] **Second Court of Robert Calcraft, 8 April 1669**

Noe Visitacons dinners to be kept.
Whereas upon the reading of the Account of William Bury Churchwarden it was observed that there was a great charge laid upon the Towne for provideing dinners at the visitacions which is by this Court held unnessarie and for the freing the Towne from the said charge for the future It is at this Court fully ordered that noe Churchwarden for the time to come shall lay out or expend any money for dinners at visitacions without an order of Court made to impower them to provide the same And all Churchwardens are to take notice thereof accordingly.

Constables to pay for their Dinners at Sessions.
Whereas also upon reading of the Chaimberlaines Account it hath beene observed that the charge of the Constables dinners at Sessions have from time to time been paid by the Chaimberlaines, and the Court takeing notice of a late Act of Parlyament that doth impower to make rates to reimburse themselves what money that shall forth upon the Account of publike affaires As also that the charg of the Constables goeing to the Sessions and serving there as Jurors is in all places paid out of the Constables Assessment by reason it is of a publike concerne And that it is very requisite the same should be done in this Towne It is therefore fully ordered at this Court that the Constables of this Burrough do from time to time at Sessions dinners pay downe their severall and respective charges and insert the same in their bill of disbursments and that upon the Account day the same shall be allowed unto them without any deniall or obstruccion whatsoever.

An Assessment of 30 li for the Church.
At this Court it is ordered that an Assessment of xxx li be forthwith laid upon this Burrough for further repaires of the Church, this Court being well satisfied that notwithstanding the last Assessment was laid out for the repaires thereof, the same is yet in great decay And that if some speedy care be not taken the repaires of the said Church will be very chargeable And to prevent the same and to speed the makeing of the said Assessment it is ordered that notice thereof be given in the Church the next Lords day.

Churchwardens Account.
At this Court William Bury Churchwarden gives up his Account both
for the Quarteridge and Church Assessment and he chargeth himselfe
with receipt of   61 03 11
And his disbursments to be   64 05 11
Remains due to him   03 02 00
Which is ordered to be paid unto him by the next Churchwarden.

Thomas Day, Thomas Sharpe, William Dickinson, Ralph Nidd made free.
At this Court came Thomas Day, Thomas Sharpe, William Dickinson, Ralph Nidd being free borne and Apprentices in the Towne and desired to be admitted freemen of this Corporacion to which this Court doth condiscend Whereupon they pay ijs vjd apiece to the Box and takes the oath incident thereto & pays the fees to the Clarke and Serjentes and are admitted freemen of this Corporacion.

John Brockhurst made free.
At this Court came John Brockhurst a Forrainer and desired to [sic] admitted a freeman of this Corporacion whose request this Court doth grant And thereupon he lays downe x li according to custome And this Court considering that he may prove a good Townsman doe give him againe 3 li 6s 8d And is admitted a freeman of this Corporacion.

[fo. 509v] **Third Court of Robert Calcraft, 3 June 1669**

The Milles lett to the Towne.
Whereas Mr Alderman this day acquainted the Court that he had taken a lease of the Milles for a yeare from the xxvth day of May last of Doctor Hurst and Mr Walton at the Rent of 70 li per Annum besides the Rent due to the Queenes Majestie and that he tooke them on the behalfe of this Towne if the Court approved thereof whereupon the Court takeing the same into their consideracions and considering that it may be a great advantage to the Towne do returne Mr Alderman thankes for his care on the behalfe of the publike affaires of this Corporacion and do accept of the said bargaine of the Milles for a yeare under the Rent aforesaid And do hereby appointe Robert Cole, Edward Paulett and John Pape to be Mill Masters for three moneths now next ensueing And to receive the proffitt of the same and to give an Account when they shall be thereunto requested.

Gentlemen appointed to treat aboute buying the Milles.
At this Court it is ordered that Mr Alderman, Mr Grant, Mr Taylor and Mr Tomlinson do treat with Doctor Hurst and the rest of the Gentlemen to whome the Milles are ingaged for the purchaseing of the said Milles or such part or parts as the said Gentlemen are aminded to sell And that they give an Account of their proceedinges thereunto to the Court at their convenience.

Anthony Ayscoghe Goodes being forfeited as a felo de se *sold to his Sonn.*
At this Court John Ayscoghe sonn of Anthony Ayscoghe of Great Paunton within this libertie and desired to compound for his fathers goodes he being found a *felo de se* by drowneing himselfe in a River within the feilds of Paunton aforesaid and died possessed of some few goodes which the Jury presented in their verdict and was this day read And this Court observing that they were goodes of noe great value do hereby bargaine and sell the said goodes to the said John Ayscoghe and all other the Personall estate to the said Anthony Ayscoghe belonging for 40s which he payes downe in open Court to the present Chaimberlaine and is thereof acquitted.

The Towne Clarke gives an Account of the Redd Lyon Suite.
At this Court the Towne Clarke gives an Account of his proceedinges at London the last terme aboute the Redd Lyon wherein he acquaints this Court that upon hearing of the cause Mr Taylor one of the Comburgesses of this Court being present the Lord Keeper did declare that there [*sic*] little or noe equitie for the Complainant Christian but in regard his father and he had beene Tennants to the said Inn for many yeares past did propound that he might be Tenant to the Inn aforesaid at the Rent of x li per Annum and to pay all the Arreares and to performe the said Covenants as formerly and to deliver up the lease which he had obtained from one Mary Fulwood one of the Heires of the late Surviveing Feoffees and then to have a lease for xxj yeares and at the Expiracion thereof to deliver up the possession and quite all his claime And that the Towne be reimbursed their money expended out of advancement of the Rent aforesaid.

[fo. 510r]

A lease lett to John Dawson.
At this Court came John Dawson and takes a lease of the House he now dwelleth in Walkergate for one and twenty yeares from and after the Expiracion of a former lease thereof yet in being paying the sume of twenty markes for a fine within a fortnight before Michaelmas next And giveing Securitie for Rent and repaires And he gives in earnest thereof xijd.

The Court of Record to be sett up.
Whereas it was this day moved in Court that there is a privilidge granted to this Corporacion of holding of a Court of pleas within this libertie for the sume of 40 li And by that Court many smale debts might be recovered at an easey charge As also that it might be very advantageous to the Towne by bringing in considerable sumes to the Alderman for the time being and other Officers belonging to this Court And by meanes thereof free the Corporacion from the severall Sallories due to them And the same being this day taken into consideracion by this Court and held to be for the good of the Towne It is ordered concluded and agreed upon by this Court that the said Court of Record be sett up and kept weekely according to the direction of the Chartor in that

behalfe and expressed And if the said Court do come to good effect then the Towne to be freed from the severall Sallories aforesaid.

For the Elleccion of the next Alderman.
For the more peaceable and orderly proceedinges at the Eleccion of the next succeeding Alderman It is at this Court ordered that upon the next eleccion day Mr George Short be sent downe into the Church to Mr Richard Holley and Mr John Lenton to make three Comburgesses there Out of which three Church [*sic*] It is likewise agreed that Mr Richard Holley be called upon the Cusheon to Mr Richard Calcraft and Mr Joseph Tomlinson to make three Comburgesses there Out of which three Comburgesses upon the Cusheon with the consent of this Court Mr Richard Calcraft is nominated Alderman for this next ensueing yeare.

Account of the Tolles.

	li	s	d
The Account of Mr Henry Humes for the tolles from the tenth day of Aprill 1669 to the first day of May Receiptes	12	15	06
His disbursments	00	15	00
Remaines due to the Towne	12	00	06
Which he payes in open Court and is discharged			
The Account of Mr Thomas Grant for the tolles from the first of May 1669 to the first day of June following Receiptes	16	03	08
His disbursments	01	15	11
Remaines due to the Towne	14	07	09
Which he payes in open Court and is discharged			
The Account of Thomas Cole as Colebuyer for the yeare past His Receipts	15	07	00
Disbursments	10	16	02
Remaines to the Towne the Stocke being increased 1 li 6s 1d the sume of	16	13	01
Which he payes to Nicholas Becke the now Overseer and is discharged.			

Mr Shorts debt paid.
At this Court it is ordered that Mr Thomas Short receive the sume of iii li js viijd of the Chaimberlaine which he is hereby ordered to be paid to him being due upon his Account of the publike concernes of this Burrough.

[fo. 510v] **Fourth Court of Robert Calcraft, 16 July 1669**

Richard Blacke paid for Sessions dinners.
At this Court it is ordered that the Chaimberlaine pay unto Richard Blacke the sume of foureteene shillinges for the charge of the Grand Juries Dinners the last Sessions And that the same be putt into the next Constables Assessment.

THE HALL BOOK OF GRANTHAM 1668–1669   129

Townes Halfe pence to passe.
Whereas the Court takeing this day into consideracion the great inconveniencie of severall sorts of brasse halfe pence in perticular mens name that are spread abroad and some of them not easely to be discerned who sett forth the same As also that the halfe pence the Corporacion hath sett out are laid up by severall Persons that their owne half pence may goe the better which is a great preiudice to this Corporacion For prevencion whereof for the future It is hereby ordered that Mr Alderman do cause proclamacion to be made in the Towne to prohibite all Persons in this Burrough from receiveing the brasse halfe pence of perticular men so that other halfe [*sic*] may not tend to the prejudice of this Corporacion.

Mr Calcraft & Mr Pooles order to save them harmles for 51 li 10s.
Whereas Mr Richard Calcraft one of the Comburgesses of this Court and one Mr John Poole a member of this Corporacion do by their bond or writeing obligatorie bearing date the [*blank*] day of [*blank*] last past stand joyntly and severally bound unto Edward Coddington of this Towne Mercer in the sume of 100 li condicioned for the true payment of 51 li 10s upon the [*blank*] day of [*blank*] next ensueing the date of the said bond or writeing obligatorie as the same relacion being thereunto had may more fully appeare Which said money was by the Gentlemen aforesaid borrowed and paid unto John Hobson Esquire for a debt oweing by this Corporacion and the Gentlemen became bound at the request and [*sic*] of this Burrough Now this Court do for themselves and their Successors firmly promise well and truly from time to time and at all times forever hereafter to save defend keepe harmles and indempnifie the said Mr Richard Calcraft & Mr John Poole and either of them their [*sic*] either of their Heires Executors & Administrators and every of them of and from all manner of payments penalties forfeitures and suites of law whatsoever that shall or may happen of the said recited bond & Condicion thereupon written.

Richard Hickson, William Grococke, John Newcombe, Henry Atkinson made free.
At this Court came Richard Hickson Apprentice to Mr Richard Calcraft to the trade of a Chandler, William Grococke Shoemaker, John Newcombe Felmonger & Henry Atkinson Taylor haveing severally served seaven yeares Apprentice to the said trades and desired to be admitted freemen of this Corporacion who [*sic*] request this Court doth grant Whereupon the said Richard Hickson John Newcombe and Henry Atkinson as Forrainers paid vs a peice to the Boxe And the said William Grococke paid ijs vjd to the Box as freeborne And paid their fees to Clarke & Serjents and tooke the oathes incident thereunto and are admitted free Burgesses of this Corporacion.

[fo. 511r] **Fifth Court of Robert Calcraft, 3 September 1669**

Account of Tolles.
At this Court Mr Michaell Taylor gives an Account of the proffitts of   li   s   d
the tolles from the fifth day of June last till the 29th June Receipts   05 09 10
Disbursments   05 02 04
Remaines due to the Towne   00 07 06
Which he payes in open Court and is discharged.

The Account of proffitts of the Milnes.
At this Court the severall Milne Masters gives an Account of the proffitts of the Milles for one Quarter of a yeare last past
Robert Cole his Receipts   09 12 06
Disbursments   02 13 06
Remaines due to the Towne   06 19 00
Besides Arreares   00 15 02
Edward Paulett his Receipts   09 16 10
Disbursments   03 00 00
Remaines to the Towne   06 16 10
Anthony Hotchkins Receipts   11 12 02
Disbursments   03 15 11
Remaines due to the Towne   07 16 03

Mill Masters appointed.
At this Court John Winge, John Turner, Edward Paulett and Anthony Hotchkin are appointed Milne Masters till the Court after the Account day next ensueing.

An Assessment of xvj li for Constable bills.
At this Court it is ordered that an Assessment of xvj li be made and laid upon the Burrough of Grantham for the payment of the Constables their bills of disbursments for the yeare past (an estimate being taken what those perticular sumes amount unto And the Cheife Constables and Under Constables are appointed Assessors and the Under Constables Collectors thereof And it is ordered that notice be given in the Church the next Sunday of the time and place of makeing the said Assessment that all such Persones as are therein concerned may if the [sic] please be there present.

Robert Cowles, Joseph Burnham, John Robinson made free.
At this Court came Joseph Burnham and John Robinson and Robert Cowles Forrainers and desired to be admitted free Burgesses of this Corporacion to whose request this Court doth condiscend whereupon they lay downe their ten pounds a peice according to Auntient custome Of which this Court tooke x li a peice of the said Joseph Burnham and John Robinson and in regards Robert Cowles doth not follow any trade in the Towne this Court restores four pounds againe And they pay their fees to Clarke and Serjents and takes the oath of freemen according to Antient custome.

[fo. 511v] **Sixth Court of Robert Calcraft, 7 October 1669**

The Account of the tolles
At this Court Mr Richard Calcraft gives an Account of the tolles for
one moneth from the xxiijth day of July last his Receipts   02 12 09
Disbursements   01 17 01
Remains due to the Towne   00 15 08
Which he payes in open Court and is discharged

At this Court Mr John Lenton gives an Account of the tolles for one
moneth from the vijth day of August last his Receipts   01 09 00
Disbursments   00 04 01
Remains due to the Towne   01 04 11
Which he payes in open Court and is discharged.

Mr Taylor paid xxxxs which he lent the Corporacion.
At this Court it is ordered that the Chaimberlaine do pay unto Mr Michaell Taylor one of the Comburgesses of this Court which he was formerly pleased to lend for the use of this Corporacion the sume of xxxxs.

Richard Blacke paid for repaires of the Gaole.
At this Court Richard Blacke brought in a bill of xxviijs & xjd which he laid out for repaireing of the Towne Hall and desired that the Court would please to order him the payment of it Whereupon it is ordered that the present Chamberlaine do pay the xxviijs & xjd unto Richard Blacke aforesaid.

Chamberlaines Account.
At this Court Thomas Ireland one of the Chaimberlaines for this
yeare accounteth for his Receipts and disbursments on the Common
affaires of this Towne and he chargeth himselfe with Receipt of   91 04 04
And his disbursments to be   89 02 00
Remaines due to the Towne   02 02 02
Which he payes in open Court and is discharged.

The Towne Clarke paid x li for the charges of the Redd Lyon.
At this Court the Towne Clarke acquainted Mr Alderman that the last terme he expended above xxx li in the suite aboute the Redd Lyon and that he received but xx li when he went up to London, and that Mr Alderman was pleased to promise to send up the other x li to London which he did know [sic] receive and therefore desired that this Court would be to order him the payment thereof Whereupon it is ordered that the Chamberlaine pay x li unto the Towne Clarke upon riseing of the Court.

[fo. 512r] Seventh Court of Robert Calcraft 21 October 1669

Mr Aldermans Account.
At this Court Mr Alderman gives an Account of all moneys by him received and disbursed upon the publike Account of this Corporacion and chargeth

himselfe with	11	05	00
And his disbursments to be	12	16	11
Remaines due to him	01	11	11

At this Court Mr Alderman also gives an Account of forty pounds

weight of Townes halfepence And he chargeth himselfe with Receipt of	19	06	06
And his disbursments to be	18	05	06
Remaines due to the Towne	01	00	06
So that upon the whole Account there Remaines to Mr Alderman	00	11	05

Which the Chaimberlaines payes to him in open Court.

Coroners Account.
At this Court Mr Thomas Short Coroner accounteth and saith that as touching Casualties happening this yeare there was one Anthony Ayscoghe of Great Paunton within this libertie found dead in the feilds of Paunton aforesaid And that the Jury impannelled to inquire how the said Anthony Ayscoghe came to his death found him a *felo de se* for that he did wilfully drowne himselfe in a River called Wytham Becke within the libertie of this Burrough And the said Coroner also saith that the Jury did find the said Anthony Ayscoghe died seized of divers goodes and Chattells mentioned in an Inventorie to the Inquisicion annexed And the said Coroner further accounteth and saith that there was one Robert Greene a young Child about three yeare old found dead at Braceby And that the Jury upon the inquirie did find that he playing aboute a little pond or river within the said Towne, and the Wind being High & he alone did accidently fall into the said pond and for want of helpe did then and there perish And the said Jury found it death by misfortune And further he hath not to account and therefore he is discharged.

Escheators Account.
At this Court Mr Henry Humes Escheator gives an Account of all monies by him received for the yeare past for light unlawfull and defective weights and measures and he chargeth himselfe

upon Statutes in that behalf made the sume of	01	04	08
And his disbursments to be	00	04	06
Remaines due to the Towne	01	00	02

Which he payes in open Court and is discharged.

At this Court the Churchwarden Chamberlaine and Collectors for Schoole Rents have further time to perfect their Accounts.

[fo. 512v]

At an Assembly holden by Mr Robert Calcraft Alderman and the Comburgesses and Burgesses of Grantham aforesaid in Corpus Christi Quire within the Prebendarie Curch [sic] there on Friday next after St Luke being 22 October 1669.

First did sitt downe upon the Cusheon or place of Election the said Mr Robert Calcraft in Corpus Christi Quire within the Prebendarie Church there
Next to him did sitt upon the Cusheon or place of Election two Comburgesses vizt Mr Richard Calcraft and Mr Joseph Tomlinson
Then was there two Comburgesses in the Church vizt Mr Richard Holley and Mr John Lenton
Then was sent downe into the Church to those two Comburgesse to make them three one other Comburgesse vizt Mr George Short
Out of which three Comburgesse in the Church one was chosen to come up and sitt upon the Cusheon or place of Eleccion one other Comburgesse vizt Mr Richard Holley
Then was there three Comburgesses upon the Cusheon or place of Eleccion vizt Mr Richard Calcraft, Mr Joseph Tomlinson & Mr Richard Holley
And then was there in the Church two Comburgesses vizt Mr John Lenton and Mr George Short
Out of which three Comburgesses upon the Cusheon or place of Eleccion vizt Mr Richard Calcraft, Mr Joseph Tomlinson and Mr Richard Holley one is to be chosen Alderman for the next ensueing yeare
And so by an unanimous consent and vote of this Assembly Mr Richard Calcraft is chosen Alderman for this next ensueing yeare
Whereupon the said Mr Robert Calcraft dischargeth himselfe from the place and office of Alderman according to Auncient custome And the said Mr Richard Calcraft now elected Alderman in his place and stead hath at this Assembly taken the oath of Alderman for this Burrough and Soake of Grantham according to the Auntient and laudable custome of the Burrough aforesaid.

And So this Assembly breakes up.

THE HALL BOOK OF GRANTHAM 1669–1670

[fo. 513r] **First Court of Richard Calcraft 29 October 1669**

First xij.   Mr Richard Calcraft Alderman
Mr Thomas Short Comburgesse   John Coddington
Mr Thomas Grant Comburgess   John Winge
Mr Thomas Hanson Comburgess   Robert Cole
Mr Michaell Taylor Comburgesse   Thomas Matkin
Mr Richard Leeming Comburgess   William Milles
Mr Robert Calcroft Comburgess   John Turner
Mr Joseph Tomlinson Comburgess   Thomas Ireland
Mr Richard Halley Comburgess   Edward Paulett
Mr John Lenton Comburgess   Christofer Thompson
Mr George Short Comburgess   William Bury
Mr Henry Humes Comburgess   Anthony Hotchkin
Mr Edward Rawlinson Comburgess   Henry Coverly

The names of the Officers

Coroner	Mr Robert Calcraft	Keybearers	Mr Alderman
Escheator	Mr John Lenton		Christofer Thompson
Churchwardens	Christopher Thompson		Edward Paulett
	Thomas Charles	Prizers of Corne	Thomas Hodgson
Chaimberlaines	Edward Paulett		Thomas Briggs
	Henry Coverly	Market Sayers	George Hanson
Collectors for	Mr Edward Rawlinson		Thomas Hatfeild
Schoole Rentes	Nicholas Becke	Leather Sealers	John Fox
Cheife Constables	Robert Cole		Edward Ulliott
	Anthony Hotchkin		Henry Wright
Marketplace	Robert Cowles		Thomas Marshall
Constables	Edward Barstow	Towne Clarke	William Hodgkinson
High Streete	John Robinson	Serjents	Thomas Calcraft
	William Dickinson		Richard Blacke
Westgate	Thomas Frith	Gaoler	Richard Blacke
	Richard Hickson	Church Clerke	William Knewstubbs
Walkergate	John Still	Bellman	Ralph Osborne
	Thomas Sharpe	Beagle	John Scott

Swinegate	Henry Godley	
	Ralph Nidd	
Castlegate	Thomas Rowley	
	Joseph Burnham	

[fo. 513v]

The Names of the Commoners of the Court there

Marketplace	Westgate
John Walker	Thomas Frith
Nicholas Becke	Edward Kenion
William Laine	Thomas Fishar
William Berriffe	Francis Bristow
Edward Leivesley	Richard Hickson
Francis Charitie	Christofer Hanson
Thomas Charles	Walkergate
Hamlett Brumpton	John Still
Thomas Cole	George Read
Edward Bristow	Thomas Gunnisson
Thomas Hodgson	Castlegate
High Streete	Thomas Rowley
Richard Hauley	
John Pape	

The Charters delivered up.

At this Court Mr Robert Calcraft late Alderman delivered up the three Chartor Boxes with all the Charters vzt

The Exemplir of Edward the 4th Chartor	King Charles the i Chartor
Henry the Eight his Chartor	King Charles the 2 Chartor
Edward the vjth his Charter & Schoole	Librarey writeinges
Elizabeth her Charter of Confirmacion	Townes Armes
Judge Dyers Award	A writing with many Seales
Stamford writeinges	
Escheators Pattent	
King James Chartor	

Accounts to be taken.

At this Court it is ordered that Mr Thomas Grant, Mr Michaell Taylor, John Turner and Edward Paulett do examine the Accounts of William Berriffe Chaimberlaine and do certifie their proceedinges therein the next Court day.

Overseers for Westgate Well appointed.
At this Court it is ordered that Francis Bristow and Marke Harnesse be Overseers for Westgate Well And that they with assistance of the Constable of the said Streete do make an assessment of xxs for repaireing of the Well aforesaid.

[fo. 514r]

Sir William Thorolds guift disposed.
At this Court it is ordered that John Turner one of the Treasurers for receiveing of the money given towards the setting of this Corporacion out of debt do lend to the Towne x li more besides the x li formerly lent to the Towne out of the xxxx li given by Sir William Thorold Knight and Barronet one of the Burgesses of the Honourable House of Commons in Parlyament for this Burrough of [*sic*] to defend the suite this terme against Christian concerning the Redd Lyon And it is this day ordered by the Court that the said x li together with the other x li formerly lent shall be repaid unto the said Treasurer by the Chaimberlaine And that the said Treasurer shall be saved harmles from all trouble or incumbrance whatsoever for or by reason of lending the said xx li to and for the use of this Corporacion.

Cheife Constable to be saved harmles against Horner.
Whereas John Turner and Edward Paulett Cheife Constables for the Corporacion for the yeare past this day acquainted the Court that they were sued by one John Horner and that what they did was in execucion of their Office for finding him and many others assembled together under pretence of religious worships & contrarey to the lawes of this Kingdome during the time of divine service at the Church they did secure the said Horner and others in prison untill Mr Alderman for the yeare past and his Brethren had the examinacion of them And that their onely indeavor was to preserve the peace of his Majestie and the peace of his Kingdome and of this Corporacion And therefore they referred themselves to this Court for the indempnifieing of them And they further acquainted the Court that the Warrants was in one Mr Seckers hands an Attorney at law and that he had beene very civill in acquainteing them with the said Warrants and if the Court pleased to approve thereof they desired Mr Secker might appeare for them Whereupon this Court considering that what the said Cheife Constables did was for a generall good do hereby order that Mr Secker do appeare And that they be saved harmles and indempnified from all charges damages and expenses whatsoever that shall or may happen for or by reason of the said suite.

The lease to Allisson tolle.
At this Court came Clement Allisson and takes a lease of the tolles of oatemeale for one whole yeare from the xxjth day of October last past paying the sume of xvjs to the Chaimberlaine for the time being.

Woolands lease of tolle.
At this Court came Robert Wollands [*sic*] and takes a lease of Denton tolle belonging to this Burrough for one whole yeare from the xxjth day of October last past paying the sume of iij li xs to the Chaimberlaine for the time being.

Coroners fee paid.
At this Court it is ordered that the present Chaimberlaine do pay xs to Mr Thomas Short Coroner and the Towne Clarke and ijs to Richard Blacke Serjent for their fees upon the Inquisicion of the Body of Anthony Ayscoghe of Great Paunton within this libertie out of the money given for the Composicion of the estate of the said Ayscoghe being found a *felo de se*.

Accounts to be examined.
At this Court ordered that Mr Thomas Grant, Mr Michaell Taylor, John Turner and Edward Paulett do examine the Account of William Berriffe Chaimberlaine and do certifie their proceedinges therein the next Court day.

Townes halfe to be sent for.
At this Court it is ordered that forty pounds weight of Townes halfepence be sent for, there being a great want of them at present.

[fo. 514v] **Second Court of Richard Calcraft, 10 December 1669**

Tomlyn's lease assigned.
At this Court came Mr John Hurst and desired to be admitted tenant to the House & land formerly demised to Thomas Tomlyn of Manthorpe he haveing the said lease assigned over to him by the Widdow and Executrix of the said Tomlyn the which this Court takeing into Consideracion as also that the said Mr Hurst is likely to prove a good Tennant do hereby admitt of the said Mr Hurst to be Tennant to the said House and land And he gives by way of Attornement ijs vjd.

Mr Alsopp debt to be paid.
Whereas Mr Alderman this day acquainted the Court that Mr Alsopp did intend to sue Mr Leeming Executrix for the fifty pounds and interest, due from the Corporacion for which Mr Leeming was bound As also that there is xx li in the hands of Robert Cole and John Turner or one of them as Treasurer for receiveing the money given towards the setting of the Corporacion out of debt And that if this Court thought convenient the said xx li might be paid in part of the said debt and take of interest untill such time as the said money with others can be laid out for the better Benefitt of the towne The which the Court takeing into consideracion as also that it is for the good of the [word missing] by saveing interest & charges It is therefore ordered that the said John Turner do pay the said xx li to the Chaimberlaine upon riseing of the Court and that the Chaimberlaine do pay the said xx li with v li more to Mr Alsopp to pay of, halfe

the debt and that the said John Turner shall be saved harmles from all trouble charges damages or incumbrances whatsoever for or by reason of paying the said xx li to and for the use of this Corporacion.

John Shootewell to receive xvs.
At this Court it is ordered that the Chaimberlaine do pay unto John Shootewell the sume of xvs due unto him for worke done on the behalfe of this Corporacion.

Mr Aldermans sallary to be paid.
At this Court it is ordered that the Chaimberlaine do pay unto Mr Alderman the sume of x li due to him for his sallary for the present yeare.

Richard Blacke money to be paid.
At this Court it is ordered that the Chaimberlaine pay unto Richard Blacke his bill for [crossed through] what he hath laid out on the behalfe of the Towne.

Accounts to be examined.
At this Court it is ordered that Mr Alderman, Mr Grant, Mr Tomlinson & Mr George Short and William Berriffe do examine the Churchwardens Account and returne their proceedinges therein the next Court day.

Christofer Hauley Accounts to be taken.
At this Court it is ordered that Christofer Hauley do bring in his Account of his Receipts and disbursments for High Streete Well the next Court day.

[fo. 515r] Third Court of Richard Calcraft, 28 January 1669/70

Accounts of the tolles.
At this Court it is ordered that the Towne Clarke draw up and Account of what proffitts hath accrued to the Corporacion out of the tolles for the yeare past.

Mr Humes Account.

	li	s	d
At this Court Mr Henry Humes gives an Account for the tolles for the moneth of November last whereby he chargeth himselfe with	02	05	05
And his disbursments to be	00	06	08
Remaines due to the Towne	01	18	09

which he payes in open Court and is discharged.

Mr Taylors Account.

	li	s	d
At this Court Mr Michaell Taylor gives an Account for the tolles for the moneth of December last whereby he chargeth himselfe with	05	09	02
And his disbursments to be	00	19	00

Remaines due to the Towne   04 09 00
which he payes in open Court and is discharged.
[*Original sum is arithmetically incorrect*]

Account of Schoole Rents.
At this Court Mr George Short gives an Account for the Schoole
Rents for the last yeare whereby he chargeth himselfe with   45 15 00
And his disbursments to Schoole masters and other sallaries   42 01 00
Arreares to gather up   01 16 08
Remaines to the Towne   02 14 00
which he payes in open Court and is discharged.

Charges to be paid.
At this Court it is ordered that Christofer Thompson the present Churchwarden do pay xvs to the Towne Clarke for charges due to him from Mr George Short as Churchwarden.

Widdow Handly to be paid.
At this Court it is ordered that Richard Handley and Charles Wetherill be appointed Overseers for High Streete Well And that they make an Assessment of forty shillings whereof xxxs of the first money that is gathered to pay Widdow Handley her bill laid out by her Husband in repaireing the said Well And the other xs to be laid out on the further repaires thereof.

[fo. 515v] **Fourth Court of Richard Calcraft, 11 March 1669/70**

Widdow Kirke to be distrained for keepeing two stalls.
Whereas upon Complaint made to the Court this day against Widdow Kirke that useth the trade of a Butcher for keepeing of two stalls upon Satterdays contrarey to the orders of the Court It is therefore ordered that a fine of xs be hereby imposed upon her And that the same be levied by distresse of her goodes to the use of this Corporacion.

The Streetes in Westgate not be raised without Mr Aldermans consent.
Whereas the Court this day taking into consideracion that the Inhabitants in Westgate do indeavor to exceed one another in the raiseing of the pavements before their doores whereby the said Streete is become very dangerous by reason of the great downe falls in many places of the said Streete As also that severall persons do pave onely the length of their Sheepe penns so as the other part lyeth low and not even with the rest of the ground there It is therefore ordered for the future that noe Person or Persons whatsoever shall raise their ground before their doores, before they give notice to Mr Alderman for the time being that care may be taken that the ground so to be raised do not exceed the next ground adjoyning on both sides And that the [*sic*] pave downe to the Channell forthwith upon notice thereof to them given so as in time the said Streete may be even and handsome upon paine for every one offending contrarey to this order to forfeite

the sume of forty shillinges of lawfull money of England to be levied of their goodes and Chattells to the use of the Corporacion.

Mr William Walles, Thomas Chirchloe made free.
At this Court came William Walles and Thomas Chirchley Forrainers & desired to be admitted free Burgesses of this Corporacion and in order thereunto did lay downe their x li apeice and also desired this Court to be kind to them The which this Court takeing into consideracion as also that they may be serviceable to the Towne do admitte of them to be free Burgesses and out of respect to them do returne them iij li vjs viijd a peice back againe And thereupon the oath of freemen and the other oathes incident thereunto according to custome and paid their fees to Clarke and Serjents and are admitted free Burgesses of this Corporacion.

William Clarke, George Read made free.
At this Court came William Clarke Apothecary who served his father as an Apprentice and George Read Cooper who served his father as an Apprentice and desired to be admitted freemen of this Corporacion to whose request this Court doth condiscend Whereupon they pay their ijs vjd as freeborne & their fees to Clarke & Serjents and takes the oath of freemen according to custome And thereupon they are admitted free Burgesses of this Corporacion.

[fo. 516Ar] **Fifth Court of Richard Calcraft, 20 May 1670**

Mr Coverly chosen on the 2nd xij.
At this Court Henry Coverly is chosen one of the Second twelve in the Roome of Mr Edward Rawlinson Comburgesse.

Mr John Coddington chosen of the first xij.
At this Court John Coddington is chosen one of the first twelve in the Roome of Mr Thomas Hanson lately deceased.

John Pape chosen on the 2nd xij.
At this Court John Pape is chosen one of the Second Company in the Roome of Mr John Coddington Comburgesse.

Mr John Winge chosen on the first xij.
At this Court John Winge is chosen one of the first Company in the Roome of Mr Richard Leeming lately deceased.

The Eleccion of the next Alderman.
For the more peaceable and orderly proceedinges at the Eleccion of the next Succeeding Alderman It is at this Court ordered that upon the next Eleccion Mr Thomas Grant [*two names Henry Humes and George Short, crossed out*] be sent downe into the Church to

Mr John Lenton and Mr George Short to make three Comburgesses there Out of which Comburgesses out of the Church It is likewise agreed that Mr John Lenton shall be called upon the Cusheon or place of Eleccion to Mr Joseph Tomlinson and Mr Richard Holley to make three Comburgesses there Out of which three Comburgesse upon the Cusheon Mr Joseph Tomlinson is nominated Alderman for the next ensueing yeare.

The sume of iij li to be allowed for the Sessions Dinner.
Whereas this Court takeing into Consideracion the Charge of Sessions Dinners as also what may be convenient to be allowed to be allowed [*sic*] for the same and haveing also examined the Chaimberlaines Booke what sume hath beene laid out formerly and the Expences formerly uncertaine this Court doth thinke it convenient to reduce it to a certaine summe Whereupon it is this day ordered that the sume of iij li be allowed and paid by the Chaimberlaine for the charge of every Sessions Dinner for the time to come And the same to be paid for Sessions Dinner from time to time to the Alderman for the time being that shall keepe the same on behalfe of this Corporacion.

The Remaineing 40 li of the Chartor money to be raised.
Whereas Mr Alderman this day acquainted the Court that there is a great necessitie for the raiseing of money for the defending for the paying of the Charge of the suite against Christian aboute the Redd Lyon it being now recovered And that it is convenient the Remaineing part of the Charter Assessment be raised Whereupon it is this day ordered that the sume of 40 li being the Remainder of the 80 li be laid upon the Inhabitants of this Towne And that Nine of the Comburgesses Six of the 2nd xij and six Comoners be Assessors thereof And the Cheife Constables Collectors of such sumes as to be paid by the first and 2d Company & Gentrie And the rest by the Petty Constables of every Ward within this Corporacion according to the order heretofore made for the Eighty pounds before mencioned.

[fo. 516Av] **Sixth Court of Richard Calcraft, 27 May 1670** [*date overwritten from 1669*]

Mr Lentons Account for tolles.
At this Court Mr John Lenton gives an Account for the tolles for the
moneth of January and he chargeth himselfe with   01 16 04
And his disbursments to be   00 06 08
Remaines which he payes in open Court and is discharged 01 19 08

Mr Tomlinsons Account for tolles.
At this Court Mr Joseph Tomlinson gives an Account for the tolles for the
moneth of Feburary last and he chargeth himselfe with   01 09 00
And his disbursments to be   00 06 00
Remaines which he payes in open Court and is discharged 01 03 00

Mr Aldermans Account for tolle.
At this Court Mr Alderman gives an Account for the tolles for the
moneth of March last and he chargeth himselfe with   09 17 06
And his disbursments to be   01 01 02
Remaines which he payes in open Court and is discharged   08 16 04

Mr Grants Account for tolle.
At this Court Mr Thomas Grant gives an Account for the tolles for the
moneth of Aprill last and he chargeth himselfe with   08 18 00
And his disbursments to be   00 15 10
Remaines to the Towne   08 02 02
which he payes in open Court and is discharged.

Nicholas Becke Account as Colebuyer.
At this Court Nicholas Becke Colebuyer gives up his Account for the yeare past
wherein he chargeth himselfe with Receipt   16 10 00
And is [sic] disbursments to be   11 19 06
Remaines to the Towne   18 12 09
Stocke increased   01 19 08

Nicholas Becke chosen Colebuyer for the next yeare.
Whereupon this Court observeing that the said Nicholas Becke hath beene very carefull and Honest in the said Office do hereby nominate him Colebuyer againe for the ensueing yeare.

[fo. 516Br] **Seventh Court of Richard Calcraft, 23 June 1670**

Halfe pence to be sent for.
At this Court it is ordered that forty pounds weight of Townes halfepence be sent for to London their being very few abroad and the Chaimberlaine dispose of the same.

Thomas Horsefeild takes a lease of the Redd Lyon for xxj yeares.
At this Court came Thomas Horefeild [sic] that married one of the daughters of Mr Thomas Hanson late one of the Comburgesses of this Court and desired to take a lease of the Redd Lyon and two Acres of land lying within the feilds of Gunnerby and Manthorpe for one & twenty yeares now to come Whereupon it is ordered that the said Thomas Horsefeild have a lease of the said Redd Lyon and land for one & twenty yeares from the feast day of St Michaell now next ensueing fully to be complete and ended yeilding and paying yearely and every yeare during the said terme the Annuall Rent of xvj li at the Annunciacion of the blessed Virgin Mary and the feast of Saint Michaell Tharchangell by even & equall porcions and giveing securitie for Rent and repaires as is accustomed by the Townes Tenants And he gives in earnest thereof ijs vjd And it is hereby further ordered and agreed upon that the Towne shall sett the said demised

premisses in good and sufficient repaires as well with pointeing slateing thatching and walling As to make gates pave and plante stables and to make any further repaires as shall be needfull and requisite and shall likewise pay all Arreares of Chimley money due till Michaelmas next And after the same so repaired and Chimley money paid the said Thomas Horsefeild shall repaire the said premisses with needfull repairacions whatsoever during the said terme and so leave the premisses sufficiently repaired and shall likewise pay the Chimley money during the terme aforesaid And it is further ordered and agreed that the said Thomas Horsefeild shall build a signe at his owne cost and charges for the said Inn And in case the Towne or the Tennant that shall next succeed will not buy the said signe of him or of his Executors or Administrators at the end of the said terme it shall be lawfull to and for him or them to take the said signe away and to dispose of it to his or their owne proper use anything heretofore mencioned to the contrarey notwithstanding.

The Towne Clarke for the Redd Lyon charges the Account to be stated.
At this Court the Towne Clarke bringes in a bill of charges expended aboute the Redd Lyon and desired for the satisfacion of the Court the same might be examined by some of the members of this and any Attorney this Court should please to make of Whereupon it is ordered that Mr Alderman, Mr Thomas Grant, Mr Michaell Taylor, Robert Cole, Edward Paulett, Thomas Cole and Thomas Fishar with the assistance of Mr William Parkins one of Attornies of the Towne do examine the said bills of charges and do state the Account And for the paying of the Towne Clarke some part at present It is ordered that the Chaimberlaine do pay the Towne Clarke xx li upon the riseing of the Court.

The dimission [sic] of Christians bill to be entred if Councill advise it.
This day the Towne Clarke acquainted the Court that if Councill thought it convenient, it would be needfull to draw up the dismission of Christians bill in Chancery to avoid him for the future Whereupon it is ordered that the Towne Clarke take advise whether it be requisite to enter the said dismission and if they advise it needfull that then the same be entred accordingly.

[fo. 516Bv] **Eighth Court of Richard Calcraft, 29 July 1670**

Mr Taylors Account for tolles.

	li	s	d
At this Court Mr Michaell Taylor accounteth for the proffitts of the tolles for the moneth of June last and he chargeth himselfe with	04	17	9 ob
And his disbursments to be	00	17	4
Remaines due to the Towne	04	0	5 ob

Which he payes in open Court and is discharged

Mr Humes Account for tolles.

At this Court Mr Henry Humes accounteth for the proffitts of the tolles for the moneth of May last and he chargeth himselfe with	03	17	01
And his disbursments to be	00	08	01

Remaines to the Towne   03 09 00
Which he payes in open Court and he is discharged

Mr Humes Account for Holly Thursday faire for tolles.
At this Court Mr Henry Humes accounteth for the proffitts of the tolles for
Holly Thursday faire and he chargeth himselfe with   05 19 04
And his disbursments to be   00 12 00
Remaines due to the Towne   05 06 06
Which he payes in open Court and is discharged

Edward Paulett Account for the Milnes.
At this Court Edward Paulett accounteth for the proffitt of the Milles and
he chargeth himselfe with Receipts   29 18 01
And his disbursments to be   26 17 04
Arreares together   01 11 03
Remaines due to the Towne   01 09 06
Which he payes in open Court.

John Turners Account for the Milnes.
At this Court John Turner accounteth for the proffitts of the Milles and
he chargeth himselfe with Receipts   27 04 10
And his disbursments to be   18 10 02
Remaines due to the Towne   08 14 08
Which he payes in Open Court and is discharged.

Mr Robert Calcrafts Account for the Millnes.
At this Court Mr Robert Calcraft accounteth for the proffitts of the Milles &
he chargeth himselfe with Receipts of   27 03 04
And his disbursments to be   24 13 00
Remaines due to the Towne   03 10 04
Which he payes in open Court and is discharged.

John Papes Account for the Milnes.
At this Court John Pape accounteth for the proffitts of the Milles and he
chargeth himselfe with Receipt of   07 03 02
And his disbursments to be   00 19 02
Remaines to the Towne   06 04 00
Which he paid to Mr Robert Calcraft the late Alderman

[fo. 517r] **Ninth Court of Richard Calcraft, 15 August 16670** [*recte* 1670]

Mr John Welbys money to be paid.
Whereas Mr Alderman this day acquainted the Court that Mr John Welby had sued Mr Grant for 130 li which this Corporacion doth [*sic*] unto the said Mr Welby and Mr Alderman also acquainted the Court that Doctor Hurst would this day pay fifty pounds into the Townes hand (the interest thereof) to be paid for ever towards the Sallary for his Schoole Dames so that if any Gentleman of this Court would be bound for a 100 li the Towne might pay xxx li and thereby cleare the said debt to Mr Welby Whereupon Mr Edward Rawlinson, Mr John Coddington and Mr John Winge for the good and Welfaire of this Corporacion are willing and contented to become [*sic*] with Mr Grant for 100 li for the use of this Burrough they haveing the like securitie for the bearing of them harmles as the rest of the Gentlemen have that are bound for the Townes debt which this Court doth promise shall be faithfully performed to them.

Mr Robert Hurst made free.
At this Court came Mr Robert Hurst sonn to Doctor Thomas Hurst and desired to be admitted a free Burgesse of this Corporacion whereunto this Court doth condiscend and according to Auntient custome the said Mr Robert Hurst laid downe his x li which said summe was frothwith [*sic*] by a Generall consent of this Court all given him againe this Court haveing a great kindnes for him both out of respect to his father and of his favors to this Corporacion And the said Mr Hurst did pay his fees to Clarke and Serjents and so was admitted and sworne free Burgesse of this Corporacion.

The Redd Lyon & the Schoole house deedes read & approved of.
At this Court the writeinges concerning Doctor Hurst Schoole House and the Settlement of the Redd Lyon for the securitie of the sallory due to the Schoole Dames was this day read and allowed and approved of the whole Court.

An Assessment of 14 li for the Constables.
At this Court it is ordered that an Assessment of xiiij li be made and laid upon this Burrough for the payment of the Constables there bills of disbursments for this present yeare an estimate being taken what those perticular sumes aboute unto And the Cheife Constables and Under Constables are appointed Assessors and the Under Constables Collectors thereof.

At this Court Anthony Hotchkin accounteth for the proffitts of the Milnes.

[fo. 517v] **Tenth Court of Richard Calcraft, 29 August 1670**

Sir Edmond Turner made free.
At this Court came Sir Edmond Turner of South Stoake within this libertie Barronett and desired to be admitted a free Burgesse of this Corporacion to which this Court

doth chearefully and freely condiscend and according to Auntient custome the said Sir Edmond Turner did lay down his x li for his freedome which said sume of money this Court with an Unanimous and free consent did returne [the sum *crossed out*] againe to the said Sir Edmond Turner but he out of his respects to this Corporacion did give the said x li to the Towne And the said Sir Edmond Turner did pay the fees to the Clarke and Serjents and so was admitted and sworne a free Burgesse of this Corporacion.

Eleventh Court of Richard Calcraft, 16 September 1670

Mr Grant, Mr Rawlinson, Mr Coddington & Mr Winge to be saved harmles from two bonds which they entred into for the Towns use.
Whereas Mr Thomas Grant & Mr Edward Rawlinson do stand joyntly & severally bound unto Richard Calcraft and Thomas Bearnes Gentleman in one obligacion bearing date the vijth day of December 1670 in the sume of 100 li Condicioned for the true payment of 51 li 10s in & upon the vijth day of March then next following And whereas also Mr John Coddington and Mr John Wing do stand joyntly & severally bound unto the said Richard Calcraft and Thomas Bearnes in one obligacion bearing date the vijth day of September 1670 in the sume of 100 li Condicioned for the true payment of 51 li 10s in & upon the vijth day of March then next ensueing All which said principall sumes of money were by the parties aforesaid borrowed and received by the Chaimberlaine of this Burrough to & for the onely proper use & behoofe of the same and paid to Mr John Welby in discharge of the bond whereon Mr Grant and other stood bound and the parties before named became bound at the intreaty & request of this Burrough Now this Court doth for themselves & their Successors firmely promise well and truly from time to time and at all times hereafter to save keepe harmeles & indempnifie the Gentlemen so bound as aforesaid & every of them their & every of their Heires Executors & Administrators of & from all & all manner of payments penalties forfeitures & suites of law whatsoever which shall or may happen arise or grow for or by reason of the said recited obligacions & Condicions thereupon written And that the Gentlemen shall be entred into the securitie of the tolles as the rest of the Gentlemen that are ingaged for the Townes Debts.

[fo. 518r] Twelfth Court of Richard Calcraft, 20 October 1670

Mr Aldermans Account.
At this Court Mr Alderman accounteth for all moneys by him disbursed upon the publike concerne of this Corporacion and that the same amounts unto xxs xd Which is paid unto him in open Court.

Coroners Account.
At this Court Mr Robert Calcraft Comburgesse & Coroner for this Burrough and Soake of Grantham for the yeare now past accounteth and saith that as Casualties happened

this yeare there was one Elizabeth Enderby who rideing in a Waine of Mr Luddington of Carleton Scroope that was loaden with mault and other Comodities goeing from Grantham to Carleton aforesaid in the feild of Londonthorpe within the libertie the Waine overthrowing and the said Elizabeth Enderby sitting on the mault with the overthrow thereof was flung a great way of from the said Waine and the said Elizabeth Enderby being very weake & infirme and not able to helpe herselfe and the said fall being great the violence thereof did take away her breath and did bruse her in severall places and by reason thereof shee suddenly died And the Jury impannelled did find the Waine Corne and other the goodes in the Waine the Narr hind horse and the Narr bullokes to be the moving instruments towards her death And the said Coroner further accounteth and saith that there was one Elizabeth Waite of Denton who was delivered of a Basterd Child which was found dead And the Jury summoned & sworne to inquire the cause of the childs death found that the Child was not timely borne and by reason thereof did languish and languishing died And that nothing did accrue thereby to the benefitt of the Burrough.

Escheators Accounts.
At this Court Mr John Lenton Escheator gives an Account of all moneys by him received for the yeare past for light Unlawfull and defective weights and measures and he chargeth

himselfe with Receipt	00 08 00
And his disbursments to be	00 04 06
Remaines due to the Towne	00 03 06

Which he payes in open Court and is discharged.

Time given for others to account.
At this Court the Churchwardens Chaimberlaine and Collectors for Schoole Rents have further time to perfect their Accounts.

Mr Lentons Account for tolle.
At this Court Mr John Lenton accounteth for the proffitts of the tolles for the moneth

of July last and he chargeth himselfe with	01 19 02
And his disbursments to be	00 06 06
Remaines due to the Towne	01 12 08

Which he payes in open Court & is discharged.

Mr Tomlinsons Account for tolle.
At this Court Mr Joseph Tomlinson accounteth for the proffitts of the tolles for the moneth

of August last and he chargeth himselfe with	01 05 01
And his disbursments to	00 04 00
Remaines due to the Towne	01 01 01

Which he payes in open Court to the Chaimberlaine and is discharged.

[fo. 518v]

At this Court Mr Alderman accounteth for the proffitts of the tolles for the moneth of September last and he chargeth himselfe with 02 07 10 ob
And his disbursments to be 00 04 08
Remaines to the Towne 02 03 02 ob
Which he payes in open Court & is discharged

At this Court the Constables gives an Account of the Constables Assessment as followeth vzt

Marketplace bill	04 17 05
Abatements	00 02 05
Collected and paid	04 15 00
High Streete bill	02 13 07
abatements	00 01 00 ob
Collected & paid	02 12 06 ob
Westgate bill	02 11 05
Abatements	00 03 02
Collected & paid	02 08 03
Walkergate	00 15 05
Abatements	00 00 09
Collected & paid	00 14 02
Swinegate	01 01 09
Collected & paid	01 01 09
Castlegate	02 01 05
Abatements	00 00 11
Collected & paid	02 00 06

[fo. 519r]

At an Assembly holden by Mr Richard Calcraft Alderman and the Comburgesses and Burgesses of Grantham aforesaid in Corpus Christi Quire within the Prebendarie there & on Friday next day after St Luke being the 21 October 1670.

First did sitt downe upon the Cusheon or place of Eleccion the said Mr Richard Calcraft in Corpus Christi Quire with in the prebendarie Church there

Next to him did sitt upon the Cusheon or place of Eleccion two Comburgesses vzt Mr Joseph Tomlinson and Mr Richard Holley

Then was there two Comburgesses in the Church vzt Mr John Lenton and Mr George Short

Then was sent downe to those two Comburgesses to make them three one other Comburgesse vzt Mr Thomas Grant

Out of which three Comburgesses in the Church one was chosen to come up and sitt on the

Cusheon or place of Eleccion one other Comburgesse vzt Mr John Lenton

Then was there three Comburgesses upon the Cusheon or place of Eleccion vzt Mr Joseph Tomlinson, Mr Richard Holley and Mr John Lenton

And then was there in the Church two Comburgesses vzt Mr George Short and Mr Thomas Grant

Out of which three Comburgesses upon the Cusheon or place of Eleccion vzt Mr Joseph Tomlinson, Mr Richard Holley and Mr John Lenton one is to be chosen Alderman for the next ensueing yeare

And so by an unanimous consent and vote of this Assembly Mr Joseph Tomlinson is nominated Alderman for the next ensueing yeare

Whereupon the said Mr Richard Calcraft dischargeth himselfe from the place & office of Alderman according to Auntient custome And the Mr Joseph Tomlinson now elected Alderman in his place and stead hath at this Assembly take [sic] the oath of Alderman of this Burrough and Soake of Grantham according to the Auntient and laudable custome of the Burrough aforesaid

And so this Assembly breakes up.

[fo. 519v] [Blank page]

THE HALL BOOK OF GRANTHAM 1670–1671

[fo. 600r] **First Court of Joseph Tomlinson 28 October 1670**

Mr Joseph Tomlinson Alderman
Mr Thomas Short Comburgesse
Mr Thomas Grant Comburgess
Mr Michaell Taylor Comburgess
Mr Robert Calcraft Comburgess
Mr Richard Calcraft Comburgess
Mr Richard Halley Comburgess
Mr John Lenton Comburgess
Mr George Short Comburgess
Mr Henry Humes Comburgess
Mr Edward Rawlinson Comburgess
Mr John Coddington Comburgess
Mr John Winge Comburgess

Robert Cole
Thomas Matkin
William Milles
John Turner
Thomas Ireland
Edward Paulett
Christofer Thompson
William Bury
Anthony Hotchkin
Henry Coverly
John Pape
John Walker

The Names of the Officers [*no post titles are given in the original*]

Mr Richard Calcraft
Mr Richard Holley
Christopher Thompson
Thomas Fisher
Anthony Hotchkin
Edward Leivesly
Mr John Coddington
Thomas Cole
Thomas Ireland
Henry Coverly
Thomas Chrichloe
William Clarke
John Robinson
Joseph Burnham
Thomas Frith
Richard Hickson
John Still
George Read
Thomas Hodgson
Francis Bristow

Mr Alderman
Christofer Tompson
Anthony Hotchkin
Thomas Briggs
Edward Archer
George Hanson
William Scott
Edward Ulliott
Henry Wright
Thomas Marshall
John Ingerson
William Hodgkinson
Thomas Calcraft
Richard Blacke
Richard Blacke
William Knewstubbs

Thomas Rowley
William Haskerd

[fo. 600v]

The Names of the Commoners
Marketplace
Thomas Chrichloe
William Clarke
Nicholas Becke
William Berriffe
Edward Leivesly
Thomas Charles
Hamlett Brumpton
Thomas Cole
Edward Bristow
Thomas Hodgson
Thomas Archer
John Robinson
High Streete
Richard Hauley
George Read Junior

Westgate
Edward Kenion
Thomas Frith
Richard Hickson
Thomas Fishar
Francis Bristow

Walkergate
George Read senior
John Still

Swinegate
Christofer Hanson

Castlegate
Thomas Rowley

Chartors delivered.
At this Court Mr Richard Calcraft the late Alderman delivered up the three Chartor Boxes with all the Chartors.

The Exemplir of Edward the 4th
Henry the Eight his Chartor
Edward the Sixth his Chartor for the Schoole
Elizabeth her Chartor of Confirmacion
Judge Dyers Award
Stamford writings
Escheators Pattent
Kinge James Chartor

King Charles the 1th [*sic*] Charter
King Charles the 2d Charter

Librarey Writeinges
Towne Armes
A writeings with many Seales

The Towne plate delivered up.
At this Court was delivered to Mr Alderman by Mr Richard Calcraft late Alderman all the Townes plate which is as followeth
The Horserace Cupp
Mr Archers Boll
Mr Wheatelye Cann

Two Tunnes
Mr Kirkbyes Boll
Mr Greenewood twelve Spounes

Mr Horsemans Boll
Mr Greenewoods Cann
Mr Batties Beaker

One Salt with Cover
One wine Boll Mr Horsemans
The waites Cognizances

Accounts to be examined.
At this Court Mr Thomas Grant, Mr Michaell Taylor, Robert Cole, Edward Paulett, Thomas Cole and William Clarke do meete upon Thursday next to examine the Account of the Churchwarden, Chaimberlaine and Collectors for Schoole Rents and to returne an Account thereof the next Court day.

[fo. 601r]

A Brasse stricke to be provided.
Whereas Mr Alderman this day acquainted the Court that by a late Act of Parlyament it is enacted that there shall be a Measure of Brasse also provided and chained in the Markett for the Measuring of Corne and graine containeing eight gallonds to the Bussell Winchester Measure and that it ought to have beene in readines before Michaelmas last as also that there is a penaltie of 5 li every Markett Day that the said Measure should be wanting and that Newarke hath bought a brasse stricke and chained it in the Markett. It is therefore ordered that a brasse stricke be sent for with all conveniencie and that the same be chained in the Market as by the said Act is limitted and directed.

A treaty to be had about the Milnes.
At this Court it is ordered that Mr Alderman, Mr Grant, Mr Robert Calcraft, Mr Richard Calcraft, Robert Cole, Edward Paulett, Thomas Cole and Thomas Archer do treat with Doctor Hurst aboute purchaseing of the Milnes and that they certifie to the Court there proceedinges therein.

A lease of Denton tolle lett.
At this Court Robert Wollands takes a lease of Denton tolle for three yeares from the last Account day at three pounds and ten shillinges per Annum And he gives in Earnest thereof xijd.

Chartor Assessment to be cleared.
At this Court it is ordered that the Constables cleare the Chartor Assessment with in three weekes upon paine of xxs a man to & for the Use of this Corporacion.

John Walker 2d xij man.
At this Court John Walker is chosen one of the Second Company.
In the Kallendar
Thomas Charles
Edward Leivesly
Thomas Archer

William Haskerd made free.
At this Court came William Haskerd Felmonger and desired to be admitted a Freeman of this Corporacion to whose request this Court doth condiscend whereupon he payes ijs vjd to the Box as Freeborne and his fees to Clarke and Serjents and takes the oath of Freeman according to Auntient custome And is admitted a freeman accordingly.

Simon Goodwin made free.
At this Court came Simon Goodwin a Forrainer & desired to be admitted a free Burgesse of this Corporacion to which this Court doth condiscend whereupon he lays downe his x li and this Court out of respect to him gives him againe 03 li 06s 08d and he payes the fees to Clarke and Serjents and takes the oath of freeman according to Auntient custome.

[fo. 601v] **Second Court of Joseph Tomlinson 4 November 1670**

A Brasse stricke to be provided.
At this Court it is ordered that a Brasin stricke be sent for ought of the Exchequer according to the directions of a late Act of Parlyament made for setling of measures and that the same be paid for by the present Chaimberlaine to be paid out of the Chartor Assessment.

Mr Allsopp debt to be paid.
Whereas Mr Alderman this day acquainted the Court that Mr Allsopp did prosecute Mrs Leeming for xxx li remaineing of the 50 li which her husband was bound for as a debt oweing by this Corporacion and that it was convenient xxx li was taken up for the payment of the said debt Whereupon this Court desired Robert Cole and Thomas Matkin that they would be pleased to become bound for the use of this Corporacion for the sume of xxx li to which they freely consented And it is ordered that they have the like securitie for the saveing of them harmles as the rest of the Gentlemen that are bound for the Townes debts.

The Church to be beautified.
Whereas also Mr Alderman further acquainted the Court that Mr Burnett the present Minister had beene with him aboute beautifieing the Church And that in order thereunto he had treated with one Thomas Troope for the doeing thereof And that he did demand xxxv li whereof xxv li to be paid in money and the other x li to be for his freedome of this Burrough And that towards the raiseing of the said money there was some Gentlemen that would give to it As also that it was very necessarie that an Assessment of xxx li was laid upon this Burrough to defray the charge of drawing the Church with lime Whereupon it is ordered than an Assessment of xxx li be laid upon this Burrough for the beautifying and repaireing of the Church according to former rules prescribed and that Thomas Troope have xxv li in money and his freedome.

Swinegate Well to be repaired.
At this Court it is ordered that an Assessment of xxxs be made for the repaireing of Swinegate Well And that the Rent of a House in Castlegate demised to William Bury be yearely paid for the repaireing of the three Wells according to the donors guift to this Corporacion.

Collectors Accounts for the Schoole Rente.
At this Court Mr Edward Rawlinson and Nicholas Becke Collectors for the Schoole Rente for the yeare past and charge themselves with Receipt of   45 15 0
And their Disbursements to be & Arrears   41 03 4
Remains to the Towne   04 10 4
Which they pay in open Court and are discharged.

[fo. 602r] **Third Court of Joseph Tomlinson, 9 December 1670**

Mr Coverly to be paid the money due upon his Account as Chaimberlaine.
At this Court it is ordered that the Chamberlaine pay unto Henry Coverly viij li xixs due to him upon his Account as Chaimberlaine And the said Henry Coverly being willing to forbeare halfe the said money for some time so as vi li may be paid unto Mr Storer in part of his interest Whereupon it is ordered that vj li be paid to Mr Storer in part of his interest upon riseing of the Court and the remainder of the debt to Henry Coverly upon the first conveniencie.

An Agreement made for the Milnes.
Whereas Mr Alderman this day acquainted the Court that he had agreed with Doctor Hurst and Mr Welby for their parts in the Mills for 180 li apeice and Mr Welbys freedome, and that they were contented to forbeare their money have personall securitie which agreement this Court doth approve of and returne thankes to Mr Alderman for his care in the concernes of this Corporacion And thereupon Mr Alderman desired Mr George Short, Thomas Ireland, Henry Coverly, William Milles, John Turner, Edward Paulett, Anthony Hotchkin, John Pape, John Walker, Thomas Charles, William Berriffe and Thomas Cole that they would be pleased to be bound for the said money having the Milnes assigned over to them for their securitie to which proposall or desire all the said Gentlemen (except William Milles and John Turner not being present in Court) did freely for the good of this Burrough thereunto [sic] It is therefore ordered that Thomas Ireland, John Turner, Edward Paulett, John Pape, John Walker and Thomas Cole be bound to Doctor Hurst for his 180 li And that Mr George Short, William Milles, Henry Coverly, Anthony Hotchkin, Thomas Charles and William Berriffe be bound unto Mr John Welby for his 180 li And that the Milles shall be assigned be assigned [sic] over to the Gentlemen aforesaid for their securitie.

Mr Cole & Mr Matkin bound for 30 li -18s.
Whereas Robert Cole and Thomas Matkin do stand joyntly and severally bound unto Thomas Walton Gent in one obligacion bearing date the xviijth day of November last in the sume of 60 li Conditioned for the true payment of xxx li xviijs in or upon the xviijth day of May then next ensueing And whereas the said sume was by the Parties aforesaid borrowed and received by the Chaimberlaine of this Burrough to and for the onely proper use and behoofe of the same And the parties before named became bound as aforesaid at the entreatie and request of this Burrough Now this Court do for themselves and their Successors firmely promise well and truly from time to time and at all times hereafter to save keepe harmles and indempnifie the said Persons so bound as aforesaid and either of them their and either of their Heires Executors & Administrators of and from all and all manner of payments penalties forfeitures and suits of law whatsoever which shall or may happen arise or grow for or by reason of the said recited obligacion thereof and Condicon thereupon written.

Mr Humes Account for Tolle.
At this Court Mr Humes accounteth for the proffitt of the tolles for the moneth of November

whereby he chargeth himselfe with Receipt	02 05 02
Disbursments	00 06 08
Remains to the Towne & paid in Court	01 18 06

[fo. 602v] **Fourth Court of Joseph Tomlinson, 6 January 1670/1**

Mr Grants Account for tolls.
At this Court Mr Grant gives an Account of the Proffitts of the tolles for the moneth of October

and he chargeth himselfe with Receipt of	05 05 02
And his disbursments to be	01 00 07
Remaines to the Towne	04 04 07

Which he payes in open Court and he is discharged.

Mr Syston to leave the Schoole.
Whereas Mr Alderman this day acquainted the Court that Mr Syston the present Schoole Master had formerly given him notice to provide a new Schoole Master against Lady day next for he was in hopes Sir John Brownlow would give him Belton Liveing and if he had it he questioned whether Sir John would let him keepe the Schoole As also that he had given notice to Mr Syston to appeare at this Court to satisfie the Court if he did desire a new Schoole Master might be provided Whereupon Mr Syston appearing in Court did declare that he thought Sir John Brownlow would not let him continue in the Schoole and haveing the liveing therefore least the Schoole should be left void he out of respect to this Corporacion did give notice to Mr Alderman to provide a new Schoole Master. But Sir John haveing since given him Belton liveing and being willing that he

have it and continue in the Schoole It is his desire to this Court that they would please to let him injoy the same and that he would keepe the orders of the Schoole and performe his duty according to the Canons of the Church And thereupon this Court doth order that the said Mr Systons do goe on in the Schoole at present And that they will peruse the Articles and Grant of the Schoole and give him a further answer the next Court day.

Richard Blacke debt to be paid.
Whereas Mr Alderman this day also acquainted the Court that Richard Blacke the present Gaoler was sent to Lincolne Gaole by Mr Glover and that he claimed viij li debt of him when in truth there was but xxiijs due to him. And that the Gaole being now void it was necessarie a new Gaoler should be chosen unlesse any of this Court would be bound with him to answer the said Accion And thereupon Mr Taylor & Mr Robert Calcraft are willing to become bound with Mr Alderman for the Appearance of the said Richard Blacke for that Accion It is therefore desired that the Eleccion of a Gaoler be putt of, till next Court day.

[fo. 603r] **Fifth Court of Joseph Tomlinson** [*no date given*]

Mr Taylors Account.
At this Court Mr Michaell Taylor accounteth for the proffitts of the tolle for the moneth of

December and he chargeth himselfe with Receipt of tolles	06 11 03
And his disbursments to be	01 02 06
Remaines due to the Towne	05 09 03

Which he payes in open Court and is discharged.

Goodes to be Apprized Chartor.
At this Court it is ordered that Richard Hickson, George Read, Edward Kenion and Joseph Burnham do apprize the Goodes distrained for the Chartor Assessment which apprizement they do make in open Court and have thereunto subscribed their hands.

Mr Richard Poole admitted Usher.
At this Court came Mr Richard Poole Minister and desired the favour of this Court that they would please to admitt him to be Usher in the Free Schoole belonging to this Corporacion and that he would serve in the said place to the utmost of his power whereupon this Court do admit the said Mr Poole to be Usher in the Schoole aforesaid.

Richard Newton admitted Gaoler.
At this Court came Richard Newton and desired to be admitted Gaoler in the Roome of Richard Blacke who still continues in Lincolne Gaole and not likely to be discharged by reason of some other Accions laid upon him Whereupon this Court do admitt of the said Nicholas Newton to be Gaoler and do ordered [*sic*] that Richard Blacke have his Headland and all the proffitts for the yeare past and the Goodes he sett downe since he came to the Gaole.

Mr Syston to leave the Schoole.
Whereas Mr Alderman this day sent for Mr Syston the Head Schoole Master and upon his Appearance in Court Mr Alderman was pleased to acquaint him that he and his Brethren had pursued the Grant and Articles of the Schoole in pursuance of an order made the last Court of which this Court hath beene also acquainted And that this Court do thinke it very necessarie and convenient that he observed the Articles of the Schoole otherwise not to continue Schoole Master And then the said Mr Syston did desire of this Court that they would please that he might continue as he did while Lady day next and then he would keepe curate at Belton and would keepe constantly at the Schoole (excepting when Sir John Brownlow was in the Countrie) which said answer of Mr Syston was noe way satisfactorie to this Court they considering the Court cannot be well followed if he continue both in the Schoole and Belton living But that he ought to part with one of them Whereupon it is this day ordered that the said Mr Syston do continue in the Schoole as Schoole Master till Lady day next he keepeing & observeing the Articles of the Schoole aforesaid.

Mr Aldermans Sallary to be paid.
At this Court it is ordered that the Chaimberlayne pay Mr Alderman his sallory upon the first receipt of money.

[fo. 603v] **Sixth Court of Joseph Tomlinson, 27 January 1670/1**

Mrs Leemings Account to be stated.
At this Court it is ordered that Robert Cole and Anthony Hotchkin do examine the Chaimberlaines Booke and state the Account of Mrs Leeming and certifie the Court thereof.

Part of the Church Wardens Payments limitted.
Whereas upon reading of the Churchwardens Account this day the Court observed that there was six shillinges for washing of the Surplice and Communion Cloth and ordering of the pewter which was thought too much And that there is ijs vjd paid yearely to Ralph Osborne Saxton for keepeing young people out of the Alyers on Shrove Tuesday which he doth neglect As also that there are great Sumes laid out for dinners at Visitacions which ought to be moderated It is therefore ordered that the Churchwardens for the future do pay foure shillinges a yeare for the Surplice washing Communion Cloth and xijd a yeare for ordering the pewter And that they forbeare paying the ijs vjd to the Saxton as formerly for Shrove Tuesday And that they shall not at any time hereafter lay out or expend above twenty shillinges at any Visitacion dinner And that this order shall be a direccion to all Succeeding Churchwardens.

Thomas Charles Account as Churchwarden.
At this Court Thomas Charles Churchwarden accounteth for the Quarteridge.
which amounts to the sume of   21 03 10
Abatements allowed of   01 09 08

Remaines to account for	19 14 02
Church lands & Bell money	13 13 04
Total	33 07 06

At this Court Thomas Charles also accounteth for the xxx li Assessment.

as followeth vizt Grantham	21 05 00
Manthorpe	02 09 08
Spittlegate	01 15 03
Total	25 09 11
The Accounts stands thus Receipts	58 17 05
Disbursments	56 02 04
Remaines	02 15 01
Arreares together	03 19 09

Christopher Thompson Account as Churchwarden.
At this Court Christopher Thompson Churchwarden gives an Account for

the Quarteridge & he chargeth himselfe with	26 17 02
And his disburments to be	29 06 10
Remaines to the Accomptant	02 09 08
Charged upon the Accomptant in Arreares	02 00 00
Remaines to him	00 09 08

[fo. 604r] **Seventh Court of Joseph Tomlinson, 9 March 1670/1**

Overseers for Swinegate Well appointed.
At this Court it is ordered that John Still and William Newton be Overseers for Swinegate Well and that they lay an Assessment of xxxxs upon the Inhabitants in Walkergate and Swinegate for the repaireing of the said Well And that the xs a yeare issueing out of a house in Castlegate demised to William Bury be for the time to come employed for the repaireing of the Common Wells of this Towne according to the donors guift.

James Long renews his lease.
At this Court came James Long and takes a lease of this Corporacion of a house in Castlegate for xxj years from and after the expiracion of a former lease thereof in being which said lease ends at Michaelmas next paying for a fine the sume of iij li vjs viijd in manner following that is to say xxxiijs upon the 24 day of June next ensueing and xxxiijs iiijd remainder of iij li vjs viijd at or upon the first day of May 1672 and giveing securitie for Rent and repaires And he gives in earnest thereof xijd.

Cheife Constables to attend Mr Alderman; fine ijs Petty Constables fine xijd.
Whereas Mr Alderman this day acquainted the Court that the Cheife Constables and Petty Constables of this Burrough did not carry their Constables Staves with them to the Church as by former orders of this Court they are injoyned and that it was by reason

the fine imposed upon them was too smale and that it convenient the fine should be raised if this Court approved thereof Whereupon it is this day ordered that the Cheife Constables do every Sunday morning and evening and upon every Christmas day the fifth day of November and the 29 day of May being Holliday do attend Mr Alderman to the Church and from the Church in their Gownes with their Staves upon paine to forfeite for every Offence ijs apeice to the use of this Corporacion And likewise that the Petty Constables do every Sunday and upon the Hollidays aforesaid carrey their Staves to the Church upon paine to forfeite xijd apeice for every Offence to the use aforesaid.

First & 2nd Company to goe to Church in their Gownes; fine xijd.
Whereas Mr Alderman also acquainted the Court that some of the first and second Company did not come in their Gownes to the Church on Sundays and Hollidays and there excuse was by reason of Raine happening sometimes And that it was very necessarie all of them should goe to the Church in their Gownes according to former order of this Court Whereupon it is ordered that the first and 2nd Company do every Sunday and upon every Christmas day upon the fifth day of November and the 29 May come to the Church constantly in the Gownes whether raine or any other foule weather happen upon paine to forfeite xijd for every Offence to the use of this Corporacion.

Redd Lyon to pay the charges of Suite
Whereas the Towne Clarke this day acquainted the Court that there was xxxviij li due to him upon his bill for the Redd Lyon and desired the Court that he might receive the Sume out of the Rent of the said Inn Whereupon it is ordered that Thomas Horsfeild the present Tenant of the Redd Lyon shall pay the sume of xxxv li to the Towne Clarke in manner following that is to say x li a yeare for three yeares now next ensueing at Michaelmas and Lady day by even and equall porcions and five pounds at the halfe yeares and after the expiracion of the said three yeares the first payment thereof to be made at Michaelmas next and the other three pounds to be abated out of his bill by and with his owne consent to this Corporacion.

[fo. 604v] **Eighth Court of Joseph Tomlinson 24 March 1670/1**

Mr Short charges as Churchwarden to be paid.
At this Court it is ordered that the Chaimberlaine receive xxixs of Thomas Charles Churchwarden due upon his Account and pay the same unto the Towne Clarke for charges of suite due from Mr George Short when he was sued by William Palmer as Churchwarden for the debts and due from William Laine as Churchwarden at the Suite of Aquilia Willbore.

Thomas Hatfeild came to pay the Townes debt.
This day Mr Richard Calcraft acquainted the Court that Thomas Hatfeild desired this Court to forbeare him the five pounds due to the Towne which was Mr Pelles guift and he would give new securitie and pay of the charges Whereupon it is ordered that Thomas

Hatfeild giveing good securitie for the said five pounds and paying of the charges he have the said money for another yeare.

William Newton, William Kirke made free.
At this Court came William Newton Baker and William Kirke Butcher both of them being free borne and haveing each of them served seaven yeares Apprenticeshipp to the said trades and desired to be admitted freemen of this Corporacion to whose request this Court doth condiscend Whereupon the said William Newton and William Kirke have paid ijs vjd apeice to the Box as freeborne and vjd apeice to the Clerk and Serjents and have taken the oath of Freemen according to the custome of this Burrough and are admitted Free Burgesses of this Borrough.

Charges aboute the Gaole.
At this Court the Chaimberlaine is ordered to pay five shillinges unto Richard Blacke which he laid downe for repaireing the Guild Hall.

Nicholas Becke Account as Cole Buyer.
At this Court Nicholas Becke Colebuyer gives an Account of the proffitt ariseing by the Cole for

the yeare past and he chargeth himselfe with receipt of	18	12	08
And his disbursments to be	14	08	00
Stocke increased and Remaines to the Towne	20	03	00

Lent the Towne out of the Colesstocke v li.
At this Court the Towne borrowes out of the Stocke of the Cole money five pounds to be paid againe by the Chaimberlaine.

William Berriffe, Thomas Cole new Cole buyer.
At this Court William Berriffe and Thomas Cole are chosen and appointed Colebuyers for the sueing yeare and paid to them.

Sandpitt laine tolle lett.
At this Court Thomas Fishar takes a lease of the tolle of Sandpitt laine for five shillinges the next Account day.

[fo. 605r] **Ninth Court of Joseph Tomlinson, 12 May 1671**

Mr Grants Account for tolle.
At this Court Mr Thomas Grant gives an Account for the proffitt of the tolles for the moneth of

Aprill last and he chargeth himselfe with Receipt of	24	07	04
And his disbursments to be	01	15	06
Remaines due to the Towne	22	12	03

Which he payes downe in open Court and is discharged. Add   00 02 04
[sums do not balance]

Mr Calcraft Account for tolle.
At this Court Mr Richard Calcraft gives an Account for the proffitt of the tolles for the moneth of
March last and he chargeth himselfe with receipt of [*no sum given*]
And his disbursments to be [*left blank*]
Remaines due to the Towne [*left blank*]
Which he payes in open Court and is discharged.

The Elleccion of the next Alderman.
For the more peaceable and orderly proceedings at the Eleccion of the next succeeding Alderman It is at this Court ordered that upon the next Elleccion day Mr Henry Humes be sent downe into the Church to Mr Thomas Grant and Mr George Short to make three Comburgesses there Out of which three Comburgesses there It is likewise agreed that Mr George Short shall be brought upon the Cusheon or place of Elleccion to Mr Richard Holley and Mr John Lenton to make three Comburgesses there Out of which three Comburgesses upon the Cusheon or place of Elleccion with a free and unanimous consent Mr Richard Holley is nominated Alderman for this next ensueing yeare.

Towne Hall to be repaired.
At this Court it is ordered that the Towne Hall be forthwith repaired by the present Chaimberlaine and that Mr Alderman and his Brethren do indeavour to get the Soake to contribute towards the repaireing of it freely of their owne good Will.

Mr Systons to resigne the Schoole.
At this Court came Mr Thomas Syston the present Schoole Master and promised to resigne the Schoole at Midsomer next and the House as soone after as possibly he could remove his goodes.

Overseers for High Streete Well appointed.
At this Court Charles Wetherill and Robert Calcraft are appointed Overseers for High Streete Well and it ordered [*sic*] that they have an Assessment of 40s upon the Inhabitants of High Streete and Castlegate for the repairing of the said Well.

[fo. 605v]

At an Assembly holden by the Comburgesses and Burgesses of Grantham aforesaid in Corpus Christi Quire with in the Prebendarie Church there on Thursday the sixth day of July Anno Domini 1671 after the decease of Mr Joseph Tomlinson late Alderman and for the Election of a new Alderman in his place and stead according to the Auntient Custome of this Burrough.

First did sitt downe upon the Cusheon or place of Eleccion Mr Richard Holley and Mr John Lenton in Corpus Christi Quire within the Prebendarie Church there

Then was there in the Church two Comburgesses vizt Mr Thomas Grant and Mr George Short.

Then was sent downe into the Church to those two Comburgesses to make them three one other Comburgesse vizt Mr Henry Humes

Out of which three Comburgesses in the Church one was chosen to come up and sitt upon the Cusheon or place of Eleccion one other Comburgesse vizt Mr George Short

Then was there three Comburgesses upon the Cusheon or place of Eleccion vizt Mr Richard Holley, Mr John Lenton and Mr George Short

And then was there remaining in the Church two Comburgesses vizt Mr Thomas Grant and Mr Henry Humes

Out of which three Comburgesses upon the Quishion or place of Eleccion vizt Mr Richard Holley, Mr John Lenton and Mr George Short one is to be chosen Alderman for the residue of this ensueing yeare for this Burrough of Grantham in the place [*sic*] Mr Joseph Tomlinson late Alderman deceased

And so by the consent and vote of this Assembly Mr Richard Holley is chosen Alderman for the residue of this yeare yet to come. And the said Mr Richard Holley being so elected Alderman as aforesaid for remainder of this yeare did at this Assembly take the oath of Alderman according to the Auntient and laudable Custome of this Burrough.

And so this Assembly breakes up.

[fo. 606r] **First Court of Richard Holley, 10 July 1671**

The Elleccion of the next Alderman.
For the more peaceable and orderly proceeding at the Eleccion of the next Succeeding Alderman It is at this Court ordered that upon the next eleccion day Mr Edward Rawlinson be sent downe into the Church to Mr Thomas Grant and Mr Henry Humes to make three Comburgesses there Out of which three Comburgesses in the Church It is likewise agreed that Mr Henry Humes be brought upon the Cusheon or place of Eleccion to Mr John Lenton and Mr George Short to make there [*rectius* three] Comburgesses there Out of which three Comburgesses upon the Cusheon with a free and unanimous consent Mr John Lenton is nominated Alderman for this next ensueing [*sic*] he haveing first promised to leave of selling of Ale and beare during the time of Aldermanshipp.

Mr Syston to leave the Schoole.
At this Court came Thomas Syston Clarke and agreed with this Court that in consideracion of Tenn pounds to be paid to him by the Towne on the five & twentieth day of this instant July he will deliver unto the Alderman and Burgesses of this Burrough peaceable possession of the Colledge House and Schoole House of Grantham now in his possession to be disposed of as they shall see Convenient.

Mr Bacon, Mr Rookesby, Henry Kellam made free.
At this Court came Francis Bacon Gent & Henry Kellam & Nathaniell Rookesby Gent & desired to be admitted free Burgesses of this Corporacion to which this Court doth consent whereupon the said Mr Bacon & Henry Kellam as free borne payes to the Box ijs vjd apiece & Mr Rookesby as a forrainer having served Mr William Parkins being a freeman Eight yeares as a Clarke pays to the Box vs & both take the oath of freemen according to custome.

Mr Walker elected Schoole Master.
Whereas Mr Alderman this day acquainted the Court that he had received a letter from Mr Walker and caused the said letter to be read in Court upon reading whereof the Court was satisfied that Mr Walker would come to be Head Schoole Master within this Corporacion if he should be freely elected thereunto Whereupon this Court taking into consideracion that he is a learned Person and a Schoole Master of great note and that it may be very advantageous to this Corporacion do with a free and unanimous consent elect the said Mr Walker Head Schoole Master within this Burrough.

Accounts to be examined.
At this Court it is ordered that Mr Thomas Grant, Mr George Short, Mr Henry Humes, Mr Robert Cole and Edward Paulet do meete and examine the Accounts of Anthony Hotchkin late Chaimberlaine and make a returne of their proceedings therein the next Court.

Mr Wing cleares his Account as Milne Master.
At this Court Mr John Wing payes iij li vs due upon his Account as Milne Master.

James Long payes part of his fine.
At this Court James Long payes in part of his fine for his lease xxxiijs iiijd.

Mr Humes Account for tolle.
At this Court Mr Henry Humes gives an Account for the proffitt of the tolles for the moneth May

last and he chargeth himselfe with receipt of	05	07	01
And his Disbursments to be	00	12	04
Remaines	04	14	09

Which he payes in open Court & is discharged.

[fo. 606v] Second Court of Richard Holley 14 July 1671

The fine imposed for revealing the Secretts of the Court.
Whereas it was this day moved in Court that some Persons of late had revealed the Secretts of the Court contrary to the orders in that behalfe made And being also moved that if part of the fines mencioned in the said orders was given to such Persons as shall

give an Account to the Court of all those that revealed the Secretts of the Court it would be an incouragment to them and a great meanes to prevent such inconveniencies Whereupon it is fully order [sic] that all and every Person and Persons who hereafter shall make appeare to this Court that any number thereof hath revealed the Secretts of this Court that then he or they shall receive one third part of all such fines and forfeitures as shall be imposed upon any Persons for the Offence aforesaid.

Mr Walker settled Schoole Master.
Whereas Mr Alderman this day acquainted the Court that Mr Walker was not willing to accept of the Head Schoole Masters place belonging to the Corporacion he haveing the proposicions performed with Mr Tomlinson the late Alderman promised him that was to have iij li vjs viijd added to this Sallary and some Roomes made convenient And that being the treatie was now likely to be concluded it was very requisite the Court should settle the said proposalls The which this Court takeing into consideracion as also that the said Mr Walker is a Worthy Person a learned Schollar and an able Schoole Master and is likely to improve the Schoole to the advantage of this Corporacion It is therefore at this Court ordered by an unanimous consent of this Court that the said Mr Walker be admitted and he is hereby admitted Head Schoole Master of this Towne Upon the same Condicions and termes as other the Head Schoole Masters of this Burrough have formerly held and injoyed the same (except termes following that is to say that he [sic] said Mr Walker shall yearely from time to time during the time he shall continue Head Schoole Master receive an Additionall Sallary of iij li vjs viijd and have some Roomes made convenient for him according to the proposicions formerly made And it is further ordered that the said Additionall Sallary of iij li vjs viijd shall not be Drawne into precedent for any succeeding Schoole Master but that the same shall be left to the Will and Pleasure of Mr Aldermans Court for the time being anything before in this order contained to the contrary notwithstanding.

Mr Robert Cole chosen of the first Company.
At this Court Mr Robert Cole was chosen of the first Company upon the death of Mr Joseph Tomlinson late Alderman.

Thomas Charles chosen of the 2d Company.
At this Court Thomas Charles is chosen of the Second Company in the Roome of Mr Robert Cole.
In the Kallendar
Edward Leivesly
Thomas Archer
Thomas Fishar

[fo. 607r] **Third Court of Richard Holley, 4 August 1671**

Mr Calcraft Account for tolle.
At this Court Mr Richard Calcraft gives an Account of the proffitts of the tolles for the moneths
of July and August and he chargeth himselfe with Receipt of   03 14 06
And his disbursments to be   00 10 04
Remaines due to the Towne   03 04 02
Which he payes in open Court and is discharged.

Anthony Hotchkin Account as Chaimberlaine.
At this Court Anthony Hotchkin Chaimberlaine for part of the yeare past gives an Account and he
chargeth himselfe with Receipt of   156 15 07
And his disbursments to be   165 09 07
Remaines due to the Accomptant   008 14 00
Which is ordered to be paid unto him by the present Chaimberlaine.

Constables Assessment.
At this Court it is ordered that an Assessment of xvj li be made and laid upon this Burrough for the payment of the Constables their bills of disbursments to Passingers for the yeare past an estimate being taken what those perticular sumes amount unto And that notice be given in the Church the next Sunday of the time and place of making the said Assessment And that the Cheife Constables and Petty Constables are appointed Assessors and the Under Constables Collectors thereof.

Richard Segrave Mercer made free.
At this Court came Mr Richard Segrave Mercer sonn of Mr Segrave of Gunnerby a Forrainer and desired to be admitted a free Burgesse of this Burrough which this Court doth condiscend And thereupon he layes downe his x li according to custome And this Court takeing into consideracion that his Ancestors have lived for many years in this Corporacion As also that he is likely to make a good Townsman do give him againe v li and he is admitted a freeman and takes his oath accordingly and payes his fees to Clarke & Serjents according to custome.

Mr Long to be paid xxxxiijs.
At this Court it is ordered that the Chaimberlaine pay unto Mr Long the sume of xxxxiijs for defraying the charge of the Alderman and Escheator for not paying their proffers in his Majesties Court of Exchequer.

John Turner & Edward Paulett charges to be paid.
At this Court John Turner and Edward Paulett brought in a bill of Mr Seckers charges which was expended in defence of Horners suite against them as Cheife Constables for what they did in the execucion of their Office which comes to 4 li 4s 2d and desires

this Court that it may be paid And thereupon it is ordered that the same be inserted into the Constables bills for this yeare And that the said money be paid unto them to discharge Mr Secker, they acting for the preservacion of his Majesties peace and good of this Corporacion.

[fo. 607v] Fourth Court of Richard Holley, 22 September 1671

Comoners Assessment to the Chartor to be paid.
At this Court it is ordered that the Comoners pay the xs due from them for the Chartor Assessment and that Henry Coverly Cheife Constable do pay xvijs due upon his Account for the Chartor Assessment.

Widdow Hauley to have xxxs upon her Account.
At this Court it is ordered that Widd Hauley have xxxs due to her late husband which he laid downe for High Streete Well as Overseer And the Arreares due upon the Assessment granted to her husband be forthwith collected.

Mrs Secker to be distrained for the Chartor Assessment.
At this Court it is ordered that Mrs Secker be distrained of for vs due upon the Charter Assessment In pursuance whereof Nicholas Newton Bayliffe of the libertie George Read and William Haskerd Constables did goe from Court and tooke two pewter dishes as a distresse for the said Assessment which said pewter dishes are delivered into the custodie of the Alderman and Burgesses of this Corporacion.

A deputacion read for the Court of pleas.
Whereas the Towne Clarke produced a deputacion drawne by Mr Skipwith deputy Recorder for keepeing of the Court of pleas and if the Court pleased to approve thereof he would waite upon the Earle of Rutland Head Recorder to obtaine the sealing of it which being this day read and the Court considering that it may be very advantageous to the Towne and a generall good and ease to the Countrie do approve of the said deputacion And order that the Towne Clarke do waite upon the Right Honorable the Earle of Rutland to obtaine his hand & seale to the said deputacion.

Roger Blankney made free.
At this Court came one Roger Blackney [sic] a Blacke Smith formerly Farrier to the Right Honorable the Lord Rosse and desired to be admitted a free Burgesse of this Corporacion To which this Court doth condiscend Whereupon he layes downe his x li as a Forrainer according to custome And this Court haveing a respect to him as being a Servant to the Lord Rosse and being likely to prove a good Townsman do give him againe iij li vjs viijd And he takes the oath of freeman and payes his fees to Clarke and Serjent and is admitted a free Burgesse of this Burrough.

Mrs Tomlinsons Account.
At this Court Mrs Tomlinson sends in an Account of her late husband concerning his Receipts
and disbursments upon the Affaires of this Towne his Receipt 15 11 03
His disbursments 11 17 01
Remaines due to the Towne 03 14 02

[fo. 608r] **Fifth Court of Richard Holley 13 October 1671**

Mr Aldermans Account.
At this Court Mr Alderman gives an Account of his disburments upon the publike concerne of this Corporacion which comes to vjs vjd and it is paid unto him in open Court.

Escheators Account.
At this Court Mr Alderman also accounteth as Escheator for part of the yeare past wherein he
chargeth himselfe for light and unlawfull Weights and Measures with
Receipt of 00 06 00
And his Disbursments at every faire to 00 02 06
To the Towne Clarke for his attendance 00 02 06
Remaines to the Towne 00 01 00
Which he pays in open Court and is discharged.

Coroners Account.
At this Court Mr Richard Calcraft Coroner accounteth and saith that as Casualties happened this yeare there was one Richard Burbidge of Belton within the libertie a Milner who letting downe the Milne stone, it fell upon him and crushed his Backe against a post And that it was the cause of his death And that the Jury impannelled to inquire after the death of the said Richard Burbidge found he was slaine by misfortune, and apprized the said stone to vjs viijd And further he hath not to account.

Time given for Accomptants.
At this Court the Churchwardens Chaimberlaines and Collectors for Schoole Rents as [*sic*] further time to give up their Accounts.

Account of the Constables Assessment
At this Court the Constables gives an Account of their Constables Assessment for the yeare past as followeth
Marketplace 05 17 03
Abatements 00 02 00
Collected 05 15 03
High Streete 03 00 07

Abatements	00 02 01
Collected	02 18 06
Westgate	02 16 00
Abatements	00 02 01
Collected	02 13 11
Walkergate cleared	00 18 03
Swinegate cleared	01 08 00
Castlegate cleared	02 12 03

[fo. 608v]

At an Assembly holden by Mr Richard Holley Alderman and the Comburgesses and Burgesses of Grantham aforesaid in Corpus Christi Quire within the Prebendary Church there &c on Fryday next after St Lukes day being 20 October 1671.

First did sitt downe upon the Cusheon or place of Eleccion the said Mr Richard Holley in Corpus Christi Quire with in the Prebendarie Church thereof
Next to him did sitt upon the Cusheon or place of Eleccion two Comburgesses vizt Mr John Lenton and Mr George Short.
Then was there in the Church two Comburgesses vizt Mr Thomas Grant and Mr Henry Humes.
Then was sent downe in to the Church to those two Comburgesses to make them three one other Comburgesse vizt Mr Edward Rawlinson
Out of which three Comburgesses in the Church one was chosen to come up and sitt upon the Cusheon or place of Eleccion vizt Mr Henry Humes.
Then was there three Comburgesses upon the Cusheon or place of Eleccion vizt Mr John Lenton, Mr George Short & Mr Henry Humes
And then was there in the Church two Comburgesses vizt Mr Thomas Grant and Mr Edward Rawlinson.
Out of which three Comburgesses upon the Cusheon or place of Eleccion vizt Mr John Lenton, Mr George Short & Mr Henry Humes one is to be chosen Alderman for the ensueing yeare.
And so by an unanimous consent and vote of this Assembly Mr John Lenton is chosen Alderman for this next ensueing yeare.

Whereupon the said Mr Richard Holley dischargeth himselfe from the place and Office of Alderman according to Auntient Custome And the said Mr John Lenton now elected Alderman in his place & stead hath at this Assembly taken the oath of Alderman for this Burrough and Soake of Grantham according to the Auntient and laudable Customes of this Burrough.

And so this Assembly breakes up.

THE HALL BOOK OF GRANTHAM 1671–1672

[fo. 609r] **First Court of John Lenton, 27 October 1671**

Mr John Lenton Alderman
Mr Thomas Short Comburgess
Mr Thomas Grant Comburgess
Mr Michaell Taylor Comburgess
Mr Robert Calcraft Comburgess
Mr Richard Calcraft Comburgess
Mr Richard Holley Comburgess
Mr Henry Humes Comburgess
Mr Edward Rawlinson Comburgess
Mr John Coddington Comburgess
Mr John Wing Comburgess

Thomas Matkin
John Walker
William Milles
John Turner
Thomas Ireland
Edward Pawlett
Christofer Thompson
William Bury
Anthony Hotchkin
Henry Coverly
John Pape
Thomas Charles

The Names of the Officers

Coroner	Mr Richard Calcraft	Keybearers	Mr Alderman
Escheator	Mr John Wing		John Pape
Collectors for	Mr Robert Cole		Henry Coverly
Schoole Rents	Robert Cowles	Prizers of Corne	Thomas Briggs
Church wardens	John Pape		Thomas Hodgson
	Thomas Fishar		
		Market Sayers	Bryan Godley
Chaimberlaines	Henry Coverly		Thomas Hatfeild
	Thomas Archer	Leather	Edward Ulliott
Cheife Constables	Thomas Matkin	Sealers	Henry Wright
	John Walker		Thomas Marshall
Market place	Edward Bristow		John Ingerson
Constables	John Robinson	Towne Clarke	William Hodgkinson
High Streete	William Haskerd	Serjents	Thomas Calcraft
	George Read		Nicholas Newton
Westgate	Thomas Frith	Gaoler	Nicholas Newton
	Richard Hickson	Church Clarke	William Knewstubbs
Walkergate	John Still	Belman	Ralph Osborne
	Simon Goodwin		
Swinegate	Francis Bristow		
	William Newton		

Castlegate   Thomas Rowley
                    John Newcome

[fo. 609v]

The Names of the Commoners
Market place   Westgate
Edward Bristow   Thomas Frith
John Robinson   Richard Hickson
Thomas Archer   Edward Kenion
William Berriffe   Thomas Fishar
Edward Leivesly   Christofer Hanson
Nicholas Becke   Francis Bristow
Hamlett Brumpton   John Newton
Thomas Cole   Walkergate
Thomas Chrichloe   John Still
William Clarke   Simon Goodwin
Thomas Hodgson   George Read Senior
High Streete   Swinegate
William Haskerd   William Newton
George Read Junior   Castlegate
Richard Hauley   Thomas Rowley
                                Joseph Burnham

Charters Delivered up.
At this Court Mr Richard Holley late Alderman delivers up the three Chartor Boxes with all Chartors vizt
The Exemplir of Edward the 4th   Judge Dyers Award
King Henry the Eight his Chartor   Stamford writeinges
King Edward the Sixth his Chartor for   Escheators Patten [sic]
Schoole
Queens Elizabeth Chartor of Confirmacion   Librarey writeings
King Charles 1 his Chartor   Townes Armes
King Charles 2d his Chartor   Awriteing with many Seales
King James his Chartor
At this Court was delivered to Mr Alderman by Mr Richard Holley late Alderman all the Townes plate which is as followeth vizt

The Townes plate delivered up.
The Horse Race Cupp   Two Tunns
Mr Archers Boll   Mr Kirkbys Boll
Mr Wheatlys Cann   Mr Greenewoods 12 Spoones
Mr Horsemans Boll   One Salt with Cover

Mr Greenwoods CannMr Horsemans Wine Boll
Mr Batties BeakerThe Waites Cognizances

The Court of pleas to be sett up.
At this Court the order made the fifth Court of Mr Richard Holley late Alderman for the setting up the Court of Record within this libertie being read is by the consent of this Court fully confirmed to all intents & purpose whatsoever.

[fo. 610r]

Clement Allissons lease tolle.
At this Court came Clement Allisson and a lease for a yeare from the Account day of the tolle of oate meale with this Corporacion paying for the same the sume of sixteene shillinges.

Townes halfe pence to be sent for.
At this Court it is ordered that forty pounds weight of Towne halfe be sent for And that Mr Robert Cole and Edward Paulett do Account out the said halfe pence and deliver them to the Chaimberlaine to be by him paid out for the Townes use.

Mrs Leemings debt to be paid.
Whereas upon the stateing and setling the Accounts of Mrs Leeming this day there appeares to be due to her 16 16 08 Whereupon it is ordered that 6 16 8 part thereof be paid to her out of the proffitts of the halfepence to be sent for as aforesaid And the other ten pounds to be paid to her at the first conveniencie And that untill such time as the said x li shall be paid shee the said Mrs Leeming shall receive interest for the same as it shall become due to her from this Corporacion.

Noe sallory to be allowed to him that Succeeds an Alderman that dyes in his yeare.
Whereas Mr Richard Holley late Alderman for part of the yeare past this day moved the Court to know if they would allow any sallory to the Succeeding Alderman in case the Alderman chosen according to the custome of this Corporacion shall happen to dye before the expiracion of his yeare And if the Court thought it not convenient to grant any sallory he for his part would be contented so as that there might be an order made that noe sallory shall be paid to any other Gentleman that may happen to succeed an Alderman in the like nature as he did Whereupon it being this day put to the vote and this Court considering that Mr Alderman that makes the feast is at a great charge and if he dye the next that succeeds is but at a little charge It is therefore ordered and agreed by and with the consent of the whole Court this day that the sallory of ten pounds paid by this Corporacion to Mr Alderman shall for ever hereafter be paid to Mr Alderman for the time being that makes the feast And if it please God he happen to depart this life before the end of his yeare That then noe sallory shall be allowed to any Gentleman

that shall succeed him as Alderman for the Remainder of the yeare any order heretofore made to the contrary thereof in any wise notwithstanding.

Overseers for the Poore to pay Colleccion.
Whereas upon reading of a former order this day for the Overseers for the Poore not to be freed above halfe a yeare for their Assessment to the Church and Poore It is now observed that the said Overseers are at little trouble and by reason thereof ought not to be freed for any time from the said charge It is therefore ordered that all Overseers for the Poore hereafter to be chosen shall from time to time pay their respective Assessments to Church and poore as the rest of the Inhabitants doth or ought to do And the said recited order as to that branch concerning the Overseers for the Poore is hereby repealed & made void to all intents and purposes whatsoever.

Robert Cowles securitie to be renewed.
At this Court Mr Richard Calcraft desired that Mr Grant, Mr Rawlinson, Mr Wing & Mr Coddington may renew their bonds to Robert Cowles for the 100 li oweing by this Corporacion for the same doth not belong to Robert Cowles but was made before to him & Mr Bearnes onely in trust.

Mr Coles Account for tolle.
At this Court Mr Robert Cole gives an Account for the proffitt of the tolles for the moneth of
September last and chargeth himselfe with Receipt of   02 18 02 ob
His disbursments   00 06 04
Remaines & paid in Court   02 11 10 ob

[fo. 610v] **Second Court of John Lenton, 27 November 1671**

Accounts to be examined.
At this Court it is ordered that Mr Thomas Grant, Mr Michaell Taylor, Mr Richard Holley, Mr Robert Cole, John Turner, Edward Paulett, Anthony Hotchkin, John Pape and Thomas Charles and William Clarke do examine the Accounts of the Churchwardens, Chaimberlaines and Collectors for Schoole Rents and certifie their proceedinges therein the next Court day.

Mr Grants Account for tolle.
At this Court Mr Thomas Grant gives an Account for the proffitts of the tolles for the
moneth of October last and that his Receipts are   06 10 05
And his disbursments are   01 01 06
Remaines due to the Towne   [sum incorrect] 05 08 01
Which he payes in open Court and is discharged.

Distresses for non Appearance at Mr Aldermans Court.
Whereas upon the Constables makeing returne of tickitts sent out against severall Persons for not makeing their Appearance at this Court they acquainted the Court and some of the said Persons wives or Servants as soone as they see them comeing to distraine do shutt their doores upon them and will not suffer them to take a distresse For the preventing of such misdemeanours for the future It is at this Court fully ordered that if any Person or Persons whatsoever being a member of this Court or his or their Wife or Wives Servant or Servants shall at any time or times hereafter shutt or cause to be shutted any doore against any Constable or Constables that shall come to take a Distresse of any Person or Persons as aforesaid for not appearing at Mr Aldermans Court for the time being or for breach of any order of this Court of Mr Alderman now made or hereafter to be made for the good proffitt well ordering & governing of this Corporacion That then all and every Person & Persons so offending by him or themselves their wife wives Servant or Servants or any Person whatsoever shall forfeite for every such of offence the sume of three shillinges and foure pence to be levied of their goodes and Chattells for the use of this Burrough according to Auntient custome.

Thomas Cole fined for Words against Mr Winge.
Whereas Mr John Winge a Justice of the peace upon the Bench acquainteing the Court this day that some of the Comoners was wagering to dismisse Thomas Cole out of this Court as a Comoner Whereupon the said Thomas Cole told the said Mr Winge he spoke false which words being spoken to a Justice o[f] peace sitting in Court were adjudged finable And a fine of 5s imposed upon him for the said Offence And upon his submission & tender of his fine this Court doth remitt the same unto him.

[fo. 611r] **Third Court of John Lenton, 15 December 1671**

Mr Humes Account for tolle.
At this Court Mr Henry Humes gives an Account of the proffitts of the tolles for the moneth
of November last and that his Receipts are	02 03 02
And his disbursments are	00 06 00
Remaines due to the Towne	01 17 02

Which he payes in open Court and is discharged.

Collectors for Schoole Rents Account.
At this Court Mr John Coddington and Thomas Cole Collectors for the Schoole Rents do gives [*sic*]
up theire Account for the yeare past their Receipts	45 14 04
Disbursments	51 10 03
Arreares	00 18 04
Remaines due to them	06 14 07

Which is hereby ordered to be paid to them out of the proffitts of the Towns halfe pence that shall be next sent for by this Corporacion.

At this Court it is ordered that Mr Michaell Taylor & Mr Robert Calcraft with the Collectors of the Schoolehouse land do divide the Pesthouse and the land thereunto belonging betwixt the two tennants so as the Rent formerly paid may be continued to this Corporacion.

Mr Grants Account for tolle.
At this Court Mr Thomas Grant gives an Account of the proffitts of the tolles for the moneth of

October last and chargeth himselfe with Receipt of	06 10 05
And his disbursments are	01 01 06
Remaines due to the Towne	05 08 11

Which he payes in open Court & he is discharged.

Streetes to be kept cleane.
Whereas upon reading the Auntient [sic] of this Court it was observed that the penaltie imposed upon such Persons as suffer Wood dirt and Rubbish to lye in the streetes against their doores is too smale as also that severall Persons do make a proffitt of the said dirt & Rubbish It is therefore ordered that the Beagle shall every Weeke give notice to all such Persons as shall suffer dirt Wood or Rubbish to lye betwixt their doores and Channell against their Houses to remove the same within a weeke following upon paine for every Person so offending to forfeite six pence to the Box to be levied by distresse & sale of goodes And if such Persons or any of them shall suffer Manure dirt & Rubbish to lye in the streetes as aforesaid by the space of a fortnight that then it shall be lawfull for any Person whatsoever to carrey the same away and convert it to his owne use without paying any thing for the same And that every Person which shall carrey the same away shall be saved harmles by this Court And it is further ordered that the Beagle do returne an Account of this order every Court day upon paine to forfeite a weekes wages.

Collectors Account for the Schoole.
At this Court Mr John Coddington and Thomas Cole gives [sic] an Account of the Schoole Rents

for the yeare past and that their Receipts are	45 14 04
Disbursements and Arreares	52 08 07

Which is ordered to be paid to them out of the proffitt of the Towns halfe that shall be next sent for.

[fo. 611v] **Fourth Court of John Lenton, 16 February 1671/2**

Cheife Constables charges to be paid.
At this Court it is ordered that the present Chaimberlaine pay unto John Turner and Edward Paulett the charges of suite expended in their defence as Cheife Constables at the suite of Horner.

Mr Aldermans Account for tolle.
At this Court Mr Alderman accounteth for the proffitt of the tolles for the moneth of January last
and that his Receipts are	01 18 10
And his disbursments are	00 06 08
Remaines due to the Towne	01 12 02

Which he payes in open Court and is discharged.

Mr Taylors Account for tolle.
At this Court Mr Michaell Taylor accounteth for the proffitts of the tolles for the moneth of
December last and that his Receipts are	06 10 03
And his disbursments are	01 02 02
Remaines due to the Towne	05 08 01

which he payes in open Court and is discharged.

Constables to be saved harmles.
At this Court it is ordered that Richard Hickson and Francis Bristow Constables be borne harmles by the Towne against Mr Edward Smith for seeing the peace kept when Mr Smith made an Assault upon one William Hickson for murder being cryed out they went to part them and to prevent further danger.

John Vincent made free.
At this Court came John Vincent Tapster at the George and desired to be admitted a Free Burgesse of this Corporacion To which this Court doth condiscend whereupon he layes downe his x li as being a Forrainer and intreated this Court to be kind to him in giveing him part of it backe againe The which this Court takeing into consideracion do returne him 40s backe againe And thereupon he is admitted a free Burgesse of this Burrough and takes the oath of Freeman and payes his fees to Clarke and Serjent according to Auntient custome.

John Poole, Robert Smith, John Fearon, William Knight, Thomas Quiningborow made free.
At this Court came John Poole Apothecary, Robert Smith, John Fearon, Cordwainers & freeborne, William Knight, Taylor and Thomas Quiningborow Stuffe Weaver & Forrainers all of them haveing served their severall Apprenticeship within this Corporacion & desired to be admitted free Burgesses thereof to which this Court doth

condiscend Whereupon the free Borne payes to the Box ijs vjd a peice & vjd every of them to the Clarke & Serjents & the Forrainers payes vs a peice to the Box and xijd apeice to the Officers And were admitted Free Burgesses of this Burrough And tooke the oaths incident thereunto.

[fo. 612r] Fifth Court of John Lenton, 10 May 1672

Mr Coddington Account for tolle.
At this Court Mr John Coddington gives an Account of the proffitts of the Townes tolle for the
moneth of February last and his Receipts are	01 11 02	
disbursments are	00 06 08	
Remaines due to the Towne	01 04 06	

which payes [sic] in open Court & he is discharged.

Colebuyers Account.
At this Court William Berriffe gives an Account as Colebuyer for the yeare past and
chargeth himselfe with Receipt of the sume of	15 03 00	
And his disbursments to be	15 16 01	
Remaines to the Towne with the increase of the stocke	15 08 10	

Which he payes to John Robinson being now elected Colebuyer for the ensueing yeare.

The Elleccion of the Succeeding Alderman.
For the more peaceable and quiet proceeding at the Church on the next Elleccion day for the succeeding Alderman It is ordered upon the next Elleccion day Mr John Coddington be sent downe into the Church to Mr Thomas Grant and Mr Edward Rawlinson to make three Comburgesses Out of which three Comburgesses in the Church It is likewise agreed that Mr Thomas Grant shall be brought upon the Chuscheon [sic] or place of Eleccion to Mr Henry Humes to make two Comburgesses there he being there alone by reason of the death of Mr George Short And it is further agreed to perfect the Eleccion that Mr John Wing be sent downe into the Church to Mr Edward Rawlinson & Mr John Coddington to make three Comburgesses there Out of which three Comburgesses in the Church It is agreed that Mr Edward Rawlinson be brought upon the Cusheon or place of Elleccion to Mr Henry Humes and Mr Thomas Grant to make three Comburgesses there Out of which three Comburgesses upon the Cusheon or place of Elleccion with a free and unanimous consent Mr Henry Humes is nominated Alderman for the next ensueing yeare.

Sandpitt tolle lett to Thomas Fishar.
At this Court Thomas Fishar takes a lease of the Tolles in the Sandpitt laine till the Account day paying for the same vijs.

Townes halfepence to be sent for.
At this Court it is ordered that forty pound Weight of Townes halfe pence be sent for the next weeke.

Monethly bread paid.
At this Court it is ordered that the Chaimberlaine pay unto Thomas Charles xijs due to him for monethly bread in the time of Edward Leivesly Chaimberlaine.

Widdow Dawsons money to be paid.
At this Court it is ordered that John Still do distraine for the money in Arreare of Swinegate Assessment for repaires of the Well and pay unto Widdow Dawson vjs in part of xix s vijd due to her for money laid downe by her husband in his life time for repaireing the said Well.

Hugh Holts Rent to be paid.
At this Court it is ordered that Hugh Holt do pay the Arreares of Rent for the peice of Ground in his possession belonging to the Towne of Grantham & cleare his Account the next Court day.

Weekes Assessment to be paid.
At this Court it is ordered that the Constables do pay the weekes Assessment and insert it into the Constable Assessment.

[fo. 612v] **Sixth Court of John Lenton, 11 July 1672**

Mr Holleys Account for tolle.
At this Court Mr Richard Holley gives an Account of the proffitts of the tolles for the moneth of

March last his Receipts	12	16	09
disbursments	01	01	06
Remaines to the Towne	11	15	03

Which he payes in open Court & he is discharged.

Mr Grants Account for tolle.
At this Court Mr Thomas Grant gives an Account of the proffitts of the tolle for the moneth of

Aprill last his Receipts	08	11	00
disbursments	00	12	07
Remaines to the Towne	07	18	05

Which he payes in open Court & he is discharged.

Mr Coles Account for tolle.
At this Court Mr Robert Cole gives an Account of the proffitt of the tolles for the moneth of

May last his Receipts	10	16	03
Disbursments	01	03	10
Remaines to the Towne [sum incorrect]	09	11	05 ob

Which he payes in open Court and he is discharged.

Towne Clarke to receive 44s for publike buisnes done.
At this Court it is ordered that the Chaimberlaine pay 44s to the Towne Clarke for money laid downe by him for takeing of the charge in the Exchequer against the Alderman and Burgesses and for buying the Acts of the two last Sessions of Parlyament.

Townes land to be inquired after.
At this Court it is ordered upon the Complaint of Mr Richard Hurst the Towns tenant of some of the Towns land being lost that a dilligent search and inquire be made for to find out the said land part of it being thought to be in Mr Edward Rawlinsons possession.

Thomas Charles Account as Churchwarden.
At this Court Thomas Charles late Churchwarden gives an Account of

his Arreares & chargeth himselfe to account	02	06	04
And that his disbursments are	02	06	04

So the Account is cleared & he discharged.

Edward Leivesly Account as Chaimberlaine.
At this Court Edward Leivesly Chaimberlaine accounteth & chargeth

himselfe with the Receipt of	91	14	09
And that his disbursments are	91	15	10
Remaines due to him	00	00	11

Which is paid unto him in open Court & he is discharged.

[fo. 613r] **Seventh Court of John Lenton 2 August 1672**

Mr Humes Account for tolle.
At this Court Mr Henry Humes gives an Account of the proffitts of the tolles for the

moneth of June last his Receipts	04	18	01
disbursments	00	16	01
Remaines to the Towne	04	02	00

Which he payes in open Court and he is discharged.

Nicholas Newton paid 2–16–10.
At this Court it is ordered that the Cheife Constables pay 2 li 16s 10d to Nicholas Newton Gaoler for charges of the men that were prest for his Majesties service at seas and that they be repaid out of the Constables Assessment.

Christofer Thompson fined for uncivill words.
Whereas Christopher Thompson a member of this Court did this day in open Court utter and declare that he cared not for the Court nor the orders of the Court in contempt of the Authoritie thereof for which offence this Court doth hereby impose a fine of iijs iiijd upon him for his uncivill speeches and do order that it be paid downe the next Court day.

Towns halfe pence to be exchanged.
Whereas Mr Alderman this day acquainted the Court that his Majestie was aboute setting forth farthings of his owne stampe and that all other halfepence would be prohibited for goeing And that till such time as the Proclamacion should come forth it was convenient that the Towne halfepence should passe in this Corporacion Whereupon it is ordered that all such Persons as take or exchange any of the Towne halfe shall have the same exchanged againe by the Chaimberlaine and shall for their so doeing be saved and kept harmles by this Corporacion.

An Assessment for repaires of the Church.
Whereas upon Complaint of the present Churchwardens that the Church is much out of repaire in some places and that there is x li due to the last Churchwarden upon his Account It is therefore by and with the consent of this Court ordered that an Assessment of thirty pounds be made and laid upon this Burrough for the further repaires of the Church and the payment of five pounds to Sir Edmund Turner and 40s to Mr Burnett and x li due to the last Churchwarden upon his Account and Nine pounds due to the Comoners from William Palmer for worke which he did in his life time at the Church which ix li the Comoners do now promise to give the Corporacion for the benefitt thereof.

[fo. 613v] **Eighth Court of John Lenton, 6 September 1672** [*1673 crossed through*]

Mr Ashtons money paid.
Whereas an Account was this day taken of the Townes halfpence that were brought in which amounts unto the sume of 108 li and it was moved by Mr Alderman that some money might be taken up for to exchange the said halfe pence and to pay Mr Ashton his 100 li Whereupon it is ordered that 200 li be taken up at interest and that some members of this Court be bound for the [*sic*] and that they have any of the Townes land in lease for their indempnitie and that they make choice of what land they please to be assigned to them for their securitie.

Towns land to be fine certaine.
Whereas it was this day moved in Court for the setting of fines certaine for the Towns land and that it would be a great incouragement to Tennants to build up their houses and might be very advantageous to the Towne Whereupon it is ordered that as the leases comes out that the fines that shall be then sett shall be a standing rule ever after for them to renew their leases so as they renew at every fifteene yeares And in default thereof that then the Court shall have power to raise the said fines at their pleasure anything in this order contained to the contrarey not withstanding.

Forty pounds taken up to exchange Halfepence.
Whereas Mr Alderman, Mr Grant, Mr Taylor and Mr Humes stand bound to Mr Edward Coddington in 40 li for the payment of 20 li with interest which was to exchang the Townes halfe pence It is therefore ordered that the 20 li & interest be paid out of the 100 li to be taken up and that they and every of them be saved harmlesse from the said bond.

Thomas Bayly, Robert Sparrow, William Bristow made free.
At this Court came Thomas Bayly, Robert Sparrow, Felmongers and William Bristow Glasier, who have severally served seaven yeares Apprenticeshipps to the said trades and desired to be admitted free Burgesses of this Corporacion to which their Desire this Court condiscend Whereupon they pay ijs vjd apeice as to the Box as freeborne and the fees to the Clarke & Serjents and take the oaths according to the custome of this Burrough.

[fo. 614r] Ninth Court of John Lenton, 20 September 1672

200 li to be taken up.
Whereas it being againe moved in Court this day that the Towne had occasion for 200 li and that a 100 li was ready if any Gentlemen of this Court would be bound for the same for the Townes use they haveing securitie from the Towne to beare them harmles Whereupon Mr Robert Calcraft, Mr Henry Humes, Edward Paulett and John Walker being present in Court are willing to become bound for the Towne for the said 100 li they haveing the Schoolehouse land formerly demised to Thomas Towers assigned to them for the terme of xxxj yeares from the Expiracion of a former lease thereof yet in being It is therefore ordered that the said land be assigned to them for xxxj yeares to beare them harmles from any such bond that they shall enter into for the use of this Corporacion.

Mr Turner lends the Towne 25 li.
At this Court John Turner is willing to lend the Towne xxv li he haveing securitie of his house in Walkergate & John Stills house and William Grococks house It is therefore ordered that the said houses be assigned to him for xxxj yeares for securitie of the said xxv li.

Constables Assessment.
At this Court it is ordered that an Assessment of xxx li be laid upon this Burrough for the Constables Assessment for the yeare past an estimate being taken what the perticular sumes amount unto And that notice thereof bee given in the Church of the time and place of makeing the Assessment.

Mr John Coddington to have Counter securitie.
At this Court Mr John Coddington and William Berriffe are contented to be bound to Robert Cowles for 51 li 10s for this Corporacion haveing a lease of Zachary Cox and Mr Wings house for 31 yeares for their Indempnitie It is therefore ordered that the said Houses be assigned to them for securitie And that there be a meeteing at the Hutch on Wednesday next to seale the said securitie and the securities abovesaid.

100 li to be taken up.
Whereas it being againe moved in Court this day that the Towne had occasion for a 100 li to exchange the Townes halfepence and that Mr Burnett would have a 100 li ready within a fortnight if any members of this Court would be bound for the same they haveing securitie from the Towne to beare them harmlesse Whereupon Thomas Ireland, Henry Coverly, William Berriffe, Thomas Fishar, Robert Cowles and John Robinson are willing to become bound for the said 100 li they haveing securitie out of the Schoolehouse land to beare them harmles It is therefore ordered that the said parties do make choice of such of the Towns land as they shall thinke fitt And that the same be made over unto them to beare them harmles from any such bond that they shall enter into for the use of this Corporacion.

[fo. 614v] **Tenth Court of John Lenton 18 October 1672**

Mr Aldermans Account for tolle.
At this Court Mr Alderman gives an Account of the proffitts of the tolles for the moneth of
August last Receipts	01 13 04
Disbursments	00 05 00
Remaines to the Towne	01 08 04

Which he payes in open Court and is discharged.

A Manufacture to be sett up.
Whereas Mr Taylor this day acquainted the Court that he and some of the Brethren hearing that the most Reverend father William Lord Bishop of Lincolne and Sir Edmund Turner were in Towne they went to waite upon them and to returne them thankes for their respects & favours to this Corporacion and that they were then pleased to declare that if a Manufacture was sett up in this Towne they would add a stocke to it and desired that the Corporacion would consider what Manufacture would be most advantageous Whereupon this Court takeing the same into their Consideracion do order and agree that a Manufacture for combeing of Wooll and converting it into yarne will be most

convenient And that a letter of thankes be returned to the Lord Bishopp and Sir Edmund Turner for their kindnes to this Corporacion.

Mr Matkin chosen of the 1 Company.
At this Court Mr Thomas Matkin is chosen one of the first Company in the Roome of Mr George Short deceased.

Edward Leivesly chosen of the 2d Company.
At this Court Mr Edward Leivesly is chosen one of the second Company in the Roome of Mr Thomas Matkin.
In the Kallender
Thomas Archer
Thomas Fishar
Thomas Cole
At this Court it is ordered that the Chaimberlaine pay xvjs ijd to Mr Henry Humes which he laid downe for charges at the suite of Mr James Ashton.

[fo. 615r] **Eleventh Court of John Lenton, 23 October 1672**

Mr Aldermans Account.
At this Court Mr Alderman accounteth for all monies laid out by him on the publike concerne of this Corporacion and that there is due to him 01 14 03 Which is paid to him by the present Chaimberlaine.

Coroners Account.
At this Court Mr Richard Holley Coroner accounteth and saith that as Casualties happened this yeare there was one Thomas Baggott an Infant of six yeares of Age the sonn in law of Edward Dickinson of this Towne payling [sic] upon the Hill in the High Streete on the side of a banke and part of the Banke on which the Child stood falling into a saw Pitt the Child fell downe with it and so was accidentely killed and the Jury found it Chance Medley And the said Coroner further accounteth and saith that theire was one Anne Pearson of this Towne spinster not haveing the feare of God before her eyes but ledd by the instigacion of the divell the fourth day of July last past did willfully Poyson herselfe And that the Jury found it willfull murder And saith noe proffitt increwed to this Corporacion this yeare And further he hath not to Account.

Escheators Account.
At this Court Mr John Wing Escheator for the yeare past accounteth for monies by him received for light defective and unlawfull weights and measures and chargeth himselfe with the
Receipts for the same the sume of 00 16 04
And his disbursments at vi d a faire and to the Towne Clarke for his
Attendance every faire 00 04 06

Remaines to the Towne 00 11 10
Which he payes in open Court and is discharged.

Mr Calcraft Account for tolle.
At this Court Mr Richard Calcraft accounteth for the proffitt of the tolles for the moneth of
September last his Receipts 02 01 04
Disbursments 00 04 06
Remaines to the Towne 01 16 10
Which he payes in open Court and is discharged.

At this Court James Long payes more in part of his fine for his lease xxs & Remaines xiijs iiijd.

At this Court Churchwarden, Chaimberlaines & Collectors for Schoole Rents have further day to account.

[fo. 615v]

At this Court the severall Constables gives an Account of the Constables Assessment for the yeare past as followeth

Market place			10 08 00
	Abatements		00 16 10
	Remaines		09 11 02
High Streete			05 12 00
	Abatements		00 09 03
	Remaines		05 02 09
Westgate			04 11 04
	Abatements		00 07 04
	Remaines		04 04 00
Walkergate			01 15 06
	Abatements		00 01 05
	Remaines		01 14 01
Swinegate			02 09 07
	Abatements		00 04 00
	Remaines	[original sum incorrect]	02 04 08
Castlegate			03 19 09
	Abatements		00 03 06
	Remaines	[original sum incorrect]	03 05 03

Thomas Wilson, John Allain, John Feilds Forrainers made free.
At this Court came Thomas Wilson Forrainer & John Allain & John Feilds Forrainers and desired to be admitted Free Burgesses of this Corporacion to which this Court doth

condiscend Whereupon the said Thomas Wilson not haveing served 7 yeares Apprentice within this Burrough layes downe his x li according to Auntient custome And the said John Allain & John Feilds haveing served their time here lays downe 5s a peice to the Box & pays their fees to Clarke & Serjents & takes the oaths incident to Freemen & are admitted Free Burgesses of this Burrough And this Court out of respect to the said Thomas Wilson do give him againe 3 li 06s 08d out of his x li.

[fo. 616r]

At an Assembly holden by Mr John Lenton Alderman and the Comburgesses and Burgesses of Grantham aforesaid in Corpus Christi Quire within the prebendary Church there &r on Fryday next after St Lukes day being 25 October 1672.

First did sitt downe upon the Cusheon or place of Eleccion the said Mr John Lenton in Corpus Christi Quire within the Prebendarie Church there &c
Next to him did sitt upon the Cusheon or place of Eleccion one Comburgesse vizt Mr ~~Edward Rawlinson~~ Mr Henry Humes
Then was there two Comburgesses in the Church vizt Mr Thomas Grant & Mr Edward Rawlinson
Then was sent downe into the Church to make them two Comburgesses three one other Comburgesse vizt Mr John Coddington
Then was there two Comburgesses upon the Cusheon or place of Eleccion vizt Mr Henry Humes and Mr Edward Rawlinson
Then was there in the Church two Comburgesses vizt Mr Thomas Grant & Mr John Coddington
Then was sent downe to those two Comburgesses to make them three one other Comburgesse vizt Mr John Winge
Out of which three in the Church vizt Mr Thomas Grant, Mr John Coddington and Mr John Wing one ~~who~~ was chosen to come up and sitt upon the Cusheon or place of Eleccion one other Comburgesse vizt Mr John Coddington
Then was there upon the Cusheon or place of Eleccion three Comburgesses vizt Mr Henry Humes, Mr Edward Rawlinson and Mr John Coddington
Then was there two Comburgesses in the Church vizt Mr Thomas Grant & Mr John Winge
Out of which three Comburgesses upon the Chusheon or place of Eleccion one is to be chosen Alderman for the ensueing yeare.
And so by an Unanimous consent and vote of this Assembly Mr Henry Humes is chosen Alderman for the next ensuing yeare.

Whereupon the said Mr John Lenton dischargeth himselfe from the place and Office of Alderman according to Auntient custome And the said Mr Humes now elected Alderman in his place and stead hath at this Assembly taken the oath of Alderman for this Burrough and Soake of Grantham according to the Auntient and laudable custome of this Burrough.

And so this Assembly breakes up.

[fo. 616v] [Blank page]

THE HALL BOOK OF GRANTHAM 1672–1673

[fo. 617r] **First Court of Henry Humes, 1 November 1672**

Mr Henry Humes Alderman
Mr Thomas Short Comburgess
Mr Thomas Grant Comburgess
Mr Michaell Taylor Comburgess
Mr Robert Calcraft Comburgess
Mr Richard Calcraft Comburgess
Mr Richard Holley Comburgess
Mr John Lenton Comburgess
Mr Edward Rawlinson Comburgess
Mr John Coddington Comburgess
Mr John Winge Comburgess
Mr Robert Cole Comburgess
Mr Thomas Matkin Comburgess

John Turner
Thomas Charles
William Milles
Thomas Ireland
Edward Pawlett
Christopher Thompson
William Bury
Anthony Hotchkin
Henry Coverly
John Pape
John Walker
Edward Leivesly

The Names of the Officers

Coroner	Mr John Lenton	Keybearers	Mr Alderman
Escheator	Mr Robert Cole		John Walker
Collectors for the	Mr Thomas Matkin		John Pape
Schoole Rents	Edward Bristow	Prizers of	Thomas Briggs
Churchwardens	John Pape	Corne	Humphrey Fishar
	John Robinson	Market	Bryan Godley
Chaimberlaines	John Walker	Sayers	Thomas Hatfeild
	Nicholas Becke	Leather Sealers	Edward Ulliott
Cheife Constables	John Turner		Henry Wright
	Thomas Charles		Thomas Marshall
Marketplace	William Clarke		John Ingerson
Constables	Simon Goodwin	Towne Clarke	William Hodgkinson
High Streete	William Haskerd	Gaoler	Nicholas Newton
	George Read	Serjent	Thomas Calcraft
Westgate	Richard Hickson	Serjent	Nicholas Newton
	Richard Segrave	Church Clarke	William Knewstubbs
Walkergate	John Still	Belman	Ralph Osborne
	Joseph Burnham		
Swinegate	William Newton		
	Thomas Bayly		

Castlegate   John Newcombe
                      Robert Sparrow

[fo. 617v]

Edward Bristow   John Still
John Robinson   George Read senior
Thomas Archer   Thomas Gunnisson
Nicholas Becke
Thomas Cole   William Newton
Thomas Chrichloe
Thomas Hodgson   Robert Cowles
William Clarke   Robert Sparrow
Simon Goodwin
                          John Newcombe
William Haskerd   Thomas Bayly
George Read
Richard Handley

Richard Hickson
Thomas Frith
Thomas Fisher
Christopher Hanson

The Chartors delivered up.
At this Court Mr John Lenton late Alderman delivered up the three Chartors Boxes with all the Chartors vizt
The Exemplir of Edward the 4th   Kings James his Chartor
King Henry the Eight his Chartor   Judge Dyers Awards
Kind Edward the sixth his Chartor for the   Stamford writing
Schoole
Queene Elizabeth Chartor of Confirmacion Escheators Pattent
King Charles the firsts Chartor   Librarey writeing
King Charles the 2d his Chartor   Towns Armes
                                       writeing with many seales

The Plate delivered up.
At this Court was delivered to Mr Alderman by Mr John Lenton Alderman all the Towns plate which is as followeth vizt
The Horse Race Cupp   Two Tunns
Mr Archers Boll   Mr Kirkbys Boll
Mr Wheatlys Cann   Mr Greenwood 12 spoones
Mr Horsemans Boll   One salt with Cover

Mr Greenewoods Cann   Mr Horsemans Wine Boll
Mr Batties Beaker   The Waites Cognizances

[fo. 618r]

The tolles lett.
At this Court Clement Alisson takes a lease of the tolle of Oatemeale for one yeare paying xvs and he gives in earnest thereof vjd.

Halfe pence to be exchanged.
At this Court Thomas Cole acquainted Mr Alderman that he had v li in Towns halfe pence in his hands and desired that if they was called in that they might be changed by this Corporacion And it is ordered that the said Thomas Cole have v li in silver for the said halfe pence when they shall be called in or discharged from passing from one to another.

Thomas Cole to have xvs.
At this Court it is ordered that the Chaimberlaine pay xvs to Thomas Cole for Wood bought of him for Swinegate Bridge by the Overseers for the High Wayes and that the same be paid againe by the Overseers of the High Wayes.

Thomas Cole dismissed the Court.
At this Court Thomas Cole a Comoner desired to be dismissed the Court and layes downe his fine of five pounds according to a former order which this Court takes of him and he is dismissed the Court upon his request and payment of his fine aforesaid.

Mr Grant called out of the body of the Church.
Whereas Mr Thomas Grant a Comburgesse of this Court was formerly sent downe into the Church by order of Court and was called upon the Cusheon in order to the quiet Eleccion of Mr Alderman And whereas the said order at the last Eleccion was made void and a great dispute aboute it in the Church and for preventing of further trouble at the next Eleccion the said Mr Thomas Grant made it his request to this Court that he might be brought out of the body of the Church The which this Court takeing into consideracion do grant him his request And it hereby ordered that at the next nominacion the Comburgesses according to their places be sent downe into the Church in order to a peaceable and quiet Eleccion of the next succeeding Alderman.

Henry Coverlys Account as Chaimberlaine.
At this Court Henry Coverly gives an Account as Chaimberlaine for
the yeare past
and he chargeth himselfe with Receipt of   140 12 10
And that his disbursments are   143 14 06

Remains due to him 003 01 08
Which is ordered to be paid unto him by the Succeeding
Chaimberlaine

Lands secured to them that are bound for the Towns debt.
At this Court it is ordered that the Schoole House land formerly demised to William Bury Esquire at Spittlegate and the Houses formerly demised to Richard Poole, Christofer Thompson, Widdow Nidd, Mr John Miller, Thomas Milles &Timothy Bristow belonging to this Corporacion be granted and set over unto Thomas Ireland, Henry Coverly, William Berriffe, Thomas Fishar, Robert Cowles and John Robinson to beare them harmles from a bond of 100 li that they are to enter into for the proper debt of this Corporacion.

[fo. 618v] **Second Court of Henry Humes, 8 November 1672**

Mr John Welbys debt to be paid.
Whereas Mr Alderman this day acquainted the Court that Mr Burnett had a 120 li ready to lend this Corporacion and had kept it by him to serve the Towne above a fortnight And if Mr Richard Holley and Mr John Lenton would become bound with the rest of the Gentlemen of this Court that are willing to be bound for the same then the 50 li due to Mr John Welby for which Mr Holley & Mr Lenton stood bound should be paid out of the said 120 li to which they condiscend Whereupon it is ordered that there be a meeteing at the Hutch to seale securitie to the said Mr Holley, Mr Lenton, Mr Bury, Henry Coverly, Williams Berriffe, John Robinson and Thomas Fishar to beare them Harmles from the said debt of 120 li And that Mr John Welbys 50 li be paid of with the interest due from this Corporacion.

Subscripcions to raise money to doe some conveniencies at the Schoole.
Whereas Mr Walker the present Schoole Master this day acquainted the Court that at his comeing to be Schoole Master that Mr Alderman which then was and some other Gentlemen of this Court that he should [*sic*] such conveniencies made him to the Schoole as were necessarie and that the Season of the yeare being very cold and he weake it would be requisite that there were a Portell to the Schoole doore and a little house build on the side of the Schoole in the Garden with a Chimley in it which Roome would be very convenient upon many occasions And if this Court would be pleased to take care that the same be done he should thinke himselfe obliged to the Towne The which this Court takeing into consideracion and that it is for a generall good do order that a Roome & portall be build to the Schoole and that the money for building of the same be raised by a Generall Contribucion of this Corporacion And for the perfecting so good a Worke some of the members of this Court do subscribe as followeth vizt

Subscripcions of the first Company.
Mr Alderman vs, Mr Grant vs, Mr Taylor vs, Mr Edward Rawlinson ijs vjd, Mr Winge ijs, Mr Robert Cole ijs vjd & Mr Matkin ijs.

By the 2d Company.
John Turner ijs, Thomas Charles ijs, Edward Paulett iiijs, Anthony Hotchkin ijs vjd, Henry Coverly ijs, John Walker ijs, Edward Leivesly ijs.

By the Comoners.
Edward Bristow ijs, John Robinson ijs, William Berriffe ijs, Thomas Chrichloe ijs Thomas Hodgson ijs, William Clarke ijs, Richard Segrave ijs, William Haskerd ijs, John Still ijs, Simon Goodwin ijs, Thomas Bayly ijs, John Newcombe ijs, Robert Sparrow ijs, Robert Cowles ijs, Joseph Burnham ijs.

Mr James Oldfeild, Thomas Oldfeild, Thomas Rawlinson, William Cole made free
At this Court came Mr James Oldfeild, Thomas Oldfeild, Thomas Rawlinson and William Cole being all freeborne within this Corporacion and desired to be admitted free Burgesses thereof to which this Court doth condiscend Whereupon they take their severall oaths of free Burgesses and pays their fees to the Clarke and Serjents and are admitted free Burgesses of the Corporacion.

[fo. 619r] **Third Court of Henry Humes, 13 December 1672**

Persons appointed to examine Accounts.
At this Court Mr Thomas Grant, Mr Michaell Taylor, Mr Robert Calcraft, Mr John Lenton, Mr Robert Cole, John Turner, Thomas Ireland, Edward Paulett and Anthony Hotchkin, Thomas Chrichloe, William Clarke, Edward Bristow, Robert Cowles, Thomas Fishar and John Robinson are ordered to meete and examine the Accounts of the Chaimberlaine, Churchwarden and Collectors for the Schoole Rents and to returne an Account of their proceeding therein the next Court day.

Mr Cole Account of the tolles for October.
At this Court Mr Robert Cole gives an Account of the profitt of the tolles for the moneth of October last and chargeth himselfe with
Receipt of   05 03 03
And his disbursments to be   00 19 00
Remaines due to the Towne   04 04 03
Which he payes in open Court and is discharged.

Mr Holleys Account for tolle for November.
At this Court Mr Richard Holley gives an Account of the profitt of
the tolles for the moneth of November last and that his Receipts are 02 16 04
And his disbursments to be   00 08 04

Remaines due to the Towne   02 08 00
Which he payes in open Court & is discharged

Mr Grants Account for the tolle for January.
At this Court Mr Thomas Grant gives an Account of the profitt of
the tolles for the moneth of January last & chargeth himselfe with
Receipt of   01 19 03
And his disbursments to be   00 07 00
Remaines to the Towne   01 12 03
Which he pays in open Court & is discharged

Thomas Archers Account as Chaimberlaine.
At this Court Thomas Archer Chaimberlaine gives an Account
of all monies by him received & laid out on the behalfe of this
Corporacion & his Receipts are   251 03 10
And his disbursments are   206 05 08 ob
Delivered to the next Chaimberlaine in Towns halfe pence   45 00 06
Remains due to the Accomptant & paid in open Court ijs iiijd & he is discharged

A lease of a peice of ground let to John Courtby.
At this Court came John Courtby and takes a lease of a peice of ground or garden place
formerly in the possession of Hugh Holt for one whole yeare from the second day of
February last at the Rent of xvjs to be paid at equall porcions at each halfe yeare And
he gives in earnest thereof vjd.

[fo. 619v] **Fourth Court of Henry Humes, 7 February 1672/3**

Mr John Coddington Account for tolles for December.
At this Court Mr John Coddington gives an Account of the profitts of
the tolles for the moneth of December and that his Receipts are   05 09 09
And his disbursments to be   00 19 00
Remaines due to the Towne   04 00 09
Which he payes in open Court and he is discharged

Mr Aldermans Account of tolle for February.
At this Court Mr Henry Humes Alderman gives an Account of the
profitts of the tolles for the moneth of February and that his Receipts are 01 15 09
And his disbursments to be   00 06 04
Remaines due to the Towne   01 09 05
Which he payes in open Court and is discharged

An order for makeing the Townes lease with provisoes.
Whereas the Court this day observeing that the lease of Hugh Holts being assigned to Sir Thomas Skipwith without the consent of this Court contrarey to a Covenant therein contained and that the same ought be forfeited to this Corporacion, but it being a Covenant and noe Provisoe it is onely a breach of Covenant and noe forfeiture It is therefore ordered for the future that the Townes leases be drawne by way of Provisoe not to assigne any of the Towne leases without the consent of Mr Aldermans Court for the time being and not by way of Covenant as formerly.

Mr Robert Parkins, Thomas Kenion, Richard Peareson, Edward Osborne made free.
At this Court came Mr Robert Parkins, Thomas Kenion, Richard Peareson and Edward Osborne being all freeborne within this Corporacion and desired to be admitted free Burgesses thereof to which this Court doth condiscend Whereupon they severally pay ijs vjd to the Box and their fees to Clarke & Serjents and takes the oaths incident thereunto and are admitted free Burgesses of this Corporacion.

Perchivall Matkin, John Benton made free.
At this Court came Perchivall Matkin, Chandler, Apprentice to Mr Richard Calcraft, And served seaven yeares as Apprentice being not freeborne And also came John Benton a Forrainer and desired to be admitted free Burgesses of this Corporacion to which this Court doth condiscend Whereupon the said Perchivall Matkin pays to the Box vs as a Forrainer & serveing an Apprenticeshipp within Burrough And the said John Benton pays his x li as a Forrainer which this Court takes and they pay their fees to the Clarke & Serjents & takes the oaths incident thereunto and are admitted free Burgesses of this Corporacion.

[fo. 620r] Fifth Court of Henry Humes, 3 April 1673

Mr Lentons Account of tolle for Aprill.
At this Court Mr John Lenton gives an Account of the proffitts of the
tolles for the moneth of Aprill last and he chargeth himselfe with   02 16 07
And his disbursments to be   00 08 08
Remaines due to the Towne   02 07 11
Which he payes in open Court and is discharged

John Robinson Account as Cole Buyer.
At this Court John Robinson Colebuyer gives an Account for the
yeare past and he chargeth himselfe with Receipt of   15 08 00
Laid out in Repaires   00 07 06
Remaines in his hands besides the 7s 6d which is increased this yeare   15 08 00
Which he payes to Thomas Chrichloe now elected Colebuyer for the ensueing yeare

An order for the Elleccion of the next Alderman.
For the more peaceable and quiett proceeding at the Elleccion of the next Succeeding Alderman It is at this Court ordered that upon the next Elleccion Mr John Wing be sent downe into the Church in the Roome and place of Mr Thomas Grant lately called up out of the body of the Church by an order made in the first Court of Mr Henry Humes the present Alderman And that Mr Robert Cole be sent downe into the body of the Church to Mr John Wing being there to make two Comburgesses in the Church And also that Mr Thomas Matkin be sent downe into the Church to Mr John Wing and Mr Robert Cole to make three Comburgesses there Out of which three Comburgesses in the Church It is likewise agreed that Mr John Winge be brought upon the Cusheon or place of Elleccion to Mr Edward Rawlinson and Mr John Coddington to make three Comburgesses there Out of which three Comburgesses upon the Cusheon or place of Elleccion Mr Edward Rawlinson is by a free and unanimous consent of this Court nominated Alderman for the next ensueing yeare.

John Pape Account as Churchwarden
At this Court John Pape as Churchwarden for the yeare past and he chargeth himselfe with the Receipt of the Quarteridge Assessment the

sume of	18 17 06
And of the xxx li Assessment	29 01 08
And for Bell money & Graves	04 17 08
And of the Rents	12 11 08
So as the Account standes thus Receipts	65 00 06
Disbursments	64 19 05
Remains due to the Towne	00 01 03

[fo. 620v] **Sixth Court of Henry Humes, 16 May 1673**

Mr Taylors Account of tolle for March.
At this Court Mr Michaell Taylor gives an Account of the profitt of

the tolles for the moneth of March last And that his Receiptes are	11 10 03
And his disbursments to be	01 08 06
Remaines due to the Towne	10 01 09

Which he payes in open Court and is discharged.

Mr Richard Calcraft Account for May.
At this Court Mr Richard Calcraft gives an Account of the proffitts of

the tolles for the month of May last And his Receipts are	11 15 08
And his disbursments to be	01 06 07 ob
Remaines due to the Towne	10 19 00 ob

Which he pays in open Court and he is discharged.

The Grants of the Corporacion to be maintained.
Whereas Mr Alderman this day acquainted the Court that he would have the rights & privilidges of this Corporacion maintained and that it was convenient to have an Attorny retained this terme to take care that noe Person or Persons whatsoever do hinder or obstruct the rights and grants of this Burrough And also whether it be in the power of this Court to alter and remove any Market within this Towne from place to place and at such times as may be convenient to the Welfare of this Corporacion which being this day put to the vote It is agreed by this Court that the privilidges of this Corporacion be maintained and that an Attorny be imployed this terme to take care thereof and that it is in the power of this Court to remove any Market belonging to this Burrough from time to time as shall be thought fitt and necessarie.

Bryan Godley elected Gaoler.
At this Court came Bryan Godley and William Cooke and severally desired to be admitted Gaoler in the place of Nicholas Newton lately deceased and being put to the vote of this Court Bryan Godley is elected Gaoler of this Burrough and Soake of Grantham and admitted accordingly.

[fo. 621r] **Seventh Court of Henry Humes, 6 June 1673**

Mr Richard Calcraft Account of tolle for June
At this Court Mr Richard Calcraft gives an Account of the profitt of
the tolles for the moneth of June last and chargeth himselfe with the   02 13 10 ob
Receipt of
And his disbursments are   00 14 10
Remaines due to the Towne   01 19 00 ob
Which he payes in open Court and is discharged.

The order for the Sheepe penns abrogated.
Whereas the Court this day tooke into consideracion an order made the xxvth day of September Anno 1612 in the time of Mr Peter Richardson Alderman for setting the sheepe penns in Westgate from Speedys Corner to the Marketplace whether it was convenient the said order should be confirmed or abrogated by reason some of the Inhabitants do claime the Sheepe penns as their right which is thought to be the privilidge of this Corporacion And being this day put to the vote of the Court It is by the Major part thereof ordered and agreed that the said order be absolutely abrogated repealed and made void to all intents & purposes whatsoever.

Widd Lewins house to be veiwed.
At this Court it is ordered that Mr Robert Calcraft, Mr Robert Cole, John Turner, Thomas Charles, Thomas Fishar and Simon Goodwin do veiw the House of Widdow Lewin and see if it be in good repaire and returne an Account thereof next Court day.

Hugh Holts lease assigned to the Towne.
Whereas Sir Thomas Skipwith this day sent word to the Court that if they pleased to have the Assignement of Hugh Holts lease paying the 5 li he paid for it he would loose his debt of above 10 li and assigne the lease to the Corporacion The which the Court takeing into their consideracion do accept thereof And do hereby order that the Chaimberlaine pay unto Sir Thomas Skipwith Bayliffe five pounds for the lease & Assignement aforesaid.

[fo. 621v] Eighth Court of Henry Humes 4 July 1673

Mr Richard Calcraft Account for tolles for June.
At this Court Mr Richard Calcraft gives an Account of the profitt of

the tolles for the moneth of June last his Receipts	02	13	10 ob
disbursements	00	14	10
Remains due to the Towne	01	19	0 ob

Which he payes in open Court and he is discharged.

The Repaires of Widdow Lewins House to be veiwed.
At this Court it is ordered that Mr Robert Calcraft, Mr Robert Cole, John Turner, Thomas Charles, Thomas Fishar and Simon Goodwin do vew the House of Widdow Lewin and see if it be in good repaires and returne an Account thereof the next Court day.

The Auntient order for the Sheepe Penns abrogated.
Whereas the Court this day takeing into consideracion an order made the xxvth day of September Anno Domini 1612 in the time of Mr Peter Richardson Alderman for setting the Sheepe penns in Westgate from Speedys Corner to the Marketplace whether it was convenient that the said order should be confirmed or abrogated by reason some of the Inhabitants do claime the sheepe penns as their right which is the privilidge of this Corporacion And being this day put to the vote of this Court It is after a long & tedious debate by the Major part of this Court ordered and agreed that the said order be absolutely abrogated repealed & made void to all intents and purposes whatsoever.

Hugh Holts lease bought for the Towne.
At this Court it is ordered that the Chaimberlaine pay 5 li to Sir Thomas Skipwith to buy in the Revercion of Hugh Holts lease for the benefitt of this Corporacion.

John Papes Account as Churchwarden.
At this Court John Pape gives his Account as Churchwarden for the

yeare past and he chargeth himselfe with Receipt of	65	00	06
And his disbursments are	64	19	03
Remaines due to the Towne	00	01	03

The said John Pape chargeth himselfe with the whole Quarteridge & Church Assessment and there is to collect of both 2 16 08 out of which the 1s 3d is due to the Towne.

Constables Assessment.

At this Court it is ordered that an Assessment of xx li be made & laid upon the Towne for the Constables bills of disbursment for the yeare past an estimate being taken what they amount And it is further ordered that notice thereof be given in the Church next Sunday of the time & place of makeinge the said Assessment.

[fo. 622r] **Ninth Court of Henry Humes, 23 October 1673**

Mr Aldermans Account.

At this Court Mr Alderman accounteth for all monies by him laid out
upon the publike concerne of this Corporacion which amounts unto   01 14 04
And it is paid unto him in open Court

Coroners Account.

At this Court Mr John Lenton Coroner accounteth and saith that as Casualties happened this yeare there was one John Beecraft and Isacke Hipwith of this Towne the xth day of September last not haveing the feare of God before their eyes did make an Assault upon one Richard Atkinson and the said Isacke Hipwith with a stone did kill the said Richard Atkinson And the Jury found it murder in the said Isacke Hipwith and in John Beecraft as Assistant And upon their tryall last Sessions the Jury of life & death found them guilty of manslaughter and that noe profitt accrewed to the Towne that yeare And further he hath not to Account.

Escheators Account.

At this Court Mr Robert Cole Escheator for the yeare past accounteth for moneys by him
received for light defective and unlawfull Weights & Measures &
that his Receipts are   [blank]
And that his disbursments at every faire vi d and to the Towne Clarke
for his attendance every faire   [blank]
Remaines due to the Towne   [blank]
Which he pays in open Court & is discharged.

Mr Holleys Account for tolles.

At this Court Mr Richard Holley accounteth for the profitts of the
tolles for the Month of August last And that his Receipts are   02 00 05
And his disbursments are   00 05 00
Remaines due to the Towne   01 15 05
Which he payes in open Court and he is discharged.

Mr Coles Account for tolles.

At this Court Mr Robert Cole accounteth for the profitts of the tolles
for the moneth July last and that his Receiptes are   01 10 01

And his disbursments are   00 05 02
Remaines due to the Towne   01 04 11
Which he pays in open Court & is discharged.

At this Court Churchwarden, Chaimberlaines & Collectors for Schoole Rents have further day to Account

At this Court it is ordered that the present Churchwarden do pay iijs iiijd due to Christofer Thompson upon his Account as Churchwarden.

[fo. 622v] [Blank page]

[fo. 623r]

At an Assembly holden by Mr Henry Humes Alderman and the comburgesses and Burgesses of Grantham aforesaid in corpus christi Quire within the Prebendary Church there &c on fryday next after St Lukes day being 22 October 1673.

First did sitt downe upon the Cusheon or place of Eleccion the said Mr Henry Humes in Corpus Christi Quire within the Prebendarie Church there &c
Next to him did sitt upon the Cusheon or placc of Eleccion two Comburgesses vizt Mr Edward Rawlinson & Mr John Coddington
Then was sent downe into the Church one Comburgesse vizt Mr John Wing, to remaine there till two more Comburgesses were sent downe into the Church Mr Thomas Grant a Comburgesse being the last yeare there by himselfe and since called out of the body of the Church by order of Court
Then was sent downe into the Church to Mr John Winge one other Comburgesse vizt Mr Robert Cole
Then was there two Comburgesses in the Church vizt Mr John Winge & Mr Robert Cole
And then was sent into the Church to those two Comburgesses to make them there one other Comburgesse vizt Mr Thomas Matkin
Out of which three Comburgesses in the Church vizt Mr John Wing, Mr Robert Cole & Mr Thomas Matkin one was chosen to come up and sitt upon the Chusheon or place of Elleccion one other Comburgesse vizt Mr John Winge
Then was there three Comburgesses upon the Cusheon or place of Elleccion vizt Mr Edward Rawlinson, Mr John Coddington & Mr John Winge
And then was there in the Church two Comburgesses vizt Mr Robert Cole & Mr Thomas Matkin
Out of which three Comburgesses upon the Cusheon or place of Elleccion vizt Mr Edward Rawlinson, Mr John Coddington & Mr John Winge one is to be chosen Alderman for the next ensueing yeare.

And so by an unanimous consent & vote of this Assembly Mr Edward Rawlinson is chosen Alderman for the next ensueing yeare.

Whereupon the said Mr Henry Humes dischargeth himselfe from the place and Office of Alderman according to Auntient custome And the said Mr Edward Rawlinson now elected Alderman in his place & stead hath at this Assembly taken the oath of Alderman for the Burrough and Soake of Grantham according to the Auntient and laudable custome of the Burrough aforesaid.

And so the Assembly breakes up.

[fo. 623v] [Blank page]

THE HALL BOOK OF GRANTHAM 1673–1674

[fo. 624r] **First Court of Edward Rawlinson, 31 October 1673**

Mr Edward Rawlinson Alderman
Mr Thomas Short comburgess
Mr Thomas Grant comburgess
Mr Michaell Taylor comburgess
Mr Robert Calcroft comburgess
Mr Richard Calcroft comburgess
Mr Richard Holley comburgesse
Mr John Lenton comburgess
Mr Henry Humes comburgess
Mr John Coddington comburgess
Mr John Winge comburgess
Mr Robert Cole comburgess
Mr Thomas Matkin comburgess

Edward Pawlett
John Pape
William Milles
John Turner
Thomas Ireland
Christofer Thompson
Anthony Hotchkin
Henry Coverly
Thomas Charles
John Walker
Edward Leivesly
Thomas Fisher

The Names of the Officers

Coroner	Mr Henry Humes	Keybearers	Mr Alderman
			Thomas Charles
			Edward Leivesly
Escheator	Mr Thomas Matkin	Prizers of Corne	Thomas Rowley
			Thomas Hodgson
Collectors for Schoole Rents	Mr Robert Calcraft
Thomas Chrichloe	Market Sayers	George Hanson
Wiliam Kirke
Churchwardens	Edward Leivesley
John Robinson	Leather Sealers	Edward Ulliott
Henry Wright
Thomas Marshall
John Ingerson
Chaimberlaines	Thomas Charles
William Clarke	Towne Clarke	William Hodgkinson
Cheife Constables	Edward Paulet
John Pape	Serjents	Thomas Calcraft
Bryan Godley
Marketplace Constables	Richard Segrave
Richard Hickson	Gaoler	Bryan Godley
Highstreete	John Vincent
Perchivall Matkin	Church Clarke	William Knewstubbe
Westgate	Joseph Burnham
Simon Grant	Belman	Ralph Osborne

Walkergate	Thomas Bayly
	Thomas Oldfeild
Swinegate	William Newton
	John Newcombe
Castlegate	Robert Sparrow
	Thomas Kenion

[fo. 624v]

Marketplace	Comoners
	High Streete
Edward Bristow	Richard Handley
John Robinson	George Read
Thomas Archer	Thomas Rowley
Nicholas Becke	
Thomas Chrichloe	Westgate
William Clarke	Christopher Hanson
Thomas Hodgson	William Haskerd
Simon Goodwin	Francis Bristow
	Thomas Frith
Castlegate	Walkergate
Robert Cowles	John Still

The Charters delivered up.
At this Court Mr Henry Humes late Alderman delivers up the three Charter Boxes with all the Charters

	Kings James his Charter
The Exemplir of Edward the 4th	Judge Dyers Award
King Henry the Eight Charter	Stamford writeings
King Edward the Sixth Chartor for the Schoole	Escheators Pattent
Queene Elizabeths Charter of Confirmacion	Librarey writeings
Kings Charles the firsts Charter	Towns Armes
Kings Charles the 2nd Charter	Writeings with many seales

The plate delivered up.
At this Court was delivered to Mr Alderman by Mr Henry Humes late Alderman All the Towns plate as followeth vizt

The Horse Race Cup	Two Tunns
Mr Archers Boll	Mr Kirkbys Boll
Mr Wheatlys Cann	Mr Greenewoods 12 spoones
Mr Horsemans Boll	One salt with Cover

Mr Greenewoods Cann   Mr Horsemans Wine Boll
Mr Batties Beaker   The Waites Cognizances

All feasts to be kept at the Redd Lyon.
Whereas Mr Alderman this day acquainted the Court that it is very requisite all publike Feasts and Dinners should be kept at the Redd Lyon for the incouragement of the present Tenant which this Court doth take to be very reasonable Whereupon it is ordered that all publike feasts for the time to come be kept at the Redd Lyon unlesse sufficient cause be shewne at Mr Alderman Court for the time being, to the contrarey and be by the said Court allowed and approved of.

Denton Tolle lett.
At this Court Robert Woollands takes a lease of Denton tolle for one wholeyeare from this present day at the Rent of vij li to be paid Quarterly And he gives in Earnest thereof xijd And he is to give sufficient securitie for payment of the said Rent at or before the Ninth day of November next or else the bargaine to be void.

[fo. 625r]

Redd Lyon Rent cleared.
At this Court Mr Horsfeild the present Tenant to the Redd Lyon gives an Account of the payment of his Rent of xvj li per Annum for three yeares at Michaelmas last the x li a yeare being deducted which he is to pay the Towne Clarke to defray the Charges in recovering the said Inn And upon Account he stands charged at vj li per Annum for three yeares and five pounds for Laydy day Rent

1671 before the Towne Clarke entred which is in all	23 00 00
And his disbursments to the Poore a yeare & halfe	10 00 00
For Repaires of the Inn as appeares by particulars	09 16 00
For the last Sessions Dinner	03 04 00
Totall	23 00 00

So the Account stands cleared till the 30th of September last past.

William Clarke chosen Chaimberlaine & refuseth the place.
Whereas the Comoners this day by a free and unanimous consent according to the Auntient custome of this Corporacion have elected and chosen William Clarke ~~one~~ a of [*sic*] Members of this Court one of the Chaimberlaines of this Burrough for the yeare to come who being severall times called to take his oath incident to the said Office did absolutely refuse to take the same or accept of the said Office for which refusall and contempt this Court by a full consent doth hereby impose a fine of five pounds upon the said William Clarke and doth give him time till next Court to give in his answer whether he will pay the said fine or accept of the said place and take his oath accordingly.

Simon Grant, William Walgrave, Bethell Briggs, William Burbridge [sic] *made free.*
At this Court came Simon Grant Woollen Draper, William Walgrave Butcher, Bethell Briggs Cordwainer and William Burbidge Butcher who had served their severall Apprenticeshipps within this Burrough and desired to be admitted Free Burgesses thereof to which this Court doth condiscend Whereupon the said Simon Grant and William Walgrave as freeborne pays ijs vjd apeice to the Box & xviijd apeice to the Clarke & Serjents And the said Bethell Briggs and William Burbidge are Forrainers pays vs apeice to the Box & xijd apeice to the Officers & are admitted Free Burgesses and tooke the oaths incident thereunto.

Mr Fishar of the 2d xij.
At this Court Thomas Fishar is chosen one of the *2d* Company
In the Kallender
Thomas Archer
John Robinson
Nicholas Becke

[fo. 625v] **Second Court of Edward Rawlinson, 8 November 1673**

Hather tolle lett.
At this Court came John Broughton and takes a lease of the tolle at Hather Hedge for one yeare from the last at the Rent of 3 li 13s 4d to be paid quarterly and to pay a quarters Rent before hand as his securitie And he gives in Earnest thereof xijd.

An order to setle the Stalls.
Whereas it was this day moved in Court that it was convenient that the Chaimberlaine should have the setling of all stalls and standings in the Market place belonging to this Corporacion And that the Freemen thereof should have the Choice of their standings and after such Choice made the Chaimberlaine for the time being to setle the rest which being taken into consideracion It is at this Court ordered that the Chaimberlaine for the time being do from time to time and at all times hereafter setle and place all the stalls and standings in the Marketplace or elsewhere within this Burrough giveing libertie as aforesaid, to Freemen to make Choice of their Ground for standings And it is further ordered that if any controversie shall arise for the future betweene any Freeman and the Chaimberlaine that then either party greived shall and may make his Complaint to Mr Alderman for the time being and two of his Brethren who are by this order authorized and impowred to end and determine the said Complaint as they in their discrecion shall thinke meete And for avoiding all differences that shall happen betweene a Freeman and a Forrainer on any Market day after any stall be set It is ordered that the Freeman shall forbid him setting of his stall in the same place the Market day after and make Complaint thereof to the then Chaimberlaine who is hereby required to remove the said stall if the party that set the same refuse so to do And it is further ordered that noe Freeman whatsoever shall pull downe any stall that shall be set up

on any Market day to make a difference in the publike Market but he shall have his remedie and releife of his greviance as is above mencioned and ordered.

[fo. 626r] Third Court of Edward Rawlinson 12 December 1673

Mr Coddingtons Account for tolle.
At this Court Mr John Coddington gives an Account of the proffitts of the tolles for the moneth of
Sept last and chargeth himselfe with Receipt of   01 19 05
Disbursments   00 04 00
Remaines due to the Towne   01 15 05
Which he payes in open Court and he is discharged.

Denton tolle lett.
At this Court Mr Robert Calcraft gives an Account of the letting of Denton tolle to William Blacke for vij li for one yeare from Martlemas last And of the tolle of Carriers goods that came to the White Lyon let to Mr Whalles for xvjs for one yeare from the said time And that both Rents are to be paid quarterly.

Thomas Fishar Account to be setled.
Whereas there hath beene formerly and still is some dispute aboute the Accounts of Thomas Fishar Churchwarden and he this day submitting himselfe to the Court and takeing xvjs viijd of from his Account this Court doth admitt thereof and doth discharge him from further answering the said Accounts.

Accounts to be examined.
At this Court it is ordered that Mr Alderman, Mr Taylor, Mr Coddington, Mr Cole, Edward Paulet, John Turner, Anthony Hotchkin, Edward Leivesly, Thomas Chrichloe, William Haskerd and Thomas Archer do examine the Accounts of the Churchwardens and Chaimberlaines and returne their proceedings therein the next Court day.

And further order to setle the stalls.
Whereas upon reading the order last Court for setling of the stalls belonging to this Burrough it was observed that for the better setlement thereof and hereby ordered that noe Person or Persons whatsoever should keepe above one stall and that not to be above ten foote in lenght [*sic*] And for the incourageing of such as keepe stalls and of other Tradsmen within this Corporacion it is ordered that noe Butchers shall goe from House to House to put their meate to saile on the Market day during the time thereof And that noe Person or Persons whatsoever being a Forrainer shall after any faire belonging to this Burrough shall continue any stall or keepe open shop after the faire be ended upon paine of xs for every such Offence And for every Butcher offending this order and for every Person keepeing above one stall & above the lenght aforesaid to forfeite iijs iiijd for every Offence to be levied by distresse and sale of goods for the use of this Corporacion.

[fo. 626v] **Fourth Court of Edward Rawlinson, 10 April 1674**

Mr Walkers Account as Chaimberlaine.
At this Court John Walker Chaimberlaine gives his Account for the yeare
past for his time and that his Receipts are   240 07 06
Disbursments   250 12 00
Remaines due to him   010 04 06
Which he is ordered to be paid upon the first Receipt of monies.

Mr Becks Account as Chaimberlaine.
At this Court Nicholas Becke Chaimberlaine passeth his Account for his time
in the yeare past his Receipts are   61 01 08
His disbursments   67 14 08
Remaines due to him   06 13 00
Which is ordered to be paid unto him by the succeeding Chaimberlaine.

John Robinsons Account as Churchwarden.
At this Court John Robinson Churchwarden passeth his Account for the yeare
past and his Receipt are   27 12 08
His disbursments   37 16 07
Remaines due to him   10 03 11

John Robinson money due upon his Account to be paid.
At this Court it is ordered for the payment of the said ten pounds 3s 11d due to the said John Robinson and for the further repaires of the Church that an Assessment of xx li be made by the present Churchwarden upon notice given in the Church of the time and place of makeing the said Assessment.

Mr Rastalls interest money to be paid.
At this Court it is ordered that Mr Robert Cole do pay out of the proffitts of the tolle he hath received iij li to Mr Rastall for interest and iiij li to the Chaimberlaine for the Rent of the tolles And that Mr Cole have the Towns halfe pence that is in his hands changed by the present Chaimberlaine except to the value of xxs.

Mr Taylors Account for tolle.
At this Court Mr Taylor gives an Account of the proffitt of the tolles for the moneth of
December last His Receipts   05 12 01 ob
His disbursments   00 17 01
Remaines due to the Towne   [sum incorrect] 04 14 00 ob
Which he payes in open Court & is discharged.

[fo. 627r]

Mr Humes Account for tolle.
At this Court Mr Henry Humes gives an Account for the proffitt of the tolles for the moneth of
Novembert [sic] last and that his Receipts are   02 17 06
Disbursments   00 08 04
Remaines due to the Towne   02 19 02
Which he payes in open Court & is discharged.

Mr Lentons Account for tolle.
At this Court Mr John Lenton gives an Account of the proffitt of the tolles for the moneth
of January last And that his Receipts are   01 18 10
His disbursments   00 08 04
Remaines due to the Towne   01 10 06
Which he payes in open Court and is discharged.

Mr Calcrafts Account for tolle.
At this Court Mr Richard Calcraft gives an Account of the tolles for the moneth of
February last And that his Receipts are   01 17 11
His disbursments   00 06 10
Remaines due to the Towne   01 11 01
Which he pays in open Court and is discharged.

Mr Robert Calcraft Account for tolle.
At this Court Mr Robert Calcraft gives an Account of the proffitt of the tolle for the moneth of
March last And that his Receipts   01 06 04
His disbursments   00 06 04
Remaines due to the Towne   01 00 00
Which he pays in open Court and is discharged.

Mr Burnet admitted Tenant to Tomlys [sic] *Cottage.*
At this Court came Mr Samuell Burnet the present Minister and desired to be admitted Tenant to a Cottage in Manthorpe belonging to this Corporacion and formerly in the possession of one Thomas Tomlyn and granted by lease to the Keybearers & Comoners of this Towne & by them assigned to the said Tomlyn and by his Executors assigned over by consent of a former order of Court to Mr John Hurst who granted the same to Mr Burnet The which this Court takeing into consideracion is also that he will be a good Tenant do hereby admitt tenant to the premisses for the Remainder of the terme yet to come & unexpired by the said originall lease he giveing securitie for the Rent of the said House & repaires.

A House in Castlegate let to Richard Poole.
At this Court Richard Poole takes a lease of a House in Castlegate late in the possession of Hugh Holt at the fine of 13 li 10s one halfe to be paid at sealing & the other halfe at Martlemas next & giveing securitie for Rent & repaires & he gives in earnest xijd And his lease to comence from Michaelmas next.

[fo. 627v] **Fifth Court of Edward Rawlinson, 16 April 1674**

A lease let to Humphery Fishar of a House in Walkergate.
At this Court came Humphery Fishar and takes a lease of a House in Walkergate wherein he now dwelleth for one and twenty yeares from Lady day last paying Eight pounds fine at two payments that is to say foure pounds upon the 24th day of June next and the xxvth day of December now next ensueing And he gives in earnest thereof xijd.

A lease let to Widdow Hawdin of a lease in High Streete.
At this Court came Widdow Hawdin and takes a lease of a House in High Streete wherein shee now dwelleth for xxj yeares from Lady day last paying two pounds & ten shillings fine at two payments vizt xxxs upon the 24th day of June next And xxs upon the xxvth day of December next And shee gives in earnest thereof xijd.

An order against Water Carts.
At this Court Mr Alderman, Mr Grant, Mr Taylor and Mr Robert Calcraft gives an Account that they had agreed with William Fearon for xxvjs viijd *per Annum* to comence at the last Court day for useing Water Carts with shodd Wheeles And it was then agreed that noe Person or Persons whatsoever should use such Carts during the time of the said William Fearon which said Agreement is allowed of and confirmed by this Court.

Persons to be distrained of for tradeing not being free.
At this Court it is ordered that George Wray junior, Thomas Poole, John Simpson, Ralph Clarke, William Handley and William Wright be forthwith distrained of for xxs a peice for tradeing a fortnight within this Corporacion not being free contrarey to the custome of this Burrough and former orders of this Court.

An order for the disposall of the xx li given yearely by Sir Edmund Turner.
Whereas Mr Alderman this day acquainted the Court that the Worshipfull Sir Edmond [*sic*] Turner of South Stoake within this libertie Barronett out of his Charitable dispocion to the Poore of this Towne and for the educateing of the Children of poore people being Freemen of this Burrough and of his good Will and affeccion to this Corporacion is pleased to send twenty pounds per Annum six pounds thereof to be distributed to Auntient decayed poore people at Christmas and foureteene pounds remainder of the said xx li for the putting the Children of poore people being freemen as aforesaid out Apprentices And that it is his desire that Mr Alderman for the time being and the rest of the Comburgesses or the Major part of them should yearely nominate & present

to the Court six poore Boyes out of which three is to be elected by the Court to be put out Apprentices with the said xiiij li In pursuance of which Mr Alderman & the Comburgesses do this day present six poore Boyes by the names of their Parents that are as followeth vizt John Robinsons Boy, Hugh Smiths Boy, John Blackes Boy, James Gibsons Boy, Edward Ulliots Boy & Widdow Hawdins Boy and by an unanimous vote upon Eleccon of them one after another it is ordered that Smith, Blacke & Gibson Boys shall be put out Apprentices this yeare And that Robinson Ulliott & Hawdins Boys be taken into consideracion the next yeare.

[fo. 628r] **Sixth Court of Edward Rawlinson, 11 May 1674**

An order for the Eleccion of the Succeeding Alderman.
For the more peaceable and quiett proceeding at the Eleccion of the next succeeding Alderman It is ordered that upon the next Elleccion day Mr Thomas Short be sent downe into the Church to Mr Robert Cole and Mr Thomas Matkin to make three Comburgesses there Out of which three Comburgesses in the Church It is likewise agreed that Mr Robert Cole be brought upon the Cusheon or place of Elleccion to Mr John Coddington & Mr John Wing to make three Comburgesses there out of which three Comburgesses Mr John Coddington by a free and unanimous consent of this Court is nominated Alderman for the next ensueing yeare.

A lease of Townes Milnes to be taken.
Whereas Mr Alderman this day acquainted the Court that Mrs Hurst, Mrs Trevillian & Mr John Welby to whome the Milles were ingaged were willing that the Towne should either buy out their title or take a lease of them for their terme at fifteene pounds per Annum apeice giveing them personall securitie for the payment thereof The which this Court takeing into consideracion and that it may be for the good and proffitt of this Corporacion It is ordered by the whole Court that a lease be taken of the said Persons for their terme at xv li apeice *per Annum* And for their securitie the Gentlemen hereafter named that is to say Mr Robert Calcraft, Mr Richard Holley, Mr Henry Humes, Mr Robert Cole, Edward Paulet, Anthony Hotchkin, Henry Coverly, Thomas Fishar, Thomas Charles, William Clarke, Thomas Chrichloe are willing and contented to become bound on the behalfe of this Corporacion And in consideracion thereof it is ordered that the said Gentlemen shall have the lease of the Milles made to them for their securitie And that they shall and may first pay the Rent due upon the lease they are ingaged in and the Overplus after the said Milles are sett in repaires to be paid to the Towne during the said lease And it is further ordered that in case any of the said Gentlemen shall depart this life during the said terme that then within two moneths after some other Person or Persons of the Court for the time being shall become bound in the Roome & place of such as shall dye And free their Executors or Administrators And in default thereof that the Executors or Administrators of such Persons dying shall stand possessed of the said Milles as to their part to their owne

use till such time as he or they shall be secured & freed from the ingagement aforesaid by this Corporacion.

Mr Coles Account for tolle.
At this Court Mr Robert Cole gives an Account of the profitt of the tolles for the moneth
of Aprill last And that his Receipts are   15 04 08
His Disbursments   01 05 06
Remaines due to the Towne   13 19 02
Which he pays in open Court and he is discharged.

[fo. 628v] Seventh Court of Edward Rawlinson 2 July 1674

Sandpitt tolle lett.
At this Court Thomas Fishar takes a lease of the tolle of Sandpitt laine for vjs *per Annum* from Mayday last to be paid at two payments halfe yearely And he gives in earnest thereof xijd.

Mr Grants Account for tolle.
At this Court Mr Thomas Grant accounteth for the proffitts of the tolles for the moneth of
June last His Receipts   05 14 06 ob
Disbursments   00 15 06
Remaines due to the Towne   04 18 00 ob
Which he pays in open Court & is discharged.

Towns leases to be assigned to Mr Robert Cole & Mr Matkin to secure them from 30 li for which they are bound for the Towne.
At this Court it is ordered that in respect Mr Robert Cole is willing to be become bound for the Milles and being bound for xxx li formerly with Mr Thomas Matkin for the use of this Burrough to Mr Walton It is ordered that Mr Cole & Mr Matkin have securitie out of the Towns lease to their content to indempnifie them from the said bond of xxx li.

William Southerne made free William Hodgson, George Wray & Thomas Poole made free.
At this Court came William Southerne who had served the Towne Clarke five yeares And William Hodgson Butcher, George Wray Tanner & Thomas Poole Bridlemaker who had severally served their Apprenticeshipp of seaven yeares and desired to be admitted free Burgesses of this Corporacion Whereupon the said William Southerne as a Forrainer lays downe his x li but this Court out of their respect to him gives him his x li againe And the said William Hodgson, George Wray & Thomas Poole paye the sume of ijs vjd to the Box as free borne And they every of them take the oath of freemen & other oaths incident thereunto And are admitted freemen of the Corporacion.

Mr Coddingtons Account for tolle.
At this Court Mr John Coddington gives an Account of the proffitts of the tolles for the moneth of
July – his Receipts   15 19 01
Disbursments   01 02 08
Remaines due to the Towne   14 16 07
Which he pays in open Court & he is discharged.

[fo. 629r] **Eighth Court of Edward Rawlinson, 29 July 1674**

Gaole bills to be paid.
At this Court it is ordered that the Constables lay downe 01 li 16s 07d for the Gaole bills due to Bryan Godley and the Cheife Constables 2 li 05s 0d due to John Shootewell for repaireing the Conduit And that they be reimbursed out of the Constables Assessment.

The fine of 40 li to be taken of, imposed up on the Towne for the Gaole.
At this Court it is ordered that the Chaimberlaine pay 06 li 13s 04d to the Towne Clarke to take of the amerciament of 40 li laid upon the Towne and Soake for not repaireing the Gaole which amerciament was estreated and compounded before the Councill of the Queene Mother And that the Chamberlaine pay 02 li 03s 00d to the Towne Clarke for charges in takeing of and compounding the said amerciament.

An Assessment for Marketplace Pumpe.
At this Court it is ordered that the Constables of the Marketplace do lay an Assessment for the repaireing of the Market place Pumpe and that they collect the same.

Mr Hurst allowed for Survaying the Towne land.
At this Court it is ordered that Mr Richard Hurst be allowed what charges he shall be at Survaying the Towns land by the Collector of the Schoole House Rents or be paid the same by the Chaimberlaine for the time.

Mr Paulet to injoy the Redd Lyon for a time.
Whereas Mr Paulet this day moved the Court that Mr Horsfeild had left the Redd Lyon and that the goodes in the House was his but if the Court pleased he would keepe open the gates for to hold that custome it had if he might injoy it without paying any Rent except what was due when Mr Horsfeild went away, till such time as the Towne can conveniently get a Tenant And then he would leave it in a weeks time Whereupon it is ordered that Mr Paulet injoy it Rent free till the Towne can get a Tenant.

Robert Barton made free.
At this Court came Robert Barton Forrainer and desired to be admitted a free Burgesse of this Corporacion to which this Court doth condiscend Whereupon he lays downe his x li and this Court out of their respecte to him doe give him againe 5 li And he takes

the oath of Freeman & the other oaths incident thereunto & pays the fees to the Clarke and Serjents & is admitted accordingly.

Mr Grant Account for tolle.
At this Court Mr Thomas Grant gives an Account of the proffitt of the tolles for the moneth

of June last And that his Receipts are	05 14 00 ob
His Disbursments	00 15 06
Remaines due to the Towne	04 18 06

Which he pays in open Court & he is discharged.

[fo. 629v] **Ninth Court of Edward Rawlinson, 25 September 1674**

Mr Rookesby to have the fine of Richard Pooles lease.
At this Court it is ordered that the 13 li 10s due for the fine of a House in Castlegate late Holts & now let to Richard Poole be paid to Mr Rookesby in part of the money due from the Towne to him in the right of his wife.

A House in Swinegate let to William Newton.
At this Court William Newton takes a lease of a House in the Vine Streete now in the tenure of Widdow Lewin for 21 yeares from Michaelmas next for x li fine five pounds part thereof to [*sic*] paid at the sealing of the lease and 5 li the Remainder at Laydy day next And he gives in earnest thereof xijd.

An Assessment to be made for the Constables bills.
At this Court it is ordered that an Assessment of 28 li be made for the Constables bills this yeare an estimate being taken what the perticular sumes amount unto and that notice be given in the Church the next Sunday of the time & place of makeing the said Assessment And it is ordered that 5 li part of the 28 li be paid unto the Towne Clarke in part of 10 li 08s 07d by him paid in defence of Richard Hickson and Francis Bristow Constables upon an Informacion in the Crowne Office against them for what they did in the execucion of their Office when Mr Edward Smith made an Assault upon William Hickson And that 5 li 8s be put in the Constables bills the next yeare to cleare the said charges.

Mr Taylors Account for tolle.
At this Court Mr Taylor gives an Account of the proffitts of the tolle for the moneth of

July last his Receipts	02 01 06
Disbursments	00 05 04
Remaines due to the Towne	01 16 02

Which he pays in open [*sic*] & is discharged.

Mr Robert Calcraft takes a lease of house in Calstlegate [sic].
At this Court Mr Robert Calcraft takes a lease of a House in Castlegate late in the possession of William Bury for 21 yeares from Michaelmas next at iiij li fine to be paid at the sealing of the lease And he gives in earnest thereof xijd.

Thomas Fishar takes Blacks Boy an Apprentice.
At this Court Thomas Fishar takes a Boy of John Blacks Apprentice for eight yeares with v li part of the money given by Sir Edmund Turner out of his Charitable disposicion for the putting out poore Children of this Towne Apprentice.

Humphrey Fishars fine to be towards makeing up Mr Pells guift.
At this Court it is ordered that the fines of Humphery Fishar lease, William Newton & Mr Robert Calcraft leases be disposed of to make up Mr Pells guift of xxx li to be let out to Tradsmen without interest.

[fo. 630r] **Tenth Court of Edward Rawlinson, 2 October 1674**

Mr Aldermans Account.
At this Court Mr Alderman gives an Account of all the proffitts he hath received upon the publike and of his disbursments and that there is due to him 01 li 04s 08d Which is paid unto him in open Court

Coroners Account.
At this Court Mr Henry Humes Coroner accounteth and saith that as Casualties happened this yeare there was [gap] of Manthorpe within this libertie who was found dead And the Jury upon their inquest found that shee had many yeares been troubled with the falling sicknes & being in a very season & haveing one of her fitts shee there perished And he saith that shee was very Poore & noe proffitt accrued to the Towne And further he hath not to Account.

Escheators Account.
At this Court Mr Thomas Matkin Escheator for the yeare past gives an Account of severall
Persons for defective Weights and Measures & that his Receipts	01 09 06
Disbursments	00 05 00
Remaines due to the Towne	01 04 06

Which he payes in open Court & is discharged.

Accounts to be examined.
At this Court the Churchwardens, Chaimberlaines and Collectors have further time to Account.

Some Constables Accounts questioned.
At this Court the severall Constables gives an Account of the Constables Assessment and of their disbursments for the yeare past And upon reading of the Account of John Vincent & Perchivall Matkin there appeares to be laid out 08 li 04s 01d which seemes very unreasonable to this Court It is therefore ordered that their bills be filed And that they bring in new bills the next Court and give further satisfaction for their laying out the said money & the other Constables

Accounts stand as followeth their Receipts	26 08 08
Disbursments	26 04 08
Remaines in the Chaimberlaines hand	00 04 00

Mr Richard Calcraft Account for tolle.
At this Court Mr Richard Calcraft gives an Account for the proffitt of the tolle for the moneth

of August last and that his Receipts are	02 06 01
Disbursments	00 05 08
Remaines	02 00 05

Mr Lentons Account for tolle.

Mr Lenton Accounts for the moneth of September his Receipts	01 15 11
Disbursments	00 04 08
Remaines	01 11 03

Mr Robert Calcraft Account for Tolle.

Mr Robert Calcraft Accounts for October His Receipts	06 17 10
Disbursments	00 12 06
Remaines	06 05 04

All which is paid in open Court & the severall Persons are discharged.

[fo. 630v] [Blank page]

[fo. 631r]

At an Assembly holden by Mr Edward Rawlinson Alderman and the Comburgesses and Burgesses of Grantham aforesaid in Corpus Christi Quire within the Prebendarie Church there &c on Friday next after St Luke day being 21 October 1674.

First did sitt downe upon the Cusheon or place of Election the said Mr Edward Rawlinson in Corpus Quire within the Presbendare [sic] Church there &c
next to him did sitt upon the Cusheon or place of Eleccion two Comburgesses vizt Mr John Coddington and Mr John Winge

Then was there in the Church two Comburgesses vizt Mr Robert Cole & Mr Thomas Matkin

Then was sent downe into the Church to those two Comburgesses to make them three one other Comburgesses vizt Mr Thomas Short

Out of which three Comburgesses in the Church one was chosen to come up and sitt upon the Cusheon or place of Eleccion vizt Mr Robert Cole

Then was there upon the Cusheon or place of Eleccion three Comburgesses vizt Mr John Coddington, Mr John Winge & Mr Robert Cole

And then was there in the Church two Comburgesses vizt Mr Thomas Matkin and Mr Thomas Short

Out of which three Comburgesses upon the Cusheon or place of Elleccion vizt Mr John Coddington Mr John Winge & Mr Robert Cole one is to [sic] chosen Alderman for the ensueing yeare

And so by an unanimous vote and consent of this Assembly Mr John Coddington is nominated Alderman for the next ensueing yeare

Whereupon the said Mr Edward Rawlinson dischargeth himselfe from the place and Office of Alderman according to Auntient custome And the said Mr John Coddington now elected Alderman in his place and stead hath at this Assembly taken the oath of Alderman for this Burrough and Soake of Grantham according to the Auntient and laudable custome of the Burrough aforesaid

And so this Assembly breaks up.

THE HALL BOOK OF GRANTHAM 1674–1675

[fo. 631v] **First Court of John Coddington, 30 October 1674**

Mr Alderman	Comburgess	Anthony Hotchkin
Mr Thomas Short	Comburgess	Thomas Fishar
Mr Thomas Grant	Comburgess	William Milles
Mr Michaell Taylor	Comburgess	John Turner
Mr Robert Calcraft	Comburgess	Thomas Ireland
Mr Richard Calcraft	Comburgess	Edward Paulett
Mr Richard Holley	Comburgess	Christofer Thompson
Mr John Lenton	Comburgess	Henry Caverly
Mr Henry Humes	Comburgess	John Pape
Mr Edward Rawlinson	Comburgess	Thomas Charles
Mr John Wing	Comburgess	John Walker
Mr Robert Cole	Comburgess	Edward Leivesly
Mr Thomas Matkin	Comburgess	

The Names of the Officers

Coroner	Mr Edward Rawlinson	Key Bearers	Mr Alderman
Escheator	Mr Thomas Shorte		Thomas Charles
Chamberlaines	John Pape		Edward Leivesly
	Edward Bristow	Prizers of Corne	Thomas Rowley
Cheife Constables	Anthony Hotchkin		Thomas Hodgson
	Thomas Fishar	Market Sayers	George Hanson
Market Place	William Haskerd		William Kirke
	Symon Grant	Leather Sealers	Edward Ulliott
High Streete	Thomas Rowley		Henry Wright
	John Newcombe		Thomas Marshall
Westgate	Thomas Bayly		John Ingerson
	Thomas Kenion	Towne Clarke	William Hodgkinson
Walkergate	Thomas Rawlinson	Serjeants	Thomas Calcraft
	John Broome		Bryan Godley
Swinegate	William Newton	Gaoler	Bryan Godley
	William Cole	Church Clarke	William Knewstubbs
Castlegate	Robert Sparrow	Bellman	Ralph Osborne
	William Kirke		

[fo. 632r] **First Court of John Coddington 30 October 1674**

Mr Calcrafts Account for Tolls.
At this Court Mr Richard Calcraft gives an Account of the proffitts of the Tolles for the month of August last and chargeth himselfe
with the Receipt of   02 06 01
Disbursements   00 05 08
Remaines to the Towne   02 00 05
Which he hath paid to William Clarke Chamberlaine and is discharged.

Allissons rent paid.
At this Court widdow Allisson payes her Rent for the Tolle of oatemeale for the yeare past And takes a new lease of the said Tolle for one yeare from this day at twenty shillings Rent and she gives in earnest thereof vjd.

Redd Lyon repaires vewed.
At this Court it is ordered that Mr Alderman, Mr Thomas Short, Mr Michaell Taylor and Mr Robert Calcraft of the first Company, Anthony Hotchkin, Thomas Fisher and Henry Coverly of the Second Company, John Robinson and Thomas Archer Comoners doe veiw the Repaires of the Red Lyon and give an Account at the next Court day.

John Still pays 4 li.
At this Court it is ordered that John Still doe pay backe the foure pounds which he received of Sir Edmond Turners guift with James Pearsons Boy for to put him out Apprentice to another.

Mr Calcraft makes good a spoone lost.
Whereas upon reading over the Townes plate this day there Appears to be one Silver Spoone wanting which was one of the thirteene Silver Spoones given by Myles Greenewood and Mr Richard Calcraft being present acquainted the Court that it was lost in his time of Aldermanshipp And that he would make it good to this Corporation.

The Milles to be setled.
Whereas Mr Robert Cole one of the ingagors for the Townes Millnes on the behalfe of this Corporation this day moved the Court that it would be very convenient that the Millers of each Millne should bring in a note in writeinge of the proffitts of the Millnes every Fryday night to Mr Alderman to be by him kept to compaire the Accounts of the Gentlemen that are ingaged which this Court doe very well Approve of and doe order that the same be done Accordingly.

[fo. 632v] **Second Court of John Coddington, [no date given]**

Persons appointed to take Accounts.
At this Court it is ordered that Mr Thomas Short, Mr Michaell Taylor, Mr Robert Calcraft, Mr Richard Holley, John Turner, Thomas Ireland, Anthony Hodgson, Thomas Fishar, William Haskerd, Richard Segrave, Thomas Archer and Thomas Oldfeild do examine the Churchwardens, Chaimberlaines and the Collectors for the Schoole Rents their severall Accounts and do make returne of their proceedings therein the next Court day.

Sir William Ellis Barronett, Thomas Harrington Esquire, Mr John Welby, Mr John Fancourts made free.
At this Court came Sir William Ellis Barronett, Thomas Harrington Esquire, John Welby Gentleman and John Fancourts being Forrainers and desired to be admitted Free Burgesses of this Corporacion to whose request this Court doth condiscend whereupon they severally lay downe the sume of ten pounds And this Court out of respect they beare to the said Sir William Ellis and Thomas Harrington they promiseing not to claime any privilidge of being tolle free do returne them their ten pounds apeice againe And this Court do also returne the 10 li againe to Mr John Welby in regard he was kind to the Corporacion upon sale of his part of the Milles and it is hereby ordered that the said Mr Welby shall have and injoy all of the prililges as other Freemen of this Burrough And this Court doth further out of respect to Mr Fancour [*sic*] by reason he hath beene very kind to some Poore Freemen within this Towne restore him his 10 li againe And they pay their severall fees to Clarke and Serjents and take the oath of free Burgesses according to the Auntient custome of this Burrough.

John Brome John Stevens Richard Sentence Robert Quew Mathew Dixon Francis Wells made free.
At this Court John Brome, John Stevens, Richard Sentence, Robert Quew, Mathew Dixon and Francis Wells who have served their severall Apprenticeshipps within this Burrough and come and desired to be admitted freemen of this Corporacion to which request this Court doth condiscend whereupon they pay their severall duties to the Towne And their fees to Clarke and Serjents & takes the oath of free Burgesses according to Auntient custome.

[fo. 633r] **Third Court of John Coddington, 27 November 1674**

Mr Welby's part of the Milnes bought.
Whereas Mr Michaell Taylor one of the Comburgesses this day acquainted Court that he hath made it a great part of his concern for the good of this Corporation for to make an Agreement with Mr John Welby for the Millnes that he hath now attainted unto if this Court please to Approve thereof. The Agreement is That Mr Welby shall have a hundred pounds at Candlemas next without interest and a hundred pounds at Candlemas twelve

month without interest and to be made Free Burgesse of this Corporation by the respect and favour of this Court and he to remitt all his share and proffitts of the Millnes since the Towne entered upon Mr Hursts and Mr Trevillians part and have securitie by bond for his money which Agreement this Court doth very well Allow and approve of and doth returne thankes to Mr Taylor for his kind respects to this Corporation And for the Securitie of Mr Welby, Mr Richard Holley, Mr Edward Rawlinson, Anthony Hotchkin and Henry Coverly out of this good intent and well to serve this Towne are here in Court willing to become bound to Mr Welby for the said money they haveing his part of the Millnes for their Securitie upon the same Termes and conditions that the Gentlemen that are ingaged for the other parts of the Millnes on the Townes behalfe Whereupon this Court returned them thankes for their readinesse to serve the publike And do hereby order that Mr Welby his part of the Millnes be secured to them according to their desire as the rest of the gentlemen that have Securitie upon the other parts on the behalfe of this Corporation.

John Still Apprentice.
At this Court it is ordered that John Still take James Gibsons boy an Apprentice out of the money of the Charitable disposition of Mr Edmund Turner And that, as he had foure pounds with Stills Boy that did not like the trade, that he have thirty shillings more with Gibsons boy.

Harrowbys payment setled.
At this Court it is ordered that what money Sir William Ellis and Sir Robert Thorold shall pay to the Church and poore it shall be divided for the future two parts to the Overseers of the Poore and the third part to the Churchwardens and which of the said officers for the time being shall receive any of the Summes aforesaid shall make the like division for the tyme to come.

John Vincent & Perchivall Matkin constables dismissed the Court.
John Vincent and Perchivall Matkin constables for the yeare past made it their request this day that they haveing great occasions this Court would be pleased to dismisse them from their Attendance Whereupon by a free consent they are dismissed this Court Accordingly.

[fo. 633v] Fourth Court of John Coddington, 11 December 1674

Mr Humes Account for Tolle.
At the Court Mr Humes gives an Account of the proffitts of the Tolles for the month of
November last and chargeth himselfe with the Receipt of	02 17 08
Disbursements	00 06 08
Remaines to the Towne	02 11 00

Which he payes in open Court and is discharged.

White Lyon tolls lett.
At this Court Mr William Walles takes a lease of the tolle of Waggons and Packhorses that lyes at his house onely and noe otherwise for one yeare from the last Account day at five and twenty Shillinges to be paid quarterly and he gives in earnest thereof twelve pence.

Denton tolls lett.
This Mr Alderman and Mr Robert Calcraft acquainted the Court that Robert Woollands hath taken of them a lease of Denton Tolle for one yeare from the last Account day at five pounds *per Annum* to be paid quarterly And that Mr William Blague stood ingaged for the said Rent And he gave in earnest thereof one shilling.

[fo. 634r] **Fifth Court of John Coddington, 15 January 1674/5**

James Long pays part of his fine.
At this Court came John [*sic*] Long and payes 13s 4d in part of the fyne of his lease. At this Court it is ordered that Mr William Warein and Robert Barton be sued for infringing the libertie And that the Towne Clarke doe prosecute the same with effect.

Redd Lyon lett.
Whereas Mr Michaell Taylor this day Acquainted the Court that the Towne Clarke was willing to take a lease of the Redd Lyon at the Rent of Fifteene pounds [*sic*] Shillinges and Eight pence if he might have a lease for Nynety and Nyne yeares and the Corporation to ingage to keepe all Sessions Dinner Venisson Feasts and Visitation Dinners at the Red Lyon dureing the said Terme And to sett the said house into sufficient repaires And that he would enter at Lady Day next and pay the Rent to the poore at Easter Whereupon this Court takeing the same into consideration doe order and agree that the Towne Clarke shall have a lease of the said Redd Lyon for Nynetie Nyne yeares at the Rent of Fifteene pounds Six shillinges and Eight pence from Lady Day next And that all Sessions Dinners Venisson Feasts and Visitation Dinners shall be kept at the said Inne dureing the said Terme And that it shall be lawfull to and for him to sett the said Inne in good and sufficient repaires out of the Rent to become due for the same to be referred to two indifferent persons one to be chosen by the Corporation And the other by the Towne Clarke And that the said Inn shall be Free from all manner of Assessments dureing the said Terme as the rest of the Townes land are And further that all and every the Clauses and agreements shall be inserted in his lease and made good to him by Covenant from this Corporation.

Edward Leiveslys Account as Churchwarden.
At this Court Edward Leivesly Churchwarden gives an Account of his Receipts and Disbursements on the behalfe of this Corporation Receipts as followeth

quarteridge and Church land	24 00 04
Bell Money	02 04 08

Spitlegate Assessment	02 11 03
Manthorpe	02 03 07
Grantham	24 10 00
Sir Robert Thorold	04 10 00
Total	59 19 10
Disbursements	59 15 06
Remaines due to the Towne	00 04 04

Which is ordered to be paid unto him by the next Churchwarden [*sic* more correctly should be paid to the town].

[fo. 634v]

Thomas Charles Account as Chaimberlaine.
At this Court Thomas Charles Chaimberlaine gives his Account for part of the yeare past

Receipts	49 05 03 ob
Disbursements	57 12 07
Remaines due to him	08 07 04

William Clarke account as Chaimberlaine.
At this Court William Clarke Chaimberlaine gives his Account for part of the yeare past

Receipts	93 17 10
Disbursements	[blank]
Remaines due to the Towne	24 14 08

[fo. 635r] **Sixth Court of John Coddington, 26 February 1674/5**

Redd Lyon to be veiwed.
At this Court it is ordered that Mr Alderman, Mr Short, Mr Taylor, William Milles, John Turner and Mr Richard Hickson doe veiw the Repaires of the Redd Lyon and give an Account thereof the next Court day.

Milles to be repaired.
At this Court Mr Robert Calcraft and Mr Robert Cole gives an Account that they had agreed with one William Glenn of North Wytham to repaire the side of the Slate Mille for Workemanshipp for Seaventeene pounds and a sack of Malt Seaven pounds to be paid dureing this tyme that he is at worke and Tenn pounds when his worke is finished to which Agreement this Court doth consent and Approve thereof.

Mr Rookesby paid 20 li.
At this Court it is order that Mr Rookeby [sic] have Twenty pounds part of the money due to his wife from this Corporation out of the proffitts of the Tolles the next faire.

[fo. 635v] **Seventh Court of John Coddington, 16 April 1675**

Streetes to be paved foure yards for their doores.
Whereas the Alderman this day acquainted the Court that he had Sir Thomas Skipwith the Recordors opinion for the paiveing of the Streetes in this Corporation it was lawfull for this Court to make an order to injoyne all householders in this Towne to paive foure yards from their houses under a penaltie And that the Streetes being much decayed it would be convenient that this Court did make an order for the paiveing of the said Streetes which being this day put to the vote of the Court It is by an unanimous consent fully agreed upon that all and every householders within this Corporation doe and shall at or before the Nyne and Twentieth day of September now next ensueing paive or cause to be paived from their severall and respective houses downe to the Channell where the Streetes are Eight yards wide and where it is above Eight yards wide then to paive foure yards and the Corporation the rest on paine of tenn Shillinges for every person neglecting to doe the same to be levyed upon their goods and Chattells to be imployed to the paiveing of such persons ground as shall soe make default in paiveing as aforesaid.

Towns land made fine certaine.
Whereas the Towne Clarke this day alsoe Acquainted the Court that in order to make the Townes lands fyne certaine he had taken an Account of the Fynes formerly sett which do Amount to Six Hundred and foure Pounds Thirteene Shillinges and foure pence or thereabouts And that if this Court would please to acquitt him of his bargaine he lately made for the lease of the Redd Lyon he would undertake to raise the said Six Hundred and four pounds Thirteene Shillinges and foure pence by Christmas next for to pay of a considerable part of the Townes debts, he haveing the full power to let all the houses and land belongeing to this Corporation according to the note given in to Mr Alderman for fyne certaines Whereupon this Court takeing the same into their consideration acquitt and discharge the Towne Clarke from his late lease of the Redd Lyon and doe order that he shall have full power to let the houses and lands belongeing to this Burrough for to raise the said Six hundred and foure Pounds Thirteene Shillinges and foure pence takeing all Securitie to the Alderman and Burgesses of this Corporation as formerly and giveing a note of three hundred pounds under his hand and Seale for the performance thereof which note is given in open Court Accordingly.

[fo. 636r]

Milles chosen of the firt [sic] *Company.*
At this Court Mr William Milles is chosen of the first Company in the roome of Mr Thomas Grant lately deceased.

John Robinson of the 2d.
At this Court John Robinson is chosen of the Second ~~twelve~~ Company in the roome of the said Mr William Milles In the Kallendar

Thomas Archer
Nichollas Becke
William Clarke

Mr Taylor Account for tolle.
At this Court Mr Michaell Taylor gives an Account of the proffitts of the Tolles for the month of
March last his Receipts	11 18 05 ob
Disbursements	01 01 04
Remains due to the Towne	10 17 01 ob

Which he payes in open Court and is Discharged.

Mr Grants Accounts for the tolle.
At this Court Symon Grant brings in an Account of the proffitts of the Tolles For February received by his Father one of the Comburgesses of this Court lately deceased
and the Receipts are	02 01 00
Disbursements	00 06 08
Remains due to the Towne	01 14 04

Which is paid in open Court.

Edward Leivesly Account as Churchwarden.
Att this Court Edward Leivesley late Churchwarden gives an Account of the Arreares of the Church Assessment for Quarteridge in his time and upon examining the said arreares there is severall abatements this day allowed of to him and upon stateing of his Account there Remaines due to him 1 14 6 which said money this Court doth order that Nicholas Becke the present Churchwarden doe payunto the said Edward Leivesly in discharge of his Account.

Francis Bristow, Marke Harnesse Overseers for Westgate.
At this Court Francis Bristow and Marke Harnesse are appointed Overseers for th'ensuing yeare for Westgate Well.

Thomas Archers Account as Colebuyer.
At this Court Thomas Archer Colebuyer for the yeare past gives an Account of the proffitts by
him made on the behalfe of this Corporacion and he charges
himselfe with	16 11 04
Disbursements	00 03 10
In his hand to be paid to the new Cole buyer	17 16 02
Stocke encreased	01 08 08

Thomas Hodgson Colebuyer.
Which money is paid to Thomas Hodgson who at this Court is Chosen Colebuyer for the yeare to come.

[fo. 636v] **Eighth Court of John Coddington, 28 May 1675**

Mr Calcraft Account for tolls for Aprill.
At this Court Mr Richard Calcraft brings in an Account of the proffitts of the tolles for the
moneth of Aprill last Receipts					08 09 00
His disbursements						01 14 04
Remaines due to the Towne
Which he pays in open Court and he is discharged.

Mr Winge nominated Alderman upon Condicion.
For the more peaceable and quiet proceedings at the Eleccion of the next Succeeding Alderman It was ordered that upon the next Elleccon Mr William Milles be sent down into the Church to Mr Thomas Short and Mr Thomas Matkin to make three Comburgesses there out of which three Comburgesses in the Church it is likewise agreed that Mr Thomas Matkin be brought upon the Cusheon or Place of Eleccion to Mr John Winge and Mr Robert Cole to make three Comburgesses there Out of which three Comburgesses Mr John Winge by a free and unanimous consent of the Court is nominated Alderman for the ensueing yeare upon Condicion that the said Mr John Winge shall at or before the next Eleccion give full satisfaccion to this Court that he shall not nor will not during the time he shall continue Alderman keepe a publike House selling Ale and Beere and if in case he doth not satisfie this Court therein by the time aforesaid Then it is at this Court further agreed to goe to a free Elleccion of an Alderman out of the three Comburgesses that shall be upon the Cusheon the day of the Elleccion And noe Aldermans feast to be provided and noe sallory to be allowed to the Gentleman that shall be elected Alderman for the ensueing yeare.

Phillip Cooke, John Jervas, John Gibson, John Goodwin, Henry Johnson made free.
At this Court came Phillip Cooke and John Jervas Forrainers & John Gibson & Henry Johnson and John Goodwin Freeborne and desired to be admitted free Burgesses of this Corporacion to whose request this Court doth condiscend whereupon the said Phillip Cooke lays downe his x li and this Court out of respect to him gives him againe 5 li And the said John Jervas payes to the Box vs And the said John Gibson and Henry Johnson ijs vjd apeice as freeborne & the said John Goodwin as a forrainer 5s and they pay their severall fees to Clarke and Serjents and are admitted & sworne freemen according to antient custome.

[fo. 637r] **Ninth Court of John Coddington, 9 July 1675**

Mr Lenton Accounts for tolles.
At this Court Mr John Lenton gives Account of the proffitt of the tolles for the moneth of
June last and that his Receipts are:				05 12 09
His disbursements						00 16 00

Remains due to the Towne   04 06 09
Which he pays in open Court and he is discharged.

Mr Cole nominated Alderman.
Whereas upon reading of the order this day made the last Court for the nominateing Mr John Winge Alderman for the ensueing yeare he being present in Court it was desired his answer whether he would leave of keepeing a publike House during the time he should continue Alderman to which he satisfied this Court he would not Whereupon it was put to the vote whether he should continue as Alderman nominated or not which was carried in this negative And the Court did proceed to a new nominacion as followeth For the more peaceable and quiet Elleccon of the next succeeding Alderman It is ordered that upon the next Elleccion day Mr William Milles be sent downe to the Church to Mr Thomas Short and Mr Thomas Matkin to make three Comburgesses and there out of which three Comburgesses in the Church It is likewise agreed that Mr Thomas Matkin be brought upon the Cusheon or place of Elleccion to Mr John Wing [*sic*] and Mr Robert Cole to make three Comburgesses there Out of which three Comburgesses Mr Robert Cole by a free and unanimous consent of this Court is nominated Alderman for the ensueing yeare.

John Smith not to be admitted a Freeman.
Whereas one John Smith whoe served his Apprenticeshipp of a Mercer and Hatter at Gainsborough within this County came this day to the Court and desired to be admitted a free Burgesse of this Corporacion with an intent to set up his trade in this Burrough and being with drawne the Court Edward Coddington, Nathaniell Garthwaite, Anthony Hotchkin and Richard Segrave Mercers & John Poole Hatter made their Applicacion to this Court and desired that Mr Alderman his Brethren and the rest of the Court would take into their consideracion that there was as many or more of that trade in the Towne already then formerly and that there was noe need of any more of that trade and desired the favour of this Court that they would not admit the said John Smith a free Burgesse of this Corporacion and by such meanes it would incourage the freeborne Burgesses to follow their trades & to take Apprentices that might be serviceable to the publike concerns of this Burrough Whereupon this Court takeing the same into their consideracion & also the disencouragement that might be to freeborne Burgesses & others that have or may serve their Apprenticeshipp in this Burrough did put it to the vote whether the said John Smith should be admitted a free Burgesse or not & it was clearly carried in the negative for which respect & favour the aforesaid Mercers & Joseph Poole did returne their harty thankes to this Court & presented five pounds for the publike affaires of this Corporacion & did also very civily & respectively treat the whole Court.

[fo. 637v] **Tenth Court of John Coddington, 20 August 1675**

Church Assessment to be made.
At this Court came Nichollas Becke Churchwarden and acquainted Mr Alderman and the Court that the Church was much out of repaires with the windowes and the leades and that the last Churchwarden Edward Leivesly had money due to him upon his Accounts and that he desired it might be paid him The which this Court takeing into consideration doe hereby order that an Assessment of twenty pounds be laid upon this parish for the further repaires of the Church and for the payment of the money due to the said Edward Leivesly upon his Account as Churchwarden And that notice thereof be given in the Church next Sunday of the tyme and place of the makeing the Assessment And it is further ordered that Mr Alderman and Mr Richard Calcraft of the first Company, John Turner and Edward Pawlett of the second Company, Symon Grant and John Broome Comoners with the Churchwardens and Overseers of the poore and such of the Inhabitants as shall meete upon notice given as aforesaid doe make and settle the said Assessment.

[fo. 638r] **Eleventh Court of John Coddington, 17 September 1675**

Account for tolles.
At this Court Mr Alderman gives an Account of the proffitts of the Tolles for the month of
August last Receipts	01 17 05
Disbursements	00 04 04
Remaines due to the Towne	01 13 01

The like.
At this Court Mr Henry Humes gives an Account of the proffitts of the Tolles for the month of
July last Receipts	02 08 02
Disbursements	00 07 00
Remaines to the Towne	02 01 02

Which he payes in open Court and is discharged.

Constables Assessment.
At this Court it is ordered that an Assessment of Six and twenty pounds be made for the payment of the Constables their bills of Disbursements for the yeare now last past an estimate being taken what they amount unto And it is also ordered that notice be given in the Church next Sunday of the tyme and place of makeing the said Assessment.

Sir Edmund Turner guift continued.
Whereas Mr Alderman this day acquainted the Court that Sir Edmund Turner was pleased to continue his favour to this Corporation and his Charitie to the Poore And that he hath sent foureteene pounds for the putting three poore Children Apprentice and that

the Ellection is to be as formerly Whereupon it is ordered that Crawshaw Robinsons and Holts Boy shall be put out Apprentices this yeare.

[fo. 638v] **Twelfth Court of John Coddington, 21 October 1675**

Coroners Account.
At this Court Mr Edward Rawlinson Coroner Accounteth and saith that as casualities happened this yeare there was one Richard Freckingham that was building of a house of Mr Batchellors in Castlegate the Scaffold broke and the said Richard Freckingham was casualities killed And the said Coroner further saith and Accounteth that there was one William Hinson building of a house in the High Streete of Mr Woodruffes the Govill Wall falling upon the said William Hinson Carpinter and casualy killed him and the Jury impannelled found the death of the Seaverall persons by Misfortune and noe proffitts accrewed to the Towne and further he hath not to Account.

Mr Aldermans Account.
At this court Mr Alderman gives an Account of all his Receipts and Disbursements upon the publike Affaires of this Corporation And that his Receipts are   01 07 10
His Disbursements   03 19 11
Remaines due to hime   02 12 01
Which is paid unto him in open Court.

Escheators Account.
At this Court Mr Thomas Short Escheator gives an Account of all monies by him received for light defective and unlawfull weights and measures and that his Receipts are 00 02 00 Which he payes in open Court and is discharged.

At this Court the Churchwarden, Chamberlaine and Collectors for the Schoolehouse Rents have further day to Account.

Mr Taylors Account for Tolles.
At this Court Mr Michaell Taylor gives an Account of the proffitt of the Tolles for the month of September   His Receipts are   02 01 10
His Disbursements   00 04 00
Remaines due to the Towne   01 17 10
Which he payes in open Court and is Discharged.

[fo. 639r]

At an Assembly holden by Mr John Coddington Alderman and the Comburgesses and Burgesses of Grantham aforesaid in Corpus Christie Quire within the Prebendarie there on Fryday next after St Luke day beinge 22 October 1675.

First did sit downe upon the Cusheon or place of Election the said Mr John Coddington in Corpus Quire within the Prebendarie Church there &c Next to him did sitt upon the Cusheon or place of Eleccion Two Comburgesses vizt Mr John Winge and Mr Robert Cole.

Then was there in the Church Two Comburgesses vizt Mr Thomas Short and Mr Thomas Matkin

Then was sent downe into the Church to those Two Comburgesses to make Them Three one other Comburgesse vizt. Mr William Milles

Out of which three Comburgesses in the Church one was Choosen to come up and Sitt upon the Cusheon or place of Election vizt Mr Thomas Matkin.

And then was there in the Church two Comburgesses vizt Mr Thomas Short & Mr William Milles out of which three Comburgesses upon the Cusheon or place of Election vizt Mr John Winge, Mr Robert Cole and Mr Thomas Matkin one is choosen Alderman for the ensuinge yeare.

And so by unanimous vote and Consent of this Assembly Mr Robert Cole is nominated Alderman for the ensuinge yeare.

Whereupon the said Mr John Coddington dischargeth himselfe from the place and office of Alderman accordinge to antient custome And the said Mr Robert Cole now elected Alderman in his place and stead hath at this Assembly taken the [oath of] Alderman for the Borough and Soake of Grantham accordinge to the antient and laudable custome of the Borough aforesaid.

And so this Assembly breaks up

[fo. 639v] [Blank page]

THE HALL BOOK OF GRANTHAM 1675–1676

[fo. 640r] **First Court of Robert Cole, 28 October 1675**

Mr Alderman
Mr Thomas Shorte Comburgesse
Mr Michael Taylor Comburgesse
Mr Robert Calcraft Comburgesse
Mr Richard Calcraft Comburgesse
Mr Richard Holley Comburgesse
Mr John Lenton Comburgesse
Mr Henry Humes Comburgesse
Mr Edward Rawlinson Comburgesse
Mr John Coddington Comburgesse
Mr John Winge Comburgesse
Mr Thomas Matkin Comburgesse
Mr William Milles Comburgesse

Christofer Thompson
Edward Leivesley
John Turner
Thomas Ireland
Edward Paulet
Anthony Hotchkin
Henry Coverly
John Pape
Thomas Charles
John Walker
Thomas Fishar
John Robinson

Names of the Officers

Coroner	Mr John Coddington	Keybearers	Mr Alderman
Escheator	Mr Michaell Taylor		Henry Coverly
Church-Wardens	Henry Coverly		Edward Leivesley
	Nicholas Becke		
Chamberlaines	Thomas Fishar	Market Sayers	George Hanson
	Thomas Chrichloe		Thomas Hatfeild
Collectors for Schoole Rentes	Mr William Milles	Prizers of Corne	William Newton
	Mr William Haskerd		Thomas Frith
		Leather Sealers	Thomas Marshall
			Asheton Lord
Cheife Constables	Christofer Thompson		Edward Ulliott
	Edward Leivesley		Henry Wright
Market place	Joseph Burnham		
	Symon Grant	Towne Clarke	William Hodgkinson
High Streete	Thomas Rowley	Serjeant	Thomas Calcraft
	John Gibson		
Westgate	William Cole	Serjeant & Gaoler	Bryan Godley
	Thomas Kenion		
Walkergate	John Broome	Church Clarke	William Knewstubbs
	John Smyth		

Swingate	William Kirke	Bellman	Ralph Osborne
	Thomas Quiningbrow		
Castlegate	John Goodwing		
	William Bristowe		

[fo. 640v]

Comoners
Marketplace
William Clarke
Edward Bristowe
Thomas Archer
Nicholas Becke
Thomas Crichloe
Thomas Hodgson
Symon Goodwing
High Streete
Richard Handley
George Read
Thomas Rowley
Christofer Hanson

Westgate
William Haskerd
Francis Bristowe
Thomas Frith

Walkergate
John Still

Castlegate
Robert Cowles

Charters delivered up in Court.
At this Court Mr John Coddington late Alderman delivers up the three Charter Boxes with all the Charters &c vizt:

The Exemplar of Edward 4th
King Henry the 8th
King Edward the 6th
Queen Elizabeth 3 Charters
King Charles the first
King Charles the second

King James
Judge Dyers Award
Stamford Writeings
Escheators Pattents
Townes Armes
Writing with many seales.

[fo. 641r]

Plate delivered up in Court.
At this Court was delivered by Mr John Coddington late Alderman to Mr Alderman that now is All the Townes Plate which is as followeth, vizt

The horse Race cup
Mr Archers Boll
Mr Wheatlyes Cann
Mr Horsemans Boll

Two Tunns
Mr Kirkby's Boll
Mr Greenwood 13 spoones
One salt with a Cover

Mr Greenwoods Cann
Mr Battyes Beaker

One Wyne Boll Mr Horsemans
The Waites cognizances

[fo. 641v] **Second Court of Robert Cole, 11 November 1675**

Mr Calcraft Account for tolles.
At this Court Mr Robert Calcraft gives an Account of the proffitts of the Tolles for the Month of October last past and that his Receipts amounts unto   07 08 07
His Disbursements   01 02 05
Remaines due to the Towne   06 06 02
Which he pays in open Court and he is discharged.

Persons appointed to take Accounts.
At this Court it is ordered that Mr Robert Calcraft, Mr John Winge, John Turner, Anthony Hotchkin, William Clarke, Richard Segrave and Thomas Archer doe examine and state the Chamberlaines, Churchwardens and the Collectors for the Scoole Rents Accounts and returne their proceedings therein the next Court day.

Tolles lett.
Mr Alderman gives an Account of Denton Tolle lett to Wollands for 5 li till the Count day.
Mr Alderman, Mr Calcraft, Towne Clarke, and Serjent to goe to Lincolne and to have charges to goe in their gownes. The pavement to goe on
An Assessement for 25 li for Westgate Well.
High Streete to have an Assessement of 40 li for the Well.
Mr Taylor to have security for 100 li
Mr Smyth Order abrogated fine 40 li.

Tolles lett.
At this Court Mr Alderman gives an Account that Denton Tolle is lett againe to Wollands Till the next Count day att the Rent of 5 li to be paid as formerly he paid the same And alsoe that Hather tolle is lett to John Broughton for 3 li per Annum from the Count day.

Sherriffe to be served with the Charter to preserve this libertie.
At this Court it is ordered That Mr Alderman, Mr Robert Calcraft, the Towne Clarke and one of the Serjeants to goe to Lincolne on Monday next beinge the first County day of the new Sherriffe to serve him with the Chartors of this Corporation to discharge him from infringinge this Liberty upon any processe whatsoever And that the present Chamberlaine doe pay their charges beinge upon the publique concerne of this Burrough

Persons to pave foure yards from their dores.
At this Court it is ordered That the Order of Sessions and the Order of Court made in the yeare of Mr John Coddington Alderman for the Inhabitants of this Towne to pave four yards from their Doores be putt in effectuall execution against all Offenders whatsoever.

At this Court Mr Alderman gives an Account that he had let Denton tolle to Roger Wollands for 5 li And Hather tolle to John Broughton for 3 li till the next Count day.

[fo. 642r] Third Court of Robert Cole, 17 December 1675

Orders to be observed.
At this Court it is ordered that the first and second doe constantly goe in their Gownes to the Church upon the dayes appointed by former Orders of this Court And also to Aldermans Court And that no excuse of rain or other pretence whatsoever shall be admitted or allowed of But That every person soe offendinge shall forfeit 2s to the Box for the use of the Corporation.

An Assessment of 4 li for High streete Well.
And this Court it is ordered That an Asessement of 4 li be made for the repaires of High streete Well upon the Inhabitants of Highstreete and Castlegate and Assessement of 40s be laid upon the Inhabitants of Westgate for the repairinge of the Well in the said Streete.

40 li fine for a free Burgesse.
Whereas Mr Alderman this day Acquainted the Court that it was very convenient That the Fine of ten pound formerly made for the Admittance of a Free Burgesse should be raised to forty pound And by such a Fine it might keepe strangers for cominge into this Burrough and be an Encouragement to the free Burgesses thereof The which this Court takinge into consideration and the benefitt of the same for the good of this Corporation do with an Unanimous consent order and Agree That no person or persons whatsoever shall hereafter be admitted a free Burgesse or Burgesses of this Burrough before he or They shall first lay downe the sume of forty pound of lawfull money of England in open Court for the use of this Corporation and after desire his or their freedome or not to be admitted And That The said order of Ten pound be hereby revoked repealed and made void to all intents and purposes whatsoever as if the same had never beene made any thing therein mentioned To the contrary thereof in anywise notwithstandinge.

John Smith made free.
At this Court came John Smyth and desired to be admitted a free Burgesse of this Burrough and beinge withdrawne the Court It was put to the vote whether the order made in the Court of Mr John Coddington against the Admittinge of the said John Smyth to be a freeman should stand in force or be abrogated And by the Major part of this Court it is ordered and Agreed that the said order be hereby abrogated and maid void to all intents and purposes whatsoever And after the said order so abrogated it was againe putt to the vote whether The said John Smyth should be admitted a free Burgesse of this Corporation And by the Major part of the said Court it was carried that the said John Smyth should be admitted a Freeman Whereupon the said John Smyth laid downe the Fine of forty pound which was taken for the use of this Corporation And he tooke the oath of a Freeman and the oaths incident thereunto and paid his fees to

the Clarke and Serjeant and is admitted a free Burgesse of this Corporation accordinge to antient custome.

Mr Chaimberlaines bond renewed.
Whereas Mr Taylor this day Acquainted Mr Alderman and the Court that Mr Chamberlaine beinge dead to whome the Corporation did owe a hundred pound for which he and some others are bound his Executors desires to have the Bond renewed and that he with the rest are willinge to become bound againe if they have counter security To which this Court do agree that Mr Taylor and the rest shall have counter security as shall be sufficient to secure Them.

[fo. 642v] **Fourth Court of Robert Cole, 6 January 1675/6**

Mr Lentons Account for tolle.
At this Court Mr John Lenton gives an Account of the proffitts of the Tolles for
the Month of November last   li   s   d
his Receipts   02 09 00
Disbursements   00 07 00
Remaines to the Towne   02 02 00
which he pays in open Court and is discharged.

Mr Chamberlaines bond renewed.
At this Court it is ordered That Mr Taylor, Mr Dalton, Mr Bearnes and Mr John Coddington who is willing to become bound with Mr Taylor Mr Dalton and Mr Bearnes in the Roome of Mr Thomas Grant deceased he beinge discharged of a bond to Mr Robert Cole for the use of this Corporation unto Mr Chamberlaine for a hundred pound due from this Burrough That They shall have a grant of the tolles to indempnifie Them from the said hundred pound That They shall be bound for to Mr Chamberlaine as aforesaid.

Constables to be saved harmles for distraineing Mr Ashton.
Whereas Mr Alderman this day acquainted the Court that Mr James Ashton did sue Thomas Rowley and John Newcombe Constables for the high streete last yeare for distraininge the Constables Assessement And that Mr Bacon his Attorny had beene often with him for an Appearance And if Mr Ashton should proceed The Constables desired they might be saved harmelesse by the Towne Whereupon it is ordered That the Town Clarke do appeare for the said Constables and That They be saved harmelesse and indempnified by this Corporation.

Persons to examine the Towne leases.
At this Court it is ordered that Mr Thomas Short, Mr Richard Holley, John Pape, Edward Pawlett, Edward Bristow, Thomas Archer do examine the Towne Leases now to be made Fine certaine That They be right as to Fines and Rents and Covenants And whereas upon one of the new Leases read in Court It was observed by Mr Alderman that

there was a Covenant not to pay the Fine certaine till the last yeare of the expiracion of the said Lease and the former orders of the Court was to pay the Fine within five yeares of the expiration of every Lease which is convenient it should continue and beinge this day put to the vote it is ordered in respect that many pay their Fines havinge sixteene yeares to come in their Leases and beinge made Fine certaine That it is sufficient to pay the Fines before the expiration of their Leases And That all former Orders of Court about the time of renewinge Leases or any other made to the contrary be and are hereby made void repealed and revoaked to all intents and purposes whatsoever.

[fo. 643r] Fifth Court of Robert Cole, 21 January 1675/6

Mr Hotchkin released of the Redd Lyon.
Whereas Anthony Hotchkin Mercer this day desired the favour of this Court that he might be released of his Bargaine of the red Lyon for what he did was intended for the good of the Towne But now Mr Smyth beinge made free he hoped this Court would Acquitt him which beinge this day put to the vote It is carried by the Major part of this Court and ordered that the said Anthony Hotchkin be released Acquitted and discharged of his Bargaine of the red Lyon aforesaid.

Leases to be sealed.
At this Court it is ordered that there bee a meeting at the Hutch in the Church at Twelve of the Clock to seale Mr Taylor, Mr Denton, Mr Walton, Mr Burnetts, John Turner, John Still, Thomas Milles, Mr Bury, Richard Poole, Thomas Cole Leases Fine certaine.

Mr Calcraft Account for tolle.

	li	s	d
Mr Calcrafts Account for Tolle for the Month of December			
Receipts	07	12	11
Disbursements	01	03	10
Remaines	06	09	01

Which is paid in open Court

Leases to be sealed.
At this Court it is ordered There be a meeting at the Hutch this afternoone at the Hutch [*sic*] in the Church at twelve a Clocke to seale Leases to Mr Robert Calcraft and Towne Clarke for fine certaine.

Mr Pawlett to sell the Red Lyon signe and to be referred to two Workemen and indifferently cheosen and to abate forty shillings.

Mr Humes Account for tolle.
At this Court Mr Henry Humes gives an Accopmt [*sic*] of the proffitts of the tolle for the Month of January last

Receipts	02	08	11
Disbursements	00	08	04
Remaines to the Towne	00	00	07

Which he pays in open Court and is discharged. [*Sum incorrect.*]

Mr Aldermans Account for tolle.
At this Court Mr Alderman gives an Account of the proffitts of the tolle for the Month of

February last Receipts	02	02	03
Disbursements	00	06	08
Remaines due to the Towne	01	15	07

Which he pays in open Court and is discharged.

[fo. 643v] **Sixth Court of Robert Cole, 10 March 1675/6**

Redd Lyon let to one Mr Stacey.
Whereas Mr Alderman this day Acquainted the Court That he had lett the Red Lyon to one Mr Mountaguue [*sic*] Stacey for seaven yeares att Ten pound per Annum from Ladyday next and for seaven yeares more from the expiration thereof, If the said Mr Stacey did like the same And it was agreed That The Towne shall sett the said Inn into repaires what is necessary to be adjudged by Two indifferent men one to be choosen by the Corporation and the other by the Said Mr Stacey And That the said Mr Stacey shall beare and pay all taxes and Assessements laid and imposed upon the said demised premisses And also that it is the desire of the said Mr Stacey That the Corporation will be as kind and respectfull to him as the last Tenant in keepinge their publique feasts at the said Inn so long as they find civill usuage All which this Court takinge into their consideration do unanimously allow and approve of the said Lease granted and do hereby order that all publique feasts shall be kept att the said Inn untill there be any cause given to keepe them at some other place.

Redd Lyon Signe to be bought.
At this Court Mr Pawlett was moved to sett a price of the signe of the Red Lyon and if he would use the Towne kindly they would buy it and have it annexed to the Inn and This Tenant should pay a yearely Rent for the same whereupon Mr Pawlett out of his good will and affection to this Corporation is unwillinge to sett a rate himselfe But if the Towne will please to chuse one indifferent Workeman he would chuse another and whatever They should judge the signe to be really worth he would abate the Towne forty shillings of the said rate The which this Court takes very kindly and doth order that the same be referred accordingly.

Townes Waites to be set up.
Whereas Mr Alderman this day also acquainted that Sir Edmund Turners Lady was aminded to present a sett of Waitts to this Corporation if They please to approve thereof to which this Court doth freely give their Consent.

Mr Rookesby receives part of his money.
At this Court it is ordered that Mr Nathaniell Rookesby hath five pound more paid him on the behalfe of his Wife and if there be not soe much due to him The Towne Clarke ingages in open Court that the remainder shall be paid backe for the use of this Corporation.

[fo. 644r] Seventh Court of Robert Cole, 23 March 1675/6

A lease to be let of the Baylywicke.
Whereas Mr Alderman this day Acquainted the Court that Mr Francis Bacon one of the Attornies of this Towne is willinge to take a Lease of the Bayliffewicke belonging to this Corporation for fees upon Arrests and Executions and will give Mr Alderman for the Time beinge for seaven yeares to come six pound per Annum for the Two first yeares and Ten pound per Annum for the other five yeares. And in pursuance thereof Mr Bacon hath given his severall propositions in writinge which beinge read in Court it was put to the vote whether The said Lease should be granted or not and if it were grantable Whereupon it was Agreed by the Court that Mr Bacon should take advice to know if such a Lease might be granted And that then the Court would consider of the said propositions delivered into the Court.

Mathew Dixon, Francis Wells made free.
At this Court came Mathew Dixon and Francis Wells who had severally served their Apprentishipps in this Towne and desired to be admitted Free Burgesses of this Corporation to which the Court doth condiscend Whereupon they pay five shillings apeece to the Box as Forraniers and their fees to Clarke and Serjeants and tooke the oath of Freemen and the other oaths incident Thereunto according to the Custome of this Burrough and are admitted Free Burgesses Accordingly.

[fo. 644v] Eighth Court of Robert Cole, 20 April 1676 [incorrectly shown as 1675]

Noe grant to be made of the Baylywicke.
At this Court Mr Bacon gives an account that he hath had Councellor Wingfield opinion about farminge the Executions Fee and Fees upon Arrest belonginge to this Corporation and his opinion is that they cannot be farmed so that he cannot goe on with his bargaine made the last Court Whereupon the said order is made void to all intents whatsoever.

John Still chosen Colebuyer.
At this Court John Still is choosen Colebuyer in the roome of Thomas Hodgson And the said Thomas Hodgson payes in Court to the Chamberlaine which was paid to the new Colebuyer the sume of eight pound and delivered to him a considerable quantity of coles and in money to the value of sixteene pound seaventeene shillings.

John Basse to pay xxs per Annum for the Water Cart.
At this Court is lett to John Basse the priviledge of goinge with a water Cart for one yeare from Mayday next at twenty shillings *per annum* to be paid halfe yearely by equall portions And it is ordered That William Fearon nor any other person shall goe with water Carts duringe the Time granted to the said John Basse.

Mr Coddingtons Account for tolles.
At this Court Mr John Coddington gives an Account of the proffitts of the Tolles for the
Month of March last Receipts   16 09 05
Disbursements   01 08 09
Remaines to the Towne   15 00 08
Which he pays in open Court and is discharged.

[fo. 645r] **Ninth Court of Robert Cole, 2 June 1676** [*incorrectly shown as 1675*]

Persons to veiw the Redd Lyon.
At this Court it is ordered that Captaine Rawdes and Mr Mallory be choosen to setle the repaires of the Red Lyon The present Tenant Mr Stacey consentinge thereunto.

Mr Turner chosen of first xij.
At this Court Mr John Turner is choosen of the first Company in the Roome of Mr Edward Rawlinson deceased.

Mr Clarke chosen of the 2nd xij.
At this Court Mr William Clarke is choosen of the second company in the roome of Mr John Turner.

Mr Matkin nominated Alderman.
For the more peceable and quiet proceedinge at the Election of the next succeedinge Alderman It is ordered that upon the next Election day Mr John Turner be sent downe into the Church to Mr Thomas Short and Mr William Milles to make Three Comburgesses there out of which Three Comburgesses in the Church It is likewise Agreed That Mr William Milles be brought upon the Cussion or place of Election to Mr John Winge and Mr Thomas Matkin by a free and unanimous Consent of this Court Mr Matkin is nominated Alderman for the ensuinge yeare.

Towne land lett upon particular securitie.
At this Court it is ordered That in regard the Townes Land is made Fine certaine and That the tenants are in the nature of purchasors for the time to come The said tenants shall only give their owne Bond for performance of Covenants and receive the like bond from the said Alderman and Burgesses & their Successors.

Persons appointed to take Accounts.
At this Court it is ordered That Mr Alderman, Mr Short, Mr Richard Calcraft, Edward Pawlett, Thomas Fishar, William Clarke, Symon Grant, Edward Bristow and John Smyth doe meete on Wednesday next to examine the Churchwardens and others Account and to returne their proceedings therein the next Court day.

In the Kallender
Thomas Archer
Nicholas Becke
Edward Bristow.

[fo. 645v] **Tenth Court of Robert Cole, 6 July 1676**

Fines for not appearing at Mr Aldermans Court.
Whereas this Court takinge into consideration this day the greate neglect of many Members of this Court in absentinge Themselves from Mr Aldermans Court when called which hath beene and is a very great hindrance and obstruction to the publique concernes of this Corporation And That the same offences are often comitted by reason of the small penalties imposed upon such offendors It is Therefore ordered by a free and unanimous consent of the whole Court for the Time to come All such persons as make default of their Appearinge att Mr Aldermans Court for the Time beinge when called by nine of the Clock in the morning exactly shall forfeit the severall penalties followinge (That is to say) every one of the first Company two shillings every one of the Second company one shillinge sixpence and every Comoner A shilling to be levied accordinge to the Custome of this Burrough for the use of the Corporation except he obtaine leave for his absence from Mr Alderman for the time beinge And That all former orders made to the contrary are hereby vacated repealed and made void to all intents and purposes whatsoever.

Noe freeman to keepe a Shope in the Countrie.
Whereas the Court this day takinge into their consideration the many abuses comitted of late by severall persons beinge freemen of this Corporation Tradinge in the Countrie and keepinge open shop there to the great prejudice of the rest of the freemen of this Borough and to the utter ruine of the Markett thereunto belonginge if some speedy care be not taken for the prevention thereof It is therefore this day by the unanimous consent of the whole Court ordered and Agreed that no Freemen or Freeman whatsoever of this Corporation shall from and after the first day of August now next ensuinge trade by sellinge of retaile any Goods in the Weeke day in the Country in any open shopp whatsoever out of the said Towne of Grantham upon paine for every such Offendor to forfeite and pay Twenty shillings a Weeke for every such offence to be levied of their goods and Chattells for the use of this Corporation.

[fo. 646r] **Eleventh Court of Robert Cole, 9 August 1676**

xx li for the Constables Assessment.
Att this Court it is ordered that an Assessement of twenty pound be made & laid upon this Borough for and towards the repaires of the Highwaies of this Towne And that Mr Alderman, Mr Thomas Short & Mr Michaell Taylor of the first Company, Thomas Ireland & Edward Pawlett of the Second Company & Symon Grant and William Haskerd Comoners be & are appointed assessors of the said Assessement & the present surveyors of the said Highwaies Collectors thereof And That the said Assessement be made upon Wednesday next at the Towne Hall & notice thereof be given in the Church the next Sunday of the Time & place of the makinge the said Assessement to the end & intent That all such persons as are therein concerned may if They please be then and there present.

Redd Lyon signe bought.
Att this Court Mr Alderman gives an Account that he & some of his Bretheren by the advice of sufficient Workemen had agreed with Mr Pawlett for the signe of the red Lyon for ten pound ten shillings if this Court approved thereof to which this Court doth condiscend and order that the present Chamberlaine do pay for the same & that the present Tenant of the Red Lyon shall pay a yearely rent for the signe aforesaid.

Mr Humes Account for tolles.
Att this Court Mr Henry Humes gives an Account for the proffittss of the Tolles for the
Month of May last & that his Receipts in the said Month came to   09 16 11
And his Disbursements to be   00 18 07
Remaines due to the Towne [*sic*]   00 18 04
which he pays in open Court and is discharged.

Mr Taylors Account for tolles.
At this Court Mr Michaell Taylor accounts for the proffitts of the Tolles for the Month
Aprill last & at [*sic*] his receipts   04 16 01
And his Disbursements are   00 09 10
Remaines due to the Towne   04 06 03
Which he pays in open Court and is discharged

Mr Lentons Account for tolles.
Att this Court Mr John Lenton gives an Account for the proffittes of the Tolles for June
last & that his receipts are   04 12 11
And his Disbursements are   00 16 02
Remaines due to the Towne   03 16 09
Which he pays in open Court and he is discharged.

[fo. 646v] **Twelfth Court of Robert Cole, 16 August 1676**

Mr Coddington Account for tolles.
Att this Court Mr John Coddington gives an Account of the proffitts of the Tolles for the
moneth of August His receipts   01 12 10
Disbursements   00 04 04
Remaines due to the Towne   01 08 06
Which he payes in open Court & is discharged.

An Assessment of xxviij li for Constables Assessment.
At this Court it is ordered that an Assessment of xxviij li be made & laid upon the Burrough for the Constables bills of disbursements for the yeare past an estimate being taken what the particular sumes amount unto And it is ordered that the Cheife Constables and Under Constables be Assessors And the Under Constables Collectors thereof And that notice be given in the Church the next Sunday of the time and place of makeing the Assessment aforesaid.

Noe freeman to retaine any Servant without Mr Aldermans consent.
Whereas the Court this day takeing into consideracion that severall Persons of late are become Inhabitants within this Towne which may hereafter be a charge to this Burrough and that by reason they are retained by Shoemakers and other freemen of this Corporacion It is therefore ordered that noe Freeman or Freemen whatsoever of this Towne shall at any time hereafter retaine or keepe any Servant or Servants that hath not formerly beene an Inhabitant within this Burrough without first acquainting Mr Alderman for the time being and obtaine his Lycence & consent to keepe such Servant and Servants upon paine for every one offending contrary to this order to forfeit ten shillings a weeke for every weeke they shall so offend to be levied of his and their goodes and Chattells for the use of this Corporacion.

Visitacion Dinners not to exceed xxiiijs.
Whereas the Court this day likewise observing that the charge of Visitacion Dinners do yearely increase and are likely to be greater if some speedy care be not taken to prevent the same It is therefore ordered that noe Churchwardens whatsoever shall lay out or expend in any Visitacion Dinner for the time to come above twenty four shillings on the publike Account of this Corporacion And if any more be expended the same shall be at the proper cost and charges of such Churchwardens as shall cause such expense and charge contrary to the true intent and meaning of this present order.

[fo. 647r] **Thirteenth Court of Robert Cole, 11 September 1676**

Mr Calcraft Account for tolle.
At this Court Mr Richard Calcraft gives an Account of the proffitts of the tolles for the

moneth of July last And that his Receipts are	02	02	08
His disbursments	00	05	00
Remaines due to the Towne	01	17	08
Which he payes in open Court and is discharged			

William Fearon to have 5 li per Annum to carry Criples away.
At this Court it is agreed by the unanimous consent thereof to and with William Fearon And the said William Fearon for and in consideracion of the sume of five pounds for one yeare now next ensueing to be paid as whereafter mencioned doth Covenant and promise to and with the Alderman and Burgesses of this Corporacion that he the said William Fearon shall and will well and truly carrey and convey all Cripples comeing to the Towne of Grantham that is to say all such as goe to Spittlegate if they come after an houre sunn sett and all such as come an houre and a halfe before sunn sett which goe to Gunnerby that he will convey them before sunn sett to either of the places aforesaid or to any other place they are to goe to, of two Myles distance from the Towne And in default thereof that he the said William Fearon shall and will pay the charges of such Cripples lying in Towne contrary to the Agreement aforesaid And the said Alderman and Burgesses doth promise and agree to and with the said William Fearon to pay him the said five pounds in manner following that is to say the Constables of Markett place to pay the two first quarters the Constables of Westgate to pay the third quarter and fourth quarter to be paid on the Account day by the Constables of Highstreete for the ensueing yeare.

Conduit to be repaired by William Bristow for 7 yeares.
At this Court it is ordered that in regard William Bristow will be at great charges in makeing new Pipes to bring the Water to the Conduit that he shall have the payment of xxxs *per Annum* performing his bargaine for seaven yeares now next ensueing.

A Chain to be in the Vinestreete.
At this Court it is ordered that for the preserving of the pavement in the Vine Streete that a Chain be sett over the said Streete.

Mr Wright securitie to be renewed.
At this Court it is ordered that Mr Henry Wright have his securitie for his 100 li and for his interest in Arreare renewed by the Towne Seale to his Sonn Mr Richard Grant.

William Pike made free.
At the same Court came William Pike Taylor who served Mr Nicholas Becke as an Apprentice & desired to be admitted a freeman of this Corporacion to which this Court doth condiscend And thereupon he payes ijs vjd to the Box and his fees to Clarke & Serjent & takes the oathe incident thereunto & is admitted a free Burgesse accordingly.

[fo. 647v] [Blank page]

[fo. 648r]

At an assembly holden by Mr Robert Cole Alderman and the Comburgesses and Burgesses of Grantham aforesaid in Corpus Christi Quire within the Prebendarie there on Friday next after St Luke day being 20 October 1676

First did sitt upon the Cusheon or place of Eleccion the said Mr Robert Cole Alderman in Corpus Christi Quire within the Prebendarie Church there &c
Next to him did sitt upon the Cusheon or place of Eleccion two Comburgesses vzt Mr John Winge and Mr Thomas Matkin
Then was there in the Church two Comburgesses Mr Thomas Short and Mr William Milles
Then was sent downe into the Church to those two Comburgesses to make them three one other Comburgesse vzt Mr John Turner
Out of which three Comburgesses in the Church one was chosen to come up and sitt upon the Cusheon or place of Eleccion vzt Mr William Milles
Then was there upon the Cusheon or place of Eleccion three Comburgesses vzt Mr John Wing, Mr Thomas Matkin & Mr William Milles
And that was there in the Church two Comburgesses vzt Mr Thomas Short and Mr John Turner
Out of which three Comburgesses upon the Cusheon or place of Eleccion vzt Mr John Winge, Mr Thomas Matkin and Mr William Milles one is to be chosen Alderman for the ensueing yeare
And so by the unanimous vote and consent of this Assembly Mr Thomas Matkin is chosen and elected Alderman for this ensueing yeare

Whereupon the said Mr Robert Cole dischargeth himselfe from the place and Office of Alderman according to Auntient custome And the said Mr Thomas Matkin now elected Alderman in his place and stead hath at this Assembly taken the oath of Alderman for this Burrough and Soake of Grantham according to the Auntient and laudable custome of the Burrough aforesaid.

And so this Assembly breakes up

[fo. 648v] [Blank page]

THE HALL BOOK OF GRANTHAM 1676–1677

[fo. 649Ar] **First Court of Thomas Matkin, 27 October 1676**

Mr Thomas Matkin Alderman
Mr Thomas Short Comburgess   Thomas Ireland
Mr Michaell Taylor Comburgess   Edward Paulet
Mr Robert Calcraft Comburgess   Christofer Thompson
Mr Richard Calcraft Comburgess   Anthony Holtchkin [*sic*]
Mr Richard Holley Comburgess   Henry Coverly
Mr John Lenton Comburgess   John Walker
Mr Henry Humes Comburgess   Thomas Charles
Mr John Coddington Comburgess   Edward Leivesly
Mr John Winge Comburgess   Thomas Fishar
Mr Robert Cole Comburgess   William Clarke
Mr William Milles Comburgess
Mr John Turner Comburgess
John Pape Cheife Constables
John Robinson

Coroner	Mr Robert Cole	Swinegate	John Goodwin
Escheator	Mr William Milles		William Bristow
Collectors for	Mr John Turner	Castlegate	Mathew Dixon
Schoole Rents	Thomas Frith		William Fearon
Chamberlaines	Henry Coverly	Keybearers	Mr Alderman
Churchwardens	Edward Bristow		Edward Leivesly
Chamberlaines	Edward Leivesly		Henry Coverly
	Richard Hickson	Prizers of	John Gibson
Market place	Simon Grant	Corne	Robert Crosfeild
Constable	John Stevens	Leather sealers	Thomas Marshall
High Streete	John Browne		Ashton Lord
	John Smith		Henry Wright
Westgate	Thomas Kenion		Anthony Taylor
	William Cole	Towne Clerke	William Hodgkinson
Walkergate	Thomas Quiningbrough	Serjents	Thomas Calcraft
	William Kirke		Bryan Godley
		Church Clarke	William Knewstubbe
		Belman	Ralph Osborne

[fo. 649Av]

Comoners
Markett place
Edward Bristow
Thomas Archer
Nicholas Berke
Thomas Chrichloe
Thomas Hodgson
Simon Goodwin
Simon Grant
Richard Segrave
John Stevenson
John Browne
John Smith
John Gibson
William Cole

Walkergate
John Still
William Kirke
Castlegate
Mathew Dixon
William Fearon

High Streete

Richard Handley
George Read
Thomas Rowley
Christofer Hanson

Westgate
Thomas Frith
William Haskerd
Thomas Kenion
Francis Bristow
Thomas Bayly
John Newcombe

Swinegate
John Goodwin
William Newton
Thomas Quiningborough

Charters delivered up in Court.
At this Court Mr Robert Cole late Alderman delivers up the three Charters Boxes with all the Charters vzt
The Exemplir of Edward the 4th
King Henry the viijth
King Edward vjth
Queene Elizabeth 3 Charters
King Charles the first
King Charles the Second

King James
Judge Dyers Award
Stamford writeings
Escheators Pattents
Towns Armes
Writing with many seales

[fo. 649Br]

Plate delivered up in Court.
At this Court was delivered by Mr Robert Cole late Alderman to Mr Alderman that now is all the Townes plate which is as followeth vzt
The Horse Race Cup
Mr Archers Boll
Mr Wheatelys Cann

Two Tunns
Mr Kirkby Boll
Mr Greenewoods 13 Spoones

Mr Horsemans Boll
Mr Greenewoods Cann
Mr Batties Beaker

One Salt with Cover
One Wine Boll Mr Horsemans
The Waites Cognizances

John Turner & John Pape lends money to the Towne.
Whereas Severall Persons moved the Court this day for monies due to them from this Corporacion & Mr John Turner & John Pape being desired by this Court to be bound for the Towne for fifty pounds intreated Mr Alderman and the Court to excuse them and Mr Turner promised to lend this Corporacon fifteene pounds and John Pape to lend Nine pounds to make up the six pounds due upon his Account as Chaimberlaine fifteene pounds Whereupon this Court doth unanimously promise and agree to and with the said Mr Turner and John Pape to pay unto them the said thirty pounds and interest for the same for one yeare now next ensueing And if either of them have urgent occasion for their money ooner giveing two moneths notice then the same shall be paid unto them or either of them within the time before mentioned

Thomas Fishars Account as Chaimberlaine.
At this Court it is ordered that Mr Alderman, Mr Shorte, Mr Richard Calcraft, Edward Paulett, Thomas Fishar, Symon Grant, Edward Bristow and John Smyth persons appointed to take Accounts as by a former order of Court they doe hereby returne an Account of Thomas Fishar Chamberlaine in the time of Mr Robert Cole Alderman and that they have firstly examined his Accounts, that they find them to be Right as they are hereafter mencioned:

His Receipts	735 06 04
disbursments	740 15 07
Remaines due to the Accomptant	05 09 03

Which is ordered to be paid unto him by the present Chamberlaine upon the first Receipt of moneys.

[fo. 649Bv] **Second Court of Thomas Matkin, 3 November 1676**

Mr Coles Account for tolle.
At this Court Mr Robert Cole gives an Account for the proffitt of the tolles for the

moneth of September last His Receipts	02 14 07
His disbursments	00 06 04
Remaines due to the Towne	02 08 03

Which is paid in open Court & he is discharged.

Mr Taylors Account for tolle.
At this Court Mr Michaell Taylor gives an Account of the proffitts of the

tolles for the moneth of October last His Receipts	06 04 05
His disbursments	00 19 08
Remaines due to the Towne	05 04 09

Which he payes in open Court & he is discharged.

Thomas Fishars Account for Westgate Well.
At this Court Thomas Fishar gives an Account as Overseer of Westgate Well
And that his Receipts amount unto 01 18 07
His disbursments 02 00 07
Remaines due to him 00 02 00
Which is ordered to be paid unto him by William Haskerd and Ducker Newball hereby appointed Overseers for the said Well for the ensueing yeare And it is further ordered that William Newton and Henry Kelham be Overseers for Swinegate Well for the time aforesaid.

Milne Masters appointed.
At this Court Edward Paulett, Thomas Charles, Simon Grant and John Smith are appointed Milne Masters for the next quarter of the yeare And it is ordered that they give up their Accounts in open Court as also all such Persons as shall succeed them And the said Milne Masters do promise to pay the money ariseing by the proffitts of the said Milnes every Quarter day.

Thomas Harrington Esquire gives a peice of plate to the Corporacion.
At this Court Mr Alderman brought in a large silver Tankerd which Thomas Harrington of Boothby Pannell in the County of Lincolne Esquire out of his respect and kindnesse to this Corporacion was pleased to give unto the Towne for ever, and further out of his kindnesse promised that he would at all times serve this Corporacon to the Utmost of his power. Whereupon this Court doth accept of the said Tankerd and that Thancke be returned for soe great a favor given to the Corporacon and that they will be ready and willing to serve him in any thing that may be in their powers.

[fo. 650r] **Third Court of Thomas Matkin, 7 December 1676**

Mr Humes Account for tolle.
At this Court Mr Henry Humes gives an Account of the proffitts of the tolles for the month of October last And that his Receipts are 05 00 09
His disbursments 02 02 07
Remaines due to the Towne 02 18 02
Which is paid in open Court and he is discharged.

Mr Lentons Account for tolle.
At this Court Mr Lenton gives an Account of the proffitts of the tolles for the moneth of November last And that his Receipts are 02 00 09
His disbursments 00 06 08
Remaines due to the Towne 01 14 01
Which is paid in open Court and he is discharged.

Mr Richard Calcraft elected Usher.
Whereas Mr Alderman this day acquainted the Court that Mr Richard Poole the present Usher haveing obtained Hough liveing did intend to leave the Schoole and had beene with him to desire to continue in the Schoole till Lady day next if this Court pleased to accept thereof And that it was very requisite to elect another Usher before that time As also that Mr Richard Calcraft Sonn of Mr Richard Calcraft one of the Comburgesse of this Court would be a very fitt person for the said place if this Court would approve thereof Whereupon it is fully ordered and agreed by this Court that the said Mr Richard Poole shall continue usher till Lady day next And that then the said Mr Richard Calcraft be admitted Usher in the place of the said Mr Poole And upon such termes as former Ushers have beene admitted to the Schoole aforesaid.

Barton vj li paid & Mr Alderman to be saved harmles.
Whereas Mr Alderman also acquainted this Court that he had lately received from the Towne Clarke an Execucion against Robert Barton the Bayliffe for vj li for infringing this libertie And that he had received the said money upon the said execucion and had the same ready in Court to pay if this Court would beare him harmles in case any trouble should hereafter arise aboute leiveing or receiveing the said money Whereupon it is this day fully ordered and agreed by the Court that Mr Alderman shall be saved kept harmles and indempnified of and from all suits charges expenses damages and incumbrances whatsoever which shall or may happen for or by reason of leiveing and receiveing of the money aforesaid upon which Agreement Mr Alderman payes the said vj li to the present Chaimberlaine.

[fo. 650v] **Fourth Court of Thomas Matkin, 2 February 1676/7**

Mr Humes Account for tolle.
At this Court Mr Henry Humes gives an Account of the proffitt of the tolles
for the moneth of May last his Receipts	05 11 11 ob
Disbursments	02 13 01
Remaines due to the Towne	02 18 10 ob

Which he pays in open Court & he is discharged.

Milne Masters appointed.
At this Court Edward Paulett, Thomas Charles, Simon Grant and John Smith are nominated & appointed Milne Masters for another quarter of a yeare now next ensueing.

Mr Richard Poole, Edward Watson, Thomas Bayly made free.
At this Court came Mr Richard Poole Minister Edward Watson Sadler & Thomas Bayly sonn of William Bayly Felmonger and desired to be admitted Freemen of this Corporacion to which this Court doth condiscend Whereupon they pay ijs vjd apeice to the Box as freeborne & xviijd apeice to Clarke and Serjents and takes the oath of a free Burgesse and the oaths incident thereunto according to Auntient custome.

Corporacion Privilidges to be performed.
Whereas Mr Alderman this day acquainted the Court that by the advice of Mr Serjent Ellis he had made severall warrants upon the Sherriffes warrants in the name of the Alderman and Burgesses And if the same pratice be continued it will ever preserve this libertie from being infringed and in time may prove a great advantage to this Corporacon And that it is very requisite and necessarie that if any trouble or suite shall happen or arise by any Sherriffe of this County aboute the Privilidge of this libertie that every Alderman and his Successors shall be secured and indempnified by the order of this Court Whereupon this Court takeing the same into their Consideracon do hereby order that the present Alderman and his Successors shall be saved kept harmles and indempnified by this Corporacon of and from all Accions suites troubles and incumbrances whatsoever which shall happen or be brought by any Sherriffe or other Person touching or concerning any thing relateing to the securing this libertie being infringed by any Person or Persons whatsoever.

[fo. 651r] **Fifth Court of Thomas Matkin, 4 May 1677**

Mr Lentons Account for tolle.
At this Court Mr John Lentons [*sic*] gives an Account of the proffitt of the tolles for
the moneth of June last His Receipts   03 16 11
Disbursments   00 14 04
Remaines due to the Towne   03 02 07
Which he payes in open Court and is discharged.

Nominacon of Alderman.
For the more peceable and quiet proceedinges of the Eleccion of the next Succeeding Alderman It is ordered that upon the next Eleccion day that Mr Michaell Taylor be sent downe into the Church to Mr Thomas Short and Mr John Turner to make three Comburgesses there Out of which three Comburgesses in the Church It is likewise agreed that Mr Michaell Taylor be brought upon the Cusheon or place of Election to Mr John Winge and Mr William Milles And by the consent of the Major part of this Court Mr Michaell Taylor is nominated Alderman for this next ensueing yeare.

Mr Aldermans sallory xx li under a limitacion.
Whereas upon the Nominacion of Mr Michaell Taylor Alderman for the next ensueing yeare Mr Alderman acquainted the Court that the sallory of ten pounds *per Annum* was very smale and inconsiderable to the great charge every Alderman was at And if this Court thought it convenient to raise it to twenty pounds *per Annum* if Mr Michaell Taylor be elected Alderman at the time aforesaid and so to continue if it goe to the senior Brethren that have beene Alderman that the same would be a great incouragement to every such succeeding Alderman Whereupon it is this day by a free and unanimous consent of this Court ordered and agreed upon that if the said Mr Michaell Taylor be elected Alderman upon the next eleccion day he shall have a sallory of twenty pounds

for his yeare And that the same shall continue and be paid to every Alderman that shall hereafter be of the senior Brethren and have formerly beene elected unto the Office of Alderman as aforesaid And that the former order of ten pounds *per Annum* be and is hereby repealed and made void to all intents & purposes whatsoever And in case any of the Junior Brethren shall be elected Alderman that have not before served in the said place that then a sallory of ten pounds *per Annum* shall be paid to him or them hereafter so elected Alderman any thing herein contained to the contrarey in any wise notwithstanding.

[fo. 651v]

Mr Taylors Account for tolle.
At this Court Mr Michaell Taylor gives an Account of the Proffitts of the Tolles for
the moneth of Aprill last   his Receipts   14 10 07
his Disbursments   01 09 02
Remaines due to the Towne   13 01 05
which he payes in open Court and is discharged.

Mr Coddington Account for tolle.
Mr John Coddingtons Account for March.
his Receipts   01 09 06
his Disbursments   00 06 04
Remaines due to the Towne   01 03 02
Which he payes in open Court and is discharged.

William Fearon to have 13 6 8 per Annum for to releive and carry away all Criples.
At this Court it is agreed by the Unanimous Consent thereof to and with William Fearon And the said William Fearon for the Consideracon of the summe of 13 6 8 for one yeare Now next ensueing to be paid as is hereafter mencioned doth Covenant and promise to and with the Alderman and Burgesses of this Corporacon that he the said William Fearon shall and will well and truly releive carry and convey all Criples comeing to this Towne of Grantham, that they be in noe wayes chargeable to the said Towne. That is to say all such as goe to Spittlegate if they come an houre after Sunsett, and all such as come an hour and a halfe before Sunsett which goe to Gonerby that he will releive and convey them before Sunsett to either of the said places or from this Towne And in default thereof that he the said William Fearon shall pay the Charges of all such Criples lyeing in the Towne And the said Alderman and Burgesses doe promise and agree to and with the said William Fearon that the Cheife Constables and petty Constables of this Corporacon shall and will pay unto the said William Fearon the said summe of 13 6 8 quarterly.

[fo. 652r]

Att an assembly holden by Mr Thomas Matkin gent Alderman and the Comburgesses and Burgesses of Grantham aforesaid in Corpus Christi Quire within the Prebandarie there on friday next after St Luke day being 19 October 1677.

First did sitt downe upon the Cusheon or place of Elleccion the said Mr Thomas Matkin Alderman in Corpus Christi Quire within the Prebandarie Church there &
Next to him did sitt upon the Cusheon or place of Elleccion two Comburgesses that is to say Mr John Winge and Mr William Milles
Then was there in the Church two Comburgesses Mr Thomas Short and Mr John Turner.
Then was sent downe into the Church to those two Comburgesses to make them three one other Comburgesse vzt Mr Michaell Taylor.
Out of which three Comburgesses in the Church one was chosen to come up and sit upon the Cusheon or place of Eleccion vzt Mr Michaell Taylor.
Then was there upon the Cusheon or place of Eleccion three Comburgesses vzt Mr John Wing, Mr Michaell Taylor & Mr William Milles.
Then was there in the Church two Comburgesses vzt Mr Thomas Short and Mr John Turner.
Out of which three Comburgesses upon the Cusheon or place of Eleccion vzt Mr John Wing, Mr William Milles and Mr Michaell Taylor one is to be chosen Alderman for the ensueing yeare.
And so by the vote and consent of this Assembly Mr Michaell Taylor is chosen Alderman for the ensueing yeare.
Whereupon the said Thomas Matkin is discharged from his place and office of Alderman And the said Mr Michaell Taylor now elected Alderman in his place and stead hath at this Assembly taken the oath of Alderman for this Burrough and Soake of Grantham according to Auntient custome.

And So this Assembly breakes up.

[fo. 652v] [Blank page]

THE HALL BOOK OF GRANTHAM 1677–1678

[fo. 653r] **At a General Assembly [sic] of Michael Taylor, 26 October 1677**

Mr Michaell Taylor Alderman
Mr Thomas Short Comburgess
Mr Robert Calcraft Comburgess
Mr Richard Calcraft Comburgess
Mr Richard Holley Comburgess
Mr John Lenton Comburgess
Mr Henry Humes Comburgess
Mr John Coddington Comburgess
Mr John Winge Comburgess
Mr Robert Cole Comburgess
Mr Thomas Matkin Comburgess
Mr William Milles Comburgess
Mr John Turner Comburgess:

Edward Paulet
Thomas Fishar
Thomas Ireland
Christofer Thompson
Anthony Holtchkin
Henry Coverly
John Walker
Thomas Charles
Edward Leivesly
John Robinson
William Clarke
Nicholas Becke

Coroner	Mr Thomas Matkin	Swinegate	Richard Owin
Escheator	Mr John Turner		Anthony Kirke
~~Chamberlaines~~	John Walker	Castlegate	James Bristow
Church Wardens	Edward Bristow		Richard Dawson
Chamberlaines	John Robinson	Keybearers	Mr Alderman
	William Haskerd		John Walker
Collectors for	Mr Richard Calcraft		John Robinson
Schoole Rents	Simon Grant	Prizers of	John Gibson
Cheife	Edward Paulet	Corn	Henry Johnson
Constables	Thomas Fishar	Market Sayers	William Walgrave
Marketplace	Nathaniel Rookesby		Christofer Hanson
Constables	William Kirke	Leather	Thomas Marshall
Highstreete	John Smith	Sealers	John Hutchin
	John Gibson		Henry Wright
Westgate	John Goodwin		Anthony Taylor
	William Fearon	Towne Clarke	William Hodgkinson
Walkergate	Henry Hubbert	Serjents	Thomas Calcraft &
	Thomas Short		Bryan Godley
		Gaoler	Bryan Godley
		Belman	Ralph Osborne

[fo. 653v]

Commoners
Market Place
Nathaniel Rooksby
William Kirke
Edward Bristow
William Cole
Thomas Archer
Thomas Chrichloe
Thomas Hudchson
Symon Goodwing
Symon Grant
Richard Segrave
John Stevenson
John Broome
John Gibson
John Smyth
John Goodwing
Henry Hubbard
Thomas Shorte
High Streete
Richard Owen
Anthony Kirke

Castlegate
None

High Streete
Richard Handley
George Read
Thomas Rowley
Christofor Hanson

Westgate

Thomas Frith
William Haskerd
Thomas Kenion
Francis Bristow
Thomas Bayly
Richard Hickson
John Newcombe
William Fearon
James Bristow

Walkergate
John Still

Swinegate
William Newton
Thomas Quiningbro
Mathew Dixon
Richard Dawson

Charters delivered up in Court.
Att this Court Thomas Matkin late Alderman delivers up the three Charter Boxes with all the Charters vizt

The Exemplir of Edward 4th
King Henry 8th
King Edward the 6th
Queen Eliz 3 Charters
King Charles the first
King Charles the second

King James
Judge Dyer's award
Stamford Writeings
Escheators Pattents
Townes Armes
Writing with many seales

Plate delivered up in Court.
Att This Court was delivered up Mr Thomas Matkin late Alderman to Mr Alderman that now is, all the Townes plate which is as followeth

The Horse Race Cupp
Mr Archers Boll

Mr Kirkeby's Boll
Two Tuns

Mr Wheatlyes Cann
Mr Horsemans Boll
Mr Greenwoods Cann
Mr Batties Beaker
Thomas Harrington Esquire his Tankerd

Mr Greenwood 13 spoones
One salt with Cover
one Wine Boll Mr Horsemans
The Waites Cognizances

[fo. 654r] **First Court of Michael Taylor, 6 November 1677**

Persons appointed to take Accounts.
At this Court it is ordered that Mr Alderman, Mr Robert Calcraft, Mr Robert Cole, Mr John Turner, Edward Paulet, Anthony Hotchkin, Thomas Fishar, Thomas Crichloe, John Smith, Simon Grant, William Haskerd, Nathaniell Rookesby or as many of them as can with conveniencie meete on Munday and Wednesday next or at any other time they do appointe to examine the Accounts of severall Officers belonging to this Corporacion and to give an Account of their proceedings the next Court day.

Henry Hubbert, Richard Dawson, Thomas Short, Anthony Kirke, Richard Owin, James Bristow, Robert Calcraft, Robert Calcraft made free.
At this Court Henry Hubbert Forrainer Apprentice to Andrew Poole Apothecary, Richard Dawson, Forrainer Apprentice to a Weaver, Robert Calcraft Wheelewright, Forrainer, Thomas Short Butcher Freeborne, Anthony Kirke Butcher Freeborne, Richard Owin Cordwainer Freeborne, James Bristow Parchment maker freeborne and Robert Calcraft Sonn of Mr Robert Calcraft one of the Comburgesses of this Court being freeborne came and desired to be admitted free Burgesses of this Corporacion to which this Court doth condiscend Whereupon they pay their severall dues to the Corporacion And their fees to the Clarke and Serjents and take the oath of Freemen and all other oaths incident thereunto and are admitted Free Burgesses of this Corporacion.

Nicholas Becke of the 2d Company.
At this Court Nicholas Berke is chosen one of the Second xij in the Roome of John Pape lately deceased
In the Kallendar
Thomas Archer
Edward Bristow
Thomas Crichloe

Mr Wrights 100 li paid.
At this Court it is ordered that the Towne Clerke pay the 100 li left in his hands of Sir Robert Carrs money to Mr Henry Wright and that interest money appeares upon an Account stated to be due to him shall be paid unto him within six moneths now next ensueing And that he have an order of Court for payment thereof and a copy of it delivered to him for his securitie.

Lawrence Barkstons Agreement for the Clocke.
Att this Court it is agreed with the Consent of Lawrence Barston [sic] that he shall have Five Shillings a yeare for keeping in Time the Towne Hall Clocke during his life, and if any accidence doe happen to the said Clocke during the said terme, the same shall be repaired by this Corporacon at their proper Costs and Charges. and the said 5s shall be paid yearely to the said Lawrence Barkston upon every Account day.

[fo. 654v]

Noe Churchwarden other Officers to refuse their places. penaltie 5 li.
Whereas the Court this takeing into consideracion that severall Officers belonging to Mr Aldermans Court have of late refused to take upon them the place & Office into which they have beene respectively chosen to the great disservice of this Corporacion It is therefore this day fully ordered and agreed upon that any Coroner, Escheator, Churchwardens, Chamberlaines and Collectors for Schoole Rents or any of them shall at any time forever hereafter being chosen into the Offices aforesaid or any of and shall refuse to accept thereof and to performe his and their Offices during the time of their continuance therein according to Auntient custome for such Officers That then every Officer as aforesaid refuseing the said Office unto which he or they shall be respectively chosen shall forfeite the sume of five pounds to be levied of their goodes and Chattells for the use of this Corporacion.

My Lord of Rutland resignes his Pattent of Recordershipp.
Whereas Mr Alderman this day acquainted the Court that he is informed that the Right Honorable the Earle of Rutland our Recordor being very Auntient and sickley hath some thoughts to Surrender up his Pattent of Recordershipp And if this Court pleased it was convenient to elect the Honorable the Lord Roos sonn and heire to the Earle of Rutland Recorder for life when there shall be occasion To which this Court doth most Unanimously and freely consent And do hereby order that a Pattent of Recordershipp for life be presented to the Honorable the Lord Roos upon Surrender of the former Pattent And that his Honour be received into this Corporacion with all the solempnities favour and respect that possible may be and as his Honours former Predecessors have beene received to the Grace of this Corparacion.

Mr Coles Account as Coroner.
At this Court Mr Robert Cole Coroner accounteth and saith that as Casualties happened this yeare there was one Mr Robert Tredway did kill one Charles Thimbleby Esquire And that the Jury impannelled found it willfull Murder and there accrued to the Towne one horse Apprized to 4 li And a sword to xijs And also that there was one Anne Woodruffe of Great Paunton wife of John Woodruffe did Willfully hang her selfe And the Jury found her a felo de se.

Severall Officers take oathes.
At this Court Mr Thomas Matkin Coroner and Mr John Turner Escheator John Walker and Edward Bristow Churchwardens John Robinson and William Haskerd Chamberlaines after the takeing the severall oaths unto their respective Offices at the same time tooke the oaths of Supremacey and Allegiance and renounced the Covenant and tooke the oath mencioned in the Act of Parlyament made in the xiijth yeare of his now Majesties Raigne according to the intent and direction of the said Act.

John Broughton Hather tolle.
At this Court John Broughton takes a lease of Hather tolle for one yeare for xxxvs the yeare ending next Account day.

[fo. 655r]

Noe Freemen to have Votes at Elleccions if they pay not to Church and Poore or ijs vjd if strangers on the Account day.
Whereas this Court takeing into consideracion the great abuses and mercenarie and [*sic*] Accions of severall Freeman of the Vulgar sort liveing out of this Corporacion many yeares and comeing to the Elleccion of Mr Alderman that now is with an intent to serve their owne private ends and interests As also of severall abuses of many Freemen within this Burrough that do not pay to Church and Poore to the great prejudice of the Publike affaires of this Corporacion It is therefore fully ordered and agreed upon by this Court that noe Freeman or Freemen whatsoever liveing out of this Corporacon and not paying scott and lott shall at any time hereafter have the freedome to vote either for an Alderman or Burgesse Unlesse such Freeman do yearely for ever upon the Account day pay two shillings and six pence apeice for the publike benefitt of this Corporacion And in default thereof they stand and are hereby disfranchized of their Freedomes to all intents and purposes whatsoever And it is further ordered and agreed upon by this Court that noe Person or Persons whatsoever shall be admitted a free Burgesse or Burgesses of this Corporacion Unlesse he or they be able to pay to the Church and Poore proportionable to his and their estates as the rest of the Free Burgesses of this Burrough any order heretofore made to the contrarey thereof in any wise notwithstanding.

None to vote against the Nominacion of an Alderman in Court that is a Member penaltie 5 li.
Whereas this Court takeing into consideracion the late great tumultuos Eleccion of the present Alderman and that the same did arise from the division of the members of this Court after the Nominacion which manner of Eleccion hath continued many yeares Unviolated and was made upon serious and good grounds and Consideracions for every Comburgesse to prepaire himselfe against the time of Eleccion in the Church As also that after the Nominacion past in the Court by the Major part thereof the rest ought to vote in the Church Unanimously with the Major so that the order of Court may not be abrogated nor the Gentleman nominated Alderman disappointed after he hath beene

at great charge and trouble It is therefore by the full and free consent of this Court ordered and agreed upon that if any Person or Persons being a Member of this Court shall at any time hereafter give his or their vote or votes at the Eleccion in the Church against the Nominacion in the Court he and they shall forfeit the sume of five pounds of lawfull money of England to be levied of his and their goodes and Chattells for the use of this Corporacion.

None to Alderman that keepes a publike Alehouse or after to be a Comburgesse.
Whereas Mr Alderman this day acquainted this Court that the great part of the trouble at the Eleccion of his being Alderman did arise by reason Mr John Wing would not leave of keeping a publike Alehouse and accept of his place of Alderman when thereunto desired by the Court And that it would be convenient to make an order that noe Comburgesse shall be capable of being Alderman that keepes a publike Alehouse nor after he hath beene Alderman to keepe the same selling of Ale during the time he continues a Comburgesse And that if Mr Wing and Mr William Milles did not leave of brewing as publike Alehouses by some certaine time this Court should appointe it is convenient they should be brought of the Cusheon & others when the time of Nominacion comes to be placed in their Roomes All which this Court taking into their Consideracions do approve thereof And do hereby order and agree that noe Comburgesse or Comburgesses for ever hereafter shall be capable of being nominated or elected Alderman that keepes a publike Alehouse nor shall be capable of being a Comburgesse or takeing his place in Court if any after being Alderman shall keepe a publike Alehouse as aforesaid And it is further ordered that if Mr Wing & Mr Milles do not leave of keepeing publike Alehouse at or before Candlemas next they shall and are hereby removed from the Cusheon that others may be there placed according to Auntient Custome.

[fo. 655v] **Second Court of Michael Taylor, 16 November 1677**

Edward Bristow chosen of the 2d Company.
At this Court Edward Bristow is chosen one of the second twelve in the Roome of Thomas Charles lately dismissed the Court and Thomas Chrichloe likewise chosen of the second twelve.
In the Kallender
Simon Grant
Richard Hickson
William Haskerd.

Mr Storeys [sic] *money to be paid.*
Att this Court it is also ordered that the Fifty pounds due to Mr Storer be paid by the present Chamberlaine on Satterday seavenight next And whereas there appeares to be due to him for interest 28 li It is hereby fully ordered that the said 28 li for interest be paid to the said Mr Storer at or before the Five and Twentieth day of December now next ensueing.

Third Court of Michael Taylor 20 November 1677

Mr Milles Account as Escheator.
Att this Court Mr William Milles Escheator for this yeare past doth give his Account for eight Unlawfull and defective Weights and measures
and that his receipts are   00 05 00
disbursments   00 05 00
Account cleared.

Persons to take Accounts.
At this Court Mr Alderman, Mr Shorte, Mr Robert Calcraft, Mr Thomas Matkin, Edward Paulet, Anthony Hotchkin, Thomas Crichloe Symon Grant are ordered to settle the Accounts of the Constables for the yeare past and returne their proceedings therein next Court day.

Mr Humes Account for tolle.
Mr Humes Accounts of Tolle for May   his Receipts   08 18 08
                                           disbursments   00 19 00
                                           Remaines   07 19 08
which he payes and is discharged.

[fo. 656r] **Fourth Court of Michael Taylor, 21 December 1677**

The Earle of Lindsey, The Lord Campden, The Lord Roos made free.
At this Court came the Right Honourable Robert Earle of Lindesey, Lord Great Chamberlaine of England, the Right Honourable Baptist Lord Campden and the Right Honourable John Lord Roos in pursuance of an order made the last Court and did very chearefully accept of this Corporacion respect & favor to admit them Free Burgesses And their Honours did severally laid downe forty pounds apeice according to a former order of this Court which was by a free harty and generall consent of the whole Court returned againe to their Lordshipps And their Honours tooke the oath of Free Burgesses according to the Auntient custome of the Burrough.

Mr Lenton Account for tolle.
At this Court Mr Lentons [*sic*] gives an Account of the Tolle for June
                                           Receipts   03 16 11
                                           disbursments   00 14 04
                                           Remaines   03 02 07
Which he payes and is discharged.

Mr Cole the like.
Mr Coles Account for the moneth of August: Receipts   01 09 03
Which he payes in open Court:, also   disbursments   00 04 00

45s 8d for a yeares Tolle of Packhorses and Wagons at the White Lyon, & he is discharged. — Remaines 01 05 03

Mr Humes the like.
Mr Humes Account for Tolle for October: Receipts   04 16 00
                                           disbursments 00 18 07
                                           Remaines   03 17 05
Which he payes and is discharged.

Sir Robert Markham made free.
At this Court came Sir Robert Markham of Sedgbrooke in this County Barronett and desired to be admitted a free Burgesse of this Corporacion to which this Court do freely consent whereupon the said Sir Robert Markham layes downe his forty pounds for his freedome which he is very chearefully willing shall goe for the use of this Corporacion and takes the oath of a freeman according to Auntient custome of this Burrough.

Persons first appointed to pay to Sir Robert Carr.
Att this Court it is ordered that Mr Robert Cole, Thomas Ireland, Thomas Fishar, and William Clarke being in the first bond of 100 li to Sir Robert Carr be and are hereby appointed Milne Masters till Midsummer next with an intent they may Receive the proffitts thereof and pay of the said bond And that yearely from Midsummer those Gentlemen that are bound to Sir Robert Carr shall Successively be Milne Masters for one yeare then next following whereby they may pay of their severall and respective bonds And it is further ordered that if the proffitts of the said Milnes fall shorte of a 100 li to pay of any bond it shall be made up by this Court And if they amount to more it shall be paid to the Corporacon and that the Milne Masters shall account quarterly in Mr Aldermans Court And it shall be lawfull for the said Milne Masters at their discretions with the aprobacion of the present Alderman to entertaine or put out any Milner or Loadsmen without any further order whatsoever.

[fo. 656v] Fifth Court of Michael Taylor, 9 July 1678

Persons to take Accounts.
At this Court Mr Alderman, Mr Shorte, Mr Cole, Mr Robert Calcraft, Anthony Hotchkin, William Clarke, Thomas Fishar, Nicholas Becke, John Smyth, Symon Grant, Richard Hickson and Henry Hubbard are appointed to meete and take the Accounts of severall persons and returne their proceedings next Court day.

Waites Elected.
At this Court came Leonard Butcher, Thomas Kelham and Thomas Tripp and desired to be admitted Waites to this Corporacon to which this Court doth Condiscend and they are hereby admitted upon the same Terms that former Waites of this Corporacion injoyed the same.

20ty for Constables Assessment.
At this Court it is ordered that an Assessment of 20^{ty} pounds be made and laid upon the Borrough for payment of the Constables their Bills of disbursments for this yeare an estimate being taken what their particular amount unto. And that notice be given in the Church the next Lords day.

Informacion against John Gibson for grinding from the Milles.
Whereas Thomas Rowley a member of this Court and now present doth Testifye that John Gibson Baker another member of this Court and here likewise present hath ground six strike of Corne from the Milles belonging to this Corporacon contrary to severall orders of this Court and contrary to the Oath of a freeman which he Tooke to observe and keep all orders made or that should be made by a free Consent for the good proffitt and honest advantage of this Borrough It is therefore at this Court in pursuance of former orders of this Court made, ordered that a Fyne of 3 shillings and Four pence a strike for every of the said six strikes be imposed and levyed upon the Goods, Chattells of the said John Gibson and that Bryan Godley the present Bayliffe of this Libertie and the proper officer in such cases is hereby ordered and forthwith required to Levey the same. And all and singular the Constables of this Corporacon are hereby likewise ordered to Be Aydeing and assisting to the said Bayliffe in putting in execucion this present order. And it is likewise ordered that the said Bayliffe and Constables shall be secured saved harmlesse and indempnified of and from all trouble charges and incumbrances whatsoever which shall or may happen for or by reason of Levyeing of the Fyne aforesaid.

[fo. 657r] **Sixth Court of Michael Taylor, 26 July 1678**

Sir Robert Markham chosen a Member of the Court.
Whereas Mr Alderman this day acquainted the Court that the Honorable Sir Robert Markham Barronett one of the Burgesses in the Honorable house for this Corporacon out of respect and kindnes which he hath to this Burrough and for to serve his Majestie and for the good & Welfare of this Corporacion is willing to become a Member of this Court Whereupon the Comoners by a free and unanimous consent do return the said Sir Robert Markham in the Kallender to Mr Alderman and his Brethren for a Second twelve man with Thomas Archer, Edward Bristow, and Thomas Chrichloe Then Mr Alderman his Brethren and Second twelve did send downe by a free and generall consent the Names of Sir Robert Markham and Thomas Archer And by all the consents of the Comoners Sir Robert Markham is chosen one of the Second Company and takes his oath accordingly And after by the unanimous consent of the first & second Company Sir Robert Markham is chosen one of the first Company and takes his oath incident thereunto and the oath of Justice of the peace according to Auntient custome and also the oaths of Supremacy & Allegiance and the oath mencioned in the Act of Parlyament made in the xiijth yeare of his now Majesties Raigne And subscribed against the Covenant as by the said Act is directed and de[c]lared.

Sir Robert Markham nominated Alderman.
And for the Elleccion of the next Succeeding Alderman It is at this Court ordered Sir Robert Markham be sent downe into the Church to Mr Thomas Short being there alone And it is further agreed that Mr Robert Calcraft be sent downe into the Church to Sir Robert Markham & Mr Thomas Short to make three Comburgesses there Out of which three Comburgesses in the Church It is agreed Sir Robert Markham be brought upon the Cusheon or place of Eleccion in the Roome of Mr John Winge lately dismissed from the said place by a former order of Court for the reasons therein mencioned And it is also agreed that Mr Richard Calcraft be sent downe into the Church to Mr Thomas Short and Mr Robert Calcraft to make three Comburgesses there. Out of which three Comburgesses it is also agreed that Mr Thomas Short be brought upon the Cusheon or place of Eleccion to Sir Robert Markham in the Roome of Mr William Milles lately dismissed from the said place in the same order made for the dismission of the said Mr Wing And it is further agreed that Mr Richard Holley be sent downe into the Church to Mr Robert Calcraft & Mr Richard Calcraft to make three Comburgesses there Out of which three Comburgesses in the Church It is also agreed that Mr Robert Calcraft be brought upon the Cusheon or place of Eleccion to make three Comburgesses there Out of which three Comburgesses upon the Cusheon or place of Eleccon Sir Robert Markham is by the free and Unanimous consent of this Court elected Alderman for this next ensueing yeare And shall on Friday after St Lukes day next take the oath of Alderman for the due Execucion of that office And all other oathes & subscripcion according to the Act of Parlyament for the Regulateing and well governing of Corporacions.

[fo. 657v] **Seventh Court of Michael Taylor, 20 September 1678**

Mr Wrights money to be paid.
Whereas Mr Alderman this day acquainted the Court that there was due to Mr Wright of Belvoyre Forty pounds from this Corporacion for which there is an order of Court that the same be paid unto him and if he might have his money before Mr Aldermans yeare was out he would present the Corporacion with a peice of plate of x li and that rather then the Corporacion lose such a kindnesse Mr Alderman Mr Robert Cole and Mr Paulett and if any more would Joyne with them and that they might be secured by this Court they would take up Forty pounds to pay Mr Wright Whereupon Mr John Lenton and and [sic] John Robinson present in Court are willing and contented to become bound with the Gentlemen aforesaid for the said Forty pounds And it is hereby ordered by a free and Unanimous consent of this Court That the said Gentlemen and every of them shall go secured saved harmelesse and indempnifyed of and from the said 40 li or any securitye they shall be bound in, or give for the same.

Gunnerby Wind Milne to be bought.
Att this Court it is ordered that Mr Alderman and some members of this Court whome he shall please to call to his Assistance doe Treat about buyng the Wyndmill on Gunerby Hill and that what bargaine they shall make shall be Ratefyed and confirmed by this Court.

Att this Court came Symon Somerby Apprentice to John Rawlinson Cordwainer, Richard Barker Apprentice to Thomas Charles Baker, William Poole and John Watson and Robert Calcraft Junior freeborne and desired to be admitted free Burgesses of this Corporacon to which this Court doth Condiscend Whereupon the said Symon Somerby and Richard Barker doe pay their Five shillings apeice to the Box and Twelve pence apeice to Clarke and Serjeants and the said William Poole John Watson and Robert Calcraft as freeborne paid 2s 6d to the Box and sixpence apeice to Clarke and Serjeants and take the Oath of free Burgesses of this Corporacion and the oathes of Supremacey and Allegiance and the Oath and subscribe the Declaracon in the late Act of Parlyament mencioned for the Regulateing and well governing of Corporacions.

[fo. 658r] **Eighth Court of Michael Taylor, 24 October 1678**

Sir Robert Markham desire to be dismissed the Court.
Whereas by an order made the fifth Court of Mr Alderman that now is the Honorable Sir Robert Markham Barronet one of the Burgesses for this Corporacion in the Honorable House of Comons in Parlyament assembled is by a free and Unanimous Consent of the said Court nominated Alderman for the next ensueing yeare And whereas the said Sir Robert Markham by his letter directed to Mr Alderman to be communicated to the Corporacion signifieing that the Parlyament meeteing aboute the time of the Ellecion he cannot possibly attend that place which letter followeth in theses words vzt These For the right Worshipfull Mr Michaell Taylor Alderman of Grantham present

His letter.   Agneho October 9 1678
Sir, The concernes that lyes upon me (in regard of the Honour I received from the Corporacon when I was last at Grantham in being so Unanimously nominated to succeed you in the Aldermanship is of so great importance that I am ready to expose all my other affaires to shew my gratefull Resentment of soe signall a Respect unto me But the Parlyament meeteing aboute the time that the Freemen do Compleate their Choice I haveing a desire to be present at the opening of the Session request the favour of the Corporacion that they will excuse my comeing downe And if it be of Consequence that they must then proceed to the Choice of another I hope they will not looke upon it as any neglect in me, but by their Concession herein oblidge me farther Sir I desire you will Communicate this to the Corporacion to whom I intreat you to present my faithfull service I am Sir your very humble Servant Robert Markham
Which excuse of the said Sir Robert Markham this Court doth freely admit of And with a free and Unanimous Consent of this Court Mr Robert Calcraft is nominated Alderman for this next ensueing yeare.

Mr Wright and Mr Storey [sic] *give two peices of plate to the Corporacion.*
At this Court Mr Alderman brought into a Court a very large silver Cupp which Mr Henry Wright of Belvoyre, out of his respect and kindnesse to this Corporacon doth give the same, and also the Tankard which Mr John Woodruffe of Corby, out of his

respects to this Corporacon doth give unto the Towne, and also one silver Cupp which Mr Edward Storer doth likewise present unto this Borrough, for the perticular Care the Corporacon tooke on him as his Guardians for his porcion in the time of his Minority, all which plate he delivers up for the use of the Corporacon which is accepted of as a very great favour and kindnesse by this Court and order that Mr Alderman returnes the Gentlemen many thanks for the same.

[fo. 658v]

At an Assembly holden by Mr Michael Taylor gentleman Alderman and the Comburgesses and Burgesses of Grantham aforesaid in Corpus Christi Quire within the Prebendarie there on Fryday next after St Lukes day being 25 October 1678.

First did sit downe upon the Cusheon or place of Elleccion the said Mr Michaell Taylor in Corpus Christi Quire within the Prebendarie Church there &c.
Next to him sit upon the Cusheon or place of Elleccion Two Comburgesses, Vizt Mr John Wing and Mr William Milles.
And soe by an Unanimous Vote and consent of this Assembly Mr John Wing is chosen Alderman for the ensueing yeare.
Whereupon the said Mr Michaell Taylor haveing discharged himselfe from his place and office of Alderman And the said Mr John Wing now Elected Alderman in his place and stead hath at this Assembly taken the Oath of Alderman for this Borrough and Soake of Grantham according to Ancient Custome and all the Oathes inciden [*sic*] thereunto.

And soe this Assembly breakes up.

THE HALL BOOK OF GRANTHAM 1678–1679

[fo. 659r] **First Court of John Wing, 24 October 1678**

Mr John Wing Alderman
Sir Robert Markham   Edward Leivesly
Mr Thomas Shorte Comburgess   William Clarke
Mr Michaell Taylor Comburgess   Thomas Ireland
Mr Robert Calcraft Comburgess   Edward Paulett
Mr Richard Calcraft Comburgess   Christofer Thompson
Mr Richard Holley Comburgess   Anthony Hottchkin
Mr John Lenton Comburgess   Henry Coverly
Mr Henry Humes Comburgess   John Robinson
Mr John Coddington Comburgess   Thomas Fishar
Mr Robert Cole Comburgess   Nicholas Becke
Mr Thomas Matkin Comburgess   Edward Bristow
Mr William Milles Comburgess   Thomas Chrichloe

The Names of the Officers

Coroner	Mr Michaell Taylor	Swinegate	Roger Blankney
Escheator	Mr Richard Calcraft	Castlegate	William Knight
Churchwardens	Thomas Chrichloe		Henry Atkinson
	John Smith	Keybearers	Mr Alderman
Chamberlaines	Thomas Fishar		Thomas Chrichloe
	Thomas Rowley		Thomas Fishar
Collectors for	Mr Richard Holley	Prizers of Corne	William Newton
Schoole Rents	John Brome		Richard Owin
Cheife Constable	Edward Leivesly	Market Sayers	Christofer Walgrave
	William Clarke		George Hanson
Market Place	John Still	Leather Sealers	Henry Wright
Constables	John Gibson		Ashton Lord
High Streete	John Goodwin		John Hutchin
	Charles Wetherill		Richard Woulds
Westgate	Henry Hibbert	Towne Clarke	William Hodgkinson
	Thomas Short	Sergents	Thomas Calcraft
Walkergate	Edward Watson		Bryan Godley
	Robert Thompson	Church Clarke	Humphery Turner
Swinegate	Richard Dawson	Belman	Ralph Osborne

[fo. 659v]

Comoners

Market Place
William Kirke
Thomas Hodgson
Simon Goodwin
Richard Segrave
William Cole
John Stevenson
John Goodwin
Henry Hubbert
Thomas Short
Anthony Kirke
Richard Owin
John Gibson
Nathaniell Rookesby

Walkergate
Edward Watson
Robert Thompson
Roger Blankney
Thomas Rawlinson
John Still
Henry Atkinson

High Streete
Richard Handley
George Read
Thomas Rowlett
Christofer Hanson
William Bristow
William Knight

Westgate
William Haskerd
Francis Bristow
John Newcombe
Thomas Kenion
James Bristow
Thomas Bayly

Swinegate
Richard Dawson
William Newton
Thomas Quiningborough
Matthew Dixon

Charters delivered up.
At this Court Mr Michaell Taylor late Alderman delivers the three Charter Boxes with all the Charters Vizt

The Exemplir of Edward 4th
King Henry the viijth
King Edward the vjth
Queen Elizabeth two Charters
King James
Escheators Pattent

King Charles the 1st
King Charles the 2d
Judge Dyers Award
Stamford writeings
Townes Armes
Writing with many seales

Mr Lenton Account for tolle.
At this Court Mr John Lenton accounteth for the proffitts of

The tolles for the moneth of October last Receipts	05	13 02
Disbursments	00	18 06
Remaines due to the Town	04	14 08

Which he payes in open Court and he is discharged.

[fo. 660r]

Plate delivered up.
At this Court was delivered by Mr Michaell Taylor late Alderman to Mr Alderman that now is all the Towns Plate which is as followeth Vzt

The Horse Race Cup	Two Tunns
Mr Archers Boll	Mr Kirkbys Boll
Mr Wheatlys Cann	Mr Greenewood – 13 Spoones
Mr Horsemans Boll	One Salt with Cover
Mr Greenewoods Cann	Mr Horsemans Wine Boll
Mr Batties Beaker	The Waites Cognizances
Thomas Harrington Esquire Cann	Mr John Woodruffes Cann
Mr Henry Wright Boll	Mr Edward Storers Cupp

Mr Humes Account for tolles.
At this Court Mr Henry Humes accounteth for the Proffitts of the Tolles for the
November and that his Receipts are   06 00 05 ob
Disbursments   00 08 00
Remaines due to the Towne   05 12 05 ob
Which he payes in open Court and is discharged.

Mr Lenton the like.
Mr Lentons Account for Tolle: his Receipts   02 00 08
Disbursments   00 06 08
Remaines   01 14 00
which he payes in open Court and is discharged.

The Accounts of the severall Milne Masters for the Milles belonging to the Towne for the years 1677 and 1678.

Mr Coles Account of the Milles.
Mr Robert Coles – his Receipts   62 11 06
His Disbursments with what he paid to Sir Robert Carr   54 07 06
Remaines due to the Towne   08 04 00

Mr Clarke the like.
Mr William Clarkes his Receipts   36 01 06
His disbursments with what he paid to Sir Robert Carr   38 01 03 ob
Remaines due to the Accomptant   01 19 09 ob

Mr Fishar the like.
Mr Thomas Fishar – his Receipts   25 02 06
His disbursments with what he paid to Sir Robert Carr   24 01 10
Remaines due to the Towne   01 00 08

[fo. 660v] **Second Court of John Wing 29 January 1678/79**

Persons to take Accounts.
At this Court it is ordered that Mr Richard Calcraft, Mr William Milles, William Clarke, Thomas Fishar, Nicholas Becke, John Smith, John Steevens, William Kirke, John Still and Thomas Rowlet do meete on Tuesday next to examine Accounts and to returne the proceedings therein next Court day.

John Newton Esquire, John Thorold Esquire, William Bury Esquire made free.
Att this Court came John Newton of Hather thorpe in the County of Lincolne Esquire Son and heyre of Sir John Newton Barronet one of the members of the Honorable house of Commons for this Corporacion and have served the same with these twenty yeares, and the said Esquire Newton desired to be admitted a free Burgesse of this Corporacion to which this Court doth Condiscend whereupon the said John Newton Esquire layes downe his 40 li for his freedome which the Court Unanimously returned him againe out of respect they beare both to his Father and himselfe.
This day also came John Thorold Esquire Son to Sir William Thorold Knight and Barronet another member of the Honorable house of Commons for this Corporacion and desired to be admitted a free Burgesse of this Borrough as freeborne to which this Court doth also condiscend. At this Court came also William Bury Esquire son and heire of William Bury of this Towne Esquire and desired to be admitted a free Burgesse here, to which the Court likewise doth consent whereupon the said John Newton Esquire ~~Will~~ John Thorold Esquire and William Bury Esquire did severally take the Oathes of a Burgesses and payes the Fees to Clarke and Serjants and are admitted accordingly.

Adam Fearon, Richard Calcraft Clerke, Thomas Matkin and Robert Thompson made free.
Att this Court came Adam Fearon son of William Fearon Senior, Richard Calcraft Clerke eldest son of Mr Richard Calcraft one of the Comburgesses of this Court and Thomas Matkin son of Thomas Matkin another of the Comburgesses of this Court and Robert Thompson son of Christopher Thompson a Member of this Court and desired to be admitted free Burgesses of this Corporacon as freeborne to which this Court doth Consent Whereupon they severally take the Oathes of free Burgesses and the generall Oathes of Alegiance and Supremacey and the Oath and subscribed the Declaracon mencioned in the late Act of Parlyament for the well governing and regulateing of Corporacions and payes 2s 6d to the Box as freeborne and Fees to Clerke and Serjeants and are admitted free Burgesses accordingly.

[fo. 661r] **Third Court of John Wing, 20 June 1679**

40li Freedome confirmed.
Whereas the Court this day takeing into Consideracon the order for 40 li for every freeman and that the same is very prejudiciall to this Corporacon it was this day put to the Vote whether the said order should be abrogated and made void or stand confirmed And it was carried by the Major part of this Court that the said order stand confirmed to all intents and purposes whatsoever.

Mr Coles Account for tolles.
Mr Robert Coles Account for Tolle for January last
His Receipts   01 15 08
Disbursements   00 06 00
Remaines to the Towne   01 09 08
which he payes in open Court and is discharged.

Mr Matkin the like.
Mr Thomas Matkins Account for February Received   01 13 07
Disbursments   00 06 08
Remaines   01 06 11
which he payes in open Court and is discharged.

Mr Milles the like.
Mr William Milles Accounts for March. His Receipts   02 10 09
Disbursments   00 08 04
Remaines   02 02 05
Which he payes in open Court and is discharged.

Mr Alderman the like.
Mr Aldermans Accounts for Aprill: his Receipts   17 11 10 ob
Disbursments   01 06 08
Remaines   16 05 02 ob

John Still Account as Colebuyer.
John Stills Account as Cole Buyer – his Receipts   19 02 00
Disbursments   04 18 00
Remaines   14 04 00

John Stevens Colebuyer.
which he payes to John Stevens now Elected Cole Buyer for the ensueing yeare.

30s for Westgate Well.
A [*sic*] this Court it is ordered that an assessment of 30s be made for the repaireing of Market place Pumpe.

[fo. 661v] **Fourth Court of John Wing, 12 September 1679**

Church to be repaired.
At this Court it is ordered that an Assessment of 30 li be made and laid upon this Parish for the Repaireing of the Church and to Reimburse severall of the late Churchwardens that have laid out money in Repaires of the Church And that notice be given in the Church of the time and place of making the said Assessment.

Constables Assessment 30 li
Att this Court it is also ordered that an Assessment of 30 li be made and laid upon this Borrough for the payment of the Constables their Bills of Disbursments for this present yeare an Estimate being Taken what the particular sumes amount unto And that notice be given in the Church of the time and place and makeing the said Assessment.

Sandpitt tolle to be paid.
Att this Court The Chamberlaine is ordered to Call of Widdow Wilson for two yeares Rent due at Michaelmas last for the house she lives in and to looke after the Tolle of Sandpitt Laine of Christopher Walgrave and of Mr Turner for the Tolle of Waggons.

Hugh Berry, Thomas Leivesly, Robert Waineman, Amos Wilkinson, John Haycocke, Thomas Hutching, Thomas Calcraft, Thomas Ulliott, James Grococke, Richard Newton, Ralph Clarke, Benjamin Lenton, Thomas Reare, John Osborne, William Osborne, Anthony Dawson, John Weaver, Thomas Brewer, William Fearon, John Simpson and William Handley. Made free.
Att this Court came Hugh Bury Butcher, Thomas Leivesley Apprentice to Edward Leivesley Butcher, Robert Waineman Apprentice to Christopher Hanson Butcher, Amos Wilkinson Apprentice to William Kirke Butcher, John Haycocke Weaver, Thomas Hutching Apprentice to John Rawlinson Cordwainer, Thomas Calcraft one of the sones of Mr Richard Calcraft one of the Comburgesses of this Court, Thomas Ulliott Apprentice to his Father a Currier, James Grococke Cordwainer apprentice to his Father, Richard Newton Felmonger Apprentice to Richard Poole and severally desired together with Ralph Clarke Cordwainer Apprentice to William Grococke senior, Benjamen Lenton Barber Apprentice to his Father, Thomas Reare Barber Apprentice to Edward Larke, John Osborne Sonn of John Osborne Glover, William Osborne Son of Ralph Osborne Glover, Antony Dawson Weaver Son of Anthony Dawson, John Weaver Cordwainer Apprentice to John Rawlinson, Thomas Brewer Weaver Apprentice to his Father, William Fearon Barber Apprentice to Edward Archer, [*words deleted*] John Simpson son of Stephen Simpson Roper, William Handley Wheelwright Son of Christofer Handley to be admitted free Burgesses of this Corporacion to which this Court doth Condiscend Whereupon they severally take the Oath of free Burgesses and the severall oaths of Supremacey and Allegiance *scilicet* this oath and subscribed the Declaracions menconed in the Act of parlament for the well governing and regulating of Corporacons and payes 2s 6d to the Box as freeborne and the Fees to the Clarke and Serjeants and are admitted free Burgesses accordingly.

[fo. 662r] **Fifth Court of John Wing, 3 October 1679**

Sir Robert Carr: Made free.
Att this Court came the Right Honorable Sir Robert Carr, Knight and Barronet Chancollor of his Majesties Dutchy of Lancaster who had Done great Kindnesses for this Corporacion, in lending them one Thousand pounds for the payment of the Townes debts and to be Repayed againe ~~by~~ in Tenn yeares by one hundred pounds per Annum without interest, and at the Request of Mr Alderman and the Rest of the Court he was pleased to doe the Corporacion that favour as to be admitted a free Burgesse thereof which is [sic] Honor was pleased to accept of. And his Honor did lay down Forty pounds according to former order of this Court which was by a free hearty and generall consent of this Court Returned againe to his Honor. And he Tooke the oath of a Free Burgesse according to the Ancient Custome of this Borrough.

Mr Bursleime, Mr Myles Long, Mr William Matkin And Mr Edward Secker Made free.
Att this Court came [blank] Bursleime gentleman Steward to the Right Honorable Sir Robert Carr being present his Honor was desired by the Court that his Steward might be admitted a free Burgesse of this Borrough to which his Honor did consent. And the said Mr Bursleime the like At this Court also came Myles Long of Sleeford in this County gent and Attorny at Law who served Mr William Parkins Senior as his Clarke for seavon yeares by way of Indenture of Apprenticeship which he produced in Court and William Matkin Brother of Mr Thomas Matkin one of the Comburgesses of this Court and Edward Secker gent an Attorny at Law as freeborne desired to be admitted free Burgesses of this Corporacion to which this Court doth Condiscend whereupon the said Mr Bursleime laid downe his forty pounds according to Custome which was by this Court unanimously given againe and the said Myles Long as a Forreiner paid his Five shillings to the Box and the said William Matkin and Edward Secker paid their 2s 6d to the Box as freeborne, and they all of them paid their Fees to Clarke and Serjeants and tooke the Oath of Free Burgesses of this Corporacion and are admitted accordingly, and also the said Myles Long, Edward Secker and William Matkin did severally take the Oathes of Supremacey And Allegiance and the Oath and subscribed the Declaracon mencioned in the Act of parlyament for the well governing and Regulateing of Corporacions.

[fo. 662v] **Sixth Court of John Wing, 10 October 1679**

Mr Waltons Account for the Milnes.
The Account of Mr Thomas Walton one of the Milne Masters for the yeares 1678 & 1680.

Sold 49 quarter 6: Strike of Mault at 20s.	49	17 06
More made of 10: quarter of at 2s quarter	01	00 00
For Molter and Mault at the Towne Mille	15	11 06
For Molter and Mault at the Slate Mille	14	19 07
Receipts	81	08 07

Paid for Millers Wages and Mille Dressing	22 02 00
Paid other necessary charges as appeares by Bill	18 01 02
Charges at Sir Robert Carrs at the Carrying over the money	00 08 00
Paid Widow Gibson her remaneing Bill left to pay in Mr Milles his time	00 06 00
Disbursments	40 17 02
To Account for	40 11 05
Paid to Sir Robert Carr	41 10 0
~~Tho~~	
Thomas Hodgson hath in his hand	03 15 00
Richard Pearson	01 06 00

Mr Milles Account for the Milnes.

Mr Milles Account for Milne Master: ~~Rec~~	
Receipts: for Mault	57 11 03
For Molter and wheate And Oatemeale making	28 12 09
Receipts	86 04 00
Disbursments	
To Sir Robert Carr	58 10 00
For Milners Wages	22 02 00
By payments	05 14 05
Disbursments	86 06 05
Remaines due to the Accomptant	00 02 05

Mr Mallory, Richard Handley made free.
Att this Court came Mr Thomas Mallory and offered to give the Court Tenn pounds for his freedome which the Court accepted of, and also Richard Handley as freeborne and desired his freedome to which the Court did consent whereupon th each of them tooke the Oathes of Freemen and paid the Fees to Clarke and Serjeants according to Ancient Custome, and the said Richard Handley and [*sic*] did at the same time take the Oathes of Supremacey and Allegiance and the Oath and subscribed the Declaracions menconed in the late Act of parlyament made for the well governing and regulating of Corporacons.

[fo. 663r]

At an Assembly holden by Mr John Wing Alderman and the Comburgesses and Burgesses of Grantham aforesaid in Corpus Christi Quire within the prebendarie Church there namely on Fryday next after St Lukes day being 24 October 1679.

First did sitt downe upon the Cusheon or place of Elleccon the said Mr John Wing Alderman in Corpus Christi Quire within the Prebendarie Church there
Next to him did sit upon the Cusheon or place of Elleccion One Comburgesse Vizt Mr William Milles.

Then was sent downe into the Church by the Unanimous Vote and consent of this Assembly, one Comburgesse (Vizt) Mr Thomas Shorte in the place of Mr John Turner lately deceased And next to him by the like free consent was sent downe one other Comburgesse, Vizt) Mr Robert Calcraft And after him by the same full Consent and agreement was sent downe one other Comburgesse, Vizt) Mr Richard Calcraft to make three Comburgesses in the Church.

Out of which three Comburgesses in the Church was chosen to come up and sit upon the Cusheon or place of Eleccion one other Comburgesse (Vizt) Mr Thomas Shorte.

Then was sent downe into the Church to Mr Robert Calcraft and Mr Richard Calcraft to make them two, three one other Comburgesse (Vizt) Mr Richard Holley

Out of which three Comburgesses in the Church one was chosen to come up and sitt upon the Cusheon or place of Eleccion to Mr William Milles and Mr Thomas Shorte to make them two, three one other Comburgesse (Vizt) Mr Robert Calcraft.

Then was there three Comburgesses upon the Cusheon or place of Eleccon (Vizt) Mr William Milles, Mr Thomas Shorte and Mr Robert Calcraft.

And then was there in the Church two Comburgesses Vizt Mr Richard Calcraft and Mr Richard Holley.

Out of which three Comburgesses upon the Cusheon or place of Eleccion Vizt Mr William Milles Mr Thomas Shorte & Mr Robert Calcraft one is to be chosen Alderman for the next ensueing yeare.

An [sic] thereupon by the Unanimous consent & Vote of this Assembly Mr William Milles is elected and chosen Alderman for this next ensuring yeare.

Whereupon the said Mr John Wing dischargeth himselfe from the place and office of Alderman according to Ancient Custome And the said Mr William Milles now elected Alderman in his place and stead hath at this Assembly taken the Oath of Alderman of this Borrough and soake of Grantham according to the Ancient and lawdable Custome of this Borrough and all Oathes and subscripcions incident to the said office as by a late Act of parlyament in that behalfe made and provided.

And soe this Assembly breakes up.

[fo. 663v] [Blank page]

THE HALL BOOK OF GRANTHAM 1679–1680

[fo. 664r] **First Court of William Milles, 31 October 1679**

Mr William Milles Alderman
Sir Robert Markham Barronet Comburgess
Mr Thomas Shorte Comburgesse
Mr Michael Taylor Comburgesse
Mr Robert Calcraft Comburgesse
Mr Richard Calcraft Comburgesse
Mr Richard Holley Comburgesse
Mr John Lenton Comburgesse
Mr Henry Humes Comburgesse
Mr John Coddington Comburgesse
Mr John Wing Comburgesse
Mr Robert Cole Comburgesse
Mr Thomas Matkin Comburgesse

John Robinson
Nicholas Becke
Thomas Ireland
Edward Paulett
Christofer Thompson
Anthony Hotchkin
Henry Coverly
Edward Leivesley
Thomas Fishar
William Clarke
Edward Bristowe
Thomas Chrichloe

Coroner	Mr John Winge	Keybearers	Mr Alderman
Escheator	Mr Michaell Taylor		John Smyth
Church Wardens	Thomas Chrichloe		William Clarke
	John Smyth	Prizers of Corne	Thomas Rowlett
Chamberlaines	William Clarke		Richard Owen
	Symon Grant	Market Sayers	Christofer Walgrave
Collectors for	Mr John Coddington		Thomas Hatfeild
Schoole Rents	George Read	Leather Sealers	Thomas Marshall
Cheife	John Robinson		John Hutching
Constables	Nicholas Becke		George Wray
Market place	William Cole		Richard Woulds
Constables	Edward Watson	Towne Clarke	William Hodgkinson
High Streete	Henry Hubbard	Serjeant	Thomas Calcraft
	William Burbidge	Serjeant & Gaol[er]	Bryan Godley
Westgate	William Fearon	Church Clarke	Humphry Turner
	Thomas Shorte	Bell man	Ralph Osborne
Walkergate	Roger Blanckney		
	Robert Thompson		
Swinegate	Anthony Kirke		
	Richard Dawson		

Castlegate   Henry Atkinson
              William Knight

[fo. 664v]

Comoners

Marketplace	Highstreete
William Kirke	Richard Handley
Thomas Hodgson	Thomas Rowley
Symon Godwing	George Read
Richard Segrave	Christofer Hanson
William Cole	William Bristowe
John Stevenson	William Knight
John Goodwing	Westgate
Henry Hubbard	William Haskerd
Thomas Shorte	Francis Bristow
Anthony Kirke	John Newcombe
Richard Owen	Thomas Kenion
John Gibson	James Bristowe
Nathaniel Rooksby	Thomas Bayly
William Burbidge	Richard Hickson
Walkergate	Swinegate
Edward Watson	Richard Dawson
Robert Thompson	William Newton
Roger Blankney	Thomas Quiningbrow
Thomas Rawlinson	Mathew Dixon
Henry Atkinson	

Charters delivered up
Att this Court Mr John Wing late Alderman delivers the three Charter Boxes with all the Charters (Vizt)

The Exemplir of Edward 4th	King Charles the 1st
King Edward the 6th	King Charles the 2nd
King Henry the 8th	Judge Dyers Award
Queene Elizabeth 2 Charters	Stamford Writeings
King James	Townes Armes
Escheators Pattents	Writing with many seales

Plate delivered up
At this Court was delivered by John Wing late Alderman to Mr Alderman that now is all the Towne plate which is as Followeth (Vizt)

The Horse Race Cup	Two Tunns
Mr Archers Boll	Mr Kirksbyes Boll

Mr Wheatlys Cann	Mr Greenwoods 13 spoones
Mr Horsemans Boll	One salt with a Cover
Mr Greenwoods Cann	Mr Horsemans Wine Boll
Mr Battyes Beaker	The Waites Cognizances
Thomas Harrington Esquire His Cann	Mr John Woodruffs Cann
	Mr Wrights Bolle
	Mr Storers Cupp

[fo. 665r]

Att an Assembly holden by the Comburgesses and Burgesses of Grantham aforesaid in Corpus Christi Quire within the Prebendarie Church there on Wednesday the 24 December 1679 after the decease of Mr William Milles late Alderman and for the Eleccion of a new Alderman in his place and stead according to the Auncient Custome of this Borrough.

First did sit downe upon the Cusheon or place of Eleccion Mr Thomas Shorte and Mr Robert Calcraft in Corpus Christi quire within the Prebendarie Church there
Then was there in the Church two Comburgesses Vizt Mr Richard Calcraft and Mr Richard Holley.
Then was sent downe into the Church to these two Comburgesses to make them three one other Comburgesse, Vizt, Mr John Coddington.
Out of which three Comburgesses in the Church one was chosen to come up and sit on the Cusheon or place of Eleccion one other Comburgesse Vizt. Mr Richard Calcraft.
Then was there three Comburgesses upon the Cusheon or place of Eleccion. Vizt Mr Thomas Shorte, Mr Robert Calcraft and Mr Richard Calcraft
And then was there remaneing in the Church two Comburgesses Vizt. Mr Richard Holley and Mr John Coddington.
Out of which three Comburgesses upon the Cusheon or place of Eleccion Vizt. Mr Thomas Shorte, Mr Robert Calcraft and Mr Richard Calcraft, one is to be chosen Alderman for the Residue of the ensueing yeare for this Borrough of Grantham in the place of Mr William Milles late Alderman deceased.

And soe by the Consent and Vote of this Assembly Mr Thomas Shorte is chosen Alderman for the Residue of this yeare yet to come. And the said Mr Thomas Shorte being soe elected Alderman as aforesaid for the Remainder of this yeare did at this Assembly take the Oath of Alderman according to the Ancient and laudable Custome of this Borrough. And the Oathes of Allegiance and supremacey And the Oath and subscribed the Declaracon mencioned in the late Act of parlyament for the well governing and Regulateing of Corporacions.

And soe this Assembly breakes up.

[fo. 665v] **First Court of Thomas Shorte, 9 January 1679/80**

Persons to take Accounts.
At this Court Mr Taylor, Mr Robert Calcraft, Mr Richard Calcraft, Mr Cole, Mr Paulett, William Clarke, John Smyth and Symon Grant are appointed to examine Accounts on Wednesday next.

Mr Holleys Account for tolles.
Mr Holleys Account for Tolle for October: his Receipts:	04	10	07
disbursments:	00	19	06
Remaines due to the Towne:	03	11	01

Which he payes and is discharged.

Mr Coddington the like.
Mr Coddingtons Account for November: his Receipts:	02	14	00
his Disbursments:	00	08	06
Remaines to the Towne:	02	05	06

Which he payes and is discharged.

Mr Wing the like.
Mr Winges Account for December: his Receipts:	04	15	01
his disbursments:	01	00	00
Remaines to the Towne:	03	15	01

Which remains as yet unpaid.

Mr Ireland, Mr Paulet, Mr Thompson chosen of the first Company.
Att this Court Mr Thomas Ireland Mr Edward Paulett and Mr Christopher Thompson are chosen of the first Company in the Roome of Mr John Lenton, Mr Henry Humes and Mr William Milles lately deceased and severally tooke the Oath of a Comburgesse and Justice of peace according to Aunciant Custome and at the same time tooke the Oathes of Allegiance and supremacey and the Oath and subscribed the declaracon and Received the Sacrament according to a late Act of Parlyament made for the well governing and Regulateing of Corporacions.

Simond Grant, William Haskerd and Richard Segrave chosen of the 2nd Company.
Att this Court Symon Grant, William Haskerd and Richard Segrave are chosen of the Second Twelve in the Roome of Mr Thomas Ireland, Mr Edward Paulett and Mr Christofer Thompson chosen of the First Company and did severally take the Oaths as of of [*sic*] the Second Company according to Ancient Custome and at the same time tooke the Oathes of Allegiance and supremacey and the Oath and subscribed the declaracion and Received the Sacrament according to the late Act of Parlyament made for the well governing and Regulating of Corporacions.

In the Kallender
Richard Hickson
John Smyth
Thomas Rowlett

[fo. 666r] **Second Court of Thomas Shorte, 16 January 1679/80**

Mr Winge Account for tolles

Mr John Wings Account for Tolle in Aprill Heareby due to the Towne	16	05	02 ob
Mr Wings Account in December the like	03	15	00
Paid to him by Thomas Rowlett Chamberlaine	03	00	00
Receipts	23	00	03 ob
Deduccions			
To him for his Sallory	10	00	00
To him for charges when Sir Robert Carr was in Towne	04	00	00
The Deduccions	14	00	00
Remaines due to the Corporacion	09	00	03 ob

Third Court of Thomas Shorte, 23 January 1679/80

Mr Wing to pay the money due upon his Account or be sued.
Whereas upon reading of the Accounts of Mr John Wing Alderman for the last yeare there appeares to be due to the Towne 9 0 3 ob his Sallory of x li and other disbursments being allowed. It is therefore ordered that the present Chamberlaine doe demand the said 9 0 3 ob. And in case the said Mr Wing doe refuse or neglect to pay the same at or upon Candlemas day next that then the said Mr Wing shall be forthwith sued at the publicke charge of this Corporacion for the 9 0 3 ob aforesaid.

Thomas Chrichloe dismissed the Court at his request. John Smyth elected in his place.
Whereas Thomas Chrichloe of the second Company haveing acquainted Mr Alderman and some other of his freinds that he had obteyned a Lycence to practice Phisicke and could not possibly attend the service of this Court and Corporacon as he ought to doe And therefore humbly desired Mr Alderman and his Freinds to acquainte this Court therewith which being this day related this Court doth approve of the said reasons and doth hereby dismisse the said Thomas Chrichloe from the place of 2d xij according to his desire. Whereupon John Smyth is chosen one of the 2d xij in his place and stead and did at this Court take the Oathes of Allegiance and Supremacey and the Oath and subscribe the Declaracon Received the Sacrament according to the Act of Parlyament made for the well governing and Regulating of Corporacions and also the Oath of 2d xij man according to Ancient Custome.

Att this Court William Kirke is Chosen Comoner Churchwarden in the Roome of John Smyth lately chosen of the second Company.

In the Kallendar
Richard Hickson
Thomas Rowlett
George Read

[fo. 666v] **Fourth Court of Thomas Shorte, 8 April 1680**

Sir Robert Markham dismissed.
Whereas upon the Reading of Robert Markhams letter wherein he desired to be dismissed from the first Company It is by this Court consented thereunto. And the said Sir Robert Markham is hereby dismissed from the said first Company accordingly.

John Broughton discharged from Hather tolles.
Att this Court John Broughton is discharged from gathering of the Tolles of all such goods as passeth by and through Highdike and Londonthorpe Feild and Mr Alderman is desired to Lett them to some other person.

Chamberlaine to receive the tolles.
Att this Court it is ordered by an Unanimous consent and agreement of the same That the Chamberlaines of this Corporacon shall take and receive all and all manner of Tolles to become due to the said Towne for the future, for and towards the payments of the debts of this Corporacon.

Mr Alderman to have x li as a Gratuitie.
Att this Court it is ordered that Mr Thomas Shorte the present Alderman shall have as a gratuity from the Corporacion the sume of Tenn pounds for his service to the Corporacon he being a Senior Brother and haveing been formerly Alderman. Notwithstanding the order made in the time of Mr Lenton late Alderman that noe gentleman that is elected Alderman upon the decease of any preceeding Alderman that might happen to dye before the expiracon of his yeare should have any Sallory, but that the Alderman that made the Feast should be paid the Sallory: provided that this be noe president For the Future nor any impeachment to the said recited order But that the same order shall stand in force for the time to come.

None but the Eldest Sonn to be free.
Itt was at this Court put to the Vote whether all the sonnes of a freeman or onely the eldest son of a Freeman of this Corporacion be borne free, and it was Voted in the negative that none but the elder Son is borne free but if the eldest sonn dye in the life of his father then his next Brother in seniority may claime his freedome.

Mr Taylors Account for tolles.
Mr Taylors Accounts for Tolles For February 1679
his Receipts 01 14 10
His disbursments 00 06 08
Remaines to the Towne 01 08 02
which he payes in open Court and is discharged.

[fo. 667Ar] **Fifth Court of Thomas Shorte, 21 May 1680**

None but the Eldest Sonn of a Freeman to be free.
Whereas at the last Court held by Mr Alderman that now is it being put to the Vote whether the eldest son of a Freeman of this Corporacion should onely have his freedome or all the sonnes of a Freeman to be in the same Capacity for their freedomes which Vote was carried by the Majority of the said Court that none but the eldest son of a Freeman should be admitted to his freedome and the Rest excluded and being this day putt to the Vote againe it was by the majority of the said Court agreed upon that the said order stand Ratefyed and confirmed to all intents and purposes whatsoever. Provided neverthelesse that if the eldest sonn should happen to dye the second should be capable of his freedome and soe the Rest of the Children of Freemen as they should be in seniority of Age, after the death of their eldest Brother and not otherwise.

Mr Aldermans Account for tolles.
Mr Aldermans Account for Tolle in January last. his Receipts 01 10 03
his Disbursments 01 05 10
Remaines due to the Towne 00 04 05
which he payes in open Court and is discharged.

Mr Calcraft the like.
Mr Robert Calcrafts account for Tolle in March last. his Receipts 13 07 05
his Disbursments 13 04 08
Remaines to the Towne 00 02 09
which he payes in open Court and is discharged.

Robert Langley, John Pape made free.
Att this Court came Robert Langley and John Pape and desired to be admitted free Burgesses of this Corporacion, and that they would willingly give their Tenn pounds apeice for the same at whose request this Court doth Condiscend whereupon they laid downe their Tenn pound apiece which is taken for the use of this Corporacion and they each of them take the Oathes of Freemen and payes their Fees to Clarke and Serjeants according to Ancient Custome and at the same time tooke the severall Oathes of Supremacey and Allegiance and the Oath and subscribed the Declaracion mencioned in the Act of parlyament made for the well governing and Regulating of Corporacions. Att this Court alsoe was James Grocock Son of William Grococke made free of this

Towne and Burrough and hath accordingly taken the Oaths of a freeman and paid his fees to Clarke and Serjeants according to Ancient Custome.

[fo. 667Av] Sixth Court of Thomas Shorte, 4 June 1680

Mr Winge to be sued for the money in his handes.
Att this Court it is ordered by the Major part of the same that order be given to Mr William Hodgkinson to send for a Writt and to prosecute suite against Mr John Wing for the moneys that are in his handes due to the Corporacion at the publicke Charge of the said Corporacion according to the order made in the third Court of Mr Alderman that now is.

William Lenton to be paid by the Chamberlaine.
Att this Court it is ordered that the Forty shillinges which is due to William Lenton for Beare drunck at the Elleccion of Mr Thomas Shorte now Alderman be paid on to him by Mr Grant Chamberlaine.

Mr Ireland nominated Alderman.
For the more peaceable and quiet proceedings at the Elleccion of the next Succeding Alderman it is at this Court agreed upon that upon the next Eleccon day Mr Edward Paulett be sent downe into the Church to Mr Richard Holley and Mr Thomas Ireland to make three Comburgesses there; out of which three Comburgesses in the Church it is likewise agreed that Mr Thomas Ireland be brought upon the Cusheon or place of Eleccion to Mr Robert Calcraft and Mr Richard Calcraft to make three Comburgesses there; Out of which three Comburgesses upon the Cusheon or place of Eleccion with a free and Unanimous Consent of this Court Mr Thomas Ireland is nominated Alderman for the ensueing yeare.

[fo. 667Br] Seventh Court of Thomas Shorte 11 June 1680

Mr Hotchkin chosen of the first Company.
Att this Court Mr Anthony Hotchkin is Chosen of the first Twelve in the Roome of Sir Robert Markham Barronet dismissed and did take the Oathes of First Twelve and Justice of peace according to Ancient Custome and the Oathes of Allegiance and Supremacey and the Oath and subscribed to the Declaracon and received the sacrament according to the late Act of parlyament made for the well governing and Regulateing of Corporacions.

William Bristow to be paid.
Att this Court Symon Grant Chamberlaine is ordered to pay to William Bristow 3 0 0 for two yeares worke for the repaireing of the Conduite, according to the Agreement

made with the said William Bristow, and the said summe is ordered to be putt in the Constables Assessment, and to be repaid unto the Chamberlaine.

Edward Watson Colebuyer.
Att this Court Edward Watson is chosen Colebuyer for the ensueing yeare, but the Cole Byer for the last yeare, hath not yet given up his Accounts.

John Marshall made free.
Att this Court came John Marshall and desired to be admitted a free Burgesse of this Corporacon, and that he would willingly give Tenn pounds for the same at whose request this Court doth Consent. Whereupon he layeth downe his Ten pounds which is taken for the Use of this Corporacion and taketh the Oath of Freeman and payes his Fees to Clarke and Serjeants according to Ancient Custome and also the Oathes of Allegiance and Supremacey and the Oath and subscribed the Declaracon menconed in the late Act of parlyament made for the well governing and Regulating of Corporacions.

[fo. 667Bv] **Eighth Court of Thomas Shorte 5 August 1680**

Widdow Wilson hath this Court paid 5li as a Fine for her lease of her house in Castlegate and this Court doth promise that her lease shall be sealed att the next opening of the Hutch.

Att this Court it is ordered that Mr Grant doe pay to Mr Critchloe 4li 8s 5d for moneys disbursed as Chamberlaine and Collector for Schoole rentes in the yeares 1676 and 1677.

Ordered An Assesment of 30 li be made for the repaires of the Markett place pumpe Markett place Constables being appointed Assessors and Collectors thereof.

Ninth Court of Thomas Shorte 25 August 1680

Mr Robert Parkins Chosen Towne Clarke.
Att this Court by a free and unanimous consent of the same Mr Robert Parkins is chosen Towne Clarke for this Borrough in the Roome and stead of Mr William Hodgkinson deceased and did at the same time take the Oath of Towne Clarke and the oathes of Allegiance and Supremacy and subscribed to the declaration according to Act of Parlyament made in the 13th yeare of his Majesties Raigne for the regulation of Corporations haveing taken the Sacrament within one yeare before.

John Gibson and William Cole to account for the last yeare.

An Assessment to be made for 22li 00 00.

[fo. 668r] **Eleventh Court of Thomas Shorte 14 October 1680**
[No Tenth Court is recorded]

Ordered that Mr Richard Hickson doe appeare on Thursday next being the Accompte day to show cause why he attendeth not the Court and accept his place in the second Twelve according to his election.

Memorandum Mr Robinson and William Kirke are to account for five pounds due to the Towne for Malt money.

Mr John Smith and Thomas Charles to account for 40 s and vi d for Malt.

William Kirke to account for 2 li 12s 0 for Malt sold.

paid to Mr Robinson 50 s in part of 3 li 3s 0 ob The Towne oweth him, and hath discharged Thomas Hodgsons debt.

[fo. 668v]

Att An Assembly holden by Mr Thomas Short gentleman Alderman and the Comburgesses and Burgesses of Grantham aforesaid in Corpus Christi Quire, within the Prebendary there On fryday next after St Lukes day being 22 October 1680.

Election
First did sitt downe upon the Cushion or place of Election the said Mr Thomas Short in Corpus Christi Quire within the Prebendary Church there
Next to him did sitt upon the Cusheon or place of Election two Comburgesses, videlicet Mr Robert Calcraft and Mr Richard Calcraft.
Then was sent downe into the Church by an Unanimous Voate and Consent of this Assembly Mr Thomas Ireland to Mr Richard Holley and Mr John Coddington, Then was there three Comburges in the Church videlicet Mr Richard Holley, Mr John Coddington and Mr Thomas Ireland
Out off [*sic*] which three Comburges in the Church was chosen to come upp and sitt uppon the Cusheon or place of Election on other Comburges videlicet Mr Thomas Ireland:
Then was there three Comburges uppon the Cushion or place of Election, videlicet Mr Robert Calcraft, Mr Richard Calcraft and Mr Thomas Ireland.
Out off [*sic*] which three Comburgesses uppon the Cusheon or place of Election videlicet Mr Robert Calcraft, Mr Richard Calcraft and Mr Thomas Ireland One is to be chosen Alderman for the ensueing yeare.

And thereuppon by the Unanimous Consent and Vote of this Assembly Mr Thomas Ireland is chosen and elected Alderman For the next ensueing yeare.

Whereuppon the said Mr Thomas Short doth discharge himselfe from the said place.

THE HALL BOOK OF GRANTHAM 1680–1681

[fo. 669r] **First Court of Thomas Ireland, 29 October 1680**

Mr Thomas Ireland Alderman
Comburgess

Mr Thomas Short
Mr Michael Taylor
Mr Robert Calcroft
Mr Richard Calcroft
Mr Richard Holley
Mr John Coddington
Mr John Wing

Mr Robert Cole
Mr Thomas Matkine
Mr Edward Pawlett
Mr Christopher Tompson
Mr Anthony Hotchine

Second twelve
Simon Graunt
John Smith
Edward Leivesly
John Robinson
Nicholas Becke
Thomas Fishar
Edward Bristow

William Hascard
Richard Seagrave

Coroner	Mr Thomas Short	Prizers of	William Newton
Escheator	Mr Robert Calcroft	Corne	Henry Johnson
Collectors of the	Mr Edward Pawlett	Leather	Richard Bristow
School Rents	John Goodwine	Sealers	Thomas Marshall
Cheife	Mr Simon Grant		Thomas Baly
Constables	Mr John Smith		Thomas Wray
Church	Richard Seagrave	Towne	
Wardens	John Stevens	Clarke	Robert Parkins
Chamberlines	Mr Nicholas Becke	Serjeante	Thomas Calcroft
	John Gibson	Gaylor	Bryan Godly
Keybearers	Mr Alderman	Church	
	Mr Richard Becke	Clarke	Humphrey Turner
	Mr Seagrave	Bellman	Ralph Osborne

[fo. 669v]

The Names of the Commoners

Market Place	Thomas Short	
	Henry Hubbard	Swinegate
	William Cole	Richard Dawson
	Richard Handly	James Bristow
	John Gibson	
	Nathaniel Rookeby	
	John Stevenson	
	John Goodwin	
Westgate	Anthony Kirke	Castlegate
	William Burbidge	John Pape
	Thomas Baly	Thomas Baly Felmonger
	John Newcome	
	Thomas Kenyon	
High Streete	William Bristow	
	Richard Owen	
	George Read	
	Thomas Rowley	
	Christopher Hanson	
Walkergate	Henry Atkinson	
	Charles Wetherill	
	Robert Thompson	
	Thomas Rawlinson	

Ordered for Mr Short and others to take the Official accompts.
At this Court was delivered by Mr Short to Mr Ireland now Alderman the severall peices of plate as followeth.

The Horse plate cupp	Mr Horsemans Boll
Thomas Archers Boll	Mr Greenwoods Cann
Mr Wheatlyes Cann	Mr Harringtons Cann
Mr Kirkbys Boll	Two Tunns
Mr Greenwoods 13 Spoons	One Salt and Cover
Mr Woodruffs Cann	Mr Wrights peice of plate
Mr Storers Cupp	Mr Horsemans wine Boll

At this Court it was ordered that Mr Thomas Short, Mr Tayler, Mr Grant, Mr Smith, Mr Fisher Mr Robinson, Mr Beck, Mr Bristow, John Stevenson, John Gibson are to take the Constables bills and other Accompts uppon Wednesday att 9 of the clocke

At this Court Mr Grant made an agreement with William Fearon for the conveyinge and releiveing of all passengers at the rate of xiij li 13s 8d per Annum and by the consent of this Court gave him Six pence in earnest

[fo. 670r] **Second Court of Thomas Ireland 14 January 1680/1**

Att this Court it is ordered that Edward Watson, Thomas Short and William Burbidge doe compleate their accompts uppon the Constables bills within one fortnight next &c and in the interim to collect and distreine for the Arreares *sub pena* xxs a man.

~~Mr Coverly Thomas Quinningborough & William Knight restored~~. [*Marginal note*]
Att this Court it is also ordered that Mr Smith Churchwarden give upp his Accompts uppon Wednesday come fortnight: Mr Robert Cole, Mr Pawlett, Mr Fisher, Mr Becke, Mr Segrave, Mr Stevens appointed to take the Accompts.

Mr Coverly, Thomas Quinningborow and William Knight restored.
Att this Court Mr Henry Coverly desiring to be restored to his place in the Second Twelve seate and Thomas Quinningborough and William Knight to be restored to their places as Comoners by the Consent of this Court were admitted and took the same, and the severall Oathes according to the Act of Parlyament, and Subscribed the Covenant etc.

Mr Nall and Francis Broome made free.
Att this Court came Marke Nall Gentleman and desired to bee admitted a free Burgesse of this Burrow, And willingly tendred in Courte the summe of Tenne pounds for his freedome which the Court taking into Consideration the same summe was payd into the hands of Mr Alderman in the absence of the Chamberlaine, and by the consent of this Court he was thereunto admitted and sworne a free-man and paid the accustomed fees to the Box and Officers, & in Courte, And alsoe tooke the severall Oaths appointed by the Act for regulateing Corporations, and subscribed the Covenant, &c.

Also Francis Broome sonne of Andrew Broome was sworne a free Burgesse of this Burrow and paid the fees in Court &c and tooke the same oathes and subscribed the Covenant &c.

[fo. 670v]

Att an Assembly holden at the Gild Hall in Grantham by Thomas Ireland Gentleman Alderman of the Towne of Grantham 20 April 1681.

Tolls to be lett.
Att this Assembly it was taken into Consideracion and agreed uppon that that [*sic*] the severall Tolls and persons that doe hire or are imployed to gather the same be so moved to appeare at the next Courte to give an Accompt of theire proceedings therein.

Redd Lyon signe.
Also at this Meeting it is agreed and concluded that the Redd Lyon the Signe and house be inquired after & that care bee taken for the speedy repaires of the said same And to inquire after the defaults of the same House.

Mr Calverly, Edward Watson, Thomas Short Collectors and Churchwardens.
Also it is Agreed that the severall Constables and other officers which are behind in there Accompts, to bee so moved to appeare and give upp the same.

The constables are Ordered to bring into the Courte the Names of such persons come into the Towne to Inhabite without licence And that care bee taken to putt the lawes and orders of this Court in Execution.

That all such Tennants as doe continue in the Towne Houses and doe not pay there rents be inquired after and care therein taken for the recovery of all Arrerages.

And that all persons Intrudeing to trayd or sett upp shopp upon Markett or other dayes within this Corporacion bee from hence removed if they cannot make it appeare they have a legall right and Authority soe to doe being Strangers and not free men of this Corporation.

[fo. 671r] **Third Court of Thomas Ireland, 23 April 1681**

Ordered at this Court the Chamberlaine demaunds of Mr John Wing the sume of Nyne pounds three pence halfe penny which he oweth to the Towne. And that the order made in the third Courtre [sic] of Mr Thomas Short late Alderman concerning the same be putt in execucion.

Ordered that a Sessment for 30 li be made for the dischargeing the churchwardens Disbursements for two yeares past.

Ordered that an Assessment for xxxs bee made for the repaires of the Markett Street Pumpe and the Constables of the same Streete gather the same.

George Bellamy sworne a Freeman.
Att this Court George Bellamy desired to bee admitted a Freeman of this ~~Burrough~~ Corporacion, And by the Consent of this B [sic] Courte he was admitted to his Freedome payd the Accustomary Fees into Courte and was sworne a freeman of the same Burrough.

[fo. 671v] **Fourth Court of Thomas Ireland, 2 September 1681**

Mr Calverlyes Accompts.
Att this Courte Mr Calverleys Accompts for the Milles was read and Allowed of. And he payd into the Chamberlines Hands three pounds Five pence remaineing due to the Towne uppon the same Accompt.

Mr Smiths Accompts.
Att this Courte Mr Smith late Churchwarden brought his Accompts into Courte which read and allowed and there remains due to the said Mr Smith from the Towne Eleaven pounds One Shilling and five pence besides Forty Shillings to bee payd by Sir William Ellis in all xiij li 01s 05d.

Ordered att this Courte Mr Alderman, Mr Taylor, Mr Cole, Mr Pawlett, Mr Leivesly, Mr Hascard, Mr Fishar, Edward Watson, William Cole, Nathaniel Rookby and Henry Hubbard doe take the Accompts of Mr Richard Calcroft, Mr Matkine for the Milles at the houre of One of the clock in the afternoone on Munday next.

Richard Hickson dismissed of the Courte.
Att this Courte Richard Hickson, being formerly chosen a Second twelve man, was called to take his place in Court but refuseing to take the same place in Courte he tendred Five poundes to the Courte and desired the Courte wold bee pleased to accept the same, which the Courte taking into Consideracion did accept of the same sume off Five pounds and the said Richard Hickson by the consent of this Courte was dismissed of this Courte.

Edward Watson chosen out of Second twelve.
Att this Courte Edward Watson was elected and Chozen to the place of a Second Twelve man and was sworne, who also tooke the several Oathes directed by severall Acts of Parliment subscribed and renounced the Covenant in Open Courte, and tooke his place in Courte.

[fo. 672r]

Mr Pawlett seated into the Boddy of the Church and uppon the Cushion.
Att this Courte it was ordered by an unanimous Voate of this Courte that Mr Edward Pawlett the next Election day bee sent into the boddy of the Church to Mr Holley and Mr Coddington and that the said Mr Pawlett be voted out of the boddy of the Church to sitt uppon the Cushion in the Church.

Richard Calcroft Nomination for Alderman.
Att this Courte by a free and unanimous Voate of this Courte Mr Richard Calcroft was Nominated Alderman for the succeeding yeare.

Thomas Rowly Chosen to the place of Second Twelve.
Att this Courte Thomas Rowley was elected a second Twelveman and desired the favour of this Courte to have liberty untill the next Courte to consider thereof and then to returne his Answer to the Courte.

Att this Courte Mr Richard Calcroft passed his Accompts for the Milles and Tolles which are as followeth:

	li	s	d
Tolles for the Mills			
Received	37	15	06
Disbursede	39	12	11
Remaines to him	01	17	06
Tolles for the Towne			
Received	30	10	07
Payed	30	16	11
Received to the Towne	00	03	07
Mr Pools Accompts			
Received	38	12	08
Payed	49	12	01
Received to him	09	07	00
Mr Matkins Accompts for the Mills			
Received	39	06	11 ob
payd	40	17	02
Received due to him	01	10	02

[fo. 672v] **Fifth Court of Mr Thomas Ireland, 30 September 1681**

Att this Court is Ordered that Fifty Pounds bee Forthwith taken upp to serve the present Occasions of this Corporacion. And that Mr Robert Calcroft, William Hascard, Edward Watson, John Newcome Charles Wetherill, and Richard Dawson become security for the same. And that they shall have the Towne Seale for there Indemnificacion.

[Amos] Sherriffe Agreed with Mr Alderman for the High Dike Tools [*sic*] under the yearly rent two poundes Thirteen shillings and foure pence.

Att the Accompt day holden the xxth of October 1681

Mr Simon Graunt as Chamberlaine passed his Accompts for his yeare past
And there remaines due to him 8 li 17s 2d.

Mr Robert Calcroft as Escheator passed his Accompts and payd downe in full discharge thereof 0 li 9s 3d.

[fo. 673r]

Att an Assembly there holden by Mr Thomas Ireland Alderman of the same Burrough, and the Comburgesses and Burgesses of Grantham aforesaid 21 October 1681

First did sitt downe uppon the Cushion or Place of Election Mr Thomas Ireland Alderman in the Prebendary Church of Grantham aforesaid.
Next to him did come uppon the Cushion two Comburgesses Mr Robert Calcroft and Mr Richard Calcroft.
Then was sent down by the Consent and Voate of this Assembly in to the boddy of the Church to Mr Richard Holley and Mr John Coddington. One other Comburgess (videlicet) Mr John Wing:–
Out of which three Comburgesses in the Church, was one chozen to sitt uppon the Cushion or place of Election be (videlicet), Mr Richard Holley.
Then was there three Comburgesses uppon the Cushion or place of Election Out of which three one is to bee chozen Alderman for the yeare next Ensueing.
And thereuppon by the unanimous Voate of this Assembly Mr Richard Calcroft is chozen Alderman for the yeare enseuing.

Whereuppon the said Mr Thomas Ireland is discharged from his place, And Mr Richard Calcroft sworne Alderman in his stead according to Auncient Custome and tooke all Oaths according to the directions of the Statutes.

And soe this Assembly breakes upp.

[fo. 673v] [Blank page]

THE HALL BOOK OF GRANTHAM 1681–1682

[fo. 674Ar] **First Court of Richard Calcroft, 28 October 1681**

Mr Richard Calcroft Alderman
First xij
Mr Thomas Short
Mr Michael Taylor
Mr Robert Calcroft
Mr Richard Holley
Mr John Coddington
Mr John Wing
Mr Robert Cole
Mr Thomas Matkine
Mr Thomas Ireland
Mr Edward Pawlett
Mr Christopher Tompson
Mr Anthony Hotchkine

Second xij
William Hascard
Edward Watson
Henry Calverly
Edward Leivesly
Thomas Fishar
John Rollinson
Nicholas Becke
Edward Bristow
Simon Grant
Richard Seagrave
John Smith

Coroner	Mr Thomas Ireland	Corn Prizers	William Newton
Escheator	Mr Richard Holley		Henry Johnson
Collectors	Mr Thompson	Markett Sayers	Thomas Hatfeild
Schoole [*sic*]	William Cole		William Scott
Cheife	Mr William Hascard	Towne Clarke	Roberte Parkins
Constables	Mr Edward Watson	Serjeant	Thomas Calcroft
Church	Richard Seagrave	Gaoler	Bryan Godley
Wardens	John Stevens	Church Clerk &	Humphrey Turner
Chamberlains	John Smith	Bellman	Ralph Osborne
	John Goodwine		
Sealers	Mr Thomas Baly		
Leather	George Wray		
	John Weaver		
	Thomas Hutchine		

[fo. 674Av]

Comoners
Markett Place
Henry Hubbard

Key bearers
Mr Alderman

Matthew Dixon
Richard Handly
William Cole
John Gibson
John Stevens
Nathaniel Rookby
John Goodwin

High streete
William Bristow
Charles Wetherill
Richard Owen
George Read
William Knight

Westgate
Henry Atkinson
John Pape
Anthony Kirke
William Burbidg
Thomas Baly
John Newcome
Thomas Kenyon

Walkergate
James Bristow
Thomas Rawlinson

Swinegate
John Marshall
Henry Broome
Thomas Quiningborow

Castlegate
Robert Langly
Thomas Leivesly

John Smith
Richard Seagrave

Callender
John Gibson
George Read
William Cole

Towne Plate delivered upp to the Present Alderman
The Horse Plate Cupp
Mr Archers Boll
Mr Wheatlys Cann
Mr Horsemans Boll
Mr Greenwoods Cann
Mr Battys Beaker
Thomas Harrington Esq his Silver Cann
Two Silver Tunns
Kirkbys Boll
Mr Greenwood xiij Spoones
One Salt and Cover
Mr Woodrooffs Cann
Mr Wright Plate
Mr Storers Cupp
Mr Horseman Wine Boll

Ordered that the Constables
doe complete there Accompts
on Wednesday next at two of
the Clocke in the afternoone
Mr Alderman, Mr Roberte Calcroft,
Mr Holly, Mr Ireland, William
Hascard, Edward Watson, John
Gibson, William Cole and Thomas Kenyon
appointed to take the same.

[fo. 674Br] **Second Court of Richard Calcroft, 16 December 1681**

The Windmill to be bought.
Att this Courte it was moved that it would be a very convenient for the Corporacion to purchase the Wind Mill Standing uppon Gunwarby Hill for the more easy grindings of all Graine and Corne within the Towne, And uppon Consideracion thereof it is Agreed

by the Courte that the same be bought, And Mr Robert Cole, Mr Edward Pawlett, Mr Christopher Tompson and Thomas Fishar Appointed to treate about the same with the Owners thereof: And to purchase the same for the use of the Corporacion, and there uppon to pay or give security for the same accordingly.

The Chamberlaine appointed to call for & receive Mr Stacys rent for his House & Signe, and the rent in Arreares from the Tanners.

Denton Toll Lett.
Denton Toll at this Courte Mr Alderman did lett to John Broughton for the yearely rent of xiijs & 4d untill the next Accompt day; And Henry Atkinson in open Courte became Ingaiged for the payment of the rent.

John Berry, James Fearon, George Hanson, Richard North, Robert Orson, Edward Scarborow & Isaack Hipworth made Free.
At this Courte John Berry, James Fearon, George Hanson, Richard North, Robert Orson, Edward Scarborow & Isaack Hipworth desired to be admitted Free men of this Burrough which the Courte Condiscended unto, and every One of them were admitted thereunto, Did take the severall Oathes of Freemen of this Corporacion in Open Courte, and payd the Fees from them respectively due & accustomed to be pay [*sic*] for the same.

Mr Pawlett passed his Accompt for the Rents of the Schoole this yeare – remaines to him 15s.

John Goodwin alsoe past his Accompt for the same & there remaines to him due 12s 2d.

[fo. 674Bv] Third Court of Mr Richard Calcroft, 20 January 1681/2

Gunwarby Mill bought for the use of the Towne.
Att this Courte Mr Cole and Mr Pawlett did acquaint the Courte that in persuance of a former Order of this Courte they have bought the Windmill for the Sume of Thirty poundes, which this Courte did well approve off, and confirmed the same And the said Mr Cole and Mr Pawlett are further desired to Inquire if the Title there of bee good: and to purchase the peece of ground whereuppon it now standeth.

Thomas Rowley Sworne on the Second xij.
Att this Corte Thomas Rowley was swore One of the Second Twelve and did take his place in Courte and the severall Oathes appointed for that purpose.

Edward Greewill made Free.
Att this Courte Edward Greewill was sworne a Freeman off this Corporation and payd downe in Courte x li, which he humbly requesting the Courte wold bee pleased to take into consideracion: The Courte was pleased to voate him Five pounds there of to be

repayed by the Chamberlaine, which was payd accordingly: He tooke all the Oathes & renounced the Covenante.

Edward Coddington made Free.
Att this Courte Edward Coddington sonne of Mr Edward Coddington, was admitted a freeman of this Corporacion tooke the severall Oathes & renounced the Covenant.

[fo. 675r] **Fourth Court of Mr Richard Calcroft, 7 April 1682**

Inmates to bee distreined.
Att this Courte Courte [sic] it is Ordered that diligent Inquiry bee made after all Sort off Inmates that have Intruded into this towne and of all all [sic] such person as have received them into there houses or habitations without leave first had and obteyned from this Courte, And that the orders of this Courte be putt in Execution and warrentts be Issued forth against all such Offenders acording to the antient and Lawdable Orders of this Courte.

John Gibson chosen on the Second xij.
Att this Courte John Gibson was elected One off the second twelve, took his Oath belonging to the same place, with the Oath off Allegiance and Supremacy & renownced the Covenant, and took his place in Courte.

Mr Edward Leivesly chosen on the first twelve.
At this Courte Mr Edward Leivesly was Elected One of the Comburges of this Corporation by an Unanimous Consent of this Courte and hath taken the Oath belonging to the same Office together with the severall Oathes appointed by the Stat, in such case provided did subscribe & renounce the Covenant.

[fo. 675v] **Fifth Court of Mr Richard Calcroft, 16 June 1682**

Att this Courte William Fearin was chosen a Petit Constable to serve in this Corporacion for the Remainder of this yeare and was sworne &c.

Christopher Smith made Free.
Christopher Smith came into this Courte, and desired the Court wold bee pleased to admitt him to his Freedome, He being the eldest sonne of Hugh Smith, which the Courte did thinke Fit and admitted him a freeburges of this Corporacion, he payd his fees & jur [sworn].

John Martines made Free
Alsoe att this Courte came John Martines being a forrainer, and craved the favour of this Courte to be admitted a Free man of this Corporacion; which the Courte takeing into

Consideration he tendring Tenne pounds in Courte, and humbly craveing the favour of this Courte to take his Condicion into there favourable Consideracion, by an unanimous Voate of this Courte he was voated a Freeman and Five pounds thereof repayd him backe againe payd his fees & jur [sworn].

Att this Courte Mr Robert Coles was by an unanimous Consent Voated to bee sent downe into the Church the next Election day to Mr John Wing and Mr John Coddington there.

Att this Courte alsoe it was Voated by an unanimous Consent, that Mr John Coddington now remaineing in the boddy of the Churche be voated to come upp and sitt uppon the cushion at the next Election Day of an Alderman for this Corporacion.

[fo. 676r]

Mr Hawley nominated Alderman.
Att this Courte it is by an Unanimous Voate and Consent for the more Regular & peaceable proceedinge to the next election of an Alderman for this Towne and Burrough Agreed uppon, And by the same Courte Mr Richard Hawley One of the Comburgesses of this Burrow is freely by an unanimous Consent of this Courte Nominated Alderman for this Towne & Burrough for the year next Ensueing. [*following line crossed through*]

Sixth Court of Richard Calcroft, 14 July 1682

Thomas Simpson made free.
Att this Courte Thomas Simpson Gentleman came and desired to be Admitted a freeman of this Corporacion which the Courte takeing into Consideracion uppon his tendring downe tenne pounds in Courte was admitted thereunto & sworne.

John Withey made free.
Alsoe John Withey eldest sonne of Mathew Withey was admitted to his Freedome, payd the accustomed fees and sworne &c.

Richard Wiles freedom denied.
Att this Courte Richard Wyles A Stranger and forrainer came into Courte and craved he might be admitted a free man of this Burrough, uppon payment of Tenne poundes for the same, But the Courte takeing it into there [*sic*] serious Consideracions, by an Unanimous Voate of this Courte his Tenne poundes was rejected, and his Freedom clearly by the Consent of the Courte denyed.

[fo. 676v] [Blank page]

[fol 677r] **Sixth [sic] [*more correctly* Seventh] Court of Richard Calcroft, 22 September 1682**

Warrants against Inmates.
Att this Courte by an Unanimous Consent of the said Courte Itt was ordered that Warrants should be made out against all Inmates that have Intruded into this Corporation and against all Those that receive them into their habitations contrary to the Ancient Customs of this Towne and the approved Orders and By Laws of this Courte.

horse Chirch yard lett to William Bilton xs per Annum.
Att this Courte the horse Church yard was letto [*sic*] William Bilton at the rent of xs a yeare he paid downe x s for the first year at the time of his entry and xs shillings per annum for aleven [*sic*] years following and payd one shilling earnest.

horse to be bought for the wind mill.
This Courte doth request Mr Cole and Mr Pawlett to buy an horse and provide a miller fit for to do the service and worke for the wind mill for the use of this Corperation.

Mr William Cole chozen [of] the second twelve.
Ordered for that William Cole being Chozen one of the Second Twelve and hath been sent for severall times to the Courte and not give in any attendance or takeing the place upon him, It is therefore ordered that the said William Cole have notice to appear at the next Courte to be holden for this Burrough and to Accept his said place of second Twelve or give other Satisfaction to the Courte or in Failer thereof the penalty for such his Contempt and refusall be Leveyed uppon his Goods and Chattells according to the Ancient Customs and orders of this Courte.

[fo. 677v] [Blank page]

[fo. 678r]

At an assembly holden by Mr Richard Calcroft Alderman and the Comburgesses and Burgesses of Grantham aforesaid 20 October beeing the Friday after Saint Lukes day 1682

First did sit downe upon the Cushion or place Election Mr Richard Calcroft Alderman in the prebendary Church of Grantham aforesaid
next to him did sit down upon the Cushion or place of Election two Comburgesses Mr Richard Hawley and Mr Robert Calcroft
Then was sent downe into the Church by an Unanimous Vote of this Assembly Mr Roberte Cole to Mr John Coddington and Mr John Wing to make up three Comburgesses in the Church

Out of which three Comburgesses was on [*sic*] Chosen to come up and sit upon the Cushion or place of Election (Vizt) Mr John Coddington

Then was there three Comburgesses upon the cushion or place of Election

[*inserted here in another hand*] Mr Hawley, Mr Robert Calcroft, Mr John Coddington

Out of which three one of them is to be chosen Alderman for the year ensueing

And thereupon by the Unanimous Voat of this Assembly Mr Richard Holley is chosen Alderman for the year ensueing

Whereupon the said Mr Richard Calcroft is discharged from his office of Alderman & the said Mr. Richard Holley sworne Alderman in his stead for this Borough of Grantham according to Ancient Customs

And so this Assembly breake upp.

[fo. 678v] [Blank page]

THE HALL BOOK OF GRANTHAM 1682–1683

[fo. 679r] **First Court of Richard Hawley, 27 October 1682**

Mr Richard Hawley Alderman
Mr Michaell Taylor   Nicholas Becke
Mr Robert Calcroft   Thomas Rowley
Mr Richard Calcroft   Thomas Fishar
Mr John Coddington   John Robinson
Mr John Winge   Edward Bristow
Mr Robert Cole   Symon Grant
Mr Thomas Matkine   William Haskard
Mr Thomas Ireland   Richard Segrave
Mr Edward Pawlett   John Smith
Mr Christopher Tompson   Edward Watson
Mr Edward Leivesly   John Gibson
Mr Anthony Hotckine   William Cole

Names of the Officers

Coroner	Mr Richard Calcroft	Swinegate	Robert Langley
Escheator	Mr John Coddington	Constables	Thomas Leivesley
Collectors	Mr Anthony Hotchkine	Walkergate	Robert Moore
for Schoole	John Newcombe	Constables	William Fearon
Church	Thomas Rowley	Castlegate	Edward Greenwood
Wardens	William Burbidge	Constables	William Fearon Junior
Chamberlains	Edward Watson	Leather	Mr Baly
	Thomas Short	Sealers	John Rawlinson
Cheife	Mr Nicholas Becke	Leather	George Wray
Constables	Mr Thomas Rowley	Sealers	Thomas Kenyon
Market place	Matthew Dixon	Corne	William Newton
Constables	John Pape	prisors	Henry Johnson
High Street	Charles Wetherill	Markett	Thomas Hatfield
Constables	Henry Atkinson	Sayors	William Scott
Westgate	Thomas Hutchine	Towne	Mr Robert Parkins
Constables	John Weaver	Clarke	

[fo. 679v]

Serjant &	Thomas Calcroft	At this Court William Cole
Gaoler	Thomas Quiningborew	being Chosen to serve this
Church Clerk	Humphrey Turner	Corporation in the office of
& Bellman	Ralph Osbourne	a second Twelve man was
Key	Mr Alderman	Sworne in Court tooke the
Bearers	Edward Watson	Severall Oaths according to
	Thomas Rowley	Law & Custome

Commoners		
Markett	Matthew Dixon	Walkergate
place	John Pape	
	Henry Hubbard	Robert Moore
	Richard Handley	William Fearon
	John Stevens	James Bristow
	Nathaniel Rookesby	Thomas Rawlinson
	John Goodwin	
		Swinegate
High	Charles Wetherill	Robert Langley
Street	Henry Atkinson	Thomas Leivesley
	William Bristow	John Marshall
	Richard Owen	Richard Dawson
	George Read	
	William Knight	
West	Thomas Hutchin	Castlegate
gate	John Weaver	
	Anthony Kerke	Edward Greenwood
	William Burbidge	William Fearon Junior
	Thomas Bally Tanner	
	John Newcombe	
	Thomas Kenyon	
	Thomas Baly Felmonger	

[fo. 680r] **Second Court of Richard Hawley, 17 November 1682**

At this Courte Wednesday next is appointed to take the Accompts off Coal byers Churchwardens & Chamberlains att two off the clock in the afternoon Mr Alderman, Mr Taylor, Mr Richard Calcroft, Mr Pawly, Mr Fisher, Mr Grant, Mr Smith, William Burbidge, Robert Langley, Thomas Hutchine are appointed to take the same accompts.

John Gasshe made free.
At this Courte John Gasshe came and desired to be admitted a Freeman off this

Corporation which the Courte takeing into Consideration upon his tendring downe tenn pounds in Court was admitted thereunto & sworne.

John Newcombe, William Barrett, Thomas Hatfield, James Hand made Free.
Allso att this Courte John Newcombe, William Barrett, James Hand & Thomas Hatfield Junior were admitted to their freedome payd their accostomed fees to Clarke & Serjeant & were sworne.

William Fearon junior sworne Constable.
Allso at this [sic] William Fearon the younger being chosen to serve this Corporation in the office off a petty Constable was sworne in Courte according to Law.

[fo. 680v] Third Court of Richard Hawly, 1 December 1682

Joseph Woods made free.
Att this Courte Joseph Woods came & desired to be admitted a Freeman off this Corporation which the Court takeing into Consideration upon his Tendring downe tenn pounds in Court was admitted thereunto & sworne.

Abraham Clarke made free.
Allso att this Courte Abraham Clarke came and desired to be admitted a Free man of this Corporation & payd downe tenn pounds into the Chamberlains hand & by an Unanimous voat off this Court five pounds was restored to him again & was sworne.

Att this Courte Mr Richard Calcroft Late Alderman deliverd up all the Towne plate to the Alderman which now is, which was received in open Courte.

[fo. 681r] Fourth Court of Richard Hawly, 2 February 1682/3

Mr Edward Leivesly chozen Collector of the Schoole rents.
Att this Court Mr Edward Leivesly one of the Comburgesses of this Burrough was sworne one of the Collectors of the Schoole house Rents.

Mr Thomas Fishar chosen of the first xij.
At this Court Mr Thomas Fishar was elected one of the Comburgesses of this Corporation by an Unanimous Consent of this Courte and hath taken the oath belonging to the same office Togeather with the severall oaths appointed by the statute in such case provided & did renounce the Covenant.

An Assessment to be made for Mr Segrave & Mr Stevens.
Att this Courte Courte [sic] it was ordered that an Assessment be made for John Stevens and Richard Segrave for xxxs for payment of their Disbursements.

Richard Wiles made Free.
Att this Court Richard Wyles [*sic*] came and craved the favor of this Court to be admitted a Freeman of this corporation which the Court takeing into consideration upon his tendring Tenn pounds in Court was admitted thereunto and sworne.

[fo. 681v] [Blank page] [no fo. 682r & v]

[fo. 683r] **Fifth Court of Richard Hawley, 8 June 1683**

The wind mill horse to be sold & another to be bought.
Att this Court it was ordered that Mr Cole and Mr Pawlett doe sell the horse belonging to the wind Mill for as much as they can, and after such Sayle to buy an other fit for the same use.

~~The Charters to be locked up in the Hutch & more Keys to be added.~~
~~Att this Courte it was ordered that the Charters before the~~ [illegible] ~~up in the hutch and two more keys added thereunto and not to be taken out of the Hutch but by~~ [illegible] ~~in the presence of such persons as are accustomed to be present at the opening thereof.~~

Mr Matkins sent downe into the church
Mr Wing to be brought upon the Cusheon
Mr Coddington nominated Alderman.
For the more peaceable and quiett proceedings at the Election of the next succeeding Alderman, it is at this Court agreed upon that upon the next Eleccion Day Mr Thomas Matkine be sent downe into the Church to Mr Robert Cole and Mr John Wing to make up three Comburgesses there out of which three Comburgesses in the Church it is like wise agreed that Mr John Wing be brought upon the Cusheon or place of Eleccion to Mr Robert Calcroft and Mr John Coddington to make up three Comburgesses there, out of which three Comburgesses upon the Cusheon or place of Eleccion Mr John Coddington is nominated Alderman for the ensueing yeare.

Mr Edward Pawlett's accompts fo[r] the Mills By the Court	Receptes	49 05 05
	Disbursments	49 02 10
	Remaines to the Towne	00 02 07
Mr Robinsons Accompts	Receiptes	46 08 05
	Disbursments	42 10 04
	Paid to the Chamberlaine	
Mr Robert Coles Accompts	Receptes	58 10 04
	Disbursments	58 06 04

	remaines	00 04 00
	2s pd to the Chamberlaine	
John Goodwine his Accompts	Receptes	58 14 00 ob
	Disbursments	41 13 01
	Remaines to the Towne	17 01 00 ob

[fo. 683v] [Blank page]

[fo. 684r] **Sixth Court of Richard Hawley, 26 July 1683**

An Assessment to be made for the Conduitt.
At this Courte it is ordered that an Assessment of Twenty pounds be made for the settinge down a new Sewsterne in the Conduitt And Mr Alderman and the two Cheife Constables are appointed Assessors and to meete on Munday at two of the Clock in the afternoone for the making of the same Assessment.

Allso an Assessment of ten shillings to be made for westgate well.

Seventh Court of Richard Hawley, 17 August 1683

George Hutchin, Amos Sherriffe, George Milner made free.
Att this Court George Hutchine, Amos Sherriffe and George Millner who have served their severall Apprentiseships within this Burrough came into Courte and desired to be admitted Freemen of this Corporacion to which request this Courte doth condiscend whereupon they pay their severall Duties to the Towne And their Fees to Clerke & Serjeantes & take the Oath of free Burgesses according to Ancient Custome.

[fo. 684v] **Eighth Court of Richard Hawley, 29 September 1683**

Att this Court the severall Constables being called to an Account concerning the Assessment for the Conduite they paid into Court the severall summs hereafter mencioned

Constables Bills
Paid by Robert Moore one of the Constables for Walkergate in parte of his Assessment	01 00 00
Paid by Matthew Dixon one of the Constables for Marketpace [*sic*] in parte of his Assessment	01 19 10
Paid by Henry Atkinson one of the Constables for Highstreet in part of his Assessment	01 00 00

Paid by Robert Langley one of the Constables
for Swinegate in part of his Assessment   01 05 00
Paid by Thomas Hutchine one of the Constables
for Westgate in part of his Assessment   03 17 00
Paid by Edward Greenwood one of the Constables
for Castlegate in part of his Assessment   01 11 06

Order for the Constables to gather upp there Assessments before the next Count Day sub pena *xxs*.
For that the Constables have beene very negligent in the gathering of the Assessment for the Conduit in their severall wards. Therefore it is ordered by this Court that the Ancient Order be confirmed, and every Constable that cleares not his Account before the next Accompt Day shall have the penalty of xxs a man leveyed upon them.

Richard Margetts made Free.
Att this Court Richard Margetts in pursuance of an Agreement made for the repaires of the Conduite was admitted to his freedome and the Chamberlaine ordered to pay 4 li residue of the sume of 14 li due upon the Agreement With the Towne & him.

[fo. 685r] **Ninth Court of Richard Hawly, 9 October 1683**

Order for Indemnicacion [sic] *of the Constables confirmed.*
Att this Courte it is ordered that the order for Indempnificacion of the Constables made in the yeare of Mr William Clarke Alderman be by this Court revived and Confirmed &c.

Thomas Hutchine & John Weaver to bee borne out in there action for false Imprizoment against Calcroft.
Allso at this Court it is ordered that Thomas Hutchine and John Weaver who were deteyned upon Suspition of fellony for no other cause but for distreyneinge of Robert Calcrofts Cow for his Assessment due for the repaires of the Conduit which he refused to pay be Indempnifyed by this Court in such Accions for the same false Imprisonment as shall by them be commenced against the said Robert Calcroft &c.

Constables of Swinegate paid in full of their Conduite Assessment 0 li 5s 3d.

The Constables of Castlegate paid in full of their Conduite Assessment 0 li 5s 7d.

[fo. 685v] [Blank page]

[fo. 686r]

Att an Assembly holden by Richard Hawley gentleman Alderman and the Comburgesses and Burgesses of Grantham aforesaid 19 October being the Fryday after St Lukes day 1685.

First did sit downe upon the Cushion or place of Election Mr Richard Hawley Alderman in the prebendary Church of Grantham aforesaid
Next to him did sit downe upon the Cushion or place of Eleccion two Comburgesses Mr Robert Calcroft and Mr John Coddington.
Then was sent downe into the Church by an Unanimous Vote of this Assembly Mr Thomas Matkine to Mr John Wing and Mr Robert Cole to make up three Comburgesses in the Church
Out of which three Comburgesses was one chosen to come up and sitt upon the Cushion or place of Eleccion (vizt) Mr John Winge &c
Then was there three Comburgesses upon the Cushion or place of Election (vizt) Mr Robert Calcroft, Mr John Coddington and Mr John Winge &c
Out of which three Comburgesses upon the Cushion or place of Election one of them is to be chosen Alderman for the yeare ensueinge

And thereupon by the Unanimous Vote of this Assembly Mr John Coddington is chosen Alderman for the yeare ensueinge.

Whereupon the said Mr Richard Hawly is discharged from his office of Alderman and the said Mr John Coddington sworne Alderman in his stead for this Burrough of Grantham According to Ancient Custome.

And so this Assembly breaks up.

THE HALL BOOK OF GRANTHAM 1683–1684

[fo. 686v] **First Court of John Coddington, 26 October 1683**

First xij	Mr John Coddington Alderman		Second xij	Mr John Smith	
	Mr Michaell Taylor			Mr John Gibson	
	Mr Robert Calcroft			John Robinson	
	Mr Richard Calcroft			Nicholas Becke	
	Mr Richard Hawley			Edward Bristow	
	Mr John Winge			Simon Grant	
	Mr Robert Cole			Richard Segrave	
	Mr Thomas Matkine			William Haskard	
	Mr Thomas Ireland			Edward Watson	
	Mr Edward Pawlett			Thomas Rowley	
	Mr Edward Leivesly			William Cole	
	Mr Thomas Fisher				

Names of the Officers

Coroner	Mr Richard Hawley	Jur	Serjeant & Gaylor	Thomas Calcroft	Jur
				Thomas Quiningborow	
Escheator	Mr John Winge	Jur	Church clark & Belman	Humfry Turner	Jur
				Ralph Osborne	
Collecters for Schoole	Mr Thomas Fisher	sworne	Key Bearers	Mr Alderman	
	Thomas Kenyon			Edward Watson	Jur
				Thomas Rowley	
Church-Wardens	Mr Edward Watson	Jur	Market place Constables	Mr Thomas Simpson	Jur
	William Burbidge			Mr Marke Nall	
Chamberlaines	Mr Thomas Rowley	Jur	High Street Constables	John Gasshe	Jur
	Richard Handley			Arthur Taylor	
Cheife-Constables	Mr John Smith	Jur	Westgate Constables	Thomas Hutchine	Jur
	Mr John Gibson			John Weaver	
Leather Sealers	George Wray		Walkergate Constables	Anthony Kerke	Jur
	Thomas Rawlinson	Jur		Thomas Baly senior	
	Thomas Marshall				
Corne Prizers	John Withey	Jur	Swinegate Constables	John Newcombe	Jur
	Robert Orson			Richard Sentence	
Markett Sayers	William Scott	Jur	Castlegate Constables	Will Fearon senior	Jur
	George Hanson			Will Fearon Junior	
Towne Clarke	Mr Robert Parkins				

[fo. 687r]

Names of the Commoners.

Marketplace		Highstreet	
	Thomas Simpson		John Gasshe
	Marke Nall		Arthur Taylor
	Matthew Dixon		Charles Wetherill
	John Pape		Henry Atkinson
	Thomas Shorte		William Bristow
	Richard Handley		Richard Owen
	John Stevens		George Read
	Nathan Rookesby		William Knight
	John Goodwine		
	Westgate		Walkergate
	Thomas Hutchine		Anthony Kerke
	John Weaver		Thomas Baly Fellmonger
	William Burbidge		Robert Moore
	Thomas Baly Tanner		James Bristow
	John Newcome Fellmonger		Thomas Rawlinson
	Thomas Kenyon		
	Swinegate		Castlegate
	John Newcome		William Fearon senior
	Richard Sentence		William Fearon Junior
	Robert Langley		Edward Greenwood
	Thomas Leivesly		
	John Marshall		
	Richard Dawson		

At this Court Mr Richard Hawley late Alderman delivered up all the Towne plate to the Alderman that now is as followeth &c

The horse race Cupp   Mr Greenwoods xiij spoones
Mr Archers Boll   One Salt & Cover
Mr Wheatlys Can   Mr Woodroffes Tankard
Mr Battys Beaker   Mr Wrights plate
Mr Harringtons Can   Mr Storeys Cup
Two Tunns   Mr Horsmans Wine Booll
Kirkbys Boll

Att this Court Mr Thomas Fishar tooke the Tolls resigned by Mr Smith att the rate of 52 li per annum for one whole yeare from this day untill the 26th day of October next to be paid quarterly.

[fo. 687v] [Blank page]

[fo. 688r] **Second Court of John Coddington, 9 November 1683**

Arthur Taylor made free.
Att this Court came Arthur Taylor and desired to be admitted a freeman of this Corporacion and by the consent of this Court he was admitted thereunto and sworne.

Vavasor Dix made free.
Allso at this Court came Vavasor Dix gent and desired to be admitted a freeman of the is Corporacion and alledging he was the son of a freeman and had served [blot] 5 yeare as a Clarke to Mr Seckar tendred downe Ten pounds in Court which the Court taking into their Consideracion were pleased by voate of this Court to returne him five pounds againe and was sworne.

Richard Fishar & Silvanus Scot made free.
Allso Richard fishar and silvanus Scott were admitted to their freedome and were sworne.

The Accompts of Mr Robert Cole for the wind mill. Disbursment	47 07 04
Recepts	43 11 10
Remaines to Mr Cole	03 15 06
Mr Watson Chamberlaine his Recepts	77 09 10
Disbursment	77 07 05
Due to the Towne	00 02 05
Thomas Short Chamberlaine his Disbursments	105 14 05
Receipts	099 05 04½
Remaine to Mr Short	006 09 01½
Thomas Rowley Churchwarden Disbursment	43 06 07
Receipts	41 05 08
Abatements	03 13 08
Remaines to him	06 14 07
Abatements	02 15 09
William Burbidge Churchwarden Disbursments	81 08 05½
Receipts	39 12 04
Remaines to him	44 11 10½
	41 16 01 ½

[fo. 688v] [Blank page]

[fo. 689r] Third Court of John Coddington 14 December 1683

Robert Craycroft, Mathew Mitchell made free.
Att this Court came Robert Craycroft and Mathew Mitchell and desired to be admitted freemen of this Corporacion and paid downe x li apeice into the Chamberlaines hands and by an Unanimous vote of this Court 5 li apeice was restored to them againe and paid their accostomed fees and were sworne.

Thomas Bacon, Thomas Osborne, August Newcome, John Woulds & Robert Clark made free.
Allso at this Court came Thomas Bacon, Thomas Osborne, August Newcome, John Woulds and Robert Clarke and craved to be admitted freemen of this Corporacion to which the Court doth condiscend paid their accustomed fees and were sworne.

An Assessment to be made for the Church.
Allso it is ordered that an Assessment of 60 li be made for and towards the Repaires of the Church and disbursments of William Burbidge and notice thereof to be given in the Church.

Fourth Court of John Coddington 18 January 1683/4

Att this Court the Bucketts belonging to this Corporacion were veiwed and it appeared that there was eight and twenty of them and the Gaylor was comanded to take care of them.

Allso at this Court Thomas Quininborrow tooke the watercarts at the yearly rent of three pounds per Annum and that William Fearon nor any other person shall goe with any watercart.

[fo. 689v] Fifth Court of John Coddington, 11 April 1684

The order against Water Carts with shod wheeles Confirmed.
Att this Court it is ordered that the Auncient Order against water Carts with shod wheeles be forthwith put in Execucion against William Fearon And John Gasshe, Arthur Taylor, Thomas Hutchine and John Weaver are appointed to distreine of the said William Fearon for his contempt the sume of Twenty Shillins *sub pena* Twenty shillings a man for their neglect.

William Still made free.
Allsoe at this Court came William Still the eldest son of Edward Still late of Grantham and desired to be admitted a free man of this Corporacion to which this Court doth condiscend he paying his accustomed fees and was sworne.

Henry Middlebrooke, Thomas Burbidge & John Becraft made free.
Allsoe at this Court came Henry Middlebrooke, Thomas Burbidge Butcher Apprentice unto John Scott and John Becraft Blacksmith Apprentice Dynnys Gibson and desired to be admitted free men of this Corporacion to which this Court doth condiscend they paying their accustomed fees and were sworne.

[fo. 690r] **Sixth Court of John Coddington, 16 May 1684**

George Read elected one of the second Twelve.
Att this Court George Read was elected one of the second Twelve tooke the oaths belonging to that place and Tooke his place in Court.

Mr Robinson elected one of the first Twelve.
Allso John Robinson was elected one of the Comburgesses of this Corporacion by an unanimous consent of this Court and tooke the oaths belonging to that office togeather with the severall oaths appointed by the statute in such case made & provided and tooke his place in Court.

Thomas Simpson elected one of the second Twelve.
Allso Thomas Simpson was elected one of the Second Twelve tooke the oaths belonging to the same place, And Tooke his place in Court.

In the Callendar	Thomas Short
	William Burbidge
	Mark Nall

Mr Robert Calcroft nominated Alderman for the yeare ensueinge.
For the more peaceable and quiet proceedings att the Eleccion of the next succeeding Alderman, it is at this Court ordered that upon the next Eleccion day Mr Thomas Ireland be sent downe into the Church to Mr Robert Cole and Mr ~~John Wing~~ Thomas Matkine to make up three Comburgesses there, out of which three Comburgesses in the Church it is likewise agreed upon that Mr Robert Cole be brought upon the Cushion or place of Eleccion to Mr Robert Calcroft and Mr John Wing to make up three Comburgesses there out of which three Comburgesses upon the Cushion Mr Robert Calcroft is nominated Alderman for the ensueing yeare.

John Wigmoore made free.
At this Court came John Wigmore a Stranger and desired to be admitted a freeman of this Corporacion which the Court takeinge into Consideracon upon his tendring downe tenne pounds was admitted thereunto and was sworne.

Joseph Challeng made free.
Allso Joseph Challenge who was an Apprentice to John Ingerson was admitted to his freedome & was sworne.

[fo. 690v] **Seventh Court of John Coddington, 13 June 1684**

Forty pounds to be taken up at Intrest.
Att this Court it is ordered that forty pounds be taken up at Interest for the use of the Corporacion, Mr Rowley, Mr Read, Mr Simpson, and John Newcombe to give Security for the same and to have the Towne Seale for their Security and Indempnificacon.

The wind mill to be sold.
Allsoe at this Court it is ordered and agreed upon that the wind mill be exposed to sayle for the best Advantage of this Corporacion.

Edward Todkill made free.
Allsoe at this Court came Edward Todkill a Stranger and craved to be admitted a freeman of this Corporacion which the Court takeinge into consideracion upon his tendring downe tenne Pounds was unanimously admitted thereunto an [sic] Sworne.

[fo. 691r] **Eighth Court of John Coddington 30 June 1684**

Mr Alderman acquainted the Court this day he received *A Venire Facias* from the Sherriffe of Lincoln to shew cause wherefore the Alderman and Burgesses do use severall Franchizes and previledges within the said Towne.

Mr Alderman and his Brethren desired a free Voat for the present Surrender of the Charter of the same Burrough unto his most gracious Majesty.

The Charter to be surrenderd as above voted &c.
Which Voat was at the same Court with an Unanimous Consent passed that the Charter should be with all convenient speed sent up and Surrendred freely to his most gracious Majesty.

Ninth Court of John Coddington, 11 July 1684

150 [li] to be taken up to mannage the proceedings of the surender.
Att this Court it is ordered that the Corporacion doe take up one hundred and fifty pounds to mannage the proceedings of the surrender, And it was allso taken into consideracion what members of court should become bound for the one hundred and fifty pounds for the Towne, And Mr John Coddington the present Alderman, Mr Michaell Taylor, Mark Nall, John Gasshe, Thomas Hutchine and John Weaver offered themselves in Court as willing to become bound for the same, And that the same Securityes be indempnifyed and secured by the Tolls and mills belonging to this Corporacion.

[fo. 691v]

Mr John Coddington Alderman & others to go to London to attend the King about a new Charter their Charge to be born.
It is allso at this Court ordered that Mr John Coddington the present Alderman, Mr Robert Cole, Mr Thomas Ireland and Mr Robert Parkins the present Town Clark do go up to attend the King at London or Windsor in order to the same. And their Charges to be paied out of the same one hundred and fifty pounds and to consult the best wayes and meanes to peticion his majesty for a new Charter for a maior Towne or Alderman as they shall be advised by such worthy persons as they shall find willing to give their Assistance therein.

[fo. 692r] Tenth Court of John Coddington, 8 August 1684

Persons appointed to take Accompts.
Att this Court it is ordered that Mr Robert Calcroft, Mr Richard Calcroft, Mr Robert Cole, Mr Thomas Ireland, Mr Grant, Mr Simpson, Thomas Hutchine, John Gasshe, Robert Langley, Thomas Short and John Newcome are appointed to take the Accompts for the mills on Munday next.

At an Assembly 11 August these severall Accompts were taken as Followeth.

		£	s	d
Mr Aldermans Accompts	Received	89	06	11
Disbursments		89	18	10
Remaines due to Mr Alderman		00	11	11
Mr Wings Accompts	Received	45	08	08
Disbursments		32	16	04 ob
Remaines due to the Towne		12	12	03 ob
Which he pais and is discharged				
Mr Thomas Coles Accompts	Received	46	12	02

Paid Sir Robert Carr	25	00	00
Remaines in his hands	21	12	02
his Disbursments	24	17	00
Due to Mr Cole	03	04	10

Which is paid him and he is discharged

[fo. 692v] Eleventh Court of John Coddington, 23 September 1684

Captain Harrington requested to take a journey to London about a new Charter.
It is ordered at this Court by an Unanimous Consent that Captaine Harrington, be requested to take a Sudden journey to London on the Behalfe of this Corporacion In order to obtaine a new Charter, And by the same Unanimous Consent Mr Robert Parkins the present Towne Clarke is apointed to attend upon him (if he so please).

An Assessment of 24 li to be levied for the Constables bills.
It is allso at this Court ordered that an Assessment of xxiiij li be made and laid upon this Burrough for the Constables Bills of Disbursments for the yeare past, an Estimate being taken what the perticuler summs amount unto And it is ordered that the Cheife Constables and under Constables be assessors, and the under Constables Collectors thereof.

Warrants against those that receive Inmates.
Allso it is ordered that Warrants be made out against those that receive Inmates and such persons as shall Intrude into this Towne without Consent or giveinge Security to Mr Alderman and his Brethren, vizet Barksdale Tomlinson widdow for receiveinge a Stranger into a poor Habitacion without Licence first had and obteyned of Mr Alderman and his Brethren contrary to the Aunceint Rules and Orders of this Court.

[fo. 693r] Twelfth Court of John Coddington 24 October 1684

Thomas Fisher takes the tolls at 52 li per annum.
Att this Court Mr Thomas Fisher tooke the Tolls at the rate of fifty two pounds *per Annum* from the six and Twentieth day of October for the Terme of one Whole yeare from thence next ensueing to be paid quarterly.

William Fearon the Cripples at 14 li per annum.
Att this Court William fearon doth agree with the Towne to carry away and releive all Passingers and Cripples from the Towne from the one and Thirtieth day of October next for and dureing the Terme of one whole yeare from thence ensueing att the rate of fourteene pounds per annum.

William Fearon & Thomas Rawlinson takes the Water Cart.
Allso att this Court William Fearon and Thomas Rawlinson tooke the Water Carts att the rate of Three pounds per annum, provided that no other persons do goe with any water Carts.

Mr Thomas Fishers Accompts for the schoole house Rents			
Receipts	21	14	08
Disbursment	21	19	02
due to Mr Fisher	00	05	06
Thomas Kenyons Accompts for the schoole house Rents	21	14	04
Recepts			
Disbursment	21	16	06
due to Thomas Kenyon	00	02	02
Thomas Rowlys Accompts as Chamberline			
Recepts	51	07	11
Disbursment	55	08	10½
due to Thomas Rowly	04	00	11½
Richard Handly Chamberline his Accompts receipts	246	08	10
Disbursments	246	09	10
Due to him	000	00	11

[fo. 693v] [Blank page]

THE HALL BOOK OF GRANTHAM 1684–1685

[fo. 694r] **First Court of Robert Calcroft, Mayor, 13 March 1684/5**

John Earle of Rutland Recorder jur

Robert Calcroft Esquire mayor			Mr Thomas Simpson		
Thomas Harrington Esquire			Mr Mark Nall		
John Thorold Esquire			Mr John Smith		
Robert Fisher Esquire			Mr Edward Watson		
John Coddington gentleman			Mr John Rollinson		
Robert Cole gentleman			Mr Samuel Prockter		
Thomas Matkine gentleman		Jur	Mr John Gasse		Jur
Thomas Ireland gentleman			Mr Thomas Hutchine		
Edward Pawlett gentleman			Mr Richard Sentance		
Thomas Fisher genttleman			Mr Thomas Baly		
John Robinson gentleman			Mr John Newcome		
Edward Bristow gentleman					
Simon Grant gentleman					

Names of the Officers

Coroner	Mr John Coddington	Jur	Markett Sayers	John Gibson	Jur
Escheator	Mr Robert Cole	Jur		John Withey	
Collectors	Mr John Robinson	Jur	Corne prizers	Thomas Hatfeild	Jur
for Schoole	Mr John Smith			George Hanson	
Church	Mr Edward Watson	Jur	Keybearers		
Wardens	Mr John Gasse				
Chamberlins	Thomas Hutchine	Jur			
	John Newcome		Church Clerke	Humphry Turner	
Cheife	Mr Thomas Simpson	Jur	& Bellman	Ralph Osborne	
Constables	Mr Mark Nall		Market place	John Marshall	Jur
Towne Clerke	Mr Robert Parkins	Jur	Constables	Edward Todkill	
Serjeant	Thomas Calcroft	Jur	High Street	Richard Bristow	Jur
& Gaylor			Constables	Robert Orson	
Leather	Richard Bristow		Westgate	William Fearon	Jur
Sealors	Thomas Baly	Jur	Constables	Thomas Reare	
	Thomas Rollinson				
	Thomas [*name erased*]				

[fo. 694v]

Walkergate Constables	John Gladwin	Jur
Swinegate Constables	Thomas Poole	
	Humfrey Fisher	Jur
	Richard North	
Castlegate Constables	Thomas Bacon	Jur
	Richard Durham	

At this Court Mr John Coddington late Alderman delivered up the Towne Plate to Robert Calcroft Esquire now major [sic] of this Corporacon as Followeth

The Horse race Cupp	Mr Kirkbys Boll
Mr Archers Boll	Mr Greenwoods 13 spoons
Mr Wheatleys Cann	one salt and Cover
Mr Horsemans Boll	Mr Horsemans wine Boll
Mr Greenwoods Cann	Mr Wrights Boll
Mr Batteys Beaker	Mr Storys Cupp
Mr Harringtons Cann	Mr Woodroffe Cann
Two Tunns	

Samuell Burnet Clerk, John Hurst, Gentleman, W Parkins, Clerk, Samuell Procter, Gent, John Theyer, Montague Stacy, John Stacy, John Calcroft, Robert Cole junior & John Gladwin made Free.

Att this Court came Samuel Burnett clerk, John Hurst gentleman, William Parkins clerk, Samuel Prockter, gentleman, John Theyer clerk, Mountague Stacy, John Stacy, John Calcroft, Robert Cole, Junior and John Gladwine into Court and desired to be admitted Freemen of this Corporacion to which this Court doth condiscend they paying their accustomed Fees and where [sic] sworne in Court &c.

George Fitzrandolph & Thomas Robinson made Free.

Allso at this Court came George Fitzrandolph and Thomas Robinson strangers and craved to be admitted Freemen of this Corporacion which the Court takeing into consideracon upon their tendring downe tenne pounds apeice where [sic] admitted thereunto and sworne in Court.

[fo. 695r] Second Court of Robert Calcroft, Mayor, 20 March 1684/5

Thomas deLign, Edward deLign, Lewis Hurst, Thomas Ashley, Hugh Ashley, Richard Hurst Junior, John Felton, Edward Hawles, Roger Herbert, William Oldes, Charles Ellis, Henry Matthew, Charles Sidgney, Francis Huddlestone & Walter Gyles made Free.

Att this Court came Thomas deLigne gentleman, Edward deLigne gentleman, Lewis Hurst gentleman, Thomas Ashley gentleman, Hugh Ashley, Richard Hurst Junior, John Felton gentleman, Edward Hawles gentleman, Roger Herbert gentleman, William

Oldes, Charles Ellis, Henry Ma[t]hews [*sic*], Charles Sedley [*sic*], Francis Huddleston and Walter Gyles and craved to be admitted Free Burgesses of this Corporacion which the Court takeing into consideracion they tendred downe tenne pounds apeice and humbly craveing the favour of the Court to be kind unto them The Court doth with an unanimous consent repay their monys back againe and were sworne in Court &c.

[fo. 695v] Third Court of Robert Calcroft, Mayor, 27 March 1685

Thomas Johnson Esquire, Decordes DeLigne Gentleman, John DeLigne gentleman, Woodroffe Gentleman, Thomas Moore Esquire, Thomas Williamson, John Moore, Savile Bradshaw Clerk, George Lasselles gentleman, John Lord clerk, Henry Knewstubs clerk, Edward Dix, Francis Coney Gentleman, Abraham Wharton, William Stillton, James Twist Clerk, William Southerne, George Winstanly & William Willson made Free.

Att this Court came Thomas Johnson Esquire, Decordes DeLigne gentleman, John DeLigne gentleman, John Woodroffe gentleman, Thomas Moore Esquire, Thomas Williamson clerk, John Moore clerk, Savile Bradshaw clerk, George Lasselles clerk, John Lord clerk, Henry Knewstubs clerk, Nathaniel Thorold gentleman, Edward Saul clerk, Richard Grant gentleman, Edward Dix gentleman, Francis Cony gentleman, Abraham Wharton clerk, William Stilton clerk, James Twist clerk, William Southerne, George Winstanly and William Wilson clerk and craved to be admitted Freemen of this Corporacion which the Court takeing into consideracion they tendred downe tenne pounds apeice and humbly craved the favour of the Court to be kind unto them The Court doth with an unanimous consent returne their monyes back again and were sworne in Court.

50li orderd to be paid to Captain Harrington for his trouble & Charge in obteining a new Charter which he returned back again to the Corporacion.

Allsoe this Court takeing into Consideracion the great Charge and trouble which Captaine Harrington hath been att in obteyning the new Charter do returne him most humble and hearty thanks, and do by an unanimous Consent order that fifty pounds be paid unto him which he doth very freely returne back againe to the Corporacion.

Fourth Court of Robert Calcroft, Mayor, 3 April 1685

Sir John Oldfeild Baronet, Christopher Berrisford, William Ambler, Edward King, William Wallet Esquire, Thomas Rastell, Martin Johnson, Robert Thornton, William Hunt, Samuell Daws, George Stow, William Eldred, Thomas Wallett, Christopher Marshall, John Walker, Richard Hardell, John Durklin, Humphrey Newton, John Clarke, Steeven Dixon, Anthony Barnes, John Farthin gent, Lewis Gwin, Robert Hardwick, Abraham Millin, Richard Cross, Gilbert Abrahall clerk, Robert Price Doctor of Divinity, John Orme Esquire, Peregrine Berty Esquire, Robert Lord Willoughby made Free.

At this Court came Sir John Oldfeild Baronet, Christopher Berrisford Esquire, William Ambler Esquire, Edward King Esquire, William Wallet Esquire, Thomas Rastell gentleman, Martin Johnson, Robert Thornton, William Hunt, Samuell Daws, George Stow, Thomas [sic] Eldred, Thomas Wallett, Christopher Marshall, John Walker, Richard Hardell, John Durkleing, Humphry Newton, John Clarke, Stephen Dixon, Anthony Barnes & John Farthin gentlemen, Lewis Gwinn Clerke, Robert Hardwick clerk, Abraham Millin clerk Richard Cross clerk, Gilbert Abrahall clerk, Robert Price Dr of Divinity, John Orme Esquire, Peregrine Bertie Esquire, Robert Lord Willoughby & desired to be admitted Free burgesses of this Corporacion which the Court takeing into consideracion they tendreing downe their tenn pounds apeece & humbly craveing the favour of the Courte, The Courte doth with an unanimous consent grant their request & returne all their money back againe & they tooke the oaths accordingly.

[fo. 696r] Fifth Court of Robert Calcroft, Mayor, 10 April 1685

Richard Handleys accompts as Chamberlin.
At this Court Richard Handley Chamberlaine passeth his accounts as followeth

Received	13 00 00
Disbursements	12 17 00
Remaining due to the Towne	00 03 00

which he payes in Court & is discharged

Armstrong Threaves, Thomas Stanser & Thomas Ellson made Free.
Allso at this Court came Armstrong Threaves, Thomas Stanser & Thomas Elston [sic] & desired to be admitted Free men of this Corporacion which the Court takeing into consideracion they tendreing tenn pounds & craveing the favour of the Court the Court doth grant their request & returne their five pounds apeece & they were sworne in Court as usually.

John Owen sent to be Keeper of the house of Correction.
Allso at this Court it is ordered that the place of Master of the house of Correction & the sallary thereunto belongeing be setled upon John Owen senior.

Sixth Court of Robert Calcroft, Mayor, 24 April 1685

James Potterton made Free.
At this Court came James Patterton [sic] & desired to be admitted a freeman of this Corporacion which the Court takeing into consideracion (he layeing down his tenn pounds) granted his request & he was sworne accordeingly.

50 li to be paid to Captain Harrington which he expended in obtaineing the Charter.
It is alsoe ordered by this Court that the Chamberlaine do pay fifty pounds to Captain Harrington which he hath expended in obteineing the Charter.

Seventh Court of Robert Calcroft, Mayor, 24 July 1685

Mr Edward Watsons accompts as Churchwarden.
Mr Edward Watson Church Warden for 1684 & 1685 passeth his Accompts as followeth

	£ s d
Receipts	050 08 06
Disbursments	074 08 02 ob
Abatements	002 00 10
& due to Mr Watson	026 00 06 ob

William Beamont Collector for 1684 & 1685 passeth his Accompts as followeth
Receipts	034 16 03
Disbursments	035 06 06
Abatements	000 03 00
Due to William Beamont	000 13 03

[fo. 696v]

James Fearon Collector passeth his Accompts as followeth
Receipts	057 01 04
Disbursments	048 19 09
Abatements	001 04 01 ob
Due to the Town	006 17 02 ob

John Marshall Colebuyer passeth his Accompts as followeth
Received	018 01 04
paid the Chamberlaine	006 00 00
Remains in his hands	012 01 04

Roger Blankney & Richard Hickson Collector passeth their Accompts as followeth
Receipts	071 16 07
Disbursments	067 19 00
Due to the Towne	003 17 01

which they pay in Court & are discharged.

Mr Samuell Procter sworne Town Clarke.
At this Court by a Free & unanimous Voat of the same Mr Samuell Procter is chosen Towne Clerke for this Burrough in the Roome & Stead of Mr Robert Parkins deceased

& did at the same Time take the Oath of Towne Clerke & the Oaths of Allegiance & Supremacy & subscribed to the Declaracion according to the Statute in such case & provided.

Mr Crichloe & Mr Taylor to take their places in the 2nd Company or pay their fines.
Allso it is ordered that Mr Thomas Crichloe & Mr Arthur Taylor have notice given them to appeare next Court to shew cause why they should not take their places in the second Company or pay their Fynes.

Mr Elwoods mony delivered to Mr Hutching.
Memorandum that at this Court Mr Elwoods bag of Mony & other things sealed up with the Townes seale were delivered to Mr Thomas Hutching Chamberlaine.

Robert Fisher Esquire dismissed the Court.
At this Court Robert Fisher Esquire desired to be dismissed from his place of Alderman which this Court with an unanimous Consent did grant unto him.

Mr John Smith sworne Alderman.
Allso at this Court Mr John Smith by an unanimous consent of the same was elected one of the Aldermen of this Corporacion & tooke the Oath belonging to the said Office & the severall Oaths appointed by the Statute.

Mr Robert Cole nominated Mayor.
Allso at this Court Mr Robert Cole is by a free consent & voat nominated Mayor of this Corporacion for the yeare ensueing

[fo. 697r] **Eighth Court of Robert Calcroft, Mayor, 25 September 1685**

At this Court Mr Robert Calcroft Mayor passeth his Accounts for the Slate mill for the yeare 1684
Received	093 14 00
Disbursment	089 01 08
Due to the Towne	004 12 04

Mr John Coddington Alderman for the yeare 1684 passeth his Accounts as followeth
Received	050 00 00
Disbursment	051 17 04
Due to Mr Coddington	001 17 04

Mr Robert Calcroft to have 15 li allowed for his sallary.
At this Court it is ordered that Mr Robert Calcroft now Mayor have the sume of Fifteene pounds allowed him for his Sallary for the yeare 1685 & it is further ordered that the

Chamberlaines do pay him the said Sume of fifteene pounds out of the first moneys they shall receive.

Mr Robert Cole passeth his Accounts for mony received to renew the Charter
Received   100 00 00
Disbursments   099 09 09 ob
Due to the Towne   000 10 02 ob

Assessment of 26 li for Constables bills.
It is ordered that an Assessment for six & twenty pounds be made for and towards the payment of the Constables Bills.

Warrant against Mr Chrichloe & Mr Tayler.
Allso it is ordered that a Warrantt be made out against Mr Thomas Crichloe & Mr Arthur Taylor to distretyne of them for refuseing to take their places in the Common Councill accordeing to his Majesties Charter.

John Rollinson, William Poole, John Calcroft & Benjamin Wheeler sworne freemen.
At this Court came John Rollinson son of John Rollinson, William Poole apprentice to Mr Becke, John Calcroft son of Mr Richard Calcroft deceased & Benjamin Wheeler Apprentice to James Gibson & craved to be admitted Freemen of this Corporacon to which this Court doth condiscend they paying their accustomed Fees & were sworne

[fo. 697v] **Ninth Court of Robert Calcroft, Mayor, 16 October 1685**

Mr Critchloe & Mr Taylor chosen two of the Common Councill.
Att this Court Mr Thomas Crichloe & Mr Arthur Taylor are both unanimously chosen two of the Common Councill of this Corporacion formally called the Second twelve.

Mrs Millers money disposed of in Courte.
Att this Court Mrs Frances Miller widdow sent a note directed to Mr Mayor & the rest of the Court desireing them to pay the interest of forty pounds which shee had formerly given to the Towne to charitable uses to these widdows following (vizt) Widdow Castle, widdow Bringhurst, Widdow Mitchell, Widdow Hoult, senior, Widdow Hollingworth & Widdow Smith in Well Lane, which was paid accordingly in open Court in the presence of Mr Burnett Minister of the said Towne.

Tenth Court of Robert Calcroft, Mayor, 20 October 1685

Mr Thomas Fisher takes the Tolls at 52 li per annum.
At this Court Mr Thomas Fisher tooke the Tolls belonging to this Corporacion for one whole yeare at the rate of 52 li per Annum & to be paid quarterly.

Eleventh & last Court of Robert Calcroft, Mayor, 23 October 1685

Mr Robert Cole elected Major [sic].
Mr Robert Cole haveing beene formerly nominated Major [sic] of this Corporacion for the ensueing yeare This Day according to his most Gracious Majesties Letters of Charter and Incorporacion to this Towne Granted he was by the unanimous vote of this Court elected and chosen Mayor for the yeare ensueing.

Mr Robert Calcroft discharged from his office of Major [sic].
Whereupon the said Robert Calcroft is discharged from his office of Major [sic] & the said Mr Robert Cole is sworne Major [sic] in his Stead in Corpus Christi Quire according to the ancient Custome of this Corporacion.

THE HALL BOOK OF GRANTHAM 1685–1686

[fo. 698r] **First Court of Robert Cole, Mayor, 30 October 1685**

Robert Cole Esquire Mayor
Thomas Harrington Esquire
John Thorold Esquire
Robert Calcroft gentleman
John Coddington gentleman
Thomas Matkin gentleman
Thomas Ireland gentleman
Edward Pawlett gentleman
Thomas Fisher gentleman
John Robinson gentleman
Edward Bristow gentleman
Simon Grant gentleman
John Smith gentleman

Mr John Rollinson
Mr Thomas Hutchin
Mr Edward Watson
Mr Thomas Simpson
Mr Samuell Procter
Mr John Gass
Mr Thomas Baily
Mr Richard Sentence
Mr John Newcombe

Coroner Escheator	Robert Calcroft gent Thomas Matkin gent	Corne Prizers	John Gibson Thomas Quiningborow
Collectors for the Schoole Church Wardens Chamberlaines	Edward Bristow gent Thomas Bayly John Gass John Weaver Mark Nall & Richard Sentence	Church Clerke & Bellman Market Place Constables High Street Constables	Humphry Turner Ralph Osborne Edward Todkill Richard Wyles George Fitzrandolp John Wigmore
Cheife Constables Towne Clerke Serjeant & Goaler Keybearers	John Rollinson & Thomas Hutchin Samuell Procter Thomas Calcroft & Robert Barton Mr Mayor John Gass & Richard Sentence	Westgate Constables Walkergate Constables Swinegate Constables Castlegate Constables Beadle	Thomas Robinson Henry Johnson William Fearon William Barrett James Fearon Robert Orson Thomas Nixon John Martine John Scott
Leather Sealers	Richard Bristow Thomas Bayly Thomas Rollinson Thomas Marshall		

Towne plate delivered.
At this Courte Mr Robert Calcroft late Mayor of this Corporacion delivered up to Robert Cole Esq the present Mayor the towne plate as followeth

The Horserace Cupp	Mr Greenwoods Cann	Mr Greenwoods 13 spoons
Mr Archers Bowlle	Mr Batteys Beaker	one Salt & cover
Mr Wheatlyes Canne	Mr Harringtons Cann	Mr Horsemans wine bow[l]
Mr Horsemans bowle	Two tunns	Mr Wrights Boll
	Mr Kirkbyes bowle	Mr Storyes [sic] Cup
		Mr Woodroffes Cann

[fo. 698v]

William Lightfoot takes a Lease of the Horse Church yard at 12s a yeare for 21 yeares.
Allso at this Court William Lightfoot takes a Lease of a peice of ground behind the Horse Mill for the Terme of one & twenty yeares at the rent of twelve Shillings per Annum & he doth condicion to Fence the same with a quick hedge & to leave the peice of ground where the horse Mill stood when the Corporacon hath occasion to make use of the same.

Mr Robert Cole late Escheator for the year past passeth his Account as followeth
Received of Thomas Mantle for a defective weight of Hemp   00 02 06
which he payes in Court to the Chamberlaine.

William Fearon to releive all Passingers & to carry away Cripples.
Att this Court William Fearon doth agree with the Towne to carry away & releive all Cripples & Passengers for the yeare ensueing at the rate of Fourteene pounds for the yeare.

Thomas Nixon made Free.
Allso at this Court came Thomas Nixon & desired to be admitted a Freeman of this Corporacion to which this Court doth condiscend he paying his accustomed Fees to the Box & to the Clarke & Serjeants was Sworne accordingly.

Second Court of Robert Cole, Mayor, 13 November 1685

Mr John Smiths accompts as Millmaster
Att this Court Mr John Smith Mill Master of the Towne Mill for the yeare 1684 passeth his
Accomps as folloeweth Received   149 12 01
Disbursed   119 08 04
Due to the Towne   030 03 09

The Waytes of this Towne to have no Lace on their Cloaks nor ribbins for their badges but at their own Charge.
It is ordered at this Court that for the Future the waytes of this Corporacion shall not have any Lace upon their Cloakes nor any Ribbon for their Badges at the Townes Charge except they buy them themselves.

Thomas Hutchine accompts as Chamberlaine.
Thomas Hutching Chamberlaine for the yeare 1685 passeth his Accounts as followeth
Received   124 06 04
Disbursed   123 13 11
Due to the Towne   000 12 03

[fo. 699r] **Third Court of Robert Cole Mayor, 18 December 1685**

All Persons refuseing to pay to Church to be presented.
Att this Court it is ordered that all persons whatsoever refuseing to pay their Severall Assessments for repaires of the Church be presented by the Church Wardens into the Sperituall Court.

John Newcombes accompt as Chamberlaine.
Att this Court John Newcome Chamberlaine passeth his Accounts as followeth
Disbursments   68 11 03
Received   65 06 10 ob
Due to the Accomptant   03 04 04 ob

John Robinson Ap[othecary], William Turner, John Coddington, James Ferman, John Newball.
Allso at this Court Mr John Robinson apprentice to Mr John Poole Apothecary, William Turner Apprentice to William Kerke Butcher, John Coddington Apprentice to Mr Edward Coddington Mercer his Father, James Ferman Apprentice to Mr Edward Leivesly Butcher & John Newball Apprentice to Duckar Newball his Father Bridlemaker came & desired to be admitted Freemen of this Corporacion to which this Court doth condiscend they paying their Accustomed Fees to the Box & to Clarke & Serjeants were Sworne accordingly.

Memorandum Mr John Smith is to account for Thirty pounds three Shillings & nine pence which remaines in his hand & upon his Millmaster Account.

One silver Tankard, one other Tankard, two tumblers one bowl & a broken spoon to be Changed.
Allso at this Court it is unanimously agreed upon that one Silver Tank[ard] weighing twenty ounces given to this Corporacion by Mr Thomas Wickliffe in the yeare of our Lord 1636 Mr Richard Cony then Alderman & one other Tankard given by Mr Miles

Greenwood weighing Eighteen Ounces in the yeare of our Lord 1638 & two Tumblers given by Mr John Batty weighing Sixteen Ounces & a quarter & one boll given by Mr Thomas Horseman & a broken Spoon weighing Six Ounces & a half be forthwith changed for other plate.

[fo. 699v] Fourth Court of Robert Cole, Mayor, 8 January 1685/6

The wife of John Scott paid to the Chamberlaine nine pounds which was due from her late husband John Wing Alderman of Grantham.
Att this Court came [*blank*] the wife of John Scott & paid in Court to the Chamberlaine the Sume of nine pounds which was due to the Corporacon from Mr John Wing her late husband & Alderman of Grantham aforesaid.

Mr Smith Ordered to account the next Court as Millmaster.
Memorandum that Mr John Smith do account the next Court for thirty pounds three Shillings & ninepence which remanes in his Hands as Mill Master.

Fifth Court of Robert Cole, Mayor, 26 February 1685/6

Mr Pawlet, Mr Fisher, Mr Grant, Mr Baily, Mr Sentance & Mr Newcombe ordered to give in their accounts.
Att this Court it is ordered that Mr Pawlett, Mr Fisher, Mr Grant, Mr Sentence, Mr Baly & Mr Newcome do Meet at the Hall on tweday next to take accounts.

Ordered when the Hutch is to be opened the Mayor 6 Aldermen 2 Cheif Constables & 4 Common Councell to be by & the penalty if notice given & present when opened.
Allso at this Court it is ordered that there shall be present at the opening of the Hutch (vizt) the Mayor for the time being six of the Aldermen the two Cheife Constables & Four of the Common Councill at the least & the penalty of any one Faileing to apeare in the Vestrie after notice given shall be for every Alderman Tenne Shillings & for every Comon Councill Man Five Shillings if there be not the Full number as aforesaid.

The plate that went to be changed produced in Court & the Charge of changing
Allso at this Court the two Tankards, two Tumblers, one Cup & a broken Spoone formerly sent up to London to be changed for other new plate was this day produced in Court the Charge of changeing & Carriage comeing to twenty Shillings.

Ordered, The red Lyon to be taken into the Towns hands for the Mayor to make his feast in; Mr Stacy to be to be [sic] *sued upon refusall to pay his rent.*
Allso it is ordered that the Red Lyon be taken into the Townes hands for every Succeeding Mayor to make his Feast in & that Mr Stacy have halfe a yeares notice given him to provide himselfe of another house & that the rent for the Red Lyon Signe

& other moneys due from Mr Stacy to the Towne be demanded of him & upon non payment thereof it is ordered that he be sued for the same.

Mr Watsons accounts as Churchwarden.
Mr Watson Churchwarden passeth his account for his Church Assesment
The Assessment comes to	25 19 04
Abatements allowed of	00 19 06½
Remaines in his hands to account for	24 19 09½

Thomas Rowlets accounts for Spittlegate Assessment for the Church.
Thomas Rowlett passeth his Accounts for Spittlegate Assessment for the church in William
Burbidges year his assesment is	10 00 00
Received of him	09 04 03
Remaines in his hands	00 15 09

[fo. 700r]

William Burbidge acounts of his Assesment For the Church for Grantham & Manthorpe.
William Burbidge accounteth for his Assesment for the Church for Grantham & Manthorpe
The Assesment comes to	54 15 01
Abatements allowed	01 08 06
Remaines due to the Towne	[sum incorrect] 00 15 06

Sixth Court of Robert Cole, Mayor, 1 April 1686

Mr Smiths accounts as Millmaster.
At this Court Mr John Smith passeth his Account for £30 3s 0d which remaines in his hands as Milmaster for the Towne Mill & for £3 16s 0 which he received of John Scott.
Received in all	33 19 00
paid	32 08 07
Remaines in his hands	01 10 05

which he is ordered to pay to Mrs Parkins Widdow to Mr Robert Parkins late Towne Clerke for the threequarters of a yeares Sallary due to him in his life time & is dicharged [*sic*].

Ordered that John Scott take Care the streets be not anoyed with dirt or swine & if he find any swine therein to have them to the pound.
It is ordered that John Scott do take care for the future that the streets of this Corporacion be not anoyed with dirt or Swine & it is ordered that if he find any Swine trespassing in the Streets that he have them to the Pound.

Seventh Court of Robert Cole, Mayor, 30 April 1686

An Assessment of 60 li to be made for defraying part of Charge of the Last Charter &c.
At this Court it is ordered by a generall Consent that an Assesment of threescore pounds be made & laid upon the Inhabitants of this Towne for & towards the defraying parte of the Charge laid out for renewing of the last Charter granted to this Corporacion & that Mr Mayor & as many of the first & second Company as can conveniently meet on Thursday next at the Guildhall shall be the Assessors & makers thereof & that the Cheife Constables of this Burrough Shall be the Collectors of so much of the said threescore pounds as is to be paid by the first & Second Company & Gentry & that the under Constables of every ward within this Burrough shall collect the Residue of the said Assessment which shall be imposed upon the rest of the Inhabitants within their respective wardes And if any person or persons being Inhabitants within this Towne shall be obstinate & refuse to pay the mony which shall so be assessed upon them or any of them that then the money due to be paid by any Such person or persons so refuseing by Force of this order & custome of this Corporacion shall be leveyed upon the said pers[on] or persones by the aforesaid Constables by distresse & sayle of the Offenders goods rendring to the party the overplus if any such be.

The Constables to provide 2 Ladders one hook & one dragg for every of their respective wards.
Allso it is ordered that the Constables do provide two Ladders one hooke & one Dragg for every of their respective Wards.

[fo. 700v]

Ordered a Table of the Benefactors to be Sett up in the Church.
And it [is] further ordered that there be a Table of the names of all Benefactors to this Corporacion be set up in the Church.

Overseers of the poor Highways & Churchwardens to meet & give up their accounts.
Memorandum that the Overseers of the poor & Highwayes & the Church Wardens do meet at the hall on Thursday next to give up their Accompts.

That the Churchwardens doe not expend above 4 nobles for their Easters Visitacion dinner & not above 1 li at Michaelmas Visitacion.
It is ordered that the Churchwardens of this Corporacion for the time being do not expend above Four nobles for their Easter Visitacion dinner & not above twenty shillings at Michaellmas Visitacion.

Charles Wetherill & William Handley Chosen overseers of the Highstreet Well &c.
Charles Wetherill & William Handley are chosen Overseers for Highstreet well & it is ordered that an Assessment of Ten shillings be made for repaires of the same.

That the overplus of 40 li of the Head Schoole masters Sallary which hath formerly been paid to Mr Walker be for the future paid to Mr Mills Assistant to the Master for his great care in Lookeing to the Schoole.

Allso it is ordered that the Overplus of Forty pounds of the Head Schoole Masters Sallary which hath formerly been paid to Mr Walker late Schoole Master be for the future paid to Mr Mills Assistant to the master of the schoole as a gratuity for the great care & paines he takes in looking to the Schoole.

Andrew Tongues accounts as Overseer of the poor.
Andrew Tong overseer for the poor passeth his accounts as followeth
his Receipts	066 14 00
his Disbursments	057 07 09
his Disbursments	002 12 00
In Andrew Tongs hands	006 14 03

Joseph Woods accounts as Overseer for the poor.
Joseph Woods Overseer for the poor passeth his accounts as followeth
his Receipts	056 11 05½
his Disbursments	044 14 08
Abatements allowed	005 04 01½
In Joseph woods hands	006 12 08

Roger Blankly, Armstrong Threaves, Edward Scarborow & Richard Taylers accounts for the Highways.
Roger Blanckney, Armstrong Threaves, Edward Scarborow & Richard Tayler passe their Accounts for the Highway Assessment
Their Assessment comes to	017 08 02
Their Disbursments come to	018 11 10
Abatements allowed of	000 15 04
Due to the Accountants	001 19 00

John Gass his accounts as Churchwarden.
John Gasse Churchwarden passeth his Account as followeth
Receipts	032 12 02
Disbursments	049 15 01
Abatements allowed	003 00 00
Due to Mr John Gasse	020 02 11

[fo. 701r] **Eighth Court of Robert Cole, Mayor, 18 June 1686**

Assessment of 20 li to be had for the repaires of the highways.
It is ordered that an Assessment of twenty pounds be made for and towards the Repaires of the highwayes of this Corporacion.

An Assessment of 20 li for the reimbursing Mr John Gass.
Allso that an Assessment of twenty pounds be made for & towards the Reimbursment of Mr John Gasse late Churchwarden.

Humphry Turner parrish Clarke to have 40s per annum added to his Sallary.
Allso it is ordered that Humphry Turner the Parish Clarke have forty Shillings per Annum added to his Sallary the first quarters wages to be paid at Midsummer next.

John Thorold Esquire nominated Mayor for the year ensueing.
At this Court John Thorold Esquire one of the Aldermen of this Corporacion is unanimously elected & nominated to be Mayor of this Corporacion for the yeare ensueing.

William Kirkes accounts for the Town Mill.
William Kerke Mill Master for the Towne Mill passeth his Accounts for the last yeare as followeth.
Receipts	129 17 06
Disbursments	098 10 11
Due to the Towne	031 06 07

Mr Becks accounts for the Slate Mill.
Mr Becke passeth his Account for the Slate Mill for the yeare last past
Receipts	090 15 02
Disbursments	098 11 02
Due to Mr Beck	007 16 00
which he is to receive of William Kerke so that there will then remaine due to the Towne from William Kerke the summe of	023 10 07

Ninth Court of Robert Cole, Mayor, 17 December [sic] 1686 [the dates of this and the following Court are probably incorrect]

Mr Gass to be paid out of a 40 li Assesment &c.
It is ordered at this Court that the Assesment of twenty pounds which was ordered last Court for the Reimbursment of Mr Gasse be increased to Forty pounds towards part of the charges of John Weaver the present Churchwarden out of which Forty pounds Mr Gasse is first to be paid.

An Assessment of 28 li to be made for reimbursing the Constables bills.
Allso it is ordered that an Assessment of Eight & twenty pounds be made & laid upon the Inhabitants of this Towne towards the payment of the Constables Bills of Disbursments.

Henry Haskard chosen promoter instead of Richard Black.
Allso at this Court the place of common promoter being vacant by the death of Richard Black is conferred upon Henry Haskard dureing the pleasure of this Court.

[fo. 701v] Tenth Court of Robert Cole, Mayor, 27 September [sic] 1686

John Marshalls accounts as Colebyer.
At this Court John Marshall Colebuyer for the yeare last past accounteth for moneys in his hands

	li	s	d
as followeth			
Money in his hands	12	01	07
Disburst thereof	04	12	10
Remaines in Mr Marshalls hands	07	08	09

which he payes to Roger Blanckney & is discharged.

Mr Thomas Fisher takes a lease of the Tolls at 52 li per annum.
At this Court Mr Thomas Fisher taketh a Lease of the Tolls belonging to this Corporacion for the ensueing yeare at two & fifty pounds to be paid to the Chamberline quarterly.

Eleventh Court of Robert Cole, Mayor 27 September 1686

Mr Thomas Matkin Elected Major [sic] instead of John Thorold Esq.
At this Court Mr John Thorold who was formerly nominated to be Mayor of this Corporacion for the yeare ensueing urgeing Severall reasons why he could not serve in the said place & Office, & allso Submitting himselfe to the auncient order of this Court in such case of Refusall This Court takeing it into their serious Consideracion have in his place & Stead unanimously elected & nominated Mr Thomas Matkin to be Mayor of this Corporacion for this yeare ensueing.

A Warrant to distrein Of Mr Arthur Taylor & Mr Chrichloe for refusing a Common Councell place.
Allso it is ordered that Warrants be made out to distreyne of Mr Arthur Taylor & Mr Thomas Crichloe for refuseing to take their places in the Comon Councell.

Twelfth Court of Robert Cole, Mayor, 12 October 1686

Mr Crichloe & Mr Taylor discharged from their Common councell Ship.
At this Court Mr Crichloe & Mr Taylor Urgeing severall Reasons why they could not serve & take their places in the Common Councell This Court thought fitt to discharge them from their said places layeing downe their Fynes which this Court doe agree to welcome them back againe.

Mr William Kirke & Mr Robert Cole junior chosen & Sworn Common Councell Men.
Allso at this Court William Kerke & Robert Cole Junior were by a Free & unanimous Consent of the Same elected & chosen of the Common Councell & were sworne in Court accordingly.

[fo. 702r] Thirteenth Court of Robert Cole, Mayor, 20 October 1686

Joseph Woods accounteth for 6 li 12s 8d.
At this Court Joseph woods accounteth for 6 li 12s 8d in his hands as Collector

In his hands	06	12	08
Disburst thereof	05	16	00
Remaines in his hands	00	16	08

Andrew Tongue accounteth for 6 li 14s 3d.
Andrew Tong accounteth for 6 li 14 s 3 d which was in his hands as Collector

In his hands	06	14	03
Disburst thereof	06	06	00
In his hands	00	08	03

which he pays in Court & is discharged.

All Officers to bring in their accounts before the next Sessions or else to be proceeded against according to Law.
It is ordered at this Court that the severall Officers of this Corporacion do bring in their severall Accompts & cleare the same before the next Sessions or else to be proceeded against according to Law.

Mr Matkins accounts as Escheator.
Mr Matkin Escheator accounteth as followeth
Received for two Defective yard Wands   00 03 06
which he pays in Court & is discharged.

Mr Chrichloe Laid down his fine for refuseing his Comon Councells place.
Allso at this Court Mr Thomas Chrichloe laid downe his Fine of tenne pounds in Court according to an Order made last Court & urgeing Severall Reasons why he could not Serve in the Common Councell this Court with an unanimous consent returned him his mony back againe.

Fourteenth & last Court of Robert Cole, Mayor, Friday next after the feast of St Luke, namely, 22 October 1686

Mr Thomas Matkin Chosen Major [sic].
Mr Thomas Matkin haveing been formerly nominated Major [sic] of this Corporacion for the ensueing yeare, This day according to his most Gracious Majesties Letters of Charter & Incorporacion to this Towne granted, he was by the unanimous Vote of this Court elected & chosen Mayor for the yeare ensueing.

Mr Robert Cole discharged from his office of Major [sic].
Whereupon the said Robert Cole is discharged from his Office of Major [sic] & the said Mr Thomas Matkin is sworne Major [sic] in his Stead in Corpus Christi Quire according to the auncient Custome of this Corporacion.

[fo. 702v] [Blank page]

THE HALL BOOK OF GRANTHAM 1686–1687

[fo. 703r] **First Court of Thomas Matkin, Mayor, 29 October 1686**

Thomas Matkin Esquire Mayor
Thomas Harrington Esquire
John Thorold Esquire
Robert Calcroft gentleman
John Coddington gentleman
Robert Cole gentleman
Thomas Ireland gentleman
Edward Pawlett gentleman
Thomas Fisher gentleman
John Robinson gentleman
Edward Bristow gentleman
Simon Grant gentleman
John Smith gentleman

Mr John Gasse
Mr John Newcome
Mr Edward Watson
Mr Thomas Simpson
Mr John Rollingson
Mr Samuel Procter
Mr Thomas Hutching
Mr Thomas Baly
Mr Richard Sentence
Mr William Kerke
Mr Robert Cole
Mr John Robinson
Mr Arthur Taylor

Names of the Officers

Coroner	Mr Robert Cole	Jur	Towne Clerke	Mr Samuell Procter
Escheator	Mr Thomas Ireland	Jur	Serjeant and	Thomas Calcroft
Collectors for	Mr Simon Grant	Jur	Gaoler	Robert Barton
Schoole House lands	Mr Richard Sentence		Leather Sealers	Richard Bristow
Churchwardens	Thomas Baly	Jur		Thomas Baly
	John Weaver			Thomas Marshall
Chamberlins	Thomas Hutching	Jur		George Wray
	William Kerke		Corne prisers	Richard Woulds
Cheife Constables	Mr John Gasse	Jur		Robert Orson
	Mr John Newcome		Overseers of	Thomas Hatfeild Junior
Market Place	Richard Wiles	Jur	the Markett	Thomas Leivesley
Constables	Thomas Robinson		Church Clerke	Robert Smith Senior
High Street	George Fitzrandolph	Jur	Bellman	Ralph Osborne
Constables	John Wigmore		Beadle	John Scott
Westgate	Henry Johnson	Jur	Key Bearors	Mr Mayor
Constables	William Barrell			Mr Baly
Walkergate	William Turner	Jur		Mr Hutching
Constables	Joseph Woods			
Swinegate	William Fearon	Jur		
Constables	Thomas Elston			

| Castlegate | Thomas Nixon | Jur |
| Constables | John Martin | |

Ordered that 40 li be taken up for the use of this Corporacion.
It is ordered at this Court that Forty pounds be taken up on Interest for the use of this Corporacion, And Mr Mayor, Mr Newcome, Mr Hutching & Mr Kerke do freely offer themselves to become bound for the said Sume.

[fo. 703v]

At this Court Mr Robert Cole late Mayor of this Corporacion delivered to Mr Matkin the Present Mayor the severall Charters following

King Edward the Sixt his Charter	Mr Wickliffes Tankard
Three Charters of Queen Elizabeth	Mr Horsmans Boll
One Charter of King James the first	Mr Greenwood Tankard
One Charter of Charles the First	Mr Battys Beaker
One of King Charles the Second	Mr Harringtons Tankard
One of King James the Second	Two Tumblers Batty &c
And Indenture & Catalogue of the	Kirkbys Boll
Books in the Library	Mr Greenwoods 13 Spoons
A Schedule Indented of the Writeings	One Salt & Cover
in the Hutch	Horsmans Wine Boll
A Book of Leases	Mr Wrights Boll
	Mr Storys Cup
The plate delivered up	Mr Woodroffe Tankard
The Horse race Cup	
Mr Archers Boll	

Francis Brown made free.
Allso at this Court came One Francis Browne a Forrainer & craved to be admitted a Freeman of this Corporacon, which this Court tooke into their Serious Consideracon, upon his paying of Ten pounds in Court was admitted thereunto & Sworne.

Second Court of Thomas Matkin, Mayor, 12 November 1686

Mr Thomas Matkin Mayor &c to be indempnified for the 40 li they became bound for.
At this court it is ordered that Mr Mayor, Mr Newcome, Mr Hutching & Mr Kirke be indempnifyed by this Corporacion for the Forty pounds which they are become bound for to Richard Sentence for the use of this Corporacion.

The Town Clerke to take the Charters up to London & to have his Charges borne.
Whereas upon reading a Rule of the Court of Exchequer for the Towne Clerke of the

Corporacion to deliver into the said Court Estreates of all Fynes Issues & Forfeitures which are by Charter granted to this Corporacion It is this day ordered that the Towne Clerke do carry with him up to London the Charters whereby the said Fynes are granted to this Coporacion & that he do waite upon Mr Halford who by a Deputacion under the Right Honourable the Earle of Rutlands hand and Seale (this day produced in Court) is nominated Deputy Recorder for this Corporacion to desire & Follow his advice and direccions for cleareing the same And that the Chamberlins do pay him what Expences he shall be at therein.

John Robinson junior & Simon Goodwin made free.
At this Court came John Robinson Junior who hath served his Appretiship with Mr John Robinson Brasier & Simon Goodwin Son of Simon Goodwin & craved to be admitted Freemen of this Corporacion which this Court takeing into their Consideracion did grant & they were Sworne accordingly.

[fo. 704r]

Mr Sentances accounts as Chamberlain.
Mr Sentence late Chamberlin accounteth as followeth
Disbursements   160 11 04 ob
Receipts   150 15 05 ob
due to Mr Sentence   009 15 11

Mr Nalls accounts as Chamberlain.
Mr Nall Chamberlin allso accounteth as followeth
Disbursements   012 17 02
Receipts   006 09 04
due to Mr Nall   006 07 10

Third Court of Thomas Matkin, Mayor, 21 January 1686/7

Mr Mills chosen Usher of the Schoole.
At this Court Mr Thomas Mills is unanimously nominated & elected Usher of this Schoole of Grantham with the proffitts thereunto belonging and that he shall enter into the said place at Lady day next ensueing untill which time Mr Calcroft the present Usher shall continue in the said place, & then receive his Sallary for the time past he desireing then to leave his said place.

The penalties of the Court to be put in execucion against John Bradfeild & Thomas Walton.
Allso it is ordered that the penalties of the auncient Court Orders be put in Execucion against John Bradfeild & Thomas Walton for tradeing not being Freemen of this Corporacion.

John Robinson Apothecary chosen a Common Councell Man.
Allso at this Court Mr John Robinson Apothecary is unanimously elected one of the Common Councill of this Corporacion formerly called the Second Twelve.

Fourth Court of Thomas Matkin, Mayor, 4 February 1686/7

Francis Bristow chosen promoter instead of Henry Haskard.
At this Court the place of Common promoter being vacant by the death of Henry Haskard is conferred upon Francis Bristow dureing the pleasure of this Court.

Mr Fisher to Lay down 10 li to prosecute Andrew Clarke & Mr Mayor to have his sallary out of the Mills.
Allso at this Court it is agreed that in consideracion Mr Fisher the present Tenant of the Tolls of this Towne doe lay downe ten pounds for the charges in prosecuteing Andrew Clarke a prisoner in this Gaole at the next Assizes that Mr Mayor shall receive his Sallary out of the First proffitts of the Mille after Midsummer next.

Mr Watson elected Alderman instead of Mr Pawlett deceased.
At this Court Mr Edward Watson is unanimously elected into the Office of one of the Aldermen of this Corporacion in the stead of Mr Pawlett deceased.

[fo. 704v]

Mr Bristow & Mr Baily accounts as Collectors of the Schoole house rents. 3 li remaines in their hands to be paid to Mr Mills.
At this Court Mr Bristow & Mr Baily Collectors for the Schoole house rents *anno* 1685 1686 account as followeth

Receippt Booke	45 08 04
paid	40 00 00
abatements allowed	02 07 10
Remaines in their hands which is ordered to be paid to Mr Mills	03 00 06

Mr Robinsons accounts as Collector of the Schoole house rents.
Mr Robinson Collector of the Schoolehouse rents Anno 1684 & 1685 passeth his Accounts as followeth

Received	45 04 02
paid	42 05 00
Abatements allowed	02 19 02
Toto	45 04 02

A warrant Ordered to distrein of Mr Robinson for refuseing his Office of Common Councellman being thereunto elected.
At this Court a Warrant is ordered to be sent to distreyne for the Summe of Ten pounds of Mr John Robinson Apothecary for refuseing to take upon him the Office of one of the Common Concill of this Corporacion he haveing the last Court been unanimously elected thereunto.

A warrant to distrein of John Bradfeild, Thomas Walton & Richard Smith for following their trades not being freemen of the Corporacion.
Allso a Warrant is granted to distreyne Thomas Walton, John Bradfeild & Richard Smith for Five Shillings apeice for exerciseing their Severall Trades within this Corporacion & not being Freemen thereof Contrary to the Custome of the same Corporacion.

That the Constables be kept harmeless for excuteing their said Warrants.
Allso it is ordered that the Constables be indempnefyed for executeing the said Warrants by this Court.

Samuel Hutchin made free.
Allso at this Court Samuell Hutching who served his Apprentiship to Matthew Dixon Currier was admitted to his Freedom & Sworne in Court according to Aunciet Custome.

Mr Arthur Tayler nominated a Common councell Man.
Att this Court Mr Arthur Taylor is nominated & elected one of the Comon Councill of this Corporacion.

Fifth Court of Thomas Matkin, Mayor, 8 April 1687

Robert Martin, Robert Fearon, Samuel Clipsham & Robert Perkins made Free.
At this Courte came Robert Martin a Foreigner & craved to be admitted a Freeman of this Corporacion & laid downe his tenn pounds allso Robert Fearon the eldest sonne liveing of his Father William Fearon, Sameul Clipsham the eldest sonne of George Clipsham & Robert Perkins eldest sonne of Mr Robert Perkins & likewise craved to be admitted Freemen which this Courte takeing into consideracion doe grant & they are Sworne accordeingly & pay their accustomed Fees.

[fo. 706r] **Sixth Court of Thomas Matkin, Mayor, 29 April 1687**

The Town Clerke to appear for the Constables at the Suite of John Robinson.
The Towne Clerke this day acquainteing the Courte that Mr Secker had brought two writts against the Constables of this towne at the suite of Mr John Robinson for distreineing the goods of the said Mr Robinson for tenn pounds for refuseing to take upon him the place of one of the Common Councill of this towne unto which he was

duely elected It is this day ordered that the towne clerke doe appeare for the said Constables & defend the said suite & that the said Constables be indempnified by this Corporacion in the said suite.

Robert Smith Chosen parish Clerk instead of Humphrey Turner.
At this Courte Robert Smith senior is chosen parish Clerke in the place of Humphrey Turner deceased.

An Assessment of 40 li to repair the Highways.
Ordered An Assessment of fourty pounds be made for the repaires of the highwaies.

Richard Smith made free.
At this Courte came Richard Smith a Forreigner & craved to be admitted a Freeman of this towne & laid downe his tenn pounds which this Courte takeing into consideracon have thought fitt to admit him a Freeman & returne him five pounds & he was sworne accordeingly.

24s intrest of 40 li Given by Mrs Millner distributed.
At this Court twenty four shilling halfe a yeares interest of 40 li given by Mrs Miller [*sic*] due at Lady day last was distributed by the Chamberlaine to widdow Holt, widdow Bringhurst, widow Castle, widdow Glover, widdow Mitchell & widdow Hollingworth in the presence of Mr Burnett minister of this towne.

Seventh Court of Thomas Matkin, Mayor, 15 July 1687

The Executors or Administrators of every one that is buried in the Church to pay 13s & 4d to the Churchwarden.
At this Courte it is ordered that whatever Corpes hereafter shall be interred in Grantham Church the Executors or Administrators of such person so deceased shall pay thirteen shillings & fourpence to the Churchwardens then in office for the breakeing up of the said ground, the said money to goe towards the repaires of the said Church & likewise that the said Executors or Admistrators, doe lay downe the same stones whole or new ones within a month next after or shall forfeit double the valew.

Mr Simpson Sworn Alderman in place of Mr Fisher.
At this Courte Mr Thomas Simpson is sworne Alderman in the place of Mr Thomas Fisher deceased.

Mr Ireland nominated Mayor.
At this Courte Mr Thomas Ireland is nominated Mayor of this towne for the yeare ensueing.

Mr Bristow & Mr Gass chosen Overseers of Market place pump & Thomas Baily & [sic].
At this Courte Mr Bristow & Mr Gass are chosen overseers for repaires of the market place pumpe & Mr Thomas Bayly & Ducker Newball for Westgate Well.

The Millmasters acquaint the Court that they had paid 100 li to Sir Robert Carr being the last due to him of the 1000 he lent the town.
The present Millmasters acquaint the Courte this day that they had paid 100 li being the last payment of the thousand pounds lately lent this towne by Sir Robert Carr all which thousand pounds has been paid out of the yearly proffitts of the mills.

[fo. 706v]

Daniel Deligne Esquire made Free.
At this Courte came Daniel Deligne Esq eldest sonne of Erasmus Deligne Esq a freeman & craved to be admitted a freeman of this Corporacion which this Courte takeing into consideracon doe grant & he is sworne accordeingly.

Eighth Court of Thomas Matkin, Mayor, 5 August 1687

The Towns debts taken into Considacion.
At this Courte the townes debts are taken into consideracon which are as follow

		li	s	d
13 July 1684	To Mrs Alice Leeming	150	00	00
9th June 1684	To the same	40	00	00
5th November 1685	To Mr Sentence	40	00	00
	To Sharpes heirs	50	00	00
	To Mrs Mary Baines	40	00	00
	To Mr Lenton	70	00	00
	Total	390	00	00

400 li to be taken up.
Ordered that four hundred pounds be taken up on security of the Mills at £5 per Cent that the aforesaid debts may be discharged.

Nathaniel Normansall, William Parker & Mathias Wing made free.
At this Courte came Nathaniel Normansell [sic] a foreigner & craved to be admitted a freeman of this Corporacon & laid downe his tenn pounds allso William Parker who had servd his apprentiship with Mr Poole the Hatter & Mathias Wing who had servd his Apprentiship with William Burbidge & craved to be admitted Freemen which this Courte takeing into consideracion doe grant & they are sworne accordeingly.

The fish shambles Channell to be amended.
Ordered that the Chanell by the fish shambles be amended by the Inhabitants thereabouts & the charges to be allowed them out of the Assessment for the highwaies & that the overseers of the Highwaies doe fill up the hole over against Robert Moores house with Rubbish.

The Collectors of the Schoole-house rents to pay the additionall Sallary to Mr Mills.
Ordered the Collectors of the Schoole-house rents doe pay to Mr Mills the Usher the additionall Sallary which was granted him before he was chosen usher for this next quarter & no longer.

Ninth Court of Thomas Matkin, Mayor, 18 August 1687

Thomas Charles accounts as Millmaster.
At this Courte Thomas Charles Millmaster of the towne Mill accounteth for the proffitts thereof
Received	97 05 00
Disbursements	89 00 08
due to the towne	08 04 04

which he paies & is discharged.

[fo. 707r]

William Coles accounts as Millmaster.
William Cole allso accounteth for the profitt of the Slate Mill as Followeth	li s d
Received	133 07 10
Disbursements	119 14 00
due to the towne	13 13 10

which he pays & is discharged.

Mr Lewis Hurst lends the Town 400 li.
This day Mr Lewis Hurst accordeing to a former promise brought into the Courte four hundred pounds which he lends to the towne at 5 li per centum to be paid at 100 li a yeare for security whereof he hath a mortgage upon the Mills as by the said mortgage beareing date this day & remaineing in the Hutch may appear.

Tenth Court of Thomas Matkin, Mayor, 2 September 1687

Ordered that the Churchwardens of Manthorpe make their Assessment &c.
At this Courte it is ordered that the Churchwardens of Manthorpe have notice forthwith to make their Assessment for the repaires of the Church & if they shall refuse to doe that then the Churchwardens of this towne doe make an Assessment upon the same.

Mrs Fisher takes the Tolls at 52 li per annum &c.
At this Courte came Constance the widdow of Mr Thomas Fisher & desires to take the tolls of this towne for the year next ensueing to begin the next court day at fifty two pounds per annum to be paid quarterly Which this Courte takeing in to consideracion doe lett her the said tolls at the said rate & Mr Dalton doe become security for the payment thereof.

Marshalls Wife & Children & a Stranger at Holme's to be Sent from this Town.
Ordered that Marshalls wife & children & the stranger at Holmes's be sent from this towne by a warrant to the place of their last abode.

An Assesment of 26 li to be made for the payment of the Constables bills.
Ordered an Assessment of twenty six pounds be made for the payment of the Constables their bills of disbursements for the year last past.

Francis Langton & Robert Frith made free.
At this Courte came Francis Langton a forreigner & laid down his tenn pounds & Robert Frith who had served his apprentiship with John Gibson baker & craved to be admitted Freemen of this corporacion which this Courte takeing into consideracion does grant & they were sworne accordeingly.

[fo. 707v] **Eleventh Court of Thomas Matkin, Mayor, 14 October 1687**

Mr Mayor to deliver to William Kirke Chamberlain 7 li 16s 0d & Six Silver Spoons.
At this Courte it is recorded that Mr Mayor delivers to William Kirke present Chamberlaine for this towne seaven pounds sixteen shillings which Mr Mayor received of one Henry Hodsons wife whereof the said chamberlaine did pay to the said woeman thirty shillings allso at this Courte Mr Mayor delivers to the said chamberlaine six silver spoons marked V : E & a rapier which was received from the said Hodson.

An Assessment of 60 li to be laid upon Grantham, Spittlegate & Manthorpe for the repaires of the Church.
At this Courte it is ordered that an assessment of threescore pounds be laid upon the Inhabitants & Freeholders of this towne Spitlegate & Manthorpe for & towards the repaires of this Church.

John Shootewell to repaire the Conduit at 1 li 10s 0d per annum.
The Chamberlaine acquaintes the Courte this day that he had made an agreement with John Shootewell a glazier for the repaireing the conduit at thirty shillings per annum for seaven yeares which this Courte does consent to.

One pound being the Intrest of Mrs Millners money distributed to 6 widdows
At this Courte 24s being halfe a yeares interest of Mrs Millers [*sic*] money was distributed to widdow Holt, widdow Bringhurst, widdow Castle, widdow Glover, widdow Mitchell, widdow Hollingworth in the presence of Mr Burnett minister of this towne.

If any person be elected Mayor & refuseth his Office he is to forfeit 20 li If an Alderman 15 li If a Common councell man 10 li &c.
At this Courte it is ordered that if it shall happen that any Freeman of this Corporacion shall be legally elected & chosen to the Major parte of this Courte to beare any office or place in this Corporacion & upon lawfull summons does not appear but refuseth to take the oath & execution of the place for such his contempt every person chosen into the place or office of Mayor of this towne so refuseing shall forfeit the sume of twenty pounds of lawful money of England every person being chosen into the office of an Alderman of this town so refuseing shall forfeit the sume of fifteen pounds of like money & every person chosen into the office or place of a common coucellor [*sic*] of this towne so refuseing shall forfeite the summe of tenn pounds of like lawfull money to be recovered by accion of debit to be prosecuted by the Mayor Aldermen & Burgesses of this Corporation for the time being for the use of this towne.

Richard Durham & James Dawson made Free.
At this Courte came Richard Durham who had served his apprentiship with Richard Durham his father & James Dawson who had served his apprentiship to Richard Sentence & craved to be admitted freemen of this Corporacion which this Courte does Grant & they are sworne accordeingly.

[fo. 708r] **Twelfth & Last Court of Thomas Matkin Mayor, on Friday next after the feast of St Luke namely 21 October 1687**

Mr Thomas Ireland elected & Chosen Mayor.
Mr Thomas Ireland haveing been formerly nominated Mayor of this corporacion for the year ensueing this day accordeing to his most gratious Majesties lettres of Charter & Incorporacion to this towne granted he is by the unanimous voate of this Courte elected & chosen Mayor of this towne for the yeare ensueing.

Mr Matkin discharged from the Office of Mayor.
Whereupon the aforesaid Mr Thomas Matkin is discharged from his office of Mayor & the said Mr Thomas Ireland is sworne Mayor in his stead in Corpus Christi Quire accordeing to the auncient custome of this corporation.

[fo. 708v] [Blank page]

THE HALL BOOK OF GRANTHAM 1687–1688

[fo. 709r] **First Court of Thomas Ireland, Mayor, 27 October 1687**

Thomas Ireland Esquire Mayor
Thomas Harrington Esquire
John Thorold Esquire
Robert Calcroft gentleman
John Coddington gentleman
Robert Cole gentleman
Thomas Matkin gentleman
John Robinson gentleman
Edward Bristow gentleman
Simon Grant gentleman
John Smith gentleman
Edward Watson gentleman
Thomas Simpson gentleman

Mr Richard Sentence
Mr Robert Cole junior
Mr John Rollingson
Mr Samuell Procter
Mr John Gass
Mr Thomas Hutchin
Mr Thomas Bayly
Mr John Newcomb
Mr William Kirke

Names of the officers

Coroner	Mr Thomas Matkin	Key Keepers	Mr Mayor
Escheator	Mr John Robinson		Mr Bayly
Collectors for	Mr John Smith		Mr Newcomb
Schools house rents	Mr Samuell Procter	Market Place	Richard Wiles
Church	Mr Thomas Baily	Constables	William Turner
Wardens	Mr John Newcomb	High Street	George Fitzrandolph
Chief	Mr Richard Sentence	Constables	John Wigmore
Constables	Mr Robert Cole	Westgate	Henry Johnson
Leather	John Owen senior	Constables	William Barrett
Sealers	Thomas Marshall	Walkergate	William Parker
	Thomas Baily	Constables	William Fearon
	George Wray	Swinegate	Thomas Rear
Corne	William Newton	Constables	Francis Brown
Prizers	Richard Woulds	Castlegate	Robert Orson
Market	Anthony Kirke	Constables	Robert Machin
Sayers	William Burbidge		
Town clerk	Samuel Procter		
Sergeant and	Thomas Calcroft		
Gaolor	Robert Burton		
Church Clerk	Robert Smith senior		
& Bellman	Ralph Osborne		

[fo. 709v]

Mr Matkin delivers up the town plate.
At this court Mr Matkin late Mayor delivers the towne plate to the present Mayor as follows

The Horserace Cup	Mr Battyes two tumblers
Mr Andrews bolle	Mr Kirkbyes boule
Mr Wickliffes tankard	Mr Greenwoods 13 spoones
Mr Horsemans Cup	One salte and cover
Mr Greenwoods tankard	Mr Horsemans wine boule
Mr Battyes Beaker	Mr Wrights boule
Mr Harringtons tankard	Mr Storyes Cup
	Mr Woodroffes tankard

As also these Chartres following
1 of King Edward the Sixth
3 of Queen Elizabeth
1 of King James the first
1 of King Charles the first
1 of King Charles the Second
1 of King James the Second

An indenture or catalogue of the books in the Library

A Booke of the towne leases

Second Court of Thomas Ireland, Mayor, 18 November 1687

William Fearon to have 14 li to Carry away the Cripples.
At this Court an agreement is made with William Fearon senior that he the said William Fearon doe convey and releive the severall criples which come to this towne for this year to come & that he have fourteen pounds paid him for the same by the Constables at the four usual quarters in the yeare.

William Fearon to pay to the Towne 3 li to go with his watercart with shod wheeles.
It is allso agreed with the said William Fearon that he have leave for this year to come to goe with his watercarte with shod wheeles payeing therefore to the use of this towne three pounds.

Third Court of Thomas Ireland, Mayor, 16 December 1687

Mr William Kirkes Accounts as Millmaster.
At this Court William Kirke accounteth for the profitts of the towne Mill from the Midsummer last to the Account day

	li	s	d
Received	34	07	10

Disbursed   23 11 00
due to the towne   10 16 10

Thomas Hutchins accounts as Millmaster.
Thomas Hutchins allso accounteth for the proffits of the Slate Mill for the same time
Received   51 06 00
Disbursed   44 01 03
due to the towne   07 04 09

[fo. 710r]

His accounts for the Wind Mill.
He allso accounteth for the Winde Mill   li   s   d
Received   00 11 10
Disbursed   04 12 06
due to Thomas Hutchin   04 00 08

His accounts as Chamberlain.
He allso accounteth as Chamberlain the last yeare
Received   121 14 06
Disbursed   127 04 01
due to Thomas Hutchin   05 10 05

William Kirke accounts as Chamberlain.
William Kirke allso accounteth as Chamberlaine
Received   526 12 01
Disbursed   538 00 11
due to William Kirke   11 08 10
more due to him which he had omitted in his account   01 00 00
                                                         12 08 10

George Burbidge made free.
At this Court came George Burbidge a Forreigner & he craved to be admitted a Freeman of this Corporacion & laid down his ten pounds which this Courte takeing into consideracion did grant & he was sworne accordeingly.

Mr Thomas Hursts Gift of 50 li.
At this Court came Lewis Hurst gentleman and acquainted the court that his Cozen Mr Thomas Hurst of London had given fifty pounds to the use of this towne which is by this Courte ordered to be distributed for the putteing forth of poore children of this towne Apprentices.

John Weavers accounts as Churchwarden.
John Weaver late Churchwarden accounteth as followeth

Received	099	01	02
Disbursed	116	00	08
Due to John Weaver	16	19	06
Abatements allowed	06	07	06
due to him in all	23	06	00

[fo. 710v]

Fourth Court of Thomas Ireland, Mayor, 10 February 1687/8

Overseers of the poore to send away Marshalls wife & Children.
Ordered that the Overseers of the poore do take care to convey Marshalls wife & children from this towne they being likely to prove chargeable to the same.

The Recorder to be consulted whether the deeds of the red Lion should be delivered to Mr Lewis Hurst or no &c.
Whereas in the yeare 1670 there was a deed or setlement made by the towne of the red Lyon Inn upon trustees in trust for the payment of twelv pounds *per annum* to the Schoolmasters & dames & for other uses in the said deed mencioned which said gift of 12 li per annum was the gift of Dr Hurst and whereas the counterparts of the said deeds have lately been delivered into the townes hands This day upon the request of Mr Lewis Hurst Grandson of the said Dr Hurst to have the same delivered into his hands It is ordered that they be reposed in the Town Clerks hands untill such time as the Recorder be consulted.

Time taken till the next Court to consider whether Mr Grant, Mr Walton and Mr Beck should have Securety given them for 250 li borrowed of Sir Robert Carr by their predecessors for the Towns use.
At this Court came Mr Grante, Mr Walton and Mr Beck & desired they might have security given them for 250 li which was formerly borrowed of Sir Robert Markham [*sic*] by their predecessors as they say for the towne use, but it not being made plainly appear to the Courte that it was not borrowed for that use they take him to consider of it while next Court day.

The Chamberlain to pay the Town Clerk his Charges he disburst the 2 Last yeares.
At this Court the Town clerk produced his bill of charges for business done for two years last past in the whole amounting to 18 li 14s 4d whereof he had received 10 li It is by this Court ordered that the Chamberlaine doe pay him the remainder.

John Bradfeild and John Draper made Free.
At this Courte came John Bradfeild and John Draper Forreigners & craved to be admitted Freemen of this Corporacion & laid down 10 li a peice which this Court takeing into consideracion doe grant and retourne them five pounds a peece back again & they are sworne accordeingly.

Fifth Court of Thomas Ireland, Mayor, 6 April 1688
Two pounds to be paid to Marshalls wife when she Comes at London.
Ordered that the Overseers of the poore doe give the carrier forty shillings to pay to Marshalls wife when she comes at London & that the carrier be agreed with to carry her & her children to London.

Joseph Hutchin and Bracebrig Green made free.
At this Court came Joseph Hutchin who had served his apprenticeship with Mr Beck & Bracebridge Green who had served his Apprentiship with Robert Smithson & craved to be admitted Freemen of this Corporacion which this Court takeing in to consideracion doe grant & they are sworne accordeingly.

[fo. 711r]

Every Freemans stall not to exceed 14 feet & every forraigner 10 feet & a penalty of 20s is to be Levyed of the Offenders.
Whereas the present Chamberlaines & the present tenants of the stalls did this day complaine to the Court that severall of the tradesmen of this towne incroached so farr with the lenghth of their stalls on the severall fair dayes that there was not roome in the faire for the stalls of the Forreigners And this Courte takeing into consideration the severall aunceint Courte orders concerneing the same doe this day unanimously agree and order that neither of the Chamberlaines nor any other person or persons whatsoever impowered to lett the stalls of this towne shall at any time hereafter lett to any person whatsoever any more than one stall, & the Court does hereby limmit the length of the Stalle of every Freeman of this towne not to exceed fourteen foote & the length of the Stall of every forreigner not to be above tenn foot upon pain that every person or persons offending against any thing conteined in this order whether he be the tenant of the stall or either of the Chamberlaines that shall lett any more stalls then one & that not above the Length aforesaid or any other person or persons whether Freeman or Forreigner that shall incroach with his or their stalls above the respective lengths hereby limited shall for every first offence forfeit to the use of the Corporacion the summe of twenty shillings of lawfull money of England to be levied by distress & sale of the offenders goods rendering the over plus if any such shall be.

Sixth Court of Thomas Ireland, Mayor, 25 April 1688

The Town Clerk to write to get an appearance enter'd in the Crown Office to a Quo Warranto *Served upon the Mayor against the Charter & a Copy thereof made.*
Whereas Mr Mayor acquainted the Court this day that the Under Sherriffe had served him in person with a *Quo Warranto* against the Charter of this towne *ret' Quinden' Pasche* [Latin – to be returned at the Quindene of Easter, that is, the fifteenth day after Easter Sunday] next. It is by this Court ordered that the Towne clerk doe write up to London to get an appearance entred in the Crowne office & that a copy of the Charter be made forthwith.

A Warrant of Attorney to be sealed by the Towne Seale to Authorize Mr Cook to appear in the Crown Office to the informacion upon the Quo Warranto.
Ordered that a warrant of Attorney be sealed with the Common Seale of this Towne to authorize Mr John Cooke one of the Clerkes in the Crowne Office to appeare to the Informacion upon the *Quo warranto*.

The Writeing concerning the red Lyon to be putt into Mr John Hursts hand.
Ordered that the writeing concerneing the red Lyon be put into Mr John Hursts hands of this towne he being one of the trustees in the said writeings mencioned.

[fo. 711v] Seventh Court of Thomas Ireland, Mayor, 4 June 1688

Thirty pounds to be taken upp sent to London for Counsell.
The Town Clerke acquainteing the Courte this day that he had received a copy of an informacion against the Charter of this towne It is at this Courte unanimously agreed that 30 li be raised & sent up to London with instruccions to the Clerke of the Crowne office who appeares for this towne in order to take Councill & get a plea drawn & putt in to the said Informacion the beginning of next terme.

The Chamberlain to gett the 30 li forthwith upon Intrest.
It is likewise ordered that the Chamberlains doe forthwith gett the said 30 li & if they have it not ready that they doe procure the same upon intrest for three months & that the said interest be allowed them & and if the said 30 li be not sufficient to pay the counsellors Fees & other fees of the Courte & other charges it is ordered the [present] Chamberlaines doe reimburse the same.

Eighth Court of Thomas Ireland, Mayor, 8 June 1688

Mr Robert Cole to go up to London with the Town Clerke and take the Charters with him and the lease of the Queens Tolle to be taken out of the Hutch.
It being agreed last Court that 30 li be raised by the Chamberlaines to be sent by to London to pay counsells fees & other charges of the Courte in defending the suite in nature of a *Quo Warranto* brought against the towne It is by the Courte ordered that Mr Robert Cole be desired to go to London with the Town clerke to take care of the same & it is unanimously agreed that the severall Charters of the towne be delivered into Mr Robert Coles hands to be carried up to London it being necessary that they be produced when the plea is putt in & that the lease of the Queens tolls be taken out of the Hutch.

An Assessment of 12 li to be laid upon this Towne toward the repaires of the Highways.
At this Court came the present overseers of the Highways of this towne & acquainted the Court they had laid money out of their own pocketts in repairing the Highways of this towne & that there still wanted more repaires. It is by this Court agreed & ordered that an Assessment of 12 li be made & laid upon this towne for & towards the repaires of the same.

Ninth Court of Thomas Ireland, Mayor, 25 June 1688

Mr Robert Calcraft, Mr Robert Cole, Mr John Robinson, Mr Edward Bristow, Mr Symon Grant & Thomas Simpson Aldermen be discharged from their offices as Aldermen by his Majesties order in privy Counsell.
Whereas Mr Mayor acquainted the Courte this day that his Majesty by his order in privy Counsell dated 7th June 1688 under the Seale of the said privy Councell had declared Mr Robert Calcroft, Mr Robert Cole, Mr John Robinson, Mr Edward Bristow, Mr Symon Grant & Thomas Simpson Aldermen to be displaced from their severall places of Aldermen accordeing to a proviso in the late Charter granted to this towne. They are accordeingly at this Courte discharged from their said severall offices or places of Aldermen.

[fo. 712r] Tenth Court of Thomas Ireland, Mayor, there near the seventh hour after noon of the same day

Mr Edward Secker, Mr Edward Coddington, Mr Nathaniel Garthwaite, Mr John Poole apothecary, and Mr John Poole Haberdasher elected Aldermen instead of Mr Robert Calcroft, Mr Robert Cole, Mr John Robinson, Mr Edward Bristow, Mr Symon Grant & Mr Thomas Sympson.
Whereas at the last Courte by his Majesties order in privy Counsell under the Seale of the said Privy Counsell Mr Robert Calcroft, Mr Robert Cole, Mr John Robinson,

Mr Edward Bristow, Mr Symon Grant & Mr Thomas Simpson [sic] were dismissed from their severall places of Aldermen of this towne. At this Court accordeing to the directions of his Majesties lettre under his signet manuall bearing date the 8th of June 1688 Mr Edward Secker, Mr Edward Codington, Mr Nathaniel Garthwaite, Mr John Poole & Mr John Poole Haberdasher are unanimously elected Aldermen of this Corporacion & tooke the accustomed oaths and the oaths of Allegience & Supremacy.

Eleventh Court of Thomas Ireland, Mayor, 20 July 1688

A warrant to distrein Mr Francis Brown for suffering townsmen to tipple contrary to the Statute.
At the Court it is ordered the warrant be made to distrein for 10s on Francis Brownes house for suffering townesmen to tipple contrary to the Statute.

An Habeas Corpus *to be procured to remove John Lambert to Nottingham.*
Ordered that a *habeas Corpus* be procured to remove John Lambert to Nottingham gaole being accused for being marryed to a second wife with the first being alive.

The Chief Constables provide a duckeing Stoole at the Town Mill.
Ordered that the Chiefe Constables doe provide a duckeing stoole at the towne Mill.

The Chamberlain to pay Mr Mayor the 2 guineas he paid Mr Evans the Kings Messenger.
Whereas Mr Mayor acquainted the Court that he had paid Mr Evans the Kings messenger 2 guineas it is ordered that the Chamberlaines doe repay him.

Twelfth Court of Thomas Ireland, Mayor, 10 August 1688

Mrs Fisher Widow takes the tolls at 52 li per annum.
At this Court came Constance Fisher widdow the present tenant of the tolls of this towne & desired to be admitted tenant to the same for one yeare after the expiracion of her present Lease being the next account day which is accordeingly granted her upon the same condicions & the same rent be [sic] 52 li to be paid quarterly.

Mr Secker and Town Clerk to go to Nottingham to advise with Serjeant Bigland about settleing the Towns mills & and other townes lands for the use of the Church & poor.
Ordered that Mr Secker & the Town clerke doe goe to Nottingham to advise with Serjeant Bigland about settleing the towns mills & other townes lands upon trustees for the use of the Church & poore.

Mr Thomas Cole chosen one of the Aldermen.
At this Court Mr Thomas Cole is chosen one of the Aldermen of this town & takes the accustomed oath & the oaths of Allegiance and Supremacy.

Mr John Coddington, Mr Burbidge & Anthony Kirke chosen Common Councellors.
At this Court Mr John Codington mercer, William Burbidge & Anthony Kirke are chosen Common Counsellors of this towne & the said William Burbidge & Anthony Kirke sworne.

[fo. 712v]

The overplus money of the schools House Rents to be paid to Mr Mills.
At this Court it is ordered that the overplus money of the Schoole house rents be paid to Mr Mills the Usher for the care he takes of the schools.

Thomas Mills and Charles Osborn made free.
At this Court came Thomas Mills eldest son of Thomas Mills & Charles Osborn who had served his Apprentiship to his father & craved to be admitted Freemen of this corporacion which this Courte takeing into consideracion doe grant & they are sworne accordeingly.

Mr Edward Secker elected Mayor.
At this Court Mr Edward Secker is unanimously elected & nominated Mayor of this Corporacion for the year ensueing.

The Chamberlain to pay the rest of the Charges to Mr Grainge in that he was at in defending the Charter.
Whereas Mr Grainge sent down his bill of charges for defendeing the charter being 34 li 00s 06 d whereof he had received 25 li it is by the Courte ordered that the Chamberlaines doe send up the other nine pounds.

Thirteenth Court of Thomas Ireland, Mayor, 28 September 1688

Sir John Brownloe Baronet made free.
At the Courte Came Sir John Brownlow Baronet & desired to be Admitted a Freeman of this Corporacion & laid downe his tenn pounds which this Court takeing into consideracion doe grant & he was sworne accordeingly.

An Assessment of 37 li to be made to pay of the Constables bills.
At this Courte it is ordered that an Assessment of thirty seaven pounds be made for & towards the payment of the Constables their bills of disbursements for the year last past.

A fine of 10 li to be laid upon Mr John Coddington junior if he refuses the Office of Common Councellor time given untill next Court.
At this Court Mr John Codington junior hath time given him whilest next Courte to take upon him the place of a Common Counsellor of this towne & if he shall then refuse to take the said place it is ordered that a fine of 10 li be laid upon him for his refusall.

John Bass, Richard Wellbourn, Andrew Poole, George Charity, John Osborne, Thomas Emerson, Charles Hotchin & William Baily made free.
At this Court came John Bass eldest son sonne of John Bass, Richard Welbourne who had served his Apprenticeship with Isabell Brumpton, Andrew Poole eldest sonne of Christopher Poole, George Charity eldest sonne of Francis Charity, John Osborne eldest sonne of John Osborne junior, Thomas Emerson who had served his Apprenticeship with John Marshall, Charles Hotchin who had served his Apprenticeship with Henry Johnson & William Bayly who had served his Apprenticeship with Thomas Baily & craved to be admitted Freemen of this Corporacion which this Courte takeing into consideracion doe grant & they are sworne accordeingly.

[fo. 713r] [The entry following is written at the bottom of the page. There is evidence that a leaf was inserted and held in place by three or more pieces of gum.]

Fourteenth & Last Court of Thomas Ireland, Mayor, Friday next after the Feast of St Luke namely 19 October 1688

Mr Edward Secker elected & chosen Mayor.
Mr Edward Secker haveing been formerly nominated Mayor of this Corporacion for the year ensueing this day accordeing to his most Gratious Majesties lettres of Charter & incorporacion to this town Granted he is by the unanimous voate of this Courte elected & chosen Mayor of this town for the year ensueing.

Mr Ireland discharged from the Office of Mayor.
Whereupon the aforesaid Mr Thomas Ireland is discharged from the office of Mayor & the said Mr Edward Secker is sworne Mayor in his stead in Corpus Christi Quire accordeing to the aunctient custome of this Corporacion.

[fo. 713v] [Blank page bearing marks that indicate a sheet had been inserted.]

[fo. 714r] Thirteenth Court of John Codington [sic], Alderman, 6 November 1688

At this Court his Majesties proclamacion being read for restoreing Corporacions to their ancient Charters Liberties rights & franchises, Accordeingly the aunctient Courte which was in being at the time of the Surrender of the late Charter Anno domini 1684 being mett by an Unanimous Vote of the said Courte Mr Edward Secker is Chosen one of the Commoners of this Courte & sworne Constable then are there remaineing in the Calendar Thomas Shorte & William Burbidge unto which two others are chosen (vizt)

Mr Edward Secker and Mr John Newcomb Fellmonger out of which Mr Edward Secker is chosen of the Second twelve & sworne accordeingly.

At this Courte Mr Edward Secker is chosen one of the Comburgesses of this towne & Sworne accordeingly.

Allso Mr Nicholas Beck, Mr Edward Bristow, Mr Simon Grant, Mr William Haskard & Mr John Smith are chosen Comburgesses & sworne accordeingly.

At this Court Mr Edward Secker, Mr Edward Leivesly & Mr John Robinson are sent as Comburgesses into the body of the Church.

Mr Edward Secker nominated Alderman.

At this Court Mr Edward Secker is unanimously nominated Alderman of this Corporacion for the year ensueing.

George Read dismissed the Courte.

At this Courte upon the reasonable request of George Read to be dismissed the Courte, he is accordeingly by consent of the same dismissed from his place.

At an Assembly held by John Codington gentleman, and the Comburgesses & Burgesses of Grantham aforesaid in Corpus Christi Quire in the Prebendary Church there 6 November 1688.

First did sitt downe upon the Cushion or place of Eleccion Mr John Codington.

Then were sent down into the body of the Church by an Unanimous Vote of this Assembly Mr Edward Secker, Mr Edward Lievesly & Mr John Robinson as three Comburgesses.

Who are all chosen to come by & sitt upon the Cushion or place of Eleccion

Then are there three Comburgesses upon the Cushion or place of Eleccion (vizt) the said Mr Secker, Mr Leivesly & Mr Robinson

Out of which three Comburgesses upon the Cushion or place of Eleccion one of them is to be chosen Alderman for the year ensueing.

And thereupon by the Unanimous Vote of this Assembly Mr Edward Secker is chosen Alderman for the year ensueing.

Whereupon the said Mr John Codington is discharged from his office of Alderman & the said Mr Edward Secker Sworne Alderman in his stead for this Burrough and Soake of Grantham accordeing to the auncient custome of the same.

[fo. 714v] [Blank page]

THE HALL BOOK OF GRANTHAM 1688–1689

[fo. 715r] **First Court of Edward Secker, Alderman, 9 November 1688**

Mr Alderman
Mr Robert Calcroft
Mr John Codington
Mr Robert Cole
Mr Thomas Matkin
Mr Thomas Ireland
Mr Edward Leivesly
Mr John Robinson
Mr Nicholas Beck
Mr Edward Bristow
Mr Simon Grant
Mr William Haskard
Mr John Smith

Mr William Cole
Mr William Burbidge
Mr Edward Watson
Mr Thomas Rouly
Mr John Gibson
Mr Thomas Simpson
Mr William Kirke
Mr Thomas Shorte
Mr John Newcomb
Mr Anthony Kirke
Mr Thomas Bayly

Names of the Officers

Coroner	Mr Ireland	Key Bearers	Mr Alderman
Escheator	Mr Leivesley		Mr Bayly
Collectors for	Mr Haskard		Mr Anthony Kirke
Schoole house rents	Mr Langley	Market Place	John Marshall
Churchwardens	Thomas Bayly	Constables	William Turner
	John Newcomb	High Street	Mathias Wing
Chamberlains	Anthony Kirke	Constables	William Fearon
	Jonathan Weaver	Westgate	William Knight
Cheife	William Cole	Constables	Thomas Leivesly
Constables	William Burbidge	Walkergate	Edward Greenall
Town Clerke	Samuell Procter	Constables	Roger Blankney
Sergeant &	Thomas Calcroft	Swinegate	Thomas Rear
Goaler	Robert Barton	Constables	Richard Owen
Leather	John Owen	Castlegate	Richard Dawson
Sealers	George Wray	Constables	William Parker
	Thomas Marshall	Town Waites	William Hickabothom
	Thomas Bayly		Leonard Butcher
Corn prizers	Thomas Rowly		John Wilcock
	John Gibson		Roger Hutchison
Market Sayer	William Turner		
	Mathias Wing		

Church Clerke &	Robert Smith senior
Bellman	Ralph Osborne
Beadle	John Scott

[fo. 715v]

Names of the Commoners

Market Place
John Marshall
William Turner

High Street
Mathias Wing
William Fearon
John Gass
Arthur Tayler
William Bristow

Westgate
William Knight
Thomas Leivesly
Thomas Hutchin
John Weaver
Thomas Bayly tanner

Walkergate
Edward Greenwood
Roger Blankney
James Bristow

Swinegate
Richard Owen
Thomas Rear
John Newcomb baker
Richard Sentence
Robert Langley

Castlegate
Richard Dawson
William Parker

William Kirke, Thomas Short, John Newcombe, William Burbidge, Anthony Kirke & Thomas Baily chosen Second Twelve.
At this Courte William Kirke, Thomas Shorte, John Newcomb, William Burbidge, Anthony Kirke & Thomas Bayly are chosen second twelve men of this Corporacion & sworne accordeingly & tooke the oaths of Allegiance and Supremacy as did all the second twelve then sitteing except John Gibson.

Samuel Procter continued Town Clerke.
At this Courte Samuell Procter the former Town Clerke is elected the continued Town clerke of this Corporacion & sworne accordeingly.

Town Plate delivered to Mr Secker.
At this Courte Mr Ireland late Mayor delivers to the present Alderman the Town Plate as Followes (vizt)

The Horserace Cupp
Mr Archers bolle
Mr Wickliffs Tankard
Mr Horsemans Cup

Mr Battys 2 tumblers
Mr Kirkebyes bolle
Mr Greenwoods 13 spoones
one Salt & cover

Mr Greenwoods Tankard
Mr Battyes Beaker
Mr Harringtons Tankard

Mr Horsemans 2 eard Cup
Mr Wrigts bolle
Mr Storyes Cup
Mr Woodroffes Tankard

and these Charters followeing
1 of King Edward the 6th
3 of Queen Elizabeth
1 of King James the 1st
1 of King Charles the 1st
1 of King Charles the 2nd
1 of King James the 2nd

[fo. 716r] Second Court of Edward Secker, 16 November 1688

Thomas Quinningbrow restored to his Goalers place.
At this Courte came Thomas Quiningborow late Goaler of this town before the surrender of the late Charter of King Charles the second & who was displaced by the Charter of King James & craved to be admitted to his former place which this Courte takeing into consideracion & his Majesties late proclamation for restoreing Corporacions to their antient rights &c & allso an order in privy Counsell concerneing the same being read It is by this Courte granted that the said Thomas Quiningbrow be admitted to his said place and time is given to Robert Barton who is now in possession of the said Goale untill Mayday next to remove his goods out of the Goale.

An Assessment of 40 li to be laid upon the town, Spittlegate & Manthorpe for the repaires of the Church.
At this Courte an Assessment of fourty pounds is order'd to be made & laid upon this town Spitlegate & Manthorpe for & towards the repaires of the Church.

George Burbidge, William Turner, Thomas Mills, William Parker, Mathias Wing, Charles Osborne, John Osborn, Robert Martin & Nathaniel Normansell made free.
At this Courte George Burbidge, William Turner, Thomas Mills, William Parker, Mathias Wing, Charles Osborne, John Osborne, Robert Martin & Nathaniel Normansell doe take the oaths of Freemen of this Corporacion.

Third Court of Edward Secker, 7 December 1688

Sir John Brownlow sworn freeman.
At this Courte Sir John Brownlow who had formerly paid his tenn pounds to this towne takes the oath of a Freeman of this Corporacion.

Counsell to be consulted whether this Town and Soake be lyable to pay to the building & repaireing the County Goale.
At this Courte it is ordered that Counsell be consulted whether this towne & Soake be lyable to pay to the buildcing & repaires of the County Goale.

The Alderman & Comburgesses, Second twelve & Town Clerk take the Oaths of Allegiance & Supremacy except John Gibson who is dismissed from his place.
At this Courte the Charter of King Charles the Second being read & therein being a clause that the Alderman, Burgesses & other ministers of this town should take the oaths of allegiance & Supremacy upon takeing upon them the said places The Alderman, Comburgesses, second twelve men & Town clerke now present in place have taken the said oaths except one John Gibson a second twelveman who refuses to take the same being tendred him who is therefore by order of this Courte dismissed from his said place.

John Wildbore, Robert Parkins, William Doughty, John Draper, Thomas Ellson, Thomas Nixon, George Charity & Richard Wellborn sworn freemen.
At this Courte came John Wildbore a forreigner & craved to be admitted a Freeman of this Corpoation & laid down his tenn pounds this Courte doe grant his request & he, Robert Parkins, William Doughty, John Draper, Thomas Elson, Thomas Nixon, George Charity & Richard Wellburne [sic] are accordeingly sworne Freemen.

The Millmasters to pay the mony arising from the Mills to Mr Lewis Hurst.
At this Courte the present Millmasters are ordered to pay the money ariseing out of the profitts of the Mills to Mr Lewis Hurst for interest.

[fo. 716v] **Fourth Court of Edward Secker, 18 January 1688/9**

Mr Alderman to Consult Counsell about the County Goale.
At this Courte it is agreed that Mr Alderman doe consult Serjeant Bigland or what other Counsell he thinks fitt whether this town & Soake be lyable to the building & repaires of the County Goale.

Overseers of the poor to repay Mr Newcombes bill disburst as Chamberlain.
Upon readeing Mr Newcombs account as Chamberlain there being some Queries about thatcheing Widdow Mawns house & the money paid for conveying Marshalls wife & children to London it is by this Courte ordered that the Overseers of the Poore doe repay the said charge.

Fifth Court of Edward Secker, 15 February 1688/9

All Inmates & others to give security or to be sent to their Last Legall abode.
At this Courte it is ordered that all inmates & others latley come to this towne doe either give security or that they be forthwith sent to the place of their last abode.

An assessment of 4 Nobles to be made for the repaires of the Marketplace pump.
Ordered an assessment of four nobles be made for the repaires of the Market place pump by Mr Bristow & Mr Gass overseers.

Mr William Kirke Late Chamberlain delivers to Anthony Kirke present Chamberlain six silver spoons & 6–6–0 in money.
At this Courte William Kirke late Chamberlaine delivers to Anthony Kirke present Chamberlain six silver spoones marked V E which were received of one Hodsons wife in Mr Matkins year & one weareing sword & six pounds & six shillings in money.

The Chamberlain to pay Phillip Cooke 30s & some other mony that was expended at the Irish Alarme.
Ordered the Chamberlaine doe pay Philip Cooke 30s & some other money which was expended in the late Irish alarme.

The Chamberlain to pay Mr Robert Cole 20s he Laid down at Belton.
Ordered that the Chamberlain doe pay Mr Robert Cole 20s which he laid down at Belton.

Ordered the Overseers of the Poore doe repay the Chamberlain the money which he laid down for lookeing to widdow Grocock.

James Catlett & Robert Idle made free.
At this Courte came James Catlett the eldest sonne of James Catlet & Robert Idle who had served his apprenticeship with John Weaver & craved to be admitted Freemen of this Corporacion which this Court doe grant & they are sworne accordeingly.

Thomas Rowlet discharged from his Office of Second Twelveman comeing to the Court disguised in drinke &c.
At this Courte Thomas Rowlett one of the second twelvemen comeing to this Courte disguised in drinke & haveing been guilty of severall other misdemeanours is by the unanimous order of this Courte dismissed from his place of Second Twelveman & discharged from his further attendance at this Courte or any hereafter.

Mr Thomas Baily to present in Lincoln Courte all person that refuse to pay his Assessment & to be kept indempnified.
Ordered that Mr Thomas Bayly the present Churchwarden doe present all such persons as refuse to pay their assessments in Lincoln Courte & if any suit or charge doe arise upon the same that he be indempnified by this towne.

No mony to be paid out of the Towns stock to Gentlemens servants.
Ordered for the future that noe money be paid out of the Towns stock to gentlemens Servants at any gentlemans house.

[fo. 717r] **Sixth Court of Edward, 1 March 1688/9**

Time given to Abraham Bell to take his freedome.
At this Courte Abraham Bell hath time while after the fair to take his freedome.

Thomas Rowlett discharged from brewing.
Ordered that a warrant be sent to discharge Thomas Rowlett from Breweing.

All Townes & Commoners land to be put in all Assessment.
Ordered that for the future all townes land & Commoners land be put in all Assessments.

John Shecraft admitted Loadsman to the Town Mill & Loadsmen to put their bells on the Mill horse necks.
Ordered that John Sheacroft [sic] be admitted Loadsman to the Slate Mill & that the Loadsmen of both mills doe put the bells on the Mill horses necks & doe constantly goe with the same.

John Bradfeilds accounts as overseer of the poor.
John Bradfeild overseer for the Poor of this towne 1688 accounteth as followeth

	li	s	d
Received	60	18	09 ob
Disbursed	56	13	08
Abatements allowed	05	06	08
	62	00	04
Due to the Accomptant	01	01	06 ob
Memorandum five shillings of Mr Taylor which was not allowed as an abatement was not diducted in his accounts	00	05	00
So there remains due to him but	00	16	06 ob

Edward Todkills accounts.

	li	s	d
Edward Todkill allso accounteth as overseer for the said year.			
Received	55	02	02
Disbursed	47	15	01

Abatements allowed	04	00	00
	51	15	01
Due to the town	03	07	01
Whereof he is to pay Mr Bradfeild	00	16	06

[fo. 717v] **Seventh Court of Edward Secker, 3 May 1689**

Mr John Newcombe Churchwarden to pay Mr Thomas Baily 25–12–2d.
At this Courte it is ordered that Mr John Newcomb the present Churchwarden doe pay to Mr Thomas Baily late Churchwarden the summe of 25li-12s-2d which is due to him & allowed upon his accompt.

The undersheriffe to be sent to about the Town & Soake serving as Jurors at Lincoln.
Ordered the Undersherriffe be sent to to [sic] allow the order of Assize for freeing the town & Soake from serveing as Jurors at Lincoln.

Dr Lambert to be sent to about Dr Hides money.
Ordered that Dr Lambert be sent to about the 20s given by Dr Hide to the Poore of this towne yearly.

Counsell to be consulted about the difference between Mr Thorold and the Town concerning the Tythe of the mille &c.
Whereas there is a difference between this town & Mr John Thorold Proprietor of the North & South Prebends of this towne about the tithe of the Mills of this towne & allso about some money which is due from the said Prebends to the Poore of this towne It is by this Courte agreed that this towne be at halfe charge in consulteing counsell with the said Mr Thorold about endeing the said difference.

All Alehousekeepers to sell their ale &c by full sealed Wincester Quarts &c.
Whereas there have been severall complaints made to this Courte of the severall abuses comitted by the pubique [sic] houses of this town & Soake in breakeing the assize of ale & beer It is by this Courte ordered that for the future after midsummer day next every Inkeeper & alehousekeeper within the said town & Liberties doe sell their ale & beer by common known full Winchester pintes quarts or gallons & by no other measure whatever & these to be sealed by the known common seale of this towne upon paine of being prosecuted at the Sessions for their severall defalts.

Robert Barton admitted & confirmed Goaler.
It is by this Courte unanimously agreed that Robert Barton the present Goaler who had time given him in the said place untill Mayday last be admitted & continued Goaler in the said place & is sworne accordeingly.

John Owen continued Master of the house of correccion.
Ordered that John Owen senior be continued in the place of Master of the house of correccion for this town & Soake.

Mr Edward Leivesly nominated Alderman.
At this Courte Mr Edward Leivesly is unanimously nominated Alderman of this Corporacion for the year ensueing.

[fo. 718r] **Eighth Court of Edward Secker, 28 May 1689**

Mrs Rookesby to be paid 30s for quartering Scotch soldiers.
Ordered that Mrs Rookesby be paid 30s by the Constables towards the charge she was at when the Scotch soldiers were in town she being charged with 34 more than her tickett.

The Chamberlain to pay Mr Aldermans sallary of 10 li.
Ordered the Chamberlaine doe pay Mr Alderman his sallary of 10 li out of the first money which comes in.

The Mill Masters to pay Mr Hurst [h]is money he having delivered an Ejectment against the mills.
Whereas Mr Alderman & the Millmasters acquaint the Courte this day that Mr Lewis Hurst had delivered declarations in ejectment against the town Mills for want of payment of his money it is by this Courte ordered that two Millmasters out of this Courte be chosen by Mr Hurst who shall enter upon the said Mills & retorne the proffitts thereof to the use of Mr Hurst onely.

One of the 1st 12 & one of the 2nd 12 to be Chosen Clerks of the market for one month & so successively two other.
Ordered that one of the first twelve being a Justice of the Peace & one of the second twelve be deputed Clerkes of the markett for one month & after that two other to continue for one month more & so successively two other to continue another month who dureing their severall & respective months shall so often as they thinke fitt weigh & examine the bread of the bakers of this town & soake & shall take care to punish the defalters.

Ninth Court of Edward Secker 14 June 1689

Personall security to be given for Mr Hurst mony by 16 persons in Court & they to have for their security the Mills & Leases of the Tolls.
Whereas Mr Alderman acquaints the Courte this day that Mr Lewis Hurst doth still insist to have his money paid in It is by this Courte ordered that personall security be given the said Mr Hurst by sixteen persons of this Courte: that is to say four & four in

a bond & it is likewise unanimously agreed by this Courte that all & every person who shall so become bound shall have for their security the Mills & the Lease of the tolls of this towne assigned to the [*sic*] them untill the same be paid.

Mr Calcroft sworn deputy Alderman for one month.
Mr Alderman being sick Mr Calcroft is sworn deputy for one month.

The Churchwardens to be indempnified by the Courte if they prosecute any persons for not paying their Assessment.
Whereas Mr Newcomb & Mr Bayly the present Churchwardens doe acquaint this Courte that they had cited William Fox of Gonerby to the spirituall Courte at Lincoln for not payeing his assessment to the repaires of the Church for his land in Manthorpe it is by this Courte ordered that if the said William Fox or any other person haveing land in Manthorpe doe refuse to pay & stand suite that then the said Churchwardens be indempnified by this Courte.

[fo. 718v] **Tenth Court of Edward Secker 28 July 1689**

William Kirkes accounts as Mill-Master.
William Kirke accounteth for the profitts of the town Mill for the year last past.

	li	s	d
Received for 64 quarter & 2 strike of Malt	62	03	06
for Moulter	24	03	00
total	86	06	06
Disburst	23	18	02
Wages	24	06	00
Allowance	03	03	00
	51	07	02
Due to the town	34	19	04

His accounts as Chamberlaine.
He allso accounteth as Chamberlaine for the last year.

Received	113	08	06
Disbursements	155	03	07
Due to William Kirke	41	15	01
so there is due to him upon the ballance of both accounts	06	15	09

Thomas Bailys accounts as Churchwarden.
Thomas Baily accounteth as Churchwarden 1688/9

Received the assessments of Grantham Manthorpe & the Spitlegate	68	18	07
The Quarteridge booke	44	04	04
for Bells & graves	05	04	00
Total	118	06	11

Disbursements	136 05 08	
Abatements allowed in the Assessments & Quarteridge	07 13 05	
	143 19 01	
Due to Thomas Bayly	25 12 02	

John Newcombes as Chamberlaine
John Newcomb accounteth as Chamberlain for the year last past

Received	84 08 07	
Disbursements	158 13 05	
Due to John Newcomb	74 04 10	

His accounts as Mill Master.
He accounteth for the profits of the Slate Mill

Received	120 01 10	
Disbursements	51 14 00	
Due to the town	68 07 10	

& for the Windmill.
he accounteth for the Windemill

Received	02 19 06	
Disbusements	06 10 04	
due to John Newcomb	03 10 10	

allso for 50 li received of Mr Hurst.
he accounteth for 50 li received of Mr Hurst being the Legacy of Mr Thomas Hurst

	50 00 00	
Disbursements	34 04 08	
due to the town	15 15 04	
due to town upon the ballance of the whole amount	06 07 06	
interest spent	00 02 01	

[fo. 719r]

Mr Hursts personall security.
At this Courte Mr Lewis Hurst delivers in his security which he had upon the town Mills by mortgage for 400 li & has personall security given him & the persons who become bound for the same receive security on the said Mills to save them indempnified And it is ordered that they doe enter upon the said Mills on monday next to raise the said money.

The persons who received the profitts of the Mills to pay Mr Hurst his interest for 100 li.
It is by this Courte ordered that those persons who doe enter upon the Mills to receive the profitts for the payment of Mr Hursts money by 100 li by the year doe likewise pay to the said Mr Hurst the full interest due for the remaineing hundred pounds.

Eleventh Court of Edward Secker, 9 August 1689

An Application to be made to the Commissioners of Sewers that they call a Session for the river Witham.
At this Courte it is ordered that Aplication be made to the Commissioners of Sewers that they will call a session of Sewers for the river Witham.

Mr Matkin &c to speake to Mr Burnet about the Schoole.
Ordered Mr Cole, Mr Matkin, Mr Ireland, Mr Leivesly, Mr Robinson, Mr Beck, Mr Grant & as many of the first & second company as can meet doe speake to Mr Burnet about the afaires of the Schoole.

The Constables to repair the Ladders of every Ward &c.
Ordered the Constables of every Ward doe repair the publique Ladders & fire Hookes in their respective wards & where any are wanteing they are to make new ones so that there be two ladders & two fire hookes for every ward And that for the future the ladders be hung under a penthouse (to be made for that purpose) in the Goale yarde.

Thomas Ellson & Henry Musson Overseers of High Street Well & Thomas Baily & John Weaver Westgate well.
Thomas Elson & Henry Musson are apointed overseers of High Street Well Mr Thomas Baily & John Weaver overseers of Westgate well.

Ordered a Commission be sent for to Lincoln to examine Wittnesses in the suit comenced against Fox for not payeing his Church Assessment.

The Chamberlain receives 3s 4d *per se* as Bucket money of Mr Alderman, Mr Beck & Mr Haskard & 1s 8d of Mr Burbidge, Mr Shorte, Jonathan Newcomb & Anthony Kirke.

The Goaler not to Lend the Town Buckets.
Ordered that for the future the Gaoler doe not lend the Common Buckits of this town to any person for any private use under pain of forfeiteing ten shillings for every Bucket so lent.

Memorandum Roger Blankney received of Jonathan Marshall late Cole byer eight pounds & tenn shillings & three pounds & tenn shillings of Mr Joseph Woods.

Ordered an Assessment of 20s be made for repaires of Westgate Well.

[fo. 719v] **Twelfth Court of Edward Secker, 20 September 1689**

Mr Fox paid his Assessment & Charges to Mr Francis.
At this Courte Mr Newcomb the present Churchwarden acquaints the Courte that whereas he had formerly caused William Fox of Gonerby to be cited to the Spirituall Courte at Lincoln for not payeing his Assessment for the repaires of the Church for his land in Manthorpe feild that the said William Fox had appeared to the citacion & stood suite but that this weeke Mr Wyatt Francis the Procter at Lincoln for the Churchwarden had sent him word that the said Mr Fox had paid the said Assessment to him & likewise his bill of charges.

An Assessment of 40 li to be made for the Constables bills.
At this Courte it is ordered that an Assessment of fourty pounds be made & laide upon the freeholders & Inhabitants of this town for the payment of the Constables their bills of disbursements.

Thirteenth Court of Edward Secker 24 October 1689

The Town Mill &c to be assigned to Mr Coddington &c who are bound to Sir John Brownlow for 400 li.
At this Courte it is ordered that the town Mill & the Slate Mill & the Queens Lease of the tolls be Assigned to trustees for the security & indempnifieing of Mr Codington & others who are become bound to Sir John Brownlow for 400 li for the Use of the town.

Mrs Fisher takes a Lease of the Tolls.
At this Courte Mrs Fisher takes a Lease of the tolls from the 26th instant to the 26th October 1690 at 52 li *per annum* to be paid by the four usuall quarterly payments. Memorandum she leaves the 40s to the curtesy of the Courte

Constables Assessments				
Marketplace	15 11 04	Swinegate	04 01 00
their bills	02 01 10	Abatements allowed	00 01 03
abated	00 04 05	their bills	02 03 10
paid the Chamberlain	13 05 01	paid the Chamberlaine	01 15 11
High Street	05 14 08	Castlegate	03 17 07
abated	00 03 02	their bills	01 18 08
their bills	01 02 06	abatements allowed	00 01 02
paid the Chamberlain	04 08 00	paid the Chamberlain	01 17 09
Westgate	08 09 10	Walkergate	03 11 08
abated	00 04 03	abatements	00 01 05

their bills	02 03 06	
paid the Chamberlain	06 02 01	
	Mr Aldermans bill	02 00 00
	Mr William Cole	06 16 00
	Mr William Burbidge	08 01 10
	Chief Constables	

[fo. 720r]

An Assembly holden by Edward Secker gentleman Alderman the Comburgesses & Burgesses of Grantham aforesaid in Corpus Christi Quire in the Prebendary Church there on the fryday next after St Luke being 25 October in the first year of the reigns of William & Mary &c 1689.

First did sit down upon the Cusheon or place of Eleccion Mr Edward Secker in Corpus Christi Quire in the Prebendary Church there
Next to him did sit down upon the Cusheon or place of Eleccion two Comburgesses vizt Mr Edward Leivesly & Mr John Robinson.
Then were sent down into the body of the Church by an unanimous vote of this Assembly three Comburgesses vizt Mr Nicholas Beck, Mr Edward Bristow & Mr Simon Grant.
Out of which Comburgesses in the body of the Church one is chosen to come up & sit upon the Cushion or place of Eleccion vizt Mr Nicholas Beck
Then are there three Comburgesses upon the Cushion or place of Eleccion vizt Mr Edward Leivesly, Mr John Robinson & Mr Nicholas Beck
Out of which 3 Comburgesses upon the Cushion or place of Eleccion one is to be chosen Alderman for the year ensueing.

Mr Edward Leivesley chosen Alderman.
And thereupon by the unanimous vote of this Assembly Mr Edward Leivesly is chosen Alderman for the year ensueing
Whereupon the said Mr Edward Secker is discharged from his office of Alderman and the said Mr Edward Leivesly sworne Alderman in his stead of this Burrough & Soake of Grantham accordeing to the aunchient Custome of the said town.

And so this Assembly breakes up.

THE HALL BOOK OF GRANTHAM 1689–1690

[fo. 720v] **First Court of Edward Leivesly 1 November 1689**

Mr Alderman Leivesly	2nd 12
Mr Robert Calcroft	Mr William Kirke
Mr John Codington	Mr Thomas Baily
Mr Robert Cole	Mr William Cole
Mr Thomas Matkin	Mr Thomas Simpson
Mr Thomas Ireland	Mr Thomas Shorte
Mr John Robinson	Mr John Newcomb
Mr Nicholas Beck	Mr William Burbidge
Mr Edward Bristow	
Mr Simon Grant	
Mr William Haskard	
Mr John Smith	
Mr Edward Watson	

Names of the Officers

Coroner	Mr Robert Calcraft	Market Sayers	Simon Goodwin
Escheator	Mr John Robinson		Thomas Hatfeild sen
Collectors of	Mr Beck	Comon Promoter	Thomas Hatfeild
the Colledg rents	Mr Thomas Baily	Market Place	Robert Cole junior
Churchwardens	John Newcomb	Constables	John Codington
	William Turner	High Street	Mr William Doughty
Chamberlaines	William Burbidge	Constables	William Fearon
	William Bristow	Westgate	William Barrett
Cheife Constables	William Kirke	Constables	John Martin
	Thomas Baily	Walkergate	Edward Todkill
Town Clerke	Samuel Procter	Constables	John Bradfeild
Serjeant	Thomas Calcroft	Swinegate	John Withey
& Gaoler	Robert Barton	Constables	Joseph Hutchin
Bailiffe of	Robert Barton	Castlegate	William Barker
the Liberties		Constables	James Ferman
Church Clerk	Robert Smith senior		
Bellman	Ralph Osborne		
Beadle	John Scott		
Leather	John Owen	Town Waites allowed	
Sealers	George Wray		William Higgabotham

	Thomas Marshall	Leonard Butcher
	Richard Woulds	John Willcock
Corn prizers	William Newton	Roger Hutchison
	Robert Orson	
	Mr Alderman	
Key bearers	John Newcomb	
	William Burbidge	

[fo. 721r]

Names of the Commoners
Market place
Mr Robert Cole junior
Mr John Codington junior
John Marshall
William Turner

High Street
Mr William Doughty
William Fearon
Arthur Tayler
William Bristow

Westgate
William Barrett
John Martin
Thomas Leivesly
Thomas Hutchin
John Weaver
Thomas Baily tanner

Walkergate
Edward Todkill
John Bradfeild
Edward Greenhall
Roger Blankney
James Bristow

Swinegate
John Withey
Joseph Hutchin
Richard Owen
Thomas Rear
John Newcomb
Richard Sentence
Robert Langley

Castlegate
William Parker
James Ferman
Richard Dawson

At this Courte Mr Secker late Alderman delivers to the present Alderman the Towne plate vizt.

The Horserace Cup
Mr Archers bolle
Mr Wickliffes Tankard
Mr Horsemans Cup
Mr Greenwoods tankard
Mr Battyes Beaker
Mr Harringtons Tankard

Mr Battyes two Tumblers
Mr Kirkbyes bolle
Mr Greenwoods 13 spoones
one Salt Cellar & Cover
Mr Horsemans boll
Mr Wrights Bolle & Cover
Mr Stories Cup
Mr Woodroffes Tankard

William Fearon to carry Cripples.
At this Courte William Fearon agrees with this town to carry all Criples & to releive all passengers for this next year for which he is to receive of the town fourteen pounds.

[fo. 721v] **Second Court of Edward Leivesly 22 November 1689**

At this Courte Mr Secker late Alderman delivers up to the present Alderman these Chartres Followeing
1 of King Edward 6th
3 of Queen Elizabeth
1 of King James 1st
1 of King Charles 1st
1 of King Charles 2nd
1 of King James 2nd

Mr Secker dismissed from Court.
Whereas Mr Edward Secker one of the Comburgesses of this towne & the present Coroner did this day acquaint the Courte of his great indisposition by the palsy whereby it was a great trouble to him and danger to his health to attend the Courte & desired the favour of this Courte to be dismissed from his further attendance, Which this Courte takeing into Consideracion doe grant his request & he is accordeingly dismissed from his said places of Comburgess & Coroner & Mr Robert Calcroft is sworn Coroner in his stead.

The Charters to be perused the Town Clerke to be kept harmeless if any damage come to him for not returning fines into the Exchequer.
At this Courte it is ordered that the severall Charters of this town be perused in open Courte & upon readeing of the same there being found a grant to the Corporacion of all Sessions fines & other forfeitures within the said Libeerties of the said Corporacion to be levyed by their own proper officers It is now the opinion of the Courte that this Corporacion has right to the said fines forfeitures &c & that the Town Clerk ought not to Estreat the same into the Exchequer & if any trouble or damage doe happen to him by reason of his not doeing the same it is hereby ordered & agreed he be indempnified & saved harmeless by this Courte.

Mr Langton to have a Warrant to distrein as Overseer of the poor.
Upon the Complaint of Francis Langton one of the overseers of the poore of this town that severall persons haveing Leases of this townes land & being tenants to Mr Moores land & the Coney Greens doe refuse to pay their several Assessments to the Poore It is ordered that a warrant be granted to distrein for the same.

William Kirke to pay 1s 8d for Buckett money.
At this Courte William Kirke one if the second twelve men of this town to pay 1s 8d for Bucket money.

John Sharpe made Free.
At this Courte John Sharpe who had served his Aprentiship to Thomas Hutchin comes & craves to be admitted a freeman of this Corporacion which this Courte doth grant & he is sworne accordeingly & payes the accustomed Fees.

[fo. 722r] **Third Court of Edward Leivesly 20 December 1689**

Mr Watson sworn Comburgess.
At this Courte Mr Edward Watson is Sworne one of the Comburgesses of this town in the place of Mr Secker lately dismissed & tooke the oaths apointed by the late act of Parliament.

Anthony Kirke Chamberlain delivers to William Burbidge 6 Silver Spoones &c.
At this Courte Anthony Kirke Chamberlain for the year last past delivers to William Burbidge present Chamberlaine six silver spones Marked V E one sword & belt & six pounds eight shillings & five pence in money.

Willson of Newarke to be distreined of for not paying toll &c.
Whereas Mrs Fisher widow & Henry Johnson the present tenants of the Tolls & Stalls of this town did at this Courte Complain that one Willson a freeman of Newarke who keeps the Marketts & Faires in this town does refuse to pay for his toll & stall to the said tenants It is this day ordered that the said Wilson be distreined on for the same & that the said tenants or Chamberlaines of this town or whosoever shall take the said distress bee indempnified by this Courte if any accion be Comenced.

A Penthouse to be built in the Goale yards.
It is ordered that the Chamberlaine doe builde a penthouse in the Goale yard for the Townes Ladders & hookes & that the charge be put in the Constables bills.

Fourth Court of Edward Leivesly 14 March 1689/90

The Towns houses be Assessed to the poor &c.
Whereas the present Overseers of the Poore & other officers of this Corporacion to whom Assessments have been granted for the reimbursement of the summes by them expended in the execucion of their offices Have at this Courte made their Complaint that the severall tenants of the houses & lands belonging to this Corporacion doe refuse to pay the severall Assessments laid upon them It is at this Courte ordered & agreed that the said Town houses & lands be Assessed for so much as they are really worth over & above the reserved rents & that if the said tenants doe refuse to pay the same that they be distreined or otherwise prosecuted for the same & that the Officers who shall doe be indempnified by this Courte.

Thomas Hatfeild senior sworn Common Promoter.
At this Courte Thomas Hatfeild senior is sworne Common Promoter for this town & Liberties in the roome of Francis Bristow lately deceased.

[fo. 722v]

John Weaman, Humphrey Turner & John Ferman made Free.
At this Courte came John Weaman who had served his apprentiship with Anthony Kirke, Humphrey Turner who had served his apprentiship with Thomas Rowly & craved to be admitted Freemen of this Corporacion as alsoe John Ferman who had served his apprentiship to Mr Edward Leivesly which this Courte takeing into consideracion does grant & they were sworne accordeingly & pay their accustomed Fees.

William Higinbotham Sworn Parish Clerk.
At this Courte William Higgabotham [*sic*] is Sworn parish Clerke in the place of Robert Smith senior lately deceased.

Sir William Ellis his 20 li to buy Wheels to imploy the poor.
Whereas Mr Kirke a member of this Courte acquainted the Courte this day that Sir William Ellis one of the members in Parliament for this Burrough had given twenty pound to sett the poore of this town on worke, It is by this Courte ordered that the same be imployed in buyeing wheeles & other necessaries & that George Chantry be apointed Overseer of the said Worke.

Anthony Kirke accounts as Chamberlain.
	li	s	d
Anthony Kirke accounteth as Chamberlain for the year last past			
Received	67	17	10
Disbursed	94	11	07
Due to Anthony Kirke	26	13	09

Allso as Millmaster
He allso accounteth for the proffitts of the Town Mill			
Received	55	07	08
Disbursed	22	05	06
Due to the Town	33	02	02
Upon the ballance of the account there remaines due to the town	06	08	05

John Weaver as Chamberlaine
John Weaver accounteth as Chamberlain for the year last past			
Received	483	17	08
Disbursed	505	05	01
Due to John Weaver	21	07	05

As Mill Master
He accounteth for the profitts of the Slate Mill
Received   69 12 08
Disbursed   40 02 08
Due to the Town   29 10 00
Upon the ballance of the account there is due to this Town   8 02 07

Richard Woulds, Richard Owen, Thomas Nixon & Nathaniell Normansell as Overseers of the Highways.
Account as overseers of the Highwayes of this Town for the year last past
Received   20 19 06 ob
Disbursed   20 17 01
Due to the Town   00 02 05 ob

[fo. 723r] **Fifth Court of Edward Leivesly, 28 March 1690**

Sir William Ellis to be Consulted about raiseing 20 li more to imploy the poor.
Upon readeing of the Proceedeings of the last Courte toucheing the twenty pounds given by Sir William Ellis, & Mr William Kirke acquainteing the Courte what wheeles & other necessaries he had provided & that he had spoke to one Mr Bradfeild a woolman to imploy the Poore in spinneing wooll &c The said Mr Bradfeild acquaints the Courte that twenty pounds was too little to keep the poore on worke above one year without a further supply Whereupon it is by this Courte ordered a letter & a copy of George Dawsons will (who gave 60 li per annum to the Poore of this town) be sent to Sir William Ellis & the rest of the Feoffees in trust for the said will desiring them to give 20 li per annum out of the said estate for the imployment of the Poore in the said woollen manufacture.

John Newcombe as Churchwarden accounteth
John Newcombe Churchwarden in the yeares 1687, 1688, 1689
Received   149 06 01
Disbursed & abatements allowed   183 00 04
Due to the accomptant   033 14 03

An Assessment of 40 li to be made for him.
Ordered by this Courte that an Assessment of 40 li be made at Mayday next for the reimbursement thereof.

Francis Musson, William Haycock, John Ingerson junior, Thomas Rollinson, Robert Durham & Thomas Palfryman made free.
At this Courte Francis Musson eldest sonn of Henry Musson, William Hacock who had served his aprentiship with John Hacock, John Ingerson junior who had served his apprentiship with his Father John Ingerson, Thomas Rollingson who had served with

his Father John Rollison, Robert Durham who had served his aprentiship with Richard Durham & Thomas Palfryman a Forreigner (who laid down his tenn pounds) & craved to be admitted Freemen of this Corporacion which this Courte takeing into consideracion doe grant & retorne the said Thomas Palfryman five pounds & they are sworne accordeingly & pay 3s apeece to the Townclerk & serjeants & 5s apeece to the box.

[fo. 723v] **Sixth Court of Edward Leivesly, 16 May 1690**

William Doughy chosen Colebuyer.
At this Courte Mr William Doughty is chosen Colebuyer for the Poore in the roome of Roger Blankney who now lies very dangerously ill & he is ordered to weigh the coales which are now in the Cole house & to take an account what money the said Roger Blankney hath in his hands.

Mr John Weaver, Robert Cole, John Coddington, Edward Todkill, William Turner, Richard Dawson chosen of the 2d Company & Sworne except Mr Coddington.
At this Courte Mr John Weaver, Mr Robert Cole, Mr John Coddington, Mr Edward Todkill, Mr William Turner & Mr Richard Dawson are chosen to be of the second Company of this Corporacion & are sworne accordeingly except Mr Codington And now remaines in the calender Thomas Baily, William Bristow & John Bradfeild.

Mr John Robinson nominated Alderman.
At this Courte Mr John Robinson is unanimously nominated Alderman of this Corporacion for the year ensueing.

Mr Clerke [sic] *takes a Lease of the Mill Pingles for 21 years.*
At this Courte Mr Clarke takes a lease of the two town Mill Pingles for one & twenty yeares from the expiracion of his present Lease & give 3 li for a fine & is to pay 20s per annum.

Widow Holt a Lease of the peice of grass ground behind the Town Mill.
Allso widow Holt junior take a lease for one year of that peice of Wast grass ground beyond the town Mill the rent 2s 6d the Mill Masters have power to dig sods for the repaire of the Mill banks.

Seventh Court of Edward Leivesly, 4 July 1690

Mr William Cole dismissed from 2d 12 man.
At this Courte Mr William Cole one of the second twelve men of this town being gone out of the town is dismissed from his said place of second twelveman & discharged from his further attendance at this Courte.

Roger Blankney accounts as Cole Buyer.
At this Courte Roger Blankney late Cole Buyer accounts
Received of John Marshall late Colebuyer & Joseph Woods   12 00 00
Left in coles ten score hundred & a halfe bought in at 9d   07 10 04 ob
Paid for weigheing   00 04 04
    07 14 08 ob
remaines in his hands   04 06 03 ob

To pay 4 li to Mr Doughty which remains in his hands.
which he is orderd to pay Mr Doughty the present Cole buyer which will make his stock 12 li 01s 00d.

An Assessment of 30 li to be made for the repaires of the Highways.
Ordered An Assessment of thirty pounds be made & laid upon the Inhabitants & Freeholders of this town for the repaires of the Highwayes of this towne.

[fo. 724r]

Judith Smith Chosen Schoole dame.
At this Courte it is ordered that Judith Smith widow & relict of Robert Smith the Church Clerke lately deceased be admitted Schooledame in the Schoolehouse given by Dr Hurst in the roome of George Hutchin who is goeing out of the said house & place.

Mr Bradfeild to be consulted about the poore work.
Ordered that Mr Alderman & who he thinks fitt of the Courte doe consult Mr Bradfeild about setteing the Poore on worke.

Mr Smith promises to give an account next Courte when he paid Mrs Parkins the thirty shillings which he was ordered to pay her or els promises to pay the same.

Also the 2d Company take the Oath made in the 1st year of their Majesties reign.
At this Courte all the second twelve men now in place tooke the oaths mencioned in an act of Parliament made in the first year of their Majesties reigne all the first Company haveing taken them before.

Eighth Court of Edward Leivesley, 29 August 1690

Fifty pounds to be taken up for the Towns Use.
At this Courte the townes debts are taken into Consideracion being 61 li. in consideracon whereof it is by this Courte ordered that 50 li be taken up at interest for six months at the rate of 5 *per Centum* & that John Weaver, Robert Cole junior, William

Turner & Richard Dawson become bound for the same And thay they have the reversion of the Mills and tolls of this town assigned to them for their Counter Security.

The Beadle to pin all Swine he shall find goeing at Large in the Town Street & so have 1d a peice for the same.
Whereas Complaint hath been made unto this Courte of the mischeife & Nusance done by Swine goeing at large in the town streets It is by this Courte ordered that the beadle for the time being doe take care to pin all swine whatsoever he shall finde goeing at large in the town streets & that he doe take of the owner 1d for every swine or pig so pinned or impounded & if he shall any wayes neglect the same that then he shall forfeit 1d for every swine or pig so taken up or impounded by any other person.

Robert Barton to remove all dunghills &c out of the first yard in the Goale & the yard to be paved.
Ordered that Robert Barton the present Gaoler doe remove all dunghills hovells & swine out of the first yard in the said Gaole & that the same be paved by the Chamberlaines & afterwards kept clean by the said Gaoler & his successors.

Mr Mills to receive what Overplus money remains out of the Schoole house rents.
At this Courte it is ordered that Mr Mills the present Usher of the Schoole shall receive what overplus money arises out of the Schoolehouse rents so long as he continues Usher.

What Bucket money is in the Chamberlains hands to be laid out in Buckets &c.
At this Courte it is ordered that what Bucket money is now in the Chamberlaines hands be laid out in bucketts & that every person of the first & second twelve companies doe take the said bucketts to their own houses.

[fo. 724v]

A person refuseing the office of Alderman to forfeit 20 li: A Comburgess 15: A Second Twelveman 10: A Commoner five pounds &c.
At this Courte it is ordered That if it shall happen that any Freeman of this Corporacion allready chosen or that hereafter shall be legally elected & chosen by the Major parte of the Aldermans Courte for the time being to bear any office or place in this Corporacion & upon lawfull Summons does not apear but refuseth to take the oath & execucion of the said place for such his contempt; every person allready chosen or hereafter to be chosen into the place or office of Alderman of this town so refuseing shall forfeit the summe of twenty pounds of lawfull money of England every person chosen or hereafter to be chosen into the place or office of a Comburgess of this town so refuseing shall forfeit the summe of fifteen pounds of like money every person allready chosen or hereafter to be chosen into the place of office of a second twelve man of this towne so refuseing shall forfeit the sume of tenn pounds of like money every person allready chosen or hereafter to be chosen into the place or office of a Comoner of this Town so

refuseing shall forfeit the summe of five pounds of like lawfull money to be recovered by accion of debt to be prosecuted by the Alderman & Burgesses of this Corporacion for the time being for the Use of the said Corporacion.

Ninth Court of Edward Leivesly, 12 September 1690

The former Court Order to be taken into Considaracion.
At this Courte it is ordered that the former Courte order be taken into Consideracion & that what orders shall be thought fit be drawn up & confirmed by the Lord Cheife Justice or other Judges as the Statute apoints.

An Assessment of 30 li be made for the Constables.
At this Courte it is ordered that an Assessment of 30 li be made & laid up on this town for the payment of the Constables their bills of disbursements for the year last past.

Thomas Alham, Hanson Hawden, Samuel Newball, William Berriff & Edward Bristow made Free.
At this Courte came Thomas Allam [*sic*] who had serv'd his aprenticeship with William Newton, Hanson Hawden, who had served his aprenticeship with Joseph Burnham, Richard Hawden who had served his aprenticeship with William Grocock, Samuel Newball, who had serv'd his aprenticeship with John Withey, William Berriff who had served his aprenticeship with Mr William Haskard & Edward Bristow eldest sonne of Richard Bristow & craved to be admitted Freemen of this Corporacion which this Court takeing into consideracion doe grante & they pay their accustomed Fees to the Town Clerk & Serjeants & are sworne accordeingly.

Mr Becks accounts as Overseer of the poor.

		li	s	d
Mr Beck accounteth as one of the overseers of the Poore for parte of the yeares 1687/1688	Received	48	19	02
Paid		48	11	04
abatements allowed		01	07	06
		49	18	10
Due to Mr Beck		00	19	08
& George Burbidge				
George Burbidge allso accounteth as overseer for the said yeares	Received	52	02	10 ob
Disbursed		54	00	01
abatements allowed		01	03	11
		55	04	00
Due to George Burbidge		03	01	01 ob

[fo. 725r] **Tenth Court of Edward Leivesley 23 October 1690**

Mrs Fisher takes lease of the tolls.
At this Courte Constance Fisher widow takes a lease of the tolls belonging to this towne for one yeare next ensueing at 56 li *per annum* to be Paid by four equall quarterly payments.

Sir Brownlows gift to the Town. [Marginal note written below the following entry]
Mr Codington & the other Mill Masters acquaint the Courte that they had paid Sir John Brownlow 100 li due the beginneing of this month upon bond being parte of the 400 li which he lent the town & that Sir John Brownlow had freely given 20 li due for the interest of the said 100 li & the remaineing 300 li to the towne to be imployed in the Woollen Manufacture.

[fo. 725v]

At An Assembly holden by Edward Leivesly gentleman Alderman the Comburgesses & Burgesses of Grantham aforesaid in Corpus Christi Quire in the Prebendary Church there on the fryday next after St Luke being 24 October 1690.

First did sit down upon the Cushions or place of Eleccion Mr Edward Leivesly Alderman in Corpus Christi Quire in the said Prebendary Church
Next to him did sit down upon the Cushions or place of Eleccion two Comburgesses vizt Mr John Robinson & Mr Nicholas Beck.
Then is sent down into the body of the Church to Mr Edward Bristow & Mr Simon Grant by unanimous vote of this Assembly one other Comburgess vizt Mr Haskard
Out of which three Comburgesses in the body of the Church one is chosen to come up & sit upon the Cushions or place of Eleccion vizt Mr Bristow
Then are there three Comburgesses upon the Cushions or place of Eleccion vizt Mr John Robinson, Mr Nicholas Beck & Mr Edward Bristow
Out of which three Comburgesses upon the Cushions or place of Eleccion one is to be chosen Alderman of this towne for the year ensueing.

Mr Robinson chosen Alderman.
And thereupon by An Unanimous vote of this Assembly Mr John Robinson is chosen Alderman for the year ensueing
Whereupon the said Mr Edward Leivesly is discharged from his office of Alderman & the said Mr John Robinson is sworne Alderman in his stead for his [*sic*] Burrough & Soake of Grantham for the year ensueing accordeing to the ancient custome of the said Burrough.

And so this Assembly breakes up.

THE HALL BOOK OF GRANTHAM 1690–1691

[fo. 726r] **First Court of John Robinson, 31 October 1690**

                                            2d 12

Mr Alderman Robinson	Mr Thomas Shorte
Mr Robert Calcroft	Mr John Newcomb
Mr John Codington	Mr Thomas Simpson
Mr Robert Cole	Mr William Kirke
Mr Thomas Matkin	Mr Thomas Baily
Mr Thomas Ireland	Mr William Burbidge
Mr Edward Leivesly	Mr Anthony Kirke
Mr Nicholas Beck	Mr John Weaver
Mr Edward Bristow	Mr Robert Cole junior
Mr Simon Grant	Mr John Codington mercer
Mr William Haskard	Mr Edward Todkill
Mr John Smith	Mr William Turner
Mr Edward Watson	Mr Richard Dawson

Names of the officers

Coroner	Mr Edward Leivesly	Market Place Constables	Richard Wiles William Doughty
Escheator	Mr Nicholas Beck	High Streett Constables	William Parker John Withey
Collectors of the Colledge rents	Mr Watson Thomas Leivesly	Westgate Constables	James Ferman William Barrett
Chamberlaines	Mr Thomas Bayly John Bradfeild	Walkergate Constables	John Ferman Samuell Hutchin
Cheife Constables Church Wardens	Mr Shorte Mr Newcomb Mr Turner Mr Codington mercer	Swinegate Constables Castlegate Constables	Joseph Hutchin Francis Langton William Baily Robert Fearon
Town Clerk	Samuel Procter	Leather Sealers	John Owen George Wray Thomas Marshall Richard Woulds
Serjeant & Gaoler	Thomas Calcroft	Corne Praizers	William Newton John Newcombe
Bailiffe of the Liberties	Robert Barton	Markett Sayers	John Ferman Samuel Rollinson

Church Clerk	William Higgabothom
Bellman	Ralph Osbourne
Beadle	John Scott
Keybearers	Mr Alderman
	Mr Bayly
	Mr Codington

[fo. 726v]

Names of the Commoners

Market Place	Walkergate
Richard Wiles	John Ferman
William Doughty	Samuell Hutchin
John Martin	Edward Greenall
John Marshall	James Bristow

Highstreet	Swinegate
William Parker	Joseph Hutchin
John Withey	Francis Langton
John Bradfeild	Richard Owen
Arthur Tayler	Thomas Rear
William Bristow	John Newcomb
	Richard Sentence
Westgate	Robert Langley
James Ferman	
William Barret	Castlegate
Thomas Leivesly	William Baley
Thomas Hutchin	Robert Fearon
Thomas Baily	

At this Courte Mr Leivesly late Alderman delivers to the present Alderman the Town plate as follow's [sic]

The Horse race Cupp	Mr Batties two tumblers	Mr Batties Salt Cellar & cover
Mr Archers bolle	Mr Batties Beaker	Mr Horsemans bolle
Mr Wickliffes tankard	Mr Harringtons Tankard	Mr Wrights bolle & cover
Mr Horsemans Cup	Mr Kirkebyes bolle	Mr Stories cup
Mr Greenwoods tankard	Mr Greenwoods 13 spoones	Mr Woodcroftes tankard

And these Chartres 1 of King Edward 6th, 3 of Queen Elizabeth, 1 of King James 1st, 1 of King Charles 1st, 1 of King Charles 2d, 1 of King James 2d.

Robert Fearon to Carry away Cripples.
At this Courte Robert Fearon engages to convey all criples that come to this towne & to releive all passengers for one yeare for 13 li to be paid him quarterly & receives 1s in earnest.

He & Richard Dawson to have their water carts goe with shod wheele.
At this Courte Richard Dawson & Robert Fearon have leave to have their water Cartes goe with shod wheeles for this next year & are therefore to pay 40s apeice & give 1s apeece in earnest.

15–12–6: given towards the buildeing of Lincoln shire house & Goale.
Ordered that 15 li 12s 6d be given by this town & soake as a gratuity & no otherwise towards the buildeing of Lincoln Shire house & Goale.

[fo. 727r] **Second Court of John Robinson 28 November 1690**

If Mr Coddington again refuse to pay the 6–1–8 an accion to be brought against him.
Whereas the Chamberlaine acquaintes the Courte this day that Mr John Coddington refuses to pay the 6 li – 1s – 8d which is due to the town by on his account as Millmaster it is ordered that the Chamblaine doe again demand the same & if then he shall againe refuse to pay the same that an accion be brought against him therefore.

Overseers of the poor to enter on widdow Grococks house &c.
Ordered that the present Overseers of the Poore doe enter upon Widdow Grococks house in this town She being mantained by colleccion & that they doe pay the interest of 20 li unto Widdow Gibson who has a mortgage for the same & give an account of the surplusage of the rent to the town.

John Newball dismissed forthwith being Commoner paying 5 li.
At this Courte John Newball a Comoner of this Courte being desirous to be dismissed from his said place paid down his fine of five pounds which his request this Courte takeing into consideracion doe grant & he is accordeingly dismissed from his said place.

Francis Langtons accounts as Overseer of the poor.
Francis Langton accounteth as one of the Overseers of the Poore for the year last past

	li	s	d
Received	49	11	06
Disbursements & abatements allowed	54	02	01 ob
Due to Francis Langton	04	10	07 ob
paid more Mr Irelands Coroners Fee for Nix & Skevinton	00	13	04

William Wright accounts as Overseer for the poor.
William Wright accounteth as overseer for the said year

Received	59	07	05
Disbursements & abatements allowed	54	05	01
Due to the town	05	02	04
The 4 Millmasters for the last year account as Follows			
Mr Robert Cole Received	50	04	09
Disbursements	59	17	11 ob
Due to Mr Cole	09	13	02 ob
Mr John Codington Received	63	07	06
Disbursements	57	05	10
due to the towne	06	01	88
Mr Matkin Recieved	52	16	10
Disbursements	51	04	04
due to the Town	01	12	06
Mr Ireland Received	66	06	08
Disbursements	54	00	06
Due to the Town	12	06	02

[fo. 727v]

William Bristows account as Chamberlaine.

William Bristow accounteth as one Chamberlaine for the year last past	li	s	d
Received	34	17	02
Disbursements	34	16	06
due to the town	00	00	08

Mr Haskards account for the Schoole.

Mr Haskard accounteth as one of the Collectors of the Schoole house Lands for part of the yeares 88 & 89 Received	21	09	02
Disbursements	21	09	02

Robert Langley for the said year.

Robert Langley accounteth for the said yeares Received	21	12	06
Disbursements	21	12	06

Third Court of John Robinson, 20 February 1690/1

William Burbidge account as Chamberlaine.

William Burbidge accounteth as the other Chamberlaine for the year last past

Received	153	02	08
Disbursements	153	16	08
Due to William Burbidge	00	14	00

A Summe Sett to be Spent upon the Recorder at the Sessions.
At this Courte it is ordered that for the future no summe exceedeing five shillings be spent upon the Recorder at the Sessions in any charges besides the dinner.

William Hutchin & Samuell Rollison made free.
At this Courte came William Hutchin who had served his apprentiship with William Cole & Samuell Rollison who had served his aprentiship to John Scott & craved to be admitted Freemen of this Corporacion which this Courte takeing into consideracion doe grant & they pay 2s 6d apeice to the Chamblaine & 3s apeece to the officers & are sworne accordeingly.

John Owen to be discharged from his Office as keeper of the house of Correccion.
At this Courte it is ordered that John Owen the present Master of the house of Correccion be discharged from his said place at Lady day next & George Chantry be apointed in his place.

A Chimny to be to be [sic] *built for the poor in their Workhouse.*
At this Courte it is ordered that William Kirke doe pay to Mr Baily the present Chamberlain the charge he will be at in buildeing a chimney at Thomas Bayly the tanners house which is now hired for a workehouse for poore people out of the 20 li given by Sir William Ellis.

Mr Smiths account as Collector of the Schoole house rents.
Mr Smith accounteth as one of the Collectors of the Schoole house rents for the year 1687
Received   21 11 00
Disbursement   21 09 01
due to the towne paid Mr Watson   00 01 11

Mr Procter the Same.
Samuel Procter accounteth as the other Collector   Received   22 11 08
Disbursements   18 15 00
Due to the Schoolemaster paid of Mr Grant by Mr Burnetts order 02 16 08

Mr Turners as Churchwarden.
William Turner accounteth as Churchwarden for the year last past
Received   90 07 05 ob
Disbursements & abatements allowed   137 15 05
due to William Turner   47 07 11 ob

[fo. 728r] **Fourth Court of John Robinson, 6 March 1690/1**

Mr Becks account as Collector of the Schoole house rents.
Mr Nicholas Beck accounteth as Collector for the Schoole house rents for the year 89

	li	s	d
Received	21	04	08
disbursements	20	05	08
due to the towne	00	19	00

Thomas Baily as the Other.
Thomas Baily accounteth as the other Collector Received	21	08	00
Disbursements	20	02	06
Due to the towne	01	05	06

Mr Burnett continued Schoole master.
At this Courte Mr Burnett is ordered to be continued Schoolemaster of this towne & to enjoy the profitts thereunto belongeing.

Mr Owen to have half of the Sallary from George Chantry as Keeper of the house of Correccion dureing his Life.
Upon the Peticion of John Owen late master of the house of Correccion to have the said place continued unto him dureing his life by reason of his olde age & poverty It is by this Courte ordered that George Chantry who the last Courte was chosen overseer of the house of Correccion doe pay to the said John Owen one moyety of the Sallary ariseing out of the said place dureing the Life of the said John Owen.

An Order concerning the Schoole Masters.
It is this day ordered that for the time to come onely the yearly Sallary of twenty pounds apeice be paid to the Schoolemaster & Usher & that what overpluss money shall arise out of the Schoolehouse rents be expended by the Collectors thereof in repaireing the house belongeing to the said Schoole.

Robert Alcock made Free.
At this Courte came Robert Allcock who had served his apprentiship with Robert Smithson & craved to be admitted a freeman of this Corporacion which this Corporacion takeing into consideracion doe grant & he is Sworne accordeingly & payes his accustomed Fees.

[fo. 728v] **Fifth Court of John Robinson, 27 March 1691**

Mr Milles resigns his Ushers place & Mr Machin chosen in his Stead.
At this Court Mr Mills [sic] the present Usher of the schoole came in person & gave the Courte his thankes for their acceptance & continuance of him in the said place untill this time & now acquaintes this Courte that he was obleiged to reside at his liveing at Newton & Freely resignes his place of usher unto this Courte Whereupon Mr Edmund Machin is elected Usher of the said Schoole in his place with all profitts & apertenances thereto belongeing.

An Order for keeping the Sessions.
At this Courte it is ordered that for the future the Genereall Sessions of the Peace & generall Goale delivery for these Liberties be kept the monday before midsummer & in the weeke after Plowday yearly.

Joseph Lowe, Anthony Hotchkin, Robert Fox, Richard Newcombe made Free.
At this Courte came Joseph Low a Foreigner & laid down his tenn pounds Anthony Hotchin eldest sonne of Anthony Hotchin deceased, Robert Fox who had served his apprentiship with Mr John Smith, Richard Newcomb who had served his apprentiship with Augustin Newcomb & craved to be admitted Freemen of this Corporacion which this Courte takeing into consideracion doe Grante & they are sworne accordeingly.

Sixth Court of John Robinson, 8 May 1691

Concerning Mrs Trevilians Annuity.
At this Courte Mrs Travilians annuity of 15 li per annum for 36 yeares from the 2nd of February 14th Charles Second 1661 being produc't it apeares that the said annuity is discharged from all taxes whatever & that there are six yeares more to come in the said Indenture from the 2nd of February last.

An Assessment of 48 li to be made for the repaires of the Church.
At this Courte it is ordered that an assessment of fourty eight pounds be laid upon the Inhabitants of this town Manthorpe & Spittlegate for & towards the repaires of the parish Church of Grantham for the yeare last past.

Mr Beck nominated Alderman.
At this Courte Mr Nicholas Beck is unanimously nominated Alderman of this Corporacion for the yeare ensueing.

[fo. 729r] Seventh Court of John Robinson, 19 June 1691

Widdow Ulliot in Swinegate to have shares of Widdow Millers money.
At this Courte Widdow Ulliot senior of Swinegate is chosen in the place of widdow Kellham deceased to have share of the interest money given by Widdow Miller late deceased.

Richard Dawsons accounts as overseer of the highwaies.

	li	s	d
Richard Dawson accounteth as overseer of the Highwaies of this town for two years last past			
Received	31	12	10
Disbursements	32	16	09

abatements allowed	01	05	00
	34	01	09
due to the accomptant: which he stopt for his water carte	02	08	11

a 30 li Assessment for the Highwaies.
Ordered that an assessment of thirty pounds be laid upon the inhabitants of this towne for the repaires of the Highwaies thereof & the reinbursment of the former overseers.

Michael Solomon Gentleman made Free.
At this Courte came Michael Solomon gentleman a forreigner who had served five years as a clarke with Mr Secker a Freeman & laid down his tenn pounds & craved to be admitted a Freeman of this Corporacion which this Courte takeing into condiseracion doe grant & retorne him five pounds & he is Sworne accordeingly.

Eighth Court of John Robinson, 3 July 1691

An Inquiry ordered to be made after Robert Langleys house for John Papes Children.
Whereas the Children of John Pape late of this towne have been chargeable to this town in being maintaind by colleccion for some years And this Courte being informed that a certain house in this towne now in the possession of one Robert Langley doth of right belong to one of the said children but is at present deteyn'd by one Richard Gibson upon pretence of a mortgage it is now by this Courte Ordered that inquiry be made into the said busines & that a course at law may be taken for recovery of the same for maintenance of the said children.

Samuell Hammond made Free.
At this Courte came Samuel Hammond a forreigner & laid down his tenn pounds & craved too be admitted a Freeman of this corporacion which this Courte takeing into consideracion doe grante & he is sworne accordeingly.

A new valuacion of the Militia to be made.
Ordered that a new valueation of the militia of this town be made some time next weeke.

[fo. 729v] **Ninth Court of John Robinson, 28 August 1691**

Samuel Hammond to have 40s out his mony he paid for his freedome.
At this Courte it is ordered that Samuel Hammond who was made free last Courte doe receive 40s out of the tenn pounds he paid the Chamberlain for his Freedome.

William Charles made Free.
At this Courte came William Charles a Forreigner & laid down his tenn pounds &

craved to be admitted a freeman of this Corporacion which this Courte taking into consideracion doe grant & he is sworne accordeingly.

Robert Barton to be paid by the Chamberlaine what mony he disbursed in defence of the accion with Everitt.
At this Courte it is ordered that the Chainberlaine [*sic*] doe pay unto Robert Barton the Bailiffe of these Liberties what money he has disburst in defence of the accion which Everitt lately brought against him.

William Kirke brings acquittances for Wheeles & reeles.
At this Courte William Kirke produces acquittances for Wheeles & reeles bought with the money Sir William Ellis lately gave this town.

Tenth Court of John Robinson, 25 September 1691

Mrs Fisher takes a Lease of the Tolls.
At this Courte came Constance Fisher widow the present tenant of the tolls of this towne & takes a lease of the same for the yeare ensueing begining the twenty sixth of October next at 56 li *per annum* to be paid quarterly & gives one shilling in earnest.

William Beamont [sic], Robert Coates & Richard Chipsham made Free.
At this Courte came William Beaumont & Robert Coates both Forreigners & laid down their ten pounds & Richard Chipsham who had served his aprentiship with Mary Chipsham which this Courte taking into Consideracion doe grant & they are sworne accordeingly & pay their accustomed Fees.

Mr Robinsons accounts as Collector for the poor.
Mr John Robinson Collector for the Poore of this towne for the yeare

	li	s	d
last past passeth his accounts as followeth			
Received	45	13	09
Disbursements	39	03	08
Abatements allowed	01	02	09
	40	06	05
due to the towne	05	07	04

Mr James Willson as the Other.
Mr James Willson the other Collector accounteth allso as Followeth

	li	s	d
Received	56	19	03
Disbursements	40	15	04
Abatements allowed	02	04	09 ob
	43	00	01 ob
due to the town	13	19	01 ob

[fo. 730r]

An Assessment of 35 li be made for the Constables.
At this Courte it is ordered that An Assessment of thirty five pounds be made for & towards the Constables their bills of disbursements for the year last past.

50 li to be taken up to pay Sir John Brownlow.
At this Courte the Millmasters informe the Courte that the proffitts of the Mills for the yeare last past would not be sufficient to pay the hundred pounds to Sir John Brownlow at the time when due & the present Chamberlaines not haveing money in their hands to satisfy the same It is by this Courte Ordered that fifty pounds be taken up at interest & that Mr John Robinson, Mr Thomas Baily & Mr John Bradfeild be bound for the same & that they have the Town Mills assured to them for their Countersecurity.

The Town Clerks Bill.
At this Courte The Town clerk produced his bill for money laid out & business done for the town amounteing to 4 li & it is ordered that the Chamberlain doe pay him the same.

Eleventh & last Court of John Robinson, 22 October 1691

Mr Simpson Chosen Comburgess.
At this Courte Mr Thomas Simpson is chosen one of the Comburgesses of this Corporation & is sworne accordeingly & takes the oaths mencioned & apointed by act of Parliament made in the first year of their present Majesties reigne.

The Constables accounts.
At this Courte the Constables account for their Assessment as followeth

	li	s	d		li	s	d
				Mr Aldermans bill is	02	04	09
				Mr Shorte Cheife Constable	08	13	08 ob
	li	s	d	Mr Newcombe Cheife Constable	03	14	10
Market place Assessment	12	00	08 ob	Walkergate Assessment	02	18	09 ob
their bills & abatements	01	05	10	bills & abatements	01	19	09 ob
paid, the Chamberlain	10	14	10 ob	Paid, the Chamberlain	00	19	00
Highstreet	05	11	04	Swinegate	03	10	10 ob
bills & abatements	03	19	00	bills & abatements	02	05	00 ob
paid, the Chamberlain	01	12	04	paid, the Chamberlain	01	05	10
Westgate	08	04	05 ob	Castlegate	03	08	03
bills & abatements	02	08	01	bills & abatements	04	16	09
paid, the Chamberlain	05	16	04 ob	due to the Constables	01	08	06

Forty Shillings Stopt with Robert Fearon.
Memorandum forty shillings was stopt with Robert Fearon one of Castlegate Constables for his water Carte goeing with shod wheeles the last yeare.

[fo. 730v]

At An Assemby holden by John Robinson gentleman Aldman [*sic*] the Comburgesses & Burgesses of Grantham aforesaid in Corpus Christi Quoire in the Prebendary Church there on the Fryday next after Saint Luke 23 October 1691.

First did sit down upon the Cushions or place of Eleccion Mr John Robinson Alderman in Corpus Christi Quoire in the said Prebendary Church.
Next to him did sit down upon the Cushions or place of Eleccion two Comburgesses vizt Mr Nicholas Beck & Mr Edward Bristow.
Then is sent down into the body of the Church to Mr Simon Grant & Mr William Haskard by unanimous vote of this Assembly one other Comburgess vizt Mr John Smith.
Out of which three Comburgesses in the body of the Church one is chosen to come by & sitt upon the Cushions or place of Eleccion vizt Mr Simon Grant.
Then are there three Comburgesses upon the Cushions or place of Eleccion vizt Mr Nicholas Beck Mr Edward Bristow & Mr Simon Grant.
Out of which three Comburgesses upon the Cushions or place of Eleccion one is to be chosen Alderman of this towne for the yeare ensueing.

Mr Beck chosen Alderman.
And thereupon by an unanimous vote of this Assembly Mr Nicholas Beck is chosen Alderman for the yeare ensueing.
Whereupon the said Mr Robinson is discharged from his office of Alderman & Mr Nicholas Beck is sworne Alderman in his stead for this Burrough & Soake of Grantham for the yeare ensueing accordeing to the aunciente custome of the said Burrough.

And so this Assembly breakes up.

THE HALL BOOK OF GRANTHAM 1691–1692

[fo. 731r] **First Court of Nicholas Beck, 30 October 1691**

1st 12	2d 12
Mr Alderman Beck	Mr Anthony Kirke
Mr John Codington	Mr William Turner
Mr Robert Cole	Mr William Kirke
Mr Thomas Matkin	Mr Thomas Shorte
Mr Thomas Ireland	Mr John Newcomb
Mr Edward Leivesly	Mr William Burbidge
Mr John Robinson	Mr Thomas Baily
Mr Edward Bristow	Mr John Weaver
Mr Simon Grant	Mr Robert Cole junior
Mr William Haskard	Mr John Codington mercer
Mr John Smith	Mr Edward Todkill
Mr Edward Watson	Mr Richard Dawson
Mr Thomas Simpson	

Names of the Officers

Coroner	Mr John Robinson	Market place Constables	Joseph Hutchin John Withey
Escheator	Mr Edward Bristow	Highstreet Constables	Robert Fox Robert Idle
Collectors of the Colledge rents	Mr Thomas Simpson William Barrett	Westgate Constables	Joseph Low Samuell Hutchin
Chamberlaines	John Newcomb John Martin	Walkergate Constables	William Charles James Ferman
Cheife Constables	Mr Anthony Kirke Mr William Turner	Swinegate Constables	Anthony Hotchin John Ferman
Churchwardens	Mr John Codington William Doughty	Castlegate Constables	James Bristow William Baily
Town clerke	Samuel Procter	Leather Sealers	George Wray John Owen Richard Woulds Thomas Marshall
Serjeants	Thomas Calcroft Robert Barton	Corn Prizers	John Newcomb William Newton
Goaler & bailiffe of the Liberties	Robert Barton	Market Sayers	Richard Hickson Samuel Rollinson

Church Clerke	William Higgabothom
Bellman	Ralph Osbourne
Beadle	John Scott
Key bearers	Mr Alderman
	Mr Bayly [sic]
	Mr Codington

[fo. 731v]

Names of the Commoners

Market Place
Joseph Hutchin
Richard Wiles
William Doughty
John Martin
John Marshall

Highstreet
Robert Fox
Robert Idle
William Parker
John Bradfeild
Arthur Tayler
William Bristow

Westgate
Joseph Low
Samuell Hutchin
William Barrett
Thomas Leivesly
Thomas Baily

Walkergate
William Charles
James Ferman
Edward Greenwood

Swinegate
Anthony Hotchkin
John Ferman
Francis Langton
Richard Owen
Robert Langley

Castlegate
James Bristow
William Baily
Robert Fearon

At this Court Mr Robinson the late Alderman delivers to the present Alderman the town plate as followeth

The Horserace Cup
Mr Archers bolle
Mr Wickliffs tankard
Mr Horsemans Cup
Mr Greenwoods tankard
Mr Batties two tumblers
Mr Batties Beaker
Mr Harringtons tankard

Mr Kirkeby bolle
Mr Greenwoods 13 Spoones
Mr Batties Salt Cellar & cover
Mr Horsemans bolle
Mr Wrights bolle & cover
Mr Stories Cup
Mr Woodroffes tankard

And likewise the Charters
1 of King Edward the 6th
3 of Queen Elizabeth
1 of King James 1st
1 of King Charles 1st
1 of King Charles 2d
1 of King James 2d

[fo. 732r]

The Constables agreement with Robert Fearon.
At this Courte the Cheife Constables agree with Robert Fearon to convey all criples that come to this towne for the ensueing yeare & he is to have 1s for every carte & 6d for every horse to the severall adjacent townes.

Mr Bradfeild to Sett the poor on work.
At this Courte it is agreed with Mr Bradfeild to set the Poore on worke in the Spinneing Schole & he is to have for this ensueing yeare 20 li.

Second Court of Nicholas Beck, 13 November 1691

Apprentices Indentures to be inrolled.
At this Courte it is ordered that the Constables of the severall wards of this town doe give notice to the severall Aprentices in their severall wardes that now are or hereafter shall be that they come in & have their Indentures Inrolled by the Town Clerke or that hereafter their Freedomes be denyed for which Inrollment onely 1s to the box & 6d to the Town Clerke shall be taken.

Robert Fearon to pay 3 li for goeing with Shod Wheeles.
At this Courte Robert Fearon hath leave to goe with the water Carte with Shod wheels for the yeare ensueing he promiseing to pay to the Chamberlaines for the use of the towne three pounds & he paies six pence parte thereof in earnest & it is agreed that not above one more shall goe in the said yeare.

Richard Dawson hath liberty to build an house.
Ordered that Richard Dawson have leave to build a small Cottage att his yards end for Robert Ferkin to inhabite.

[fo. 732v] **Third Court of Nicholas Beck, 11 December 1691**

Mr Bristow dismissed from Comburgess.
Att this Court Mr Edward Bristow one of the Comburgesses of this town desired the Court to bee dismissed from his further Attendance upon this Court & laid down Fifteene pounds as the Customary fine into the Chamberlains hands which this Court takeing into consideracion doe grant & he is accordingly discharged from his said place of a Comburgess & his further attendance upon this Court.

Thomas Rear discharged as Commoner.
Att this Court also Thomas Rear a Commoner of this town alleadging his condicion in haveing a great charge of Children & that his attendance upon this court was a great hindrance to his businesse & desired to bee discharged from his said place, which this Court taking into consideracion doe grant his request, & he is accordingly discharged from his said place.

Richard Sentance, John Newcombe & Thomas Hutchin as Commoners discharged from Court.
Att this Court also Richard Sentence [sic] Thomas Hutchin & John Newcomb Commoners of the Court came & desired to bee dismissed from their said places, which this Court taking into consideracion doe grant & they are accordingly dismissed from their said places.

Mr Coddington accounts as Church Wardan.

Att this Court Mr John Codington [sic] accounteth as Church Warden for the year last past.	li	s	d
Received	54	11	00
Disbursed	60	03	07
Abatements	00	16	04
	60	19	11
due to the accomptant	06	08	11

Mr Leivesleys accounts as Mill Master.

Mr Edward Leivesly [sic] also accounteth as one of the Mill Masters for half a yeare att the Slate Mill	li	s	d
Received	48	11	00
Disbursments	47	05	10
due to the town paid the Chamberlain	01	05	02

Anthony Kirkes as Mill Master.

Anthony Kirk [sic] also accounteth as one of the Mill Masters for one half yeare att the towne Mill	li	s	d
Received	38	19	00
disbursments	23	11	08

& to Sir John Brownloe *per* the Chamberlain	15 00 00
total	38 11 08
due to the towne	00 07 04

Mr Becks the same.
Mr Beck also accounteth for one half yeare for the Slate Mill

	li s d
Received	41 14 00
Disbursements	41 10 00
due to the town	00 04 00

Robert Cole the same.
Robert Cole also accounteth for the town Mill

Received	29 11 09
disbursments	29 07 10
due to the town	00 03 11

[fo. 733r]

John Bradfeild accounts as one Chamberlaine.
John Bradfeild also accounteth as one of the Chamberlains for the yeare last past

	li s d
Received	206 11 10
disbursments	213 03 04
due to the accomptant	006 11 06

Thomas Baily the Other.

Thomas Baily also accounteth as the other Chamberlaine. Received	111 19 04
disbursments	113 11 07
due to the accomptant	001 12 03

Fourth Court of Nicholas Beck, 5 February 1691/2

Thomas Quinningbrow chosen Goaler.
Att this Court Thomas Quiningborow who was formerly Goaler of this town came and desired to bee admitted Goaler of this towne & Baliffe of the liberties thereto belonging being vacant by the death of Robert Barton late deceased which this Court takeing into consideracion do grant, & he takes the accustomed oathes belonging to the said places.

Time Given to Widow Barton.
Att this Court time is given to Widow Barton to continue in the Goale to sell her ale, & dispose of her goods untill May day next.

Robert Quinningbrow made Free.
Att this Court came Robert Quiningbrow who had served his Apprentiship with Mr Nicholas Beck senior & desired to bee admitted a freeman of this Corporacion, which this court taking into consideracion doe grant & he is sworne accordingly & pays 5s to the box & 3s to the officers.

Fifth Court of Nicholas Beck, 13 May 1692

Robert Quinningbrow to give securety.
Att this Court It is ordered that Robert Quiningbrow doe give security to this towne for the maintenance of such children as were borne before he came to inhabite in this towne.

Mr Wiles Colebuyer.
Att this Court Mr Richard Wyles is chosen Cole buyer for the yeare ensueing.

Isaac Garner, Thomas Fisher made Free.
Att this Court came Isaac Garner a forreyner craved to bee admitted a freeman of this Corporacion & laid down his tenn pounds, & Thomas Fisher eldest sonn of Thomas Fisher deceased desired the same which this court taking into consideracion doe grant, & they are sworne according, & pay their accustomed Fees.

Mr Grant nominated Alderman.
Att this Court Mr Simon Grant is unanimously nominated Alderman of this corporacion for the yeare ensueing.

Mr Watson accounts as Collector for Schoole house rents.
Mr Edward Watson accounteth as one of the collectors of the Schooll house rents

	li	s	d
for the year last past			
Received	21	03	01
disbursments	21	03	01

Thomas Leivesley the other.
Thomas Leivesly also accounteth as the other Collector

Received	21	06	02
disbursments	20	05	00
due to him from the town	01	01	02

[fo. 733v] Sixth Court of Nicholas Beck, 29 July 1692

Thomas Rollinson Chosen Serjeant.
Att this Court Thomas Rollinson is chosen one of the Serjeants of the Mace of this towne by Mr Alderman & his bretheren & is sworne accordingly.

Order concerning the Tolls.
Att this Court it is ordered that the tenants of the tolls of this towne do distreyn of such persons as refuse to pay the same, & that they bee indempnifyed by the town for so doing.

Mr John Coddington Chosen a 2:12 man but refuses his Office.
Att this Court Mr John Codington Mercer is chosen one of the second twelve men of this Corporacion according to the ancient custome of the said town, who being required to take upon him the said place & the oath for the execucion of the said place being tendred to him, he refused to take the same.

Seventh Court of Nicholas Beck, 23 September 1692

Mr Doughtys accounts as Cole Buyer.
Att this Court William Doughty late Cole buyer for this towne accounteth as followeth

	li	s	d
Received in money & coales 11 li 16s 00 made of them	12	15	04 ob
Disbursments and other charges	01	09	03
Delivered to Mr Wyles the next Cole buyer in coles & money	11	06	01 ob
	12	15	04 ob

Mr William Kirke chosen Comburgess.
Att this Court Mr William Kirke is chosen one of the Comburgessess in this towne & sworne accordingly & took the oath of a Justice of peace & the oaths appointed by Act of parliament made in the first yeare of their Majesties reigne.

fivety pounds to be taken up for the use of the Town.
Att this Court the townes debts being taken into consideracion it is ordered that 50 li bee taken up att interest & that Mr Watson, Mr Simpson Mr Todkill & Mr Low bee found for the same, & have counter security given.

A 34 li Assessment to be made for the Constables bills.
Att this Court an assessment of 34 li is ordered to bee laid upon this town of Grantham for the payment of the Cheif Constables & Constables their bills of disbursments for the yeare last past.

Mr Charles Chosen a Second twelve man but refuses of Office.
Att this Court Mr William Charles is chosen one of the second twelve men of this Corporacion according to the ancient custome of the said towne & the oath for the execucion of the said place being tendred to him he refused to take the same.

Eighth & last Court of Nicholas Beck, 20 October 1692
[*No entries shown under this heading.*]

[fo. 734r]

An Assembly holden by Nicholas Beck Gentleman Alderman the Comburgesses & Burgesses of Grantham aforesaid in Corpus Christi Quoire in the prebendary Church there on fryday next after St Luke being 21 October 1692.

First did sitt downe upon the Cusshions or place of eleccion Mr Nicholas Beck Alderman in Corpus Christi Quoire in the said prebendary Church.
Next to him did sitt downe upon the Cusshion or place of eleccion one Comburgess vizt Mr Simon Grant.
Then is sent downe into the body of the Church to Mr William Haskard & Mr John Smith by uanimous vote of this assembly one other Comburgesse vizt Mr Edward Watson.
Out of which Comburgesses in the body of the Church and is chosen to come up to sitt upon the Cusshion or place of eleccion vizt Mr William Haskard.
Then likewise is sent downe into the body of the Church to Mr John Smith & Mr Edward Watson by uanimous [*sic*] vote of this assembly one other Comburgesse vizt Mr Thomas Simpson.
Out of which three Comburgesses in the body of the Chruch one other is chosen to come up & sitt upon the cusshions or place of eleccion vizt Mr John Smith.
Then are there three Comburgtesses upon the cusshions or place of eleccion Mr Grant, Mr Grant [*sic*], Mr Haskard & Mr Smith.
Out of which three Comburgesses upon the cusshions or place of eleccion one is to bee chosen Alderman of this town for the year ensueing.

Mr Grant chosen Alderman.
And thereupon by an uanimous [*sic*] vote of this assembly Mr Simon Grant is chosen Alderman for the yeare ensueing.
Whereupon the said Mr Beck is discharged from his office of Alderman & Mr Simon Grant is sworne Alderman in his stead for this Borough & Soake of Grantham for the yeare ensueing according to the ancient custome of the said Borrough.

And so this Assembly breaks up.

THE HALL BOOK OF GRANTHAM 1692–1693

[fo. 734v] **First Court of Simon Grant 28 October 1692**

Mr Alderman Grant
Mr Codington
Mr Robert Cole
Mr Thomas Matkin
Mr Thomas Ireland
Mr Edward Leivesly
Mr John Robinson
Mr Nicholas Beck
Mr William Haskard
Mr John Smith
Mr Edward Watson
Mr William Kirke
Mr Newcomb

Mr Robert Cole
Mr Joseph Low
Mr William Burbidge
Mr Anthony Kirke
Mr Thomas Baily
Mr William Turner
Mr Richard Dawson
Mr George Codington
Mr William Charles
Mr John Bradfeild

Names of the officers

Coroner	Mr Robinson	Markett place	Anthony Hotchkin
Escheator	Mr Bristow	Constables	Francis Langton
Collector of the	Mr Simpson	High street	Robert Fox
Colledge rents	William Barrett	Constables	Robert Idle
Chamberlains	Mr Newcomb	Westgate	John Calcroft
	John Martin	Constables	James Ferman
Cheif Constables	Mr Anthony Kirke	Walkergate	Richard Owen
	Mr Turner	Constables	John Ferman
Church Wardens	Mr John Codington	Swinegate	Robert Fearon
	Mr William Doughty	Constables	William Hutchin
Town Clerk	Mr Procter	Castlegate	Thomas Nixon
Goaler & Serjeant	Robert Barton	Constables	William Quincey
	Thomas Calcraft		
Church Clerk	William Higabothom		
Bellman	Ralph Osborne		
Beadle	John Scott		
Leather Sealers	George Wray		
	John Owen		
	Richard Woulds		
	Thomas Marshall		

Corn prizers	John Newcomb
	William Newton
Markett Sayers	Richard Hixson
	John Rollison
Key Keepers	Mr Alderman
	Mr Newcomb
	Mr Doughty
Town waits	William Higabothom
	Leonard Butcher
	John Wilcocks
	Roger Hutchison

[fo. 735r]

Names of the Commoners

Markett place	Anthony Hotchkin	Walkergate	Richard Owen
	Francis Langton		John Ferman
	Joseph Hutchin		Edward Greenwood
	Richard Wyles		
	William Doughty		
	John Martin		
	John Marshall		
Highstreet	Robert Fox	Swinegate	Robert Fearon
	Robert Idle		William Hutchin
	Arthur Tayler		Robert Langley
	William Bristow		
Westgate	John Calcroft	Castlegate	Thomas Nixon
	James Ferman		William Quincey
	Samuell Hutchin		
	William Barrett		
	Thomas Leivesly		
	Thomas Baily		

James Bristow & William Baily dismissed from Court as Comoners.
Att this Court James Bristow and William Baily Comoners represented to Mr Alderman and the court the inconveniencys they attended having a great charge in attending this Court and desired to bee dismissed from their further attendance on the said Court it is by this Court ordered that they bee accordingly dismissed from their further attendance on the said Court.

27 Buckets in the hall.
Att this Court an account is taken how many bucketts are in the Hall and there now are seaven and twenty.

6 Ladders and Six Hookes.
There are likewise six ladders and six hookes.

William Martin, William Quincey, Anthony Rowley made Free.
Att this Court came William Martin a forreigner & craved to be admitted a freeman of this town & laid downe his tenn pounds also William Quincey who had served his Apprentiship with John Gibson & Anthony Rowley eldest son of Thomas Rowley & desired the same which this Court taking into consideracion doe grant & they are sworne accordingly & pay the accustomed Fees.

Thomas Swinglers promise.
Thomas Swingler promises to give security to the towne.

Town Plate delivered.
Att this Court Mr Beck late Alderman delivered to the present Alderman the town plate as following   And likewise the Charters

The Horserace Cup	Mr Kirkeby bolle	1 of King Edward 6th
Mr Archers Bolle	Mr Greenwood 13 spoones	3 of Queen Elizabeth
Mr Wickliffs tankard	Mr Batties salt cellar & cover	1st of King James 1st
Mr Horsemans Cup	Mr Horsemans Bolle	1st of King Charles 1st
Mr Greenwoods tankard	Mr Wrights bolle & cover	1st of King Charles 2nd
Mr Batties two tumblers	Mr Stories cup	1st of King James 2nd
Mr Batties beaker	Mr Woodroffes tankard	
Mr Harringtons Tankard		

[fo. 735v] **Second Court of Simon Grant, 11 November 1692**

John Lockton, Christopher Walgrave and Joseph Baily made Free.
Att this Court came John Locton a forreigner & craved to bee admitted a freeman of this Corporacion & laid down his tenn pounds which this Court taking into consideracion doe grant and he with Christopher Wallgrave who had served his apprentiship to his Mother widow Alice Wallgrave and Joseph Bayly who had served his apprentiship to Thomas Quiningbrow a freeman of this Corporacion took the accustomed oaths & pay their accustomed fees.

Robert Fearons Agreement with the town.
Att this Court an agreement is made with Robert Fearon to releive all passengers & to convey all criples that come to this towne for one yeare from the 16th of this instant

November & he is to have for the same the summe of nineteene pounds out of which he is to repay to the town three pounds for leave for his Watercart to goe with shod Wheeles one shilling given by the cheif Constables to Robert Fearon and one shilling paid by Robert Fearon to the Alderman in earnest.

Thomas Short chosen Goaler instead of Thomas Quinningbrow.
Att this Court came Thomas Quinningbrow the present Goaler and accquainted the Court of his great indisposicion insomuch that he was att present unable to execute the said office and did Freely resigne the said place unto this Court. Whereupon by unanimous vote of this Court Mr Thomas Shorte is chosen Goaler Serjeant att the Mace and Baliffe of the Liberties in his roome and is sworn accordingly.

Att this Court John Newcombe overseer of the poor accounteth as followeth:

	li	s	d
Received	57	00	00
disbursed	53	12	07
Abatements allowed	1	09	02¾
due to the town	2	00	02¼

Robert Orson accounts as Overseer of the poor.
Robert Orson the other Overseer of the poor accounteth as followeth

Received	50	17	09
disbursed	50	15	08
due to the town	00	02	01

[fo. 736r] **Third Court of Simon Grant, 9 December 1692**

William Parker a Comoner dismissed from Court paying his 5 li.
Att this Court came William Parker a Comoner of this Court & told the court with his occacions would not permitt him to attend this Court without a great prejudice to his other busines & laid down his five pounds as a fine which this Court taking into consideracion do grant & he is accordingly dismissed from his said place & further attendance on this Court.

Fourth Court of Simon Grant, 13 January 1692/3

Mr Simpsons accounts.
Att this Court Mr Thomas Simpson one of the Collectors for the School house rents for the year past.

	li	s	d
Received	24	18	04
Disbursed	26	00	00
due to the acomptant	01	01	08

William Barretts accounts.
William Barrett also accounteth as the other Overseer.

John Newcombes accounts as Chamberlaine.
John Newcomb Felmonger accounteth as one of the Chamberlains for the yeare last past.

	li	s	d
Received	53	11	09
Disbursed	54	01	05
Due to the accomptant	00	09	08

John Martin the same.
John Martin also accounteth as the other Chamberlain.

	li	s	d
Received	77	19	01
Disbursed	78	01	02
Due to the accomptant	00	02	01

William Doughty accounts as Churchwarden.
William Doughty accounteth as Church Warden for the year last past.

	li	s	d
Received	52	16	08
Disbursed	77	11	10
Due to the accomptant	54	15	02

[fo. 736v] Fifth Court of Simon Grant, 28 February 1692/3

An Assessment of 35 li to be made to reimburse Mr Turner &c as Churchwardens.
Att this Courte it is agreed and ordered that an assessment of 35 li be laid upon the Inhabitants of this towne Manthorpe and Spittlegate for the Reimbursment of Mr Turner, Mr Codington & Mr Doughty the late Church Wardens of this parish for what money they have laid out in repaires of the Church for the 3 last yeares.

The Wind Mill Sold.
At this Courte Mr Alderman acquainted the Courte that he had sold the Wind Mill for 46 li 15s to Major Williams of Denton which this Courte doe agree to.

Sixth Court of Simon Grant, 23 March 1692/3
[*No entries shown under this heading.*]

Seventh Court of Simon Grant, 4 May 1693

Mr Wiles chosen Comoner Chamberlain.
At this Courte Richard Wiles is chosen Comoner Chamberline in the roome of Mr Joseph Low who is chosen one of the Cheife Constables in the place of Edward Todkill deceased and Sworne accordingly.

Thanks to paid to Captain Smith for his Cla[s]pes he gave to the Alderman for the Tippit.
Ordered that Captain Smith have the thanks of this Courte for the Claspes he gave to the Alderman and his successors for the Tippitt.

John Newcombe chosen Comburgess.
Att this Courte Mr John Newcombe is chosen one of the Comburgesses of this Corporacion in the place of Mr Thomas Simpson deceased & tooke the oath of the said place and the oath of Justice of the Peace & the other oaths Ist William and Marie.

John Weaver dismissed from Courte.
At this Courte John Weaver upon his request that he was unable to attend the service of this Courte is dismissed from his place of a second Twelveman & his further attendance in this Courte.

Mr Bradfeild chosen Second Twelve man.
At this Courte John Bradfeild is chosen one of the second twelvemen of this Corporacion according to ancient custome and Sworne accordingly.

Mr Haskard nominated Alderman.
At this Courte Mr William Haskard is unanimously elected & nominated Alderman of this Corporacion for the yeare ensueing.

[fo. 737r] Eighth Court of Simon Grant, 19 September 1693

Mr Beck for the Mace & 2 ladders.

An Assessment of 30 li for the Constables bills be made.
Ordered An assessment of 30 li be made for the payment of the Constables bills of disbursements for the yeare last past.

Five pounds to be allowed to the Deputy Recorder for his Sallary.
At this Courte Mr Alderman moved the Courte that the present Sallary paid to the Deputy Recorder vizt 40s per annum for his advice and 40s per annum for keepeing sessions was very small And this Courte taking the same into Consideracion do agree & order that for the future 5 li per annum be allowed to the said Deputy Recorder for his said Sallary.

A Vote passed wether the money Mr Alderman paid was the Towns debt or not.
Att this Court Mr Alderman Grant, Mr Beck, Mr Clarke and Widdow Dalton came and desired to have security from the Towne for 250 li for which old Mr Doughty, Mr Towne, Mr Clarke, Mr Beck & Mr Dalton were bound and had paid the same & the same put to the vote whether this Courte thought the same was the townes debt or not or ought to be paid by the towne it was by the major parte of this Courte carryed on the negative.

Benjamin Wheelers accounts as Collector for the poore and Mr Normansalls as the same.
At this Courte Mr Normansall and Benjamin Wheeler as Collectors for the poore accounted.

Mr Normansalls Receipts	57 13 09
Weekely payments	45 01 02
by payments and abatements allowed	04 13 10½
	49 15 00½
due from the account to the towne	07 18 08½
Mr Wheelers Receipts	60 08 09
his disbursements: weekely payments	42 16 08
by payments	06 18 03
abatements allowed	03 15 11½
	53 10 10½
due to the towne	06 17 10½

Ninth Court of Simon Grant, 13 October 1693

Joseph Oliver and Francis Barriffe made Free.
At this Courte came Joseph Oliver who had served his apprentiship with William Newton, And Francis Berriffe a forreigner who laid downe his tenn poundes & craved to be admitted Freeman of this Corporacion which this Courte takeing into consideracion doe Grant and retorne fifty shillings to the said Francis Berriffe and they are sworne accordingly.

At this Courte a Lease of the Tolls for one [year] to comence from the Twenty sixth of this instant October is Lett to Constance Fisher Widdow at 56 li per annum 1s paid in earnest.

At An Assembly holden by Simon Grant gentleman Alderman And the Comburgesses and Burgesses of Grantham aforesaid in Corpus Christi Quoire in the Prebendary Church there on the Fryday next after St Luke being 20 October 1693.

First did sit downe upon the Cushions or place of Eleccion Mr Simon Grant Alderman in Corpus Christi Quoire in the said prebendary Church.

Next to him did sitt downe upon the Cushions or place of Eleccion two other Comburgesses vizt Mr William Haskard and Mr John Smith.

[fo. 737v]

Then are sent downe into the body of the Church to Mr Edward Watson by unanimous vote of this assembly two other Comburgesses vizt. Mr William Kirke and Mr John Newcombe out of which Three Comburgesses in the body of the Church one is chosen to come up & sitt upon the Cushions or place of Eleccion vizt Mr Edward Watson.

Then are there three Comburgesses upon the Cushions or place of Eleccion vizt Mr Haskard, Mr Smith and Mr Watson

Out of which three Comburgesses upon the Cushions or one is to be chosen Alderman of this towne for the yeare ensueing.

And thereupon by an unanimous vote of this assembly Mr William Haskard is chosen Alderman for the yeare ensueing.

William Haskard Sworn Alderman.

Whereupon the said Mr Simon Grant is discharged from his office of Alderman and Mr William Haskard is Sworne Alderman in his stead for this Burrough and Soake of Grantham for the yeare ensueing according to the Ancient Custome of the said Burrough.

And so this Assembly breakes up.

THE HALL BOOK OF GRANTHAM 1693–1694

First Court of William Haskard, 27 October 1693

Mr John Calcroft & Mr William Doughty chosen Second Twelvemen.
At this Courte Mr John Calcroft & Mr William Doughty are chosen Second Twelve men of this Corporacion according to the Ancient Custome of the same & Sworne accordingly.

Town plate and Charters delivered.
At this Courte the late Mr Alderman Grant delivers to the present Alderman the Townes plate as followes.

The Horserace Cup	Mr Batties 2 tumblers	Mr Batties salt celler & cover
Mr Archers bolle	Mr Batties beaker	Mr Horseman bolle
Mr Wickliffs tankard	Mr Harringtons tankard	Mr Wrights Cup & cover
Mr Greenwoods tankard	Mr Kirkbyes Bolle	Mr Stories Cup
Mr Horsemans Cup	Mr Greenwoods 13 Spoones	Mr Woodroffs tankard

And the Charters 1 of Edward 6th, 3 of Queen Elizabeth, 1 of King James 1st, one of King Charles 1st, one of King Charles 2nd, one of King James 2nd.

Mr Charles agrees as Cheif Constable agrees with Robert Fearon.
At this Courte Mr Charles Cheife Constable by consent of the Courte agrees with Robert Fearon to convey all Criples & releive passingers for the yeare ensueing and gives him 21 li out of which 3 li is to be deducted out for his water carte.

Coroner	Mr Grant	Church clerk	William Higgabotham	Markett place Constables	Francis Langton John Ferman
Escheator	Mr Smith	Bellman	Ralph Osborne		
Collectors of the Schoolhouse rents	Mr Newcombe Samuel Hutchin	Beadle	John Scott & Silvester Scott	High Street	Robert Fox Robert Idle
Chamberlins	Joseph Law James Ferman	Leather Sealers	John Owen Richard Woulds Thomas Marshall Thomas Baily	Westgate Walkergate	William Hutchin Isaac Garner Thomas Fisher George Miller
Cheife Constables	Mr Charles Mr Bradfield	Corne prizers	William Quincey Robert Orson	Swinegate	Robert Fearon Thomas Rallison

Churchwardens	Mr Charles	Markett Sayers	Thomas Leiveseley	Castlegate	Thomas Nixon William Quincey
	Mr Hotchin		Richard Hickson	Towne Waites	William Higgabotham
Town clerk	S. Procter	Key keepers	Mr Alderman Mr Charles		Leonard Butsher John Wilcock
Serjant & Goaler	Thomas Rawlinson Thomas Shorte		Mr Low		Roger Hutchinson

[fo. 738r] **Second Court of William Haskard, 17 November 1693**

Bucket money to be paid by Mr William Kirke &c.
At this Courte these persons following pay their buckett money vizt Mr William Kirke 3s 4d, Mr Newcombe 3s 4d, Mr Turner 1s 8d, Mr Dawson 1s 8d, Mr Charles 1s 8d, Mr Bradfeild 1s 8d, Mr Low 1s 8d, Mr Doughty 1s 8d, Mr Calcroft 1s 8d.

Sir John Brownlows Gift & Kind Offer to the Town.
At this Courte Mr Alderman and the late Millmasters for the yeare last past acquaint the Courte that that [sic] last weeke they had beene at Sir John Brownlows to pay him the last hundred pounds of the 400 li. the Towne had formerly borrowed of him and that Sir John Brownlow had beene pleased to returne the towne 30 li to be imployed in the woollen manufactuary and to acquaint Mr Alderman that at any time if the Towne had occasion he would be ready to furnish them with what money they had occasion for, For which his kind & favourable intention to this towne this Courte doe returne him their unanimous thanks & that Mr Alderman be pleased to doe the same in the name of the Courte.

Mr Kirkes account as Mill Master.
November 28 1693 Mr Kirke accountes as Millmaster for the towne Mill for 27 weeks.

	li	s	d
Received	41	08	00
Disburst	42	03	10
due to the Accomptant	00	15	10

Mr Shortes the Same.
Mr Thomas Shorte alsoe accounteth as Millmaster for the Slate Mill for the said time

Received	75	04	09
Disburst	60	15	08
more disburst	02	00	06
	62	16	02
due to the towne	12	08	07

Mr Newcombe the Same.
Mr Newcombe alsoe accounteth as Millmaster for the Towne Mill for 26 weekes.
Received   50 02 07
Disburst   46 04 07
due to the towne   3 18 00

Mr Burbidge the Same.
Mr Burbidge accounteth as Millmaster for the Slate Mill for the said time.
Received   61 01 04½
Disburst   50 03 05
due to the towne   10 17 11½

Mr Kirke as Collector for the Schoole.
Mr Kirke Accounteth as Collector of the Schoole house rents
for the yeare last past.   Received   21 03 02
Disburst   32 02 10
due to the Accomptant   10 19 08
of which he receives a bond for 8 li of Nicholas Quire of   08 00 00
& of Joseph Hutchin   01 13 04
                                                      09 13 04
Soe due to the Accomptant upon this account   01 06 04

Joseph Hutchins Accompts as the other Collector of the Schoolehouse rents.
Received   22 02 02
Disburst   20 10 04
due to the towne which he paid to Mr Kirke   01 13 04

Mr Turner accountes as Chamberlaine.
for the yeare Last past   Received   197 06 04
Disburst   194 08 01
due to the towne   02 18 03

Mr Wiles accountes as the other Chamberlaine
for the said yeare.   Received   55 06 08
Disbursements   54 14 05
due to the towne   00 12 03

Mr Charles accounteth as the Church Warden for the yeare Last past.
                                                      li s d
Received for quarter   29 00 04
for rents   05 05 08
for bells   09 16 00
totall   44 02 00

Disburst	104	14 02½
abatements allowed & a farther bill	101	11 04
	106	05 06½
due to the accomptant upon ballance	62	03 06½

[fo. 738v] Third Court of William Haskard, 19 January 1693/4

A Church Assessment of 64 li to be made.
At this Courte it is ordered that an assessment of Sixty Four pounds be laid upon the [*sic*] of this towne Spittlegate & Manthorpe for the payment of Mr Charles late Churchwarden of the said parish his disbursements for the last yeare in repaires of the Church and other ornaments of the same.

Forty pounds to be taken up for the Use of the Town.
At this Courte it is ordered that forty pounds be taken up at interest for the use of this town to purchase the Assignement of the Mortgage of Widdow Gibson upon the house of William Grocock late deceased & that Mr Alderman, Mr Cole, Mr Kirke be bound for the same & have Counter Security from this towne upon the Mills.

Thomas Fearon & Gabriel Barker made Free.
At this Courte came Thomas Fearon Eldest sonn liveing of Thomas Fearon late deceased and Gabriell Barker a foreigner who laid downe his ten pounds and craved to be admitted Freemen of this Corporacion which this Courte takeing into Consideracion doe grant and returne 6 li to Gabriell Barker & they are sworne accordingly & pay their accustomed Fees.

Fourth Court of William Haskard, 31 May 1694

Isaac Garner dismissed from Court.
At this Courte Mr Isaac Garner a Commoner of this Courte Laid downe his fine of Five pounds and desired to be dismissed from his further attendance on this Courte which his request by the Courte is granted and he is accordingly dismissed from his said place and further attendance.

William Hutchin chosen Coale Buyer.
At this Courte Mr William Hutchin is chosen Colebyer.

Mr Smith nominated Alderman.
At this Courte Mr John Smith is unanimously nominated Alderman of this Corporacion for the yeare ensueing.

Mr William Burbidge & Mr Anthony Kirke chosen Comburgesses.
At this Courte Mr William Burbidge & Mr Anthony Kirke are chosen Comburgesses of this Corporacion in the roome of Mr Thomas Matkin & Mr Edward Watson deceased.

Mr Parkers account as Overseer of the poor.
5th June 1694
	li	s	d
William Parker overseer of the poore for the last yeare accounteth			
Received	47	07	01
Disburst	47	06	08½
Abatement allowed	01	14	09½
	49	01	06
Due to the Accomptant	01	14	05

William Mastin the Same.
William Martin the other Overseer of the poore for the said yeare accounteth
	li	s	d
Received	58	02	00½
Disburst	50	15	07
Abatements Allowed	03	15	11½
	54	11	06½
Due to the towne	03	10	06

Mr Wild as Colebuyer.
Richard Wild accounteth as Cole Buyer
	li	s	d
Received	14	07	08
Disburst	02	01	01
Due to the towne	12	06	07

[fo. 739r] **Fifth Court of William Haskard, 3 August 1694**

The Chamberlaine to pay Ann Gibson & Ann Fisher, Widdow Bringhurst & Widdow Mitchell Share of Mrs Millers money.
At this Courte came Ann Gibson Widdow and Ann Fisher Widdow & desired by consent of this Courte & of Mr Burnet the present Minister of the Corporacion they might be admitted to receive the Share of Mrs Millers money in the roome of Widdow Bringhurst & Widdow Mitchell deceased which is accordingly granted and the Chamberlaine is ordered to pay them their said Share.

Sixth Court of William Haskard, 21 September 1694

	li	s	d			li	s	d
Mr Alderman	00	14	00	Westgate	Thomas Fisher	01	10	10
Mr Charles Cheife Constable	08	00	00		George Miller	01	09	08

Mr Bradfeild Cheife Constable	03	10	00	Swinegate Robert Fearon	02 04 06
Francis Langton	01	11	06	Thomas Rawlinson	01 15 07
Markett Place John Ferman	01	11	03	Castlegate William Quincy	01 09 06
Robert Fox	01	10	08	Thomas Nixon	01 15 00
High Streete Robert Idle	01	12	00	Conduite	03 00 00
William Hutchin	02	05	00		33 19 00

An Assessment of 36 li to be made for the Constables.
At this Courte it is ordered and agreed upon by the whole Courte that an Assessment of Thirty six pounds be made and laid upon the Inhabitants of this Towne for the payment of the Constables their bills of disbursements for the yeare last past for the conveyance of Criples and providing carriages for their Majesties use.

Seventh Court of William Haskard, 18 October 1694

Mrs Fisher takes the Tolls.
At this Courte a Lease of the tolls of this towne is let to Constance Fisher *vidua* for one yeare to Commence from the 26th day of this instant October at the rate of 56 li. to be paid quarterly.

Mr Thomas Baily chosen Comburgess
At this Courte Mr Thomas Baily is chosen one of the Comburgesses of this town in the roome of Mr Thomas Ireland deceased and sworne accordingly and likewise tooke the oaths apointed in the first yeare of their Majesties Raigne.

Constables accounts as Follows.

	li s d		
Markett place	11 13 02	Swinegate	03 17 05
their bills & abatements	03 09 01½	their bills & abatements	03 16 08½
paid the Chamberlaine	08 04 00½	paid the Chamberlaine	00 00 08½
High Streete	04 17 10	Castlegate	03 10 09
their bills & abatements	03 06 05	their bills & abatements	03 01 01
paid the Chamberlaine	01 11 05	paid the Chamberlaine	00 09 08
Westgate	07 02 01		
their bills & abatements	02 14 04½	paid Mr Alderman	00 15 00
paid the Chamberlaine	04 07 04½	paid Mr Charles	09 00 06
		paid Mr Bradfeild	04 03 04
Walkergate	03 00 01½		
their bills & abatements	03 03 00½		

[fo. 739v]

At An Assembly holden by William Haskard Alderman and the Comburgesses and Burgesses of Grantham aforesaid in Corpus Christi Quoire in the prebendary Church there on the fryday next after St Luke being 19 October 1694.

First did sit downe upon the Cushions or place of Eleccion Mr William Haskard Alderman in Corpus Christi Quoire in the said prebendary Church
Next to him did sit downe upon the Cushions or place of Eleccion one other Comburgess vzt Mr John Smith
Then is sent down into the body of the Church to Mr William Kirke & Mr John Newcombe one other Comburgess vizt Mr Robert Cole
Out of which 3 Comburgesses in the body of the Church one is chosen to come up and sitt upon Cushions or place of Eleccion vizt Mr Robert Cole.
Next is sent downe into the body of the Church to Mr Kirke & Mr Newcombe one other Comburgesses vizt Mr Leivesley
Out of which Three Comburgesses in the body of the Church one other is chosen to come up & sit upon the Cushions or place of Eleccion vizt Mr Leivesley.
Then are their [*sic*] Three Comburgesses upon the Cushions or place of Eleccion vizt Mr Smith, Mr Cole, Mr Leivesley
Out of which Three Comburgesses upon the Cushions or place of Election one is to be chosen Alderman of this Towne for the yeare ensueing
And there upon by unanimous vote of this Assembly Mr John Smith is chosen Alderman for the yeare ensueing.

Mr Smith Sworne Alderman.
Whereupon the said Mr William Haskard is discharged from his office of Alderman & Mr John Smith Sworne Alderman in his stead for this Burrough and Soake of Grantham for the yeare ensueing according to the Ancient Custome of the said Burrough.

And so this Assembly breakes up.

THE HALL BOOK OF GRANTHAM 1694–1695

[fo. 740r] First Court of John Smith, 26 October 1694

Mr John Coddington discharged from the Court.
Att this Court came Mr John Coddington who was formerly chosen to serve as a second Twelve man of this Corporacion but had neglected to take the oath for the execucion of the said place and this day laid down his Fine of Tenn pounds & desired he might be dismissed from his said place of a 2nd twelve man & his further Attendance upon this Court which this Court taking in Consideracion doe grant and he is accordingly dismissed from his said place & his further attendance upon this Court.

Robert Idle & Thomas Hixon dismissed from the Court.
At this Court came Robert Idle one of the Comoners of this Court & Thomas Hixon one other of the said Commoners and complained to this Court that their attendance upon this Court was a very great Injury to their Trades and desired the Favour of this Court that they might be discharged from their further attendance on the said Court which this Court taking into Consideracion doe grant & they are accordingly by the unanimous vote of this Court dismissed from their said places of Comoners & their further attendance on this Court.

[fo. 740v] [Blank page]

[fo. 741r] Second Court of John Smith, 2 November 1694

Att this Court Mr Alderman acquainted the Court that he and the Cheif Constables had made a Bargain with Robert Fearon to convey and relieve all Passengers coming to this Town for this year next ensueing for which the Town is to allow him to goe with the Water Cart this year free.

Mr Anthony Hotchin, Mr Richard Wyld, Mr Francis Langton & Mr William Bristow chosen 2nd Twelve men.
At this Court Mr Anthony Hotchin, Mr Richard Wyldes [sic], Mr Francis Langton and Mr William Bristow Comoners of this Court by Unanimous Consent and according to the ancient Custome of this Court are chosen to be of the second twelve men of this Corporacion and took their oaths and places accordingly.

Third Court of John Smith, 30 November 1694

Place of Master of the House of Correccion removed.
At this Court it is ordered that the place of Master of the House of Correccion be removed from George Chantry who is the present Master thereof to the Goale & Mr Short is ordered to be Master thereof and he is hereby ordered to receive the whole Sallary belonging to the said place & that all necessaryes be provided for the said place.

Persons chose in the office of Comburgesses or Second twelve men to provide themselves Gowns within 6 weeks after such Eleccion.
The Penalty.
At this Court it is ordered that every person who shall hereafter be elected & chosen into this Office of one of the Comburgesses of this Towne doe within six weekes next after their Eleccion into the said place provide themselves one New Gown faced with Velvet & with Sleeves tufted with Silke & that every person who shall hereafter be chosen into the office of a Second Twelve man of this Corporaccon doe within the said time after their Eleccion provide themselves one Good Gowne faced with Fur and trimmed with Ribbands upon pain that every Comburgess soe offending shall forfeit 20s for every month and every second twelve man 10s for every month to be leavyed by distress for the Use of this Corporaccion.

Chimes to be put into good repair and to be kept in good order.
At this Court it is ordered that the present Churchwarden Doe sett the Chimes which are now out of repaire into good Repaire and that he and the Succeeding Churchwardens doe take Care that the said Chimes for the future be kept in good repair.

Wednesday Markett to be proclaimed and kept.
Att this Court it is ordered that the Markett which by the Charters is granted to this Corporaccion to be kept on the Wednesday in every weeke be proclaimed the next Markett day and next Fair day and that the same be kept and continued every Wednesday following.

[fo. 741v] **Fourth Court of John Smith, December 1694** [*No date given*]

Att this Court it is ordered that (in pursueance of a former order of Court made the third Court of William Haskard gentleman the late Alderman) 40 li be taken up att Interest to purchase the Assignment of the Mortgage of the Widdow Gibson upon the House of Widdow Grocock in Highstreet.

Fifth Court of John Smith, 24 May 1695

Lease to be granted to William Fox of a house &c in Manthorpe.
Upon the Application of Mr William Fox of Gonerby to this Court for the renewing of a Lease formerly granted by this Corporacion to Mr Samuel Burnett Clerk of a Messuage or Tenement & Commons of pasture with the appurtenances in Manthorp which Lease the said Mr Burnett hath assigned to the said Mr Fox under the reserved rent of 13s & 4d & the Fine certain of three pounds twelve shillings and six pence It is this day by this Court ordered that the said Mr Fox be admitted Tenant to this Corporacion for the said Messuage &c for the Term of one and twenty yeares from the expiracion of the said Lease.

No Churchwarden to bargain with the Ringers without Leave.
Att this Court is ordered that for the Future noe Churchwarden of this Towne doe make any bargain with the Ringers for the yearly ringing to Church before they have leave from this Court.

An Assessment of 45 li to be made to reimburse Mr Hotchin his expenses as Churchwarden.
At this Court it is ordered that an Assessment of 45 li be made & laid upon the Inhabitants of this Town, Manthorp, & Spittlegate for the reimbursing of Mr Anthony Hotchkin [sic] the Churchwarden for the year past his expenses in Execucion of his said Office.

Att this Court it is ordered that 50 li which is now due from the Town to James Freeman upon Bond be paid in and that the same be borrowed again of him & that Mr Alderman Smith, Mr Robert Cole Junior, Mr William Turner & Mr Joseph Lowe be bound for the same & that they be indempnified by this Court for entering into the said Security.

Mr Robert Cole Senior nominated Alderman for the next yeare.
At this Court Mr Robert Cole Senior is nominated Alderman of this Corporacion for the year ensueing.

Widdow Hawden & Widdow Toms to receive the share of Widdow Millers Interest money.
At this Court by Consent of this Court & of Mr Burnett the present Minister of this Towne Widdow Hawdon & Widdow Toms are chosen to receive the Share of Widdow Millers Interest money of 40 li in the room of Widdow Holt & widdow Castle deceased.

Mr John Sharp made free.
At this Court came John Sharp Inholder a Forreigner and Craved to be admitted a Freeman of this Corporacion & laid down his 10 li as a Fine which this Court taking into Consideracion doeth grant & return him 20s & he is sworn accordingly.

[fo. 742r] **Sixth Court of John Smith, 23 August 1695**

Mr Hutchin Coalbuyer.
At this Court William Hutchin is continued Coal buyer for the year ensueing.

Att this Court it is ordered that the Chamberlain doe pay the Gold smith for the Chains he made for the Town Waytes.

William Bristow discharged from the Court.
At this Court William Bristow one of the second Twelve Company of this Town being gone out of the Towne is discharged from his said place of a Second Twelve man and his further Attendance upon this Court.

Mr Hotchkin discharged from further attendance upon this Court.
At this Court Mr Anthony Hotchkin one of the second Twelve men of this Corporacion laid down his Fine of tenn pounds & desired to be dismissed from his said place and he is accordingly dismissed from his said place and further Attendance on this Court.

James Firman chosen 2nd twelveman.
At this Court James Firman is chosen one of the second Twelve men of this Towne according to the ancient Custome.

John Firman chosen 2nd twelveman [entry repeated].
At this Court John Firman is chosen one of the second Twelve men of this Town according to the ancient Custome.

40 li to be taken up to pay the Town debts.
At this Court it is ordered that 40 li be taken up to pay the Townes debts & that Mr Leivesley & Mr Beck be bound for the same and that they have Counter Security from the Towne for indempnifying them for being bound for the same.

[fo. 742v] **Seventh Court of John Smith, 20 September 1695**

John Firman & James Firman take the oaths of 2nd 12 men.
At this Court James Firman and John Firman who were chosen second Twelve men of this Corporacion the Last Court took upon them the Oaths of the said place.

Assessment of 40 li for paying Constables bills.
At this Court it is ordered that an Assessment of Forty pounds be made and laid upon the Inhabitants of this Towne for reimbursing of the Constables Bills of Disbursements for the year last past.

Bartholomew Yeomans
Francis Wilson
Thomas Keale eldest Son of Joseph Keale   made free of
John Holmes   this Corporacion
William Handley
Anthony Brewer
William Gibson eldest Son of [blank] Gibson

At this Court Mr William Fox father of Robert Fox late one of the Chamberlains of this Town payes to John Bradfeild the present Chamberlain 4 li 2s 3d which the said Robert Fox had received for the Use of this Corporacion.

[fo. 743r] Eighth Court of John Smith, 18 October 1695

At this Court John Newball and Samuell Newball [sic] past their Accounts as Overseers of the poor of Grantham for the year last past

	li	s	d
John Newballs Receipts	44	09	00
John Newballs Disbursements	48	11	02
Abatements	01	14	07
	50	05	09
Due to the Accomptant	05	16	09
Samuel Clipshams Receipts	79	17	03
His Disbursements	62	16	03
Abatements	02	19	10½
	65	16	01½
Due to the Town	14	01	01½

Ninth & last Court of John Smith 24 October 1695

At this Court a Lease of the profitts of the Tolls belonging to this Corporacion is lett to Constance Fisher widdow for one year to comence from the 26 of October at 56 li per Annum to be paid quarterly.

The Constables Accounts as follows.

Markett place Constables Receipts	14 15 11½	Castlegate Received	03 16 05
Disbursements	03 07 00	Constables Disbursements	03 19 06
Abatements	00 11 03½	Abatements	06 00 08
	03 18 03½		04 00 02
Due to the Town	10 15 08	Due to the Constable	00 03 09
Highstreet Constables Receipts	05 07 10		
Disburst	03 04 06	Mr Aldermans Bill	03 13 10

Abatements	00 00 07½	Mr Calcroft Cheif Constable	08 09 00
	03 05 01½	Mr Doughty	02 16 11
Due to the Town	02 02 08½		
Westgate Constables received	07 12 04		
Disbursements	03 06 09		
Abatements	00 05 10		
	03 12 07		
Due to the Towne	03 09 09		
Walkergate Constables Received	04 01 07½		
Disbursements	03 02 00		
Abatements	00 07 11		
	03 09 11		
Due to the Town	00 11 08½		
Swinegate Received	03 18 04		
Constables Disbursements	03 10 06		
Abatements	00 09 01		
	03 19 07		
Due to the Constables	00 01 03		

[fo. 743v]

Att an Assembly holden by John Smith Gentleman Alderman & the Comburgesses & Burgesses of Grantham aforesaid in Corpus Christi Quoir in the Prebendary Church there on the Fryday next after Saint Luke being 25 October 1695.

First did sit down upon the Cushions or place of Eleccion Mr John Smith Alderman in Corpus Christi Quoire in the said Prebendary Church.
Next to him did sit down upon the Cushions or place of Eleccon two other Comburgesses vizt Mr Robert Cole senior & Mr Edward Leivesley.
Then is sent downe into the body of the Church to Mr William Kirke and Mr John Newcomb one other Comburgess vizt Mr John Robinson.
Out of which three Comburgesses in the body of the Church one is chosen to come up & sit upon the Cushions or place of Eleccion vizt Mr John Robinson.
Then are there three Comburgesses upon the Cushions or place of Eleccion vizt Mr Cole, Mr Edward Leivesliey and Mr John Robinson.
Out of which three Comburgesses upon the Cushions or place of Eleccion one is to be chosen Alderman of this Towne for the year next ensueing.
And thereupon by unanimous Vote of this Assembly Mr Robert Cole is chosen Alderman for the year ensueing.

Mr Cole chosen Alderman.
Whereupn the said Mr John Smith is discharged from his Office of Alderman & Mr Robert Cole sworn Alderman in his Stead for this Burrough and Soake of Grantham for the year ensueing according to the Ancient Custome of the said Burrough.

And soe this Assembly breaks up.

THE HALL BOOK OF GRANTHAM 1695–1696

First Court of Robert Cole 1 November 1695

At this Court Mr Smith the Late Alderman delivers to the present Alderman the Towne plate vizt:
[*no details given*]

Mr Thomas Matkin discharged the Court.
At this Court came Mr Thomas Matkin a Commoner of this Court and laid down his Fine of Five pounds and desired to be dismissed from his office of a Commoner and his further Attendance on this Court which is accordingly granted and he is hereby dismissed from his further Attendance on this Court.

[fo. 744r] Second Court of Robert Cole senior, 15 November 1695

Robert Fearon to goe with water Cart one year for 3 li.
At this Court Robert Fearon has leave to goe with his Water Cart with Wheels shod With Iron for the year ensueing att the rate of three pounds and payes one shilling in Earnest.

Alsoe at this Court the Cheif Constables doe agree with the said Robert Fearon to convey and releive all Cripples and poor Passengers coming to this Towne att the rate of twenty pounds for the year ensueing & receives one Shilling in Earnest.

Att this Court Mr. Smith the late Alderman delivers to the present Alderman the following Charters vizt.
One of King Edward the 6th   One of King Charles 1st
Three of Queen Elizabeth   One of King Charles 2nd
One of King James 1st   One of King James 2nd
and Mrs Millers Deed of guift for 40 li.

The Grange to be assessed for all Town dutyes & to be leavyed by distress.
At this Court Mr Alderman acquainted the Court that Robert Fisher Esquire who now lives at the Grange in Grantham had refused to pay any Assessment or Town dutyes to the Towne of Grantham for the said Grange on Pretence the said Grange was exempted from payment thereof and that the said Mr Fisher was desirous the same might be tried by Accion at Law in his Life time that his wife and Children hereafter might not be troubled about the same And this Court taking the same into Consideracon doe vote that the said Grange be assessed for all Town dutyes and that if any Accion be brought

against any of the Officers of this Towne for collecting the same that they doe appeare & defend the said Accion or Accions and that they be therein indempnifyed by this Court.

Third Court of Robert Cole senior, 13 December 1695

Assessment of 6d the pound for the Highways.
At this Court it is ordered that an Assessment at the Rate of six pence the pound be made & laid upon the Inhabitants of this Towne for the paying the Surveyors of the Highwayes of this Towne their Disbursments in the execucion of their offices for the year last past.

Assessment of 80 li for repairs of the Church.
At this Court upon the examinacion of the Accounts of Mr Robert Cole late Churchwarden of this Town it is ordered that an assessment of four score pounds be made & laid upon the Inhabitants of this Town Manthorp & Spittlegate for the money by him disbursed in the repaires of the parish Church of this Towne for the year last past.

Mr Leivesleys Accounts as Collector of the School house rents 1694 and 1695	£	s	d	Robert Cole Junior his Accounts as Churchwarden for the year last past			
Receipts	45	07	08	Received for Church rents Bells & Graves	11	05	04
Disburst	40	00	00	For Quarterage money	30	07	08
				Received for rents to be given to the poor	08	10	00
					50	03	00
				Disburst	123	00	01½
				Abatements allowed	001	09	08
					124	09	09½
				Due to Mr Cole	074	06	09½
Mr Newcombs and Samuel Hutchins Accounts as Collectors of the Schoolhouse rents for part of the years 1693 & 1694							
Recieved	45	07	08	Mr Robert Cole his Account as Escheator for the year last past			
Disbursment	40	00	00	Received of William Johnson of Bourn for a defective Yardwan [sic]	00	02	06
Due to the Town	05	07	08				
Abatements to be allowed	01	09	10				
Due to the Town	03	17	10				

[fo. 744v] **Fourth Court of Robert Cole 31 January 1695/6**

The Town Clerk to treat with the Queens Counsell about renewing the Lease of the Tolls.
At this Court it is ordered that Mr Procter the present Town Clerke doe further treat with the Queens Councell about the Renewall of the Lease of the Tolls to this Corporacion and that he search for & if possible get a Coppy of Bishopp Foxes Will or Deed for the Endowment of the Free school of this Towne. Ordered that a Lettre be sent to Sir John Brownlow to give him Thanks for his Kindness in giving 10 li to the poor of this Town and likewise to desire him & Sir William Ellis to assist the Towne Clerk in getting the Court Orders which were formerly ordered to be confirmed, to be confirmed by the Lord Keeper and Lords Cheife Justices.

At this Court John Bradfeild Chamberlain for the year last past accounteth
Received	330 12 00
Disburst	334 08 00
Due to the Accomptant	003 16 00

Fifth Court of Robert Cole, 6 March 1695/6

William Wing made free.
At this Court came William Wing who had served his Apprenticeship to John Newcomb and moved to be admitted a Freeman of this Corporacion which this Court does grant and he is sworn accordingly.

Sixth Court of Robert Cole, 24 April 1696

Att his Court Mr William Haskard accounteth as Millmaster for the last year from the 3rd December 1694 to 27th May 1695.
Received	40 09 09
Disburst	27 05 03
Due to the Town	13 04 06

Mr William Kirk accounteth as Millmaster for the said time for the Slate Mill.
Received	56 05 04
Disburst	34 09 10
Due to the Town	21 15 06

Att this Court Mr Anthony Kirk accounteth as Millmaster for the Town Mill from 3rd June 95 to the 2nd December 95.
Received	40 14 09½
Disburst	24 11 03
Due to the Town	16 03 06½

Mr Burbidge accounteth for the Slate Mill for the same time
Received   44 05 09
Disburst   28 11 00
Due to the Towne   15 14 09

[fo. 745r] **Seventh Court of Robert Cole, 19 May 1696**

Joseph Hutchin Chose Coalbuyer.
At this Court Joseph Hutchin is chosen Colebuyer for the year ensueing in the room of William Hutchin late Coalbuyer
Paid to him by William Hutchin [*no amounts given*].

Samuel [sic] *to keep the Conduit in repair one year and to have 30s.*
At this Court the Chamberlain makes a bargain on the behalf of this Corporacion with Samuel Clipsham a Plumber to repair the Conduit Pipes and the Conduit Cisterns for the year next ensueing to commence from MidSumer next at the rate of 30s. The Chamberlain to set the Cistern in good repaires and Samuel Clipsham to leave it in the same repair at the end of the said year one shilling given in earnest.

Comburgesses & 2nd 12 men to wear their Gowns on Sundays & Constables to walk with their Staffs.
At this Court it is ordered that the Twelve Comburgesses of this Town for the time being & the second twelve Company doe every Sunday, every Aldermans Court day, every Christmas day & the fifth day of November attend Mr Alderman in their gowns according to a former Court order made the thirtyeth day of November 1694 Under the Pain that every Comburgess shall for every default pay two Shillings six pence Every second Twelve man one Shilling six pence for the Use of the Corporacion to be leavyed by Distress & Sale of the Goods of the person soe offending and every Constable to pay Six pence that does not bring his Staff each of the said dayes to be leavyed as aforesaid.

Mr Edward Leivesley nominated Alderman.
At this Court Mr Edward Leivesley is Unanimously nominated Alderman of this Corporacion for the year ensueing according to the ancient Usage of this Corporacion.

Edward Lomax & Henry Smith made free.
Att this Court came Edward Lomax who had served his apprenticeship to Richard Hixson and Henry Smith who had served his apprenticeship to his Father Robert Smith and craved to be admitted Freemen of this Corporacion which this Court does grant and they are sworne accordingly.

Eighth Court of Robert Cole, 24 July 1696

Books Staff and Coulours reposed in Mr Aldermans hands to be delivered from Alderman to Alderman.
Now are reposed in Mr Aldermans hands one New Statute Booke at Large one old Statute Book at Large One Daltons Justice of the peace one Leading Staff and the Coulours which formerly belonged to the Company in the Militia of this Towne & Soake which are ordered to be delivered from Alderman to Alderman Successively at the time the plate and Charters of this Towne are delivered over.

Forty shillings to be Assessed upon the Markett Place for repair of the pump there.
Ordered an Assessment of 40s be laid upon the Inhabitants of the Market place for the reimbursment of Mr Richard Sentence the Oversees [*sic*] of the Market place Pump what money he has laid out this last year in the Repair of the said Pump.

[fo. 745v] **Ninth Court of Robert Cole, 28 August 1696**

New Lease to be granted to Mr Thorold of Johnsons house.
Ordered that a New Lease be granted to Mr Thorold of Johnsons House in Manthorp for the Terme of one and twenty yeares to comence from Michaelmas next ensueing Upon the Fine certaine of Twenty pounds & the reserved rent of twenty Five shillings *per Annum.*

Tenth Court of Robert Cole, 18 August 1696 [date appears incorrect]

30 li to be Assessed to pay Constables bills.
At this Court it is ordered that an Assessment of Thirty pounds be made and laid upon the Inhabitants of this Towne for the payment of the Constables of this Town their Disbursments in the Execucion of their offices for the year last past.

Eleventh & last Court of Robert Cole, 22 October 1696

The Tolls lett to Mrs Fisher.
At this Court a Lease of the profitts of the Tolls of this Corporacion is lett to Constance Fisher widdow for one year to comence from the 26th October 1696 at the rate of 50 li to be paid quarterly And in Consideracion that she now complains that she had a hard pennyworth the last year it is now ordered that the Chamberlain do abate her six pounds in her rent.

The Constables Accounts as Follows	li	s	d		li	s	d
Markett Place Received	10	01	00	Mr Aldermans Bill	00	04	02
Constables Disburst	03	06	10	Mr Turner Cheif Constable	04	02	04
Abatements allowed	00	11	02	Mr Wiles Cheif Constable	03	14	08
Paid the Chamberlain	06	03	00				
High street Received	03	13	02	Castlegate Received	02	18	04
Constables Disburst	03	12	04	Constables Disburst	03	15	07
Abatements allowed	00	01	06	Abatements allowed	00	01	02
	03	13	10	Paid the Constables	03	16	09
	00	00	08		00	18	05
Westgate Received	05	05	03	Walkergate Received	05	00	10
Constables Disburst	03	08	06	Constables Disburst	03	12	09
Abatements allowed	00	05	08	Abatements allowed	00	01	10
Paid the Chamberlain	03	14	02	Paid the Chamberlain	03	14	07
	01	11	01		01	06	03
Swinegate Received	02	15	00	At this Court Thomas Rookesby eldest			
Constables Disburst	03	06	06	son of Nathaniel Rooksby and craved			
Abatements allowed	00	02	08	to be admitted a Freeman of this			
Paid the Constables	03	09	02	Corporacion which this Court does			
	00	14	02	grant & he is sworn accordingly.			

[fo. 746r]

At an Assembly holden by Robert Cole senior Gentleman Alderman and the Comburgesses and Burgesses of Grantham aforesaid in Corpus Christi Quoir in the Prebendary Church there on Fryday next after St. Luke being 23 October 1696.

First did sit down upon the Cushions or place of Eleccion Mr Robert Cole Alderman in Corpus Christi Quoir in the said Prebendary Church.
Next to him did sit down upon the Cushions or place of Eleccion two other Comburgesses vizt Mr Edward Leivesley and Mr John Robinson.
Then is sent down into the body of the Church to Mr William Kirk & Mr John Newcomb one other Comburgess vizt Mr Beck.
Out of which three Comburgesses in the body of the Church one is chosen to come up & sitt upon the Cushions or place of Eleccion vizt. Mr Beck.
Then are there three Comburgesses upon the Cushions or place of Eleccion viz. Mr Edward Leivesley, Mr John Robinson & Mr Beck.
Out of which three Comburgesses upon the Cushions or place of Eleccion one is to be chosen Alderman of this Towne for the year ensueing.

Mr Edward Leivesley chose Alderman.
And thereupon by unanimous Vote of this Assembly Mr Edward Leivesley is chosen Alderman for the year ensueing.

Whereupon the said Mr Robert Cole is discharged from his Office of Alderman and Mr Edward Leivesley sworn Alderman in his stead for this Burrough and Soake of Grantham for the year ensueing according to the Antient Custome of the said Burrough.

And soe this Assembly breakes up.

Thomas Rooksby made free.
[No text is written adjacent to this marginal note – see above fo. 745v]

THE HALL BOOK OF GRANTHAM 1696–1697

[fo. 746v] [Blank page] [this is presumably the page on which details of the First Court of Edward Leivesley would have been entered]

[fo. 747r] **Second Court of Edward Leivesley 13 November 1696**

Att this Samuel Clipsham payes Mr Robert Cole two pounds tenn shillings in full discharge of the remainder of the money due upon his Accounts as late Overseer of the poor of this Towne which money the said Mr Cole has expended in Conveying downe one Thomas Kellam a poor distracted man of the Towne from Bethlem Hospitall.

Att this Court it is ordered that four score pounds be taken up at Interest for the Use of this Corporacion for the Renewall of the Lease of the Tolls of this Corporacion & Soake from the Queen Dowagers Councell att the fine of 65 li lately contracted for by the Town Clark & the charges in passing the Lease & that Mr Joseph Lowe, Mr Francis Langton, Mr Robert Cole Junior & Mr Richard Wyld doe become bound for the same & that they be indemnifyed by this Towne either by Assignment of the said Lease or otherwise for their soe being become bound.

Third Court of Edward Leivesley, 18 December 1696

At this Court Mr Robert Cole Junior accounteth as Millmaster for the Towne Mill from the 9th of December 1695 to the 25th May 1696

	li	s	d
His Receipts	45	00	01
Disburst	38	14	06
Due to the Towne	06	05	07
Mr William Turner also accounteth as Millmaster for the Slate Mill for the said time			
Received	61	02	05
Disburst	37	05	02
Due to the Towne	23	17	03
John Martin accounteth as Churchwarden for the last year			
Received	50	12	04
Disburst	75	08	02½
Due to the Acomptant	24	15	10½

At this Court it is ordered that an Assessment of 26 li be laid upon the Inhabitants of the parish vizt. Grantham Manthorpe & Spittlegate for the reimbursement of John Martin the late Churchwarden such summes as he laid out in the repaires & ornaments of the Parish Church of Grantham for the year last past.

At this Court it is ordered that for the future the Churchwarden doe not make any Visitacion dinner but that 2s 6d be allowed for the Ministers ordnary and 2s apiece for Grantham & 1s 6d for Manthorpe and Spittlegate Churchwardens & noe more.

At this Court it is ordered that for the future there be not made any publick Sessions Dinners but that every person who shall dine there shall pay their own ordnary.

[fo. 747v] **Fourth Court of Edward Leivesley, 22 January 1696/7**

Att this Court Robert Cole Junior complains that in the Accounts he passed the last Court as Millmaster he had forgett a Bill of forty three shillings and two pence which he had paid to the Smith which being made to appear by his Accounts he is allowed the said Bill and there now remains due from him to the towne 4 li 2s 5d.

	li	s	d
At this Court Mr John Coddington accounteth as one of the Overseers of the poor for the year last past			
Received	42	08	03
Disburst	51	12	06½
Abatements allowed	01	19	00
	53	11	06
Due to the Accomptant	11	11	03½
William Newton alsoe accounteth as the other overseer for the said yeare			
Received	66	11	06½
Disburst	62	06	05
Abatements allowed	03	16	03½
	66	02	08½
Due to the Town	00	08	09½

Fifth Court of Edward Leivesley, 5 March 1696/7

	li	s	d
Att this Court Mr William Kirk accounteth for the	21	15	06
Paid by order of the Chamberlain to Mr Sharpe	02	17	04
To Mrs Storey	07	09	00
To Mr Clark	04	09	00
To Widdow Young	01	00	00
paid to Mr Greenwood Chamberlain	04	08	00

paid to Mr Wyles Chamberlain	01 10 00	
paid the same	00 02 02	
	21 15 06	
Mr Doughty accounteth as Chamberlain for the last year		
Received	59 17 04	
Disburst	60 19 03½	
Due to the Accomptant	01 01 11½	
Mr Edward Greenwood accounteth as Chamberlain for the said year		
Received	124 11 11	
Disburst	114 02 02	
Due to the Town	010 09 09	

Att this Court William Gunby who had served his Apprenticeship to Henry Atkinson and craved to be admitted a Freeman of this Corporacion which this Court does grant & he is sworn accordingly.

[fo. 748r] Sixth Court of Edward Leivesley, 16 April 1697

At this Court Notice is given to the severall Inkeepers of this Towne that for the future they doe not hire any Hostler or Chamberlains for any longer terme than by day or by weeke that hereafter they may not claime a Settlement in the Towne.

Seventh Court of Edward Leivesley, 21 May 1697

At this Court came Thomas Frith who served his Apprenticeship to Thomas Hutchin, Joseph Winter who served his Apprenticeship to Thomas Archer and William Gulston a Forreigner (who laid down his tenn pounds) & craved to be admitted Freemen of this Corporacion which this Court does grant & they are sworne accordingly.

At this Court Mr John Robinson is unanimously nominated Alderman of this Corporacion for the year ensueing.

Eighth Court of Edward Leivesley, 11 June 1697

At this Court it is ordered that Mr Alderman and Mr Beck doe continue Millmasters untill Martlemas next & that they doe out of the profitts thereof pay the Arreares of rent due to Sir Edmond Turnor & the Executors of Mrs Trevillian.
At this court Widdow Read in the presence of Mr Burnett Minister of this Towne is nominated one of the six widdows to receive the yearly money given by Mrs Miller widdow deceased.

Att this Court Samuel Hammond posts his Accompts as Overseer of the
poor for the year last past

	li	s	d
Received	51	01	06
Disburst	49	01	02
Abatements allowed	01	02	08
Due to the Town	00	17	08

Mr Garner accounteth as the other Overseer for the said Towne

	li	s	d
Received	69	11	07
Disburst	74	03	06
Abatements allowed	02	15	09
Due to Mr Garner	07	07	08

[fo. 748v] **Ninth Court of Edward Leivesley, 17 September 1697**

At this court Mr Alderman acquainting the Court that Mr Machin the present Usher of the Schools was leaving the Town to be Curate to Mr Smith Rector of Westborow and goeing to reside there upon the Request of Mr Samuel Coddington by his Friends in Court to Supply the said place he is unanimously chosen Usher of the Schoole of the said Towne and to enter upon the said place and perquisites at Michaelmas next.

Att this court it is ordered that an Assessment of 35 li be made and laid upon the Inhabitants of this Towne for the payment of the Constables of this Towne their Disbursements in the Execucion of their offices for the year last past.

Att this Court came Sir John Thorold Baronet a Forreigner and craved to be admitted a Freeman of this Corporacion and laid down his Forty pounds which this Court taking into Consideracion doe admit him to his freedome and he is sworne accordingly and payes the accustomed Fees & one shilling for the stamp paper.

Tenth Court of Edward Leivesley, 21 October 1697

At this Court came Constance Fisher widdow & desired to take a Lease of the Tolls of this Town for the year ensueing which this Court taking into Consideracion doe grant the same at the rate of £50 2s 6d paid in earnest.

The Constables Accounts as follows:			li	s	d
Market Place	Received		11	05	05
	Disburst		03	12	05
	Abatements Allowed		00	18	00½
	Due to the Towne		06	14	11½
High Street	Received		03	17	00
	Disburst		03	05	00

	Abatements allowed	00 03 06
	Due to the Towne	03 08 06
Westgate	Received	05 08 04
	Disburst	03 04 10
	Abatements allowed	00 01 08½
	Due to the Towne	02 01 08½
Castlegate	Received	02 08 03
	Disburst	04 02 09
	Abatements allowed	00 01 02½
	Due to the Constables	00 15 08½
Swinegate	Received	03 01 01
	Disburst	03 03 06
	Abatements allowed	00 03 00
	Due to the Constables	00 05 05
Walkergate	Received	05 19 08
	Disburst	03 06 04
	Abatements allowed	00 04 06
	Due to the Chamberlaine	00 08 09½

	li s d
Mr Alderman's Bill	0 09 00
Mr Lowe Chief Constable	6 10 06
Mr Langton Chief Constable	7 11 03

[fo. 749r]

At an Assembly holden by Edward Leivesley Gentleman Alderman and the Comburgesses and Burgesses of Grantham aforesaid in Corpus Christi Quoire in the Prebendary Church there on the Fryday next after St Luke being 22 October 1697.

First did sit down upon the Cushions or place of Eleccion Mr Edward Leivesley Alderman in Corpus Christi Quoire in the said Prebendary Church.
Next to him did sitt down upon the Cushions or place of Eleccion two other Comburgesses vizt Mr John Robinson & Mr Nicholas Beck.
Then is sent down into the body of the Church to Mr William Kirke and Mr John Newcomb one other Comburgess vizt Mr Simon Grant.
Out of which three Comburgesses in the body of the Church one is chosen to come up and sitt upon the Cushions or place of Eleccion vizt Mr Grant.
Then are three Comburgesses upon the Cushions or place of Eleccion vizt Mr Robinson, Mr Beck and Mr Grant.
Out of which three Comburgesses upon the Cushions or Place of Eleccion one is to be chosen Alderman for the year ensueing.

And thereupon by Unanimous vote of this Assembly Mr John Robinson is Chozen Alderman for the Year ensueing.

Whereupon the said Mr Edward Leivesley is discharged from his Office of Alderman Alderman [*sic*] & Mr John Robinson sworn Alderman in his stead for this Burrough and Soak of Grantham for the Year ensueing according to the ancient Custome of the said Burrough.

And so this Assembly breakes up.

THE HALL BOOK OF GRANTHAM 1697–1698

[fo. 749r] **First Court of John Robinson, 29 October 1697**
[The names of the First and Second Twelves and Commoners are not given.]

Att this Court Mr Leivesley the late Alderman delivers to the present Alderman the Towne plate as follows

The Horserace Cup	Mr Harringtons Tankard
Mr Archers Bowle	Mr Kirkbyes Boll
Mr Wickliffs Tankard	Mr Greenwoods thirteen Spoons
Mr Greenwoods Tankard	Mr Battyes Salt Cellar & Cover
Mr Horsemans Cup	Mr Storeys Cup
Mr Battyes two Tumblers	Mr Woodruffs Tankard
Mr Battyes Beaker	Mr Wrights Cup & Cover
& these Charters	And the Statute book at large
One of King Edward the 6th	Daltons Justice of the peace
Three of Queen Elizabeth	The Leading Staff
One of King James the 1st	The Coulours belonging to the
One of King Charles the 1st	Militia Company of this Towne and Soake &
One of King Charles the 2d	One old Statute Booke
One of King James the 2d.	

Att this Court Mr Fisher the present Churchwarden made a bargain with Edward Dickenson to keep the Hall Clock in good repair at 5s *per Annum* And one shilling paid in Earnest.

[fo. 749v]

Names of the officers

Coroner	Mr Edward Leivesley	Jur	Markett Place Constables	Francis Wilson and Thomas Fearon
Escheator	Mr Nicholas Beck	Jur		
Collectors of the Schoolhouse rents	Mr Simon Grant & George Miller	Jur	High Street Constables	William Matkin and Robert Orson
Chamberlains	Mr Francis Langton John Goodwin	Jur		
Chief Constables	Mr William Charles & Mr John Firman	Jur	Westgate Constables	George Charity and William Matkin

Churchwardens	Mr James Firman & Mr Thomas Fisher	Walkergate Constables	Edward Lomax and Thomas Rooksby
Towne Clerk	Mr Samuel Procter		
Sergeants and Gaoler and Bailiff of the Liberties	Anthony Taylor & Thomas Short	Swinegate Constables	Samuel Clipsham Joseph Rawlinson
Church Clerke	William Higginbottom		
Bellman	Ralph Osborne	Castlegate	Robert Fearon and
Beedle	John Scott	Constables	William Wing
Leather Sealers	[blank] Hutchin John Newball George Miller and Thomas Rawlinson	Towne Waytes	William Higginbotton Leonard Butcher John Wilcock and Roger Hutchinson
Cornprizers	Robert Orson & William Wing		
Market Sayers	Joseph Lowe and John Calcroft		
Keykeepers	[blank]		

[fo. 750r] **Second Court of John Robinson, 2 January 1697/8**

At this Court Mr John Coddington one of the Comburgesses of this Towne acquainted this Court with the Inconveniencyes that he received in the Attendance of this Court in the said Office of Comburgess and desired to be dismissed from his said place and further attendance att this Court which this court takeing into Consideration doe grant and he is hereby dismissed from his said place and further attendance att this Court without paying any fine.

At this Court Mr William Kirke acquainted the court that Sir William Ellis Baronet had ordered him to receive of his Bailiff 25 li towards the Charge of New Casting the fifth bell which is now broke for which this Court doe give Sir William their Unanimous thanks and desire Mr Kirke to doe the same in the name of the Towne.

At this Court came Gabriel Rawlinson who served seaven years Apprenticeship to John Shootwell and William Martin who served seaven years Apprenticeship to Mr Edward Leivesley and craved to be admitted Freemen of this Corporacion which this Court does grant and they are sworne accordingly.

Att this Court Mr Robert Cole Junior and Mr William Turner are unanimously chosen Comburgesses of this Corporacion in the room of Mr Nicholas Beck deceased and Mr Coddington who has leave to depart this Court and were sworne accordingly and took the oaths of Allegiance and Supremacy appointed by Act of Parliament.

Att this Court Mr Thomas Fisher and Mr John Goodwin are chosen of the second Twelve Company in the room of Mr Robert Cole Junior and Mr William Turner according to antient Custome and sworne accordingly.

Third Court of John Robinson 18 February 1697/8

At this Court of the Sallary of George Chantry as keeper of the house of Correction and teacher of the Jarsey Schoole is taken from him by reason he has not for some time past had any Schollars and likewise has neglected his duty as Master of the said house of Correccion and he is discharged from the said place at Lady Day next.

Ordered that the Town Clerk doe demand of John Newball the money he received more than he ought to doe in pretence of the Kings tax laid upon the Town Mill when Mr Beck was Millmaster.

	£	s	d
At this Court Mr Richard Wiles accounteth as Chamberlain of this Towne for the year past			
Received	72	13	02
Disburst	74	07	07
Due to Mr Wiles	1	14	05
Mr Barratt accounteth as the other Chamberlain			
Received	97	04	08
Disbursements	97	05	11½
Due to Mr Barratt	00	01	03½

	£	s	d
At this Court Mr Lievesley accounteth as Millmaster for the Slate Mill from 5th of June 1696 to January the 3rd 1697			
Received	177	18	01
Disburst	166	19	01½
Due to the Town	010	18	01½

[fo. 750v] Fourth Court of John Robinson, 18 March 1697/8

Att this Court Mr Alderman acquainting the Court that Mr Richard Dawson one of the second twelve men of this Towne desired to be dismissed from his said place of second twelveman and his further Attendance of this Court. And Mr John Marshall one of the Commoners of this court desireing the same by reason they are both of them sent by their buisiness to be out of Town It is by this Court ordered that they be dismissed from their said places and further attendances att this Court without paying any Fine.

Att this Court it is ordered that a Clause be putt into the Oath hereafter to be administred to every person hereafter claiming to be admitted Freemen of this Corporacion that they shall grind such Malt and Corne as they Use in their Houses att the Mills of this Towne according to antient Custome.

Fifth Court of John Robinson, 27 May 1698

At this Court Mr Thomas Baily is chosen one of the second Twelve men of this Corporacion and sworn accordingly.

At this Court Mr Joseph Lowe and Mr William Charles are chozen Comburgesses of this Town in the room in the room [sic] of Mr John Newcomb and Mr Robert Cole Junior lately deceased and tooke the Oaths for Execucion of their Offices and the oaths appointed by Act of Parliament made in the first year of the reign of his Majestie King William and the late Queen Mary.

At this Court Mr Richard Wiles is sworne Cheif Constable for the ensueing part of the year in the room of Mr Charles who is chozen one of the Comburgesses of this Corporacion.

Att this Court Mr Francis Wilson is chosen one of the Second twelve men of this Corporacion.

At this Court came Mr Edward Parker a Forreigner and laid down his Tenn pounds as a Fine and craved to be admitted as Freeman of this Corporacion which this Court taking into Consideracion doe grant and he sworne accordingly and pays the accustomed Fees. Att this Court came John Benton eldest son of John Benton and Richard Read who had served his Apprenticeship with William Bristow and craved to be admitted Freemen of this Corporacion which this Court takeing into Consideracion doe grant and they are sworne accordingly.

Att this Court Mr Simon Grant is Unanimously nominated Alderman of this Corporacion for the Year ensueing.

[fo. 751r] Sixth Court of John Robinson, 24 June 1698

At this Court Mr John Smith one of the Comburgesses of the Town having been informed against upon the Oath of his Servant that he had begotten her with Child of which she was afterward brought to bed which evil doing was Contrary to former order of the Court. This Court takeing the same into Consideracion and Mr Smith being present in Court and not offering anything materiall in his owne defence he is by order of this Court discharged from his said office of Comburgess and his further Attendance of this Court according to the said former order.

Att this Court Mr John Bradfeild is chosen one of the Comburgesses of this Towne in the room of Mr John Smith lately discharged from the said place for the Misdemeanour of Fornication according to a former order of this Court.

Thomas Matkin accounteth as Overseer of the poor of this town for the last year s d

	Received	69 00 00
	Disburst	57 14 10
	Abatements allowed	02 06 08
		60 01 06
	Due to the Town	09 01 00
Robert Quiningborough accounteth as the other Overseer	Received	90 07 07
	Disburst	68 02 10
	Abatements allowed	03 04 09
		71 07 07
	Due	19 00 00

Seventh Court of John Robinson, 19 August 1698

Att this Court it is ordered that for the future all such persons as shall hereafter be intrusted by the Town as Millmasters shall every Monday morning during such time as they shall continue Millmasters deliver to Mr Alderman for the time being a note in writing of all such wheat and Moulter and the price thereof as shall be weekly delivered & likewise the Quantity of Malt that shall be weekly delivered out.

At this court it is ordered John Owen senior shall for the future after Michaelmas next be discharged from receiving the 40s out of the Sallary due to the Master of the house of Correccion for the town and Soake.

Mr Haskard accounteth as Millmaster for the Town Mill from November 22d 1697 to the 16th May 1698		£ s d
	Received	51 08 01
	Disburst	43 18 09
	Due to the Town	07 09 04

At this Court came Richard Bullimore a Forreigner and laid down his tenn pounds, John Lenton eldest son of William Lenton, Nehemiah Wilson eldest Son of Thomas Wilson, John Crichloe eldest Son of Thomas Crichloe, John Burman eldest Son of Joseph Burman, Thomas Poole eldest son of John Poole, Nicholas Newton eldest Son of William Newton, John Coddington eldest Son of John Coddington, Mr Edward Secker who had served seaven years with Thomas Buck, John Goodborne who has served seaven years with Mr Robert Cole Junior, George Durham who had served seaven years with Richard Durham, Edward Garthwaite who had served seaven years with his father Mr Nathanial Garthwaite came and desired to be admitted Freemen of this Corporacion which this court taking into consideracion coe grant and they are sworne accordingly and pay their accustomed fees.

[fo. 751v] **Eighth Court of John Robinson, 16 September 1698**

At this Court it is ordered that the Overseers of the poor doe take Care to provide for Anne Pearson an Apprentice Girle with Widdow Eston she being unable to keep her any longer.

Whereas Thomas Brown of Allington att this Court produced an Assignment of the Lease from this Corporacion to George Road of a Tenement in Walkergate and desired the said Lease might be renewed in his Name under the Usuall rent and Fine in the said Lease mencioned. It is by this court ordered That the said Lease be renewed to the said Thomas Brown for the Term of one and Twenty yeares from the expiracion of the said Terme in the said recited Lease.

At this Court Mr Robert Quiningbrough one of the Overseers of the poor of this Towne complained that severall persons have refused to pay their severall Assessments for releife of the poor of this Towne and threatened to sue him in Case he distrein for the same. It is by this Court ordered that these Overseers doe distrein for the same and that they be indempnified for soe doing by this Corporacion.

At this Court it is ordered that an Assessment of Threescore and Five pounds be made for the reimbursement of the Constables Bills of disbursements for the year last past according to the

Accounts given in.		£	s	d
Constables Accounts		03	17	00
Mr Wyles				
Mr Firman	Cheif Constables	00	15	00
& Mr Charles		21	00	00
Mr Bullimore		00	11	04
Francis Wilson		02	10	00
Thomas Fearon		02	12	00
Thomas Rawlinson		02	12	06
Robert Orson		02	10	00
George Charity		02	12	00
William Matkin		02	12	00
Edward Lomax		02	15	00
Thomas Rooksby		02	12	00
Samuel Clipsham		02	11	00
Joseph Rawlinson		02	12	00

Robert Fearon		05 10 00
William Wing		02 12 00
		60 03 00

At this Court came William Kirkham who served his Apprenticeship with Widdow Short and desired to be admitted a freeman of this Corporacion which this Court taking into consideracion doe grant and he is sworne accordingly.

Ordered that Mr Anthony Kirke be continued Millmaster of the Town Mill for the next half year.

[fo. 750Ar] **Ninth Court of John Robinson, 20 October 1698**
[fo. 750A follows fo. 751]

At this Court came Constance Fisher Widdow and desired to be admitted Tenant of the Tolls of this Corporacion as formerly which this Court taking into Consideracion doe grant and accordingly they doe lett her the profitts of the said Tolls for this Year ensueing att the rate of 50 li to be paid Quarterly one Shilling paid in Earnest.

Att this Court came William Mercer a Forreigner and laid down his tenn pounds and craved to be admitted a Freeman of this Corporacion Which this Court taking into Consideracion doe grant and he is sworn accordingly and pays the accustomed Fees.

The Constables Account as followeth:		£ s d
Markett place	Received	21 04 08
Constables	Disburst	05 09 00
	Abatements allowed	01 13 03½
		07 02 03½
	Due to the Towne	14 02 04½
High Street	Received	07 14 07
Constables	Disburst	05 02 02
	Abatements allowed	00 05 06
		05 07 08
	Due to the Town	02 06 11
Westgate	Received	11 04 11
Constables	Disbursements	05 02 00
	Abatement allowed	00 09 01½
		05 11 01½
	Due to the Town	05 13 09½
Walkergate	Received	11 12 06
Constables	Disburst	05 08 03
	Abatements allowed	00 07 10½
		05 16 01½

	Due to the Town	05 16 04½
Swinegate	Received	05 05 07½
Constables	Disburst	05 01 06
	Abatements allowed	00 01 01½
		05 02 07
	Due to the Town	00 03 00
Castlegate	Received	06 06 07
Constables	Disburst	02 17 04
	Abatement allowed	00 01 04½
		02 18 08½
	Due to the Town	03 07 11

[fo. 750 Av]

At an Assembly held by John Robinson Gentleman Alderman of Grantham aforesaid the Comburgesses and Burgesses of the said Towne in Corpus Christi Quoire in the Prebendary Church there the Friday next after St Luke being 21 October 1698.

First did sitt downe upon the Cushion or place of Eleccion Mr John Robinson Alderman in Corpus Christi Quoire in the said Prebendary Church.
Next to him did sitt downe upon the Cushions or place of Eleccion one other comburgess vizt Mr Simon Grant.
Then are sent down into the Body of the Church to Mr William Kirke there two other Comburgesses vizt Mr Haskard and Mr Burbidge
Out of which three Comburgesses in the body of the Church one is chosen to come up and sitt upon the Cushion or place of Eleccion vizt Mr Haskard
Then is sent downe into the body of the Church to Mr William Kirke and Mr Burbidge one other comburgess vizt Mr Anthony Kirk.
Out of which three Comburgesses in the Body of the Church one other is chosen to come up and sitt on the Cushions or place of Eleccion vizt. Mr William Kirke
Then are those three Comburgesses upon the Cushion or place of Eleccion vizt. Mr Grant, Mr Haskard and Mr William Kirke
Out of which three Comburgesses upon the Cushions or place of Eleccion one is to be chosen Alderman for the Year ensueing
And thereupon by unanimous Vote of this Assembly Mr Simon Grant is chosen Alderman for the year ensueing

Whereupon the said Mr Robinson is discharged from his Office of Alderman and Mr Simon Grant sworne Alderman in his stead for this Burrough and Soake of Grantham for the year ensueing according to the antient Custome of the said Burrough.

And soe this Assembly breaks up.

THE HALL BOOK OF GRANTHAM 1698–1699

[fo. 751Br] **First Court of Simon Grant, 28 October 1698**

At this Court Mr Robinson the late Alderman delivers to the present Alderman the Towns Plate and Charters as follows

The Horserace Cup	Mr Harringtons Tankard
Mr Archers Boll	Mr Kirkbyes Boll
Mr Wickliffs Tankard	Mr Greenwoods 13 Spoons
Mr Greenwoods Tankard	Mr Battyes Salt Cellar and Cover
Mr Horsemans Cup	Mr Storyes Cup
Mr Battyes two Tumblers	Mr Woodruffs Tankard
Mr Battyes Beaker	Mr Wrights Cup and Cover

These Charters

One of King Edward the 6th:	One of King Charles the 1st
Three of Queen Elizabeth	One of King Charles the 2nd
One of King James the 1st	One of King James the 2nd

[fo. 751Bv] **Second Court of Simon Grant, 18 November 1698**

At this Court Mr Richard Sentence Overseer of the Marketplace pump complained that he has disburst about the repaires of the said pump Twenty eight shillings It is this day ordered that an Assessment be made for the same.

Third Court of Simon Grant, 20 January 1698/9

At this Court came Robert Smithergall a Forreigner and laid down his Tenn pounds and craved to be admitted a Freeman of this Town which this Court taking into Consideracion doe grant and return him Five pounds in Consideracion whereof he obledges himself to dress all Publick Aldermans Dinners and Suppers all Chief Constables feasts and the Sessions Dinners att the Guildhall during his life and is sworne accordingly.

[fo. 752r] **Fourth Court of Simon Grant, 10 March 1698/9**

At this Court it is ordered that the Churchwardens of this Towne for the time being doe allow to William Higginbottom the present Church Clerk Five shillings a Quarter during the time he shall continue Church Clerk as an Addition to his Sallary.

At this Court came George Read eldest son of George Read, William Hayes eldest son of William Hayes, William Marshall eldest son of Thomas Marshall and craved to be admitted Freemen of this Corporacion which this Court taking into Consideracion doe grant and they are Sworn accordingly.

Fifth Court of Simon Grant, 26 May 1699

At this Court Mr William Haskard is Unanimously nominated Alderman of this Corporacion for the Year ensueing.

Mr Fisher accounteth as Churchwarden for part of the yeares 1697 & 1698

	li	s	d
Received	063	18	02
Disburset	156	13	01
Abatements allowed	001	17	04
	158	10	05
Due to Mr Fisher	094	12	03

[fo. 752v] **Sixth Court of Simon Grant, 9 July 1699**

Mr Bristow accounteth as Overseer of the poor for 6 months in the Last year

	li	s	d
Received	53	02	06
Disburst	50	15	07
Abatements allowed	01	15	05
	52	11	00
Due to the Town	00	11	06

Mr Vincent accounteth as the other Overseer

Received	62	04	03
Disburst	58	09	06
Abatements allowed	02	12	01½
	61	01	07½
Due to the Town	01	02	04½

At this Court the share of Mrs Millers interest money is ordered to be paid to Widdow Lowe in the room of Widdow Read deceased in the presence of Mr Burnett Minister of the Towne.

At this Court came George Mills who had served his Apprenticeship with Mr Thomas Fisher and desired to [sic] admitted a Freeman of this Corporacion which this Court taking into consideracion doe grant and he is sworne accordingly.

At this Court it is ordered that an Assessment of Ninety four pounds and twelve shillings & threepence be laid upon the Inhabitants of this Town Manthorp and Spittlegate for the payment of Mr Thomas Fisher his Disbursements as Churchwarden for the year last past.

[fo. 753r] **Seventh Court of Simon Grant, 22 June 1699**

	li	s	d
At this Court Mr Joseph Hutchin late Cole buyer accounteth for money put in his hands	10	10	00
for Coals sold	20	18	04
	31	08	04
Disburst	23	07	03
Due to the Towne	08	01	01

Which he is ordered to pay to Mr Lomax for the Use aforesaid.

At this Court came William Quincey a Commoner of this Court and desired that in consideracion his occasions required him to be often out of Towne and that his Attendance att this Court would be prejudiceall to him it is now ordered that he be dismissed from his said place of a Commoner and further Attendance att this Court.

At this Court came Thomas Robinson who had served his Apprenticeship with Richard Quincey and desired to be admitted a Freeman of this Corporacion which this Court does grant and he is sworn accordingly and payed the accustomed Fees to the box and officers.

At this Court came Mr Samuel Coddington the Usher of the School and acquainted the Court that by reason of his goeing to a Living in the Countrey he could not attend the School att such times as necessary and desired to be dismissed from the said place which is accordingly granted and Mr Charles Burnett being here in Court and desiring to be admitted to the said place it is accordingly granted him with the Sallary thereto belonging.

At this Court it is ordered that the Redd Lyon Inne be rebuilt.

Eighth Court of Simon Grant, 21 July 1699

Att this Court came Thomas Cole who had served his Apprenticeship with his father Mr Robert Cole, Edwin Halam eldest son of John Halam, Thomas Walgrave who had served his Apprenticeship with his Mother Alice Walgrave, John Thorold who had served his apprenticeship with Mr Edward Bristow, Thomas Brown who served his Apprenticeship to Mr William Haskard and John Kirk [sic] eldest son of Mr William Kirke and desired to be admitted Freemen of this Corporacion which this Court taking into consideracion doe grant and they are sworne accordingly.

[fo. 753v] Ninth Court of Simon Grant, 21 September 1699

At this Court came Abraham Beveston a Forreigner and craved to [be] admitted a Freeman of this Corporacion and laid down his Tenn pounds as a Fine which this Court taking into Consideracion doe grant and he is Sworne accordingly alsoe John Grocock eldest son of William Grocock, John Spottswood who had served his Apprenticeship to John Woulds a Freeman of this Corporacion and William Everitt who had served his Apprenticeship with Mr William Burbidge and craved to be admitted Freemen of this Corporacion which this Court taking into Consideracion doe grant and they were sworn accordingly.

Tenth Court of Simon Grant, 3 October 1699

The Constables Disbursements

	li	s	d
Mr Calcroft	03	19	06
Mr Bullimore	03	00	00
Thomas Fearon	03	06	09
Joseph Rawlinson	03	17	05
John Benton	03	04	01 ½
Samuel Clipsham	02	17	03
William Matkin	03	02	07
Edward Lomax	02	16	05
Edward Parker	02	13	00
William Wing	03	04	06
Robert Fearon	03	00	00
Francis Berriff	01	06	00
George Charity	03	10	00
Thomas Rooksby	03	04	00 ½
Due to Mr Alderman	01	00	00
	44	01	07

[fo. 754r] **Eleventh Court of Simon Grant, 19 October 1699**

At this Court came Constance Fisher widdow and desired to be admitted Tenant of the Tolls of this Corporacion as formerly which this Court taking into Consideracion doe grant and accordingly they doe lett her the profits of the said Tolls for this year ensueing att the rate of fifty pounds to be paid Quarterly 1s paid Mr Alderman in Earnest.

The Differences between the Town and Mr Newball by consent of the Court and Mr Newball is referred to Mr Procter and Mr Seckar.

Constables Accounts		li	s	d
Markett place Constables	Received	17	13	03½
	Disburst	06	09	04
	Abatements allowed	01	00	02½
		07	09	06½
	Due to Town	10	03	09
High Street Constables	Received	06	02	09½
	Disburst	06	06	09½
	Abatements allowed	00	01	06½
		06	08	04
	Due to Constables	05	08	06½
Westgate Constables	Received	08	02	10½
	Disburst	07	00	00
	Abatements allowed	00	01	09
		07	01	09½
	Paid the Chamberlain	01	01	01
	Mr Smith	00	03	06
		00	17	07
Walkergate Constables	Received	09	14	02
	Disburst	04	09	08
	Abatements allowed	00	06	04
		04	15	00
	Paid the Chamberlain	04	19	02
Castlegate Constables	Received	04	15	09
	Disburst	06	05	03
	Abatements allowed	00	00	07½
		06	05	10½
	Due to Constables	01	10	01½
Swinegate Constables	Received	03	13	10½
	Disburst	05	05	04
	Abatements allowed	00	01	11
		05	07	03

Due to Constables	01 13 04½
more	00 05 00
	01 18 04½

[fo. 754v]

At an Assembly holden by Simon Grant Gentleman Alderman of Grantham aforesaid and the Comburgesses and Burgesses of the said Town in Corpus Christi Quoir in the prebendary Church there the Fryday next after St Luke 20 October 1699.

First did sit down upon the Cushions or place of Eleccion Mr Simon Grant in Corpus Christi Quoir in the said Prebendary Church Next to him did sitt down upon the Cushions or place of Eleccion two other Comburgesses vizt Mr William Haskard and Mr William Kirke
Then is sent down to the body of the Church to Mr William Burbidge and Mr Anthony Kirke one other Comburgess vizt Mr Turner
Out of which three Comburgesses in the body of the Church one is chosen to come up and sit upon the Cushions or place of Eleccion vizt Mr William Burbidge
Then are three Comburgesses upon the Cushions or place of Eleccion vizt Mr William Haskard, Mr William Kirke and Mr William Burbidge
Out of which three Comburgesses upon the Cushions or place of Eleccion on is chozen Alderman for the ensueing year vizt Mr William Haskard.

Whereupon the said Mr Grant is discharged from his office of Alderman and Mr William Haskard sworne Alderman in his stead for this Burrough and Soake of Grantham for the year ensueing according to the Antient Custome of the said Burrough.

And so this Assembly breaks up.

THE HALL BOOK OF GRANTHAM 1699–1700

[fo. 755r] **First Court of William Haskard, 26 October 1699**

At this Court Mr Bullimore upon request (he goeing to leave the Town) is discharged from his office of Second Twelveman and further Attendance on this Court.

At this Court Mr Grant the late Alderman delivers to the present Alderman the Town plate & Charters as follows:

The Horserace Cup	Mr Harringtons Tankard
Mr Archers Boll	Mr Kirkbyes Boll
Mr Wickliffs Tankard	Mr Greenwoods 13 Spoons
Mr Greenwoods Tankard	Mr Battyes Salt Cellar and Cover
Mr Horsemans Cup	Mr Storyes Cupp
Mr Battyes two Tumblers	Mr Woodrufts Tankard
Mr Battyes Beaker	Mr Wrights Cup and Cover

These Charters

One of King Edward 6th	One of King Charles the 1st
Three of Queen of [sic] Elizabeth	One of King Charles the 2nd
One of King James the 1st	One of King James the 2nd

At this Court Mr Thomas Rawlinson and Mr John Benton are chosen second Twelve men and Sworne accordingly.

[fo. 755v] **Second Court of William Haskard, 15 December 1699**

At this Court it is ordered that an Addicional Assessment be made for the relief of the poor.

At this Court came Thomas Stanser eldest son of Thomas Stanser, Edward Elson who had Served his Apprenticeship to William Knight and George Short eldest son of Thomas Short and craved to be admitted Freemen of this Corporacion which this Court taking into Consideracion doe grant and they are Sworne accordingly.

Third Court of William Haskard, 19 January 1699/1700

John Firman accounteth as Chamberlain for the last year

Received	62 04 02
Disburst	84 02 04
Due to the Accomptant	21 18 02

Thomas Rawlinson accounteth as the other Chamberlain for the said year

Receipts	132 14 04
Disbursements	163 04 09½
Due to the Accomptant	030 10 05½

Fourth Court of William Haskard, 9 February 1699/1700

Mr Anthony Kirk accounts as Millmaster from May 98 to 5 February 1699. [*No details given*].

[fo. 756r] Fifth Court of William Haskard, 7 March 1699/1700

At this Court the Church Clock being broke Edward Dickenson undertakes to mend it for tenn shillings.

Nicholas Quiver being informed against for selling Nales and Laths and other things which he ought not to doe is by Consent of the Court ordered to come and take his freedome or else to be proceeded against according to Law.

It is alsoe ordered by Consent of the whole Court that the redd Lyon Inne be this Spring pulled downe and rebuilt soe farr as is necessary and Convenient William Niccolls to be bound to his good behaviour and care to be taken if possible to turn him out of Town if he will not come and take his freedome.

Sixth Court of William Haskard, 28 May 1700

At this Court Mr John Calcroft by Unanimous Vote of this Court is chosen one of the Comburgesses of this Town in the room of Mr Simon Grant late deceased.

At this court Mr William Kirk is unanimously nominated Alderman of this Town for the Year ensueing.

At this Court came Richard Ellis Esquire and laid down forty pounds and desires to be admitted a Freeman of this Corporacion Which this Court taking into Consideracion doe grant and he is sworn accordingly.

Mr Patrick Spottswood a forreigner also at this Court laid down his Fine of of [*sic*] tenn pounds and desired to be admitted a freeman of this Corporacion Which this Court taking into Consideracion doe grant and he his sworn accordingly.

[fo. 756v] **Seventh Court of William Haskard, 10 June 1700**

At this Court Mr William Kirk accounteth as one of the Collectors of
the Schoolhouse Rents	Received	22 10 00
Disburst		20 19 05
Due to the Town		01 10 07

Robert Owen accounteth as followeth	Received	22 15 00
Disburst		20 11 02
Due to the Town		02 03 10

Mr Langton accounteth as Churchwarden for the last year
Received	53 03 10
Disburst	87 05 10
Abatements allowed	02 07 08
	89 13 06
Due to the Accomptant	36 09 08

Ordered that an assessment of forty pounds be made and laid upon the Inhabitants of this Town Manthorp and Spittlegate for reimbursement of the said Churchwardens.

Eighth Court of William Haskard, 20 September 1700

At this Court Mr William Doughty accounteth as Millmaster for the Town Mill from the
12th February last for 32 weeks	Received	48 00 11
	Disburst	36 15 11
	Due to the Town	11 05 00
Mr Calcraft also accounteth for the said time	Received	69 08 09
	Disburst	54 19 04
	Due to the Town	14 09 05

At this Court Widdow Wray and Widdow Handley are chosen to receive Mistress Millers guift in the presence of Mr Burnett the Minister of the Towne in the room of Widdow Toms and Widdow Glover deceased.

Ordered that an Assessment of twenty six pounds be laid upon the Inhabitants of this Town for the payment of the Constables Bills of Disbursements for the part of the last year untill Mid-Summer last	Mr Alderman	01	01	09
	Mr Fisher	01	11	00
	Mr Firman	01	18	02
	James Smith	01	17	07
	John Osborn	02	13	01
	Mr Greenwood	01	07	11
	Mr Lomax	01	09	02
	Mr Clipsham	00	14	00
	Francis Berriff	01	15	00
	William Wing	01	01	00
	Edward Barber	00	18	00
	John Bass	01	10	00
	Thomas Robinson	00	19	00
	George Charity	00	19	06
	Thomas Rooksby	00	15	00

At this Court Mr William Doughty is chosen one of the Comburgesses of this room of Mr William Turner who is lately gone to live out of Towne and desired to be discharged from the said place.

[fo. 757r] **Ninth Court of William Haskard, 17 October 1700**

At this Court Mr John Calcraft is Unanimously chosen Towne Clarke for the Burrough and Soak of Grantham in the room of Mr Procter late deceased and is sworne accordingly.

Tenth & last Court of William Haskard, 24 October 1700

At this Court the Tolls of Grantham were lett to Constance Fisher to comence from the 26th Instant for one Year at 50 li payable Quarterly Gave Mr Alderman in Earnest one shilling.

[fo. 757v]

At an Assembly Holden by William Haskard, Gentleman, Alderman of Grantham aforesaid & the Comburgesses & Burgesses of the said Town in Corpus Christi Quoire in the Prebendary Church there the Friday next after St Luke 25 October 1700.

First did sitt down upon the Cushions or place of Eleccion Mr William Haskard in Corpus Christi Quoire in the said Prebendary Church
Next to him did sitt down upon the Cushions or place of Eleccion two other Comburgesses vizt. Mr William Kirke and Mr William Burbidge

Then is sent downe to the body of the Church to Mr Anthony Kirke and Mr William Turner one other Comburgess vizt. Mr Joseph Lowe

Out of which three Combugesses in the body of the Church one is chosen to come up and sitt upon the Cushions or place of Eleccion vizt Mr Anthony Kirke

Then are there three Comburgesses upon the Cushions or place of Election vizt Mr William Kirke, Mr William Burbige and Mr Anthony Kirke

Out of which three Comburgesses upon the Cushions or place of Eleccion one is chosen Alderman for this yeare vizt. Mr William Kirke

Whereupon the said Mr William Haskard is discharged from his office and Mr William Kirke sworne Alderman in his stead for this Burrough and Soake of Grantham for the year ensueing according to the Antient Custome of the said Burrough.

And soe this Assembly breaks up.

THE HALL BOOK OF GRANTHAM 1700–1701

[fo. 758r] **First Court of William Kirke, 1 November 1700**

Att this Court Mr Haskard the Late Alderman delivers to the present Alderman the Towne Plate and Charters as followeth

The Horserace Cup	Mr Harringtons Tankard & Mr Kirkbys
Mr Archers Bowle	Tankard
Mr Wickliffs Tankard	Mr Greenwoods 13 Spoons
Mr Greenwoods Tankard	Mr Battyes Salt Cellar and Cover
Mr Horsemans 2 Cups	Mr Storeys Cup
Mr Battyes two Tumblers	Mr Woodrooffs Tankard
Mr Battyes Beaker	Mr Wrights Cup and Cover

These Charters

One of King Edward 6th	Three of Queen Elizabeth
one of King James 1st	One of King Charles 1st
One of King Charles the 2nd	One of King James 2nd

Att this Court Mr William Doughty is chosen one of the Comburgesses of this Town in the room of Mr William Turner who desired to be discharged being he is gone to live in the Countrey and the said Mr Doughty is Sworne accordingly.

Mr William Kirk Alderman

	2nd Twelve
Mr Robert Cole	Mr John Firman
Mr Edward Leivesley	Mr Thomas Rawlinson
Mr John Robinson	Mr Richard Wyld
Mr William Haskard	Mr Francis Langton
Mr William Burbidge	Mr James Firman
Mr Anthony Kirke	Mr Thomas Fisher
Mr Thomas Baily	Mr Thomas Baily
Mr Joseph Lowe	Mr Francis Wilson
Mr William Charles	Mr Robert Langley
Mr John Bradfeild	Mr John Benton
Mr John Calcroft	
Mr William Doughty	

[fo. 758v]

Names of the officers

Mr William Haskard	Coroner	Andrew Rudkin	Beadle
Mr William Burbidge	Escheator	Thomas Cole and Thomas Walgrave	Market Sayers
Mr Anthony Kirke and Samuel Clipsham	Collectors of the Schoolhouse Rents		
Mr Thomas Fisher & Mr Edward Barber	Chamberlains	Robert Orson & William Wing	Corn Prizers
Robert Langley & Robert Orson	Churchwardens	John Weaver Richard Woulds & Thomas Marshall	Leather Serchers
Mr John Firman & Mr Thomas Rawlinson	Chief Constables	Mr Alderman Mr Thomas Fisher	Key Keepers
Mr John Calcroft	Towne Clerk	Mr Robert Langley	
George Short	Gaoler	John Osborn	Promoter
George Short & Richard Bristow	Serjeants	William Higginbottom Leonard Butcher John Wilson & Roger Hutchinson	Town Waites

Constables

William Wing & Edward Lomax	Market Place
Thomas Robinson & John Osborn	High Street
Thomas Cole & John Short	Westgate
William Martin & John Lenton	Walkergate
Thomas Walgrave John Kirk	Swinegate Castlegate

Ralph Osborne — Sexton

[fo. 759r] **Second Court of William Kirke, 15 November 1700**

Thomas Rooksby discharged the Court.
Att this Court Thomas Rooksby desired by Mr John Benton to be discharged from any further attendance att this Court and the Court upon Consideracion grants the same accordingly.

Cornelius Lenton & John Read made free.
Att this Court Cornelius Lenton son of William Lenton late of Grantham aforesaid Shoemaker deceased formerly free of this Corporacion and alsoe John Read the Son of

George Read having served Seaven yeares Apprenticeship came into Court & craved to be admitted Freemen of this Corporacion which the Court agreed to upon Cornelius Lenton his laying down 10 pounds for his Freedome which he did & upon a Vote of the Court he had five pounds returned & they were sworn accordingly.

Att this Court Mr Robert Cole was chosen Treasurer for the yeare ensueing to receive & take such Summes of money as shall be collected for the Conveyance of Passengers pursueant to the Late Act of Parliament.

Mr Thomas Wilson Chief Constable for the Soake discharged.
At this Court it is ordered and agreed that Thomas Wilson of Harlaxton be discharged from the Office of Cheif Constable for the Soake and att the same time elected Mr Gabriel Wilkinson of Londonthorp Cheif Constable in his place.

At this Court John Basse, Thomas Hutchin, William Parker and Henry Johnson Overseers of the Highwayes of Grantham for the yeare ending att Christmas last and John Thorold, Robert Smithergall, Leonard Camock and Abraham Beveston Overseers for this present yeare desire to have an order to collect such summes as they have disburst for Repairs of the Highwayes & the Court has ordered that they shall have an Assessment of 6d per pound to defray the said Charge.

[fo. 759v] **Third Court of William Kirke, 26 November 1700**

Joseph Rawlinson Chamberlain passes his Accounts.

	li	s	d
Att this Court Joseph Rawlinson presented his Accounts as Chamberlain:			
His Receipts amounted to	451	07	08
His Disbursements amounted to	488	15	11
Rests due to the Chamberlain	037	08	03

Upon the Account above written there is due to Mr Joseph Rawlinson 37 li 8s 3d which this Court orders Mr Thomas Fisher the present Chamberlain to pay to him.

Fourth Court of William Kirke, 13 December 1700

Att this Court upon complaint of Mr Joseph Rawlinson that there was 13s omitted in his Last Accounts as Chamberlain it is now ordered that Mr Fisher the present Chamberlain doe pay the same to him.

Mr Hotchkin accounteth as overseer of the poor from September 24th 1699 to March 31st 1700.

	li	s	d
His Disbursements amount to	161	18	11
His Receipts amount to	157	17	00¾

Abatements to be allowed	008 02	11
Due to accomptant	018 04	09¼

Mr John Poole accounteth as the other Overseer

His Receipts	72 01	10½
His Disbursements	69 08	00
Remains due to Mr Poole	02 13	10½

Judith Langley widow to receive Mrs Millers guift.
Agreed that Judith Langley widow be allowed the payment given by Mrs Miller deceased instead of Widow Bignall deceased.

Robert Clark and Alexander Mason made Free.
Att this Court came Robert Clarke and Alexander Mason forreigners & desired to be made Free of this Corporacion & have laid down tenn pounds a peice and the Court upon Consideracion ordered forty shillings a peice to be paid them back & then they were Sworn Freemen of this Corporacion & the 16 li was received by the Chamberlain.

Ordered that noe more persons be made free untill next Eleccion of Burgesses be over.

[fo. 760r] **Fifth Court of William Kirke, 26 December 1700**

All the matters att the last Court were confirmed att this Court.

The Honourable Thomas Baptist Maners made free.
Att this Court the Honourable Thomas Baptist Maners Esq. desired to be sworne a Freeman of this Corporacion and accordingly he was sworne and paid forty pounds into Mr Alderman's hands.

Sixth Court of William Kirke, 24 January 1700/1

Mills to be a Security to Mr Alderman and Mr Leivesley for 100 li by them borrowed.
Att this Court it is ordered that the Mills be a Security to Mr Alderman & Mr Edward Leivesley to indempnifye and reimburse one hundred pounds which they have borrowed of Catherine Threaves of Belton in the said County of Lincolne widow for the Use of the Corporacion in discharging a Debt due to John Stafford of four score pounds & Interest.

Ordered that a Lettre be writt about the repaires of the Schoole.

Richard Atkin, Mr Mills, John Martin, Henry Musson, William Burbidge, John Greenwood, Anthony Fisher and Thomas Quinningborow made free.
At this Court Richard Atkin, William Mills, John Martin, Henry Musson, William

Burbidge, John Greenwood and Anthony Fisher having served their Apprenticeships of seaven years and Thomas Quinningborow eldest son of Thomas Quinningborough a Freeman of this Corporacion coming into this Court desiring their Several Freedomes the Court thought the same fitting and they were Sworne accordingly.

At this Court it is ordered that John Calcraft Gentleman the present Town Clarke hath a Right to Freedome and that he shall be made Free if he thinks fitt the next Court and that his Eldest son John Calcraft shall att any time after he attains the Age of one and twenty yeares be Sworne Freeman of this Corporacion if he require it.

[fo. 760v] Seventh Court of William Kirke 7 March 1700/1

Wilsons Lease to be renewed.
Ordered that a New Lease be made to Thomas Wilson of the house in Castlegate which Susannah Wilson had a lease of for 21 yeares.

Persons made free in the reign of King James 2nd not claiming their freedome by Birth &c to have no benefitt thereby.
Att this Court it is declared and ordered that all persons who were made free in the reigne of the Late King James the Second and had not a right of Freedome by Birth, Service of Apprenticeship or purchase shall have noe benefitt by that Freedome granted to them.

John Fox to be made free.
At this Court came John Fox a Whitesmith and desired to be sworne a Freeman of this Corporacion and upon his offering to give Security for the Keeping the Church Clock and Chymes there and the Town Clock is good order for seaven years it is ordered that soe soon as he hath given Security in manner as aforesaid he shall be Sworne a Freeman.

Thomas Newcome made free.
At this Court came Thomas Newcome eldest Son of John Newcome late of Grantham aforesaid Felmonger deceased and desired to be sworne a Freeman of this Corporacion which this Court thought fitt & he was sworne accordingly.

Ordered that John Martins Abatements of 36 shillings be allowed & paid him by Robert Orson the present Churchwarden.

Ordered that Mr Thomas Fisher the late Chamberlain be paid 7 li 19s 6d by Robert Orson the present Churchwarden there being so much due to him upon the ballance of this Account.

Eighth Court of William Kirke, 21 March 1700/1

Carr Brown and James Musson made free.
At this Court came Carr Browne and desired to be sworn a Freeman of this Corporacion having Served Seaven yeares Apprenticeship to Mr John Robinson & also att the same time James Musson came in and desired his Freedome having served his Apprenticeship to Robert Smith which the Court agreed to and they were sworne accordingly.

[fo. 761r] Ninth Court of William Kirke, 11 April 1701

At this Court Thomas Hatfeild was sworne promoter.

Tenth Court of William Kirke, 23 May 1701

It is this day ordered that every person that shall have the Black Cloth to lay over the Coffin att the Buryall of any person shall pay six pence to the Churchwarden for the Use of the Towne.

Mr William Burbidge elected Alderman.
At this Court Mr William Burbidge is unanimously elected according to antient Custome to serve as Alderman for the year next ensueing.

Eleventh Court of William Kirke, 6 June 1701

At this Court George Millner passed his Accounts as Collector of the Schoolhouse rents for the

	li	s	d
year 1697.			
His Receipts amount to	22	16	08
His Disbursements amount to	20	12	08
Rest to be paid to the Chamberlain	02	04	00

[fo. 761v] Twelfth Court of William Kirke, 25 July 1701

Assessment of 50 li to be made to defray Robert Orson Churchwarden.
At this Court it is ordered that an Assessment of Fifty pounds be made to defray Robert Orson the late Churchwarden of Grantham for the moneyes which he hath expended in and about the Repairs of the Church and alsoe for him to pay 7 li 13s 6d to Mr Robert Fisher and 36s to John Martin thereout.

John Fox, John Barret and William Briggs made Free.
At this Court John Fox having given Security for the keeping the Church Clock and Chimes and the Town Clock in good repaires and John Barrett having served seaven years Apprenticeship to Mr Anthony Kirk and William Briggs having served seaven years Apprenticeship to Henry Johnson desired to be made Free Burgesses of this Corporacion which the Court agreed unto and they were Sworne accordingly.

Thirteenth Court of William Kirke, 29 August 1701

Widow Poole to receive part of Mistress Millers Dole.
At this Court it is ordered that Elizabeth Poole the elder widow doe receive 8s per annum out of the Charity given by Mistress Miller.

Agreed and ordered that the Summe of fifty shillings in the hands of Mr William Haskard for Sessions Fines be demanded of him by Mr Edward Parker the present Chamberlain and he to receive the same and alsoe fifty shillings for the fine upon renewing Thomas Wilsons Lease.

Joseph Clarke, James Grocock and John Vincent made free.
Joseph Clarke Apothecary having served seaven yeares Apprenticeship to his father William Clarke, James Grocock having served seaven yeares Apprenticeship to Mr John Rawlinson and John Vincent the eldest Son of John Vincent of Grantham came in att this Court and desired to be admitted Free Burgesses of this Corporacion which the Court agrees to and they were Sworne accordingly.

[fo. 762r] **Fourteenth Court of William Kirke, 26 September 1701**

Ordered that an Assessment be made at 6d per pound for defraying the Constables bills for carrying away Vagabonds this present yeare ending at St Luke next.

Fifteenth Court of William Kirke, 3 October 1701

Att this Court Nathaniel Garthwaite and Mr Richard Sentence the Collectors for the Poor brought in their accounts the totall summes whereof are as underwritten.

	li	s	d
Charge upon Mr Garthwaite is			
By moneyes received for 6 months & 2 weeks upon the Assessment for the poor amounts to	096	09	05
By moneys received of Sir Thomas Rolt	004	10	00
By moneys received for Lively Palmer	003	00	00
Of Mrs Todkill	000	10	00

Of Outners	000	10	10
	105	00	03
His Disbursements amount to	100	18	00
His abatements amount to	003	07	09¾
	104	05	09¾
Charge	105	00	03
Discharge	104	05	09¾
Rests to balance which Mr Garthwaite is to pay to Mr Sentence.	000	14	05¼

Charge upon Mr Sentence

	li	s	d
By moneyes received by him for 7 months and one week upon the poor Assessment att 14 li 16s 10d per month amounts to	107	11	00½
Yearly payment which he received amount to	005	17	04
By money received of Mr Garthwaite	002	02	05
And by more to be received of Mr Garthwaite	000	14	05¼
	116	05	02¾
Totall of his Disbursements amount to	117	19	09
His Abatements	005	10	06
Totall of his Discharge	123	10	06
His Charge	116	05	02¾
Rests due to Mr Sentance	007	05	00¼

At this court the Accounts of Mr Garthwaite & Mr Sentence were stated and allowed and upon the whole Accounts there remaines due to Mr Richard Sentence Seaven pounds and tenn shillings which this Court orders Mr Richard Hickson the present Collector to pay to Mr Sentence.

[fo. 762v] **Sixteenth Court of William Kirke, 23 October 1701**

At this Court Constance Fisher widow tooke the Tolls of this Towne for the yeare next ensueing to commence from the 26th instant at 56 li per Annum and she gave 1s in Earnest and pays quarterly.

Ordered that Mr Edward Parker the present Chamberlain pay Mr Alderman Kirke his bill of Charges amounting to twenty Five shillings And alsoe that he pay to Mr John Calcraft the present Town Clarke his bill amounting to 6 li 6s 4d.

Nicholas Pyke, Joseph Challands
At this Court came Nicholas Pyke Eldest son of William Pyke late a Freeman of this Corporacion deceased and Joseph Challands the eldest son of Joseph Challands late alsoe a Freeman of this Corporacion & desired to be sworne Freeman of this Corporacion which this Court though fitt and they were sworne accordingly.

The Account of the Constables Assessments
Marketplace Constables	06 11 09½
Highstreet	02 11 01
Westgate	03 07 06
Walkergate	02 01 06
Swinegate	02 00 08
Castlegate	01 17 09½
The Conygreens & Mr Smiths grounds	02 11 02
	21 01 00

Disbursements
Mr Alderman	00 15 11
Mr John Firman	02 05 06½
Mr Rawlinson	01 13 09½
Mr Thomas Fisher	02 02 10
Mr James Firman	02 08 10
William Wing	02 10 09
John Thorold	01 06 02
Thomas Walgrave	01 03 04
Thomas Cole	01 00 07
John Kirk	01 01 06
William Martin	01 08 00
John Lenton	01 07 05
John Osborn	01 01 02
Thomas Robinson	01 02 06

[fo. 763r]

Att an Assemby holden by William Kirke gentleman Alderman of Grantham aforesaid and the Comburgesses and Burgesses of the said Towne in Corpus Christie Quoir in the Prebendary Church there the Friday next after Saint Luke being 24 October 1701.

First did sit down upon the Cushions or place of Eleccion Mr William Kirke in Corpus Christie Quoire in the said Prebendary Church.
Next to him did sitt downe upon the Cushions or place of Eleccion two other Comburgesses vizt Mr William Burbidge and Mr Anthony Kirke.
Then is sent down to the body of the Church to Mr Joseph Lowe two other Comburgesses vizt Mr William Charles and Mr John Bradfeild.
Out of which three Comburgesses in the body of the Church one is chozen to come up and sitt upon the Cushions or place of Eleccion vizt Mr Joseph Lowe.
Then are there three Comburgesses upon the Cushions or place of Eleccion vizt Mr William Burbidge, Mr Anthony Kirk and Mr Joseph Lowe.

Mr William Burbidge chozen Alderman.
Out of which three Comburgesses upon the Cushions or place of Eleccion one is chosen Alderman for this year vizt: Mr William Burbidge.

Whereupon the said Mr William Kirke is discharged from his office and Mr William Burbidge sworne Alderman in his Stead for this Burrough and Soake of Grantham for the year ensueing according to the Antient Custome of the said Burrough.

And soe this Assembly breaks up.

THE HALL BOOK OF GRANTHAM 1701–1702

[fo. 763v] **First Court of William Burbidge 31 October 1701**

At this Court Mr William Kirke the late Alderman delivers to the present Alderman the Towne Plate and Charters as followeth

The Horserace Cup	Mr Harringtons Tankard
Mr Archers Bowle	Mr Kirkbyes Bowle
Mr Wirkliffs Tankard	Mr Greenwoods 13 Spoons
Mr Greenwoods tankard	Mr Battyes Salt Celler & Cover
Mr Horsemans 2 Cupps	Mr Storyes Cup
Mr Battyes two Tumblers	Mr Woodruffs Tankard
Mr Battyes Beaker	Mr Wrights Cup and Cover

These Charters
One of King Edward, Three of Queen Elizabeth, One of King James 1st, One of King Charles 1st, One of King Charles 2d, One of King James 2d.

Francis Wilson discharged the Court.
At this Court Francis Wilson as was alleadged by Mr Joseph Lowe desiring to be discharged from any further Attendance att this Court as one of the second twelve The Court agreed thereto and ordered that he be discharged accordingly.

Ordered that the Millmasters, Collectors of the Schoolhouse rents, Chamberlains and Churchwardens Accounts be taken on Wednesday next the 5th of November att one of the Clock in the Afternoon and the Arms finders doe appear and bring in their Armes.

Mr William Burbidge Alderman

1st 12	Mr Robert Cole	2d 12	Mr Thomas Fisher
	Mr Edward Leivesley		Mr John Benton
	Mr John Robinson		Mr Richard Wyld
	Mr William Haskard		Mr James Firman
	Mr William Kirke		Mr John Firman
	Mr Anthony Kirke		Mr Thomas Baily
	Mr Thomas Baily		Mr Robert Langley
	Mr Joseph Lowe		Mr Thomas Rawlinson
	Mr William Charles		
	Mr John Bradfeild		
	Mr John Calcroft		
	Mr William Doughty		

[fo. 764r]

Names of the officers			
Coroner	Mr William Kirke	Beadle	Andrew Rudkin
Escheator	Mr Anthony Kirke	Markett	John Kirke
Collectors of the Schoolhouse rents	Mr Joseph Lowe John Bass	Sayers Cornprizers	William Martin Robert Orson
Chamberlains	Mr Thomas Rawlinson William Wing	Leather Serchers	William Wing John Weaver
Churchwardens	Robert Langley		Richard Woulds Thomas Marshall
Chief Constables	Mr Thomas Fisher Mr John Benton	Keykeepers	Henry Smith Mr Alderman
Town Clark	Mr John Calcraft		Mr Thomas Rawlinson
Goaler	George Short		Mr Robert Langley
Serjeants	George Short Richard Bristow	Promoter	Thomas Hatfeild Senior William Higginbottom
Markett place	Thomas Cole		Leonard Butcher
Constables	Thomas Robinson	Town waites	John Wilcox
Highstreet	John Osborn		Roger Hutchinson
Constables	Robert Smithergall John Thorold	Parish Clarke Sexton	William Higginbottom William Osborne
Westgate	Alexander Mason		
Walkergate	William Martin Thomas Stanser		
Swinegate	Thomas Walgrave John Lenton John Kirk		
Castlegate	Abraham Beveston		

[fo. 764v] **Second Court of William Burbidge, 13 November 1701**

George Charity to pay 3 li for his Water cart goeing about.
At this Court it is ordered that Mr George Charity should pay three pounds for his Watercart going on the Streets the year next ensueing to be paid quarterly paid Mr Mr [*sic*] Alderman 1s in Earnest.

Edward Parker discharged the Court.
At this Court came Edward Parker a Commoner and desired to be dismissed the Court whereupon his paying five pounds to the Chamberlain he was accordingly discharged.

Ordered that Mr Edward Leivesley and Mr William Kirke the present Millmasters doe give a Note under their hands to Robert Fysher Esquire for the payment of 15 li which has been due to him from the Towne severall yeares for his Charges to London in Carrying an Address to his late Majestye King James.

Third Court of William Burbidge, 9 January 1701/2

All proceedings att the last Court are confirmed at this.

At this Court Robert Langley past his Accounts as Churchwarden for the last year and the same are as under written

	li	s	d
Charge			
For Quarteridge of Seals in the Church as his book of particulars makes appear	31	18	04
Received for Bells & Graves	08	14	10
Received for a yeares Rent of Severall people as the Rentall makes appear	13	15	04
	54	08	06
Discharge			
A bill of Disbursments amounting to	117	19	07½
paid the Chamberlain for the poor on St Thomas day & good Fryday	008	10	00
His Abatements amount to	001	03	04
	127	12	11½

Disburst 127 12 11½
Received 054 08 06
Due to the Accomptant 073 04 05½

[fo. 765r]

Whereof twenty six pounds is to be taken of which is to be paid to William Bristow in the Assessment to be made for the Church for the next yeare Soe as there remains due to Mr Langley 47 li 04s 05½d.

It is att this Court ordered that an Assessment be made to raise 50 li for the repaires & other things belonging to the Church to reinburse Mr Langley.

	li	s	d
At this Court Mr Thomas Fisher accounted as Chamberlain for the last yeare			
His Receipts amount to	125	07	07
His Disbursments	114	12	07½
Due from Mr Fisher to the Town	010	14	11½

At this Court Mr John Calcraft past his Accompts as Mill master

His whole receipts amounted to	26 18 08 ½
His Disbursments amounted to	26 19 04
Due to Mr Calcroft	00 00 08 ½

At this Court Mr William Doughty past his Accompts as Millmaster which are as under written

His whole receipts amounted to	30 11 01 ½
His Disbursments amount to	30 11 03 ½

At this Court Mr Edward Parker the late Chamberlain past his Accompts which are as Under written

His Receipts amount to	119 10 07 ½
His disbursments are	130 18 10
Rests due to the Accomptant	011 08 02 ½

Joseph Whittacre, William Steevens, William Parnham made free.
At this Court came Joseph Whittacre having served his Apprenticeship to John Gibson Baker, William Steevens eldest Son of John Steevens Malster a Freeman of this Corporacion, William Parnham eldest Son of Henry Parnham Blacksmith and desired to be admitted Freemen of this Corporation which this Court thought fitt and they were sworne accordingly.

At this Court it is ordered that Mr Thomas Fisher doe pay 10 li 14s 11½d being the Ballance of his Accompt to Mr Edward Parker the late Chamberlain & that Mr Rawlinson the present Chamberlain do pay him 13s 3d more being the ballance of the Accompts of the said Edward Parker.

[fo. 765v] **Fourth Court of William Burbidge 27 February 1701/02**

At this Court the proceedings of the last Court are ordered to stand confirmed.

Ordered that Robert Orson doe pay the 7 li 13s 4d formerly ordered to be paid to Mr Fisher on or before Lady day next or else to be proceeded against according to Law.

At this Court Mr Samuel Burnett the Elder the present Schoolmaster of the Freeschoole of this Corporacion proposing to resigne the same into the hands of the Corporacion att our Lady day next And this Court accepting of his Resignation have thought fitt and doe order the present Chamberlain to pay the said Mr Burnett twenty pounds as a Gratuity for his voluntary resigning the said Schoole And this Court do further order that a Message be sent to Mr Norwell of Ingoldsby to acquaint him that the place of Schoolmaster of the said School is now vacant And this Court doe further order and agree that Mr Charles Burnett the present Usher be continued in that place.

At this Court Mr William Wing, Mr Thomas Cole and Mr Edward Greenwood were chosen to be the second Twelve and were sworne and took their places.

At this Court Mr Richard Wyld was chosen one of the Comburgesses of this Corporacion.

At this Court Mr Alderman Burbidge past his Accompts as Collector of the Schoolhouse rents for the year due Michaelmas 1700
The whole yeares rent amounts to	45 04 04
His Disbursments to the Schoolmaster and about Widow Hawdings house amounts to	47 19 03
Rests due to Mr Alderman	02 14 11

At the same Court Mr Anthony Kirk past his Accompt as Collector of the same rents for half a year due att Lady day 1701
The half yeares rent due att Lady day	22 10 00
His Disbursments & abatements amount to	20 17 00
Rests due from Mr Kirk	01 13 00

[fo. 766r] **Fifth Court of William Burbidge, 8 April 1702**

Ordered that all officers doe appeare att the Church every Fair day by eight of the Clock in the Morning to walk the Fair.

At this Court John Troughton of Lowestoft in the County of Suffolke Clerke was unanimously elected Schoolmaster of the Free Schoole of this Corporacion of Grantham Mr Burnett the late Schoolmaster having resigned the same And it is agreed by the said Mr Troughton that he accepts of the same place Subject to the same Condicions as Mr Wilkinson, Mr Stokes and Mr Syston accepted of the same.

Sixth Court of William Burbidge, 30 April 1702

Robert Southern, Christopher Hanson, William Knight, Thomas Sherriffe, Edward Hatfeild.
At this Court Robert Southern eldest Son of William Southerne [sic] a Freeman of this Corporacion, Christopher Hanson eldest Son of Christopher Hanson a Freeman of this Corporacion, William Knight eldest Son of William Knight a Freeman of this Corporacion, Thomas Sherriffe eldest Son of Amos Sherriffe a Freeman of this Corporacion and Edward Hatfeild having served seaven yeares Apprenticeship to his Father Thomas Hatfeild Butcher came in and desired to be sworne Freemen of this Corporacion which the Court thought fitt and they were Sworne accordingly.

At this Court it is ordered that tenn Shillings be paid to the Towne Waites for their Attendance to play the Proclamacion and Coronacion day of Queen Anne.

At this Court it is ordered and agreed that fifty pounds be taken up for the Use of the Towne and be paid into the Chamberlains hands and that Mr William Kirke and Mr John Calcroft be bound for the same and that security be given for their Security by the Town Mills.

[fo. 766v] **Seventh Court of William Burbidge, 22 May 1702**

Ordered that the Collectors of the poor and the overseers of the Highwayes the Collectors of the Schoolhouse rents and the Millmasters doe pass their Accompts on Wednesday the 3d day of June next.

At this Court it is ordered that Mr Samuel Burnett the late Schoolmaster of Grantham shall receive four pounds *per Annum* out of the Schoolhouse rents to be paid quarterly by the Collector of those rents for three yeares next ensueing if the said Mr Burnett live soe long the first payment to beginn and be made att Midsummer next.

Ordered that Mr Robert Cole, Mr William Haskard, Mr Anthony Kirke, Mr John Calcroft and Mr William Doughty doe attend att the Guildhall in Grantham Wednesday the 3d day of June to take the Accompts aforesaid and all other persons belonging to the Court doe attend at that time if they think fitt.

Thomas Dawson.
At this Court came in Thomas Dawson having served his Apprenticeship for Seaven yeares to Mr Richard Hickson of Grantham aforesaid and desired to be made free of this Corporacion which this Court thought fitt and he was Sworne accordingly.

At this Court Mr Anthony Kirk is unanimously elected to serve as Alderman for the year next ensueing for this Corporacion of Grantham.

Mr William Wing elected to serve in buying and selling Coles for the Use of the poor.

[fo. 767r] **Eighth Court of William Burbidge, 3 July 1702**

At this Court it is ordered that Samuel Prince and his wife be sent to the Town of Sapperton by a Warrant their last Settlement being there.

Ordered that this present Alderman and every Alderman for the future shall receive twenty pounds a yeare for a Sallary from the Towne.

Ordered that every man that attends the Sessions if he dine with the Recorder shall bear his own Charges.

Ninth Court of William Burbidge, 18 September 1702

Thomas True, Thomas Cole, William Poole.
At this Court came in Thomas True of Grantham aforesaid Carpinter and desired to be sworne a Freeman of this Corporacion which this Court taking into Consideracion agreed upon his paying downe five pounds to the Chamberlain for the Use of the Corporacion and giving a Note to pay five pounds more within 6 months At the same Court came in Thomas Cole the eldest Son of Thomas Cole a Freeman of this Corporacion and William Poole the eldest Son of Thomas Poole a Freeman of this Corporacion and desired their freedome which this Court thought fitt & agreed hereto and the said Thomas True, Thomas Cole and William Poole were sworne accordingly. And this Court ordered the Chamberlain to deliver the said Thomas True his Note again.

[fo. 767v] Tenth Court of William Burbidge, 25 September 1702

At this Court the Cheif Constables and Constables produced their severall Bills for conveying of Passengers & other Charges belonging to their office and the same amounting to above 20 li it is this day ordered that an Assessment of 9d in the pound be made & laid towards discharging this said moneyes soe expended.

At this Court it is agreed by Mr Alderman, Mr William Haskard, Mr William Kirke, Mr Anthony Kirke, Mr Joseph Lowe, Mr John Bradfeild Mr John Calcroft, Mr John Firman, Mr Thomas Cole, Mr William Wing, Mr Edward Greenwood and Mr Thomas Rawlinson that whereas there is 300 li or thereabouts now due and owing upon Security from this Corporacion they will become Security for the same and they are to have Counter Security to indempnifye them by having an Assignment of the Town Mills and Tolls.

At this Court Mr James Firman was elected to serve as a Comburgess of this Corporacion in the room of Mr Edward Leivesley deceased and the oath of a Comburgess being tendered to him he absolutely refused to take the same.
It is therefore ordered that the said James Firman doe pay fifteen pounds for refusing to serve in the said place and if he refuse to pay the same when demanded it is ordered that a due Course of Law be taken against the said James Firman for recovery of the same.

John Fisher, Robert Osborne.
At this Court came John Fisher and desired his Freedome having served seaven yeares to John Sharp Cordwainer a Freeman of this Corporacion and Robert Osborne having served seaven yeares to his Father John Osborne Glover a Freeman of this Corporacion

and desired to be sworne Freemen of this Corporacion which this Court thought fitt and they were sworne accordingly.

[fo. 768r] Eleventh Court of William Burbidge, 9 October 1702

William Niccolls.
At this Court William Niccolls of Grantham aforesaid came in and desired to be sworne a Freeman of this Corporacion which this Court thought fitt upon his paying five pounds into the Chamberlains hands and giving a Note to pay five pounds more att sic months end which Note this Court thought fitt to give him again and he was sworne a Freeman of this Corporacion.

At this Court it is ordered that the Town Clarke doe forthwith proceed att Law against Mr James Firman for recovering the fifteen pounds upon his refusall to serve as a Comburgess of this Corporacion.

Twelfth Court of William Burbidge, 22 October 1702

At this Court Mr James Firman acquainting the Court that he having considered of his being sworne a Comburgess of this Corporacion (after his having refused to serve) att two former Courts, and that he is now willing to serve if this Court think fitt Whereupon this Court taking the same into Consideracion doe order that the former orders made against the said James Firman for recovering of the 15 li against him for refusall to serve in the said office be void and of none effect and that the said James Firman be sworne a Comburgess and the said James Firman was sworne accordingly.

At this Court Mrs Jane Leivesley accompted for the profitts of the Slate Mill received by her late husband Mr Edward Leivesley and her Selfe and her Receipts and Disbursments are as underwritten

	li	s	d
The totall of the Receipts of Mr Leivesley as his first accounts and these of Mrs Leivesley makes appear amount to	123	13	05
Their Disbursments amount to	100	14	11½
Rest due to the Town to ballance which was paid into the hands of Mr William Wing	022	18	05½

At this Court Mrs Constance Fisher tooke the Tolls of this Towne for the yeare ensueing to comence from the 26th instant att 56 li *per Annum* payable quarterly and gave 1s in earnest.

John Davye.
At this Court John Davye Felmonger came in and desired to be Sworne a Freeman of this Corporacion which this Court agreed to upon this Condicion that he payd ten pounds to the present Chamberlain which he did and was sworne accordingly.

[fo. 768v] [Blank page]

[fo. 769r]

At an Assembly holden by William Burbidge gentleman Alderman of Grantham aforesaid and the Comburgesses and Burgesses of the said Town in Corpus Christi Quoire in the Prebendary Church there the Fryday next after Saint Luke 23 October 1702.

First did sitt down upon the Cushions or place of Eleccion Mr William Burbidge in Corpus Christi Quoire in the said Prebendary.
Next to him did sitt down upon the Cushions or place of Eleccion two other Comburgesses vizt Mr Anthony Kirke and Mr Joseph Lowe.
Then is sent downe to the body of the Church to Mr John Bradfeild two other Comburgesses vizt Mr John Calcroft and Mr William Doughty.
Out of which three Comburgesses in the Body of the Church one is chosen to come up and sitt upon the Cushions or place of Eleccion vizt Mr John Bradfeild.
Then are there three Comburgesses upon the Cushions or place of Eleccion vizt Mr Anthony Kirke, Mr Joseph Lowe and Mr John Bradfeild.
Out of which three Comburgesses upon the Cushions or place of Eleccion one is chozen Alderman for this yeare vizt Mr Anthony Kirke.

Whereupon the said Mr William Burbidge is discharged from his Office and Mr Anthony Kirke sworne Alderman in his stead for this Burrough and Soake of Grantham for the yeare ensueing according to the Antient Custome of the said Burrough.

And soe this Assembly breaks up.

THE HALL BOOK OF GRANTHAM 1702–1703

[fo. 769v] **First Court of Mr Anthony Kirke, 30 October 1702**

Mr Anthony Kirke Alderman
Coroner   Mr Robert Cole
Escheator   Mr John Robinson
First 12   Mr William Haskard
               Mr William Kirke
               Mr William Burbidge
               Mr Thomas Baily
               Mr Joseph Lowe
               Mr John Bradfeild
               Mr John Calcroft
               Mr William Doughty
               Mr Richard Wyld
               Mr James Firman

2nd 12   Mr William Wing
               Mr Thomas Cole
               Mr John Firman
               Mr Thomas Baily
               Mr Robert Langley
               Mr Thomas Rawlinson
               Mr John Benton
               Mr Edward Greenwood
               Mr Thomas Robinson
               Mr Alexander Mason

[fo. 770r]
Names of the officers
Coroner   Mr William Burbidge   Beadle   Andrew Rudkin
Escheator   Mr Joseph Lowe   Markettsayers   William Martin
Collectors of the   Mr John Bradfeild   Thomas Walgrave
Schoolhouse rents   Mr George Charity   Cornprizers   Robert Orson
Chamberlains   Mr Edward Greenwood   Joseph Whittacrer
                     Thomas Robinson   Leather   John Weaver

Churchwardens	Robert Langley	Searchers	Richard Woulds
	Alexander Mason		Thomas Marshall &
Cheif Constables	Mr William Wing		Henry Smith
	Mr Thomas Cole	Keykeepers	Mr Alderman
Town Clark	Mr John Calcraft		Mr Edward Greenwood
Goaler	George Short		Mr Robert Langley
Serjeants	George Short &	Promoter	Thomas Hatfeild
	Richard Bristow	Towne Waites	Leonard Butcher
Market place	Robert Smithergall		John Wolcock
Constables	John Thorold		Roger Hutchinson
High street	John Lenton		James Higginbottom
	William Gibson	Bellman	William Osborne
Westgate	Cornelius Lenton	Parish Clark	William Higginbottom
	Thomas Walgrave		
Walkergate	William Martin		
	Thomas Stanser		
Swinegate	Abraham Beveston		
Castlegate	John Fox		

[fo. 770v]

At this Court Mr Burbidge the late Alderman delivers to the present Alderman the Town Plate & Charters as followeth

The Horserace Cup
Mr Archers Bowle
Mr Wickliffs Tankard
Mr Greenwoods Tankard
Mr Horsemans 2 Cupps
Mr Battyes 2 Tumblers
Mr Battyes Beaker

Mr Harringtons Tankard
Mr Kirkbyes bowle
Mr Greenwoods 13 Spoons
Mr Battyes Salt Cellar & Cover
Mr Storyes Cup
Mr Woodruffs Tankard
Mr Wrights Cup & Cover

These Charters
One of King Edward 6th Three of Queen Elizabeth One of King James 1st One of King Charles 1st One of King Charles 2nd One of King James 2nd.

Charles Sutton
Att this court came Charles Sutton who having served seaven years Apprenticeship to George Read the elder of Grantham Cooper a Freeman of this Corporacion & desired his Freedome which this Court thought fitt & he was sworne accordingly.

Second Court of Antony Kirke, 27 November 1702

At this Court it was agreed that a New Lease be made to Mr Robert Calcroft of a house in Walkergate in the Occupacon of John Marshall for one and twenty yeares commencing att Lady day next he having paid 19 li 4s 2d to the Chamberlain as a Fine.

Att the same Court a Lease was ordered to be Sealed to William Long of two Tenements in Well Lane for one & twenty yeares comencing from Michaelmas last he having paid 5s Fine.

Att the same Court a Lease was ordered to be Sealed to Michael Allt of the house he lives in in Swinegate for one & twenty yeares comencing from Lady day next att 1 li 3s 1½d Fine.

[fo. 771r] **Third Court of Antony Kirke, 18 December 1702**

	li	s	d
At this Court Mr Langleyes Accounts were taken as Churchwarden for the year 1702 His Receipts amount to	055	07	00
His Disbursments amount to	124	14	00½
Due to Mr Langley	069	07	00½

At this Court it is ordered that an Assessment of Seaventy pounds be made and laid to defray Mr Robert Langley the moneys expended by him in repairs & other Charges relating to the Church of Grantham.

At the same Court Mr Thomas Rawlinsons Accounts were taken as Chamberlain for the year 1701 & there was due to the Town from him three pounds nine shillings & seaven pence which he paid to Mr Greenwood the present Chamberlain.

At the same Court Mr William Wings Accounts were taken as Chamberlain for the year 1702 And there was due to the said Mr Wing twenty pounds four shillings and tenn pence which the Court orders the present Chamberlain to pay to him.

At this Court Mr Joseph Lowe's Accounts were taken as Collector of the Schoolhouse rents for half a yeare due att Lady day 1702.

Receipts	£	s	d	Disbursments		£	s	d
Markett place	02	00	00	paid the Schoolmaster		20	00	00
High street	01	10	00	Abatements for rent never paid		00	10	00
Walkergate	05	07	06	Sallary		00	02	06
Swinegate	08	07	06	spent att Mr Marshalls 8d Taxes 2s:		00	02	08
Castlegate	01	17	04		£ s d	20	15	02
Manthorpe	02	10	00	Receipts	22 11 08			

| Spittlegate &c | 00 19 04 | Disbursments | 20 15 02 |
| | 22 11 08 | Rests to ballance | 01 16 06 |

The Accounts of John Bass Collector of the same Rents for half a yeare due att
Michaelmas 1702   £   s   d
His Receipts as the other particuler of Rents above amount to   22 11 08
The rents payable yearly amount to   00 05 00
                                                                                              22 16 08

Disbursments
paid the Schoolmasters Sallary   20 00 00
Abatements for rent not gott   00 10 00
paid Mr Wing the Chamberlain   02 00 00
For Sallary   00 02 06
Spent at Marshalls   00 00 08
Taxes for the Pesthouse   00 03 00
                                                                                              22 16 02

Receipts   22 16 08
Disbursments   22 16 02
Due from the Acomptant   00 00 06

[fo. 771v] **Fourth Court of Antony Kirke, 5 February 1702/3**

Mr John Chambrey.
Att this court Mr John Chambrey being lately becom'd an Inhabitant of this Corporacion desired to be admitted a Freeman of this Corporacion whereupn he paying tenn pounds for his Freedom to the present Chamberlain Mr Greenwood he was sworn accordingly.

At this Court John Davye, George Fitzrandolph and John Chambrey were sworn Constables for this Corporacion for the Yeare ensueing or untill they shall be lawfully discharged from their said offices.

At this Court John Davye desired to be discharged from any other Attendance att this Court and tendered to pay his Five pounds as a Fine for a Discharge pursueant to former orders made in this Court which said summe this Court accepted of & ordered the same to be paid to Mr Greenwood which was done & the said John Davye discharged accordingly.

At this Court the said John Chambrey desired to be discharged from any further Attendance and paid his Fine of Five pounds to the Chamberlain & he was discharged accordingly.

At this Court Mr Alderman Kirke paid one pounds thirteen Shillings to the present Chamberlain being the ballance of his Accounts as Collector of the Schoolhouse rents taken att a Court held the 27th February 1701.

At this Court it is ordered that the present Chamberlain doe pay to Mr William Burbidge 2 li 14s 11d being the ballance of his accounts as Collector of the Schoolhouse rents taken att a Court held the 27th February 1702.

[fo. 772r] **Fifth Court of Antony Kirke 5 March 1702/3**

At this Court it is by a Generall Consent ordered and agreed that any Freeman of this Corporacion already elected and chosen or that hereafter shall be legally elected and chosen att any Court already held or hereafter to be held by the present Alderman Comburgesses & Burgesses of the said Towne or Burrough of Grantham aforesaid or their Successors into any of the places hereinafter particularly mencioned and upon lawfull summons to appeare att any of the said Courts doth or doe refuse to appeare there or if any such person or persons doe appeare and refuse to take upon him or them the oath & execucion of any such place or places or any of them that then and in every such Case every such person or persons neglecting or refusing to appear att the Aldermans Court for the time being to be held for the said Towne or Burrough or if he or they doe appear there and refuse to take upon him or them the execucion of the place or places as he or they shall be elected to serve in that then and in every or any the Cases aforesaid every such person or persons soe neglecting or refusing as aforesaid shall forfeit the severall and respective Summes hereinafter particularly mencioned and expressed (that is to say) every person already elected or hereafter to be elected & chosen to serve as a Comburgess for the Corporacion aforesaid being lawfully summoned to appear att the said Court & neglecting to appear there or appearing and refusing to take upon him the execucion of that office shall forfeit the summe of Fifteen pounds of lawfull money of England And alsoe every person already elected or hereafter to be elected and chosen to serve in the place or Office of a Second Twelve man of this Town or Burrough being lawfully summoned to appear att the said Court and neglecting to appeare there or appearing and refusing to take upon him the Execucion of that office shall forfeit the Summe of Tenn pounds of like money And alsoe every person already elected or hereafter to be elected & chosen to serve in the office of a Constable for this Towne or Burrough being lawfully summoned to appear att the said Court and refusing or neglecting to appear there or if he appear there and refuse to take upon him that office shall forfeit the summe of Five pounds of like money And it is hereby ordered and agreed that if any person or persons shall att any time

[fo. 772v]

hereafter pay any of the Fines above ordered as aforesaid By such payment he or they so Fined shall be excused from the Service of such of the offices to which he or they was or were elected for one yeare only and noe longer And every such person after the end of such yeare shall be lyable to be elected and chosen att any other Court into any of the Offices aforesaid and upon his refusall to serve therein shall be lyable to the Forfeitures above mencioned in like manner at if he or they had never paid any Fine The said severall Summes to be recovered by Accion of debt to be prosecuted by the Alderman Comburgesses & Burgesses of this Corporacion for the time being or to be leavyed by Distress for the Use of the said Corporacion.

Att this Court Elizabeth Taylor widow desired to be accepted in the roome of Alice Hawding widow deceased to receive the Charity of 8s per Annum setled by Mrs Frances Millner widow deceased which this Court thought fitt and ordered the said Widow Taylor to receive the same accordingly

At this Court Samuel Clipsham past his Accounts as Collector of the Schoolhouse rents

	li	s	d
Charge For the half yeares rent	22	16	08
Discharge Paid to the Schoolmaster & Usher half a yeares Sallary	20	00	00
His Abatements for rent Sallary & Taxes	00	15	11
By moneyes paid to Mr Wing	01	15	00

At this Court George Charity paid 1 li 10s to Mr Alderman for his Water Cart for the Yeare ended att Martinmas last and att the same Court was agreed that he should be permitted to goe on with his Watercart from Martinmas last for a year paying 40s for the same & that money to be applyed towards repaires of the Highwayes.

At this Court it is ordered that the Tolls & Mills be made Security to Mr Alderman and the other persons that have given Security for moneys for the Use of the Corporacion.

[fo. 773r] **Sixth Court of Antony Kirke, 30 April 1703**

William Halam
At this Court William Halam Son of John Halam of Grantham aforesaid desired to have his Freedome having served seaven yeares Apprenticeship to his Father which this Court thought fitt and he was sworne accordingly.

At this Court Mr John Marshall was agreed with for the Cole house in his Yard att 10s per Annum & he to be Cole Master for the year ensueing.

Seventh Court of Antony Kirke, 28 May 1703

	li	s	d
At this Court Mr William Wing past his accounts as Coalmaster			
The Charge upon him was	10	12	06
His Discharge			
By Disbursments	01	19	11
By moneyes paid to Mr Marshall	05	15	07
By 57 hundred of Coals weighed to Mr Marshall	02	17	00
	10	12	06

At this Court a New Lease was granted to William Bristow of a Messuage in the Highstreet in Grantham for one & twenty yeares comencing att Lady day next att 16s *per Annum* & under a Fine of 4 li 8s Fine certain forever.

At the same Court a New Lease was granted to Mrs Elizabeth Pawlett of a Messuage in Castlegate in Grantham for one and twenty yeares comencing from Lady day last for 8s *per Annum* & under a Fine of 1 li 03s 01½d Fine certain forever.

At this Court security was given by a Lease of the Mills to Mr William Haskard, Mr William Kirke, Mr William Burbidge, Mr Joseph Lowe, Mr John Bradfeild & Mr John Calcroft Comburgesses of Grantham aforesaid and Thomas Rawlinson, William Wing, Thomas Cole & Edward Greenwood.

At this Court Mr Joseph Lowe was unanimously elected to serve as Alderman for this Corporacion for the yeare ensueing.

[fo. 773v] **Eighth Court of Antony Kirke, 9 July 1703**

At this Court Mr Joseph Hutchin desired to be discharged from any further Attendance att this Court which was agreed to and he is discharged accordingly.

At this Court Mr John Thorold tooke William Hayes's house at forty five shillings *per Annum* The Town to pay nothing but Queens Taxes & to putt it into good repair and the Tenant to keep it soe and pay all Townes Dutyes & other Assessments.

At this Court it was ordered that noe Abatements shall be allowed in Mr Hutchins & Mr Clarks Assessment for the poor but for those houses that stand empty.

Ordered that Mr Hutchins and Mr Clark pay three pounds to Mr Robert Cole and three pounds to Mrs Jane Grant upon Account of moneys due to them from the Towne.

[fo. 774r] **Ninth Court of Antony Kirk, 13 August 1703**

	li	s	d
At this Court Mr Robert Clark past his Accounts as Collector for the poor			
His receipts to Easter last amounted to	031	06	01
His Disbursments amounted to	016	16	11½
Rests due to the Towne	014	09	01½

Which 14 li 09s 01½d was paid to Mr William Bristow the present Overseer of the poor.

At this Court Mr Thomas Hutchin past his Accounts as overseer of the poor
His receipts to Easter last amounted to 20 14 10
His Disbursments amounted to 19 02 06
Rests due to the Towne 01 12 04
Which was paid to William Bristow.

John Hutchin, William Pillsworth, Francis Scarborow.
At this Court Mr John Hutchin eldest son of Thomas Hutchin of Grantham Cordwainer & William Pillsworth Cordwainer & Francis Scarborow who have served their severall Apprenticeships within this Burrough and craved to be admitted Freemen of this Corporacion which this Court taking into consideracion agreed to & they were sworne accordingly.

	li	s	d
At this Court Mr William Kirke past his Accounts as Millmaster			
Due to the Towne upon his last Accounts	01	19	01
His receipts to this present time amounted to	78	07	07
His disbursments amounted to	78	07	09
Rests due to the Towne	01	18	11

which he is to pay to the present Chamberlain at the next Court.

At this Court John Fisher was elected to serve as Constable for Swinegate And William Pillsworth chosen Constable for Castlegate.

[fo. 774v] **Tenth Court of Antony Kirke, 3 September 1705 [sic]**

	li	s	d
Att this Court Mr William Burbidge past his Accounts as Millmaster for the Slate Mills from the 12th October 1702 to 23th August 1703			
His receipts amounted to	59	16	02
His Disbursments	58	09	09
Rests due to the Towne	01	06	05

At this Court it is unanimously agreed that all Malt hereafter to be ground att the Town Mill shall be ground att 12d per quarter & noe more and soe proporcionably for a greater or lesser quantity.

Eleventh Court of Antony Kirke, 24 September 1703

At this Court it is ordered that the Names of the Benefactors to this Towne be entered and sett up in a Frame and plact in the Church.

Ordered that Forty pounds be taken up by Mr William Wing and Mr Thomas Cole Millmasters and that the Mills be made a Security for indempnifying them.

Thomas Mills, Edmund Smith
At this Court came Thomas Mills a Foreigner and laid down his Ten Pounds and Edmund Smith eldest son of Mr John Smith (a Freeman of this Burrough) & craved to be admitted Freemen of this Corpracion which this Court taking into Consideracion doe grant and they were sworne accordingly.

[fo. 775r] Twelfth Court of Antony Kirke, 21 October 1703

At this Court it is ordered that the Town Clarke shall proceed att Law against Mr William Haskard for the recovery of moneyes in his hands which belongeth to this Corporacion if he doe not pay the same to the present Chamberlain Thomas Robinson on or before Saturday next.

At this Court Mr William Kirke paid the ballance of his Accounts as Millmaster to Thomas Robinson Chamberlain the same being Eight & thirty Shillings & Eleaven pence.

Whereas at the last Court it was ordered that Forty pounds should be taken up by Mr William Wing and Mr Thomas Cole Millmasters and that the profitts of the Mills be made a Security for indempnifyeing them And whereas the occasions of the Towne required a greater summe And whereas the said William Wing & Thomas Cole have borrowed Fifty pounds of Mrs Anne Scott widow for the Use of the Corporacion It is now ordered that the Town Mill and Slate Mill doe stand a Security to the said William Wing and Thomas Cole to indempnify them their heires and Assignes against the said Bond.

At this Court Constance Fisher took a Lease of the Tolls belonging to this Towne for one year next ensueing att 52 li per Annum to be paid quarterly & they are 12d in Earnest & there being 32s 6d now due to Mrs Fisher from Mr John Coddington the Court agreed & ordered that the same shall be allowed to her out of her rent if Mr Coddington doe not pay her the same.

The Constables Accounts.				Received	Abatements
	li	s	d		
Markett Place Assessment amounted to	05	04	01½	04 14 05	00 09 08½
Highstreet	02	02	01½	01 12 06	00 09 07
Westgate	02	04	06	02 00 00	00 04 06
Walkergate	03	09	09	03 05 00	00 04 09
Swinegate	01	14	09½	01 11 06	00 03 03½
Castlegate	01	13	06½	01 06 00	00 07 06½

Moneyes paid thereout

Mr Aldermans Bill		01 00 06
John Thorolds bill		00 13 09
Robert Smithergalls bill		00 10 02
William Gibson		00 19 07
Cornelius Lenton		00 09 02
Thomas Walgrave		00 09 07
William Martins bill		00 11 08
Thomas Stanser		00 13 06
Abraham Bevestone		00 15 06
John Fisher		00 05 00
George Fitzrandolph		00 06 04½
William Pillsworth		00 05 06
John Fox		00 14 01
Mr Calcraft the Town Clark his bill		02 03 06
Mr Wings		03 02 05½
Mr Thomas Cole		02 03 06

[fo. 775v]

At an Assembly holden by Antony Kirke gentleman Alderman of Grantham aforesaid and the Comburgesses & Burgesses of the said Towne in Corpus Christi Quoire in the prebendary Church there the Fryday next after Saint Luke 22 October 1703.
First did sitt downe upon the Cushions or places of Eleccion Mr Anthony Kirke in Corpus Christi Quoire in the said Prebendary Church
Next to him did sitt downe upon the Cushions or place of Eleccion two other Comburgesses vizt Mr Joseph Lowe & Mr John Bradfeild
Then is sent downe to the body of the Church to Mr John Calcroft and Mr William Doughty one other Comburgess vizt Mr Thomas Bayly
Out of which three Comburgesses in the Body of the Church one is chosen to come up and sitt upon the Cushions or place of Eleccion vizt Mr Thomas Baily [*sic*]
Then are there three Comburgesses upon the Cushions or place of Eleccion vizt Mr Joseph Lowe, Mr John Bradfield & Mr Thomas Baily [*sic*]

Out of which three Comburgesses upon the Cushions or places of Eleccion one is chosen Alderman for this year vizt Mr Thomas Bayly

Whereupon the said Mr Anthony Kirke is discharged from his Office and Mr Thomas Baily sworne Alderman in his Stead for this Burrough and Soake of Grantham for the yeare ensueing according to the Antient Custome of the said Burrough

And soe this Assembly breaks up.

THE HALL BOOK OF GRANTHAM 1703–1704

[fo. 776r] **First Court of Thomas Baily, 29 October 1703**

Mr Thomas Baily Alderman

1st 12	2nd 12
Mr Robert Cole	Mr Robert Langley
Mr John Robinson	Mr Alexander Mason
Mr William Haskard	Mr John Firman
Mr William Kirke	Mr Thomas Baily
Mr William Burbidge	Mr Thomas Rawlinson
Mr Anthony Kirke	Mr John Benton
Mr Joseph Lowe	Mr William Wing
Mr John Bradfeild	Mr Thomas Cole
Mr John Calcroft	Mr Edward Greenwood
Mr William Doughty	Mr John Thorold
Mr Richard Wyld	Mr Thomas Robinson
Mr James Firman	

Names of the officers

Coroner	Mr Anthony Kirke	Swinegate	John Fox and John Fisher
Escheator	Mr John Bradfeild		
Collectors of the Schoolhouse rents	Mr John Calcroft William Martin	Castlegate	William Pillsworth Thomas True
Chamberlains	Mr Thomas Cole & John Bass	Markett sayers	William Martin Thomas Walgrave
Churchwardens	Mr Alexander Mason Mr William Wing	Beadle Corn prizers	Andrew Rudkin Thomas Robinson
Cheif Constables	Mr Robert Langley Mr Alexander Mason	Leather Searchers	Robert Orson John Weaver, John Woulds, Thomas Marshall and Henry Smith
Town Clarke	Mr John Calcraft [sic]		
Goaler	George Short		
Bailiff of the Libertyes	The same		
Serjeants	George Short and Richard Bristow	Keybearers	Mr Alderman Mr Thomas Cole Mr William Wing
Market place	Mr Thomas Mills		
Constables	Mr Edmund Smith	Promoter	Thomas Hatfeild senior
Westgate	Cornelius Lenton Thomas Walgrave	Town Waite	Leonard Butcher John Wilcock

High Street	Abraham Beveston		Roger Hutchinson &
	William Gibson		James Higginbottom
Walkergate	Thomas Stanser	Parish Clarke	William Higginbottom
	George Fitzrandolph	Sexton	Ralph Osborne

[fo. 776v]

At this Court Mr Anthony Kirke the Late Alderman delivered to the present Alderman the Town Plate and Charters as followeth

The Horserace Cup	Mr Harringtons Tankard
Mr Archers Bowle	Mr Kirkbyes Bowles
Mr Wickliffs Tankard	Mr Greenwoods 13 Spoons
Mr Greenwoods Tankard	Mr Battyes Salt Cellar & Cover
Mr Horsemans 2 Cupps	Mr Storers Cup
Mr Battyes 2 Tumblers	Mr Woodruffs Tankard
Mr Battyes Beaker	Mr Wrights Cup & Cover

These Charters:
One of King Edward 6th; Three of Queen Elizabeth; One of King James 1st; One of King Charles 1st; One of King Charles 2nd; One of King James 2nd.

At this Court Mr William Burbidge late Millmaster paid to Mr Thomas Robinson the present Chamberlain one pound six shillings and five pence being the ballance of his Accounts taken the 3rd day of September last past.

At this Court Mr Alexander Mason, Mr John Thorold and Mr Thomas Robinson were chosen to serve as Second Twelve men and were Sworne accordingly.

At this Court Mr William Haskard paid 50s to Thomas Robinson in full of Fines received by him when he was Alderman.

At this Court Mr Anthony Kirke paid 7 li 0s 6d to the said Thomas Robinson in full of Fines received by him when Alderman.

And Mr Lowe Escheator for the year last past paid him 19s 2d for Fines received by him as Escheator.

[fo. 777r] **Second Court of Thomas Baily, 10 December 1703**

At this Court Thomas True was sworne Constable for the Burrough.

Third Court of Thomas Baily, 12 May 1704

At this Court Edward Greenwood past his Accounts as Chamberlain for half a year beginning October 1702.

	li	s	d
His Receipts amounted to	135	17	03½
His disbursements amounted to	139	09	07
Rests Due to Mr Greenwood	003	12	03½

Which sum was paid to him by Mr Thomas Robinson

Att this Court Thomas Robinson posts his Accounts as Chamberlain for half a year beginning in May 1703

His Receipts amounted to	133	03	00½
His disbursements amounted to	128	10	04½
Due to the Town	004	12	08

which the Court now orders shall be paid to Mr Thomas Cole

Ordered that Mr Thomas Cole doe pay to Mr Edward Greenwood Seventeen Shillings & a penny which he had paid to Mr Sharpe & Thomas True

At this Court Mr William Bristow posts his Accounts as Overseer of the poor for the year 1703

His Receipts amounted to	91	19	10½
His disbursements amounted to	84	06	05¼
Due to the Town	07	13	05¼

Whereof Mr Bristow paid to Mr Doran 02 li 10s 06½d & paid Mr Parker 05 li 02s 11¼d

At this Court Mr Charles Doran posts his Accounts as Overseer to the poor for the year 1703

His Receipts amounted to	89	05	03
His disbursements	91	15	09½
Rests due to Mr Doran	02	10	06½

Which was paid to him as above by Mr Bristow.

[fo. 777v]

Att this Court Widow Elston was chozen to receive the Charity given by Mrs Millers will in the room of widow Ray deceased.

Ordered that Henry Parnham have a Blew Coat out of Mr Blythes Charity in the room of Robert Allanson deceased.

William Baily, John White, Mark Durham, Edward Nix, Daniel Neale, Edward Newcome, William Hatfeild.
At this Court came William Baily eldest Son of Mr Thomas Baily and John White, Mark Durham, Tayler Edward Nix Glazier, Daniel Neale Cooper, Edward Newcome of Caythorp Shoemaker and William Hatfield Butcher who had served their Severall Apprenticeshipps of Seaven yeares within this Burrough and craved to be admitted

Freemen of this Corporacion which this Court taking into Consideracion doe grant and they were sworne accordingly.

Fourth Court of Thomas Baily, 28 July 1704

At this Court it is ordered and agreed that the summe of sixty pounds be taken up att Interest and that Mr John Calcroft, Mr John Firman and Mr Alexander Mason be bound for the Same and that a Counter Security be made to them of the Lease of the Tolls of this Corporacion for their Indemnity. It is now also ordered and agreed that the said summe of sixty pounds be paid into the Chamberlains Hands.

It is now alsoe ordered and agreed that a New Stable be built at the Redd Lyon at the Charge of the Corporacion.

Henry Lightfoot, Benjamin Rowley, John Baxter, Charles Osbourn, John Marshall.
Att this Court came Henry Lightfoot Cooper, Benjamin Rowley Baker, John Baxter Courrier, Charles Osborn Shoemaker (who had served their severall Apprenticeships of seaven years within this Burrough) and John Marshall Barber eldest son of John Marshall a Freeman of this Corporacion and craved to be admitted Freemen of this Corporacion which this Court taking into Consideration agreed to and they were sworne accordingly.

Att this Court it was ordered that the Millmasters doe pass their Accounts on Tuesday the 8th of August and that Mr Alexander Mason and Robert Orson doe pass their Accounts at the same time.

John True
Att this court came John True a Forreignor and laid down his Five pounds & craved to be admitted a Freeman of this Corporacion which this Court taking into Consideration agreed to upon his giving a Note under his hand for payment of Five pounds more to Mr John Calcraft for the Use of this Corporacion on the 24th of June next and he was sworne accordingly.

[fo. 778r] **Fifth Court of Thomas Baily, 1 September 1704**

Att this Court Mr Thomas Cole past his Accounts as Millmaster beginning August 17th
1703 and ending 7th August 1704   li   s   d
His Receipts amounted to   60   14   00¾
His disbursements amounted to   38   15   09
Rests due to the Town   21   18   03¾
Which this Court orders shall be paid to the present Chamberlain.

Ordered that the present Chamberlain doe take a Distress for yeares rent due for a lease in the High Street now in the occupation of Mr Olliver Rolt att 6s 8d per Annum and that if any suit arise about taking the said Distress the Charges and Damages (if any happen thereby) shall be paid by the Chamberlain out of the Corporacion Stocks.

And it is also ordered that a distress to be taken upon Wilsons house or houses in the Occupacion of Mr Simon Grant and others for Arreares of rent due to this Corporacion and that the Churchwarden be indemnifyed by this Court for taking the said distress.

At this Court Mr Alexander and Mr Mason past his Accounts as Churchwarden for the year 1703
His Receipts amounted to   49 12 03
His disbursements amounted to   64 02 09
Rests due to Mr Mason   14 10 06
Which this Court ordered should be paid to him by the present Churchwarden
And the present Churchwarden to have an Assessment.
Att this court Mr William Wing past his Accounts as Millmaster for the Slate Mill beginning 31st August 1703 & ending the first day of August 1704
His Receipts amounted to   93 09 07½
His disbursements amounted to   60 01 04½
Rests due to the Towne   33 08 03
Which summe this Court orders the said Mr Wing to pay to the present Chamberlain.

Att this Court a New Lease was granted to Mr Edmund Smith of a house in Walkergate formerly John Stills for one and twenty yeares commencing from Lady Day last att three pounds *per Annum* payable Quarterly and upon the fine of four pounds eight shillings.

[fo. 778v]

Att this Court it is ordered that 2 li 17s 6d be paid by the present Churchwarden to Robert Orson the Late Churchwarden out of the next Assessment to be made for the repaires of the Church and that what Charges the said Robert Orson was att in prosecuting any person or persons for not paying their Assessment be borne by the said Robert Orson. The said prosecucion being begunn and carryed on without any order of this Court.

Sixth Court of Thomas Baily, 6 October 1704

At this Court it was ordered that an assessment 4d per pound be made and laid upon the Inhabitants of this Towne for reimbursing the Constables the moneyes by them expended expended [*sic*] this year in Conveying of Vagrants.

John Newton, William Newton.
At this Court came John Newton and William Newton sons of William Newton the Elder baker who had served seaven years Apprenticeship to their Father and craved to be admitted Freemen of this Corporacion which this Court taking into Consideracion agreed to and they were sworne accordingly.

[fo. 779r] **Seventh Court of Thomas Baily, 19 October 1704**

At this Court the tolls of this Town were lett to Constance Fisher widow for one yeare to commence from the 26th of October instant at 52 li per annum payable quarterly and she gave 1s in Earnest.

John Cole
At this Court came John Cole Victualer a Forreigner and laid down his Five pounds and craved to be admitted a Freeman of this Corporacion which this Court upon Consideracion agreed to upon his giving a Note under his hand for payment of 5 li more for the Use of this Corporacion att Lady Day next and he was Sworne accordingly.

At this Court Mr John Coddington mercer is elected to be a Comburgess of this Corporacion in the room of Mr Richard Wild deceased and being summoned to this Court to take the Office upon him the said Mr Coddington appeared and refused to take upon him the said Office or place of a Comburgess.

At this Court the Constables of this Towne accounted as followeth	£	s	d
Market Place Constables received	03	03	03½
Disburst	00	15	01
Due to the Town	02	08	02½
Highstreet Constables received	00	19	00½
Disburst	01	04	03
Due to the Constables	00	05	02½
Westgate Constables received	01	09	07½
Disburst	00	18	06
Due to the Town	00	11	01½
Walkergate Constables received	01	19	02
Disburst	00	17	04
Due to the Town	01	01	10
Castlegate Constables received	00	17	01¼
Disburst	01	11	07
Due to the Constables	00	14	05¾
Swinegate Constables received	00	19	03½
Disburst	01	07	03
Due to the Constables	00	07	11½
Mr Alderman's Bill	00	06	08

Mr Langleyes	00	15	04
Mr Masons	00	10	02
The Assessment making	00	06	00
Robert Lyons Bill for the house of Correccion	00	12	00
George Fitzrandolph for a Ladder	00	06	00

[fo. 779v] [Blank page]

[fo. 780r]

Att an Assembly holden by Thomas Baily Gentleman Alderman and the Comburgesses and Burgesses of Grantham aforesaid in Corpus Christi Quoire in the Prebendary Church there on the Freyday next after St Luke being 20 October 1704.

First did sitt downe upon the Cushions or place of Election Mr Thomas Baily Alderman in Corpus Christi Quoire in the said prebendary Church.
Next to him did sitt downe upon the Cushions or place of Election two other Comburgesses vizt. Mr Joseph Lowe and Mr John Bradfeild.
Then is sent downe into the Body of the Church to Mr John Calcroft and Mr William Doughty one other Comburgess vizt. Mr James Firman.
Out of which three Comburgesses in the Body of the Church one is chosen to come up and sitt upon the Cushions or place of Election vizt Mr John Calcroft.
Then are there three Comburgesses upon the Cushions or place of Election vizt Mr Joseph Lowe, Mr John Bradfeild and Mr John Calcroft.
Out of which three Comburgesses upon the Cushions or place of Election one is to be chosen Alderman of this Towne for the year next ensueing.
And thereupon by Unanimous Vote of this Assembly Mr Joseph Lowe is chosen Alderman for the year ensueing.

Whereupon the said Mr Thomas Baily is discharged from his Office of Alderman and Mr Joseph Lowe sworne Alderman in his stead for the Burrough and Soake of Grantham for the Year ensueing according to the Ancient Custome of the said Burrough.

And soe this Assembly breaks up.

[fo. 780v] [Blank page]

APPENDIX 1: COURTS AND ASSEMBLIES 1662–1704

Year	Alderman (Mayor 1684–87)	Pages	Items	Courts	Assemblies
1662	Michael Taylor	21	86	12	0
1663	Robert Calcraft	17	86	16	0
1664	Thomas Mills/John Watson	19	88	12	1
1665	Thomas Hanson	18	78	12	0
1666	Richard Leeming	14	67	10	0
1667	Thomas Short	21	93	16	0
1668	Robert Calcraft	10	39	7	0
1669	Richard Calcraft	13	66	12	0
1670	Joseph Tomlinson/Richard Holley	18	85	14	1
1671	John Lenton	17	68	11	0
1672	Henry Humes	12	50	9	0
1673	Edward Rawlinson	15	61	10	0
1674	John Coddington	17	51	12	0
1675	Robert Cole	16	60	13	0
1676	Thomas Matkin	7	24	5	0
1677	Michael Taylor	12	38	8	1
1678	John Wing	9	24	6	0
1679	William Milles/Thomas Short	10	41	11	1
1680	Thomas Ireland	9	33	5	0
1681	Richard Calcraft	8	30	7	0
1682	Richard Hawley	13	32	9	0
1683	John Coddington	12	43	12	0
1684	Robert Calcraft (mayor)	8	36	11	0
1685	Robert Cole (mayor)	9	57	14	0
1686	Thomas Matkin (mayor)	11	52	12	0
1687	Thomas Ireland (mayor)/Jn Coddington	11	53	15	0
1688	Edward Secker	12	72	13	0
1689	Edward Leivesley	11	53	10	0
1690	John Robinson	12	55	11	0

APPENDIX 1

Year	Alderman (Mayor 1684–87)	Pages	Items	Courts	Assemblies
1691	Nicholas Beck	7	33	7	0
1692	Simon Grant	7	35	9	0
1693	William Haskard	5	26	7	0
1694	John Smith	7	31	9	0
1695	Robert Cole	6	29	11	0
1696	Edward Leivesley	6	24	10	0
1697	John Robinson	8	39	8	0
1698	Simon Grant	8	22	11	0
1699	William Haskard	6	25	10	0
1700	William Kirke	12	46	16	0
1701	William Burbidge	11	49	12	0
1702	Anthony Kirke	14	49	12	0
1703	Thomas Baily	9	32	7	0
	Grand totals	488	2061	444	4
	Mean per Aldermanic Year	11.62	49.07	10.57	

Notes

[1] The folios in the Hall Book are numbered but some pages jump and others are given the same number. Some pages are left blank and these have been excluded from the above data.

[2] The figures for Assemblies exclude the annual Assembly held in St Wulfram's Church on the Friday following St Luke's Day at which the Alderman for the ensuing year was usually chosen.

APPENDIX 2: LIST OF ALDERMEN, COMBURGESSES AND SECOND TWELVEMEN 1662–1704

Family Name	Christian Name	Date first appointed Commoner	Second Twelve	Comburgess	Alderman (or Mayor)	Date of Dismissal/ Resignation/Death	Approx age in 1663	Lincoln Wills	Lincoln Inventories
Baily	Thomas (I)	1677*	1685–94	1694– post 1704	1703			W 1690/17 tanner	
Baily	Thomas (II)	1677*	1698– post 1704	1698– post 1704					
Beck	Nicholas	1668	1677–84	1688–98	1691	Died before 2 January 1698			
Bradfield	John	1689	1692–98	1698– post 1704	(1705)				
Bristowe	Edward	1666	1677–85	1685–91		Discharged then restored 1688; desired to be dismissed 11 December 1691			
Bristowe	William	1675	1694–95			Discharged 11 August 1695 'being gone out of the Towne'			
Burbidge	William	1679	1688–94	1694– post 1704	1701				
Bury	William	1662	1667–72				c23		
Calcraft	John	1692	1693–1700	1700– post 1704	(1706)				
Calcraft	Richard	1653	1657–61	1661–84	1669, 1681	Died before 3 December 1684	35	W 1684/ ii/90 gent	I 162(a)/92

Family Name	Christian Name	Date first appointed Commoner	Second Twelve	Comburgess	Alderman (or Mayor)	Date of Dismissal/Resignation/Death	Approx age in 1663	Lincoln Wills	Lincoln Inventories
Calcraft	Robert (I)	pre-1630	pre-1633	1637–47 & 1661–66	1642, 1663–64	Dismissed as royalist 1647; restored 1661; died before 12 October 1666	68		
Calcraft	Robert (II)	1660		1662–1691	1668, 1684 (part)	Died 1691	37		
Chantler	Gilbert	pre-1630	1637–45	1646–47 & 1661–66		Dismissed as royalist 1647; restored 1661; dismissed 27 April 1666 'in gaol for debt'	c53–58		
Charles	Thomas	1666	1671–77			Dismissed (no reason stated) on or before 16 November 1677			
Charles	William	1691	1692–98	1698–1701					
Chrichloe	Thomas	1670	1677–80			Resigned 23 January 1680 as obtained licence to practise Phisicke & declined place 1685			
Clarke	William	1670	1676–80						
Coddington	Edward (I)	1653	1656–63			Died before 31 July 1663	c31		
Coddington	Edward (II)			1688					
Coddington	John (I)	1654	1662–70	1670–97	1674, 1683	Discharged owing to inconveniences in attendance 2 January 1698	30		
Coddington	John (II)	1689	1690–92			Neglects to take oath & is dismissed 26 October 1694			
Cole	Robert (I)	1660	1663–72	1672–c1704	1675, 1685, 1695	Died in or after 1704	26		

Family Name	Christian Name	Date first appointed Commoner	Second Twelve	Comburgess	Alderman (or Mayor)	Date of Dismissal/Resignation/Death	Approx age in 1663	Lincoln Wills	Lincoln Inventories
Cole	Robert (II)	1685	1686	1686–87 & 1690–98		Died before 27 May 1698			
Cole	William	1674	1682–83, 1688–90						
Coverly	Henry	1667	1669–81						
Cox	Zachary	1656	1659–67			Requested dismissal from 2nd XII 18 October 1667; died before 26 April 1675	c29	W 1675/61, woollen draper	1177/49
Dawson	Richard	1677	1690–98			Dismissed 'sent by their buisiness to be out of Town' 18 March 1698			
Doughty	William	1689	1693–1700	1700–post 1704					
Ferman (Firman)	James	1689	1695–1702	1702–post 1704	(1709)				
Ferman (Firman)	John	1690	1695–post 1704						
Fisher	Robert			1685		Appointed Alderman under 1685 Charter; desired to be dismissed July 1685			
Fisher	Thomas (I)	1665	1673–83	1683–87		Died before 15 July 1687			
Fisher	Thomas (II)	1693	1698–1702						
Gasse (Gasshe)	John	1683	1685–88						
Goodwin	John		1698			A John Goodwin was a Commoner 1675–83			

Family Name	Christian Name	Date first appointed Commoner	Second Twelve	Comburgess	Alderman (or Mayor)	Date of Dismissal/ Resignation/Death	Approx age in 1663	Lincoln Wills	Lincoln Inventories
Gibson	James	1675	1682–83, 1688			Refused to take oath of allegiance & dismissed 7 December 1688			
Grant	Simon	1673	1680–85	1685–1700	1692, 1698	Died before 28 May 1700			
Grant	Thomas	1644	1648–56	1656–75		Died (buried 7 April 1675)	c40		
Hanson	Christopher	pre-1630	1634–41	1641–50 & 1661–68	May–Oct 1646	Dismissed as royalist 7 June 1650; restored 1661; dismissed 8 July 1668 'very weake and auntient' & died 1670	c54–60	W 1671/i/246 butcher	I 173/341
Hanson	Thomas	1640		1662–70	1665	Re-admitted 14 June 1661; died before 20 May 1670	44	W 1669/ ii/439 innholder	
Harrington	Thomas			1685–88		Appointed Alderman under Charter of 1685			
Haskard	William	1671	1680–84	1688– post 1704	1693, 1699				
Holley (Hawley)	Richard	1647	1655–65	1665–84	1671 (part), 1682	Died before 19 December 1684	c37–40		
Hotchkin(s)	Anthony (I)	1663	1668–80	1680–83		Died before 26 February 1683	21		
Hotchkin(s)	Anthony (II)	1691	1694–95			Paid £10 & desired to be dismissed 23 August 1695			
Humes	Henry	1656	1662–67	1667–80	1672	Died before 9 January 1680	c28		

Family Name	Christian Name	Date first appointed Commoner	Second Twelve	Comburgess	Alderman (or Mayor)	Date of Dismissal/ Resignation/Death	Approx age in 1663	Lincoln Wills	Lincoln Inventories
Hutchin	Hugh	1653	1657–66	1666–67		Did not take his place as Comburgess, distrained and dismissed 4 October 1667	c31	W 1673/135 shoemaker	I 174/133
Hutchin	Thomas	1682	1685–88						
Ireland	Thomas	1664	1666–1680	1680–94	1680, 1687	Died before 18 October 1694			
Kirke	Anthony	1677	1688–94	1694– post 1704	1702				
Kirke	William	1674	1686–92	1692– post 1704	1700				
Langton	Francis	1690	1694–1700						
Leeming	Richard	1661		1662–69	1666	Died before 20 May 1670	29	W 1669/i/175 gent	I 169/505
Leivesley	Edward	1663	1672–82	1682–85 & 1688–1702	1689, 1696	Died before 25 September 1702	c21		
Lenton	John	1640	1655–66	1666–79	1671	Died before 19 November 1679	c44–45	W 1679/ ii/515 gent	I 180(2)/425
Lowe	Joseph	1691	1692–98	1698– post 1704	1704				
Matkin	Thomas	1655	1663–72	1672–99	1676, 1686	Died before 4 December 1699	c29		
Mills	Thomas	pre-1630	1634	1641–64	1644, 1653, 1664	Died in office before 5 November 1664	c53–56	W 1664/533 fellmonger	
Mills	William	1662	1664–75	1675–79	1679	Died in office before 24 December 1679	c22		
Nall	Mark	1683	1685						

Family Name	Christian Name	Date first appointed Commoner	Second Twelve	Comburgess	Alderman (or Mayor)	Date of Dismissal/ Resignation/Death	Approx age in 1663	Lincoln Wills	Lincoln Inventories
Newcom(b)e	John	1671	1685–93	1693–98		Died before 27 May 1698			
Oldfield	Thomas	1653	1656–63			Requested dismissal from 2nd XII 26 June 1663	c32–37	W 1671/i/277 yeoman	I 173/231
Pape	John	1667	1670–77			Died before 6 November 1677	c30–40	W 1670/ii/480, Hester, w of William, woollendraper	I 187/250
Pawlett	Edward	1664	1666–80	1680–87		Died February 1687; probate inventory dated 2 March 1687			
Poole	Andrew	1661	1662			Distrained for refusal to take place on 2nd XII October 1663; died June 1677	30	W 1677/288 apothecary	I 219A/249
Poole	John (haberdasher)			1688		Appointed 25 June 1688 and then voided by Court on 6 November 1688			
Poole	John (apothecary)			1688		Appointed 25 June 1688 and then voided by Court on 6 November 1688			
Procter	Samuel		1685–88			Town Clerk in 1685 & continued as Town Clerk until his death October 1700			
Rawlinson	Edward	1658	1662–67	1667–76	1673	Died before 28 February 1676	c26		
Read	George	1670	1684–88			Requested to be dismissed 6 November 1688			

Family Name	Christian Name	Date first appointed Commoner	Second Twelve	Comburgess	Alderman (or Mayor)	Date of Dismissal/Resignation/Death	Approx age in 1663	Lincoln Wills	Lincoln Inventories
Robinson	John	1670	1675–84	1684–post 1704	1690, 1697				
Rollinson	John		1685–88			Nominated Common Council Man in Charter of 1685			
Rowley	Thomas	1668	1681–83 & 88–89			Dismissed as 'disguised in drinke' & guilty of 'other misdemeanours'			
Segrave	Richard	1676	1680–83						
Secker	Edward		1685–88	1688–89	1688	Dismissed owing to 'great indisposition by the palsy'			
Sentence	Richard	1683	1685–88			As Commoner, desired to be dismissed 11 Dec 1691			
Short	George	1653	1661–67	1667–72		Died before 18 October 1672	22		
Short	Thomas (I)	pre-1630	1661	1661–80	1667, 1679 (part)	Dismissed as royalist 1647; restored 1661; last reference 29 October 1680	c54–60		
Short	Thomas (II)	1677	1688–92						
Simpson	Thomas	1683	1684–87 & 88–91	1687 & 1691		Died before 4 May 1693			
Smith	John	1675	1680–85	1685–98	1695	Discharged 24 June 1698 'having begotten his servant with child'			
Taylor (Tailer)	Michael	1648	1654–59	1659–85	1662, 1677	Died before 15 January 1685	c35–40	W 1684/ii/160 gent	I 185(a)/86

Family Name	Christian Name	Date first appointed Commoner	Second Twelve	Comburgess	Alderman (or Mayor)	Date of Dismissal/ Resignation/Death	Approx age in 1663	Lincoln Wills	Lincoln Inventories
Taylor	Arthur	1683	1686			Nominated Common Council Man in Charter of 1685 but refused			
Thompson	Christopher	1665	1667–80						
Thorold	John			1685–88		Appointed Alderman under Charter of 1685; nominated Mayor but refused			
Todkill	Edward	1689	1690–91						
Tomlinson	Joseph	1653	1657–62	1662–71	1670	Died before 6 July 1671	c25	W 1671/ii/619 gent	
Turner	John	1660	1665–76	1676–78		Died before 24 October 1679	c24–25		
Turner	William	1686	1690–1698	1698–1700					
Walker	John	1660	1670–78				c24–25		
Watson	Edward	1678	1681–87 & 89–94			Died before 31 May 1694	c24–25		
Watson	John			1662–67	1664	Re-admitted 14 June 1661; died before 23 April 1667	c35–45	W 1667/i/307 gent	Ad 1667/243
Weaver	John	1681	1690–93			Dismissed on his request 14 May 1696			
Wilson	Francis		1698–1701			Discharged further attendance 31 October 1701			
Wing	John	1657	1662–70	1670–85	1678	Died before 16 March 1685	27		
Wyld (Wiles)	Richard	1686	1694–1702	1702–04		Died before 19 October 1704			

Note
* There were two men called Thomas Bayly, one a tanner and the other a fellmonger, and their identification is unclear prior to 1677.

INDEX OF PERSONAL NAMES

Abrahall, Gilbert   313, 314
Alham (Allam), Thomas   373
Allain, John   183, 184
Allanson, Robert   481
Allcock (Alcock), Robert   380
Allisson
  Clement   136, 171, 188
  Widow   215
Allt (Ault), Robert   470
Alsopp, Mr   137, 153
Ambler, Richard   313, 314
Anne, Queen   lv
Archer
  Edward   101, 115, 150, 266, 271
  Mr   4, 26, 45, 66, 87, 151, 170, 187, 228, 242, 250, 263, 282, 289, 303, 312, 320, 331, 342, 353, 366, 377, 388, 397, 403, 430, 438, 444, 449, 459, 469, 480
  Thomas   15, 25, 26, 41, 44, 45, 50, 63, 66, 69, 87, 91, 101, 102, 121, 151, 152, 164, 169, 170, 182, 187, 191, 200, 202, 203, 215, 216, 221, 228, 229, 231, 236, 242, 250, 251, 257, 426
Armestead, Richard   12
Ascough (Ayscoghe)
  Anthony   12, 68, 69, 70, 127, 132, 137
  John   127
Ashby, Widow   53
Ashley
  Hugh   312
  Thomas   312
Ashton, James   12, 114, 179, 182, 231
Atkin, Richard   452
Atkins, William   xlii
Atkinson
  Henry   131, 261, 262, 271, 282, 289, 290, 295, 296, 298, 299, 303, 426
  Richard   196

Babbington, Mr   12

Bacon
  Francis   163, 231, 234
  Thomas   305, 312
Baggott, Thomas   182
Baily (Baly, Bayly)
  Joseph   397
  Thomas (I) (Alderman 1703–04)   xlvii, 180, 186, 187, 190, 200, 214, 242, 244, 250, 262, 271, 281, 282, 288, 289, 295, 296, 302, 303, 311, 319, 322, 330, 333, 336, 340, 352, 353, 357, 358, 359, 362, 365, 376, 377, 380, 381, 385, 387, 388, 391, 395, 408, 449, 459, 468, 477, 478, 479, 480, 481, 482, 483, 484, 485, 487, 488
  Thomas (II) (fellmonger)   282, 296, 303, 319, 330, 341, 350, 352, 366, 371, 377, 396, 403, 433, 449, 459, 468, 479, 488
  Thomas (III)   245, 311
  William (I)   9
  William (II)   350, 376, 377, 387, 388, 396
  William (III)   481
Baines, Mrs Mary   336
Ball, Sir Peter   xxxix
Barker
  Gabriel   406
  Richard   259
  William   365
Barkston (Barston), Lawrence   252
Barnes, Anthony   313, 314
Barrett (Barret)
  John   455
  William   297, 319, 341, 365, 366, 376, 377, 387, 388, 395, 396, 399, 432
Barstow, Edward   134
Barton
  Robert   211, 218, 245, 319, 330, 352, 354, 358, 365, 373, 376, 384, 387, 391, 395
  Widow   391

Basse (Bass)
  John (I)   235, 350
  John (II)   350, 447, 451, 460, 471, 479
Batchellor, Mr   225
Battic (Batty), Mr John   4, 26, 45, 66, 87,
    152, 171, 188, 201, 229, 243, 251, 263,
    272, 282, 289, 303, 312, 320, 322, 331,
    342, 353, 354, 366, 377, 388, 397, 403,
    430, 438, 444, 449, 459, 469, 480
Baxter, John   482
Beamond (Beamont)
  John   95, 101, 123
  William   315, 384
Bearne (Bearnes, Bearns), Thomas   69, 70,
    109, 146, 172, 231
Beck(e)
  Mr   35, 49, 81
  Nicholas (Alderman 1691–92)   xxxvi,
    liv, 102, 111, 115, 121, 123, 124, 128,
    134, 135, 142, 151, 154, 160, 170,
    186, 187, 200, 202, 204, 221, 224,
    227, 228, 236, 239, 242, 249, 251,
    256, 261, 264, 270, 281, 282, 283,
    288, 295, 302, 317, 326, 345, 351,
    352, 362, 364, 365, 374, 375, 376,
    380, 382, 386, 387, 389, 390, 391,
    392, 393, 394, 395, 397, 400, 401,
    413, 422, 426, 428, 430, 431, 432,
    487, 488
  Richard   281
Becraft
  John (I)   196
  John (II)   306
Bell, Abraham   357
Bellamy, George   284
Bennett, Henry   xl
Benton
  John (I)   192, 433, 444, 449, 450, 459,
    460, 468, 479
  John (II)   433, 441
Beriffe (Barriffe, Berriffe)
  Francis   441, 447
  William (I)   xxxvii, 4, 21, 23, 26, 41, 44,
    45, 50, 66, 69, 73, 83, 87, 102, 103,
    123, 124, 135, 137, 138, 151, 154,
    160, 170, 176, 181, 189, 190
  William (II)   374, 401
Berrisford, Christopher   313, 314
Berry
  Henry   xlii
  John   290
Bertie (Bartue, Berty)
  Mr   55
  Peregrine   313, 314
  Robert. *See* Lindsey, Robert.
Beveston, Abraham   441, 451, 460, 469,
    477, 480
Bigland, Serjeant   348, 355
Bignall, Widow   452
Bilton, William   293
Black (Blacke)
  John   207, 211
  Richard   xxv, 3, 7, 21, 25, 44, 51, 56, 65,
    86, 91, 101, 116, 123, 128, 131, 134,
    137, 138, 150, 156, 326
  William   203
Blague, William   218
Blankney (Blackney, Blanckney, Blankly),
    Roger   166, 261, 262, 270, 271, 315,
    325, 327, 352, 353, 362, 366, 371, 372
Blithe (Blith)
  Mr   481
  Widow   93
  William   6, 17
Bradfield (Bradfeild), John   lix, 332, 334,
    345, 357, 358, 365, 366, 370, 371, 372,
    376, 377, 385, 388, 389, 391, 395, 400,
    403, 404, 408, 414, 419, 434, 449, 457,
    459, 465, 467, 468, 474, 477, 479, 485,
    488
Bradshaw, Savile   313
Branston, Richard   11, 86
Breilsford, Widow   14, 46
Brewer
  Anthony   414
  Thomas   265
Briggs
  Bethell   202
  George   xx
  Thomas   134, 150, 169, 186
  William   455
Bringhurst, 339
  Widow   317, 335, 407
Bristowe (Bristow)
  Edward (I)   xlvii, liv, 87, 88, 102, 121,
    124, 135, 151, 169, 170, 186, 187,
    190, 200, 214, 228, 231, 236, 241,
    242, 243, 249, 250, 251, 253, 257,
    261, 270, 281, 282, 288, 295, 302,
    311, 319, 330, 333, 336, 347, 348,

351, 352, 355, 364, 365, 375, 376, 386, 387, 390, 395, 441, 488
Edward (II)   88
Edward (III)   374
Francis   124, 135, 136, 150, 151, 169, 170, 175, 200, 210, 221, 228, 242, 250, 262, 271, 333, 369
James   249, 250, 251, 262, 271, 282, 289, 296, 303, 353, 366, 377, 387, 388, 396
Richard   61, 66, 84, 86, 94, 96, 281, 311, 319, 330, 374, 450, 460, 469, 479, 481
Thomas   98, 111, 112, 114
Timothy   189
William   61, 87, 88, 102, 121, 180, 228, 239, 241, 262, 271, 277, 278, 282, 289, 296, 304, 353, 365, 366, 371, 377, 379, 388, 396, 410, 413, 433, 439, 461, 474, 475, 488

Brockhurst, John   126
Bromwich, Andrew   xlii
Broome (Brome)
Andrew   4, 7, 17, 21, 283
Francis   283
Henry   289
John   214, 216, 224, 227, 250, 261
Broughton, John   202, 229, 230, 253, 275, 290
Brown(e)
Carr   454
Francis   331, 341, 348
John   241, 242
Mr   37
Thomas   435, 441
Brownlow (Brownloe)
Sir John (I)   liv
Sir John (II)   xxxiv, liv, lix, 155, 157, 349, 354, 363, 375, 385, 391, 404, 419
Brumpton
Hamlett   56, 66, 84, 86, 87, 101, 102, 121, 124, 135, 151, 170
Isabell   350
Buik, Thomas   434
Bullimore
Mr   435, 441, 444
Richard   434
Burbidge (Burbridge)
George   343, 354, 374
Richard   167

Thomas   306
William (I) (Alderman 1701–02)   lii, 202, 270, 271, 282, 283, 289, 295, 296, 302, 303, 305, 306, 323, 336, 341, 349, 350, 352, 353, 362, 364, 365, 366, 368, 376, 379, 387, 395, 405, 407, 420, 437, 441, 443, 447, 449, 450, 454, 457, 458, 459, 460, 461, 462, 463, 464, 465, 466, 467, 468, 469, 472, 474, 475, 479, 480, 487, 488
William (II)   452, 453
Burnet(t)
Charles   xxxvii, 440, 462
Rev Samuel   xxx, xxxvi, xxxvii, 153, 179, 181, 189, 205, 232, 312, 317, 335, 339, 362, 380, 381, 407, 412, 426, 440, 446, 462, 463, 464
Burnham (Burman)
John   434
Joseph   130, 135, 150, 156, 170, 186, 190, 199, 227, 374, 434
Bursleime, Mr   xliii, 267
Burton, Robert   341
Bury (Berry)
Hugh   265
Sir William   xlii, 262
William (I) (carpenter)   xxvii, 3, 4, 12, 23, 25, 26, 38, 40, 44, 45, 54, 57, 60, 66, 68, 75, 76, 78, 79, 82, 87, 92, 96, 98, 101, 106, 110, 111, 123, 125, 126, 134, 150, 154, 158, 169, 186, 211, 488
William (II) (lawyer)   xxxix, xlii, lvi, 32, 51, 53, 54, 78, 89, 92, 189, 232, 264
Butcher, Leonard   256, 352, 366, 396, 404, 431, 450, 460, 469, 479
Butler, Richard   54, 71

Calcraft (Calcroft)
John (I)   xi, xix, lv, 312, 317, 395, 396, 403, 404, 431, 445, 446, 447, 449, 450, 453, 456, 459, 460, 462, 463, 465, 467, 468, 469, 474, 477, 479, 482, 485, 488
John (II)   453
Richard (I) (Alderman 1669–70 & 1681–82)   xxv, xxxvi, xlii, xliii, l, 3, 5, 10, 12, 14, 18, 25, 34, 35, 44, 48, 49, 51, 52, 53, 58, 60, 65, 75, 77, 78,

INDEX OF PERSONAL NAMES

    84, 85, 86, 91, 94, 98, 99, 100, 101, 103, 105, 106, 109, 112, 122, 123, 126, 128, 129, 131, 133, 134, 137, 138, 139, 140, 141, 142, 143, 145, 146, 147, 149, 150, 151, 152, 159, 161, 165, 167, 169, 172, 183, 186, 192, 193, 194, 195, 199, 205, 212, 214, 215, 222, 224, 227, 236, 238, 241, 243, 245, 249, 258, 261, 263, 264, 269, 270, 272, 273, 277, 279, 281, 285, 286, 287, 288, 289, 290, 291, 292, 293, 294, 295, 297, 302, 308, 317, 486, 488

  Richard (Usher)   xxxvi, xlii, xliii, 264, 332

  Robert (I) (Alderman 1642–43 & 1663–64)   xxiii, xxv, 3, 12, 14, 17, 19, 24, 25, 27, 28, 29, 31, 32, 36, 37, 38, 39, 40, 41, 42, 43, 44, 45, 48, 49, 51, 52, 53, 55, 58, 60, 65, 67, 68, 71, 75, 77, 80, 486, 489

  Robert (II) (Alderman 1668–69 & Mayor 1685)   xxv, xlvii, l, li, 3, 6, 12, 14, 25, 30, 33, 35, 44, 51, 59, 64, 65, 75, 77, 78, 83, 91, 98, 100, 101, 103, 112, 122, 123, 130, 131, 132, 133, 134, 135, 144, 147, 150, 152, 156, 169, 172, 174, 180, 186, 190, 194, 195, 199, 203, 205, 206, 207, 211, 212, 214, 215, 216, 218, 219, 227, 229, 232, 241, 242, 249, 251, 255, 256, 258, 259, 261, 269, 270, 272, 276, 277, 279, 281, 287, 288, 289, 293, 295, 298, 301, 302, 306, 308, 311, 312, 313, 314, 315, 316, 317, 318, 319, 320, 330, 341, 347, 352, 365, 367, 376, 470, 486, 489

  Robert (III)   259, 300

  Thomas   xliii, 4, 21, 23, 25, 26, 27, 28, 41, 44, 45, 66, 84, 85, 86, 87, 89, 94, 101, 111, 134, 150, 161, 169, 186, 199, 214, 227, 241, 249, 261, 266, 270, 281, 288, 296, 302, 311, 319, 330, 341, 352, 365, 376, 387, 395, 415, 441

Camock, Leonard   451
Campden, Baptist, Lord   xl, 255
Carr, Sir Robert   xxv, xxxix, xl, xli, xliii, xliv, 251, 256, 263, 267, 268, 274, 309, 336

Castle, Widow   317, 335, 339, 412
Catlet(t)
  James (I)   356
  James (II)   356
Challands
  Joseph (I)   456
  Joseph (II)   456
Challeng(e), John   307
Chamberlaine, Robert   70, 114, 231
Chambrey, John   471
Chantler, Gilbert   3, 4, 5, 8, 12, 14, 22, 24, 25, 34, 44, 49, 65, 77, 82, 489
Chantry, George   lix, 369, 380, 381, 411, 432
Charity (Charitie)
  Francis   3, 4, 14, 15, 17, 23, 25, 26, 27, 28, 33, 35, 41, 45, 50, 65, 66, 69, 84, 86, 87, 102, 121, 124, 135, 350
  George   350, 355, 430, 435, 441, 447, 460, 468, 473
Charles
  Thomas (I)   44, 61, 65, 86, 87, 88, 101, 102, 112, 118, 121, 123, 124, 134, 135, 151, 152, 154, 157, 158, 159, 164, 169, 172, 177, 178, 186, 190, 194, 195, 199, 207, 214, 219, 227, 241, 244, 245, 249, 254, 259, 279, 489
  Thomas (II)   88, 337
  William   383, 387, 388, 393, 395, 403, 404, 405, 406, 407, 408, 433, 435, 449, 457, 459, 489
Charles I, King   xvii, xliii
Charles II, King   xxiii, xxxii, xliv, xlv, xlvi, xlix, l, li, lx
Chomeley (Chomley), Mr   114
Chrichloe (Chrichley, Critchloe)
  John   434
  Thomas   xlvii, xlix, 140, 150, 151, 170, 187, 190, 192, 199, 200, 203, 207, 227, 228, 242, 250, 251, 254, 255, 257, 261, 270, 274, 278, 316, 317, 327, 328, 434, 489
Christian, Edward   lvi, lvii, lviii, 51, 55, 89, 90, 91, 95, 98, 109, 136, 141, 143
Clark(e)
  Abraham   297
  Andrew   333
  John   313, 314
  Joseph   34

Joseph (II)   455
Mrs   114
Ralph   206, 265
Robert (I)   7
Robert (II)   305
Robert (III)   452, 475
William (I)   xxii, 49, 51, 300
William (II)   140, 150, 151, 152, 170, 172, 186, 187, 190, 199, 200, 201, 207, 215, 219, 221, 228, 229, 235, 236, 241, 249, 256, 261, 262, 263, 270, 273, 371, 401, 425, 455, 474, 489

Clipsham
George   334
Mary   384
Richard   384
Samuel   334, 414, 420, 424, 431, 435, 441, 447, 450, 473

Coates, Robert   384
Coddington (Codington)
Edward (I)   3, 489
Edward (II)   li, 129, 180, 223, 291, 321, 347, 348, 489
Edward (III)   291
John (I) (Alderman 1674–75, 1683–84 & 1688)   xlv, xlvi, xlvii, lii, liii, 3, 8, 12, 14, 17, 20, 21, 101, 111, 123, 134, 141, 145, 146, 150, 169, 172, 173, 174, 176, 181, 184, 186, 191, 193, 197, 199, 203, 207, 209, 212, 213, 214, 215, 216, 217, 218, 219, 220, 222, 224, 225, 226, 227, 228, 229, 230, 231, 235, 238, 241, 247, 249, 261, 270, 272, 273, 279, 281, 285, 287, 288, 292, 293, 294, 295, 298, 301, 302, 304, 305, 306, 308, 309, 311, 312, 316, 319, 330, 341, 350, 351, 352, 363, 365, 376, 377, 378, 379, 387, 388, 390, 395, 399, 425, 431, 486, 489
John (II)   321, 349, 366, 371, 376, 387, 393, 410, 434, 476, 489
John (III)   434, 484
Samuel (Usher)   xxxvi, 25, 44, 47, 65, 75, 86, 427, 440

Cole
Henry   36
John   484

Robert (I) (Alderman 1675–76 & 1695–96; Mayor 1685–86)   xxx, xxxvi, xlvi, xlvii, li, 3, 4, 20, 25, 29, 30, 33, 38, 39, 41, 44, 58, 62, 65, 68, 71, 75, 83, 86, 88, 89, 91, 94, 101, 103, 109, 111, 113, 123, 126, 130, 134, 137, 143, 150, 152, 153, 155, 157, 163, 164, 169, 171, 178, 186, 190, 193, 194, 195, 197, 199, 203, 204, 207, 208, 213, 214, 215, 219, 222, 223, 226, 230, 231, 232, 233, 235, 236, 237, 238, 240, 241, 243, 249, 251, 252, 255, 256, 258, 261, 263, 265, 270, 273, 281, 283, 285, 288, 290, 293, 295, 298, 301, 302, 304, 306, 307, 308, 309, 311, 316, 317, 318, 319, 320, 321, 322, 323, 324, 325, 326, 327, 328, 329, 330, 331, 341, 347, 352, 356, 362, 365, 376, 379, 387, 395, 406, 409, 412, 415, 416, 417, 418, 419, 420, 421, 422, 423, 424, 441, 449, 451, 459, 464, 468, 474, 479, 486, 487, 489
Robert (II)   312, 328, 330, 341, 352, 366, 371, 372, 376, 387, 391, 395, 412, 418, 424, 425, 431, 432, 433, 434, 490
Thomas (I)   lii, 37, 65, 86, 102, 109, 111, 114, 118, 121, 124, 128, 135, 143, 151, 152, 154, 160, 170, 173, 174, 182, 187, 188, 233, 308, 348
Thomas (II)   441, 450, 457, 460, 463, 465, 468, 469, 474, 476, 477, 479, 481, 482
Thomas (III)   465
William   190, 214, 227, 232, 241, 242, 250, 262, 270, 271, 278, 282, 285, 288, 289, 293, 295, 296, 302, 337, 352, 364, 365, 371, 380, 490

Coleman, Edward   xlii
Coney (Cony)
Francis   313
Richard   321
Cook(e)
John   345
Philip   223, 356
Richard   194
Courtby, John   191
Coverly (Coverley, Calverly, Calverlye, Caverly), Henry   11, 102, 108, 109,

INDEX OF PERSONAL NAMES 501

121, 123, 134, 140, 150, 154, 169, 181, 186, 188, 189, 190, 199, 207, 214, 215, 227, 241, 249, 261, 270, 283, 284, 285, 288, 490
Cowles, Robert   130, 134, 169, 172, 181, 187, 189, 190, 200, 228
Cox, Zachary   3, 6, 7, 12, 14, 15, 17, 22, 25, 27, 28, 33, 35, 36, 38, 44, 65, 86, 98, 112, 181, 490
Craddin, James   38
Crawshaw   225
Craycroft, Robert   305
Crosfeild   241
Cross, Richard   313, 314
Crostwaite, Samuel   99

Dalton
  Maurice   xx, 49, 51, 61, 65, 69, 70
  Mr   338, 401
Danby, Lord High Treasurer   xlii, l
Dann, Luce   30, 93
Darker, Mrs   91
Darnil(e)   12, 68
Davye, John   467, 471
Daws, Samuell   313, 314
Dawson
  Anthony   265
  George   lix, 370
  James   339
  John   4, 26, 127, 313
  Richard   249, 250, 251, 261, 262, 270, 271, 282, 286, 296, 303, 352, 353, 366, 371, 373, 376, 378, 382, 387, 389, 395, 404, 432, 490
  Thomas   464
  Widow   177
Day, Thomas   126
De Ligne (deLign)
  Daniel   336
  Decordes   313
  Edward   312
  Erasmus   17, 336
  Thomas   312
Denton, Mr   232
Dickenson (Dickinson)
  Edward   xxxiii, 182, 430, 445
  William   126, 134
Dix
  Edward   13, 91, 313
  Vavasor   304

Dixon
  John   216
  Mathew   234, 242, 250, 262, 271, 289, 295, 296, 299, 303, 334
  Stephen   313, 314
Doran, Charles   481
Doughty
  Old Mr   401
  William   355, 366, 371, 372, 376, 377, 387, 388, 393, 395, 396, 399, 403, 404, 415, 426, 446, 447, 449, 459, 462, 464, 467, 468, 477, 479, 485, 490
Draper, John   345, 355
Ducker, Mr   93
Durham
  George   434
  Mark   481
  Richard (I)   30, 312, 339, 371, 434
  Richard (II)   339
  Robert   370
Durklin (Durkleing), John   313, 314
Dye
  John   17, 77, 114
  Widow   114
Dyer, Judge   88, 103, 124, 135, 151, 187, 200, 228, 242, 250, 262, 271

Edward IV, King   xvii
Edward VI, King   xviii
Eldred
  Thomas   314
  William   313
Ellis (Ellys)
  Charles   312, 313
  Richard   446
  Serjent   246
  William   xxiv, xxvi, lvi, 56, 62, 68, 72, 75, 89
  Sir William   xxxix, xl, xli, xlii, xliii, xliv, xlix, l, liv, lix, 216, 217, 285, 369, 370, 380, 384, 419, 431
Elston (El(l)son)
  Edward   444
  Thomas   314, 330, 355, 362
  Widow   435, 481
  William   8
Elwood, Mr   20, 316
Emerson, Thomas   350
Enderby, Elizabeth   147

Evans, Mr 348
Everitt 39, 384

Fancourt
  James 113
  John 216
  Mr 114
Farthin, John 313, 314
Fearon
  Adam 264
  James 290, 315, 319
  John (I) 61
  John (II) 175
  Robert 334, 376, 377, 378, 386, 388, 389, 395, 396, 397, 398, 403, 408, 410, 417, 431, 436, 441
  Thomas (I) 406, 435
  Thomas (II) 406, 430, 438
  William (I) 105, 106, 206, 239, 241, 242, 247, 248, 249, 250, 264, 270, 282, 295, 296, 302, 303, 305, 309, 310, 334, 341, 342, 365, 367
  William (II) 266, 295, 296, 297, 302, 303, 311, 319, 320, 330, 352, 353, 366
Felton, John 312
Ferkin, Robert 389
Ferman (Firman, Furman)
  Henry 69
  James (I) 17, 18, 81
  James (II) 321, 365, 366, 376, 377, 387, 388, 395, 396, 403, 413, 431, 449, 457, 459, 465, 466, 468, 479, 485, 490
  John 376, 377, 387, 388, 395, 396, 403, 408, 413, 430, 445, 449, 450, 457, 459, 465, 468, 479, 482, 490
  Mr 435, 447
Fields, John 183, 184
Fiennes, Celia xvi
Filding, Christopher 110
Fisher (Fishar, Fysher)
  Ann 406
  Anthony 452, 453
  Constance 338, 348, 363, 368, 375, 384, 401, 408, 414, 421, 427, 436, 442, 447, 456, 466, 476, 484
  Humphrey 46, 186, 206, 211, 312
  John 465, 475, 477, 479
  Robert xlvii, xlix, 311, 316, 417, 430, 454, 460, 490

Thomas (I) xlvii, 61, 65, 66, 76, 80, 84, 86, 87, 91, 94, 102, 103, 124, 135, 150, 160, 164, 169, 170, 176, 181, 182, 187, 189, 190, 194, 195, 199, 202, 203, 207, 208, 211, 214, 215, 216, 227, 236, 241, 243, 244, 249, 251, 256, 261, 263, 270, 281, 282, 283, 285, 288, 290, 295, 296, 297, 302, 303, 304, 309, 310, 311, 317, 319, 322, 327, 330, 333, 335, 338, 392, 490
  Thomas (II) 392, 403, 406, 431, 432, 439, 440, 447, 449, 450, 451, 453, 457, 459, 460, 461, 462, 490
Fitzrandolph, George 312, 319, 330, 341, 471, 477, 480, 485
Fleck, John 1
Foster, Captain xxv, 51
Fox(e)
  John (I) 134
  John (II) 453, 455, 469, 477, 479
  Richard, Bishop of Winchester 419
  Robert 382, 387, 388, 395, 396, 403, 408, 414
  William 360, 363, 412, 414
France, William 291
Francis, Wyatt 363
Freckingham, Richard 225
Frisby, Richard 3, 4, 23, 114
Frith
  Robert 338
  Thomas (I) 61, 87, 102, 121, 124, 134, 135, 150, 152, 169, 170, 187, 200, 227, 228, 241, 242, 250
  Thomas (II) 426
Fuller, William, Bishop of Lincoln 181, 182
Fulwood, Mary lvii, 127

Gardner, William 11
Garner, Isaac 392, 403, 406, 427
Garthwaite
  Edward 434
  Nathaniel xxiv, li, 76, 223, 347, 348, 435, 455, 456
Gass(e) (Gasshe), John xlv, xlvii, 296, 302, 303, 305, 308, 311, 319, 325, 326, 330, 336, 341, 353, 490
Gibson
  Ann 406

Dynnys   306
James   207, 217, 317, 490
John   xxii, liv, 222, 227, 241, 242, 249, 250, 257, 261, 262, 271, 278, 281, 282, 289, 291, 295, 302, 311, 319, 338, 352, 353, 355, 397, 462
Richard   383
Robert   65, 66, 71, 76, 84, 86, 87, 94
Widow   268, 378, 406, 411
William   414, 469, 477, 479
Gladwin(e), John   312
Glenn, William   219
Glover
  Mr   156
  Widow   334, 339, 446
Godley (Godly)
  Bryan   115, 169, 186, 194, 199, 209, 214, 227, 241, 249, 257, 261, 270, 281, 288
  Henry   115, 124, 135
Goodborne, John   434
Goodson
  John   4
  Widow   56
Goodwin(g)
  John   222, 228, 241, 242, 249, 250, 261, 262, 271, 281, 282, 288, 289, 290, 296, 299, 303, 430, 432, 491
  Simon (I)   153, 169, 170, 186, 187, 190, 194, 195, 200, 242, 250, 262, 271, 332, 365
  Simon (II)   332
Gorge, Arthur   xxxviii, 90
Grainge, Mr   349
Grant (Graunt)
  Mrs Jane   474
  Richard   239, 313
  Simon (I) (Alderman 1692–93 & 1698–99)   xix, xxxvi, xlvii, li, 199, 202, 214, 221, 224, 227, 236, 237, 241, 242, 243, 244, 245, 249, 250, 251, 254, 255, 256, 270, 273, 277, 278, 281, 282, 286, 288, 295, 296, 302, 308, 311, 319, 322, 330, 341, 347, 348, 351, 352, 362, 364, 365, 375, 376, 380, 386, 387, 392, 394, 395, 397, 398, 399, 400, 401, 402, 428, 430, 433, 437, 438, 439, 440, 441, 442, 443, 444, 445, 487, 491
  Simon (II)   483

Thomas   3, 6, 7, 14, 21, 22, 25, 27, 28, 31, 35, 39, 41, 44, 45, 47, 48, 54, 57, 58, 65, 68, 69, 70, 75, 77, 80, 86, 89, 91, 101, 103, 105, 111, 112, 115, 119, 123, 126, 128, 134, 135, 137, 138, 140, 142, 143, 145, 146, 149, 150, 151, 152, 154, 160, 161, 162, 163, 168, 169, 172, 174, 176, 177, 184, 186, 188, 190, 191, 193, 197, 199, 206, 208, 210, 214, 220, 231, 491
Green(e)
  Bracebridge (Bracebrig)   345
  John   99
  Robert   xlii, 133
Greenall (Greenhall), Edward   352, 366, 377
Greenwood (Greenewood)
  Edward   295, 296, 300, 303, 353, 396, 425, 426, 447, 463, 465, 468, 469, 470, 471, 474, 479, 481
  John   452, 453
  Mr Miles   4, 12, 26, 87, 151, 152, 170, 171, 187, 188, 200, 201, 228, 229, 242, 243, 251, 263, 272, 282, 289, 303, 312, 320, 322, 331, 342, 353, 354, 366, 377, 388, 397, 403, 430, 438, 444, 449, 459, 480
  Myles   215
Greewill, Edward   290
Grocock(e)
  James (I)   266, 276
  James (II)   455
  John   441
  Widow   356, 378, 411
  William   3, 25, 44, 65, 129, 180, 266, 276, 375, 406, 441
Gulston, William   426
Gunby
  Edward   110
  Willaim   426
Gunnisson (Gunnesson), Thomas   45, 61, 66, 69, 84, 86, 87, 102, 124, 135, 187
Gwin, Lewis   313, 314
Gyles, Walter   312, 313

Haire
  Henry   xxxvii, 8, 9, 30, 32, 34, 35, 36, 37, 39, 42, 46, 49, 55, 67, 73
  John   8, 37, 39, 42, 63, 67
  Simon   63, 67

Halam
  Edwin   441
  John   441, 473
  William   473
Halford, Mr   332
Hall, Isaac   115
Hammond, Samuel   384, 427
Hand, James   297
Handley (Handly)
  Christopher   266
  Richard   139, 187, 200, 228, 242, 250, 262, 268, 271, 282, 289, 296, 302, 303, 310, 314
  Widow   139, 446
  William (I)   206, 266, 325
  William (II)   414
Hanson
  Christopher (I) (Alderman 1646)   3, 8, 9, 12, 14, 17, 18, 24, 25, 34, 42, 43, 44, 47, 48, 49, 59, 61, 64, 65, 78, 84, 85, 86, 94, 100, 101, 112, 113, 122, 491
  Christopher (II)   3, 4, 21, 22, 26, 40, 49, 65, 66, 102, 124, 135, 151, 170, 187, 200, 228, 242, 249, 250, 262, 265, 272, 282, 463
  Christopher (III)   463
  George (I)   77, 79, 86, 123, 134, 150, 199, 214, 227, 261, 302, 311
  George (II)   290
  Thomas (Alderman 1665–66)   xxv, lvi, lviii, 3, 12, 14, 15, 17, 22, 25, 34, 38, 39, 40, 42, 43, 44, 47, 48, 51, 56, 57, 58, 59, 63, 64, 69, 72, 73, 76, 77, 78, 79, 80, 81, 82, 84, 85, 86, 87, 89, 92, 98, 99, 101, 123, 134, 140, 142, 486, 491
Hardell, Richard   313, 314
Hardwick, Robert   313, 314
Harnesse, Mark   10, 108, 136, 221
Harrington, Captain Thomas   xlvi, xlvii, xlix, l, lvi, 6, 17, 216, 244, 251, 262, 272, 282, 289, 303, 309, 311, 312, 313, 315, 319, 320, 330, 331, 340, 342, 354, 366, 377, 388, 397, 403, 430, 438, 444, 449, 459, 469, 480, 491
Haskard (Haskerd, Hascard)
  Henry   327, 333
  Thomas   25
  William (Alderman 1693–94 & 1699–1700)   liv, 151, 153, 169, 170, 186, 187, 190, 200, 203, 214, 216, 227, 228, 237, 242, 244, 249, 250, 251, 253, 254, 262, 271, 273, 281, 285, 286, 288, 289, 295, 302, 351, 352, 362, 365, 374, 375, 376, 379, 386, 387, 394, 395, 400, 402, 403, 404, 406, 407, 408, 409, 411, 419, 434, 437, 439, 441, 443, 444, 445, 446, 447, 448, 449, 450, 455, 459, 464, 465, 468, 474, 476, 479, 480, 487, 491
Hatfield (Hatfeild)
  Edward   463
  Thomas (I)   3, 4, 23, 25, 26, 40, 42, 45, 47, 57, 66, 114, 115, 123, 134, 159, 160, 169, 186, 227, 270, 288, 295, 311, 365, 369
  Thomas (II)   297, 330, 364, 454, 460, 463, 469, 479
  William   481
Hawdin(g) (Hawden)
  Hanson   374
  Richard   374
  Widow Alice   206, 207, 412, 463, 473
Hawles, Edward   312
Haycocke
  John   266, 369
  William   370
Hayes
  William (I)   61, 439, 474
  William (II)   439
Herbert, Roger   312
Hickabotham (Higabothom, Higgabothom, Higgabothom, Higginbottom, Higginbotton, Higinbotham)
  James   469, 480
  William   352, 365, 369, 377, 395, 396, 403, 404, 431, 439, 450, 460, 469, 480
Hickson (Hixon, Hixson)
  Richard   129, 134, 135, 150, 151, 156, 169, 170, 175, 186, 187, 199, 210, 219, 241, 250, 254, 256, 271, 274, 275, 279, 285, 315, 387, 388, 396, 404, 420, 456, 464
  Thomas   410
  William   175, 210
Hide, Dr   358
Hill, Lawrence   xlii
Hinson, William   226

INDEX OF PERSONAL NAMES

Hipwith (Hipworth)
  Isaac (Isacke) (I)   196
  Isaac (Isaack) (II)   290
Hobson, John   12, 105, 129
Hodgkinson, William   xi, xviii, xix, xxv, xxxiii, xxxvii, xli, lv, lviii, lx, 3, 25, 44, 65, 86, 101, 123, 134, 150, 169, 186, 199, 214, 227, 241, 249, 261, 270, 277, 278
Hodgson (Hudchson)
  Anthony   216
  Thomas   78, 89, 101, 123, 124, 134, 135, 150, 151, 169, 170, 187, 190, 199, 200, 214, 221, 228, 234, 242, 250, 262, 266, 271, 279
  William   208
Hodson
  Henry   338
  Hodsons wife   338, 356
Holley (Halley, Hawly, Hawley, Hauley)
  Christopher   57, 138
  Richard (I) (Alderman 1671 & 1682–83)   xxxiv, 3, 4, 12, 23, 25, 26, 30, 35, 38, 39, 41, 44, 45, 46, 47, 48, 52, 53, 56, 57, 58, 59, 65, 66, 68, 72, 77, 80, 86, 92, 94, 101, 103, 112, 114, 119, 122, 123, 128, 133, 134, 141, 149, 150, 161, 162, 163, 165, 166, 167, 168, 169, 170, 171, 172, 177, 182, 189, 190, 196, 199, 207, 214, 216, 217, 227, 231, 241, 249, 258, 261, 269, 270, 272, 273, 277, 279, 281, 285, 287, 288, 289, 292, 293, 294, 295, 296, 297, 298, 299, 300, 301, 302, 303, 486, 491
  Richard (II)   80, 87, 102, 107, 124, 135, 151, 170
  Widow   166
Hollingworth, Widow   317, 335, 339
Holme   338
Holmes, John   414
Holt (Hoult)
  Hugh   31, 38, 177, 191, 195, 206, 225
  Widow (I)   317, 335, 339, 412
  Widow (II)   371
Horner, John   xxxi, xxxii, 136
Horsefield (Horefeild, Horsfield), Thomas   lxviii, 142, 143, 159, 201, 209
Horseman, Mr Thomas   4, 26, 45, 66, 87, 152, 170, 171, 187, 188, 200, 201, 228, 229, 242, 243, 251, 263, 272, 282, 289, 303, 312, 320, 322, 331, 342, 353, 354, 366, 377, 388, 397, 403, 430, 438, 444, 449, 459, 469, 480
Hotchkin(s) (Hodgkins, Hodgson, Holtchkin)
  Anthony (I)   xxviii, 8, 25, 26, 40, 44, 45, 47, 65, 66, 68, 69, 80, 86, 87, 92, 99, 101, 102, 103, 105, 108, 112, 123, 130, 134, 145, 150, 154, 157, 163, 165, 169, 172, 186, 190, 199, 203, 207, 214, 215, 217, 223, 227, 229, 232, 241, 249, 251, 255, 256, 261, 270, 277, 281, 288, 295, 382, 491
  Anthony (II)   382, 387, 388, 395, 396, 410, 412, 413, 451, 491
  Charles   349
Hubbert (Hubbard, Hibbert), Henry   249, 250, 251, 256, 261, 262, 270, 271, 282, 285, 288, 296
Huddlestone, Francis   312, 313
Hudson
  Richard   15
  Widow   15
Humes, Henry (Alderman 1672–73)   xxviii, 3, 6, 11, 12, 14, 25, 29, 34, 35, 38, 39, 41, 44, 65, 86, 98, 99, 101, 115, 119, 123, 128, 132, 134, 138, 140, 143, 144, 150, 154, 161, 162, 163, 168, 169, 173, 176, 178, 180, 182, 184, 186, 189, 191, 193, 194, 195, 197, 198, 199, 200, 205, 207, 214, 217, 224, 227, 232, 237, 241, 244, 245, 249, 255, 256, 261, 263, 270, 273, 486, 491
Hunt, William   313, 314
Hurst
  John   lviii, 137, 205, 312, 346
  Lewis   lviii, 312, 337, 343, 344, 355, 359, 361
  Mr   217
  Mrs   207
  Richard (I)   54, 71, 75, 178, 209
  Richard (II)   312
  Robert   145
  Dr Thomas   xxxviii, 12, 30, 39, 54, 71, 80, 81, 90, 126, 145, 154, 344, 361, 372
Hussey, Bridget   11, 14
Hutchin(e) (Hutching, Hutchkin)
  [blank] Hutchin   431
  George   xxxviii, 299, 371

Hugh   4, 7, 12, 14, 25, 30, 44, 56, 65, 68, 75, 80, 82, 90, 96, 97, 98, 492
John (I)   249, 261, 270
John (II)   475
Joseph   345, 365, 366, 376, 377, 387, 388, 396, 405, 420, 440, 474
Mr   404
Samuel   334, 376, 377, 387, 388, 396, 403, 418
Thomas   xlv, xlvii, 266, 289, 296, 297, 301, 303, 304, 305, 308, 311, 316, 320, 322, 331, 332, 341, 343, 353, 366, 368, 377, 390, 426, 451, 475, 492
William   395, 396, 403, 406, 408, 413, 420
Hutchison (Hutchinson), Roger   352, 366, 396, 404, 431, 450, 460, 469, 480

Idle, Robert   356, 387, 388, 395, 403, 408, 410
Inkerson (Ingerson)
    John (I)   3, 25, 44, 65, 86, 150, 169, 186, 199, 214, 307, 370
    John (II)   370
Ireland, Thomas (Alderman 1680–81; Mayor 1687–88)   xxxvi, xliv, xlvi, xlvii, li, lii, 39, 44, 45, 50, 53, 56, 57, 58, 63, 66, 68, 69, 71, 75, 82, 86, 94, 101, 123, 131, 134, 150, 154, 169, 181, 186, 189, 190, 199, 214, 216, 227, 237, 241, 249, 261, 270, 273, 277, 279, 280, 281, 283, 284, 286, 287, 288, 295, 306, 308, 311, 319, 330, 335, 339, 340, 341, 342, 344, 345, 346, 347, 348, 349, 351, 352, 361, 364, 375, 377, 378, 395, 408, 486, 492

James II, King   xliii, xliv, xlvi, xlviii, xlix, l, li, lii, lx
James, Christopher   99
Jervas, John   222
Johnson
    Henry   222, 249, 281, 288, 295, 319, 330, 341, 350, 368, 451, 455
    Martin   313, 314
    Thomas   313
    William   418
Jordan, William   86

Katherine, Mrs   46, 53

Keale
    John   38, 76
    Joseph   414
    Thomas   414
Kel(l)ham
    George   29
    Henry   163, 244
    Thomas (I)   256
    Thomas (II)   424
    Widow   382
Kenion (Kenyon)
    Edward   4, 26, 45, 49, 66, 87, 102, 115, 124, 135, 151, 156, 170
    George   115
    Thomas   192, 200, 214, 227, 241, 242, 250, 262, 271, 289, 295, 296, 302, 303, 310
King, Edward   313, 314
Kirchival, James   65
Kirkby (Kirkbye, Kerkby,), Mr   4, 151, 170, 187, 200, 228, 242, 250, 263, 271, 282, 289, 303, 312, 331, 353, 366, 378, 388, 397, 403, 430, 444, 449, 459, 469, 480
Kirke (Kerke, Kirk)
    Anthony (Antony) (Alderman 1702–03)   lii, 249, 250, 251, 262, 270, 271, 282, 289, 296, 302, 303, 341, 349, 352, 353, 356, 362, 368, 376, 387, 390, 395, 419, 436, 437, 443, 448, 449, 450, 455, 457, 458, 459, 460, 463, 464, 465, 467, 468, 470, 471, 472, 473, 474, 475, 476, 477, 478, 479, 480, 487, 492
    John   441, 450, 457, 460
    Widow   139
    William (Alderman 1700–01)   lix, 160, 199, 214, 228, 241, 242, 250, 262, 266, 271, 275, 279, 321, 326, 328, 330, 331, 338, 341, 342, 343, 352, 353, 356, 360, 365, 367, 369, 370, 376, 384, 387, 393, 395, 402, 404, 405, 406, 409, 415, 419, 422, 425, 428, 431, 437, 443, 444, 445, 447, 448, 449, 450, 451, 452, 453, 454, 455, 456, 457, 458, 459, 460, 464, 465, 468, 474, 475, 476, 479, 487, 492
Kirkham, William   436
Knewstubbs (Knewstubbe)
    Henry   313

William   7, 29, 96, 102, 124, 134, 150,
    169, 186, 199, 214, 227, 241
Knight
    William (I)   175, 262, 272, 283, 289, 296,
        303, 352, 353, 463
    William (II)   463

Laine(s) (Lane), William   lvii, 3, 4, 21, 23,
    25, 26, 41, 44, 45, 50, 65, 66, 69, 73, 75,
    76, 80, 83, 86, 87, 101, 102, 105, 107,
    108, 111, 112, 113, 124, 135, 159
Lake, Sir Edward   32
Lambert
    Dr   358
    John   348
Langley
    Judith   452
    Robert   276, 289, 295, 296, 300, 303,
        308, 352, 353, 366, 377, 379, 383,
        388, 396, 449, 450, 459, 460, 461,
        468, 469, 470, 479, 485
    William   30
Langton, Francis   338, 367, 377, 378, 388,
    395, 396, 403, 408, 410, 424, 428, 430,
    446, 449, 492
Larke
    Edward   266
    William   249
Lasselles, George   313
Laxton, Zachary   xxviii, 30
Leeming
    Mrs Alice   153, 157, 171, 336
    Richard (Alderman 1666–67)   xxiii,
        xxxviii, lvi, lvii, 3, 6, 12, 14, 15, 16,
        17, 20, 21, 22, 25, 32, 33, 44, 47, 48,
        59, 64, 73, 75, 77, 78, 84, 85, 86, 90,
        91, 94, 95, 96, 97, 98, 99, 100, 101,
        102, 103, 105, 106, 123, 125, 136,
        137, 140, 486, 492
    Walter   lvi, 77
Leivesley (Leivesly)
    Edward (Alderman 1689–90 & 1696–97)
        xxxvi, 3, 25, 26, 41, 45, 50, 65, 66,
        69, 76, 84, 86, 102, 124, 135, 150,
        151, 152, 164, 170, 177, 178, 182,
        186, 190, 199, 203, 214, 218, 221,
        224, 227, 241, 249, 261, 266, 271,
        281, 285, 288, 291, 295, 302, 321,
        351, 352, 359, 362, 364, 365, 368,
        369, 370, 371, 372, 373, 375, 376,
        377, 387, 390, 409, 413, 415, 418,
        420, 422, 423, 424, 425, 426, 427,
        428, 429, 430, 431, 432, 449, 452,
        459, 460, 465, 466, 486, 487, 492
    Jane   466
    Thomas   266, 289, 295, 296, 303, 330,
        352, 353, 366, 376, 377, 388, 392,
        396, 404
Lenton
    Benjamin   266
    Cornelius   450, 469, 477, 479
    John (I) (Alderman 1671–72)   xxx, lvii,
        3, 14, 16, 25, 44, 57, 63, 65, 68, 71,
        73, 74, 80, 82, 86, 91, 92, 101, 108,
        122, 123, 128, 131, 133, 134, 141,
        147, 149, 151, 161, 162, 168, 169,
        172, 173, 175, 176, 177, 178, 179,
        180, 181, 182, 184, 186, 187, 189,
        190, 191, 196, 199, 205, 212, 214,
        222, 227, 231, 237, 241, 244, 246,
        249, 255, 258, 261, 262, 263, 270,
        273, 275, 336, 486, 492
    John (II)   434, 450, 457, 460, 469
    William   277, 434, 450
Lewen(s) (Lewin), Widow   194, 195, 210
Lightfoot
    Henry   482
    William   320
Lindsey, Robert, Third Earl of   xxv, xxvi,
    xl, xli, xliv, xlvi, xlix, 51, 53, 54, 55,
    255
Little, Robert   30
Lockton, John   397
Lomax, Edward   420, 431, 435, 440, 441,
    447, 450
Long (Longe)
    James   98, 158, 163, 165, 183
    John   218
    Myles   xliii, 267
    William   470
Lord
    Ashton   227, 241, 261
    John   314
Louis XIV, King of France   xlv
Low(e)
    Joseph   382, 387, 388, 393, 395, 400, 403,
        404, 412, 424, 428, 431, 433, 448,
        449, 457, 459, 460, 465, 467, 468,
        470, 474, 477, 479, 480, 485, 492
    Widow   440

Luddington, Mr   147
Lyon, Robert   485

Machin
　Edmund (Usher)   xxxvi, 381, 427
　Robert   341
Mallory, Thomas   235, 268
Manners (Maners), Thomas Baptist   452
Mantle, Thomas   320
Margetts, Richard   300
Markham, Sir Robert   xl, xli, xlii, lvi, 6, 12, 35, 49, 51, 256, 257, 258, 259, 261, 271, 275, 277, 344
Marshall
　Christopher   314, 315
　John   279, 297, 304, 312, 316, 328, 350, 352, 353, 362, 366, 372, 377, 388, 396, 432, 470, 473, 474, 482
　Thomas   102, 124, 135, 151, 170, 187, 200, 215, 228, 242, 250, 271, 282, 290, 303, 320, 331, 341, 352, 376, 387, 395, 403, 439, 450, 460, 469, 479
　wife and children   339, 344, 345, 355
　William (I)   50, 52
　William (II)   439
Martin(e)(s)
　John   292, 332, 365, 366, 377, 387, 388, 395, 396, 398, 424, 425, 452, 453, 454
　Robert   335, 354
　William   397, 431, 450, 457, 460, 468, 469, 477, 479
Mary, Queen   lv
Mason, Alexander   452, 460, 468, 469, 479, 480, 482, 483
Mastin, William   407
Mat(t)hew(s), Henry   312, 313
Matkin
　Percival (Perchivall)   193, 200, 213, 218
　Thomas (I) (Alderman 1676–77; Mayor 1686–87)   xxxvi, xlii, xlvii, xlix, 3, 4, 18, 20, 25, 29, 41, 44, 57, 65, 75, 86, 101, 103, 111, 117, 120, 123, 134, 150, 153, 154, 169, 182, 186, 190, 193, 197, 199, 207, 208, 213, 214, 222, 223, 226, 227, 235, 240, 241, 243, 244, 246, 248, 249, 250, 253, 255, 261, 265, 267, 270, 281, 285, 286, 288, 295, 298, 301, 302, 306, 311, 319, 327, 328, 329, 330, 331, 332, 333, 334, 335, 336, 337, 338, 339, 340, 341, 351, 355, 361, 364, 375, 378, 387, 395, 417, 486, 492
　Thomas (II)   xlii, 263, 434, 435
　Widow   114
　William (I)   xliii, 267
　William (II)   430, 441
Mawn, Widow   354
Mercer, William   436
Meres
　Nathaniell   83, 108
　Widow   109
Michin   115
Middlebrooke, John   115
Miller (Millner)
　George   403, 407, 430, 431
　John   39, 58, 62, 119, 189
　Mrs Frances   317, 335, 339, 382, 407, 412, 417, 426, 440, 446, 452, 455, 473, 481
Millin, Abraham   313, 314
Mills (Milles)
　George   440
　Thomas (I) (Alderman 1644–45, 1653–54 & 1664)   3, 7, 11, 14, 24, 25, 34, 42, 43, 44, 47, 48, 486, 492
　Thomas (II) (Usher)   xxxvi, 6, 12, 189, 232, 325, 332, 333, 337, 348, 372, 380
　Thomas (III) (Fellmonger)   46, 348, 353
　Thomas (IV)   476, 479
　William (I) (Alderman 1679)   xlii, 3, 4, 6, 7, 12, 14, 16, 20, 21, 23, 25, 26, 27, 28, 34, 35, 38, 39, 41, 42, 44, 47, 50, 65, 68, 72, 86, 88, 90, 93, 101, 123, 134, 150, 154, 169, 186, 199, 214, 219, 220, 222, 223, 226, 227, 235, 240, 241, 246, 248, 249, 254, 255, 258, 260, 261, 263, 265, 268, 269, 270, 272, 273, 486, 492
　William (II)   452
Milner, George   299, 454
Mitchell
　Mathew   305
　Widow   317, 335, 339, 407
Modena, Maria of   xliii
Monmouth, James, Duke of   1
Moore
　James   29

John 313
Mr 366
Robert 95, 295, 296, 299, 303
Thomas 313
Mounson, Sir John 11
Mountague, Robert xxv, 30, 53, 54, 55
Musson
  Francis 370
  Henry (I) 362, 370
  Henry (II) 452
  James 454

Nall (Nalle), Mark xlv, xlvii, xlix, 283, 302, 303, 306, 308, 311, 319, 332, 492
Neale, Daniel 481
Newball
  Duckar (Ducker) 244, 321, 336
  John 321, 378, 414, 431, 432, 442
  Samuel 374, 414
  William 3, 25, 44, 65, 86
Newcom(b)e
  August(ine) 305, 382
  Edward 481
  John (I) xlvii, 129, 170, 187, 190, 200, 214, 231, 242, 250, 262, 271, 282, 286, 289, 295, 296, 297, 302, 303, 307, 308, 311, 319, 321, 322, 330, 331, 341, 350, 351, 353, 355, 358, 360, 361, 362, 363, 365, 366, 370, 375, 376, 381, 385, 387, 390, 395, 396, 400, 402, 403, 404, 405, 409, 415, 418, 419, 422, 433, 493
  John (II) 353, 376, 377, 396, 398, 399, 453
  Richard 382
  Thomas 453
Newdigate, Serjent xxvi, 56
Newton
  Humphrey 313, 314
  Sir Isaac xxvi, xxxiii
  Sir John xxvi, xlii, xliii, xliv, xlv, xlix, l, 17, 54, 55, 264
  John (I) xxxix, xlii, xlix, 264
  John (II) 30, 170
  John (III) 484
  Nicholas (I) 156, 166, 169, 179, 186, 194
  Nicholas (II) 434
  Richard (I) 156
  Richard(II) 265

William (I) 158, 160, 169, 170, 186, 187, 200, 210, 211, 214, 227, 242, 244, 250, 261, 262, 271, 281, 288, 295, 341, 366, 374, 376, 387, 396, 401, 425, 434, 484
William (II) 484
Niccolls, William lix, 445, 466
Nidd
  Ralph 126, 135
  Widow lvii, 98, 110, 189
Nix 378
  Edward 481
Nixon, Thomas 319, 320, 331, 355, 370, 395, 396, 404, 408
Noble, Eleanor 99
Normansell (Normansall), Nathaniell (Nathan) 336, 354, 370, 401
North, Richard 290, 312
Norwell, Mr 462

Oates, Titus xlii
Oldes, William 312, 313
Oldfield (Oldfeild)
  James 190
  Sir John 313, 314
  Thomas (I) 3, 19, 493
  Thomas (II) 190, 200, 216
Oliver, Joseph 401
Orme, John 313, 314
Orson, Robert 290, 302, 311, 319, 330, 341, 366, 398, 403, 430, 431, 435, 450, 453, 454, 460, 468, 479, 482, 483
Osborne
  Charles (I) 349, 353
  Charles (II) 482
  Edward 192
  John (I) 266
  John (II) 350
  John (III) 350, 354, 447, 450, 457, 460, 465
  Ralph 3, 25, 44, 66, 87, 95, 102, 124, 134, 169, 186, 199, 214, 228, 241, 249, 261, 270, 281, 288, 296, 302, 311, 319, 330, 341, 353, 365, 377, 388, 395, 403, 431, 450, 480
  Robert 465
  Thomas 305
  William (I) 266
  William (II) 460, 469

Owin (Owen)
  John   314, 341, 352, 359, 365, 376, 380, 381, 387, 395, 403, 434
  Richard   249, 250, 251, 261, 262, 270, 271, 282, 289, 296, 303, 351, 352, 365, 369, 376, 388, 395, 396
  Robert   446

Palfryman, Thomas   370, 371
Palmer
  Lively   455
  William   4, 9, 26, 37, 45, 49, 55, 62, 66, 87, 88, 89, 93, 96, 99, 110, 111, 159, 179
Pape
  John (I)   65, 101, 102, 118, 121, 124, 126, 135, 140, 144, 150, 154, 169, 172, 186, 193, 195, 199, 214, 227, 231, 241, 243, 493
  John (II)   276, 282, 289, 295, 296, 303, 383
Parham, Jonathan   31, 38, 46, 77, 91
Parker
  Edward (I)   433, 441, 455, 456, 460, 462
  Edward (II)   447, 460
  William   336, 341, 352, 353, 354, 366, 376, 377, 388, 398, 407, 451
Parkin, Widow   74
Parkins (Perkins)
  Mrs   323, 372
  Robert (I)   xi, xviii, xix, xxv, xxvi, xlvi, xlvii, lv, 4, 11, 13, 14, 15, 26, 33, 68, 192, 278, 281, 288, 295, 302, 308, 309, 311, 315, 323
  Robert (II)   334, 355
  William (I)   xxiii, xliii, lvi, 6, 15, 41, 50, 52, 56, 95, 143, 163, 267
  William (II)   95, 314
Parnham
  Henry   462, 481
  Thomas   108, 109
  William   462
Pateman, John   108, 117, 119
Pawlett (Pauley, Paulet, Paulett, Pawly)
  Edward   xix, xx, xxviii, xxix, xxxi, xlii, xliv, xlvii, lvii, lviii, 25, 26, 27, 28, 38, 40, 44, 45, 46, 47, 48, 50, 52, 53, 55, 56, 57, 65, 69, 75, 77, 79, 80, 82, 86, 91, 96, 101, 103, 113, 123, 125, 126, 130, 134, 135, 136, 137, 143, 144, 150, 152, 154, 163, 165, 169, 171, 172, 175, 180, 186, 190, 199, 203, 207, 209, 214, 224, 227, 231, 232, 233, 236, 237, 241, 243, 244, 245, 249, 251, 255, 258, 261, 270, 273, 277, 281, 283, 285, 288, 290, 293, 295, 296, 298, 302, 311, 319, 322, 330, 333, 493
  Mrs Elizabeth   474
  Robert   xxxv, xlii
Paxtons, Richard   16
Peareson (Pearson)
  Anne (I)   182
  Anne (II)   435
  James   215
  Katherine   99
  Richard   192, 268
Peeke   74
Pell (Pelle), Walter   15, 56, 88, 114, 159, 211
Pike, William   239
Pillsworth, William   475, 477, 479
Plummer (Plumer), John   xxviii, 44, 65, 66, 75, 76, 84, 86, 87, 94, 101, 112, 114, 117, 118, 119, 125
Poole
  Andrew (I)   3, 19, 21, 27
  Andrew (II)   251
  Andrew (III)   350
  Christopher   350
  Elizabeth   455
  John   109, 129
  John (apothecary)   li, 175, 321, 346, 347, 348, 434, 452, 493
  John (haberdasher)   li, 223, 336, 346, 347, 493
  Joseph   223
  Rev Richard (Usher)   xxxvi, 156, 245
  Richard   50, 80, 189, 206, 210, 232, 266, 286
  Thomas (I)   206, 208, 312, 465
  Thomas (II)   434
  William (I)   259, 317
  William (II)   465
Portwood, Lambert   95
Potterton, James   314
Price, Robert   313, 314
Prince, Samuel   464
Procter (Prockter, Proctor), Samuel   xi, xviii, xix, xlvii, liv, lv, 92, 311, 312, 315,

INDEX OF PERSONAL NAMES

319, 330, 341, 352, 353, 365, 376, 380, 387, 395, 404, 419, 431, 442, 447, 493
Pyke
  Nicholas   456
  William   456

Quew, Robert   216
Quincey
  Richard   440
  William   395, 396, 397, 403, 404, 408, 440
Quiningborow (Quiningborew, Quiningbro, Quiningbrow, Quiningborough, Quiningbrough, Quinningborough, Quinningbrow)
  Daniel   37
  Robert   392, 434, 435
  Thomas (I)   175, 228, 241, 242, 250, 262, 271, 283, 289, 296, 302, 305, 319, 354, 391, 395, 398, 453
  Thomas (II)   452, 453
Quire, Nicholas   405
Quiver, Nicholas   445

Rastall (Restell)
  Mr   204
  Thomas   313, 314
Rawdes, Captain   235
Rawlinson (Rallison, Rollinson, Rollingson)
  Edward (Alderman 1673–74)   3, 25, 38, 39, 41, 44, 57, 65, 101, 118, 123, 134, 145, 146, 150, 154, 168, 169, 176, 178, 184, 186, 190, 193, 197, 198, 199, 202, 203, 204, 207, 209, 210, 212, 213, 214, 217, 225, 227, 235, 486, 493
  Gabriel   431
  John   259, 266, 295, 319, 370, 396
  Joseph   431, 435, 441, 451
  Samuel   375, 379
  Thomas (I)   190, 214, 262, 271, 282, 289, 296, 302, 303, 310, 311, 319, 392, 403, 404, 408, 431, 435, 444, 445, 449, 450, 457, 459, 460, 462, 465, 468, 474, 479
  Thomas (II)   370
Ray, Widow   481
Read
  George (I)   3, 4, 23, 26, 44, 45, 65, 66, 69, 72, 84, 86, 87, 102, 124, 135, 150, 151, 169, 170, 186, 187, 200, 228, 242, 250, 262, 270, 271, 275, 282, 289, 296, 302, 306, 351, 439, 469, 493
  George (II)   140, 151
  George (III)   439
  John   450
  Richard   433
  Widow   426
Rear(e), Thomas   266, 311, 341, 352, 353, 366, 377, 390
Richardson
  Jermin   61
  Peter   194, 195
Riseing, William   3, 4, 14, 15, 17, 23, 25, 26, 40, 44, 45, 69
Roades (Rhodes), Samuel   3, 19, 21, 25, 44, 65, 86, 90, 101, 123
Robinson   11
  John (I) (Alderman 1690–91 & 1697–98)   xxxvi, xlvii, li, 130, 134, 150, 151, 169, 170, 176, 181, 186, 187, 189, 190, 192, 199, 200, 202, 204, 207, 215, 220, 225, 227, 241, 249, 253, 258, 261, 270, 279, 281, 282, 288, 295, 298, 302, 306, 311, 319, 330, 332, 333, 335, 341, 347, 351, 352, 362, 364, 365, 371, 375, 378, 379, 380, 381, 382, 383, 384, 385, 386, 387, 395, 415, 422, 426, 428, 429, 430, 431, 432, 433, 434, 435, 436, 437, 438, 449, 454, 459, 468, 479, 486, 487, 494
  John (II)   321, 330, 332, 333
  Thomas   312, 319, 330, 440, 447, 450, 457, 460, 468, 476, 479, 480, 481
Robson, Widow   30
Rollinson (Rawlinson)
  James   387
  John   xlvi, xlvii, 311, 317, 319, 330, 340, 494
Rolt
  Olliver   483
  Sir Thomas   455
Rookesby (Rookby, Rookeby)
  Mrs   359
  Nathaniell (Nathan)   163, 210, 219, 234, 249, 250, 251, 262, 271, 285, 289, 296, 303, 422, 441
  Thomas   422, 423, 431, 435, 447, 450

Roos (Rosse), Lord   xxiv, xl, xli, 166, 252, 255. *See also* Rutland, John, Ninth Earl of
Rowley (Rouly, Rowlet, Rowlett, Rowly)
  Anthony   397
  Benjamin   482
  Thomas   115, 124, 135, 151, 170, 200, 214, 227, 228, 231, 242, 250, 257, 261, 270, 271, 274, 275, 282, 286, 290, 295, 296, 302, 304, 307, 310, 323, 352, 356, 357, 397, 494
Rudd, Edward   30
Rudkin
  Andrew   450, 460, 468, 479
  Henry   lvii, 9, 35, 58, 59, 80, 95, 103, 105, 106, 107, 108, 114, 115, 119
Rutland
  John, Eighth Earl of   xxiv, xxv, xxvi, xxxiii, xliv, 13, 15, 29, 53, 166, 252
  John, Ninth Earl of   xlix, 332

Sanderson
  Dr   92
  Dr Robert, Bishop of Lincoln   13
Sandford, John   79, 81
Saule
  Edward   313
  Mr   35, 37, 39, 42, 55, 57
Scarborow
  Edward   290, 325
  Francis   475
Scot (Scott)
  Anne   476
  John   3, 10, 66, 95, 116, 124, 134, 306, 319, 322, 323, 330, 353, 365, 377, 380, 388, 395, 431
  Silvanus   304
  Silvester   403
  William   44, 45, 50, 66, 69, 84, 86, 87, 102, 150, 288, 295, 302
Secker
  Edward (I) (Alderman 1688–89)   xxii, xliii, li, lii, liv, 136, 165, 166, 267, 304, 334, 346, 347, 348, 349, 350, 351, 352, 353, 354, 355, 356, 358, 359, 360, 362, 363, 364, 366, 367, 368, 383, 434, 442, 486, 494
  Edward (II)   434
  Mrs   xxiv, xxxii, 166

Segrave (Seagrave), Richard   165, 186, 190, 199, 216, 223, 229, 242, 250, 262, 271, 273, 281, 283, 288, 289, 295, 297, 302, 494
Selbie (Selby)
  Hellen   xxvii
  Widow   74
Sentance (Sentence), Richard   xlvii, 216, 302, 303, 311, 319, 322, 330, 332, 336, 339, 341, 353, 366, 377, 390, 421, 438, 455, 456, 494
Shaftesbury, Earl of   xliii, xliv
Sharp(e)
  John (I)   368
  John (II)   412
  Mr   425, 481
  Sharpes heirs   336
  Thomas   126, 134
Sheacroft (Shecraft), John   357
Sherriffe
  Amos   299, 463
  Thomas   463
Shootewell, John   118, 138, 209, 339, 431
Short(e)
  George (I)   3, 5, 9, 12, 14, 25, 27, 28, 33, 35, 44, 61, 63, 65, 68, 83, 86, 88, 89, 91, 93, 98, 101, 120, 123, 128, 133, 134, 138, 139, 140, 141, 149, 150, 154, 159, 161, 162, 163, 168, 182, 494
  George (II)   444, 450, 460, 469, 479
  Thomas (I) (Alderman 1667–68 & 1679–80)   xxviii, xliii, xliv, 3, 18, 24, 25, 34, 37, 38, 42, 43, 44, 47, 48, 49, 59, 61, 63, 64, 65, 75, 77, 78, 84, 86, 91, 94, 98, 100, 101, 104, 106, 107, 111, 112, 113, 115, 116, 117, 118, 121, 123, 124, 128, 132, 134, 137, 150, 169, 186, 199, 207, 213, 214, 215, 216, 219, 222, 223, 225, 226, 227, 231, 235, 236, 237, 240, 241, 243, 246, 248, 249, 250, 251, 255, 258, 261, 262, 267, 269, 270, 272, 273, 274, 275, 276, 277, 278, 279, 280, 281, 282, 288, 486, 494
  Thomas (II)   262, 271, 282, 283, 284, 295, 303, 304, 306, 308, 350, 352, 353, 365, 376, 387, 398, 404, 431, 444, 494
  Widow   436

INDEX OF PERSONAL NAMES 513

Sidgney (Sedley), Charles 312
Simpson
  John xx, 206, 265
  Mr 9, 15
  Stephen 69, 95
  Thomas xlvii, xlix, li, 292, 302, 303,
    306, 311, 319, 330, 335, 341, 347,
    348, 352, 365, 376, 385, 387, 393,
    394, 395, 398, 400, 494
  Widow 74, 94
Skevinton 378
Skipwith, Thomas xxxix, lvi, 30, 57, 72,
  89, 166, 192, 195, 220, 306
Slater
  Thomas 76
  Widow 4
Smith (Smyth)
  Captain 400
  Christopher 291
  Edmund 476, 479, 483
  Edward 175, 210
  Henry 420, 460, 469, 479
  Hugh 113, 207
  James 447
  John (Alderman 1695–96) xlvii, liv, 223,
    227, 229, 230, 232, 236, 241, 242,
    243, 244, 249, 250, 251, 256, 261,
    263, 270, 274, 279, 281, 282, 283,
    285, 289, 291, 295, 296, 302, 303,
    311, 316, 319, 320, 321, 322, 323,
    330, 341, 351, 352, 353, 365, 372,
    376, 380, 382, 385, 387, 394, 395,
    402, 403, 406, 409, 410, 412, 413,
    414, 415, 416, 417, 433, 434, 442,
    476, 487, 494
  Judith xxxviii, 317, 371
  Mr 427, 457
  Richard 334, 335
  Robert xxxviii, 3, 25, 36, 44, 65, 86,
    101, 175, 330, 335, 341, 353, 365,
    369, 372, 420, 454
Smithergall, Robert 438, 451, 460, 469, 477
Smithson, Robert 345, 381
Snow, Leonard 78
Solomon, Michael 383
Somerby, Simon 259
Sooley, Hugh 82
Southern(e)
  Robert 463
  William 208, 313, 463

Sparrow, Robert 180, 187, 190, 200, 214
Speedy
  Henry xxvii
  Joan xxvii
  Richard xxvii
Spottswood
  John 441
  Patrick 446
Stacey (Stacy)
  John 312
  Mountague lviii, 233, 235, 290, 312,
    322, 323
Stafford, John 452
Staley, William xlii
Stanser
  Thomas (I) 314, 444, 477
  Thomas (II) 444, 460, 469, 480
Starkey, Mr 37
Stevens (Steevens)
  John 216, 241, 262, 265, 281, 283, 288,
    289, 296, 297, 303, 462
  William 462
Stevenson, John 242, 262, 271, 282
Still
  Anne (widow) 11, 38, 55, 62
  Edward 55, 73, 81, 306
  John 102, 119, 121, 124, 134, 135, 150,
    152, 158, 169, 170, 177, 180, 186,
    187, 190, 200, 215, 217, 228, 232,
    234, 242, 250, 261, 262, 264, 265,
    483
  William (I) 55
  William (II) 306
Stilton, William 313
Stokes, Henry xxxiii, xxxiv, xxxvii, 28, 463
Storer (Storey, Storie)
  Edward 254, 260, 263, 272, 282, 289,
    303, 312, 320, 331, 342, 354, 377,
    388, 397, 403, 430, 438, 444, 449,
    459, 469, 480
  Mrs 425
Stow, George 313, 314
Sunderland, Robert, Second Earl of xxv
Sutton, Charles 469
Swingler, Thomas 397
Syston, Rev Thomas xxxiii, xxxiv, xxxvii,
  28, 29, 155, 156, 157, 161, 162, 463

Taylor (Tayler, Tailer)
  Anthony 241, 249, 431

514   INDEX OF PERSONAL NAMES

Arthur   xlvii, xlix, 302, 303, 304, 305,
    316, 317, 327, 330, 334, 353, 356,
    366, 377, 388, 396, 495
Elizabeth   473
John   3
Michael (Alderman 1662–63 & 1677–78)
    xx, xxi, xxiii, xxiv, xxv, xl, xli, xlv,
    lvi, 1, 8, 10, 11, 13, 15, 16, 20, 22, 24,
    25, 26, 28, 30, 32, 33, 34, 35, 38, 39,
    40, 41, 44, 47, 49, 51, 56, 63, 65, 68,
    69, 75, 77, 78, 94, 98, 101, 105, 115,
    119, 123, 126, 127, 130, 131, 134, 135,
    137, 138, 143, 150, 152, 156, 169, 172,
    174, 175, 180, 181, 186, 190, 193, 199,
    203, 204, 206, 210, 215, 216, 217, 219,
    221, 225, 227, 229, 231, 232, 237, 241,
    246, 247, 248, 249, 251, 254, 255, 257,
    258, 259, 260, 261, 262, 270, 273, 276,
    281, 282, 285, 288, 295, 296, 302, 308,
    486, 494
Michael (baker)   95
Richard   325
Thomas   15, 25, 26, 40, 42, 45, 47, 48,
    57, 66, 70, 87, 89, 102
Theyer, John   312
Thimbleby, Charles   252
Thompson (Tompson)
    Christopher   xliv, 14, 20, 26, 38, 45, 60,
    66, 75, 82, 98, 99, 101, 109, 123, 134,
    139, 150, 158, 169, 179, 186, 189, 197,
    199, 214, 227, 241, 249, 261, 263, 264,
    270, 273, 281, 290, 295, 495
    Robert   264, 270, 271, 282
Thornton, Robert   313, 314
Thorold (Thorrold)
    John   xlii, xlvii, xlix, l, lvii, 264, 311,
    319, 326, 327, 330, 341, 358, 421,
    427, 441, 450, 451, 457, 460, 469,
    474, 477, 479, 489, 495
    Nathaniel   313
    Robert   63, 68, 89, 94, 217, 219
    Sir William   xx, xxxix, xlii, xlix, lvii, 17,
    106, 136, 264
Threaves
    Armstrong   314, 325
    Catherine   452
Todkill
    Edward   307, 311, 319, 357, 365, 366,
    371, 376, 387, 393, 400, 495
    Mrs   455

Tomlinson
    Joseph (Alderman 1670–71)   xxiv, xxxiv,
    xxxv, 3, 10, 12, 14, 25, 27, 28, 30, 32,
    33, 34, 35, 36, 38, 44, 45, 46, 49, 52,
    53, 54, 57, 58, 65, 67, 75, 77, 80, 86,
    91, 94, 100, 101, 103, 112, 113, 122,
    123, 126, 128, 133, 134, 138, 141, 148,
    149, 150, 153, 154, 155, 156, 157, 158,
    159, 160, 161, 162, 164, 486, 495
    Mrs   167
    Widow Barksdale   309
Tomlyn
    Thomas   89, 113, 137, 205
    Widow   137
Toms, Widow   412, 446
Tonge (Tong, Tongue)
    Andrew   325, 328
    Israel   xlii
Towers, Thomas   54, 71, 180
Tredway, Robert   252
Trevillian
    Mr   35, 49, 53, 217
    Mrs   207, 382, 426
Trigge, Francis   lv
Tripp, Thomas   256
Troope, Thomas   153
Troughton, Rev John   xxxvii, 463
True
    John   482
    Thomas   465, 479, 481
Trueman, John   93
Turner
    Humphrey   262, 271, 282, 289, 297, 303,
    312, 320, 336
    John   xxxi, 3, 4, 6, 12, 20, 26, 30, 38,
    44, 45, 46, 48, 50, 53, 55, 57, 58, 60,
    75, 86, 94, 101, 111, 113, 123, 125,
    130, 134, 135, 136, 137, 138, 144,
    150, 154, 165, 169, 172, 175, 180,
    186, 190, 194, 195, 199, 203, 214,
    216, 219, 224, 227, 232, 235, 240,
    241, 243, 246, 248, 249, 251, 253,
    269, 495
    William   321, 330, 341, 352, 353, 354,
    365, 366, 371, 373, 376, 380, 387,
    395, 399, 404, 405, 422, 424, 431,
    432, 447, 448, 449, 495
Turnor (Turner), Edmund   xv, xl, lix, 146,
    179, 181, 182, 206, 211, 215, 217, 224,
    233, 426

INDEX OF PERSONAL NAMES

Twist, James 313
Tyerman, Mr 6
Tyrwhit (Terrwhit), Mr 11

Ulliott (Ulliot)
  Edward 3, 25, 44, 65, 86, 101, 123, 134, 150, 169, 186, 199, 207, 214, 227
  Thomas 266
  Widow 382

Vincent
  John (I) 175, 199, 217, 439, 455
  John (II) 455

Waineman
  Robert (I) 25, 44
  Robert (II) 266
Waite
  Elizabeth 147
  Richard 83, 108, 117, 119
Walgrave
  Alice 397, 441
  Christopher (I) 3, 261, 265, 270
  Christopher (II) 397
  Thomas 441, 450, 457, 460, 468, 469, 477, 479
  William 202, 249
Walker
  John 4, 7, 17, 25, 26, 30, 33, 35, 45, 46, 60, 63, 65, 66, 68, 75, 77, 79, 80, 82, 99, 102, 112, 119, 124, 150, 152, 154, 169, 180, 186, 190, 199, 204, 214, 227, 241, 249, 253, 495
  Rev William xxxiv, xxxv, xxxvi, 163, 164, 189, 325
Walles (Whalles), William 91, 140, 203, 218
Wallet(t)
  Thomas 313, 314
  William 313, 314
Walpoole, John 99
Walton, Thomas xxviii, 126, 232, 267, 332, 334, 344
Warein, William 218
Watson
  Edward (I) 58
  Edward (II) xlvii, 245, 261, 262, 270, 271, 278, 283, 284, 285, 286, 288, 289, 295, 296, 302, 304, 311, 315, 319, 323, 330, 333, 341, 352, 365, 368, 376, 379, 380, 387, 392, 393, 394, 395, 402, 407, 495
  John (I) (Alderman 1664) xxiii, xxiv, xxv, 3, 6, 7, 11, 12, 14, 18, 24, 25, 32, 33, 34, 42, 43, 44, 47, 48, 49, 50, 52, 53, 55, 56, 58, 60, 61, 62, 63, 64, 65, 66, 67, 68, 75, 77, 82, 86, 486, 495
  John (II) 259
  Martha (Mrs) 6, 58, 62
Weaver, John xlv, xlvi, 266, 288, 295, 296, 300, 302, 303, 305, 308, 319, 330, 344, 352, 353, 356, 362, 366, 369, 371, 372, 376, 387, 400, 450, 460, 468, 479, 495
Welbourne, Richard 350, 355
Welby
  John 12, 16, 39, 57, 68, 145, 154, 189, 207, 216, 217
  William lvi, 6, 12, 114
Weld, Mr 12
Wells
  Francis 234
  John 21
Wetherill, Charles 42, 139, 261, 282, 286, 289, 295, 296, 303, 324
Wharton, Abraham 313
Wheately (Wheatelye, Wheatly), Mr 4, 26, 45, 66, 87, 151, 170, 187, 200, 228, 242, 251, 263, 282, 289, 312, 320
Wheeler, Benjamin 317, 401
White
  John (I) 12, 20
  John (II) 481
Whittacre, Joseph 462, 468
Wickliffe, Thomas 321, 353, 366, 388, 397, 403, 430, 438, 449, 459, 469, 480
Wigmoore (Wigmore), John 307, 319, 340
Wilcock(s), John 352, 366, 396, 404, 431, 450, 460, 469, 479
Wildbore, John 355
Wiles (Wild, Wyld, Wyldes, Wyles), Richard 292, 298, 319, 330, 341, 376, 377, 388, 392, 396, 400, 405, 407, 410, 422, 424, 426, 432, 433, 435, 449, 459, 463, 468, 484, 495
Wilkinson
  Amos 265
  Gabriel 451
  Hugh xi, xxxvii, 28
  Mrs xxxvii, 97
Willbore, Aquilia 159

William (of Orange) III, King   liv, lv, lx
Williams, Major   399
Willoughby
　Peregrine   1
　Robert, Lord   1, 313, 314
Wilson (Willson)   368, 483
　Francis (I)   314
　Francis (II)   414, 430, 433, 435, 449, 459
　James   384
　Nehemiah   434
　Susannah   453
　Thomas   183, 184, 434, 451, 453, 455
　Widow   266, 278
　William   313
Wing (Winge)
　John (I) (Alderman 1678–79)   xli, xlii, xliii, l, lvi, 3, 10, 12, 25, 32, 44, 65, 75, 78, 86, 101, 123, 130, 134, 140, 145, 146, 150, 163, 169, 172, 173, 181, 182, 184, 186, 190, 193, 197, 199, 207, 212, 213, 214, 222, 223, 226, 227, 235, 240, 241, 246, 248, 249, 254, 258, 260, 261, 263, 264, 266, 267, 268, 270, 271, 273, 274, 277, 281, 284, 287, 288, 293, 295, 298, 301, 302, 306, 308, 322, 486, 495
　John (II) (of Denton)   110
　Mathias   336, 352, 353, 354
　Widow   110
　William   419, 431, 436, 441, 447, 450, 457, 460, 463, 464, 465, 466, 468, 469, 470, 471, 473, 474, 476, 479, 483
Wingfield, Counsellor   234
Winstanly, George   313
Wintor (Winter)
　Joseph   424
　Richard   4

Wollands (Woolands)
　Robert   137, 152, 201, 229
　Roger   230
Wood, Sir Henry   xxxix
Woodruffe (Woodroffe, Woodruft)
　Anne   252
　John   252
　Mr John   225, 259, 263, 282, 289, 303, 312, 313, 320, 331, 341, 354, 366, 377, 388, 397, 403, 430, 438, 444, 449, 459, 469, 480
Woods, Joseph   297, 325, 328, 330, 362, 372
Woulds
　John   305, 441, 479
　Richard   270, 330, 341, 366, 370, 376, 387, 395, 403, 450, 460, 469
Wray
　George (I)   101, 123
　George (II)   206, 208, 270, 288, 295, 302, 330, 341, 352, 365, 376, 387, 395
　Thomas   281
　Widow   446
Wright (Wrigt)
　Elizabeth   22
　Henry   123, 134, 150, 169, 186, 199, 214, 227, 239, 241, 249, 251, 261
　Mr Henry   12, 16, 22, 258, 259, 263, 272, 282, 289, 303, 320, 331, 342, 354, 366, 376, 388, 397, 403, 430, 438, 444, 449, 459, 469, 480
　William   206, 378
Wythey (Withey)
　John   292, 302, 311, 365, 366, 374, 376, 377, 387
　Matthew   xx, 6, 10, 11, 14, 292

Yeomans, Bartholomew   414
Young, Widow   425

INDEX OF PLACES

In Lincolnshire unless otherwise described.

Allington   110, 435
Aswardby   xl
Ayno (Agneho), Northants   260

Barkston   xiii
Belton   xiii, xxxiv, liv, 8, 22, 155, 157, 167, 356, 452
Belvoir (Belvoyre)   xli, 258, 259
Bethlem Hospital, Moorfields, London   424
Boothby Pagnell (Pannell)   xlvi, xlix, lvi, 244
Boston   xxii, xxviii, xxxii, xxxvii, xlvi, xlvii, lii, 21
Braceby   xiii, 132

Cambridge   xxvi
Carlton (Scroop)   147
Collyweston   xvi
Colsterworth   xiii, xxvi, xxxv, xxxvi
Culverthorpe (Hather thorpe)   264

Denton   xiii, lvi, 80, 83, 108, 110, 117, 119, 137, 147, 152, 201, 203, 218, 229, 230, 290, 399, 412
Dunsthorpe   63

Easton   xiii
Edinburgh   xxviii

Gainsborough   223
Gonerby (Gunnerby, Gunwarby)   xiii, lviii, 8, 54, 142, 165, 239, 247, 258, 289, 290, 360, 363
Grantham, streets and places within
  Angel Inn   xiii, xxxi
  Castlegate   xiii, xvi, xxxvii, xxxix, 4, 5, 23, 26, 41, 45, 57, 66, 69, 79, 84, 87, 88, 102, 104, 106, 107, 108, 121, 124, 135, 148, 151, 154, 158, 161, 168, 170, 183, 187, 200, 206, 210, 211, 214, 225, 228, 230, 241, 242, 249, 250, 261, 271, 278, 282, 289, 296, 300, 302, 303, 312, 319, 331, 341, 352, 353, 363, 365, 366, 376, 377, 385, 386, 387, 388, 395, 396, 404, 408, 414, 422, 428, 431, 437, 442, 450, 453, 457, 460, 469, 470, 474, 475, 477, 479, 484
  Church Lane   54, 75
  Conduit   xxxix, lix, 33, 35, 36, 37, 38, 42, 94, 96, 105, 107, 109, 118, 119, 209, 239, 277, 299, 300, 339, 408, 420
  Coney Greens   367, 457
  Corpus Christi Choir   xvii, liv. *See also* St Wulfram's Church
  Dimsdale House   xlvi, 13, 16, 17, 62
  Earlsfield   xiii
  Finkin (Finkle) Street   xiii
  George Inn   xiii, 39, 175
  Grammar School   xviii, xxxiii, xxxv, 190. *See also Index of Subjects*
  Guild Hall   xvii, xviii, xxxiii, 160, 324
  High Street   xiii, xvi, xvii, 3, 4, 5, 23, 25, 26, 40, 42, 44, 45, 57, 61, 65, 66, 69, 79, 84, 86, 87, 88, 101, 102, 107, 121, 123, 124, 134, 135, 138, 139, 148, 151, 161, 166, 167, 169, 170, 182, 183, 186, 199, 200, 206, 214, 225, 227, 228, 229, 230, 231, 239, 241, 242, 249, 250, 261, 262, 270, 271, 282, 289, 295, 296, 299, 302, 303, 311, 319, 324, 330, 341, 352, 353, 362, 363, 365, 366, 376, 377, 385, 387, 388, 395, 396, 403, 408, 411, 414, 422, 427, 430, 436, 442, 450, 457, 460, 469, 470, 474, 477, 480, 483, 484
  Horse Churchyard   293, 320
  Market Place (Street)   xiii, xvi, xix, 3, 4, 5, 7, 23, 25, 26, 36, 38, 40, 44, 45, 61, 65, 66, 69, 76, 78, 79, 83, 86, 87, 88, 92,

96, 101, 102, 104, 107, 121, 123, 124, 134, 135, 148, 151, 152, 167, 169, 170, 183, 186, 194, 199, 200, 202, 209, 214, 227, 228, 239, 241, 242, 249, 250, 261, 262, 265, 270, 271, 278, 282, 284, 288, 295, 296, 299, 302, 303, 311, 319, 330, 336, 341, 352, 353, 356, 363, 365, 366, 376, 377, 385, 387, 388, 395, 396, 403, 408, 414, 421, 422, 427, 430, 436, 438, 442, 450, 457, 460, 469, 477, 479, 484

Mill Pingle   8, 12, 71, 75
Pest House   xxvi, xxvii, 16, 32, 75, 92, 174, 471
Red Lion (Lyon) Inn   v, xix, xlvi, lv, lvi, lviii, lix, 6, 11, 51, 72, 75, 77, 78, 89, 90, 91, 95, 97, 107, 109, 110, 127, 131, 136, 141, 142, 143, 145, 159, 201, 215, 218, 219, 220, 232, 233, 235, 237, 285, 322, 344, 346, 440, 445, 482
Sand Pit Lane   xxxii, 160, 176, 208, 266
Slate Mill (North Mill)   lix, 8, 16, 30, 38, 45, 220, 267, 316, 326, 337, 343, 357, 361, 363, 370, 390, 391, 404, 405, 419, 420, 424, 432, 466, 476, 483
St Catherine's Road   xiii
St Wulfram's Church   xiii, xvii, xviii, xxxi, xxxii, xxxiii, xxxix, xlvii, xlviii, lv, 13, 15, 31, 32, 37, 74, 93, 94, 106, 108, 111, 112, 113, 125, 126, 153, 173, 179, 204, 224, 266, 305, 321, 324, 335, 338, 354, 360, 362, 363, 382, 406, 418, 445, 454, 455, 461, 476, 483. *See also* Corpus Christi Choir
Swinegate   xiii, xvi, xxxvii, 3, 4, 5, 23, 25, 26, 32, 41, 45, 46, 49, 53, 66, 69, 73, 79, 84, 86, 87, 88, 102, 104, 110, 121, 124, 136, 148, 152, 154, 158, 168, 169, 170, 177, 183, 186, 188, 200, 210, 214, 228, 241, 242, 244, 249, 250, 261, 262, 270, 271, 282, 289, 295, 296, 300, 302, 303, 312, 319, 330, 341, 352, 353, 363, 365, 366, 376, 377, 382, 385, 387, 388, 395, 396, 403, 408, 415, 422, 428, 431, 437, 442, 450, 457, 460, 469, 470, 475, 477, 479, 484
Vine Street   210, 239

Walkergate (Watergate)   xiii, xvi, lv, 3, 4, 5, 7, 23, 25, 26, 40, 44, 45, 65, 66, 69, 73, 79, 84, 86, 87, 88, 102, 104, 109, 119, 121, 124, 127, 134, 135, 148, 151, 158, 168, 169, 170, 180, 183, 186, 200, 206, 214, 227, 228, 241, 242, 249, 250, 261, 262, 270, 271, 282, 289, 295, 296, 299, 302, 303, 312, 319, 330, 341, 352, 353, 363, 365, 366, 376, 377, 385, 387, 388, 395, 396, 403, 408, 415, 422, 428, 431, 435, 436, 442, 450, 457, 460, 469, 470, 477, 480, 483, 484
Well Lane   xvi, 317, 470
Well Lane (Wellaine, Welham) Mill (South Mill, Town Mill)   lix, 8, 17, 30, 38, 46, 52, 267, 320, 323, 326, 337, 342, 348, 357, 360, 363, 369, 371, 390, 391, 404, 405, 419, 424, 432, 434, 436, 446, 475, 476
Westgate   xiii, xvi, xxxvii, 3, 4, 5, 9, 23, 25, 26, 27, 40, 44, 45, 65, 66, 69, 84, 86, 87, 88, 97, 102, 104, 108, 121, 124, 134, 135, 136, 139, 148, 151, 168, 169, 170, 183, 186, 194, 195, 199, 200, 214, 221, 227, 228, 229, 230, 239, 241, 242, 244, 249, 250, 261, 262, 265, 270, 271, 282, 289, 295, 296, 299, 300, 302, 303, 311, 319, 330, 336, 341, 352, 353, 362, 363, 365, 366, 376, 377, 385, 387, 388, 395, 396, 403, 407, 408, 415, 422, 428, 430, 436, 442, 450, 457, 460, 469, 477, 479, 484
Wharf Road   xiii
White Lion (Lyon) Inn   xiii, 21, 203, 256
Grimsby   xlvi, lii

Harlaxton   xiii, 451
Harrowby   xiii, 63, 217
Heydour (Hather)   xlii, 202, 229, 230, 254, 264
High Dyke (Dike)   275, 286
Hough   xxxvi, 245
Houghton & Walton   xiii

Kesteven   xxxix, xliv

Lancaster   xl, 267

INDEX OF PLACES

Leicester   xxii
Lincoln   xxii, xxiii, xxv, xxviii, xxxii, xxxvi, xlv, xlvi, xlvii, liv, lix, 13, 67, 156, 181, 229, 244, 264, 307, 357, 358, 360, 362, 363, 379, 452
London   xxiii, xxiv, xxvi, xxvii, xxix, xxx, xxxi, xxxv, xlii, xlvi, li, liv, lx, 4, 17, 26, 33, 34, 37, 52, 54, 57, 58, 59, 73, 92, 93, 105, 109, 120, 127, 131, 142, 308, 309, 322, 331, 332, 343, 345, 346, 347, 355, 461
Londonthorpe   xxiii, xxxvii, 147, 275, 451
Loughborough, Leics   xxii
Louth   xxviii, xxxv
Lowestoft, Suffolk   xxxvii, 463
Lyme Regis, Dorset   l

Manthorpe (Manthorp)   xiii, xxvi, lviii, 58, 89, 137, 142, 158, 205, 211, 219, 323, 338, 354, 360, 363, 382, 399, 406, 412, 418, 421, 425, 440, 446, 470
Marston   xxxix, xlix
Melton Mowbray, Leics   xxxiii, 28
Morton   70
Mowbeck stream   xiii, lix

Newark, Notts   xlii, xlvii, 152, 368
Newton   381
Nocton   liv
Northampton   xxii
Nottingham   36, 348

Oxford   xliv, xlv

Panton   xl

Ponton (Paunton), Great, Little   xiii, 127, 132, 137, 252

Rippingale   57

Sapperton   xiii, 82, 464
Scotland   xliv
Sedgebrook   xl, lvi, 256
Sedgemoor   l
Sleaford   xliii, li, liv, 267
Somerby   108
Spalding   xxviii
Spittlegate (Spitalgate)   xiii, 38, 76, 111, 112, 158, 189, 219, 239, 247, 323, 338, 354, 360, 382, 399, 406, 412, 418, 425, 440, 446, 471
Stamford   xxviii, xliv, xlvi, xlvii, 88, 103, 106, 124, 135, 151, 170, 187, 200, 228, 242, 250, 262, 271
Stoke, South   145, 206
Stoke Rochford   xiii
Stowe, Bucks   xl

Taunton, Somerset   l
Torbay, Devon   liv

Westborough   xxxvi, 427
Westminster, London   xviii, xxiii, xliii, xliv
Windsor   xlvi, 308
Winthorpe, Notts   36
Witham (Wytham), River   xiii, xxvi, xlii, lix, 362
Woolsthorpe (by Colsterworth)   xxvi

York   xxviii

INDEX OF SUBJECTS

The names of the Alderman, Comburgesses (First Twelve) and Second Twelve, officers including Coroner, Escheator, Church Wardens, Chamberlains, Collectors of School-house rents, Chief and Ward Constables, Key Bearers, Prizers of Corn, Market Sayers, Leather Sealers, town and church clerks, bailiff, gaoler, beadle, and others as well as Commoners are generally given at the First Court in each Aldermanic Year (see pages xvii, xix, xx, xxi). The First Courts are as follows: 3, 4, 25, 26, 44, 45, 65, 66, 86, 87, 101, 102, 123, 124, 134, 135, 150, 151, 169, 170, 186, 187, 199, 200, 214, 227, 228, 241, 242, 249, 250, 251, 261, 262, 270, 271, 272, 281, 282, 288, 289, 295, 296, 302, 303, 311, 312, 319, 320, 330, 331, 341, 342, 352, 353, 365, 366, 376, 377, 387, 388, 395, 396, 403, 404, 410, 417, 424, 430, 431, 438, 444, 449, 450, 459, 460, 468, 469, 479, 480. The First (or occasionally Second) Courts normally include the handing over of the town plate and the borough charters. For the period 1685–1688, the terms Mayor, Aldermen and Common Councilmen replaced Alderman, Comburgesses and Second Twelvemen respectively.

accounts. *See under* Alderman/Mayor; Chamberlains; Churchwardens; Coal-buyers; Collectors of School house rents; Constables; Coroner; Escheator; Mill-masters

Alderman/Mayor   xiv, xxi. *See also Index of Persons and Appendix 2*
  accounts of   4, 22, 24, 40, 67, 82, 103, 119, 120, 132, 146, 167, 182, 196, 211, 225, 308, 316
  arrangements for election of   xvii, 18, 59, 78, 94, 112, 128, 140, 141, 161, 162, 176, 188, 207, 222, 235, 246, 253, 254, 258, 277, 292, 298, 306, 318, 326, 327, 329, 339, 349, 350, 400, 454, 464, 474
almshouses   xxxviii, 30, 31, 81
arms, town   xxviii, xxix, xxxi, 57, 71, 88, 103, 105, 124, 135, 151, 170, 187, 200, 228, 242, 250, 262, 271
assembly   xvi, 24, 42, 43, 47, 48, 64, 84, 85, 100, 121, 122, 133, 148, 149, 161, 162, 168, 184, 185, 197, 198, 212, 213, 225, 226, 240, 248, 260, 268, 269, 272, 279, 280, 287, 293, 294, 301, 351, 364, 375, 386, 394, 401, 402, 409, 415, 416, 422, 423, 428, 429, 437, 443, 447, 448, 457, 458, 467, 477, 478, 485. *See also*

Alderman/Mayor, arrangements for election of

Bailiffs of the Liberties   xviii, xxv, 3, 51, 56, 96, 166, 257, 365, 376, 384, 387, 391, 398, 431, 479
behaviour in Court, uncivil   118, 179
borough halfpence   xxviii, xxix, xxx, xxxi, 105, 108, 112, 120, 129, 132, 137, 142, 171, 174, 177, 179, 180, 181, 188, 191, 204
bucket money   367, 373, 404
buckets   xviii, 31, 305, 362, 373, 397
Burgesses in Parliament   xxiii, xxv, xxxviii, xxxix, xl, xli, xlii, xliii, xliv, xlv, xlix, l, liv, lx, 54, 136, 259, 369

Chamberlains, accounts of   5, 29, 41, 50, 72, 90, 103, 105, 120, 121, 125, 131, 154, 165, 178, 188, 189, 191, 204, 219, 243, 278, 286, 304, 310, 314, 321, 332, 343, 355, 360, 361, 369, 379, 391, 399, 405, 419, 426, 432, 445, 451, 452, 453, 461, 462, 470
charters of incorporation, renewal and replacement of   xxii, xxiii, xxiv, xxv, xlv, xlvi, xlvii, xlix, l, li, lii, liv, lvi, lviii, lx, 37, 56, 78, 79, 83, 84, 141, 166, 307,

INDEX OF SUBJECTS 521

308, 309, 313, 315, 317, 324, 346, 347, 349, 350
Churchwardens, accounts of   5, 9, 10, 29, 30, 37, 41, 73, 91, 92, 113, 126, 157, 158, 159, 178, 193, 195, 197, 204, 218, 219, 221, 285, 304, 315, 323, 325, 344, 358, 360, 361, 370, 380, 390, 399, 405, 406, 418, 424, 439, 446, 461, 470, 481, 483
cloaks   7, 29, 321
cloth market   14
Coal-buyers (Coalmasters), accounts of   18, 79, 80, 96, 114, 128, 142, 160, 176, 192, 221, 265, 315, 327, 372, 393, 407, 440, 474
Collectors of School house rents, accounts of   10, 46, 92, 139, 154, 173, 174, 278, 290, 310, 315, 328, 333, 379, 380, 381, 392, 398, 399, 405, 418, 446, 454, 463, 470, 471, 473
Comburgesses. *These are normally listed under First Courts above; see also Appendix 2*
common box, opening of   15, 37, 47, 115, 121
common work (common day)   16
Commoners. *These are normally listed under First Courts above*
Constables. *These are normally listed under First Courts above*
accounts of   5, 6, 7, 23, 26, 27, 40, 42, 69, 83, 84, 88, 104, 117, 121, 148, 168, 183, 212, 299, 300, 363, 364, 385, 408, 414, 415, 422, 427, 428, 435, 436, 437, 441, 442, 443, 457, 477, 484, 485
Coroner, accounts of   xvii, 22, 40, 67, 82, 83, 99, 132, 137, 146, 147, 167, 182, 196, 211, 225, 252, 378

defective weights and measures. *See* Escheator
dinners   lviii, 201
   choice   19, 438
   lecturers   12, 22
   sessions   53, 72, 73, 91, 107, 116, 117, 120, 125, 128, 141, 201, 218, 380, 425, 438
   visitations   74, 91, 125, 157, 218, 238, 324, 425

distraint of goods   xviii, xxiv, xxvii, xlix, li, 19, 20, 21, 27, 50, 52, 59, 63, 75, 76, 83, 94, 96, 97, 118, 139, 156, 166, 173, 174, 177, 203, 206, 231, 283, 291, 300, 305, 317, 324, 327, 334, 345, 348, 367, 368, 393, 411, 417, 420, 435, 473, 483

Escheator. *These are normally listed under First Courts above*
   accounts of   xvii, 22, 23, 40, 67, 83, 99, 120, 132, 147, 167, 182, 183, 196, 211, 225, 255, 286, 320, 328, 418, 480

fire   xviii, xxxvii, 18, 81, 92, 97, 362
First Twelve. *See* Comburgesses *and Appendix 2*
freedom
   actions against those not being free   206, 332, 334, 389, 445
   admissions to   lv, 8, 10, 11, 15, 30, 31, 37, 39, 42, 56, 61, 88, 93, 95, 115, 118, 126, 129, 130, 140, 145, 146, 153, 160, 163, 165, 166, 175, 176, 180, 183, 184, 190, 192, 202, 208, 209, 210, 216, 222, 230, 234, 239, 245, 251, 255, 256, 264, 266, 267, 268, 276, 278, 283, 284, 290, 291, 292, 296, 297, 298, 299, 300, 304, 305, 306, 307, 312, 313, 314, 315, 317, 320, 321, 331, 332, 334, 335, 336, 339, 343, 345, 349, 350, 354, 355, 356, 357, 368, 369, 370, 371, 374, 380, 381, 382, 383, 384, 392, 397, 401, 406, 412, 414, 419, 420, 422, 423, 426, 427, 431, 433, 434, 435, 436, 438, 439, 440, 441, 444, 446, 450, 451, 452, 453, 454, 455, 456, 462, 463, 464, 465, 466, 467, 469, 471, 473, 475, 476, 481, 482, 484

gaol, gaoler   xviii, xxv, xxxii, liv, 6, 7, 11, 12, 54, 55, 77, 91, 131, 156, 160, 179, 194, 209, 333, 348, 362, 373, 489. *See also First Courts above*

hooks and ladders   xviii, 16, 20, 32, 49, 71, 324, 362, 368, 397
house of correction   314, 359, 380, 381, 411, 432, 434

Hutch, Common   xix, lvi, 11, 22, 38, 39, 55, 60, 62, 79, 82, 96, 104, 181, 189, 232, 278, 298, 322, 331, 337, 347

inmates   xvi, 291, 293, 309, 356

Kallendar for Second Twelve   20, 38, 60, 82, 99, 112, 118, 152, 164, 182, 202, 220, 236, 251, 254, 257, 274, 275, 350, 371

Keybearers (Keykeepers). *See First Courts above*

Leather Sealers (Searchers). *See First Courts above*
lectures, weekly   11, 12, 17, 20, 22, 37
loans to the Corporation   xvii, xxxix, 12

mace   xviii, xxii, 400
Mandamus, writ of   xx, 71
manufacture, woollen (scheme to set the poor on work)   lix, 181, 370, 375, 404
Market Sayers. *See First Courts above*
Mayor. *See First Courts above and Appendix 2*
Mercers' Company   11, 20
Mill-masters, accounts of   10, 17, 45, 46, 52, 53, 60, 130, 144, 145, 163, 215, 263, 267, 268, 285, 286, 298, 299, 304, 316, 320, 321, 323, 326, 337, 342, 343, 360, 361, 369, 370, 378, 379, 390, 391, 404, 405, 419, 420, 424, 432, 434, 445, 446, 462, 466, 475, 480, 482, 483
mills
　horse mill   9, 320
　water mills. *See in the Index of Places under* Grantham: Slate Mill (North Mill); Well Lane Mill
　windmill   258, 289, 293, 298, 304, 307, 343, 399

Overseers of the Highways   188, 324, 337, 347, 370, 383, 451, 464
Overseers for the Poor   xxviii, xxxi, 53, 54, 63, 68, 69, 74, 75, 112, 172, 217, 224, 324, 344, 345, 355, 356, 367, 368, 374, 378, 414, 425, 435, 464, 475, 481

plague (pestilence)   xvi, xxvi, xxvii, xxviii, 16, 32, 48, 59, 62, 75, 78, 92, 174, 471

poor relief and support   xxxviii, 80, 81, 90, 105, 113, 206, 207, 211, 325, 343, 356, 369, 370, 372, 378, 380, 389, 417, 419, 424, 435, 464. *See also* Overseers for the Poor
population   xvi, xxxii, lx
Promoter   327, 333, 365, 369, 450, 454, 460, 469, 479
pumps   54, 76, 78, 79, 92, 96, 107, 209, 265, 284, 336, 356, 358, 421, 438. *See also* wells
Puritanism   xx, xxii, xxxviii, lx

Quo Warranto, writ of   xxiii, xlv, li, 32, 346, 347

Recorder, Deputy Recorder   xxiii, xxiv, xli, xlvii, l, lviii, 30, 57, 116, 166, 252, 311, 332, 344, 380, 400, 465
refusal to take office   xxii, xlix, li, 5, 6, 19, 20, 21, 27, 96, 97, 98, 201, 252, 274, 285, 293, 317, 327, 328, 334, 335, 339, 349, 355, 373, 374, 393, 465, 466, 472, 473, 484, 491, 493, 495

scavenger   3
schoolmaster   xviii, xxxiii, xxxiv, xxxv, xxxvi, xxxvii, xliv, 28, 29, 47, 155, 157, 161, 163, 164, 189, 325, 381, 462, 463, 464, 470, 473
Second Twelve. *These are normally listed under First Courts above; see also Appendix 2*
Sergeant (Serjeant)-at-Mace   xviii, 19, 22. *See also First Courts above*
Sexton   450, 460, 480. *See also First Courts above*
Sheriff   xxii, xxv, xlv, li, 229, 246, 307, 346, 358
shoemakers, company of   12
soke of Grantham   xiii, xv, xvii, xxv, xxvi, lx, 11, 13, 22, 29, 42, 51, 52, 53, 54, 55, 56, 57, 58, 62, 68, 74, 82, 95, 146, 161, 194, 209, 355, 358, 359, 379, 421, 424, 430, 434, 451
soldiers   8, 359
stalls   xviii, 12, 139, 202, 203, 345, 368
streets in Grantham. *See Index of Places under* Grantham
　cleansing of   174

INDEX OF SUBJECTS 523

paving of   lix, 106, 139, 220, 229, 239

tithes   11, 15, 48, 358
tokens   xxviii, xxix, xxx, xxxi. *See also* borough halfpence
tolls (including accounts)   xviii, xix, xxiii, xxxix, xlv, lvi, 9, 10, 12, 28, 29, 35, 41, 58, 59, 78, 79, 80, 95, 97, 103, 104, 105, 106, 107, 114, 115, 116, 117, 119, 128, 130, 131, 136, 137, 138, 141, 142, 143, 144, 146, 147, 148, 152, 155, 156, 160, 161, 163, 165, 171, 172, 173, 174, 175, 176, 177, 178, 181, 183, 188, 190, 191, 192, 193, 194, 195, 196, 201, 202, 203, 204, 205, 208, 209, 210, 212, 215, 216, 217, 218, 219, 221, 222, 224, 225, 229, 230, 231, 232, 233, 235, 237, 238, 243, 244, 245, 246, 247, 253, 255, 256, 262, 263, 265, 266, 273, 274, 275, 276, 283, 286, 290, 303, 308, 309, 317, 327, 333, 338, 347, 348, 359, 360, 363, 368, 373, 375, 384, 393, 401, 408, 414, 419, 421, 424, 427, 436, 442, 447, 456, 465, 466, 473, 476, 482, 484. *See also in the Index of Places:* Denton; Grantham, Sand Pit Lane; Harlaxton; Heydour; Ponton
town plate   215, 244, 258, 259, 260, 321, 322. *See also First Courts above*
town properties
  leases of   xviii, xix, xxvi, xxxvii, xxxviii, lv, lvi, lvii, lviii, lix, 7, 8, 11, 30, 31, 36, 38, 48, 51, 54, 58, 60, 61, 62, 63, 71, 72, 73, 76, 77, 78, 79, 81, 82, 89, 91, 97, 98, 109, 110, 111, 112, 113, 114, 117, 119, 126, 127, 137, 142, 158, 163, 179, 180, 181, 183, 191, 192, 195, 205, 206, 207, 208, 210, 211, 218, 220, 232, 233, 278, 320, 331, 342, 363, 367, 371, 412, 421, 435, 453, 455, 470, 474, 483
  viewing of   lvi, 54, 194, 195, 215, 219, 235
town solicitor   xxiii, xxv, 15
trades and occupations   xxv, xxvi
  alehouse keeper   254, 358
  apothecary   li, 21, 27, 140, 175, 251, 321, 333, 334, 347, 455, 493
  attorney   xxv, xliii, li, lvi, 32, 53, 54, 89, 136, 143, 194, 231, 234, 267
  baker   61, 88, 95, 115, 160, 257, 259, 338, 353, 359, 462, 482, 484

  barber   262, 482
  blacksmith   166, 306, 462
  brazier   xxviii, 332
  bridlemaker (bridler)   208, 321
  butcher   61, 95, 115, 139, 202, 203, 208, 251, 266, 306, 321, 463, 481, 491
  carpenter   xxvii, 57, 75, 76, 78, 79, 92, 96
  chandler   129, 192
  cooper   61, 140, 469, 481, 482
  cordwainer   xlvi, xlvii, 61, 73, 175, 202, 251, 259, 266, 465, 475
  currier   266, 334
  draper (woollendraper)   202, 490, 493
  farrier   166
  fellmonger   46, 72, 123, 129, 153, 180, 245, 266, 282, 296, 303, 351, 399, 453, 467, 492, 495
  glazier   115, 180, 339, 481
  glover   266, 465
  goldsmith   413
  haberdasher   li, 347, 348, 493
  hatter   223, 336
  hostler   426
  innholder (innkeeper)   358, 426, 491
  loadsman   256, 357
  mercer   xxviii, li, 8, 129, 165, 223, 232, 321, 349, 376, 387, 393, 484
  miller (milner)   167, 215, 256, 268, 293
  parchment maker   251
  plumber   118, 420
  roper   95, 266
  sadler   56, 58, 115, 245
  shoemaker   xxxii, 129, 238, 450, 481, 482, 492
  smith   425
  tailor   115, 129, 175, 239
  tanner   12, 61, 71, 74, 208, 290, 296, 303, 353, 366, 380, 488, 495
  victualler   484
  vintner   21
  weaver (stuff weaver)   175, 251, 266
  wheelwright   251, 266
  whitesmith   453

usher   xviii, xxxiii, xxxv, xxxvi, xxxvii, 156, 245, 332, 337, 349, 373, 381, 427, 440, 462, 473. *See also* schoolmaster

vestry   322
vicar   xxxvi, 13

waits   lv, 4, 7, 21, 26, 29, 45, 66, 87, 152, 171, 188, 201, 229, 233, 243, 251, 256, 263, 272, 321, 352, 365, 396, 404, 413, 431, 450, 460, 464, 469, 479

wards   xiii, xvi, xviii, 18, 27, 36, 59, 60, 71, 300, 324, 362, 389. *See also in the Index of Places under* Grantham: Castlegate; High Street; Market Place; Swinegate; Walkergate; Westgate

wells   xviii, lix, 9, 54, 57, 107, 108, 136, 138, 139, 154, 158, 161, 166, 177, 221, 229, 230, 244, 265, 299, 324, 336, 362. *See also* pumps